This book is dedicated to John C. Wright,
who served as a mentor to many of those
who contributed to this volume.

Children and Television

Fifty Years of Research

Edited by

Norma Pecora
Ohio University

John P. Murray
The Mind Science Foundation, San Antonio
Center on Media and Child Health, Children's Hospital Boston
Harvard Medical School

Ellen Ann Wartella
University of California, Riverside

LAWRENCE ERLBAUM ASSOCIATES, PUBLISHERS
2007   Mahwah, New Jersey   London

Lawrence Erlbaum Associates, Inc., Publishers
10 Industrial Avenue
Mahwah, New Jersey 07430
www.erlbaum.com

Cover design by Tomai Maridou

Library of Congress Cataloging-in-Publication Data

Children and television : fifty years of research / edited by Norma Pecora,
John P. Murray, Ellen Ann Wartella.
     p. cm.
     Includes bibliographical references and index.
ISBN 0-8058-4138-5 (cloth) – ISBN 0-8058-4139-3 (pbk.) 1. Television
and children–Bibliography. 2. Television and youth–Bibliography.
I. Pecora, Norma Odom. II. Murray, John P. III. Wartella, Ellen.
Z7164.C5C512 2006
[HQ784.T4]
016.30223'45'083–dc22

                                                            2005044942

Books published by Lawrence Erlbaum Associates are printed on acid-free paper,
and their bindings are chosen for strength and durability.

Printed in the United States of America
10 9 8 7 6 5 4 3 2

Contents

    Michael Rich

6   Advertising and Consumer Development   149
    Nancy A. Jennings and Ellen A. Wartella

7   TV Violence: Research and Controversy   183
    John P. Murray

8   Health, Drugs, and Values   205
    Elizabeth P. Lorch

    Bibliography   233
    Author Index   363
    Subject Index   379

Series Foreword

Jennings Bryant
University of Alabama

Most scholarly books that become "classics" do so after years of use by generations of teachers and learners. But occasionally a book comes along that was born to be a classic. Such is Pecora, Murray, and Wartella's *Children and Television: Fifty Years of Research.*

What is the basis of this claim?

1. Consider the chapter authors. The case could well be made that the senior scholar of each chapter is the respective "dean" of his or her specialized field of inquiry. I may get in trouble for revealing the relative antiquity of so many of my academic heroes who are represented in this esteemed group of scholars, but the research programs they represent have, indeed, been "decades in the making." For many years, these dedicated scholars have fostered the best of programmatic research in their respective domains of inquiry into television and children.

2. The moment is propitious. Sufficient time has expired to permit a comprehensive assessment of the field. Looked at from the perspective of more timeworn disciplines within the academy, 50 years is a relatively short life span; however, it is sufficient to permit the aggregation of a reliable, revealing body of literature. The last few years have witnessed numerous meta-analyses, major specialty handbooks, and other forms of productive synthesis within the mass communication discipline. The chapters in this

volume have productively incorporated such accumulated knowledge and acquired wisdom.

3. The two main cornerstones of this volume are extremely sturdy. In many ways, this volume is the intellectual heir of Murray's (1980) *Television & Youth: 25 Years of Research & Controversy*. Building a new classic on the foundation of another is not a bad way to begin. Moreover, the second foundation—the bibliography that anchors this volume—will prove to be an invaluable resource for the next generation of media-and-children scholars. Thank goodness some people are such organized packrats!

4. The authors have proven to be Solomon-like in consistently distinguishing between the forest and the trees. When your foundational bibliography comprises literally thousands of peer-reviewed articles, books, chapters, and other documents, that is a lot of "trees," and they constitute one very dense forest. But as I reviewed this volume, I was constantly amazed by how well the contributors had extracted the big picture, the major trends, and the pivotal moments from the bounteous morass that constituted their literature reviews.

5. The time is right. We are suffiently within the portals of the information age that we are routinely overwhelmed by the expansiveness of the literature in active research areas like television and children. Therefore, we need all the help we can get in terms of one of the traditional functions of media—editorialization. For such productive interpretation, tribal elders are required. In a real sense, only the current slate of contributors could so compellingly tell the stories of television and children in such an elegant manner.

6. The topic is right, but our moment may be passing. As a perusal of several of the more current resources listed in this volume's bibliography will affirm, recent surveys that have provided normative data on contemporary media use by children and youth reaffirm the fact that television remains the most widely used medium by today's youngsters. However, "the times they are a-changin'," and who knows what tomorrow's medium or media of choice of childhood will be? In that sense, this book may well serve not only to summarize the wisdom of the ages (i.e., the first 50 years), it may also function as a benchmark from which to ascertain the new beginnings of the next revolution of media and youth.

The editors and authors of this seminal volume are to be commended for their sagacity and applauded for their vigilance. On behalf of your grateful consumers, thank you.

Foreword

Lloyd N. Morrisett
Children's Television Workshop

If anyone still harbors the belief that television viewing by children is a playful and innocuous use of time without consequence, reading this book will almost surely change that belief. The very large body of research that has been directed at television and children over these 50 years leads to some inescapable conclusions. Among them are:

- Most children watch a great deal of television. They spend more time watching television than in any other discretionary activity.
- Many children begin watching television at a very early age, often less than 12 months.
- At whatever age they begin watching television, children learn from it.
- Both the amount of time children spend watching television and what they watch affect learning and behavior in important ways.
- If children watch programs that are designed to be educational, they learn what is being taught.
- If children watch programs that have significant violent content, they are likely to show increases in aggressive behavior both immediately and as much as 10 years later.
- Television often reinforces social stereotypes of gender, race, ethnicity, age, and disability.

When Joan Cooney and I began working on *Sesame Street* in 1966, we knew that children spent much of their free time watching television.

Sesame Street was created as an experiment to find out if television could be used to teach young children some of the skills they would need to succeed in school. It was a time when the attention of the nation was focused on the educational needs of young children and little television programming was created specifically to meet those needs.

Now, 40 years later, there has been an enormous increase in available television content with the growth of cable and the rise of satellite television. Many people have the choice of hundreds of channels. As part of that expansion there has been an increase in the amount of programming for children, but it is questionable if the proportion of television created for children is any greater now than in 1969. Newton Minow would almost certainly say now, as he did in 1961, that television is a "vast wasteland." He might add that there are oases in the desert of television, but it takes a determined person to seek those out.

The increase in children's programming is primarily the result of children, including preschool children, being seen as a profitable market. Ironically, the very success of *Sesame Street,* an educational program created by a nonprofit company, undoubtedly contributed to the recognition of the "child market." This market-driven increase in children's television is not benign. The staff of Sesame Workshop recently completed a study surveying child development experts, teachers, and parents, to identify and rate the needs of children that could be met by media. One of the major clusters of needs that was identified is "protection of childhood," and the single most cited need in that group that is not being met is "protection from too much marketing."

I like to think that the course of our concern with television and children might be analogous to what happened with smoking. Over many years the evidence piled up that smoking was often a key precursor to lung cancer. Although people still smoke, the dangers of smoking are common knowledge, and society has taken steps to discourage smoking— smoke-free workplaces, high taxes on cigarettes, and widely distributed educational materials.

Unfortunately, with television we do not have the obvious levers of policy to make the changes that would improve the educational outcomes for children. The First Amendment places limits on the control of television content, although those limits have not been really tested when applied to television and children. The Federal Communications Commission (FCC) has, for the most part, abrogated its responsibility in this area. There seems to be little leadership in Congress or the administration on these issues.

Public broadcasting has the potential to become the educational destination for children and young people. The children's offerings on public television are of high quality and very popular with Congress. It often seems that federal funding for public television continues only because of children's programming. A dream of mine would be for public television to become a children's service. The obstacles to that dream are a fragmented system and vested interests in the status quo. If, however, the competitive position of public broadcasting continues to erode, leaders might see that a new direction, concentrating on the needs of children, can offer a road to public broadcasting health. A freely and universally available educational television channel for children would be a wonderful contribution to our society and a magnificent accomplishment for public television.

Preface

This project that led to this book began in 1996 in Texas, of all places!

John Murray was in San Antonio, Texas, serving as a Scholar-in-Residence at the Mind Science Foundation in San Antonio and a Visiting Scholar at the University of Texas (UT) at Austin. As a result of conversations with colleagues at UT, particularly Ellen Wartella who was Dean of the College of Communication, and John Wright and Aletha Huston in the Human Ecology program at UT, we decided that the time was ripe for a review of the past 50 years of research on the topic of children and television.

Norma Pecora had just published an excellent review of the research and policies relating to the economics of children's television programming and had worked with Ellen Wartella in the mid-1990s to update the 25-year review of research published by John Murray in 1980. Thus the "natural" team of Pecora, Murray and Wartella was born!

Projects of the scope of this book—reviewing more than 2,000 research reports, published since 1955—require large amounts of footwork and vast amounts of collaboration. We set our sights on 2005 as the 50th anniversary of the publication of the earliest commentaries on the topic of children and television; the Congressional testimony of Paul Lazarsfeld and Eleanor Maccoby, a sociologist and psychologist, respectively, who sketched the future of a research program for the social sciences.

We have arrived with our offering, *Children and Television: Fifty Years of Research*. Along the way, we received tremendous support from our colleagues and our institutions.

The institutional support consisted of our respective universities: Ohio University and the University of Texas. In addition, John Murray benefited from the strong institutional and financial support of The Mind Science Foundation in San Antonio, which provided support for sabbatical research and writing in 1996–97, as well as the Department of Health and Human Services (with the support of Senator Sam Brownback), which provided research support for a sabbatical at Harvard Medical School, Center on Media and Child Health during 2004–05.

The support of our colleagues is manifested in the outstanding contributions that they have made to this book by writing chapters that provide state-of-the-art summaries of research in their areas of expertise in children's television. One of our colleagues, John C. Wright, had a special part to play in his role as a mentor to many of the contributors in this book. Indeed, he launched the careers of numerous students in the field of children's television and his tragic accidental death was a great loss. For these reasons, we have dedicated this book to his memory.

—Norma Pecora
John P. Murray
Ellen Wartella

Introduction

Norma Pecora

Three boys, aged nine, eleven, and thirteen years, who had recently seen depicted the adventures of frontier life including the holding up of a stage coach and the lassoing of the driver, spent weeks planning to lasso, murder and rob a neighborhood milkman, who started on his route at four o'clock in the morning. They made their headquarters in a barn and saved enough money to buy a revolver, adopting as their watchword the phrase "Dead Men Tell No Tales." One spring morning the conspirators, with their faces covered with black cloth, lay "in ambush" for the milkman. Fortunately for him, as the lariat was thrown the horse shied, and, although the shot was appropriately fired, the milkman's life was saved. Such a direct influence of the theater is by no means rare . . .

—Jane Addams (1909/1972, p. 93)

Thus began our quest to understand children's relationship to entertainment media. For more than 50 years, the focal point of that quest has been television. This book is an attempt to bring together the academic research conducted in the United States addressing questions about children and their television. Some of the questions have considered the content of programming, children's responses to television, regulation concerning children's television policies, issues of advertising, and concerns about sex and race stereotyping. For the most part, the questions asked modeled the earlier research on children and movies or radio with initial questions about media preferences or use and the quality of programming. Many voiced the concerns articulated by Addams that children's entertainment be held to a higher standard. Perhaps most interesting is the idea that public debate, beginning with Addams, has helped shape the research agenda on children's media. As described by

Wartella and Reeves (1985), in one of the earlier publications from this bibliography, "the origin of research about children [and the questions asked] lies in concern expressed by the public about each medium as it was introduced" (p. 120). From motion pictures to current questions about the Internet there is a pattern of research studies that move from "media use to increasing emphasis on issues of physical and emotional harm, and changes in children's knowledge, attitudes, and behaviors" (Wartella & Reeves, 1985, p. 126). They went on to say there are recurring studies about violence, sex, and advertising.

This project has been a labor of love, sometimes, that brings together the two seminal works in the field. The first is the publication of Murray's (1980) *Television & Youth: 25 Years of Research and Controversy*; and the other, an undertaking that has remained in boxes as Ellen Wartella and I moved from place to place over the last 20 years. *Television & Youth* has been an important resource for anyone interested in children and television. It offers a far-reaching analysis of the questions and concerns of early television. In addition, the bibliography offered a comprehensive review of the literature for those first 25 years of television.

In the early 1980s, while working as Wartella's graduate assistant, I walked into her office one day and she said, "Have I got a project for you." With that we began to collect a bibliography of all the academic research on children and their media. The first citations are dated from 1911 and are concerned with the way children's leisure time is affected by the movies. Over the years the project has been supported by various grants and numerous undergraduate and graduate students as we would periodically update the database. This was not a project to keep an idle graduate student busy, but came from Wartella's frustration over policy debates of the time. Although there was a growing and compelling scholarship on children and their media, it rarely seemed to inform or change public policy. The intent of the project, then as now, was to see where we had been in an attempt to shape a future agenda.

To begin, this project is a comprehensive bibliography of the research on children and television that starts with Lazarsfeld's testimony before Congress in 1955 and ends in 2002, covering almost 50 years of academic research. Note that the bibliography is included both in print format at the end of the volume, and on the CD-ROM accompanying this volume.) More important, in addition to this bibliography, the book offers essays by those who have been involved in some of the most important questions addressed by this research.

Using a wide range of resources, both formal and informal, we have culled the academic literature for any research that speaks to children and television. *Children* is defined as ages birth to 18 and *television* has been defined broadly as entertainment. The works included here are studies of content, effects, and policy; research that has been conducted by both social scientists and those in the growing field of cultural studies. We began by combining the work in Murray's *Television & Youth* and the historical bibliography accumulated by Wartella and Pecora and updated both using the primary resources for any literature search: *Communication Abstracts*, *Educational Abstracts*, *ERIC*, *Medline*, *PAIS*, *PsycINFO*, and *Sociological Abstracts*. Once we located a book or journal article, we then used the bibliography of that work to add to the database of existing citations.

This project is not a complete bibliography—to those whose work was somehow missed, we apologize. Every effort has been made to incorporate all the research that has been conducted, but, for whatever reason, you might not find your name in this bibliography. The study of children's television offers some interesting challenges. As demonstrated by the authors of the chapters here, this research is interdisciplinary by nature and draws on many academic traditions. Scholars working in communication studies, psychology, sociology, education, economics, and medicine are among those who have contributed to our understandings of children and their television. Thus the net was cast widely.

The book does not attempt to address international work on children's television. Although there are interesting studies that occasionally make their way into the U.S. academic literature, it was beyond the scope of this work to include a comprehensive list of international research. In addition, television was defined as primarily the commercial broadcast and cable networks, excluding educational programming such as *Sesame Street*. Also not included is the body of work carried out under the auspices of the federal government, such as the seminal work of the Surgeon General's Scientific Advisory Committee on Television and Social Behavior in the early 1970s or the National Television Violence Study funded by the cable industry in 1997. Finally, there is a growing body of research by organizations such as Children Now, the Kaiser Foundation, the Annenberg Public Policy Center of the University of Pennsylvania, and the Pew Charitable Trust Fund that are not a part of this book but certainly have contributed to our knowledge of children's television. However, the intent of the bibliography is to incorporate work that is readily available in the public domain of academic research; hence the focus is on journals and books.

Finally, this book is about television, which is only one part of children's media environment. As technology brings the Internet and Web pages into children's playgrounds, we leave the next volume to others.

The book begins with Pecora's chapter, which offers an overview, by decade, of the social and cultural context during which this research was conducted, including the landscape of children's television, public debate and policy of the time, and the research questions addressed. As Wartella and Reeves (1985) pointed out, issues of violence, sex, and advertising recur often in response to the public debate of the time. This chapter attempts to put into context those debates and the shifting focus of research and increasing complexity of the questions asked.

Huston and Wright (chap. 2, this volume) have been in the forefront of the research on children's learning from television. Their chapter, written with Bickham and Lee, brings us a history of their important work conducted at the Center for Research on the Influences of Television on Children (CRITC). Among other issues, over the past fifty years the formal features of children's television have changed from live action and simple animation to the fast pace that dominates contemporary children's entertainment. This has consequences on the way children process information. As outlined in the chapter, their work has "attempted to understand how TV's form and content guide children's attention to television, how children come to understand the medium, and how characteristics of the medium affect what children learn from it" (p. 41).

Although *Sesame Street* is not included in this bibliography, the contribution of Sesame Workshop (formerly the Children's Television Workshop) is represented by the work of Daniel R. Anderson. His chapter, written with Marie Evans Schmidt (chap. 3, this volume), offers us an overview of the research on cognitive development and educational achievement. For far too long we have tried to keep separate children's formal learning from informal, outside-the-classroom, learning. However, Anderson and Schmidt's work brings together the compelling body of literature that examines academic accomplishment as they are associated with both educational television such as *Sesame Street* and other viewing experience. Gordon L. Berry (chap. 4, this volume), who has been a leader in the work on social and cultural images, looks back through the "use and misuse" of television to help understand the contribution of its imagery to children's comprehension of their world. The social concerns of the 1960s are reflected in the research on children and youth in the 1970s, when we began to address the socialization of minority children through television. Research on gender and minorities becomes a part of our lexicon.

From Rich (chap. 5, this volume) we have a part of the debate that is seldom included in discussions about children's television—the medical community. His chapter also demonstrates the interdisciplinary nature of the field. Physicians have long been concerned about the media as a part of children's general health and well-being. Through an analysis of specifically the medical literature, we come to understand their apprehensions.

The next three chapters address the dominant issues that have defined contemporary research on children's television: advertising and consumer behavior, violence, and health choices. The work by Jennings and Wartella (chap. 6, this volume) offers a historical review of the research on advertising and marketing practices aimed at children and youth. Theirs is a comprehensive discussion of both the socialization process and the way we have come to understand it in the context of consumerism. The chapter by Murray (chap. 7, this volume) is not only a review of the past, but also an insight into the current cutting-edge work in physiological research on responses to media violence. Finally, Lorch (chap. 8, this volume) offers an analysis of the research on television's role in health choices that includes not only substance abuse but also the growing concern for adolescent sexuality. Placed in a theoretical context, her work demonstrates the significance of a growing body of literature that helps to understand the choices children and adolescents make when it comes to health issues.

REFERENCES

Addams, J. (1972). *The spirit of youth and city streets.* Urbana: University of Illinois Press. (Original work published 1909)

Murray, John P. (1980) *Television & youth: 25 years of research and controversy.* Boys Town, NE: The Boys Town Center for the Study of Youth Development.

Wartella, E. A., & Reeves, B. (1985). Historical trends in research on children and media: 1900–1960. *Journal of Communication, 35*(2), 118–133.

1

The Changing Nature of Children's Television: Fifty Years of Research

Norma Pecora
Ohio University

While television was in its infancy *Paul Lazarsfeld* (1955),[1] in testimony before the Kefauver Committee on Juvenile Delinquency, called for a comprehensive program to study not only the effects of the new medium of television, but other "unorthodox kinds of studies which would add to our understanding" of these effects (p. 247). Unorthodox studies, according to Lazarsfeld, included collaborative and long-term research and studies of the family and of those involved in the creative process. Lazarsfeld argued for a well-funded, centralized organization or foundation to carry this agenda forward. Unfortunately, although the Surgeon General's studies published in the 1970s were no doubt the model Lazarsfeld had in mind, rarely have his words been heeded. As we see here, much of the research in the field of children and television has been underfunded, short-term, isolated, uncoordinated studies carried out in the kind of seclusion he called "the accidental initiative of individual scholars" (p. 244). There are exceptions, of course, as illustrated by several of the contributors to this book, who have built organizations and institutes within their universities. We in the field tend to collaborate

---

[1]Citations in italics can be found in the master bibliography.

where possible with students, mentors, and colleagues—a process made more possible by the Internet—but for the most part Congress ignored Lazarsfeld's appeal and left the research on this "burning social issue" (p. 244) to the vagaries of the academic climate.

However, what we do have is a body of research cumulated over the past 50 years by a diverse group of scholars. Their work reflects some underlying concerns we as a society have about youth and the media at different points in time. From the beginning we have worried about the effect of television on children, questions carried over from motion pictures, radio, and comic books, and we have been troubled by television's ubiquitous nature. Two recent studies have looked back on media research in general (Bryant & Miron, 2004) and specifically funded research on children ages 0 to 6 (Rideout, Roberts, & Foehr, 2005). Bryant and Miron (2004) analyzed the literature of mass communication for the theoretical and scientific paradigms that have been "developed by communication scholars or imported from . . . various cognate disciplines" (p. 664). Although their work addressed theories, in general, and not specifically to the literature on children and the media, Bryant and Miron's work is useful in understanding the theories that have informed our discipline. Most relevant is Piaget's cognitive development theory that is central to much of the research on children and media. In the mass communication journals, Piaget was first used in 1971 "with a fairly even distribution use over time thereafter" (Bryant & Miron, 2004, p. 679). The Kaiser Family Foundation study analyzed funded research on children 0 to 6 that was published in peer-reviewed publications. They found that the first of this research was conducted in the early 1960s and has been grounded in social learning theory from the work of Bandura and others.

These concerns and questions have occurred in, according to *Wartella and Reeves* (1984) "the nexus of social values, political exigencies, and the cultural context of how media have been incorporated into American life" (p. 28). In this chapter we look at the more than 2,000 studies that address youth and television.[2] Organized around decades, this chapter will consider the studies in (a) the context of children's culture for the decade; (b) the landscape of television; and (c) the research questions addressed during the decade.

---

[2]These studies include a comprehensive list of all academic research, books and journals, published in the United States using the keywords *children* and *television*. *Children* is defined as ages 0 through college and *television* is defined as commercially distributed (not public or school based).

Before beginning, it is important to place the questions asked about children and television in a historical context. These questions, and the theoretical and methodological foundations that inform them, did not raise full cloth out of the academic world but rather are grounded in a long tradition of social concerns about youth and the media. In 1909, Jane Addams wrote, "The theater becomes to them [youth] a 'veritable house of dreams' infinitely more real than the noisy streets and crowded factories" (Addams, 1909/1972, p. 76). Her words reflected a growing disquiet over the new medium of motion pictures and her alarm over the "effects" of the dream palaces set the agenda for research that followed. As each new medium was introduced, researchers have asked much the same question.

In their analysis of a selected sample of an earlier version of the database for this project,[3] examining the years 1900 through 1960, *Wartella and Reeves* (1985) found that research questions have been similar as each new medium was introduced to the child audience. Their review of the preliminary database found "a progression from early attention studies of media use to increasing emphasis on issues of physical and emotional harm, and changes in children's knowledge, attitudes, and behaviors (p. 120). In addition," Wartella and Reeves pointed out that "studies about violence, sex, and advertising recur" (p. 126). Media use and audience preference studies most likely come in the first years of the introduction of a medium, followed by research that reflected the public debate about the impact of new technologies. They also commented on research that was conducted by a diverse population of scholars from the disciplines of psychology, sociology, education, communication, and social work. Indeed, there are more than 400 journals represented in this bibliography.

In an earlier article, *Wartella and Reeves* (1984) also examined how the research agenda on children and television changed over the years from 1955 to 1980. They found that there was a change in the nature of the child viewer with research that was more grounded in cognitive theory and developmental studies. During the 1970s "there [was] a . . . concern with the ways in which children of different ages make sense of and utilize the messages of television (p. 27). They identified the cycles of research as, first, the children's use and preference of the medium, often followed by (or concurrent with) a concern for physical and emotional

---

[3]The full bibliography for this project includes research on motion pictures, radio, and comic books from 1900 through 2002. The database for this 1983 publication was for research from 1900 through 1960 and included 242 entries. The earliest citations are from 1911.

health effects. Last, according to Wartella and Reeves, researchers turned their attention to the "effects of media content on children's knowledge, attitudes and behavior" (p. 27). The role of television in children's lives becomes defined by content areas such as violence and sex. In their analysis of these 25 years of children's television research, Wartella and Reeves pointed out that research studies were often policy driven. For example:

> The first minor rumble in the number of violence citations occurred in 1961, the same year that Senator Dodd held Judiciary subcommittee hearings that included testimony on television and juvenile delinquency . . . also the year that FCC Chairman Newton Minow labeled television "a vast wasteland." (p. 29)

According to them, both children's research and media policy debates were limited until 1969 when the issue began to reach a zenith. In that year, the Surgeon General's committee was established and research funding was awarded for a comprehensive examination of children and media. In 1972, the Surgeon General's report was issued, and academic work in the area reached an all-time high. According to *Wartella and Reeves* (1984), advertising research showed a similar peak during Federal Trade Commission (FTC) hearings on children's Saturday morning cartoons in 1978 and 1979.

Using the work of Reeves and Wartella (1982), in the first presentation of these bibliography data, *Meadowcroft and McDonald* (1986) analyzed a random sample of 163 studies on youth and the media from 1911 to 1980. Like Wartella and Reeves, they found there were peaks in the distribution of studies across the years. According to Meadowcroft and McDonald the first peak, 1925 to 1947, coincided with policy debates driven by the establishment of the Federal Radio Commission in 1927 and the Federal Communications Commission (FCC) in 1934. The second peak, 1969 to 1979, occurred during the time of the Commission on Obscenity and Pornography and the National Commission on the Causes and Prevention of Violence in the late 1960s and the Surgeon General's studies published in 1972. They argued, counter to Reeves and Wartella, that there was not a cyclical trend to the research on children and media as each new medium entered the culture. Meadowcroft and McDonald found, instead, that,

> [w]ithin the first 10 years of research on any medium, research topics include: individual characteristics, viewing conditions, media content and learning of media content. Three initial research questions seem to emerge, therefore, in

the first 10 years on children and an innovative medium: (1) What is the content of the medium? (2) How does the content affect different children? And (3) How do these effects vary, according to viewing contexts . . . research on each medium seems to address research topics independent of other media topic agendas. (p. 479)

For television, *Meadowcroft and McDonald* (1986) claimed variables were introduced into the research agenda in the following pattern:

Years 1–5:	Media content; individual characteristics; viewing conditions; attitudes and interests; learning.[4]
Years 11–15:	Bad behaviors; home/peer.
Years 16–20:	Individual characteristics; advertising; attitudes/interest displacement.
Years 21–25:	Antisocial-psychological; other psychological.
Years 31–35:	Good behaviors
Years 36–40:	Medium characteristics; unhealthy mental effects.

This chapter is not an attempt to prove or disprove either position; rather, the debate is offered as an example of the problematics that center around any attempt to characterize research variables. In other words, this is not a critique of the questions we have asked but rather the context in which we have asked them.

As we can see from Table 1.1, there have been an ever increasing number of studies throughout the five decades considered here, with the peak in the 1970s.

The number of research studies conducted over the past 50 or so years has increased dramatically. In the first decade there were fewer than 100 studies; since 1970 we have averaged at least five times that number per year. Certainly the Surgeon General's study, in part, accounts for increased attention to this topic in the 1970s. We can only speculate as to why interest in this research has been sustained. In part, those who contributed to the Surgeon General's studies made their reputation in the field and continued to build an expertise in the field; the growing academic community in all disciplines has meant an increase in research and books and journals in all disciplines; a rise in the research on children, in general, and children and media as an area of study; and, no doubt, those

---

[4] This category may reflect an error in the presentation of the data as the years 6 through 10, represented in their reporting on motion pictures and radio, appears to be missing. It is of no consequence to the discussion here.

TABLE 1.1
Distribution of Research Studies by Decade
Children and Television

Decade	Total Studies	Average Number of Studies per Year
1949	5	5
1950–59	88	8.8
1960–69	127	12.7
1970–79	565	56.5
1980–89	677	67.7
1990–99	602	60.2
2000–02	233	74.3

of us who have grown up with television find it an intellectual challenge. This has presented a formidable body of research, unfortunately, with little of the "systematic and overall planning" Lazarsfeld (1955, p. 244) called for. What follows here is an attempt to bring some coherency to the studies that have been done over the past 50 years and place them in the context of the time.[5]

TELEVISION IS INTRODUCED: THE LATE 1940S

Television was introduced in the late 1940s as American industry shifted production from tools of war to tools of leisure and tried to meet the growing demand for household goods. The technology of television had been ready prewar but was put on hold. After World War II, it was quickly introduced. By 1954, 7 years after its introduction, 55% of households had television. Women who had taken the place of men in the workforce during the war years were encouraged to return to the home, which was often now in a new suburban development, and to raise a family. This idealized image of the family—White, middle-class, suburbia with mom in the kitchen and dad at work—was often perpetuated by the new television programs, such as Father Knows Best. Preschool was a limited concept and many children did not enter school until first grade. When children did reach school age, they often walked home for lunch, arriving in time

---

[5]This is in no way a comprehensive analysis of the research done during these decades but rather a look at the trends and themes that emerged. For a more thorough discussion Luke's (1990) Constructing the Child Viewer is recommended. The reader is also encouraged to browse the full bibliography.

to eat peanut butter sandwiches on Wonder Bread while watching one of the many locally produced noontime cartoon shows.

History has it that the first network children's television program was *Movies for the Small Fry* in 1947, later *Small Fry Club* on the DuMont network, followed closely by *Juvenile Jury* on NBC and two puppet shows: *Judy Splinters* and *Puppet Playhouse*. A few programs at that time had limited network distribution but most were locally produced or syndicated (Davis, 1995; Erickson, 1995; Grossman, 1987; Hollis, 2001). *TeleComics,* later *NBC Comics,* was the first network cartoon series (Erickson, 1995), with westerns, action-adventures, storyteller, and variety shows dominating the schedule (*Turow, 1981*). According to Grossman (1987) and *Turow* (*1981*) there were no Saturday morning programs scheduled until about the mid- to late 1950s; most children's programming was aired weekdays during the lunch hour, after school, or on Saturday or Sunday evening (*Turow, 1981*). *Oky Doky Ranch, Small Fry Club, Junior Jamboree,* and the *Puppet Playhouse* were all broadcast during the early evening hours (Grossman, 1987). Several have speculated that the television industry used children's programming as a way of introducing television into the home (*Melody & Ehrlich, 1974; Turow, 1981*) and, certainly, using these kinds of programs in the early evening, family hours, would be a way to do so.[6] In addition, *Palmer* (*1988*) presented us with three reasons early television broadcasters "eagerly" programmed for children: (a) to attract young families, (b) to fill otherwise useless hours with inexpensive programming, and (c) to demonstrate a public-service orientation.

The Research

The five earliest studies identified from the 1940s demonstrate that from the beginning questions addressed issues of media preference, social concerns, and health. According to Grossman (1987), much of the early criticism came from physicians concerned with the physical effects of this new medium. Symptoms ranged from "frogitis," caused by children sitting in front of the television with their knees folded to the side; "TV bottom" or an ache in the tailbone caused by sitting too long; or "TV tummy," which

---

[6]According to Gomery (2001), early television programmed sports to attract the male audience but family size was one of the best variables to describe early adoption of television. He stated, "Suburbanites with baby boom families embraced TV as soon as stations went on the air and dealers offered sets for sale at $200 or less" (p. 124).

was the consequence of becoming too excited during action-adventure shows. One of the earliest research studies in this bibliography was on the potential of television to damage the eye (*Rones, 1949*). Of the five television studies, all conducted in 1949, the focus was on issues that reflect today's concerns: television's potential for social good or as a "cure" for juvenile delinquency (*Hutchinson, 1949; Riley, Cantwell, & Ruttiger, 1949*) and television's relationship to education (*Lewis, 1949; Rehage, 1949*). They were found in publications as diverse as *Sight Saving Research*, *Public Opinion Quarterly*, and *The Elementary School Journal*.

SELLING TELEVISIONS: THE 1950s

During this decade, the postwar baby boom was making its way through the educational system, teens were becoming identified as a consumer market, and experts like Dr. Spock were encouraging parents to allow their children more freedom and responsibility (Mintz, 2004; *Pecora, 1998*).

Television came of age in the 1950s with four national networks: DuMont, ABC, CBS, and NBC, although DuMont folded by 1955. Initially, a freeze on license applications imposed between 1948 and 1952 kept the medium from growing until issues such as interference were sorted out. Once they were, television quickly became a part of the American landscape. *Witty (1966)* reported that in the Chicago area, in 1949 and 1950, 43% of the children had a television set in their home; by 1959, 99% had a television. It had become the leisure activity of choice for families and children. Radio responded by changing formats because many radio programs, including children's shows, made the exodus to television.

The 1950s were called, by some, the golden age of children's television because of the quantity and quality of programming available. During the 1950s, children's television programming went from 2.5 hours per week to a high of 37 hours in 1956 on the three national networks (*Shelby, 1964, p. 248*).[7] In a comprehensive study of children's programming *Turow (1981)* demonstrated a shift in the number of hours of programming from 10 programs in 1948–49 with an average of 20 programs from 1950 through 1959.

---

[7]*Witty and Bricker (1952)* also reported that children watched many of the adult programs offered in prime time. A 1950 survey found that by sixth grade children's preference was for adult variety shows and sports.

During the first part of the 1950s programming was still found during the lunch hour, after school, or in the early evening, but by the end of the decade Saturday morning was becoming the daypart of choice for children. While television was young, local programming featuring Uncle Bobs and Captain Neds was cheap and easy to produce. Eventually, economies of scale made national network distribution and syndication a more viable option. By 1957, two of the three networks (CBS and NBC) had begun to program children's entertainment on a more competitive basis and moved it from the evening hours to Saturday morning (Grossman, 1987). Beginning at 9:30 a.m., CBS carried *Captain Kangaroo*, *Mighty Mouse*, several variety programs, and the *Lone Ranger*. NBC, in the meantime, had *Howdy Doody*, *Gumby*, and several action-adventure shows (Grossman, 1987). According to Davis (1995), *Fury*, one of the action-adventure shows on NBC Saturday morning was one of the first action-adventure shows to encourage prosocial themes. Although most of these programs were aimed at the younger child, *American Bandstand* debuted nationally in 1957 as afternoon programming for teens (Davis, 1995). The mid-1950s brought us the first of Disney on television with *The Wonderful World of Disney*. Cartoons became an important part of local lunchtime and after-school shows as first Warner Brothers and then Paramount opened their library of movie cartoons like *Looney Tunes* and *Popeye* (Erickson, 1995; Hollis, 2001). By the end of the decade, however, Hanna Barbera designed a process for animation to make it more affordable for television: *Ruff and Ready* (1957) was the first of such cartoons, soon followed by *Huckleberry Hound* (1958).

There were a number of early efforts to use television as an educational tool: *Ding Dong School* (1952) and *Romper Room* (1953) were representative of such programs in large television markets. *Ding Dong School* was, according to Davis (1995), viewed by 95% of the country's preschoolers. The show combined educational lessons with play activities for children in the home audience, and its host, Miss Frances, was an educator and head of education at Roosevelt College in Chicago (Davis, 1995). *Romper Room*, a franchised program, also used educational experiences with activities for the home audience, although in this case these activities usually involved supplies available at the local toy store (Hollis, 2001). Other educational programming of the 1950s included *Mr. Wizard* and *Mr. I Magination*, *Captain Kangaroo*, *Jon Gnagy: Learn to Draw*, and *Zoo Parade*.

One typical example of both the format for children's television and early educational programming came from WBNS-TV in Columbus,

Ohio. A CBS affiliate that went on the air in 1949, the station carried several locally produced children's programs in the first years including *Aunt Fran and Her Playmates*. Predating both *Ding Dong School* and *Romper Room*, Fran Norris, the creator and host of the show, conceived of the idea for a "kindergarten of the air" while she watched her young daughter sing commercial jingles. The program was on from 1950 to 1957 and had a wide following in the Columbus market. Using the tools Norris learned while training to be a teacher, the program included crafts, storytelling, cartoons, finger play, and musical games—the things of kindergarten. Reflecting the commercial nature of children's programs of the time, the children had milk from a local dairy for their snack time and Aunt Fran sold dolls for the local toy story (Pecora & Mack, 2001).

Although early children's programming was often sustaining (i.e., the network or station financed the cost of the show's production), others followed the model established by radio and were fully sponsored by an advertiser. For example, during this decade, *Matty's Funday Funnies* was brought to us by Mattel Toys and *Kellogg's Cereal Presents* was presented by Kellogg's Cereal. Nabisco continued its sponsorship of *Sky King* as it had on radio (*Barcus, 1977*).

Government Policy

The 1950s brought the Kefauver Hearings where Lazarsfeld gave his testimony leading to the comments that began this chapter. These government hearings were the first to include television, as previous hearings on youth media addressed primarily issues of violence in other media such as comic books or motion pictures.[8] According to Rowland (1983), "by the end of commercial television's first decade of full national service, politicians, broadcasters, and social scientists had begun to map out the terms of an alliance for approaching the issue of policymaking for the medium" (p. 113). Indeed Congress, again according to Rowland, "could use the rhetoric of science to transmit to broadcasters the opinions, whether real or perceived, that television programming was too often challenging the tolerances of national taste" (p. 113). We should not overlook the fact that

---

[8]It should be noted that there is also a long tradition of industry self-regulation represented by codes of conduct adopted by the networks and established by professional organizations such as the National Association of Broadcasters (NAB). These have generally been in response to public outcry. We are interested here only in government regulation because that is what is more likely to generate academic research.

the Kefauver Hearings, where Lazarsfeld testified on the state of research, were charged with identifying the "causes and contributing factors" of juvenile delinquency (cited in Rowland, 1983, p. 101). These hearings were the consequence of social concern over movies such as *Black Board Jungle* and *Rebel Without a Cause* and rock and roll music entering the youth culture, just as previous hearings were primarily concerned with the contribution of media content to children's potential for violence (*Pecora, 1998*; Rowland, 1983). With the encouragement of social scientists like Lazarsfeld there was now the promise of an answer. Scholars and entertainers alike were called to testify before Congress about this relationship between the mass media and the "youth problem." Kefauver was quoted as saying, in response, that the experts "are important in our investigation of this kind" (cited in Reeves & Baughman, 1983, p. 543).

The Research

The 1950s provided a series of firsts in research on children's television. Although there was a body of literature generated by earlier scholars working in radio and motion pictures, there was in fact little comparative research. *Bogart's* (*1956/1972a*) essay on early research is one exception. Consequently we know television, but not in comparison to previous children's media. Of the 88 studies from this decade, in the master bibliography, only slightly more than 15% consider children's media environment (*Banning, 1955; Barrow & Westley, 1959a, 1959b; Freidson, 1953; Kefauver, 1956; Lyness, 1951, 1952; Marx, 1953; Pittman, 1958; Roody, 1952; Witty, 1952a; Witty & Bricker, 1952*); the majority look at television in isolation. Unlike the first years of research, here only two studies could be considered to look at health: television causing bad dreams (*Ervy, 1952*) or addiction (*Meerlo, 1954*). Although the majority were concerned with use and preference or the impact on school, grades, and reading, a few take into account social variables such as gender (*Bailyn, 1959; Balogh, 1959; Lyness, 1952*), social status (*Albert & Meline, 1958; Banning, 1955; Freidson, 1953*), and ethnicity [Polish-American] (*Freidson, 1954*). *Guest* (*1955*) gave us one of the first studies on brand loyalty. *Maccoby's* (*1951*)[9] comprehensive study of "television" children and "nontelevision" children was based on interviews with 332 mothers. Maccoby examined questions of family TV ownership, children's viewing

---

[9]This study was presented by Maccoby to the Kefauver Committee.

including social context of experience, TV and homework, and displacement of other activities. She found, among other things, that TV viewing is not done as a children's group activity, that it interferes very little with homework, and that much of the viewing time is taken from play time rather than other activities. She went on to discuss the implications for children's psychological well-being and the implications for future work.

In one of the few comparative studies, Bailyn (1959) turned her attention to the cognitive effects of the media. Her concern was with the "specific cognitive aspects of the child: stereotyping, perception of threat, projected self-image, and passivity" (p. 2). She found two clusters of media users in her sample of more than 600 fifth- and sixth-grade children: those who were more likely to listen to radio and read books (the nonpictoral group) and those who were attracted to the pictoral media of television and motion pictures. Girls were more likely the former and boys the latter. Bailyn found there were gender and social class differences across the four dimensions studied. Her conclusion: "Such an effect [on cognitive functions] seems to exist when exposure is accompanied by certain psychological characteristics in the children themselves" (p. 37). In other words, there was some effect on some children under some conditions.

Although the academic research on youth and television during this decade was a relatively new phenomenon, many of the questions reflected our contemporary concerns: How much television do children view? What are its effects on children's cognitive skills? What is the relationship among television, youth, and violence? What are children's content preferences? What are the effects of advertising on issues of parental purchasing and brand loyalty?

TELEVISION COMES OF AGE: THE 1960s

The decade of the 1960s brought an era of social concern and turmoil that had interesting repercussions for the television industry. For the most part the industry continued to be dominated by the three networks; however, by the end of the decade public broadcasting became an alternative available in most homes. Notions of a Great Society brought us *Sesame Street* on the new public broadcasting outlets, an experiment in using television for social change; public broadcasting also brought *Mister Rogers' Neighborhood*. Both programs became the standard for children's preschool programming.[10] In addition, color television was introduced in the mid-1960s, among other consequences, making black-and-white theatrical cartoons obsolete and making way for the animation technique introduced by Hanna and Barbera in the late 1950s. This significantly reduced the cost of animation and moved cartoons from movie houses and adult fare to Saturday morning children's entertainment.

The Programs

In the early 1960s, according to *Shelby* (*1964*), the networks programmed an average of 23 hours per week of children's shows, a third of which were variety shows, more than half of them on weekdays. Also using the New York City market, *Palmer* (*1988*) reported an average number of 34 hours of programming per week.[11] What is striking about Palmer's figures, reinforced by *Turow* (*1981*), is the sharp decline in weekday programming. In the 1960 New York market, programming was almost equally divided between weekdays and Saturdays; by 1970, only 5 hours of programming could be found on weekdays and almost all programming for children was now on Saturday. *Turow* (*1981*) found that 61% of 1960 programming was on Saturday but by 1968–69, 83% was on Saturday. At the beginning of the decade, children's television was primarily live action, often studio productions, broadcast during many of the hours when children had free time.

By the end of the decade children were watching cartoons, but the 1960s began with a continuation of the programs of the 1950s that were often previously theatrical releases or similar serial adventures— *Adventures of Rin Tin Tin, The Lone Ranger, Annie Oakley,* and *Sky King* and *Captain Jet*. From 1960 to 1965 there were several educational programs: *Watch Mr. Wizard, Young People's Concerts, Discovery,* and *Captain*

---

[10]Most significant, the 1960s bring *Sesame Street* and a national public broadcasting system. The success of *Sesame Street* illustrated that educational programming could be entertaining and exciting— but best served commercial free. Created as a part of the social movement of the time and the Great Society President Lyndon Johnson hoped to build, the show was an immediate success. However the focus here is on commercial programming, as that is more often the subject of research. For a discussion of the contribution of *Sesame Street* see, for example, Fisch and Truglio (2001) or Mitang (2001).

[11]It is difficult to account for this discrepancy but it indicates a problem of doing meta-analysis. Shelby used listings obtained from *Broadcasting* and *Sponsor* magazines for January of each year and the data were a part of his Ohio State University doctoral dissertation; Palmer used data reported by ACT with no attribution of source.

Kangaroo. Puppet shows also still dominated the marketplace with *Howdy Doody, Kukla Fran and Ollie, Shari Lewis*, and *Fireball XL-5*. However, it was in this decade that cartoons came to be defined as children's entertainment. With the introduction of a new "limited animation" technique from Hanna-Barbera, the number of cartoons during children's television hours increased from 23% of the children's series in 1960–61 to 86% of these programs in 1968–69. Gone were the cowboys and space cadets to be replaced by an animated version of the Beatles, *The Flintstones*, and *George of the Jungle*. Nonfiction and variety shows were replaced by action-adventures; westerns were replaced by police dramas (*Turow 1981*). At the local level, Captain Jim or Big Brother Bob continued to sell peanut butter with the cartoons at lunchtime or after school and the franchised *Romper Room* filled the local station hours.

Most interesting, perhaps, was the shift in advertising support. By the late 1950s there were no longer sustaining programs; all children's television programs were supported by advertising dollars. According to *Shelby* (1964), this was the consequence of increased advertising budgets in the toy industry. *Turow's* (1980) research supported this shift in advertising and programming relationships demonstrating that, during the 1950s there was a steady decline in sustaining support by the networks; by the 1960s there was virtually none. Full sponsorship of a show declined from 61% in 1960–61 to 4% by 1968–69. Turow argued this shift was the result of increased television ownership (the industry no longer needed to woo children), the increased availability of advertising dollars for children's television, and the rising cost of television programming making it necessary to share the cost among more players.

Shelby (1964), in one of the few early studies of the children's television industry, argued that there was a "period of adjustment" between 1958 and 1963 when the industry responded to an increasing government concern with the lack of quality in children's television, particularly after the "vast wasteland" speech by FCC Chairman Newton Minow. The speech, presented to the National Association of Broadcasters in May 1961, reminded broadcasters of their public interest mandate, raising a concern for the violent content of television. In a footnote, Shelby pointed out that, in part, the demand for improved television quality was the outcome of social pressures not only from Minow and organizations like the National Parent–Teachers Association but also from the press. Congress was also pressuring the television industry to improve the quality of children's television, calling for a "far reaching" study that was an outcome of the subcommittee on juvenile delinquency headed by

Senator Thomas J. Dodd (Tougher Than It Seems, 1962). In announcing this study the Secretary of the Department of Health, Education, and Welfare stated:

> Out of this project, we hope, will come a better understanding of the effects of television upon young people, and data indicating how its rich potentials can best be utilized to help fulfill the special needs of children in this complex and changing world. (Tougher Than It Seems, 1962, p. 30)

Television was barely a decade old and already there were calls for reform. Debates on media violence carried over from the motion picture industry and concerns for the quality of children's television were the consequence of unmet possibilities of television as educator. Although there were threads of concern about the "quality" of children's programming, for the most part, the issues were defined around the violent nature of television.

The programs made for children in the 1960s were filled with super-heroes (*Mighty Mouse, Super Six,* and *Spiderman*) or variety shows (*The Banana Splits, Lunch With Soupy Sales*) but the television children watched in prime time was increasingly filled with news of rioting cities and the Vietnam War or police dramas.

Government Policy

This decade is perhaps most significant for more formally bringing together academics and policymakers, a carryover from the investment of social science during World War II (Rowland, 1983). Rowland (1983) argued that "members of Congress could use the rhetoric of science to transmit to broadcasters the opinion, whether real or perceived, that television programming was too often challenging the tolerance of national taste" while researchers found in Congress "the authoritative instrument for further legitimation of their normal science activities" (pp. 113–114). We were moving closer to the well-funded, centralized organization or foundation *Lazarsfeld* (1955) called for in his congressional testimony. As the 1960s ended the Senate Subcommittee on Communications, headed by Senator Joseph Pastore, agreed to support a study of television violence modeled on the Surgeon General's research on cigarette smoking.[12]

---

[12]The history of these events is best developed in other resources (Cooper, 1996; Murray & Salomon, 1984; Reeves & Baughman, 1983; Rowland, 1983).

The growing relationship between academics and policymakers was reflected in the proliferation of studies published in the literature. Using the data from an earlier version of this bibliography, Wartella and Reeves (1984) found the number of citations on the effects of television violence surged from less than ten between 1955 and 1970 to more than 40 after 1970. Although it is difficult to demonstrate a clear relationship between public concerns and academic interests, intuitively it would be obvious that the growing social violence of the 1960s would be manifest in academic research.

The Research

This bibliography demonstrates there is indeed an increase in the number of published research studies during the 1960s, with an average of eleven studies for the first 9 years and 22 published studies in 1969. More important, during the first years of the 1960s, academic attention was on the relationship of family and television (*Appell, 1960; Becker & Wolfe, 1960; Belson, 1960; Blood, 1961; Mehling, 1960; Niven, 1960*) by the end of the 1960s attention had turned toward violence and aggression (*Arnold, 1969; Bandura, 1968; Cowden, Bassett & Cohen, 1969; Geen, 1968; Geen & Berkowitz, 1967; Gordon, 1969; Klapper, 1968; Larsen, 1966; Larsen, Gray, & Fortis, 1968; Littner, 1969; Osburne & Hale, 1969; Zusne, 1968*).

One of the seminal works that made important contributions to the policy debate during this time was *Television in the Lives of Our Children* (*Schramm, Lyle, & Parker, 1961b*). The study surveyed almost 6,000 students, some who did not yet receive television, and about 2,000 parents. According to Reeves and Baughman (1983), FCC Chairman Newton Minow read the book and used its conclusions as his platform that television was not "realizing its full potential as a carrier of ideas and information" (Schramm, et al., 1961, cited in Reeves & Baughman, 1983, p. 545). *Television in the Lives of Our Children* was one of the last studies that could compare non-TV homes because, by 1960, almost 90% of the homes in the United States had a television receiver.

This decade also saw the beginnings of research on children as consumers with the work of *Gilkison* (1965) on teen buying decisions and *Well's* (1966) and *McNeal's* (1969) work on children's consumer behavior. Although there was some attempt to describe children's consumer behavior during the days of radio and market research firms for teens were established in the 1950s, these were the first attempts to understand television as a marketing tool (*Pecora, 1998*). Academics were also responding to the social climate of the time as they considered questions about class (*Keller, 1963*), or race as a variable (*Fletcher, 1969; Gerson, 1966*), and children's reactions to the Kennedy assassination (*Sigel, 1965*). Only two studies examined the media industries: The first was the *Shelby (1964)* study of programming and the second was the report on local television programming from the Television Information Office (*Garry, Rainsberry, & Winick, 1962*).[13]

In addition to the *Schramm et al.* (*1961*) study, perhaps one of the major contributions of this decade was the research of *Bandura* (*1965, 1968*), which has served as the dominant model for the continued research on social learning both in the context of aggressive behavior and later socialization research on gender and consumerism.

ACCOMMODATION AND ADJUSTMENT: THE 1970s

The 1970s saw little change in the economics or structure of broadcast television and Saturday morning continued to rule children's television. It was a period in television history of "accommodation and adjustment" (Sterling & Kittross, 1990, p. 373). However, although little changed in programming format, it was an active period of debate within Congress and the FCC. In the mid-1970s the FCC instituted the PrimeTime Access Rule (PTAR) and the Financial and Syndication Ruling (Fin-Syn) in an attempt to break up the networks' control over prime-time programming and the syndication market. This resulted in the growth of independent television stations, those not affiliated with the networks and a strong syndication market. In 1975 there were fewer than 100 independent stations; 10 years later there were more than 600 stations all needing programming to fill their on-air hours (*Pecora, 1998*). This had little consequence on the children's market during the 1970s but it set the stage for major changes in the 1980s—more on that later.

No doubt, the most important influence on children's television during the 1970s was Action for Children's Television (ACT), a citizen's advocacy group, founded in the winter of 1967. The group submitted their first petition to the FCC in 1970 requesting age-specific programming and advertising limits in children's television viewing (*McGregor*,

---

[13]The Television Information Office report was included here even though it does not strictly meet the criteria for inclusion because there were so few reports on the industry structure or programming decisions.

1986; Sarson, 1970). They had done their homework by analyzing the commercials on the popular *Romper Room* and found that, as one mother said, "That's no program—that's one long commercial" (Sarson, 1970, p. 51). This experience, and the recognition that violence and conflict were used to get children's attention, led the group to a series of actions. Among these were their testimony at Senate hearings appointing new FCC commissioners and at the hearings held by Senator Pastore to amend the Communications Act (Sarson 1970). Throughout the 1970s, in response to the ACT petitions, the FCC held hearings and conducted research[14] on the implications and consequences of regulating children's television. Unfortunately by the end of the decade it was evident that, for the most part, the government's strategy was industry compliance, not regulation. In addition to the petition filed with the FCC (Docket 19142), ACT was instrumental in bringing advertising practices to the attention of the FTC (*Kunkel & Roberts, 1991*). Causality is difficult to prove; however there is no doubt that the work of ACT changed the public agenda on children's television research. Violence was still a part of that debate, but throughout the 1970s academic researchers turned their attention to developmental and cognitive questions and the investigation of children's advertising content.

In the meantime, The Surgeon General's report was released in 1972. This five-volume report contained 40 papers that addressed the issue of violence on television. One can't do justice to the magnitude of work that came from the Surgeon General's report but its consequences are far reaching.[15] In many ways it has defined the discipline for several generations because the scholars involved in the Surgeon General's Study went on to research and write in the field of children's television. These scholars, in turn, have trained the next generation of scholars. A second outcome of the Surgeon General's report was the introduction of the concept of "prosocial" television. Although this was not the first time television (or radio) was discussed in the context of "doing good," it was the beginning of the debate framed as prosocial. One social scientist of the time, in a speech to the American Psychological Association, argued that the

---

[14]During the 1970s the FCC commissioned a number of reports, the most comprehensive of which came from the Children's Television Task Force. This five-volume report included an analysis of programming aired during the 1973–74 and 1977–78 season; nonprogram material aired on Saturday mornings and program separators; an economic analysis of advertising-supported television; alternative media and technologies; and an review of the research on the relationship between age and television.

[15]There are a number of summaries available, for example, *Atkin, Murray, and Nayman (1971).*

term was making its way into discussions of what television ought to be (Milavsky, 1974). As he stated:

> The new exhortation is that television programming be more pro-social. The idea that television can be more pro-social is a seductive and disarming prospect, both to those within and to those outside of the industry. At a time when it appears to many that our institutions are failing to cope with our many social problems, either out of the short comings of those occupying positions in control of the institutions, or out of the institutions' failure to adapt to a change society, the prospect that television could help is a very appealing one. (p. 8)

He went on to point out that his concern was not with television doing good but with the dangers of scoring programs based on the content categories of one's notion of good.

Milavsky's concern aside, prosocial has become the catchphrase for children's television programming.[16]

The Programs

Little of substance changed in early 1970s children's programming. Saturday was still prime viewing time and cartoons continued to be the program of choice with an occasional live action-adventure or old, off-network situation comedy. In 1970, only one regularly scheduled commercial program was broadcast on weekdays (*Captain Kangaroo*) and almost 80% of the programming was animation (*Turow, 1981*).[17] By the latter part of the decade the number of live action programs doubled (15% compared to 36%) and the previous half-hour-length programming had been replaced by 60- or 90-minute shows that served as an umbrella for several stand-alone series (*All New Superfriends Hour, The Batman/Tarzan Adventure Hour*, and *Scooby's Laff-a-Lympics*; Grossman, 1987; *Turow, 1981*).

Perhaps in response to the climate of the time, CBS (*In the Know*) and ABC (*Multiplication Rock*, later *Schoolhouse Rock*) programmed educational interstitials during Saturday mornings (*Turow, 1981*). According to Turow these 5-minute, commercial-like segments appeared in

---

[16]It must be remembered that *prosocial* was not a word used to describe children's television in the early 1970s. Even *Sesame Street* was concerned with children's cognitive skills, not altruism or socialization.

[17]Turow's work on television programming was an extension of his contribution to the Surgeon General's report.

1971—coincidentally the year of the first FCC hearings responding to ACT. Live action returned briefly with *Shazam*, *Land of the Lost*, *The Secret of Isis*, *Far Out Space Nuts*, and *Run Joe Run*. The networks saw the live action, situation comedies like *Far Out Space Nuts* as the "best alternatives to the violent cartoon shows"; unfortunately they seldom lasted more than a season (Davis, 1995, p. 107). For the most part, parents and children turned to the Public Broadcasting System (PBS) for alternative programming, where the success of *Sesame Street* and *Mister Rogers' Neighborhood* beget *Zoom* and *The Electric Company*.

Milavsky's prophecy about prosocial television was coming true, as previously well-established cartoons like *Popeye* and *Mighty Mouse* ended their episodes with useful advice like avoiding electrical sockets and encouraging viewers to vegetables (Erickson, 1995).

Diversity, if you will, came in the form of *The Harlem Globetrotters* on CBS in 1970, the first cartoon series to star African American characters. ABC followed the next year with *The Jackson Five* (Davis, 1995). Minorities were increasingly represented in what was once an all-White world: a Native American in *Sealab 2020*; *Kid Power*; *I Am the Greatest*, an animated program featuring Muhammad Ali; and Bill Cosby's *Fat Albert* (Erickson, 1995; Grossman, 1987). Gender diversity was also a part of this decade. During the 1950s and 1960s the title character or host was almost always male; by 1978 only 47% of the series had a male host (*Turow, 1981*). This is not to say that the other 53% were female but that the decline in male hosts reflected the number of series that had no title character and the number in which there were both a female and male title character (*Archie and Sabrina*, *Shazam/Isis Hour*, or *Super Friends*; Turow, 1981). The few programs in which girls were the host or title character included *Josie and the Pussycats*; *Sabrina, the Teenage Witch*; *Super Witch*; and *Pebbles and Bamm Bamm*: a rock star, two witches, and a toddler. Clearly, the changes in 1970s children's television reflected both the political and social events of the time.

New things were happening by the end of the decade with the introduction of the Cartoon Network, Nickelodeon, and the Disney Channel on cable television, but for the most part, these new venues did little to change children's television until the 1980s.

The Research

Academic publications presented in the bibliography demonstrate the swell of research conducted during the 1970s. Not including the 40 projects generated by the Surgeon General's report, more than 550 studies were published on children and television between 1970 and 1979, compared to 126 in the 1960s. There were an average of 13 studies per year in the decade of the 1960s and an average of 56 studies per year in the 1970s; from 18 research projects in 1970 before the publication of the Surgeon General's report to 105 in 1979.

The work of academics during this decade very much reflects the findings of *Luke* (1990), who argued that this decade "began a subtle shift toward theoretical positions that conceptualized TV (and other mass media) as cultural product and audiences as embedded within and socialized by a cultural apparatus, of which TV was only one, albeit influential, socializing agency"(p. 174). This translated into the concept of an active audience and led to a cognitive model of childhood. Research during this era began to apply Piaget's cognitive development theory and Bandura's social learning (Bryant & Miron, 2004). Although traditional effects research did not disappear, much of it was replaced by attempts to understand and give credibility to children as active participants in the media experience.[18]

Violence and aggression were still a part of the questions addressed during this decade, although only a small percentage of the research by the end. In 1970, over 25% of the studies were on violence; in 1979, only 5% of the studies were on violence. The concern for media violence was replaced by variables on race, class, gender, or advertising and consumer behavior. Continuing the trend from the 1960s, throughout the decade a number of academics used social class and race as a content variable or socializing agency. As *Luke* (1990) found, during this decade,

> The audience was reexamined and found to represent subgroups previously unaccounted for, and effects were reconceptualized from short-term behavioral outcomes to long-term socializing influences on morals, values, attitudes, and perceptions of social reality. Toward the end of the decade, the child viewer underwent a subtle reconceptualization, from a behavioral response mechanism to one who interacted from TV's form and content on the basis of, inter alia, developing cognitive abilities. (p. 174)

Questions such as media functions among low-income adolescents (*Dominick & Greenberg, 1970; Gorn & Goldberg, 1977*) or the urban poor (*Greenberg, Dervin, Dominick, & Bowes, 1970*) or studies on the effects of

---

[18]*Luke* (1990) also acknowledged, but gave no explanation for, the tremendous growth and diversity of research during this decade.

race in social learning (*Donohue, 1975a, 1975b; Hayes, McWilliams, & Hayes, 1977; Neeley, Heckel, & Leichtman, 1973; Nicholas, McCarter, & Heckel, 1971a, 1971b; Thalen, 1971*) represent some of the 30 studies that interrogated these issues. In 1974, attention turned to issues of gender in children's television with eight studies in that year where almost none had occurred previously. Content variables such as sex-role stereotyping and images were the first questions explored (*Beuf, 1974; Busby, 1974, 1975; Long & Simon, 1974; O'Kelly, 1974; Seidenberg, 1974; Sternglanz & Serbin, 1974*). Images dominated the research for the rest of the decade (*Busby, 1975; Dohrmann, 1975; Friedman, 1977; Lemon, 1977; Mathes, 1976; Miles, 1975; O'Kelly & Bloomquist, 1976; Verna; 1975*); a few studies asked the question of what girls were recognizing or learning from these role models (*Davidson, Yasuna, & Tower, 1979; Lull, Hanson, & Marx, 1977*). This was the beginning of assumptions of an active audience.

Research on advertising and commercial content also increased during this time. In the 1950s there were only two studies on television advertising (*Brumbaugh, 1954; Eakin, 1955*). During the 1960s, only two specifically addressed children's advertising (*Masson, 1965; Thompson, 1964*) and three considered children (*McNeal, 1969; Wells, 1966*) or teens (*Gilkison, 1965*) as consumers. However, in the 1970s, 57 or almost 10% of the research was on advertising or consumer behavior. This included research on health and medicines (*Korn, 1978; Lewis & Lewis, 1975; Milavsky, Pekowski, & Stipp, 1975–1976; Payne, 1976; Robertson, Rossiter, & Gleason, 1979a, 1979b; Seidenberg, 1974*) and parental mediation (*Burr & Burr, 1977a; Reid & Frazer, 1979*).[19] Also, children came to be defined as consumers during this decade particularly with the work of Rossiter, Wackman, Ward, and Wartella, (*Calder, Robertson, & Rossiter, 1975; Churchill & Moschio, 1979; Moore & Stephens, 1975; Stampfl, Moschis, Lawton, 1978; Ward & Wackman, 1971; Ward, Wackman, Faber, & Lesser, 1974; Ward, Wackman & Wartella, 1977; Wartella, Wackman, Ward, Shamir, & Alexander, 1979*).

Milavsky's (1974) concern about the consequences of prosocial research came to be as fourteen studies addressed prosocial television— no doubt more addressed the issue but these were the studies that used the term as a part of the title, giving it credibility. According to Milavsky, the term came from work by *Friedrich and Huston-Stein* (1973) that was part of the Surgeon General's report. In the bibliography here it is cited as

---

[19]To remind the reader, this is not a definitive list of the work in the field but a representative sample of the research.

"Aggressive and Prosocial Television Programs and the Natural Behavior of Preschool Children," published as a monograph by the Society for Research in Child Development. *Morris, Marshall, and Miller* (1973) used the term prosocial in their work, "The Effect of Vicarious Punishment on Prosocial Behavior in Children."

McLuhan's theory of the media found its way to children's television research with the work of *Balance, Coughlin, and Bringmann* (1972) titled "Examination of Social Context Effects Upon Affective Responses to 'Hot' and 'Cool' Communication Media." Early media literacy research is evident in the publications of "Children's Literate Television Viewing" (*Cohen & Salomon*, 1979) and "The Relationship of Visual Attention to Children's Comprehension of Television" (*Lorch, Anderson, & Levin*, 1979). Although a media-literate society was not a new concept, *Witty and Bricker* (1952) offered parents ways to help children "build critical judgment," and little had been done to address the topic in children's television until this time.

Finally, it should be noted that several of the projects in the bibliography were commissioned by ACT, primarily the work of F. Earle Barcus and *Melody's* (1973) book, *Children's Television: The Economics of Exploitation*. This book was one of the first and only studies of children's television to investigate the economic structure of the industry and the relationship between advertisers and networks.

As we go into the next decade, television is well established as a part of children's lives and children's television is defined as advertiser-supported, network animated programs mostly on Saturday morning and sometimes Sunday. The Surgeon General's report, like the Payne Fund studies of the 1930s, set the agenda for the decade, not so much for the questions asked but for the way children are considered. Academic research is less driven by questions of effects and media violence but now more likely to think of children as active participants in the interpretation and construction of meaning in the viewing experience. Interestingly, no doubt in response to the growing feminist movement, there was a particular point in time (1974) when gendered research appeared. Perhaps most remarkable was the introduction of the concept of prosocial and the limited attention paid to the economics of the industry.

CABLE AND HOME VIDEO COME OF AGE: THE 1980s

According to Wartella and Mazzarella (1990), the 1980s were marked by a series of books that explored the changing nature of childhood (e.g.,

Elkind, 1981; Meyrowitz, 1985; Postman, 1982). Building on the work of these authors, who argued children's leisure was at once becoming commodified and dominated by television, Wartella and Mazzarella (1990) wrote, "During the twentieth century independent, autonomous youth cultures developed around leisure activities, and that the mass media became the social catalysts promoting, sustaining, and commercializing the leisure of each succeeding youth culture" (p. 173). Comparing research on children's leisure beginning at the turn of the century and through the 1980s they found that over time children's leisure had indeed become commodified as the media "intrudes into other parts of their leisure time by providing the source and objects of their play" (p. 188) reinforced by the introduction of home video viewing during this decade. They also pointed to the changing nature of childhood, as increasingly peers and peer-oriented popular culture gain in importance. This concept of youth culture as "increasingly autonomous, peer-oriented, and commercialized" (p. 189) became even more evident during the 1980s when videocassettes, and cable, and toy-based programs entered the landscape of children's media.

During this decade, policy debates on children's television initiated by ACT in 1970 were put to rest when Mark Fowler was appointed Chairman of the FCC. The *Report and Order*, issued in 1984, closed the debate (*Uscinski, 1984*). Although Fowler believed there should be quality children's programming (Clark, 2004) it was his argument that market demand would create a place for it. Unfortunately he had not read the work of *Roberson* (*1981*) and *Valdez* (*1981*), who maintained that there was no economic incentive to program for children. Regulatory debates during this period continued, however, with particular attention paid to the practice of product tie-ins, much like host-selling of earlier days. Even as legislation about children's television continued to be introduced in Congress, ACT took the debate to the federal courts challenging the FCC's inaction (*Aufderheide, 1989*). By the end of the decade, with Fowler no longer chairman, the FCC again turned its attention to children's television. In the meantime, Congress was working on The Children's Television Act to legislate what the FCC failed to accomplish.

Violence was still very much a part of the public debate, with hearings in both the House and Senate. In the mid-1980s, antitrust regulation that constrained the major networks from working together was set aside after a contentious fight so the networks could develop policies limiting television violence (Cooper, 1996). During this time the American Psychological Association and the American Academy of Pediatrics also released reports pointing to the dangers of television violence (Cooper, 1996). However, for the most part, Congress and the FCC were quiet on the issue of children's television regulation although the concern for more age-specific programming was being met by the industry itself.

The Programs

For the first 30 years, the network broadcast stations dominated the children's television industry. Strong local independent stations like WGN in Chicago offered some competition or counterprogramming for the weekday afternoon but for the most part the child audience belonged to the networks. Then along came cable.

Writing just after an FCC ruling that called for cable operators to originate programming "in the public interest," Tropp (1970) encouraged for cable operators to address the needs of two constituents: communities and children. It took almost 10 years for the first children's cable network, Nickelodeon, to be launched, bringing network television serious competition for children. Cable's initial growth was slow as access to cable was dependent on a number of factors. For example, when Tropp was writing, only 8% of American homes had cable, which was then serving primarily as a distribution outlet for network signals. In 1979, when Nickelodeon was first aired, only 18% of homes had cable; by the middle of the 1980s about half of all homes had cable service (Sterling & Kittross, 1990). By the end of the 1980s, both Nickelodeon and the Disney Channel were well established as children's television venues and cable joined syndication in offering "alternatives" to network programming (Pecora, 2004).

Most noteworthy during this decade was the introduction of the Smurfs on NBC Saturday morning television and their influence on the television and toy industries. Although merchandising licensing agreements were not new, none had met with the success of the Smurfs. A series of events including Reagan-era economics and the growth of independent television stations, set the stage for the bond between the television and toy industries (*Erickson, 1998; Pecora, 1998*). Within the decade the number of children's cartoons on independent television stations tied to merchandising grew from none in 1982 to nine 3 years later (*Pecora, 1998*). Although the FCC's "no-host selling" regulation kept such programming to a minimum on the networks, the public debate during this decade came to be defined around licensed characters. Reagan's appointment to the FCC, Mark Fowler, closed down Docket 19142, which had been introduced by ACT in the early 1970s, arguing that the marketplace would determine children's programming needs (*McGregor, 1986*). To an extent, he was right: Children's programming came into demand because of the growing number of new, independent stations that relied on syndicated programming. By the end of the decade, the children's television and toy markets were dominated by story lines built around multiple characters designed to sell—programming became a showcase for licensed products. Programs such as *Care Bears, Rainbow Brite*, and *The Snorks* built on the success of *The Smurfs*.

The Research

Research on children and television during the 1980s continued to grow, with 118 studies in 1980, the most in any single year under consideration here, and an average of 68 studies per year over the decade. In part, this spike is accounted for by an increase in the number of edited books specifically on children and television published in 1980 (*Adler et al., 1980; Palmer & Dorr, 1980; Withey & Abeles, 1980*); these edited volumes accounted for 22 of the 1980 studies. Prior to then, there had been only two edited books on children and television research (*Kline & Clarke, 1971; Wartella, 1979*). It would seem that book publishers began to recognize a growing market for this work and were willing to invest in its publication.

The research during this decade reflected, in many ways, the work that had come before: media effects and viewing patterns, violence, advertising, and race and gender. Television was now a well-established medium and several retrospectives were published during this decade including the foundation to this book, Murray's (1980) book, *Television and Youth: 25 Years of Research & Controversy*. Anticipating more current concerns, one study addressed television's role in childhood obesity (*Dietz & Gortmaker, 1985*) and another focused on video games[20] (*Dominick, 1984*).

Again, as with previous decades, many of the questions asked about children and television in the 1980s were concerned with the violent nature of the medium. During the 1980s these questions addressed content areas (*Boemer, 1984; Celozzi, Kazelskis, & Gustch, 1981; Cohen & Adoni, 1980; Comstock, 1986; Cramer & Mecham, 1982; Dominick, 1984;*

---

[20]The parameters for this bibliography were television and children, therefore only those studies that were comparative would have appeared in any search. However, this 1984 study is certainly among the first of any of the research on video games.

Gadow & Sprafkin, 1987; Gerbner & Gross, 1980; Liss & Reinhardt, 1980), antisocial behavior (Doolittle, 1980; Gadow & Sprafkin, 1989; Huesmann & Malamuth, 1986; Lovelace & Huston 1982; Roloff & Greenberg, 1980), and gendered differences, although some research unfortunately assumed no differences between male and female response to aggression (Cantor & Orwant, 1980; Donnerstein, 1980). Several reviews were produced that allowed us to place these concerns in context including Adler (1980), Comstock (1980a, 1980b), Gerbner and Gross (1980), O'Bryan (1980), Rubinstein (1980), Turow (1980), Withey and Abeles (1980), Collins (1981a), Meyer and Nissen (1981), Turow (1981), Wolf, Hexamer, and Meyer (1982), Fosarelli (1984), Wartella and Reeves (1985), Friedrich-Cofer and Huston (1986), Hearold (1986), Meadowcroft and McDonald (1986), Freedman (1988), and Heath, Bresolin, and Rinaldi (1989).

Research on advertising and commercialization also dominated the work of this decade. As in the 1970s, several studies addressed the issue of drugs both over the counter and tobacco and alcohol (Martin & Duncan, 1984; Orlandi, 1989; Rossiter & Robertson, 1980; Sheiman, 1980). Others were concerned with the nutritional value of food advertised to children (Bolton, 1983; Dawson, Walsh, & Jeffrey, 1988; Galst, 1980; Jeffrey, McLellarn, & Fox, 1982; Lambo, 1981; Palmer & McDowell, 1981) and one of the first studies on the relationship between children and obesity was Jeffrey, McLellarn, and Fox's (1982) study on television and children's eating habits. Two other studies on obesity that were prescienct were the work of Dietz and Gortmaker (1985) and Dietz (1986). Alperowicz (1984) and Kunkel (1988a, 1988b) were among the few that reflected a concern with the relationship between the licensed toy and television industries.

Gender and race continued to be important questions throughout the 1980s. Building on research initiated during the 1970s, questions of gendered images continued to be addressed during this decade. An average of three projects a year spoke to program content (Barcus, 1983; Feldstein & Feldstein, 1982; Harris & Voorhees, 1981; Riffe, Goldson, Saxton, & Yu, 1989) or children's modeling of gendered roles (Christenson & Roberts, 1983; Durkin, 1985; Eisenstock, 1984; Jeffries-Fox & Jefferies-Fox, 1981; Morgan, 1987). Those doing research on diversity were most likely to consider a group's television preferences (Liss, 1981; Newby, Robinson, & Hill, 1980; Weber & Fleming, 1984) or television as a socialization agent (Atkin, Greenberg, & McDermott, 1983; Berry & Mitchell-Kernan, 1982; Meyer & Hexamer, 1981; Stroman, 1984). Although neither gender (4%) nor race (3%) was a major part of the research during this decade, these projects contributed to the growing body of work on television's role in socialization.

Although there had long been an attempt to understand visual literacy as we did print literacy and to teach children to 'read' visual images,[21] such ideas were not part of the research on children and television until the 1980s. The first such study appears to have been conducted by *Sudano* (*1978*). However, by 1989, a further 15 research projects promoted the idea of a television literacy. These were seen as intervention programs (*Collins, 1982; Feshbach, Feshbach, & Cohen, 1982; Roberts, 1982*) for middle school children (*Bilowit & Ganek, 1980; Rapaczynski, Singer, & Singer, 1982*), high school students (*Hall, 1980*), emotionally disturbed children (*Sprafkin, Gadow, & Kant, 1987*), and the gifted (*Abelman, 1995a*). *Liebert, Sprafkin, and Davidson* (*1982*) identified the work of *Dorr, Graves, and Phelps* (*1980*) as among the first of these attempts to develop these critical intervention curricula in the classroom.

Theoretically and methodologically, the research on children's television began to be influenced by the growing paradigmatic shift brought about by a growing body of research in cultural studies. *Alexander, Ryan, and Munoz's* (*1984*) ethnography of sibling viewing, *Dunn and Cardwell's* (*1984*) use of symbolic interaction, *Kinder's* (*1984*) analysis of audience as spectator, and *Lemish* (1987) and *Messaris* (1987a) were all early examples of this work. *Wartella* (*1987a*), in her commentary on qualitative research on children's media, noted that there is a history of qualitative work beginning with the early Chicago School; however, in children's media research the field has been dominated by the traditions of social science. The work of those previously mentioned, and particularly Lemish and Messaris, according to Wartella, return us to the intellectual traditions of naturalistic observation associated with the Chicago School. Throughout the 1980s qualitative research and cultural studies began to establish a place in the discipline including research on children and television.

Overall, the 1980s saw continued growth in the research on children and television with a wide range of questions addressing television's effects on behavior, attitudes, and cognitive skills. Advertising and consumerism and television violence were persistent questions joined by concerns with prosocial behavior and issues of race and gender. During the 1980s scholars turned their attention to ways that children could be inoculated against what was seen as the unplanned educational curriculum (*Berry, 1980a*) of television. However, the questions raised by Lazarsfeld were still seldom addressed. It would appear only *Palmer* (*1987a*) examined

---

[21]Among others, the Payne Fund studies of the early 1930s promoted the idea of teaching children to learn to "read" the motion pictures.

the creative process, although several researchers considered the role of the economic marketplace (*Valdez, 1981; Watkins, 1987*) and several focused on the regulatory process (*Aufderheide, 1989; Goff & Goff, 1982; Kunkel, 1988a, 1988b; Kunkel & Watkins, 1987; Rubinstein, 1983; Tucker & Saffelle, 1982*). Perhaps in an interesting case of hubris, one study examined the television viewing rules in the homes of media scholars (*Bybee, Robinson, & Turow, 1982*). For the most part, the 1980s brought little new in the way of research on children and television.

TELEVISION AS CULTURE: THE 1990s

Between the late 1940s and the early 1990s both television and children had changed dramatically. Where children of the early television era were not likely to begin school until they were 5 or 6, by 1990 almost half of the children in the United States were enrolled in a preschool program (U.S. Department of Education, 2001). Social changes such as this increase in school enrollment, the introduction of school busing, and the rise of the dual-income family all contributed to the changing nature of the child audience. For the most part, during this time young children's lives were much more structured around after-school programs and organized activities (Mintz, 2004). According to Mintz, in 2004 "about 44% of sixteen- and seventeen-year-old males and 42% of females [held] jobs, compared to 29% of boys and 18% of girls in 1953" (p. 348). Most of their jobs were low-paying work in the service industries, but these positions allowed them the disposable income that contributed to the growing commercialization of this population. According to one report, spending by and for children rose from $60 billion in 1989 to $75 billion 2 years later (Heuton, 1990).

During the 1990s we saw the continued consumerization of childhood, as junior brands of many adult products and merchandise were available for children or marketed to them. As in the 1950s, automobile manufacturers marketed their cars to children and young adults. In addition, a new market was identified—tweens who were seen as consumers for a wide range of products from computers and automobiles to personal care products to fast foods. For example, fast-food advertisers increased their spending 64% in 1 year (Freeman, 1992).

Children's programming in the 1990s continued to expand. We entered the decade with cable and home video well established: 56% of homes had cable and they received about 33 channels; VCR ownership rose to 65% of all television households (Sterling & Kittross, 2002).

However, during this decade other forms of technology, particularly the Internet, changed the landscape. Whereas at the beginning of the decade two thirds of all viewers watched the networks and about 20% of viewers watched pay and basic cable, by the late 1990s network viewing was down to 54% and cable accounted for 41% of television viewing (Sterling & Kittross, 2002). In addition to Saturday morning on the traditional networks, children now had available a growing syndication market, Nickelodeon, the Disney Channel, the Fox Children's Network (FCN), and the Cartoon Network. This competition created a demand that was being met by new production houses (Freeman, 1992; Heuton, 1990). Programming and program availability was at an all-time high.

The new tween audience created a genre of programming and a return to live action after years of programming dominated by animation and old reruns. For example, Nickelodeon introduced Nick at Nite, a series of original half-hour, live-action programs for the tween audience. One could begin to see the networks abdicate their programming responsibilities to public broadcasting and cable as ABC scheduled a 2-hour adult morning talk show during Saturday morning programming and others debated following ABC's lead.

Policy Issues of the 1990s

Most notable during this decade was the passage of the 1990 Children's Television Act. After more than 4 decades of hearings, meetings, and lobbying going back to the Kefauver Hearings, Congress finally passed a bill setting standards for children's television. The Act called for age-specific programming, deemed FCC-friendly, and limits on advertising minutes. The FCC was to provide oversight and review a station's contribution to "educational and informational programming" at license renewal time. In late 1993 the FCC began hearings to revisit the Act after concern about the broadcasters' interpretation of the provisions. By the mid-1990s, more rigorous guidelines were established both for the quantity and quality of programming required to meet the guidelines. The Three-Hour Rule was put in place in the mid-1990s, to strengthen the Children's Television Act and define educational programming (McAvoy, 1993). Other legislative events occurred during this decade, including the passage of the Telecommunications Act of 1996, which required manufacturers to include a V-chip in all new televisions allowing for blocking programs parents felt were inappropriate. However, none had the impact of the Children's Television Act. Although the Act was to encourage new and creative "FCC-friendly" programs, in fact, by the end of the decade children's broadcast television had changed little.

Research of the 1990s

The rate of research declined slightly during the 1990s, with about 600 studies reported compared to the high of approximately 670 during the 1980s. As in previous years, the research was reported in a wide range of journals from many disciplines. During this decade scholars continued to address the concerns of television violence in terms of content (*Anderson, 1997; Rajecki et al., 1994; Valkenburg & Janssen, 1999*), but far more often the focus was on effects of such content (e.g., *Derksen & Strasburger, 1996; Donner 1990; Gadow & Sprafkin, 1993; Huesmann & Miller, 1994; Kalamas & Gruber, 1998; Krcmar & Valkenburg, 1999; Murray, 1994; Wood, Wong, & Chachere, 1991; Zillmann, Bryant, & Huston, 1994*). In addition, Kelly (*1999*) produced a comprehensive guide to the literature on violence and several studies in this area were international in scope (*Chiland, Young, & Kaplan, 1994; Palermo, 1995*). Only one study set out to distinguish gender differences in television violence viewing (*Eron, 1992*). Perhaps most notable was the increase in work that addresses policy responses to media violence. As Congress debated the Telecommunications Act of 1996, several projects reviewed the efficacy of the V-chip (*Abelman, 1999; Cantor, 1998a, 1998c; Healy, 1995; McDowell & Maitland, 1998; Sneegas & Plank, 1998*). Others debated policy consequences on the First Amendment (*Ballard, 1995; Benedek & Brown, 1999; Minow & LaMay, 1995; Schneider, 1994*).

Prior to 1990, five studies addressed policy issues relating to children's television and for the most part they came from the Surgeon General's report. During the 1990s, in addition to the V-chip and First Amendment, approximately 25 studies considered the implications for government policy including advertising (*Lewin, 1990; Manrai, Manrai, & Murray, 1994; Martin, 1997; Riecken & Yavas, 1990*). Analysis of the Children's Television Act of 1990 is best represented by the work of *Kunkel (1991, 1993, 1998), Hayes (1994), Knell (1995), Snyder (1995),* and *Sullivan and Jordan (1999)*. Other exemplars of policy research include *Palmer and MacNeil (1991), Murray (1995),* and *Wilcox and Kunkel (1996)*.

Gender and race and ethnicity research (more than 100 studies) received much more attention during this decade than did violence and aggression (80 studies). Two edited books, *Media, Sex and the Adolescent*

(Greenberg, Brown, & Buerkel-Rothfuss, 1991) and *Children and Television: Images in a Changing Sociocultural World* (Asamen & Berry, 1993) contributed to this debate. As in the past, many of these studies addressed television content (Kolbe, 1990; Moore, 1992; Remafedi, 1990; Thompson & Zerbinos, 1995) or socialization (Berry, 1998; Bush, Smith, & Martin, 1999; German, 1994; Griffin, Shaikat, & Plotkin, 1994; Milkie, 1994;). Studies of body image and eating disorders, both gendered issues, began to appear during this decade (Botta, 1999; Dietz, 1993; Fingerson, 1999; Myers & Biocca, 1992; Ogletree, Williams, Raffeld, Mason, & Fricke, 1990), as did work on adolescent sexuality represented by the work of Bearinger (1990), Brown, Childers, and Waszak (1990).

John (1999) contributed a comprehensive retrospective on consumer socialization in her analysis of research from 1974 to 1999. Although research on marketing to children existed previously (e.g., Guest, 1955), she claimed the publication of the *Journal of Consumer Research* and the work of Ward (1971) gave a "focus to a new generation of researchers and an emerging field of study pertaining to children as consumers" (p. 183).

Comparative work on new technologies and television was still minimal (Calvert, 1999a; Coffey & Stipp, 1997; Kinder, 1991; Kubey, 1996; Kubey & Larson, 1990), although as *Wartella and Reeves* (1984) pointed out, when a new technology enters, the research agenda shifts from the older to the newer technology so one would expect to find few comparative studies. Nonetheless, in the 1990s television began to be replaced by other forms of technology and initial research was concerned with displacement (Brown, Childers, Bauman, & Koch, 1990; Coffey & Stipp, 1997; Dorr & Kunkel, 1990; Huston, Wright, Marquis, & Green, 1999) and, for example, children and parental beliefs about video games (Sneed & Runco, 1992). As a challenge to displacement, Coffey and Stipp (1997), using 1996 data, argued that home PC use for children 2 to 11 was so low that it did not "support the assumption that there is a new, computer-savvy generation that is turning away from television . . . and for the foreseeable future, PC-based activities will not have a strong impact on TV viewing" (p. 64).

The most significant changes that occurred in the 1990s were the central role qualitative work began to take during this decade. Although it was hinted at during the 1980s, work that approached the cultural context of childhood and a youth culture became much more established in the academy. A growing body of work represented by Henry Giroux, Larry Grossberg, and Lisa Lewis influenced by British cultural studies challenged the traditional assumptions in social science, and television was considered but one part of a youth culture. According to *Jenkins* (*1998*) this approach offers "a more complex account of children's own cultural lives" (p. 2). It is an approach that considers children as actively engaged in the construction and reception of the images offered up by television among other forms of popular communication. In this bibliography *Brown, Childers, and Waszak* (*1990*), *Brown and Newcomer* (*1991*), *Brown and Schulze* (*1993*), *Milkie* (*1994*), and *Lemish* (*1997*) spoke to new ways of considering children's reception of television and *Fisherkeller* (*1997*), among others, addressed the use of television to construct identity. *Lee* (*1991*), *Acland* (*1992*), and *Seiter* (*1990*) considered representations of race and gender. *Kline* (*1993*) and *Seiter's* (*1993*) classic texts of this decade began to frame our understanding of the construction of children as consumers, while *Chan-Olmsted* (*1996*), *Pecora* (*1998*), and *Hendershot* (*1994, 1998*) considered the political and economic nature of children's entertainment. *Luke* (*1990, 1991*) presented a history of the research on children's television as a construction of political, social, and cultural forces that serves as an ideal.

Throughout this decade, the research agenda established in the early days of television continued with a concern for television content and its effect on children. However, social changes are also reflected in this agenda with an increasing interest in gendered and minority programming and the growing interest in a concern for children as consumers. However, the concerns of Lazarsfeld were still not addressed. The only well-funded, collaborative, centralized research project during the 1990s was the National Television Violence Study (1997), funded by the cable companies. Researchers still appear to be as interested in families on television (*Berry, 1998; Douglas, 1996; Douglas & Olson, 1996; Moore, 1992; Larson, 1993; Weiss & Wilson, 1998*) as in how families use television (*Alexander, 1994; Krcmar, 1998; Robinson, 1990; Strouse, Buerkel-Rothfus, & Long, 1995*)

ENTERING A NEW MILLENNIUM

As we enter the new millennium, digital technology has brought dramatic changes to the landscape of children's television as the Internet and video games vye for attention. Although children and young adults still spend about 6 hours a day with the media, a figure that has remained constant over several years, they now spread those hours over other technology. In a study of 8- to 18-year-olds, Rideout et al. (2005) found that these young people now spend their time media multitasking: 1 hour of exposure to media including DVDs, video games, and computers translates to only 3 more minutes of media use. However, television is still the dominant medium, although it is no longer simply television; television content and characters can now be found in video games, books, CDs, DVDs, and Web sites. No self-respecting television program is without a Web site where children and young people can go to continue their TV relationship. Consequently television programming is designed to incorporate multiple platforms and television programming has become a growth area—a synthesis of such programming is beyond the scope of this chapter as new concepts are pitched at a heady rate. The media landscape of the year 2000 was one of both more and different. Not only was television ubiquitous but by 2000, 85% of U.S. households had a VCR in the household and between 1998 and 1999 the sales of DVD players more than tripled (Sterling & Kittross, 2002). In the study of 8- to 18-year-olds, Rideout et al. (2005) found that in 1999 only 47% of homes had Internet access; by 2004 that number was 74%.

Children of the new millennium are considered both sophisticated consumers and technologically savvy. Now, not only are snack foods and cereals sold to these consumers in training but Disney and Nickelodeon, for example, pair up with computer manufacturers to sell monitors with Mickey Mouse's ears or the Blue's Clues signature paw print. The technology of computers and child-friendly keyboards and mouses make adult technology accessible to even the youngest. LeapFrog, an interactive educational program, encourages children to be comfortable with the technology while they learn their ABCs. In addition, even younger children were now a part of this landscape as parents are encouraged to play Beethoven and Mozart and read, prebirth, using CDs and books produced by Baby Einstein.

In Rideout et al. (2005), leisure time among these young people was likely to be spent at the computer playing games, visiting websites, or communicating with friends. However, television was still an important part of their lives; according to Rideout et al., children and youth watch an average of 3 hours compared to about 1.25 hours spent on a computer. However, commercial television and Internet connections are not the only option for children of the new millennium. The ability to control viewing and to watch programs repeatedly has made videocassettes and, more recently, DVDs popular viewing for both younger children and teens. When Roberts, Foehr, Rideout, and Brodie (1999) first conducted a comprehensive media survey for the Kaiser Family Foundation, DVDs were not even a part of the landscape. Three years later the DVD was one of the most frequently used forms of media.

Research of the New Millennium

This project covers only the first 3 years of the new century (2000–2002), yet, on average, these years represent a significant increase in research on children and television. During the 1950s when *Lazarsfeld* (*1955*) called for a systematic study of children and television, there was an average of almost 9 studies each year; in the years 2000 to 2002 there were on average 74 per year. Although one would like to attribute this increase to a recognition of the seriousness of the scholarship and the importance of the questions, it no doubt reflects the growth of academic research in general.

As with previous decades, the research here reflected traditional concerns of media violence including *Cantor's* (*2000*) meta-analysis, several studies on effects (*Bushman & Huesmann, 2001; Nathanson & Cantor, 2000*) and other work on impact and aggression (*Kelley & Beauchesne, 2001; Scharrer, 2001*); although *Jones* (*2002*) offered an alternative reading of the value of make-believe violence. Several studies examined television content for violence (*Wilson, Colvin, & Smith, 2002; Wilson, Smith, et al., 2002*). At the beginning of this decade a number of these studies placed violence within the larger social and cultural context (*Brown & Witherspoon, 2002; Manno, Bantz, & Kauffman, 2000*) or a new sense of "hypermasculinity" (*Scharrer, 2001; Waxmonsky & Beresin, 2001*). *Krcmar* (*2001*) offered a rare opportunity to understand the way media violence plays out in young people's understanding of morality. Although representations of war have been a concern since the 1970s (e.g., *Hollander, 1971; Tolley, 1973*), a frightening new term came into our lexicon as we now must consider the consequences of terrorism (*Atwood & Donnelly, 2002; Duggal, Berezkin, & John, 2002; Pfefferbaum et al., 2001*).

Race and gender were, as they had been since the 1970s, important questions to address and almost a quarter of the projects in the first 3 years of this decade attempted to do so. Many of the studies during this time frame used race or gender as variable measures. Of the studies that considered race and ethnicity, representation (*Cortes, 2000; Larson, 2002; Li-Vollmer, 2002*) and media socialization (*O'Connor, Brooks-Gunn, & Graber, 2000*) among African American children were the major issues addressed; only one study during these years considered other ethnic minorities (*Thompson, 2002*). Overwhelmingly, issues of gender dominated the research on representation (*Calvert, Kondla, Ertel, & Meisel, 2001; Jarvis, 2001; Johnson & Young, 2002; Klein, Shiffman, & Welka, 2000; Klinger, Hamilton, & Cantrell, 2001; Leaper, Breed, Hoffman, & Perlman, 2002;*

Powell & Abels, 2002) and socialization (*Brown & Witherspoon, 2002;
Chapin, 2000; Cope-Farrar & Kunkel, 2002; Ward, Gorvine, & Cytron-
Walker, 2002; Witt, 2000*).

Health concerns such as weight and drug and alcohol use dominate the
literature during this time. Of the studies on body image, nine were concerned with obesity and eight with thinness and image. The act of television
viewing and its sedentary nature is blamed in all studies of childhood obesity and considered a major risk factor in most (*Crespo et al., 2001;
Dennison, Erb, & Jenkins, 2002; Epstein, Paluch, Gordy, & Dorn, 2000; Faith
et al., 2001; Gable & Lutz, 2000; Harrison, 2000a, 2000b; Horn, Paradis,
Potvin, Macaulay, & Desrosiers, 2001; Miller, 2001; Robinson, 2001*),
whereas thinness appears to be linked to ideals established by program
content (*Harrison, 2000a, 2000b, 2001; Harter, 2000; Jambor, 2001; Polce-
Lynch, Myers, Kliewer, & Kilmartin, 2001; Posavac, Posavac, & Weigel, 2001;
Young, McFatter, & Clopton, 2001*).

Substance abuse, such as abuse of alcohol, cigarettes, and drugs, was a
small part of this literature with only three studies addressing these concerns[22] (*Andsager, Austin, & Pinkleton, 2002; Gidwani, Sobol, DeJong,
Perrin & Gortmaker, 2002; Saffer, 2002*). On the other hand, during the
three years under consideration here, there was an increase in the number of projects that looked at the success and effect of using television to
change such behavior through public service announcements. Prior to
the year 2000, there were only four such studies (*Bauman, La Prelle,
Brown, Koch, & Padgett, 1991; Blosser & Roberts 1985; Frenette, 1999;
Galst, 1980*). From 2000 to 2002 there were nine (*Andsager, Austin, &
Pinkleton, 2001; Bernhardt, Sorenson, & Brown, 2001; Cappella, Fishbein,
Ahern, Kirkland, & Sayeed, 2001; DeJong & Hoffman, 2000; Palmgreen,
Donohew, Lorch, Hoyle, & Stephenson, 2001, 2002; Pinkleton, Austin, &
Fujioka, 2001; Siegel & Burgoon, 2002; Worden & Flynn, 2002*).

New areas of research include family or coviewing and parental mediation. As with public service announcements there is also a disproportion-
ate increase in the number of studies during this time. From 1950 to 1999
less than 2% of the studies examined the results of parental mediation or
coviewing on children's understanding of television while from 2000 to
2003, almost 7% of the studies addressed parental mediation or coviewing
(e.g., *Nathanson, 2001a, 2001b, 2002; Tan et al., 2000; Van den Bulck &*

---

[22]There is no doubt that other studies consider such questions as part of a larger project; the focus
here is on those that emphasize such health issues.

Van den Bergh, 2000; Warren, Gerke, & Kelly, 2002). As ratings systems are imposed by industry or government, they too are studied. In the 1970s it was the violence ratings (Coffin & Tuchman, 1973; Eleey, Gerbner, & Tedesco, 1972) and in the 1990s the research was on the success of content ratings (Abelman, 1999; Cantor, 1998a, 1998b; Krcmar & Cantor, 1997; Sneegas & Plank, 1998). Only two such studies were conducted in the years under discussion (Abelman, 2001; Krcmar & Albada, 2000).

Although teens and adolescents are not a new phenomenon and one of the first studies conducted was on TV and teenagers (P. Lewis, 1949), the research of these last years reflects the continuing influence from cultural studies. This growing body of literature is seen in the research on teens (Brooker, 2001; Campbell, 2001; Fisherkeller, 2000; Hymowitz, 2001; Jarvis, 2001; Ward, Gorvine, & Cytron-Walker, 2002), as well as recent work on young children (Cook, 2000) and preschoolers (Hendershot, 2000; Tobin, 2000). Jones (2002) offered a new interpretation of mediated violence as Heins (2001) and Hendershot (2002) rethought regulatory issues using new paradigms for understanding.

As in the past, we continue to be concerned with the physiological effects of television including the consequences of magnetic fields (Kaune et al., 2000), falling sets (DiScala, Barthel, & Sege, 2001; Scheidler, Shultz, Schall, Vyas, & Barksdale, 2002), and the development of a child's sight patterns (Gerhardstein & Rovee-Collier, 2002).

FIFTY YEARS OF RESEARCH

Fifty years after Lazarsfeld's testimony before the Kefauver Commission, it is time to stop and address the state of children's television research. Much has changed since Lazarsfeld testified before Congress and the world is a very different place. His call was for a well-funded centralized organization to support long-term collaborative research on not only the effects of this new medium but also studies of the family and of the institutions that create children's television. As the citations in this bibliography demonstrate, many have heeded his call, although with several notable exceptions rarely in any systematic way. Unfortunately, one of the most important of his requests—a foundation or organization to carry an agenda forward—was never realized. Government agencies and organizations like the Ford or Markel Foundation, Children Now, and the Kaiser Family Foundation have funded a significant number of studies but there has never been any long-term constant funding. One of the variables in the earliest stages of this project was to consider the funding source and the author's research institution. It soon became obvious that it was difficult to gather the information on funding as records were variable and reporting inconsistent. Funding, particularly from the government, appeared to occur at the whim of those in office or the vagarities of public opinion. The comprehensive Surgeon General's study was well funded, but it stands alone. There are some organizations and institutions that have supported a comprehensive research agenda such as CRITC at the University of Texas, Austin and more recently the Center on Media and Child Health at Harvard University. However, for the most part, we toil alone or with coauthors dependent on the kindness of strangers and our university or college for support—what Lazarsfeld (1955) termed "the accidental initiative of individual scholars" (p. 244).

This body of research, cumulated over 50 years, has nonetheless led us to a more complex understanding of the role of television in the lives of children and youth. Although we still worry about children's eyesight (Gerhardstein & Rovee-Collier, 2002; Rones, 1949), because of the work of hundreds of academics we now understand a wide range of issues about children and youth and their television. During the early days of this discipline, the questions were more likely to address media preference, social concerns, and health-related issues. In the 1950s research on viewing preference, impact on schooling, and comparisons between homes with television and those without was the focus of scholars. Bailyn (1959) was one of the first to consider the cognitive aspects of television. Bandura's work in the early 1960s on imitation gave us social learning theory and a body of literature that has been concerned with the way children model what television offers. One of the first and among the few studies on television as an institution was Shelby's analysis of network programming. The 1960s also brought the initial work on children as consumers from Wells (1966) and McNeal (1969), which was further developed by the work of Ward and others in the 1970s. The social unrest of the 1960s was reflected in the research of the 1970s that considered race (Nicholas, McCarter, & Heckel, 1971a, 1971b; Thalen, 1971) and gender (Busby 1974; Long & Simon, 1974; Nicholas, McCarter, & Heckel, 1971a, 1971b) as central variables to socialization. Each of these studies, along with others, both broadened the debate and added to our body of knowledge.

With the 1980s came a renewed interest in the concept of media literacy with the early work of Dorr, Graves, and Phelps (1980), Finn (1980), Hall (1980), Abelman (1984); and continued work on race represented by the research from Berry (1980b), Dates (1980), Newby, Robinson, and Hill (1980), Atkin, Greenberg, and McDermott (1983), and Stroman (1984); and gender, from *McGhee and Freuh (1980) and Alexander (1981)*. The 1990s brought a theoretical and paradigmatic shift in the way we research children and youth and television. Building on the work of cultural studies and political economy that gained ground in media studies during the 1980s, and the growing body of literature on youth studies, these projects were concerned with television as a part of children's popular culture in the classroom (*Fisherkeller, 1997; Lee, 1991*) or as a part of their everyday lives (*Jenkins, 1998; Kinder, 1999; Kline, 1993; Seiter, 1993*). Issues of representation and interpretation gained prominence in the discussion.

As we enter the new millennium, television competes with other technologies for children's time and attention. Video games, computer and interactive technology, and instant messaging all are now also a part of children's culture. This is perhaps a good time to reflect back on the advice of Lazarsfeld.

REFERENCES

Addams, J. (1972). *The spirit of youth and city streets*. Urbana: University of Illinois Press. (Original work published 1909)

Bryant, J., & Miron, D. (2004). Theory and research in mass communication. *Journal of Communication, 54*(4), 662–704.

Clark, N. (2004). The birth of an advocacy group. *Journalism History, 30*(2), 66–75.

Cooper, C. (1996). *Violence on television*. Lanham, MD: University Press of America.

Davis, J. (1995). *Children's television, 1947–1990*. Jefferson NC: McFarland.

Elkind, D. (1981). *The hurried child: Growing up too fast too soon*. Reading, MA: Addison-Wesley.

Erickson, H. (1995). *Television cartoon shows: An illustrated encyclopedia, 1949 through 1993*. Jefferson, NC: McFarland.

Fisch, S., & Truglio, R. (Eds.). (2001). *G is for growing*. Mahwah, NJ: Lawrence Erlbaum Associates.

Freeman, M. (1992, August 31). Majors use blocks to build audience. *Broadcasting,* pp. 35–40.

Gomery, D. (2001). Finding TV's pioneering audiences. *Journal of Popular Film & Television, 29*(3), 121–129.

Grossman, G. H. (1987). *Saturday morning TV*. New York: Arlington House.

Heuton, C. (1990, September 10). Kids biz no child's play. *Channels, 10*(12), 46–47.

Hollis, T. (2001). *Hi there, boys and girls!: America's local children's TV programs*. Jackson: University Press of Mississippi.

McAvoy, K. (1993, July 26). FCC gets into the children's act. *Broadcasting & Cable, 123*(30), 42.

Meyrowitz, J. (1985). *No sense of place*. New York: Oxford University Press.

Milavsky, J. R. (1974, September 1). *Some cons as well as pros in the new concern for pro-social television*. Paper presented at the annual meetings of the American Psychological Association, New Orleans, LA.

Mintz, S. (2004). *Huck's raft: A history of American childhood*. Cambridge MA: Belknap.

Mitang, L. D. (2001). *Big Bird and beyond*. New York: Fordham University Press.

Murray, J. P., & Salomon, G. (Eds.). (1984). *The future of children's television*. Boys Town, NE: Boys Town in cooperation with John and Mary Markle Foundation.

National Television Violence Study (Vols. 1–3). (1997). Thousand Oaks, CA: Sage Publications.

Pecora, N. (2004). Nickelodeon grows up: The economic evolution of a network. In H. Hendershot (Ed.), *Nickelodeon nation*. New York: New York University Press.

Pecora, N. (Executive Producer), & Mack, J. (Writer/Producer). (2001). "Aunt Fran and her playmates: A social history of children's television" [video documentary] Athens: Ohio University.

Postman, N. (1982). *The disappearance of childhood*. New York: Delacorte.

Reeves, B., & Baughman, J. (1983). Fraught with such great possibilities: The historical relationship of communication research to mass media regulation. In O. Gandy, P. Espinosa, & J. Ordover (Eds.), *Proceedings of the 10th annual Telecommunications Policy Research conference*. Norwood, NJ: Ablex.

Reeves, B., & Wartella, E. (1982, May). *For some children, under some conditions: A history of research on children and media*. Paper presented to the International Communication Association, Boston, MA.

Rideout, V., Roberts, D., & Foehr, U. G. (2005, March) *Generation M: Media in the lives of 8–18-year-olds*. A Kaiser Family Foundation Study. Retrieved 4/10/05 from www.kff.org

Roberts, D., Foehr, U. G., Rideout, V., & Brodie, M., (1999, November) *Kids & media @ the new millennium*. A Kaiser Family Foundation Report. Retrieved 2/15/05 from www.kff.org

Rowland, W. D. (1983). *The politics of TV violence*. Beverly Hills, CA: Sage.

Sarson, E. (1970). Growing grass roots in viewerland. *Television Quarterly, 9*(3), 50–58.

Sterling, C., & Kittross, J. M. (1990). *Stay tuned* (2nd ed.). Belmont CA: Wadsworth.

Sterling, C., & Kittross, J. M. (2002). *Stay tuned* (3rd ed.). Mahwah NJ: Lawrence Erlbaum Associates, Inc.

The Kaiser Family Foundation. (2005). *Issue brief*. Washington, DC: Author.

Tougher than it seems—The tv kid show problem. (1962, August 6). *Sponsor* (pp. 29–33, 50).

Tropp, S. (1970). Children's programs on CATV. *Television Quarterly, 9*(3), 30–37.

U.S. Department of Education, National Center for Educational Statistics. (2001). *Digest of Education Statistics 2000* (Rep. No. NCES 2001–034). Washington, DC: Author.

Wartella, E., & Mazzarella, S. (1990). A historical comparison of children's use of leisure time. In R. Butsch (Ed.), *For fun and profit* (pp. 173–194). Philadelphia: Temple University Press.

Wartella, E., & Reeves, B. (1984). Trends in research on children's television. In J. P. Murray & G. Salomon (Eds.), *The future of children's television* (pp. 23–35). Boys Town, NE: The Boys Town Center for the Study of Youth Development.

Wartella, E., & Reeves, B. (1985). Historical trends in research on children and the media: 1900–1960. *Journal of Communication, 35*(2), 118–133.

2

From Attention to Comprehension: How Children Watch and Learn From Television

Aletha C. Huston
David S. Bickham
June H. Lee
John C. Wright*
University of Texas, Austin

In this chapter, we present an overview of some of the research on children's attention and comprehension of television, relying particularly on our own work conducted over the last 25 years at the Center for Research on the Influences of Television on Children (CRITC). There have been two overriding objectives guiding our research. First, we have tried to understand the ecology of developing children's media use—that is, to investigate developmental patterns and changes in media use and to understand the influences of the family and contexts on children's use of television and other electronic media. Second, we have examined the content and forms of television as influences on children's cognitive processing of televised information. In this work, we have attempted to

*John C. Wright was originally scheduled to be the first author of this chapter. After his sudden death the other authors completed the chapter, but his thinking and his research are central to much of the material presented here.

understand how TV's form and content guide children's attention to television, how children come to understand the medium, and how characteristics of the medium affect what children learn from it. To achieve these objectives, we have conducted naturalistic, longitudinal studies of children's television use as well as laboratory investigations of children's attention and comprehension of selected bits of television. The ultimate goals of this work are to gain a better understanding of cognitive and social development and the more practical objective of determining how television can be used to enhance that development.

We begin the chapter with basic information about the development of viewing patterns, examining some of the influences of family and other ecological contexts on viewing. We then turn to theory and research designed to help us understand how and why some of these developmental changes come about, considering the relations of television form and content to attention and comprehension. In the last section, we present investigations of what children learn from educational television content in their everyday lives.

DEVELOPMENTAL CHANGES IN TELEVISION VIEWING

As children develop, both the amount and content of their television diets change. Children's cognitive abilities, structural factors in their lives, and personal preferences combine to determine duration of viewing and program choices. Individual characteristics (e.g., gender) affect television use, as does the larger sociocultural context. Children from different socioeconomic backgrounds and different ethnic groups use television differently throughout their childhood.

Total Amount of Television Viewing

The amount of time children spend with television has been a primary concern for years among parents, caregivers, pediatricians, and others concerned with the healthy development of young people. Numerous reports have documented the prominence of television in children's lives. For many children, television consumes more time than any other activity except sleep (Comstock & Paik, 1991). Even with the proliferation of new electronic media, television is a strongly preferred leisure activity for many children, and understanding patterns of its use is essential to understanding development.

Television viewing starts in infancy, when familial viewing patterns and controls determine exposure. In recent years, the viewing habits of children under 2 years old have been the center of national attention. At least one TV program has been designed with this age group as its target audience (*Teletubbies*), and the American Association of Pediatricians recently recommended that parents completely prohibit television viewing for children this young. This and other concerns about infant viewing, however, are based more on conjecture than research. Considering the paucity of reliable information about very young children's television use, the fact that children as young as 12 months can learn from television (Meltzoff, 1988), and the tendency for viewing habits to be set early in life and remain stable (Huston, Wright, Rice, Kerkman, & St. Peters, 1990; Tangney & Feshbach, 1988; Wright & Huston, 1995), research describing how very young children use television can provide valuable insight into the inception of its use.

Data from the Panel Study of Income Dynamics Child Development Supplement (PSID-CDS) lend themselves well to investigating television viewing among young children. During 1997, parents in this nationally representative study completed two time-use diaries for their children ages 0 to 12 years in which they accounted for all of the child's activities over 1 weekday and 1 weekend day (see Hofferth & Sandberg, 2001, for a description of CDS methods). Whenever the child watched television or played video or computer games, parents reported the titles of the program or game being used. Our analyses of these data revealed that children aged 2 and younger watched on average 10 hours and 45 minutes of television a week, significantly less than did older children (Wright, Huston, Vandewater, et al., 2001).

In the Early Window Study, we also described the media habits of very young children. For this project we followed a sample of approximately 240 children from low-income families over the course of 3 years, one group from age 2 through 5 and another from age 4 through 7, collecting repeated time-use diaries about their television viewing. Viewing was classified as a primary activity if it was named first as a description of the child's activity, but TV could also be a secondary activity, performed concurrently with playing, eating, or other activities. Very young children (2–3-year-olds) had high levels of secondary viewing of general-audience programs (an average of 80 minutes per day), suggesting that they were exposed to a great deal of television that adults and older children were watching (Huston, Wright, Marquis, & Green, 1999). Similarly, very young children in the PSID study had more secondary viewing than did older children (Wright, Huston, Vandewater, et al., 2001).

Cross-sectional studies show that viewing generally increases during the preschool years and peaks in early adolescence. Although earlier studies found a slight decline around age 6 when children enter school

(Comstock, Chaffee, Katzman, McCoombs, & Roberts, 1978; Comstock & Paik, 1991; Comstock & Scharrer, 2001), two more recent studies with large representative samples show fairly steady amounts of viewing from the preschool years into the early elementary years. It is possible that school entry represents less change in time away from home than in earlier years because most preschool children spend time in child care or early education programs. Both studies showed increases between about ages 8 and 13, and declines during later adolescence (Roberts, Foehr, Rideout, & Brodie, 1999; Wright, Huston, Vandewater, et al., 2001).

Longitudinal designs allow for an examination of the stability of individual viewing habits over time. In our Topeka Study, conducted in the early 1980s, we followed cohorts of young children over a 2-year period (Huston et al., 1990). From ages 3 to 5, total viewing increased slightly from 19.2 hours a week to 20.8. Between ages 5 and 7, viewing declined from 19.2 hours a week to 15.5, perhaps illustrating the effects of school entry. Individual differences in both amounts and types of programs viewed were stable over 2 years, and preschool viewing was modestly associated with total viewing 10 years later (Anderson, Huston, Schmitt, Linebarger, & Wright, 2001). Children apparently acquire television habits very early in life and maintain them at least through their early school years.

Explaining Developmental Differences in Viewing

Cognitive developmental change constitutes one basis for increases and decreases in viewing with age. As children grow, they become increasingly capable of decoding the audio and visual messages of television, making time with the medium both more pleasurable and more informative. This cognitive change is also indicated by the fact that the percentage of time children pay attention to the screen while in the room with a television increases with age until about age 10 (Anderson, Lorch, Field, Collins, & Nathan, 1986). The peak in viewing at early adolescence or late elementary school age may also be a result of developing cognitive processes. It is at or around the age of 10 that the format and pace of television most completely match the abilities and sophistication of the child viewer (Anderson & Smith, 1984). When the child is slightly older than this, he or she is a "master television viewer" and sees the medium as a primary source of knowledge and relaxation. In subsequent years other sources of information and entertainment (e.g., music and magazines) may be perceived as more engaging and may partially replace television.

Television Content

With age, children also make shifts in the types of content viewed, often choosing more cognitively challenging programming. In the Topeka Study, we coded television programs for redundancy of scenes and characters and for the amount of temporal integration required by the content, both measures of cognitive demand. Between ages 3 and 7, children moved from less demanding to more demanding programs, according to these indicators (Huston et al., 1990).

The amount of time children spend watching child-informative television drops dramatically as they progress from preschool into kindergarten and beyond (Huston et al., 1999; Huston et al., 1990; Wright, Huston, Vandewater, et al., 2001). What is a popular choice among 3- to 5-year-olds for 4 hours a week is significantly less preferred among 9- to 12-year-olds, who watch educational television only about 1.5 hours a week (Wright, Huston, Vandewater, et al., 2001). This is probably attributable to the fact that most educational programs target preschool children as their primary audience (Huston et al., 1990). Viewing cartoons also declines with age, albeit a little later than the decline in viewing educational programs.

Televised violence is often linked to features of the medium that attract young children's attention. In cartoons designed for children, both humor and violence are seamlessly merged with quick pace and animation to ensure the most attention and attraction to the images. As children age, they move away from cartoons, but continue to be attracted to comedy (e.g., situation comedies) and to violence (e.g., action-adventure; Wright, Huston, Vandewater, et al., 2001). Despite these shifts in genre, there are stable individual differences. Young children who watch age-appropriate humorous programs such as cartoons or educational shows watch situation comedies at a later age. Children who watch a lot of cartoons in the early years watch more action-adventure in later years (Huston et al., 1990). This stability may indicate lasting preferences and individual differences in the perceived function of television as a source of humor and entertainment.

The violent content of many children's favorites has been a concern since the medium's inception. The established relations between media violence and aggression, criminal activity, and other antisocial behaviors justify extensive research attention to this issue (see Bushman & Huesmann, 2001 for a review). In fact, a recent meta-analysis found that the link between violent television viewing and aggressive behavior is almost as strong as the relation between smoking and lung cancer (Bushman & Anderson, 2001). Therefore, understanding developmental patterns of viewing violence is especially important to understanding who is at risk for these consequences.

CHILDREN'S CHARACTERISTICS AS INFLUENCES ON VIEWING

Children's abilities and interests are likely to affect their choice of television as an activity and their choice of content to view. Boys and girls have different interests and preferences, but there is surprisingly little evidence of large gender differences in overall TV use. Among preadolescents, some studies find slightly more viewing by boys than by girls, but others do not. In one study (Roberts et al., 1999) boys watched 20 minutes more a day than did girls (a statistically reliable difference), whereas in two others (Huston, et al., 1999; Wright, Huston, Vandewater, et al., 2001) there were no overall gender differences.

There are gender differences, however, in preferred content, particularly as children reach late childhood and early adolescence. In the PSID study, among 9- to 12-year-olds, girls watched more comedy and relationship dramas, and boys watched more sports programs. The decline in viewing cartoons occurs at an earlier age for girls than for boys (Wright, Huston, Vandewater, et al., 2001). All of these differences are consistent with the idea that viewing specific genres of television is one of many gendered activities that dominate the time of early adolescents. Programs that include older characters and social relationships are attractive to girls in this age group because maturity and social interactions are themes that traverse all areas of their lives. Similarly, cartoons and sports contain subject matter relevant to boys entering adolescence.

ECOLOGICAL INFLUENCES ON VIEWING

Television viewing occurs in an ecological context of the family, which is in turn affected by the social and cultural institutions surrounding that family (Kotler, Wright, & Huston, 2001; Wright, St. Peters, & Huston, 1990). Parents' and siblings' viewing choices affect the kinds of programs that children watch. For children under age 7, most viewing of general audience programs occurs with an adult, usually a parent. In our analyses of coviewing patterns, it appeared that parents' preferences affected the programs that they viewed with their children more than children's preferences did (St. Peters, Fitch, Huston, Wright, & Eakins, 1991). Similarly, children with younger siblings were more likely to watch educational TV than were children with older siblings, probably because of sibling preferences (Caplovitz, 2002; Piñon, Huston, & Wright, 1989).

School and child care are institutional influences, affecting children's time at home and exposure to television. Children who attend school or center-based child care are less likely than those who are at home to have opportunities to watch television on weekdays (Huston et al., 1999; Piñon et al., 1989). In the analysis of the PSID data, weekday viewing peaked among 3- to 5-year-olds and was lower for school-age children. Weekend viewing was highest among 6- to 8-year-olds and 9- to 12-year-olds, suggesting that school-age children may compensate with increased viewing on the weekends (Wright, Huston, Vandewater, et al., 2001). The drop in viewing during adolescence may also be a result of increased involvement in school, out-of-school activities, and time with peers away from home (Comstock & Paik, 1991). The medium is not only less appealing cognitively than it was when they were younger, but also more interesting activities are more available and socially essential.

Both socioeconomic status and ethnic group are markers of sociocultural influences on media use. Children from families with relatively high levels of parent education and income watch less television overall, but not necessarily less educational television, than do children whose parents have less education and income (Huston & Wright, 1997; Truglio, Murphy, Oppenheimer, Huston, & Wright, 1996). In general, African American children watch more than White children, and there are smaller differences associated with parent education and income among African American than among White children (Bickham et al., 2002). Hispanic American children's viewing falls somewhere between the other two groups (Bickham et al., 2002; Roberts et al., 1999; Tangney & Feshbach, 1988). Developmental changes in viewing appear to vary slightly across ethnic groups. In our analyses of the PSID data, there were no age differences in total television viewing for African American children, but, for both White and Hispanic American children, older children watched more than did younger children (Bickham et al., 2002). In another large sample, older Black children watched about 2 hours of television more a day than their younger counterparts, whereas older White children watched only 1 hour more than younger White children (Roberts et al., 1999).

SUMMARY OF VIEWING PATTERNS

Overall, television is a popular activity for children at all points along the developmental path. They watch television when they can find the time and begin to lose interest in it as social activities and other life events begin to take precedence in their lives. Children are, however, never nonviewers. Even very young children and older adolescents watch enough to experience both its positive and negative effects.

THE MECHANISMS OF DEVELOPMENTAL CHANGES IN TELEVISION VIEWING

Children's naturally occurring use of the medium as a whole and the types of programming it delivers correspond broadly to the cognitive changes and to structural features of their lives. Children appear to be attracted to the medium when they understand and are excited by its form. They seek out content that they find entertaining and relevant to their current situation. A more precise understanding of the processes guiding children's uses of TV can be gained by moving from the natural environment to the laboratory, examining the ways in which children process the information they encounter on TV.

Children Use Television Actively

The early models of television effects, which implied a passive child being manipulated by the media environment, long ago gave way to models of a child who uses, processes, and makes decisions about the media information that is available. Children make decisions about when and how they watch television. At a more microscopic level, they make moment-to-moment decisions about when to attend, when to look away, and when to monitor sound for an interesting moment. They integrate and interpret content according to the intellectual skills and schemata that they possess.

Exploration–Search

Television as a medium presents information in particular forms and formats. In fact, much of the criticism of the medium is based on its forms. Critics have argued that it is inherently superficial or overwhelming to children because information is presented at a rapid pace that cannot be altered by the viewer. Others have asserted that the visual qualities of the medium lead to visual information processing that interferes with language development (Healy, 1990) or imagination (Singer & Singer, 1981).

Much of our early research was devoted to gaining a better understanding of children's responses to and knowledge of the forms and formats of television (see Huston & Wright, 1989). The initial work was guided by Wright and Vlietstra's (1975) exploration–search model of information getting. In that model, microgenetic developmental changes in information getting are proposed as a sequence moving from exploration to search. When an individual confronts a new stimulus environment, exploration dominates. Exploration is characterized by somewhat disconnected, brief attention to various parts of the environment. The most perceptually salient aspects are likely to be noticed first and to get attention. As the stimulus becomes more familiar, attentional processes become more systematic, goal directed, and intentional as the person searches for particular aspects of the stimulus based on her individual goals and existing knowledge or schemata. This microgenetic process can occur for people of all ages when they encounter new situations. For example, an adult arriving in Paris for the first time might be in the exploration mode, wandering the streets, noticing many features of the environment and moving from one to the next with little in the way of preexisting guidelines. A person who is familiar with Paris, on the other hand, might be in search mode, making directly for a particular museum or landmark chosen in advance.

Many microgenetic exploration–search sequences accumulate to a macrogenetic pattern because, as children get older, they are less likely to encounter completely new stimulus environments and are more likely to be in environments that are at least partially familiar. They also gain skill in regulating, planning, and guiding their own activities. Hence, overall, children move from attention patterns that are predominantly exploration in infancy and the early preschool years to attention patterns that are predominantly search by middle childhood.

Wright and Huston (1983) applied this theory to children's processing of televised information. We assumed that such processing was a function not only of the content presented by the medium but also of the particular forms, or formal features, that characterize the presentation. Formal features are characteristics of the televised presentation that are relatively independent of content (e.g., animation). Many of the formal features used in children's programming are perceptually salient (e.g., high action, visual special effects, and auditory effects); others are less striking perceptually but relay program-specific information (e.g., moderate action and dialog).

We predicted initially that younger children would attend more to salient formal features and older children would attend more to informative features, but for the most part, these predictions were not supported (Huston & Wright, 1989). Children did attend to salient features, but there was little change with age. Anderson and Lorch's (1983) studies of children's attention to television demonstrated that children attended to content that was comprehensible, even when it was presented without perceptually salient formal features. They proposed that children learn that certain formal features are regularly associated with child-oriented content (e.g., child and female voices), and attend because they expect the content to be comprehensible. That is, formal features serve as *signals* for content.

Stimulus Sampling Model

Wright (see Huston & Wright, 1983) expanded this idea by proposing that viewers confronted with a television program sample bits of the program with quick looks (or by listening) and make fairly rapid judgments about whether or not the content is likely to be comprehensible, interesting, entertaining, or relevant. Wright argued that it was logically impossible for comprehensibility to affect later attention to the content already comprehended. Instead, the content and form at one point in time lead children to have expectations about what is likely to come next, and those expectations influence subsequent attention. Formal features often guide these judgments because one can recognize them almost instantly. For example, one can detect animation immediately, whereas it would take longer to determine whether or not the content presented dealt with a topic of interest. If the stimulus sample suggests the content is worth viewing, attention continues. If not, attention quickly moves to something else and can be rerecruited by auditory cues or by loss of interest in the alternative activity.

Developmental changes in this process come about through familiarization. What is comprehensible and interesting changes not only with cognitive development, but also with repeated exposure. Attention and interest are likely to be greatest when content is neither too easy nor too hard; that is, it is moderately familiar and understandable. If content is too easy or familiar, it will be boring; if it is too difficult, it will hold little interest. Over time, with increasing cognitive sophistication and knowledge,

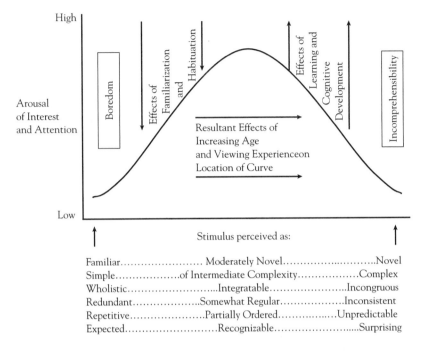

FIG. 2.1. The traveling lens model. From "The Forms of Television: Effects on Children's Attention, Comprehension, and Social Behavior," by M. L. Rice, A. C. Huston, and J. C. Wright, p. 32, 1982, Washington, DC: U.S. Government Printing Office. Reprinted with permission.

the optimal point of moderate familiarity or comprehensibility changes. What was very difficult before becomes moderately difficult and therefore interesting; what was moderate before becomes easy and less interesting. This process is illustrated in Fig. 2.1 (Wright & Huston, 1983).

FORMAL FEATURES GUIDE COGNITIVE PROCESSING OF TELEVISION

Getting the Content Message

The stimulus sampling hypothesis implied that formal features that signal interesting or comprehensible content, independent of the actual content, would guide children's attention. To test that prediction, Campbell, Wright, and Huston (1987) designed a set of televised segments presenting nutritional information in two formats: (a) a "child" format that was animated, had sprightly music, and was narrated by a cartoon-character voice using second-person pronouns ("You are stronger when you eat X"); and (b) an "adult" format that used live photography, sedate music, and was narrated by an adult male using third-person pronouns ("People are stronger when they eat X"). Messages at three levels of difficulty were constructed in each format, but within each difficulty level, content was virtually identical. Hence, format and difficulty were independent of one another.

The feature signal hypothesis led to the prediction that children would attend more to the child format than to the adult format, and the data strongly supported that prediction. Children also recalled more information from the child format segments than they did from adult format segments with identical content. It appears that the child formal features attracted children to the content (or adult forms repelled them) and that they learned more from it as a result (Campbell et al., 1987).

Formal features that elicit attention can also serve as guides helping children to distinguish important from unimportant content. In one investigation, targeted items of content in *Fat Albert and the Cosby Kids* were classified as central or incidental to the plot. Some of these were marked by visual special effects or sound effects; others were not. Overall, children understood and recalled the content that was central to the story better when it was marked with salient formal features than when it was not. This finding was more true for younger (5–6-year-olds) than for older (8–9-year-olds) children (Calvert, Huston, Watkins, & Wright, 1982).

Interpreting Content Connotations

Formal features signal much more than the level and interest of the content. Producers use filmic and video conventions as implicit cues to appeal to particular audiences or to convey particular connotations. For example, advertisements for sex-typed toys are made with different forms. Commercials for boys' toys are made with rapid action, quick cuts and scene changes, and loud sound effects; commercials for girls' toys are made with dreamy or tinkling music, scene changes marked by dissolves, and quiet sound (Welch, Huston-Stein, Wright, & Plehal, 1979). Children recognize these sex-typed cues, judging televised segments as sex-typed even when the content of the segment is neutral (Huston, Greer, Wright, Welch, & Ross, 1984).

Judging Reality

Formal features guide children's judgments about fiction and reality— whether what they are seeing is real or not. In recent years, reality programs, infomercials, and other new genres have blurred the line between fiction and reality partly by using formal features. The features that were once reliable markers of reality may now confuse adults as well as children. For example, staged reconstructions of crimes are shown with handheld cameras, running commentary, and other features that characterize live broadcasts of real events.

Perceptions of reality occur on two dimensions: factuality ("Did it happen in the unrehearsed real world?") and social realism ("How like real life is it, even if it is fictional?"; Wright, Huston, Reitz, & Piemyat, 1994). Judgments about *factuality*—whether the content shown exists in the real world outside television or whether it is constructed and scripted for TV—occur in a fairly regular developmental sequence. For example, 7-year-olds understand better than 5-year-olds that fictional characters do not retain their TV roles in their off-TV lives. The older children also understand that fictional shows are scripted, rehearsed, made up, and synthetic. In the preschool years, children argue that animated content is not real, but that other content is. By about age 8 or 9, children are about as accurate as adults in judging whether a television program is presenting fiction or fact. Individual differences between children appear to be a function of overall levels of cognitive development, as indexed by measures of general intellectual ability, rather than experience with television itself (Wright et al., 1994).

Children make factuality judgments primarily on the basis of genre (e.g., news is factual; drama is not), which in turn depends primarily on formal production features (e.g., talking heads and onscreen graphics indicate news or documentaries; Fitch, Huston, & Wright, 1993). Children ages 9 through 12 who were interviewed just after the *Challenger* shuttle disaster initially knew the televised events were factual and not just space fiction partly by noting the formal features characteristic of live news and not simply by judging the plausibility of the content (Wright, Kunkel, Piñon, & Huston, 1989). When children perceive that a program is factual, they process the information presented more extensively and deeply, but they also learn social information from fiction. Third- and fourth-grade children who perceived the content of a TV story as factual recalled more complex, inferential content, and more psychological and emotional states of characters than did those who perceived the story as fictional (Wright, Huston, Alvarez, et al., 1995).

When children have real-world information about an occupation, they can make distinctions between reality and the images seen on fictional TV. In one study, different groups of children were asked what real police officers do, what real nurses do, what TV police officers do, and what TV nurses do; their answers were different in predictable ways. For example, they said that TV police officers catch criminals and engage in car chases and real-world police have to work hard (Wright, Huston, Truglio, et al., 1995).

When occupations are unfamiliar, however, children use both factual and fictional TV as a source of information. In one experiment, we showed children documentaries or fictional stories about unfamiliar occupations. When asked what people in that occupation do, they responded with the actions they had seen. Those who had seen documentaries were a little more likely to think the content was accurate, but those who saw fictional content often thought it presented a realistic view of the occupation (Huston, Wright, Fitch, Wroblewski, & Piemyat, 1997).

The second dimension of perceived reality—*social realism*—has to do with the child's perception that the television portrayals of unfamiliar people and places are plausible and true to life. Judgments about the social realism of television do not decline with age. Children judge social realism primarily on the basis of content cues, often comparing the actions they see on television to their knowledge about the real world, but formal features (e.g., a laugh track) can also contribute to these perceptions. The more television one has habitually watched, the more socially realistic one believes TV in general to be, and the more one finds information in entertainment programming to be applicable to, and useful in, the real world (see Huston & Wright, 1997). Analogous results have been obtained regarding perceptions of the reality of televised violence (Huesmann, Lagerspetz, & Eron, 1984). Children who judged television as both factual and socially realistic were the ones whose beliefs about real-world occupational roles were most like television portrayals of those occupations (Wright, Huston, Truglio, et al., 1995).

SUMMARY

The work summarized here represents only a small part of existing knowledge about how children use television to acquire information and knowledge. The medium of television offers a range of forms and formats in which to present content. Children use these forms and formats as guides to attention, aids to comprehension, and guides to the type of content being presented. Even in the very early years, children make moment-to-moment decisions about attending or not attending on the basis of their judgments about the likely comprehensibility and interest of the content. With development, they learn to use the conventions of the medium as one basis for those judgments. They are not passive recipients or victims of irresistible perceptual onslaughts, but active users of the medium. And, most important for the real world of children's experiences, children can learn and retain a range of information from television. When this information is age-appropriate, relevant, educational content, children are likely to learn its messages. We turn now to the exploration of the effects of viewing this type of program.

Developmental Changes in Learning Educational Content From Television

There is strong, consistent evidence that age-appropriate educational television has positive and enduring effects on children's development. This body of research has largely centered on preschool children, for whom the most prominent and successful example of educational programming is *Sesame Street*. Its influence has been a frequent subject for inquiry over the last three decades.

Evidence of the Positive Educational Effects of Sesame Street. *Sesame Street* was the first children's program to address an educational curriculum with detailed, specified goals. It pioneered the use of formative research to inform production and evaluated the program's effectiveness with extensive summative research (Palmer & Fisch, 2001). Numerous assessments of *Sesame Street*, using methods ranging from experimental studies (Ball & Bogatz, 1970; Bogatz & Ball, 1971) to national surveys (Zill, 2001) to longitudinal studies, have confirmed its positive impact among young audiences (see Fisch & Truglio, 2001).

We conducted a 2-year longitudinal study, the Topeka Study, with 271 children ages 3 and 5 to explore the implication of television viewing for early learning skills. We found that watching *Sesame Street* contributed to preschoolers' vocabulary development, independent of parent education, gender, the presence of older siblings, parental encouragement of *Sesame Street* viewing, and parental attitudes toward television viewing (Rice, Huston, Truglio, & Wright, 1990). This benefit, however, was limited to the younger cohort. Three-year-olds who were frequent viewers of *Sesame Street* showed more improvement in vocabulary scores by age 5 than did infrequent viewers. *Sesame Street* viewing at age 5 was not related to vocabulary development by age 7. In fact, analyses showed children in the older cohort who had higher vocabulary scores were marginally less likely to watch *Sesame Street* at age 7, suggesting that these children may have advanced beyond the level of the program.

The Early Window, a second comprehensive longitudinal study of the relations between television viewing and academic skills, conducted with children from low-income families, demonstrated similar results (Wright, Huston, Murphy, et al., 2001). This study was a 3-year longitudinal assessment of the relations between viewing different categories of television content and academic competencies in two cohorts of children (followed from ages 2–5 and 4–7). The sample was ethnically diverse and consisted of children from low- to moderate-income families. The children's viewing information was collected in repeated 24-hour time-use diaries. All programs were coded according to their content and intended audience, yielding the following categories: (a) child-audience, informative or educational; (b) child-audience, noninformative cartoons; (c) child-audience, other programs; and (d) general-audience programs. We controlled for the quality of the home environment and the primary language spoken at home (English or Spanish).

An array of dependent measures was examined: school readiness (e.g., knowledge of colors, shapes, spatial and size relations), reading skills, number skills, and vocabulary. Path analyses, conducted separately for each cohort, indicated that 2- to 3-year-olds who watched more child-audience informative programs scored higher on all four academic measures at age 3 than did those who watched less. Viewing such programs at later ages, however, did not contribute to performance on these measures beyond viewing in the initial period. That is, viewing child-audience informative programs at ages 4 to 5 did not predict test scores at age 5. For the older cohort, viewing at ages 4 to 5 and 6 to 7 were not related to academic skills at ages 5 and 7, respectively. By contrast, viewing child-audience cartoons and general-audience programs at an early age tended to predict low academic skills (Wright, Huston, Murphy, et al., 2001).

With reference to *Sesame Street* specifically, viewers at ages 2 to 3 had an advantage over nonviewers on academic measures at ages 3, 4, and 5, controlling for maternal education, family income-to-needs ratio, the quality of the home environment, the primary language spoken at home, and the child's initial language skills (Wright, Huston, Scantlin, Kotler, 2001). From ages 4 to 7, however, no benefits from viewing were apparent. These two studies were consistent in substantiating the value of educational television for children from varied backgrounds, but there appears to be an early window of opportunity during which its effects are strongest.

Effects of Preschool Educational Viewing.   Most educational programming has emerged from the PBS Ready to Learn initiative. More recently, commercial efforts have given rise to innovative educational programs. *Blue's Clues*, a cable program designed to teach cognitive skills and prosocial behavior, has been enormously popular among preschoolers (Anderson et al., 2000). As with *Sesame Street, Blue's Clues* has been successful in fulfilling its educational goals for its target age group. Three- to five-year-old viewers outperformed nonviewers on various measures of cognitive development, including riddles, Gestalt closure, and matrices (nonverbal skills and problem-solving ability). Viewing did not influence scores on expressive vocabulary or self-esteem measures. Viewers' caregivers rated them as more flexible thinkers, better problem solvers, and more prosocial compared with ratings of nonviewers. The advantages enjoyed by viewers grew over the 2-year measurement period (Anderson et al., 2000). Whether these positive findings were consistent across ages was unclear, as the investigators did not differentiate between effects on younger and older preschoolers. However, the unique use of episode repetition and layering in *Blue's Clues* (Crawley, Anderson, Wilder, Williams, & Santomero, 1999) may extend its effects to a wider age range.

Early television viewing appears to have long-term consequences for children's achievement. In the Recontact Study (Anderson et al., 2001), we tracked 570 adolescents whose media use and family characteristics were studied in detail when they were 5 years old in one of two locations—Topeka, Kansas, or Springfield, Massachusetts. The frequencies of viewing three types of television—informative, violent, and all other programming—in the preschool years and in adolescence were calculated. Teens' television viewing diets and the total time they had spent watching television as preschoolers were used to predict academic achievement, achievement motivation, leisure reading, extracurricular activities, aggression, health behavior, and self-image in adolescence. Child and family variables known to affect the relation between viewing and outcomes (gender, site, parent education, birth order, and gender-by-site interaction) were statistically controlled.

Analyses showed that viewing child informative programs as preschoolers predicted academic success in adolescents, but more strongly for boys. Boys who had watched child informative programs frequently in preschool earned higher grades in English, math, and science in high school than did those who watched infrequently. Among girls, viewing and grades were positively, but not significantly, associated. For both sexes, adolescents who had viewed educational programming, particularly *Sesame Street*, as preschoolers reported spending more time reading books not required for school. This contradicts theorists who argue that such programming reduces interest in reading and books. Preschool-aged viewers of child informative programs also perceived themselves as more competent in math and science, and the boys among them placed more value on achievement, particularly in math and science, than did infrequent viewers. We proposed that boys may stand to gain more from the academic and prosocial content in educational shows because such content runs counter to other sex-typed socializing influences for boys.

The processes that translate educational viewing to academic success in adolescence clearly do not involve simple learning of content. Although preschoolers who watched educational programs may have maintained their interest in educational content and gone on to watch informative programs as adolescents, our analyses did not find evidence to support such a path (Anderson et al., 2001). Rather, it seems more likely that early educational viewing initiated a trajectory of learning. Viewers of educational programs master early learning skills, are interested and motivated learners, and, when they enter school, are perceived favorably by teachers. These predispositions set up children for early academic success, and they are magnified over time; as a result, the children become efficacious learners and high achievers as adolescents (Anderson et al., 2001). That is, as young viewers, children learn school readiness skills and positive attitudes toward learning, acquired in part through educational programming, and these carry forward into adolescence (Anderson et al., 2001).

Older Children's Educational Viewing.   Compared with studies of preschoolers' educational viewing, assessments of educational programming aimed at older age groups have been scarce. Where research exists, it indicates that educational programs with well-designed curricula can offer benefits for older children's academic skills (Huston & Wright, 1997). For example, an evaluation of *Square One TV*—a mathematics show aimed at 8- to 12-year-olds—demonstrated that viewers scored higher in the number and variety of problem-solving heuristics used, as well as the mathematical completeness and complexity of their solutions (Hall, Esty, & Fisch, 1990).

Overall, however, relatively little is known about older children's learning from educational television. Several factors could explain this gap in our knowledge. The role of television in children's learning changes according to the interplay between viewers' ages and program content and form (Rice et al., 1990). Children may simply lose interest in—or be less receptive to—educational programming during the school years, partly due to a lack of age-appropriate programs for older children, and partly due to the possibility that learning academic skills from television plays a less important role in children's lives once they enter school and receive formal instruction (Wright, Huston, Scantlin, et al., 2001).

With regard to program content and form, television is particularly well suited to convey certain kinds of content, such as letters, numbers, words and their meanings, shapes, colors, and so on—content that is most fitting for younger children. The combination of the medium's strengths (e.g., an emphasis on visual presentation, ability to focus attention through production techniques, repetition) and young children's preferences (e.g., repetition; their focus on concrete, visual aspects of content) may make it particularly effective for young children.

Compared with younger children, as noted earlier, older children favor programs with increasing complexity and continuous narratives, themes, or plots (Huston et al., 1990). Older children (10–11-year-olds) are also more interested in fictional dramatic programs and programs rich in verbal humor, satire, and male–female relationships (Mielke, 1983). Programs such as *Square One TV, Ghostwriter,* and *3-2-1 Contact* have appealed to these preferences by incorporating dramatic storylines into certain program segments. For older children, however, television may be more useful for piquing their interest in subjects (e.g., science, geography, society, literature) than for teaching academic content directly (Wright, Huston, Scantlin, et al., 2001). This may explain the absence of effects among older children in studies using only academic skills (rather than, for instance, interest in specific subjects or achievement motivation) as dependent measures.

Currently, educational television remains in the domain of preschool audiences, among whom the strongest relations with learning seem to exist for the younger preschoolers. There is no reason to believe that its benefits are limited to young children, but its potential has yet to be fully realized for older children.

CONCLUSION

We understand a great deal more about how children use television, what engages their attention, and how and what they learn from television than we did 25 years ago. The old view of the zombie child mesmerized in front of the television set has been replaced with a model of a child who actively sifts, judges, and uses television content. Even as new electronic media proliferate, television remains a central part of children's lives, and they watch it almost from birth onward. Cognitive developmental changes lead to changes in viewing and in preference for different types of content. From quite an early age, children begin to learn the forms and formats of the medium; they use these as well as content to make judgments about what is attention-worthy, entertaining, and real or fictional. They spend a great deal of time with content that has no known value to their development, but when they watch programs designed to provide education and information, they can profit considerably. Young preschool children are particularly likely to learn preacademic skills from well-designed television, and early viewing has lasting associations with academic achievement.

REFERENCES

Anderson, D. R., Bryant, J., Wilder, A., Santomero, A., Williams, M., & Crawley, A. M. (2000). Researching *Blue's Clues*: Viewing behavior and impact. *Media Psychology, 2,* 179–194.

Anderson, D. R., Huston, A. C., Schmitt, K. L., Linebarger, D. L., & Wright, J. C. (2001). Early childhood television viewing and adolescent behavior: The Recontact Study. *Monographs of the Society for Research in Child Development, 66*(1, Serial No. 264).

Anderson, D. R., & Lorch, E. P. (1983). Looking at television: Action or reaction? In J. Bryant & D. R. Anderson (Eds.), *Children's understanding of television: Research on attention and comprehension* (pp. 1–33). New York: Academic.

Anderson, D. R., Lorch, E. P., Field, D. E., Collins, P. A., & Nathan, J. G. (1986). Television viewing at home: Age trends in visual attention and time with TV. *Child Development, 57,* 1024–1033.

Anderson, D., & Smith, R. (1984). Young children's TV viewing: The problem of cognitive continuity. In F. Morrison, C. Lord, & D. Keating (Eds.), *Advances in applied developmental psychology* (Vol. 1, pp. 115–163). New York: Academic.

Ball, S., & Bogatz, G. A. (1970). *The first year of Sesame Street: An evaluation.* Princeton, NJ: Educational Testing Service.

Bickham, D. S., Vandewater, E. A., Huston, A. C., Lee, J. H., Gilman Caplovitz, A., & Wright, J. C. (2002). Predictors of children's media use: An examination of three ethnic groups. Manuscript submitted for publication.

Bogatz, G. A., & Ball, S. (1971). *The second year of "Sesame Street": A continuing evaluation.* Princeton, NJ: Educational Testing Service.

Bushman, B. J., & Anderson, C. A. (2001). Media violence and the American public: Scientific facts versus media misinformation. *American Psychologist, 56,* 477–489.

Bushman, B. J., & Huesmann, L. R. (2001). Effects of televised violence on aggression. In D. G. Singer & J. L. Singer (Eds.), *Handbook of children and the media* (pp. 223–254). Thousand Oaks, CA: Sage.

Calvert, S. L., Huston, A., Watkins, B. A., & Wright, J. C. (1982). The relation between selective attention to television forms and children's comprehension of content. *Child Development, 53,* 601–610.

Campbell, T. A., Wright, J. C., & Huston, A. C. (1987). Form cues and content difficulty as determinants of children's cognitive processing of televised educational messages. *Journal of Experimental Child Psychology, 43,* 311–327.

Caplovitz, A. G. (2002). *The influence of siblings on children's television viewing.* Unpublished master's thesis, University of Texas, Austin, TX.

Comstock, G., Chaffee, S., Katzman, N., McCoombs, M., & Roberts, D. (1978). *Television and human behavior.* New York: Columbia University Press.

Comstock, G., & Paik, H. (1991). *Television and the American child.* New York: Academic.

Comstock, G., & Scharrer, E. (2001). The use of television and other film-related media. In D. G. Singer & J. L. Singer (Eds.), *Handbook of children and the media* (pp. 47–72). Thousand Oaks, CA: Sage.

Crawley, A. M., Anderson, D. R., Wilder, A., Williams, M., & Santomero, A. (1999). Effects of repeated exposures to a single episode of the television program *Blue's Clues* on the viewing behaviors and comprehension of preschool children. *Journal of Educational Psychology, 91,* 630–637.

Fisch, S. M., & Truglio, R. T. (2001). *"G" is for growing: Thirty years of research on children and Sesame Street.* Mahwah, NJ: Lawrence Erlbaum Associates.

Fitch, M., Huston, A. C., & Wright, J. C. (1993). From television forms to genre schemata: Children's perceptions of television reality. In G. L. Berry & J. K. Asamen (Eds.), *Children and television: Images in a changing sociocultural world* (pp. 38–52). Thousand Oaks, CA: Sage.

Hall, E. R., Esty, E. T., & Fisch, S. M. (1990). Television and children's problem-solving behavior: A synopsis of an evaluation of the effects of *Square One TV. Journal of Mathematical Behavior, 9,* 161–174.

Healy, J. (1990). *Endangered minds: Why our children don't think.* New York: Simon & Schuster.

Hofferth, S. L., & Sandberg, J. F. (2001). How American children spend their time. *Journal of Marriage & the Family, 63,* 295–308.

Huesmann, L. R., Lagerspetz, K., & Eron, L. D. (1984). Intervening variables in the TV violence-aggression relation: Evidence from two countries. *Developmental Psychology, 20,* 746–775.

Huston, A. C., Greer, D., Wright, J. C., Welch, R., & Ross, R. (1984). Children's comprehension of televised formal features with masculine and feminine connotations. *Developmental Psychology, 20,* 707–716.

Huston, A. C., & Wright, J. C. (1983). Children's processing of television: The informative functions of formal features. In J. Bryant & D. R. Anderson (Eds.), *Children's understanding of TV: Research on attention and comprehension* (pp. 37–68). New York: Academic.

Huston, A. C., & Wright, J. C. (1989). The forms of television and the child viewer. In G. A. Comstock (Ed.), *Public communication and behavior* (Vol. 2, pp. 103–158). New York: Academic.

Huston, A. C., & Wright, J. C. (1997). Mass media and children's development. In W. Damon, I. Sigel, & K. A. Renninger (Eds.), *Handbook of child psychology: Vol. 4. Child psychology in practice* (5th ed., pp. 999–1058). New York: Wiley.

Huston, A. C., Wright, J. C., Fitch, M., Wroblewski, R., & Piemyat, S. (1997). Effects of documentary and fictional television formats on children's acquisition of schemata for unfamiliar occupations. *Journal of Applied Developmental Psychology, 18*, 563–585.

Huston, A. C., Wright, J. C., Marquis, J., & Green, S. B. (1999). How young children spend their time: Television and other activities. *Developmental Psychology, 35*, 912–925.

Huston, A. C., Wright, J. C., Rice, M. L., Kerkman, D., & St. Peters, M. (1990). Development of television viewing patterns in early childhood: A longitudinal investigation. *Developmental Psychology, 26*, 409–420.

Kotler, J. A., Wright, J. C., & Huston, A. C. (2001). Television use in families with children. In J. Bryant & A. Bryant (Eds.), *Television and the American family* (2nd Ed., pp. 33–48). Mahwah, NJ: Lawrence Erlbaum Associates.

Meltzoff, A. N. (1988). Imitation of televised models by infants. *Child Development, 59*, 1221–1229.

Mielke, K. W. (1983). Formative research on appeal and comprehension in *3-2-1 CONTACT*. In J. Bryant & D. R. Anderson (Eds.), *Children understanding of television: Research on attention and comprehension* (pp. 241–263). New York: Academic.

Palmer, E. L., & Fisch, S. M. (2001). The beginnings of *Sesame Street* research. In S. M. Fisch & R. T. Truglio (Eds.), *"G" is for growing: Thirty years of research on children and Sesame Street* (pp. 3–24). Mahwah, NJ: Lawrence Erlbaum Associates.

Piñon, M., Huston, A. C., & Wright, J. C. (1989). Family ecology and child characteristics that predict young children's educational television viewing. *Child Development, 60*, 846–856.

Rice, M. L., Huston, A. C., Truglio, R., & Wright, J. (1990). Words from "Sesame Street": Learning vocabulary while viewing. *Developmental Psychology, 26*, 421–428.

Rice, M. L., Huston, A. C., & Wright, J. C. (1982). The forms of television: Effects on children's attention, comprehension, and social behavior. In D. Pearl, L. Bouthilet, & J. Lazar (Eds.), *Television and behavior: Ten years of scientific progress and implications for the eighties: Vol. 2. Technical reports* (pp. 24–38). Washington, DC: U.S. Government Printing Office.

Roberts, D. F., Foehr, U. G., Rideout, V. J., & Brodie, M. (1999). *Kids and media at the new millennium*. Menlo Park, CA: Kaiser Family Foundation.

Singer, J. L., & Singer, D. G. (1981). *Television, imagination, and aggression: A study of preschoolers*. Hillsdale, NJ: Lawrence Erlbaum Associates.

St. Peters, M., Fitch, M., Huston, A. C., Wright, J. C., & Eakins, D. J. (1991). Television and families: What do young children watch with their parents? *Child Development, 62*, 1409–1423.

Tangney, J. P., & Feshbach, S. (1988). Children's television viewing frequency: Individual differences and demographic correlates. *Personality and Social Psychology Bulletin, 14*, 145–158.

Truglio, R. T., Murphy, K. C., Oppenheimer, S., Huston, A. C., & Wright, J. C. (1996). Predictors of children's entertainment television viewing: Why are they tuning in? *Journal of Applied Developmental Psychology, 17,* 475–494.

Welch, R., Huston-Stein, A., Wright, J. C., & Plehal, R. (1979). Subtle sex-role cues in children's commercials. *Journal of Communication, 29,* 202–209.

Wright, J. C., & Huston, A. C. (1983). A matter of form: Potentials of television for young viewers. *American Psychologist, 38,* 835–843.

Wright, J. C., & Huston, A. C. (1995, June). *Effects of educational TV viewing on lower income preschoolers on academic skills, school readiness, and school adjustment one to three years later.* Report to Children's Television Workshop, Center for Research on the Influences of Television on Children, University of Kansas, Lawrence, KS.

Wright, J. C., Huston, A. C., Alvarez, M., Truglio, R., Fitch, M., & Piemyat, S. (1995). Perceived television reality and children's emotional and cognitive responses to its social content. *Journal of Applied Developmental Psychology, 16,* 231–251.

Wright, J. C., Huston, A. C., Murphy, K. C., St. Peters, M., Piñon, M., Scantlin, R., et al. (2001). The relations of early television viewing to school readiness and vocabulary of children from low-income families: The Early Window Project. *Child Development, 72,* 1347–1366.

Wright, J. C., Huston, A. C., Reitz, A. L., & Piemyat, S. (1994). Young children's perceptions of television reality: Determinants and developmental differences. *Developmental Psychology, 30,* 229–239.

Wright, J. C., Huston, A. C., Scantlin, R., & Kotler, J. (2001). The Early Window Project: *Sesame Street* prepares children for school. In S. M. Fisch & R. T. Truglio (Eds.), *"G" is for growing: Thirty years of research on children and* Sesame Street (pp. 97–114). Mahwah, NJ: Lawrence Erlbaum Associates.

Wright, J. C., Huston, A. C., Truglio, R., Fitch, M., Smith, E. D., & Piemyat, S. (1995). Occupational portrayals on television: Children's role schemata, career aspirations, and perceptions of reality. *Child Development, 66,* 1706–1718.

Wright, J. C., Huston, A. C., Vandewater, E. A., Bickham, D. S., Scantlin, R. M., Kotler, J. A., et al. (2001). American children's use of electronic media in 1997: A national survey. *Journal of Applied Developmental Psychology, 22,* 31–47.

Wright, J. C., Kunkel, D., Piñon, M., & Huston, A. C. (1989). How children reacted to televised coverage of the space shuttle disaster. *Journal of Communication, 39,* 27–45.

Wright, J. C., St. Peters, M., & Huston, A. C. (1990). Family television use and its relation to children's cognitive skills and social behavior. In J. Bryant (Ed.), *Television and the American family* (pp. 227–252). Hillsdale, NJ: Lawrence Erlbaum Associates.

Wright, J. C., & Vlietstra, A. G. (1975). The development of selective attention: From perceptual exploration to logical search. In H. W. Reese (Ed.), *Advances in child development and behavior* (Vol. 10, pp. 195–239). New York: Academic Press.

Zill, N. (2001). Does *Sesame Street* enhance school readiness?: Evidence from a national survey of children. In S. M. Fisch & R. T. Truglio (Eds.), *"G" is for growing: Thirty years of research on children and* Sesame Street (pp. 115–130). Mahwah, NJ: Lawrence Erlbaum Associates.

3

The Impact of Television on Cognitive Development and Educational Achievement

Marie Evans Schmidt
Daniel R. Anderson
University of Massachusetts, Amherst

Two opposing trends have characterized discussions of children's television viewing and its' relationship to educational achievement. First, there has been a popular belief that television viewing, regardless of its content, may be detrimental to cognitive and educational development. The second and contradictory trend has been widespread popular support for the use of TV at home as an educational tool.

This chapter addresses the impact of television on cognitive development and academic achievement. We conclude that educational television has a substantial positive impact and that entertainment television has a negative impact, primarily due to displacement of reading in the early elementary school years and the effects of violent content. Effects of television independent of content have not, for the most part, been demonstrated. We first deal with the effects of content, and then with the effects of television as a medium.

EDUCATIONAL CONTENT

Beginning in the late 1960s, American children were exposed for the first time to a professionally produced TV program explicitly designed to help prepare them for school while entertaining them. *Sesame Street* was like no other program produced for children and it quickly became popular with children and parents. Perhaps because of its success, it also generated criticism. Critics feared that the program would render children intellectually passive, reduce their ability to comprehend sustained arguments, induce a desire that education be as entertaining as television, reduce interest in language and reading, and shorten attention spans (e.g., Healy, 1990; Mander, 1978; Moody, 1980; Singer, 1980; Winn, 1977). The program's supporters hoped it would better prepare children for school. Because *Sesame Street's* goals are explicitly educational, and because the program has been popular, controversial, and long running, it has been the subject of more research than any other program. The research has established fairly conclusively that children learn from *Sesame Street* and that the impact is positive and of long duration. Because smaller amounts of research on other educational programs have generally produced similar findings, we conclude that educational television has a positive impact on educational achievement.

Numerous large- and small-scale evaluation studies and experiments have found that preschoolers by and large learn the specific intended lessons from *Sesame Street* as measured through testing of various kinds (e.g., Ball & Bogatz, 1970; Lorch, Anderson, & Levin, 1979). This learning prepares preschoolers for elementary school. In a survey of more than 10,000 parents, Zill, Davies, and Daly (1994) reported that *Sesame Street* viewing was associated with emergent literacy and numeracy skills, particularly for low-socioeconomic-status (SES) children, even after numerous statistical controls were considered (e.g., parent education and income, race, frequency of parent reading to child, participation in a preschool program). Children who watched *Sesame Street* before starting school were also better readers in early elementary school (Zill, 2001; Zill et al., 1994).

These findings were verified in a longitudinal study reported by Wright et al. (2001). They found that educational viewing (particularly *Sesame Street*) was related to letter–word and number skills, vocabulary, and school readiness for children from low to moderate SES families (they did not study children from more favored circumstances).

Other research found that *Sesame Street* viewing is accompanied by vocabulary learning. Rice and Woodsmall (1988), in an experiment, showed that preschoolers could readily learn vocabulary from *Sesame Street* and Rice, Huston, Truglio, and Wright (1990) verified this finding in a longitudinal field study. They found that 3-year-olds who watched more *Sesame Street* had higher Peabody Picture Vocabulary Test (PPVT) scores at age 5. This was true even after variables such as parental education and initial PPVT scores were controlled.

Does this early positive impact of *Sesame Street* have effects traceable beyond the early elementary school years? The answer is yes. Anderson, Huston, Schmitt, Linebarger, and Wright (2001) studied adolescents whose TV viewing had been intensively investigated when they were preschoolers. *Sesame Street* viewing at age 5 years predicted better high school grades in English, math, and science. This relationship held even after controls for other types of viewing and background factors such as parent education and child cognitive status were applied.

It is clear that *Sesame Street*, the longest running TV program with an explicitly academic curriculum, has short-term positive effects on vocabulary and school-readiness and that these have long-term positive consequences. No other curriculum-based program has been as intensively studied, but numerous evaluations and other kinds of studies have found positive effects for many other curriculum-based programs consistent with those found for *Sesame Street*. Television that is designed to teach does so, with long-term positive consequences.

ENTERTAINMENT CONTENT

The impact of entertainment television on cognitive development and education is somewhat more difficult to pin down than is the impact of educational television. The primary reason is that the vast majority of studies relating TV viewing to achievement have failed to determine the actual content of programs the children viewed. In most of these studies, time spent watching TV was examined in relation to indexes of cognitive development or achievement, with little or no regard to whether the content was educational, violent, light entertainment, or intended for adults. Only a few studies have specifically distinguished between types of content.

That said, the viewing diets of most children, especially during the school-age years, consist largely of entertainment programming without obvious educational content. Relationships of overall television viewing to achievement are therefore primarily relationships to entertainment content. Typically, a curvilinear relationship of viewing time to achievement is found, with increasing achievement as viewing increases up to about 10 hours a week, and decreasing achievement with viewing beyond that (e.g., P. A. Williams, Haertel, Walberg, & Haertel, 1982).

Such relationships, of course, are notoriously difficult to interpret in terms of whether television plays a causal role in achievement. It could be, for example, that children who watch large amounts of television come from poor and ethnic minority backgrounds that are themselves associated with lower academic achievement. A large amount of television viewing may thus simply be a marker for other factors that put a child at risk for academic failure. When such factors are taken into account, some studies find that the relationship between viewing and achievement disappears (e.g., Gaddy, 1986; Keith, Reimers, Fehrmann, Pottebaum, & Aubey, 1986), and others find that the relationship changes form (e.g., Fetler, 1984). For example, TV viewing tends to be negatively associated with achievement in children from economically advantaged families but is positively associated (or not associated at all) with achievement for low-SES children or children with limited proficiency in English (California Assessment Program, 1981, 1982). Comstock and Paik (1991) interpreted these results as follows: Television viewing, when it displaces intellectually rich experiences, has a deleterious effect on children's achievement, but it is beneficial to children when it provides such experiences. Unfortunately, without a clear sense of the content of the television programs watched by the children in these studies, the relationships between achievement and viewing are somewhat murky. Some kinds of television content are obviously more valuable for cognitive development and academic achievement than are others.

When content is taken into account, the picture becomes clearer. In a Swedish study, preschool viewing of general entertainment content was negatively associated with subsequent school performance (Rosengren & Windahl, 1989). Viewing of educational programs, on the other hand, was associated with better performance on school tests in first grade, and later in sixth grade. Wright et al. (2001) found an analogous pattern of results for American preschoolers from poor to moderate-income families such that educational viewing positively predicted school readiness and vocabulary, whereas general entertainment viewing negatively predicted these outcomes. In both of these studies, knowing what the children watched on television provided much stronger relationships than simply knowing how much time the children watched television.

VIOLENT CONTENT

There is some indication that the negative impact of entertainment programming is primarily due to violence. Anderson et al. (2001), in predicting high school achievement from preschool television viewing, found no relationship for viewing of nonviolent entertainment programming but did find a negative relationship for viewing of violent entertainment programming (girls only). Huesmann and Eron (1986) hypothesized that early violence viewing causes aggressive behavior in children, which in turn initiates a pattern of habitual negative interactions with teachers and peers at school. Failure at school may frustrate children, leading to more aggression and isolation, which, in turn, leads to more television viewing. Similarly, Singer and Singer (1981) argued that violent TV content induces impulsivity and aggression in young children. Huesmann and Eron (1986) found a significant negative correlation between achievement (as measured by California Achievement Test scores) and both aggression and violence viewing for a large sample of first- and third-grade children. Although there were confounds in the data set (low achievement was related to low SES and lack of parental education, themselves correlated with aggression), the correlation between aggression and academic achievement was one of the highest for aggression.

Longitudinal research by Huesmann, Eron, Lefkowitz, and Walder (1984) suggested that aggression most likely causes lowered academic performance, rather than vice versa. Huesmann and Eron (1986) hypothesized that 6 to 11 may be a critical age range for children's susceptibility to the negative effects of violence viewing, because habitual aggressive behaviors formed during this phase of development are hard to extinguish and may continue into adulthood.

Earlier violence viewing may also put children at academic risk. As noted earlier, Anderson et al. (2001) found that preschool violence viewing predicted lower academic achievement in girls but not boys. They argued that girls are ordinarily better socialized for school than are boys and that girls typically watch less violence on TV than boys. Girls who watch more violence as preschoolers, on the other hand, become more aggressive and impulsive and thus are less socially prepared to enter school. In a sense, Anderson et al. hypothesized that watching violence on television brings girls down to boys' level of socialization relevant to school.

It should be noted that Anderson et al. (2001) also found that preschool educational television viewing was negatively associated with adolescent aggression. Because programs such as *Sesame Street* teach strategies of impulse control and conflict resolution, it can be argued that part of the positive impact of educational programs on achievement is due to their positive effect on social behaviors, including reduced aggression.

EFFECTS OF TELEVISION AS A MEDIUM

It is often claimed that television viewing, per se, is inimical to cognitive development and education. This claim is difficult to maintain in the face of clear evidence that educational television viewing enhances achievement. Nevertheless, a substantial amount of research and theory has been directed at this issue. We pose commonly asked questions concerning the effects of the medium and summarize the research that attempts to answer them.

Does Television Viewing Displace More Valuable Cognitive Activities?

In its simplest form, the time displacement hypothesis holds that if a child spends an hour watching television, that child of necessity spends an hour less in some other activity. If that other activity is more valuable to cognitive development and academic achievement than watching television, then this displacement may have a negative impact. We conclude that the overall evidence for a negative impact of displacement is weak.

For the displacement hypothesis to be correct, TV viewing has to displace activities considered intellectually valuable. Studies of the introduction of television found that TV, in fact, replaced activities functionally similar to TV viewing, such as radio listening, comic book reading, and moviegoing (Himmelweit, Oppenheim, & Vince, 1958; Schramm, Lyle, & Parker, 1961). Unstructured "marginal fringe activities" (e.g., hanging out) were also displaced (Himmelweit et al., 1958; Mutz, Roberts, & van Vuuren, 1993). Surprisingly, there were no substantial changes in time spent in book reading. Mutz et al. (1993) found that the introduction of television in South Africa reduced fifth to 12th graders' leisure reading time by less than 3 minutes per day. In most studies, homework time was not significantly altered by the introduction of television, either.

The majority of studies conducted long after television was introduced have not found that time spent watching television reduces time spent in activities related to school (e.g., reading, homework). Most cross-sectional correlational studies, for instance, have not found a significant relationship between television and reading (Beentjes & van der Voort, 1988), but there is, nevertheless, some evidence that TV viewing during first and second grade may be inimical to reading acquisition, as we review later.

There is some evidence that increased television viewing is associated with reduced participation in extracurricular activities (Anderson et al.,

2001; Gentile & Walsh, 2002; Huston et al., 1992; Mutz et al., 1993; Willits & Willits, 1986) and that involvement in these kinds of activities is associated with decreases in school dropout rates (Mahoney, 2000). However, other studies have not found that TV viewing is related to participation in other activities (Carpenter, Huston, & Spera, 1989; Timmer, Eccles, & O'Brien, 1985), so the evidence is not conclusive.

At this point, if there are straightforward negative effects of time displacement, they have yet to be demonstrated. Although some have argued that comic book reading or radio listening may have been more cognitively valuable activities than television viewing, no research has demonstrated the short- or long-term positive effects on academic achievement of these older media.

Does Television Viewing Reduce Reading Achievement?

Among others, Healy (1990) argued that television, as a visual medium, reduces children's attention to and interest in language. Over time, she hypothesizes, this inattention to language reduces interest and practice in reading. She argues that *Sesame Street* is particularly damaging because it is so visually attractive. Others have argued that, especially for early readers, reading is difficult and effortful, whereas television viewing is easy. Consequently, given the choice, children will choose to watch television rather than read. This slows down reading acquisition.

Healy's (1990) argument is easily dealt with. As described earlier, a series of investigations have found that *Sesame Street* viewing leads to increased vocabulary, school readiness, and early reading. In addition, Anderson et al. (2001) found that *Sesame Street* viewing predicted better high school grades in English and increased book reading in adolescence. Language learning is not limited to *Sesame Street*. Singer and Singer (1998) found that preschoolers who watched 10 episodes of *Barney and Friends* over a 2- to 3-week period learned unfamiliar words from the program, as measured in a vocabulary test.

The argument that early elementary school children may avoid reading when they can watch TV instead is more plausible. There is some evidence that this may retard reading development. First, however, we describe research with older children.

In the Anderson et al. (2001) research, teenagers who watched a lot of entertainment content on television read fewer books but they did not read fewer magazines. Watching sports predicted reading the newspaper sports sections and reading sports magazines. Watching a lot of documentary and news programs, on the other hand, had no relationship to book reading, but it did predict more newspaper reading. These findings suggest that content interests frequently connect television viewing and reading. In older children, therefore, simple displacement effects are implausible. Unfortunately, the vast majority of studies that examine the relationship between TV viewing and reading have not taken TV or text content into account.

In a longitudinal panel study, Morgan and Gross (1982) found a positive correlation between time spent watching television in sixth through ninth grade and time spent reading 3 years later. Mutz et al. (1993) concluded that, overall, there was no significant relationship between TV viewing in the fifth grade and time spent reading in Grades 6 through 12. Ritchie, Price, and Roberts (1987) found that changes in reading achievement over 3 years were unrelated to earlier television viewing from the third grade on. These and other studies suggest that by about the third grade, television viewing is unrelated to reading achievement and time spent reading.

When first-and second-grade children are examined, however, the case for a negative impact of television becomes stronger. In a longitudinal panel study of Dutch children, Koolstra and van der Voort (1996) found a negative relationship between TV viewing in Grades 2 through 4 and later book reading. In a landmark study of the arrival of TV in Canada, second graders who had grown up without television (TV had not yet come to their town due to its geographical location) scored higher on measures of reading skills (with controls for IQ) than children living in similar towns with TV. Four years after the arrival of TV, however, their skills were equivalent to their peers who had grown up with television (Corteen & Williams, 1986). This quasi-experimental study provides what is probably the strongest evidence that television may reduce reading acquisition.

The relationship between reading acquisition and television viewing appears to be mediated by content. Huston, Wright, Marquis, and Green (1999) found that viewing entertainment content displaced reading and educational activities in preschool and early elementary school children; no such effects were observed for viewing educational content. T. M. Williams (1986a, 1986b) proposed that first- to third-grade children in Stage 2 of reading acquisition (learning to decode print) are uniquely vulnerable to displacement effects of television, because reading practice (outside of school) is required for print decoding to become automatic. Less capable children may be particularly at risk. Becoming a fluent reader lays the foundation for later reading enjoyment. If reading is difficult for slower children, they might start to watch more TV than fluent readers do. By thus depriving themselves of further reading practice, or lowering the quality of their practice (if they combine it with television viewing), heavy Stage 2 TV viewers may fall behind their peers. These initial differences in reading skills could lead to later gaps in reading achievement scores between light and heavy TV viewers (Corteen & Williams, 1986).

Another mechanism proposed to account for the possibly negative relationship between television viewing and early reading achievement has been called the reading depreciation hypothesis (Koolstra & van der Voort, 1996), or more generally, the entertainment and mental effort hypothesis (Anderson & Collins, 1988). According to the reading depreciation hypothesis, television viewing leads children to see television as an easy and pleasurable form of entertainment, which provides more direct satisfaction than books. A preference for television develops and reading declines (van der Voort, 2001). Koolstra and van der Voort (1996) tested this hypothesis in their 3-year Dutch panel study. Television negatively affected second- to fourth-grade children's attitudes about reading, as well as the number of books read (at Years 2 and 3) but not reading achievement. However, TV viewing did not influence the children's estimates of mental effort during reading, suggesting that this hypothesis may be weak.

Another proponent of the mental effort theory, although in slightly different form, is Salomon (1984), who claimed that children perceive television as easy and therefore invest less mental effort in processing television content. This attitude, he suggested, could be transferred to other cognitive tasks, essentially cultivating a style of shallow, "mindless" processing, which might lead children to seek out less challenging reading material. Salomon (1984) demonstrated that American school-aged children have preconceived notions that television is easy. There is also evidence that amount of mental effort can be experimentally increased with instructions that change the context of the task (e.g., "You'll be tested on this later") and that the increase leads to learning gains (Beentjes, Vooijs, & van der Voort, 1993; Field & Anderson, 1985). However, evidence is lacking as to whether lower mental effort in TV viewing really does carry over to other tasks, especially reading. Research is inconclusive on this matter (e.g., Roberts, Bachen, Hornby, & Hernandez-Ramos, 1984).

Wright et al. (2001) proposed an interesting variant of the mental effort hypothesis. General entertainment television viewed by young children may be largely incomprehensible to them. If the content is too difficult, they may be less engaged by it, which might affect their expectations about the medium of television. Watching incomprehensible content, as opposed to comprehensible educational content, deprives young children of positive learning experiences with television and may establish early preferences for less cognitively demanding TV programs (Wright et al., 2001). Conversely, an opposite effect might occur for children exposed to age-appropriate educational children's programs. Early experience with these programs could lead children to form expectations that television is supposed to be challenging and stimulating. This hypothesis is supported by the fact that *Sesame Street* viewers read more books as adolescents (Anderson et al., 2001).

In summary, the relationships between reading and television viewing are complex. In older children, who are already established readers, there appears to be no substantially negative effect of television viewing. Rather, television content, in relation to the child's interests, may stimulate reading, and text content may stimulate interest in certain classes of TV programs. For preschool children, the clearest finding is that educational TV viewing predicts greater reading at older ages. In early school-age children, for whom reading is still a mentally demanding activity, there is some evidence that entertainment television may have a displacement effect and therefore a negative impact on reading acquisition. This latter effect should clearly not be extended to include educational programs such as *Reading Rainbow, Ghostwriter,* and *Between the Lions* that are designed to enhance literacy and reading skills in first and second graders. Evaluations of these programs indicate that they promote reading and literacy in their viewers (e.g., Linebarger, Eskrootchi, Sai Doku, Larsen, & Kosanic, 2001).

Does Television Interfere With Homework?

Time spent on homework is strongly related to achievement. In American studies, amount of television viewing is generally unrelated to homework time (e.g., Anderson et al., 2001; Keith et al., 1986). This lack of a trade-off may be due in part to the fact that many children do homework while at the same time watching television (Beentjes, Koolstra, & van der Voort, 1996). Does this background television reduce the quality of homework? It can surely impair performance on intellectual tasks by increasing the attentional load during challenging activities. Armstrong and his colleagues have demonstrated such short-term negative effects of background television on cognitive tasks (Armstrong, Boiarsky, & Mares, 1991; Armstrong & Greenberg, 1990). Pool, van der Voort, Beentjes, and Koolstra (2000) found that Dutch eighth graders did less well on a homework assignment when they completed it with a Dutch-language soap opera in the background (although their performance was unchanged by an English-language music video in the background). Because homework is often combined with television viewing, it is possible that the distracting effects of television could, over time, impair school performance, if combining homework and television viewing became a habit (Armstrong & Greenberg, 1990; van der Voort, 2001). This has been tested in only one investigation. Anderson et al. (2001) found no indication that high school students who did homework with television received lower grades than students who did homework in silence. In both cases, however, total time spent doing homework strongly predicted grade point average. It is not clear why doing homework with television in this study did not have a negative impact. It may be that students do the least demanding forms of homework with television and more demanding forms in silence. There also may be individual learning styles such that some students can be productive in a divided attention situation whereas other students are not. The latter students may choose to do their homework without media.

Does Television Make Children Intellectually Passive?

The argument has frequently been made that television viewers become intellectually passive (e.g., Kubey & Czikszentmihalyi, 1990; Mander, 1978; Singer, 1980). This view stems from the apparently passive nature of television viewing itself. Viewing requires little overt behavior, programs are visually explicit and require little visual imagination, and the medium is not interactive. In contrast, several theorists have argued that this passivity is more apparent than real. They argue that the cognitive activities involved in interpreting television images and content are substantial and that the child is of necessity cognitively active if he or she is to comprehend typical television content (e.g., Anderson & Lorch, 1983; Anderson & Smith, 1984; Huston & Wright, 1983, 1989).

There are no studies that attempt to directly determine whether television viewing makes children cognitively passive, either in the short or long term. The closest is found in the Anderson et al. (2001) investigation of the relationship between early television viewing and adolescent behavior. Assuming that participation in organized extracurricular activities is a form of being "active," they concluded that their "analyses provide no support for the hypothesis that early television viewing fosters a general passivity" (p. 98).

Other investigations have tended to focus on the nature of television viewing itself. Whereas adults frequently use television as a means of mood management and a means for relaxation (e.g., Anderson, Collins, Schmitt, & Jacobvitz, 1996), children appear to be cognitively active during TV viewing. A number of investigations have indicated that children's attention to television is strategic in nature and in service to the comprehension of content and is not merely passively gained and lost by salient production features (e.g., Anderson, Lorch, Field, & Sanders, 1981; Lorch et al., 1979). Other studies have shown the necessity of active inferential processes in comprehending television (Smith, Anderson, & Fischer, 1985). In addition, observations during viewing indicate that children frequently ask questions and discuss the content of programs (Alexander, Ryan, & Munoz, 1984).

The theory that children are cognitively active during television viewing (Anderson & Lorch, 1983) has led to the design of a new generation of preschool educational TV programs, including *Blue's Clues* and *Dora the Explorer* (Gladwell, 2000). These programs, among other things, explicitly invite the viewers to be active in problem solving and communication while they watch. Experienced viewers of *Blue's Clues*, for example, yell out answers to cognitive problems, point to correct places on the screen in perceptual problem solving, and the like (Crawley, Anderson, Wilder, Williams, & Santomero, 1999). These active viewing behaviors transfer during the viewing of other programs the children had never previously seen (Crawley et al., 2002). Although the research on the impact of television viewing on active cognition is mostly nonexistent, research on the nature of television itself, plus the findings of Anderson et al. (2001) with respect to participation in extracurricular activities, indicates that the passivity hypothesis as yet has no support.

Does Television Shorten Children's Attention Spans or Cause Hyperactivity?

One of the persisting claims about television is that it shortens children's attention spans and causes hyperactivity. Again, *Sesame Street* has been claimed to be chief among the offenders in causing these problems (Halpern, 1975; Hartmann, 1996; Healy, 1990; Winn, 1977). The reasoning seems to be that television's frequent visual changes and *Sesame Street's* short segments model a sporadic attentional style that is in some way incorporated by the child.

There is no evidence that short television segments or frequent visual change on television influences children adversely, although there is very little research on the issue. In the only empirical test of whether fast-paced programs induce hyperactivity or reduce children's ability to sustain attention while problem solving, Anderson, Levin, and Lorch (1977) manipulated the pace of an episode of *Sesame Street* by editing together the most rapidly paced sequences from a number of programs into one program. Children who watched the rapidly paced version did not perform any differently on tasks assessing persistence or impulsivity than children who watched a very slowly paced version or children who read storybooks with their parents. Because children who watch *Sesame Street* do generally better in school, including subjects that require intensely sustained attention, such as math, this hypothesis appears to be wrong.

An alternative hypothesis gets more support. Friedrich and Stein (1973) and Singer and Singer (1981) noted that aggressive portrayals on television provide frequent models of impulsive, restless behavior. They argued that, through observational learning, children who watch violent television may incorporate such impulsive and restless styles in their own behavior. A handful of studies have provided support for this hypothesis. As examples, Singer, Singer, and Rapaczynski (1984) showed that young children may have more difficulty sitting still after watching violent content, and a field experiment showed that educational or prosocial programming (*Mister Rogers Neighborhood*) can improve preschoolers' persistence and tolerance for delay, whereas aggressive action programs have the opposite effect (Friedrich & Stein, 1973).

CONCLUSIONS AND FUTURE DIRECTIONS

To us it is clear that most of the effects of television on cognitive development and academic achievement stem from the particular content viewed. There is little question but that educational television programs teach, and that this teaching has beneficial short- and long-term consequences for schooling. These consequences are due not only to academic content and skills learned from the programs, but also from the social teaching of impulse and aggression control. Most of the negative effects of television stem from entertainment programs, particularly those with violent content. These negative effects include reading displacement in the early elementary school years, and modeling of aggression, restlessness, and impulsivity. The bottom line of this review is that the medium of television is neither harmful nor beneficial to children; rather, the content viewed determines television's effects. As Anderson et al. (2001) put it, "the medium is not the message; the message is the message" (p. 134).

There are many issues related to the cognitive and educational impact of television that remain to be substantially explored by researchers. The long-term positive benefits of educational television depend, in part, on whether children can learn abstract knowledge or problem-solving skills and transfer them to new situations. Although it is clear that children, at various ages, can learn specific facts and information from television, very little research has specifically investigated whether transfer occurs, and if, so, by what possible mechanisms. Evaluations of educational television shows have provided mixed evidence for transfer. For instance, children understood the educational content of CRO, a program for 6- to 11-year-olds that focused on science and technology. However, they could not transfer underlying principles (e.g., about the dynamics of flight) learned from the program to problems with a different set of stimuli (e.g., a new group of "flying machines"; Fay, Teasley, Cheng, Bachman, & Schnakenburg, 1995). Five- and 6-year-old children could not apply a problem-solving strategy learned from *Sesame Street* to a new problem, even though they could replicate the strategy with a problem very similar to the one on the show. More promising results have come from studies of the math series *Square One*. In one study, some of the children transferred problem-solving skills learned from the program to new problems. However, transfer performance was worse than performance on recall and comprehension measures. In another study, viewing *Square One* in schools for 6 weeks led to improved performance, for fifth graders, on math problems not shown on TV (Hall, Esty, & Fisch, 1990). Finally, research on the impact of the program *Blue's Clues* demonstrated that preschoolers could answer far-transfer questions, in which concepts or strategies from an episode were tested with different stimuli than those on the program (Crawley et al., 1999). Nevertheless, the design principles by which transfer is most readily achieved have not been clearly elucidated for educational television. It should be noted that this problem is not limited to television but is an issue for education in general.

There is almost no research on the impact of television on children under 3 years of age. Infants and toddlers are routinely exposed to television produced for older children and adults, and increasingly, programs are being directed at them. Anderson and Evans (2001) argued that television could have both negative and positive effects on very young children. As an example of potential negative effects, exposure to large amounts of "background" television may have disrupting influences on toy play and on parent–child interactions as both the child and the parent are distracted by TV. What little evidence exists suggests that exposure to background television is detrimental to cognitive and language development (Carew, 1980; Nelson, 1973). On the other hand, educational television may have its greatest positive impact on very young children, as well. In their study of children from lower income families, Wright et al. (2001) found the greatest beneficial effects of educational TV were on the youngest children in their study, 2- and 3-year-olds.

Research has also failed to adequately address dynamic process variables in the home (rather than static variables like SES), which may be implicated, at every step, in children's experiences with television. Because it has been established that a child's background influences television viewing choices and expectations for the medium, theory and research should address how these early patterns are formed as part of the family and school systems (Neuman, 1995). In a recent study, Gentile and Walsh (2002) examined how family media habits influence children's performance in school. They found significant relationships between family media use and children's academic achievement. Families that used media in "healthy ways" (e.g., educational television viewing, not watching TV while doing homework) had children who performed better in school (as reported by parents). In addition, parents who were knowledgeable about media and its effects and who engaged in more alternative activities (other than using media) with their children were more likely to have academically successful children (Gentile & Walsh, 2002).

Finally, it is clear to us that when television programs are designed with a research-based knowledge of how children use and understand television, and when they are designed to incorporate systematic academic or social curricula, children benefit. When they are designed merely to entertain through action and violence, children suffer. There is evidence that the quality of children's television has improved through the 1990s as a consequence of the Children's Television's Act of 1990 mandating a minimal amount of beneficial programming, (Schmitt, 1999) and as a consequence of federal funding of public broadcasting through programs such as Ready to Learn. As television is transformed to a digital medium, and as regulation and funding are reconsidered as a consequence, we believe that it is of the utmost importance to adopt policies that maximize children's exposure to beneficial programming and minimize exposure to programming that is harmful.

REFERENCES

Alexander, A., Ryan, M., & Munoz, P. (1984). Creating a learning context: Investigations on the interactions of siblings during television viewing. *Critical Studies in Mass Communication, 1*, 345–364.

Anderson, D. R., & Collins, P. A. (1988). *The influence on children's education: The effects of television on cognitive development*. Washington, DC: U.S. Department of Education.

Anderson, D. R., Collins, P. A., Schmitt, K. L., & Jacobvitz, R. S. (1996). Stressful life events and television viewing. *Communication Research, 23*, 243–260.

Anderson, D. R., & Evans, M. K. (2001). Peril and potential of media for toddlers. *Zero to Three, 22*(2), 10–16.

Anderson, D. R., Huston, A. C., Schmitt, K., Linebarger, D. L., & Wright, J. C. (2001). Early childhood television viewing and adolescent behavior: The recontact study. *Monographs for the Society for Research in Child Development, 66*(Serial No. 264).

Anderson, D. R., Levin, S. R., & Lorch, E. (1977). The effects of television program pacing in behavior of preschool children. *Communication Research, 25*, 159–166.

Anderson, D. R., & Lorch, E. P. (1983). Looking at television: Action or reaction? In J. Bryant & D. R. Anderson (Eds.), *Children's understanding of TV: Research on attention and comprehension* (pp. 1–33). New York: Academic.

Anderson, D. R., Lorch, E. P., Field, D. E., & Sanders, J. (1981). The effect of television program comprehensibility on preschool children's visual attention to television. *Child Development, 52*, 151–157.

Anderson, D. R., & Smith, R. (1984). Young children's television viewing: The problem of cognitive continuity. In F. Morrison, C. Lord, & D. Keating (Eds.), *Advances in applied developmental psychology* (pp. 115–163). New York: Academic.

Armstrong, G. B., Boiarsky, G. A., & Mares, M. L. (1991). Background television and reading performance. *Communication Monographs, 58*, 235–253.

Armstrong, G. B., & Greenberg, B. S. (1990). Background television as an inhibitor of cognitive processing. *Human Communication Research, 16*, 355–386.

Ball, S. J., & Bogatz, G. A. (1970). *The first year of Sesame Street: An evaluation*. Princeton, NJ: Educational Testing Service.

Beentjes, J. W. J., Koolstra, C. M., & van der Voort, T. H. A. (1996). Combining background media with doing homework: Incidence of background media use and perceived effects. *Communication Education, 45*, 59–72.

Beentjes, J. W. J., & van der Voort, T. H. A. (1988). Television's impact on children's reading skills: A review of research. *Reading Research Quarterly, 23*, 389–413.

Beentjes, J. W. J., Vooijis, M. W., & van der Voort, T. H. A. (1993). Children's recall of televised and printed news as a function of test expectation. *Journal of Educational Television, 19*, 5–13.

California Assessment Program. (1981). *Student achievement in California schools. 1979–1980 annual report: Television and student achievement*. Sacramento: California State Department of Education. (ERIC Document Reproduction Service No. ED 195 559)

California Assessment Program. (1982). *Survey of sixth grade school achievement and television viewing habits*. Sacramento: California State Department of Education.

Carew, J. V. (1980). Experience and the development of intelligence in young children at home and in day care. *Monographs for the Society for Research in Child Development, 45*(6–7), (Serial no. 187).

Carpenter, C. J., Huston, A. C., & Spera, L. (1989). Children's use of time in their everyday activities during middle childhood. In M. Bloch & A. Pellegrini (Eds.), *The ecological context of children's play.* Norwood, NJ: Ablex.

Comstock, G. A., & Paik, H. J. (1991). *Television and the American child.* Orlando, FL: Academic.

Corteen, R. S., & Williams, T. M. (1986). Television and reading skills. In T. M. Williams (Ed.), *The impact of television: A natural experiment in three communities* (pp. 39–85). Orlando, FL: Academic.

Crawley, A. M., Anderson, D. R., Santomero, A., Wilder, A., Williams, M., Evans, M. K., et al. (2002). Do children learn how to watch television? The impact of extensive experience with *Blue's Clues* on preschool children's television viewing behavior. *Journal of Communication, 52,* 264–280.

Crawley, A. M., Anderson, D. R., Wilder, A., Williams, M., & Santomero, A. (1999). Effects of repeated exposures to a single episode of the television program *Blue's Clues* on the viewing behaviors and comprehension of preschool children. *Journal of Educational Psychology, 91,* 630–637.

Fay, A. L., Teasley, S. D., Cheng, B. H., Bachman, K. M., & Schnakenburg, J. H. (1995). *Children's interest in and their understanding of science and technology: A study of the effects of CRO.* Pittsburgh, PA: University of Pittsburgh Children's Television Workshop.

Fetler, M. (1984). Television viewing and school achievement. *Journal of Communication, 35,* 104–118.

Field, D. E., & Anderson, D. R. (1985). Instruction and modality effects on children's television comprehension and attention. *Journal of Educational Psychology, 77,* 91–100.

Friedrich, L. K., & Stein, A. H. (1973). Aggressive and prosocial television programs and the natural behavior of preschool children. *Monographs for the Society for Research in Child Development, 38,* 1–64.

Gaddy, G. D. (1986). Television's impact on high school achievement. *Public Opinion Quarterly, 50,* 340–359.

Gentile, D. A., & Walsh, D. A. (2002). A normative study of family media habits. *Applied Developmental Psychology, 23,* 157–178.

Gladwell, M. (2000). *The tipping point: How little things can make a big difference.* Boston: Little, Brown.

Hall, E. R., Esty, E. T., & Fisch, S. M. (1990). Television and children's problem-solving behavior: A synopsis of an evaluation of the effects of *Square One TV. Journal of Mathematical Behavior, 9,* 161–174.

Halpern, W. (1975). Turned-on toddlers. *Journal of Communication, 25,* 66–70.

Hartmann, T. (1996). *Beyond ADD: Hunting for reasons in the past & present.* Grass Valley, CA: Underwood.

Healy, J. M. (1990). *Endangered minds: Why our children don't think.* New York: Simon & Schuster.

Himmelweit, H. T., Oppenheim, A. N., & Vince, P. (1958). *Television and the child.* London: Oxford University Press.

Huesmann, L. R., & Eron, L. D. (1986). *Television and the aggressive child: A cross-national comparison*. Hillsdale, NJ: Lawrence Erlbaum Associates.

Huesmann, L. R., Eron, L. D., Lefkowitz, M. M., & Walder, L. O. (1984). The stability of aggression over time and generations. *Developmental Psychology, 20*, 1120–1134.

Huston, A. C., Donnerstein, E., Fairchild, H., Feshbach, N. D., Katz, P. A., Murray, J. P., et al. (1992). *Big world, small screen: the role of television in American society*. Lincoln: University of Nebraska Press.

Huston, A., & Wright, J. (1983). Children's processing of television: The informative functions of formal features. In J. Bryant & D. R. Anderson (Eds.), *Children's understanding of television: Research on attention and comprehension* (pp. 35–68). New York: Academic.

Huston, A. C., & Wright, J. C. (1989). The forms of television and the child viewer. In G. Comstock & G. A. Comstock (Eds.), *Public communication and behavior* (Vol. 2, pp. 103–158). New York: Academic.

Huston, A. C., Wright, J. C., Marquis, J., & Green, S. B. (1999). How young children spend their time: Television and other activities. *Developmental Psychology, 35*, 912–925.

Keith, T. Z., Reimers, T. M., Fehrmann, P. G., Pottebaum, S. M., & Aubey, L. W. (1986). Parental involvement, homework, and TV time: Direct and indirect effects on high school achievement. *Journal of Educational Psychology, 78*, 373–380.

Koolstra, C., & van der Voort, T. (1996). Longitudinal effects of television on children's leisure time reading: A test of three explanatory models. *Human Communication Research, 23*, 4–35.

Kubey, R., & Czikzentmihalyi, M. (1990). *Television and the quality of life: How viewing shapes everyday experience*. Hillsdale, NJ: Lawrence Erlbaum Associates.

Linebarger, D. L., Eskrootchi, P., Sai Doku, N., Larsen, R., & Kosanic, A. (2001, April). *Summative evaluation of* Between the Lions: A new educational TV show for young children. Poster session presented at the biennial meeting of the Society for Research in Child Development, Minneapolis, MN.

Lorch, E. P., Anderson, D. R., & Levin, S. R. (1979). The relationship of visual attention and comprehension of television by preschool children. *Child Development, 50*, 722–727.

Mahoney, J. L. (2000). School extracurricular activity participation as a moderator in the development of anti-social patterns. *Child Development, 71*, 502–516.

Mander, G. (1978). *Four arguments for the elimination of television*. New York: Morrow.

Moody, K. (1980). *Growing up on television: The TV effect*. New York: Times.

Morgan, M., & Gross, L. (1982). Television and educational achievement and aspiration. In D. Pearl, L. Bouthilet, & J. Lazar (Eds.), *Television and behavior: Ten years of scientific progress and implications for the eighties: Vol. 2. Technical reports* (pp. 78–90). Washington, DC: Department of Health and Human Services.

Mutz, D. C., Roberts, D. F., & van Vuuren, D. P. (1993). Reconsidering the displacement hypothesis: Television's influence on children's time use. *Communication Research, 20*, 51–75.

Nelson, K. (1973). Structure and strategy in learning to talk. *Monographs of the Society for Research in Child Development, 38*(1–2).

Neuman, S. B. (1995). *Literacy in the television age: The myth of the TV effect* (2nd Ed.). Norwood, NJ: Ablex.

Pool, M. M., van der Voort, T. H. A., Beentjees, J. W. J., & Koolstra, C. M. (2000). Background television as an inhibitor of performance on easy and difficult homework assignments. *Communication Research, 27,* 293–326.

Rice, M. L., Huston, A. C., Truglio, R., & Wright, J. C. (1990). Words from *Sesame Street:* Learning vocabulary while viewing. *Developmental Psychology, 26,* 421–428.

Rice, M. L., & Woodsmall, L. (1988). Lessons from television: Children's word learning when viewing. *Child Development, 59,* 420–429.

Ritchie, D., Price, V., & Roberts, D. F. (1987). Television, reading, and reading achievement. *Communication Research, 14,* 292–315.

Roberts, D., Bachen, C., Hornby, M., & Hernandez-Ramos, P. (1984). Reading and television: Predictors of reading at different age levels. *Communication Research, 11,* 9–50.

Rosengren, K. E., & Windahl, S. (1989). *Media matter: TV use in childhood and adolescence.* Norwood, NJ: Ablex.

Salomon, G. (1984). Television is "easy" and print is "tough": The differential investment of mental effort in learning as a function of perceptions and attributions. *Journal of Educational Psychology, 76,* 647–658.

Schmitt, K. L. (1999). *The three-hour rule: Is it living up to expectations?* (Report No. 30). Philadelphia: University of Pennsylvania, Annenberg Public Policy Center.

Schramm, W., Lyle, J., & Parker, E. B. (1961). *Television in the lives of our children.* Stanford, CA: Stanford University Press.

Singer, J. L. (1980). The power and limits of television: A cognitive-affective analysis. In P. Tannenbaum (Ed.), *The entertainment function of television* (pp. 353–396). Hillsdale, NJ: Lawrence Erlbaum Associates.

Singer, J. L., & Singer, D. G. (1981). *Television, imagination, and aggression: A study of preschoolers.* Hillsdale, NJ: Lawrence Erlbaum Associates.

Singer, J. L., & Singer, D. G. (1998). *Barney & Friends* as entertainment and education: Evaluating the quality and effectiveness of a television series for preschool children. In J. Asamen & G. Berry (Eds.), *Research paradigms, television, and social behavior* (pp. 305–367). Thousand Oaks, CA: Sage.

Singer, J. L., Singer, D. G., & Rapaczynski, W. (1984). Family patterns and television viewing as predictors of children's beliefs and aggression. *Journal of Communication, 34,* 73–89.

Smith, R., Anderson, D. R., & Fischer, C. (1985). Young children's comprehension of montage. *Child Development, 56,* 962–971.

Timmer, S. G., Eccles, J. S., & O'Brien, K. (1985). How children use time. In F. T. Juster & F. P. Stafford (Eds.), *Time, goods, and well-being.* Ann Arbor: University of Michigan, Institute for Social Research.

van der Voort, T. H. A. (2001). Television's impact on children's leisure-time reading and reading skills. In L. Verhoeven & C. Snow (Eds.), *Literacy and motivation: Reading engagement in individuals and groups* (pp. 95–119). Mahwah, NJ: Lawrence Erlbaum Associates.

Williams, P. A., Haertel, E. H., Walberg, H. J., & Haertel, G. D. (1982). The impact of leisure time television on school learning: A research synthesis. *American Educational Research Journal, 19,* 19–50.

Williams, T. M. (1986a). Background and overview. In T. M. Williams (Ed.), *The impact of television: A natural experiment in three communities* (pp. 1–38). New York: Academic.

Williams, T. M. (1986b). Summary, conclusions, and implications. In T. M. Williams (Ed.), *The impact of television: A natural experiment in three communities* (pp. 395–430). New York: Academic.

Willits, W. L., & Willits, F. K. (1986). Adolescent participation in leisure activities: "The less, the more" or "the more, the more"? *Leisure Sciences, 8*, 189–206.

Winn, M. (1977). *The plug-in drug: Television, children, and the family.* New York: Viking.

Wright, J. C., Huston, A. C., Murphy, K. C., St. Peters, M., Pinon, M., Scantlin, R., et al. (2001). The relations of early television viewing to school readiness and vocabulary of children from low-income families: The early window project. *Child Development, 72,* 1347–1366.

Zill, N. (2001). Does *Sesame Street* enhance school readiness?: Evidence from a national survey of children. In S. M. Fisch & R. T. Truglio (Eds.), *"G" is for growing* (pp. 131–146). Mahwah, NJ: Lawrence Erlbaum Associates.

Zill, N., Davies, E., & Daly, M. (1994). *Viewing of Sesame Street by preschool children in the United States and its relation to school readiness.* Rockville, MD: Westat.

that is now in some 98% of all U.S. households as well as its growth as an industry. Comstock noted the following:

> Five decades ago, at the beginning of the introduction of television in the United States in 1946, two networks offered a total of 11 hours of programming *weekly* over a handful of outlets to about 10,000 households. Four years later, four networks—the familiar American Broadcasting Company (ABC), Columbia Broadcasting Systems (CBS), and National Broadcasting Company (NBC), as well as the short-lived DuMont Television Network (DTN)—were broadcasting 90 hours over about 100 stations to about 10.5 million households. Today, broadcast outlets typically exceed 18 hours of programming, daily, cable networks offer 24-hour services, the three major networks have been joined by a fourth (FOX) and several neophytes, and independent stations are plentiful. (p. 12)

The Annenberg Public Policy Center (1997) reported in a survey of more than 1,000 parents and 300 of their 10- to 17-year-old children the following: (a) nearly 80% of the households with children have an average of 2.5 working television sets per household; (b) two in five (40.7%) of the children have television sets in their bedrooms; (c) the VCR is the most common media delivery system in the homes with televisions; and (d) only half the households surveyed reported having a subscription to a daily newspaper, but nearly two thirds have video game equipment. Of the nine in-home activities measured, after sleeping (8.8 hours), watching television was the most common use of time by children, according to their parents. Children 2 through 17 spend on average 2.1 hours in front of the television, more than doing schoolwork (1.3 hours), reading a book (.99 hours), using the home computer (.87 hours), playing video games such as Sega or Nintendo (.75 hours), or reading a magazine or newspaper (.38 hours). Children also spend an average of 1.1 hours per day in front of their sets watching videotapes. Later findings suggest that U.S. homes and children continue to have an increasingly diverse media environment. Children between the ages of 2 and 7 are already using media for 3.5 hours each day (Kubey & Donovan, 2001). Nevertheless, even as the use of nontelevision electronic media is increasing, television has remained the dominant medium in the home (Woolf, 1999).

Any analysis of the development of television over the last few decades, its prevalence in the home, parental attitudes toward it, and the use and misuse of this medium must also have factored into its tremendous presence the increasing growth of the cable companies and independent media groups that have challenged the major networks for a share of their viewers. In addition, computer technology associated with

4

Television, Social Roles, and Marginality: Portrayals of the Past and Images for the Future

Gordon L. Berry
University of California–Los Angeles

It is axiomatic to state that the medium of television is firmly rooted in the culture of American society. These cultural roots are not, however, benign, ordinary, and commonplace, as the "hula hoop" or the "pet rock" that had their time in the hearts and minds of American children and then faded, perhaps to be seen again in a corner of the Smithsonian Institute. This medium came into American society to be a serious contender with those traditional agents of socialization known as the family, school, religious institutions, and even the peer group. Television and its messages did not have to play by the historical rules of the traditional socializing agents, but it quickly embraced their old cultural messages and proceeded to carve out its own unique ways of characterizing, portraying, and interpreting the customs, values, and beliefs that were so much a part of American life. Thus, television was not only able to absorb the storytelling capacity to pass along the cultural values of the United States, but it also established its own media-based subcultural landscape, a landscape of sight, sound, people, and values that were so highly attractive that its ubiquity in the United States and the power of its messages make it one of the emerging socializers of the young, as well as an informational base point for shaping the attitudes of the old. Comstock (1998) captured the ubiquitous nature of this medium the television set, and a number of its electronic cousins, have all come together with the traditional broadcast outlets to form a dynamic communication reservoir: a type of message-laden communication holding tank where the real and unreal portrayals and positive and negative images can attract like a magnet to our memory to form a system of personal cognitive schemas.

Both the prevalence and power of television in American society have helped to inform the two foci of this chapter. First, I discuss a narrow range of social role portrayals in television programs that relate to race and ethnicity and sex and gender. Social class issues are woven into the discussion because of their natural ability to serve as social role descriptors of both race and gender. It discusses these social roles within the historical antecedents and present-day context of the development of personal schemata that could ultimately give rise to many of the culturally marginalized social role portrayals in television programs. Second, the chapter, through the principles of social learning, demonstrates the potential for children to acquire culturally marginalized views of selected social roles in our society. Thus, the chapter turns both on the past and present experiences, attitudes, and perceptions of various social groups by those who create the social roles and those who receive them.

The concept of a social role is based on the principle that each individual tends to occupy or is perceived to be in a position in groups to which he or she belongs, and other people tend to behave and agree on certain expectations concerning his or her behavior (Goldenson, 1994). Social psychologists would, for example, suggest that the position the individual occupies is termed his or her *role category* (e.g., police officer, and in the case of this chapter, a person of color or men and women), and the attitudes and behavior associated with that category are termed *role expectations* or *role behaviors*. McConnell (1980) argued that a social role is a more or less stereotyped set of responses that a person makes to related or similar situations. Social roles become important, whether you select the social descriptors yourself or have them thrust on you, because any social system can be viewed as a group of related social roles where they are defined by reference to others, related roles, or counterpositions, and to the rights and obligations that each role possesses in the social system (Goldenson, 1994).

Clearly, selecting the examples of social roles to be race and gender was a purposeful attempt to narrowcast the breadth of these complicated concepts. Social roles in a larger context would also include portrayals of the elderly, the disabled, sexual orientation, and a wide range of religious groups with roots in this country and abroad. In fact, there is a natural interrelationship to many of the images in television programs and how various roles are portrayed and frequently marginalized. The concept of media marginalization of social roles is a process by which an egocentric creative perspective consciously or unconsciously, unfairly or inaccurately, provides ethnic, class, religious, and gender cultural portrayals and images that stereotype and misrepresent them (Berry & Reimert, 1994). In addition to selecting a narrow range of social roles to discuss, it should be noted that I am aware of the inherent problems in using certain terms interchangeably, such as race and ethnicity, as well as sex and gender. Looking at the concept of race, for example, we note that it technically refers to biological differences and ethnicity describes groups in which members share cultural heritage from one generation to another (Baruth & Manning, 1991; Pedersen, 1988).

Both of the foci in this chapter related to social roles and marginalization are modest on one level and important on another: modest in the sense that the chapter revisits in a theoretical and broad-based fashion those past and present socialization type experiences that can potentially drive the marginalized images that eventually characterize many of the social roles in television programs. They are important because of the positive potential and even the beauty of the medium of television, when properly used by children, to be a developmentally meaningful social and cultural force for entertainment, information, and education, a medium that is both a communicator and mediator that can teach about and portray the dynamic nature of the various social roles in society. Social role portrayals should be crafted by creative professionals with all of the freedom to show their realistic and human foibles, balanced enough to demonstrate their strengths and weaknesses, and creatively rich enough to illustrate the challenges and values of various roles in a culturally diverse country and world. Thus, there is nothing in this article that should be construed as being contrary to the values inherent in First Amendment rights, creative license, and the ability of professionals to invent stories and characters as part of the creative process. There is an assumption throughout the chapter that children represent a special audience, and adults have a responsibility to play a role in the process of their media socialization.

TELEVISION, SOCIAL ROLES, AND MARGINALITY: CULTURAL ANTECEDENTS AND MEDIA PORTRAYALS

Broadcasters in any country design program content to reflect the viewing patterns of the country and even communities where they are based.

After all, television in the United States is an entertainment medium and a business. These broadcasters must face the challenges of the push and pull of meeting the needs of the viewing audience, adherence to government regulatory agencies, and recognition of the concerns of social action groups. They must also respond to the general competitive environment in which this business enterprise must survive. Broadcasters are further challenged by the need to program for the changing level of cultural diversity that is now a fact of life in the United States. One aspect of the cultural diversity picture can be seen in the growth rates for racial minority groups that census figures revealed for the decade between 1970 and 1980. According to Wilson and Gutierrez (1985), the census figures showed that the minority group growth rates had outpaced the national averages and, as a result, minorities substantially increased their share of the national population in the 10-year period. The biggest growth was found in the Latino and Asian/Pacific Islander groups, although African Americans and Native Americans also posted percentage gains. Between 1970 and 1980 Latinos grew from 4.5% to 6.4% of the U.S. population, Asian and Pacific Islanders from 0.8% to 1.5%, African Americans from 11.1% to 11.7%, and Native Americans from 0.4% to 0.6% (Hauser, 1981; Wilson & Gutierrez, 1985). As of 2003, Hispanics or Latinos represent the largest minority group in the United States.

The 1990 U.S. Census projections showed that by the year 2000, more than one third of the population will be racial and ethnic minorities, and by the year 2010, racial and ethnic minorities will become a numerical majority (Berry, 1993; Sue, Arrendondo, & McDavis, 1992). This "diversification" of the United States can be seen to be more dynamic by data showing that the population is increasingly aging, people with disabling or handicapping conditions are seeking more opportunities, and women presently represent one of the growing groups entering the labor force.

A couple of major reasons have driven the increase statistics over the last two decades and they can account for the accelerated growth of groups of color in the United States. First, there is some evidence that most of the so-called minority groups have a younger median age than the overall population and thus are within the childbearing and family-rearing ages. Second, there has been a particular increase in immigration from Asia and Latin America, and people from other parts of the world continue to be drawn to the United States by the reputation it acquired as a place of refuge for the oppressed. These two reasons and others to explain the increase in the number of culturally diverse groups in the United States mean that our past and present attitudes about racial and cultural differences must be better understood as the country moves toward the future.

It is against the backdrop of the historical attitudes that this country and many places in the world have held about race and color as well as sex and gender that we must understand the early belief systems that emerged about being different. We must also understand how these beliefs about race and gender tended to set the stage for the social role portrayals in the medium of television today. Rivlin (1973) offered the problems of understanding the meaning of being different in a culturally diverse country. He argued, in part, that one of the most difficult words for people to understand when they look at various cultures or subcultures is *different*, because different means different; it does not mean better than or worse than. Although we must ultimately come to grips in this country with what appears to be systemic and unresolved issues of race and ethnicity, gender, and class, the roots of differences have long tentacles into the souls of men and women. Indeed, before there were mass media the very early history of humankind surely had various groups of people waging war because of the differences in tribal beliefs. In addition, one can speculate that in many of these early cultural groups the role of women was also restricted. In 1758 in his classic, *Sytema Naturae*, the Swedish botanist Carolus Linnaeus established the taxonomic (classification) systems for various forms of life. He listed four categories that he labeled as "varieties" of human species. To each he attributed inherited biological as well as learned cultural characteristics. He described *Homo European* as light-skinned, blond, and governed by laws; *Homo American* was cooper colored and regulated by customs; *Homo Asiatic* was sooty and dark-eyed and governed by opinions; and *Homo African* was black and indolent and governed by caprice or whim (*Academic American Encyclopedia*, 1997). It is not difficult to see the clear racial bias in this early view of different groups. Classical Athens frequently relegated women to a status just above slaves and children, and to a life dominated by men.

Slavery in the American colonies was able to survive because of religious, social, political, and economic beliefs that Africans brought to these shores were inherently inferior and could be classified as property along with the other animals. Native American people were virtually annihilated because of a belief in the superiority of people of European descent over these indigenous groups. During the early westward movement, restrictive and oppressive laws were instituted related to Asian and Hispanic people.

An entire array of early events related to race, color, sex, gender set the stage for a number of terms that are a part of the lexicon today, and they are reflective of what can and has driven some of the media portrayals.

Stereotypes, prejudices, racism, and sexism are concepts that emerge when one attempts to understand the genesis of so many images in the early media. Lum (1986) defined stereotyping as the prejudicial attitude of a person or group that superimposes on a total race, sex, or religion a generalization about behavioral characteristics. Hamilton and Rose (1980) stated:

> Stereotypic judgments can be viewed as expressing the perceiver's belief regarding a correctional relationship between two variables, one having to do with group membership and the other being a psychological attribute. Thus, for example, the statement "Blacks are lazy" does not mean that "Blacks, just like everyone else, are lazy"; rather, it states a relationship between blackness and laziness that by implication includes the assertion that non-blackness is associated with lesser degrees of laziness. (p. 833)

Part of this view can be explained by the perspective from Cosby (1994) when she suggested that in relationship to perception and cognitive functioning, humans categorize objects to simplify their environment.

Stereotypes all too often contribute to racism, sexism, and other prejudiced views about people, places, and things in American and other cultures. Jones (1997) suggested that prejudice is a negative attitude toward a person or group based on a social comparison process in which the individual's own group is taken as a reference point. Thus although stereotyping per se may have merit in popular literature and the arts, argued Wilson and Gutierrez (1985), combined with prejudice it poses a devastating obstacle to human development and understanding in a multicultural society.

Racism is often defined as the domination of one social or ethnic group by another. Racism also refers to a theory that inherited physical characteristics, such as skin color, facial features, and even hair texture determine behavior patterns, personality traits, and intellectual abilities. We attribute a number of stereotypic and prejudicial views to race despite the fact that in people or *Homo sapiens*, it has little, if any, biological significance.

The struggle for women's rights that began in the mid-19th century faced a number of difficult obstacles, similar to the issue of race. Butler and Paisley (1980) in their book, *Women and the Mass Media: Sourcebook for Research and Action*, cited a statement made by Elizabeth Cady Stanton in 1860 before the New York legislature, where she drew a parallel between sexism and racism:

> The woman has no name. She is Mrs. Richard Roe or Mrs. John Doe, just whose Mrs. she may chance to be . . . Mrs. Roe has no right to her earnings;

she can neither buy nor sell, make contracts, nor lay up anything that she can call her own . . . Mrs. Roe has no legal existence; she has not the best right to her own person. The husband has the power to restrain and administer moderate chastisement. (p. 25)

Sexism and the ideology of the superiority of one sex over another have shaped American institutions, and impacted the social role of women in profound ways. Thus, wrote Williams (1974), "Women have been seen as incarnations of both the highest good and the basest evil, of chaste and of lust, of virtue and deceit, and of the sacred and the profane" (p. 1).

Prejudiced attitudes, stereotypes, racism, and sexism were all a part of the American psyche as the country was founded, developed through the colonial period, struggled through the Civil War and Reconstruction periods, created a dynamic society through the industrial period, and moved with unparalleled creativity into this age of mass communication. It was not surprising, therefore, that the early forms of popular culture, namely the theater, cinema, newspapers, and magazines, would reflect the attitudes that were held about the role of people of color and women in a developing United States. That is to say, if minority groups and women had to cope with a series of de facto and de jure laws that denied them equal access to a good education, limited employment opportunities, and restricted political rights, it was natural that their social status would reflect the quality of life that they were forced to live. This quality of life became a fertile source of news, storytelling, stage productions, and general hegemony that attempted to tell something about the life and culture of people of color and women.

Images of Black Americans as happy, lazy, dull-witted, and comic buffoons were part of the minstrel shows as late as the 1930s. After all, African Americans in parts of the country were unable to have full voting rights until some 100 years after the signing of the Emancipation Proclamation in 1863. Restrictive legislative and general community practices prevented Hispanic, Native, and Asian Americans from enjoying many of the rights of citizenship. Indeed, even the negative policies toward European immigrants reflected a developing country's fears about ethnic and religious groups, as well as people who were felt to be lower class. Some of these fears about race were later translated into action with this country's internment of Japanese Americans during World War II.

Early progressive newspapers, radio, and journals did make some attempts to be socially responsive to the plight of minority groups and women, but generally speaking, these media followed patterns based on marginalized belief systems that stereotyped or simply ignored them. Of course, many of the so-called progressive and liberal papers also maintained discriminatory hiring practices for minority groups and women. It remained for the Black press and other media to carry much of the fight for equality. Along with the progressive media, significant new coalitions involving African Americans, Jewish Americans, religious groups, organizations of women, White philanthropic groups, and others emerged as early as the 1920s to address some of the problems facing minority groups in various aspects of American life. For example, some of these same groups fought against the David Mark Griffith and Thomas Dixon film, *The Birth of a Nation,* in 1915. This film was designed to establish the principle of White supremacy and to celebrate slavery. These two producers portrayed African Americans in the film as slavish, vicious, sexless and lustful, and corrupt and loyal (Dates & Barlow, 1990).

It remained for a new medium known as television with its initial broadcast reportedly taking place in 1927, to come on the scene and profoundly shape the perception of social roles in the United States. Television in today's world is the medium of choice for children and adults. The images and portrayals of social roles that compose the content of television today, like its early electronic, print, and theatrical relatives, utilized historical and present-day perceptions of them drawn from the way a creative person views, feels, and thinks about his or her role in society. Much of the way people think about others who are similar and different from themselves grows out of their early experiences associated with the socialization process in the home, school, and community, as well as many of the images communicated to them by television and other media. The images on television are drawn from the stored memories and knowledge of the individuals who are creating the social roles, and they tend to represent their understanding of the culture of that ethnic and gender group. It is from this base of personal understandings, whether right or wrong, limited or profound, that the personal, social, intellectual, economic, political, and aesthetic attributes are selected and crafted for the social role portrayals. The combining, organizing, and structuring of bits of information from one's own background is a way of processing it and of making sense of the knowledge about race, class, gender, and a host of other sociopsychological factors in the world. This way of cognitively processing information from a set of beliefs, experiences, and media images can be referred to as *schemas.*

Eggen and Kauchak (1997) suggested that theorists do not agree on a single definition, but most think of schemas as complex knowledge structures that represent one's understanding of events and objects. These schemas are also able to guide a person's actions. Schema theory is based on the assumption that people use the regularities of their experience actively to construct knowledge and expectations about people, places, objects, and events (Fitch, Huston, & Wright, 1993). Knowledge about social roles, groups, and events has been conceptualized as social schemas (Fiske & Taylor, 1984; Fitch et al., 1993). Social role schemas in particular carry certain expectations for behavior, and are one of the plausible ways to account for racial or ethnic stereotyping (Mancuso, 2001).

Social researchers employ a concept called *social psychological distance* to refer to the possible similarities and differences between people. Social psychological distance is a concept that embraces the gap in cultural, social, and individual characteristics and perspectives that separates one person from another, making difficult the development of shared meanings about life's crucial experiences. In the context of this chapter, social psychological distance, socializing experiences, and the level of schematicity can all play a part in the manner and types of social roles that are created and communicated, as well as how they are eventually received by the viewer. To take this position on the potential creative impact of psychological distance and the other psychological constructs does not mean that culturally sensitive social role portrayals must grow out of a similarity of race, sex, and class of those who create them. Nothing could be further from the truth. It is fair to argue that the greater the social psychological distance of those who create and those who receive the social roles, the greater the potential is for prior experiences to cause, consciously or unconsciously, stereotypes to emerge.

Blocher (1987) identified four kinds of systematic biases that this chapter modified to show how they can reflect negatively on social role portrayals when employed in television programs. These assumptions or biases are as follows:

- *Social pathology or deviance assumption.* This view ignores variation in behavior patterns within a given cultural group, and assumes that social problems are rooted in their attitudes, customs, and beliefs.
- *Social disorganization assumption.* This view tends to interpret differences between behavior patterns of dominant and minority groups as a product of social disorganization or disintegration of the minority group.
- *Cultural deficit assumption.* This view of social, ethnic, and cultural differences tends to assume that members of minority groups suffer from deficits as a result of their cultural heritage.

- *Genetic deficiency model.* This view basically asserts that differences between culturally diverse groups in intellectual matters are due to basic genetic differences.

A type of selective reporting and racial hegemony need not be limited to any special type of television program. The local news has been studied by several people to ascertain how the issue of race was reported, and these research efforts demonstrated that some aspects of the biases previously discussed were uncovered. According to Graber (1990), several aspects of the crime reporting of the news implied that Blacks were more dangerous than Whites. For example, accused Black criminals were usually portrayed in mug shots or by footage of them being led around in handcuffs, their arms held by uniformed White policemen. This type of crime coverage may invoke Whites' fear of Blacks by showing Black criminals more than White criminals connected to symbols of menace. On the other hand, none of the accused violent White criminals during the week studied were shown in mug shots or in physical custody. The difference may have been due to the fact that most Whites were alleged organized crime figures of high economic status. They could raise bail money, secure good legal representation, and seek advice on how to handle the press. Thus, the contrast in portrayals of Black and White criminals reflects at least in part underlying differences in the social class of offenders, and is an instance of the unintended class bias of local TV news (Entman, 1990; Graber, 1990).

Concern of developmentalists with the types of subtle or overt intrusions of cultural biases might be due to the extent that they are a part of the legitimate storytelling act, and to what degree they are reflected in largely unconscious processes that negatively skew the cultural messages about various social roles in society. Negative and restricted roles occur from biases that can cause faulty learning experiences about self and others, and eventually confuse our special group of television viewers, developing children.

CHILDREN, SOCIAL ROLES, TELEVISION, AND THE LEARNING PROCESSES

Television is an audiovisual medium with content that can cause, overtly and imperceptibly, learning to take place. Many of the images on television involving race, gender, and class call for the type of mental processing from the children where they acquire experiences about these social roles that can be positive or negative. The social roles being portrayed on television, along with the general personal environmental experiences of children, serve as a type of model from which they can interpret and gain meaning from the roles being portrayed. Central to this type of social cognitive theory is the idea that people learn through interacting with and observing each other, a process referred to as *modeling*. Modeling relates to the changes that result from observing the actions of others (Eggen & Kauchak, 1997). A central proposition on which this type of social learning is based is that children can and do learn behaviors through observations of models who perform such behaviors without direct reinforcement. The combination of the prevalence, importance, and attractiveness of so many role models on television makes the content a potential force for symbolic learning such as that acquired from television. As a result of the prestige that people, places, and things on television hold in the life of the child, it is fair to assume that its models can cause new behaviors and reinforce those that are already a part of his or her behavioral and experiential repertoire.

Johnson (1977) spoke very early to the power of the teaching and learning potential of television by suggesting that this medium is more than a casual communicator; it is the greatest communications mechanism ever designed; it provides us with an unending stream of information, opinion, aesthetic taste and moral values. Leifer, Gordon, and Graves (1974) concluded that children change their attitudes about people and activities to reflect those encountered in television programs. They concluded that television is not only an entertainer of children, it is also an important socializer of them.

It is important at this stage to pause long enough to point out that to advance some of the principles of social learning to account for what takes place when the child is processing and attending to the television content is not to embrace the notion that the viewing process is totally "reactive" in nature. Clearly, the level of cognitive attention and processing given to the content coming from the television is far more complicated to suggest that models, even along with a host of attractive formal features, are the driving teaching and learning forces that simply impact on a passively receptive viewer who is watching this medium. Murray (1980) observed that most of the early research on the topic of television and children focused on the effects rather than the uses of this medium. To Murray, this meant that the research question asked most often was, "What does television do to the viewer?" The question that also needed an answer was, "What does the viewer do to (or with) television?" Although it is fair when considering the impact of the principles of social learning and modeling on the attitudes of children when social roles are portrayed, their cognitive behaviors during the viewing of television are active processes driven by present and past schemata, socializing experiences, and developmental factors that are guiding the levels of learning and understanding of the meanings associated with those roles. Thus, argued Anderson and Lorch (1983), efforts to account for the impact of television should consider what the viewer brings to the television at least as much as it brings to the viewer. Nevertheless, to utilize the principles of social learning as simply one of the theoretical basics for trying to understand the types of learning processes that children utilize to acquire meaning from social role portrays seem to be a reasonable position.

Two realistic questions to ask are what the general nature of the social role or social group portrayals on television is, and what distorted and marginalized attitudes developing children are likely to acquire from them. For example, on the issues associated with the effect and affect of violence on children, we know a great deal because of the long history of research in this area. Violence and the "mean world syndrome" are not, however, the only kinds of influences one would expect on attitudes and values because the content of television drama distorts the distribution of individuals by sex, occupation, and race (Condry, 1989; Signorielli, 1987). Both the extent of television in our lives and its prestige as a communicator of social status have a way of valuing and devaluing social groups. Analysts of television content point out that devaluation and stereotyping of social groups can occur in two ways: by ignoring them entirely or by presenting negative images when they are portrayed (Huston et al., 1992). An early publication by the organization Action for Children's Television (1983) highlighted some of the concerns related to the devaluation of certain groups:

> The "scalp-hunting Indian" . . . the "Mexican bandit" . . . the "crotchety old man". . . the "buxom black mama". . . the "inscrutable Oriental" . . . the "helpless female" . . . all images that are not now part of a more prejudiced past, right? Wrong. Minorities and women have been protesting these tired stereotypes for years. Yet they're all still there in living color on the TV screen, teaching children lessons about the world that countless speeches about racial harmony and sexual equality could scarcely correct . . . What kind of message is TV sending by leaving those who are "different" out of the picture? What does it teach the young Chicano if the Hispanic characters on television are most often criminals? Equally important, what does it teach the young white child about Hispanics—especially if he has no personal contact with them to help him form his own opinions? (p. 1)

Several researchers looking at the issues of the presence or absence of people of color on television have commented on the status of these social groups and their roles. Geiogamah and Pavel (1993) noted that after endless decades of arrogant, insensitive, and greedy misuse of the Native image, the media have in the past several years fallen into a pattern of neglecting, shutting out, and ignoring Natives peoples' pleas for fair representation and a role in shaping what goes out on the airwaves. Hamamoto (1993) discussed the concept of the "controlling images" of Asian Americans where they are portrayed as the evil genius, benign mystic, sidekick, helping professional, and newscaster (female only). Subervi-Vélez and Colsant (1993) pointed out that Hispanic characters are particularly absent from commercial entertainment television; a middle-class Hispanic family has rarely been featured on prime-time, only once some 10 years ago. Graves (1993), although recognizing the increased number of African Americans in some television programs over the years, concluded that the characters are more likely to be presented in a highly stereotyped manner than are White characters in terms of occupational level, social role assignments, and behavioral characteristics. More recent studies of entertainment television have found that some African American characters, like White characters, now are more likely than their counterparts in the real world to occupy high-status lifestyles (Center for African American Studies Research Report, 2002). Finally, it appears that Middle Eastern groups have become a new favorite target for showing religious, political, and related negative ethnic portrayals.

Sex role socialization and the impact of the medium of television must be, as this chapter has argued, considered within the framework of how racial and ethnic groups have been portrayed. Women on television are likely to be younger than men, tend to be cast in traditional and stereotypical roles, and are more likely to have blond or red than black or brown hair (Davis, 1990; Signorielli, 1993). Naturally, most people can easily cite five, six, or more examples of women who are not stereotyped, and it is easy to forget that the majority of female characters in prime time are found in more traditional roles (Signorielli, 1993). One can conclude, as did Graves (1993) and an American Psychological Association task force (Huston et al., 1992), that people of color are underrepresented, are segregated in specific types of content, and rarely engage in cross-ethnic interactions.

The brief sketches of some of the ways in which people of color and women are portrayed must be seen and understood within the context of the child's age, previous experiences, and a host of other sociopsychological factors. As previously noted, television viewing is not a one-way experience for children. Children bring various cognitive skills and abilities to the television viewing experience at different ages that will influence what they attend to, perceive, and understand of what they have viewed (Doubleday & Droege, 1993). Thus, a crucial question for any discussion of content turns on the extent to which the medium is able to provide meaning.

The national policy organization Children Now answered some of the questions on what the medium communicates and the meaning acquired by children and a cohort of teenagers. This group commissioned a study involving a national poll of 1,200 children aged 10 to 17. Their research demonstrated that children get messages about race by seeing how and how often its members are portrayed in television programs. This study found that across all races, children are more likely to associate positive characteristics with White characters, and negative characteristics with minority characters (Children Now, 1998). For example, children associated the following characteristics more often with White characters on television:

- Having lots of money.
- Being well educated.
- Being a leader.
- Doing well in school.
- Being intelligent.

These characteristics were more often associated with minority characters:

- Breaking the law.
- Having a hard time financially.
- Being lazy.
- Acting goofy.

Significantly, race and social class were tightly connected in the minds of the children who participated in this study, and this relationship can be seen in the data summary from the Children Now research.

Children Now and the Kaiser Family Foundation (1997) issued an equally insightful research report related to how females were portrayed in television programs and other media. Although this research was commissioned to examine female characters across a range of media, the findings about television seem to be consistent with some of the research suggested by scholars over the years. For example, the qualities children in this study associated with female television characters were the following: (a) worrying about appearance, (b) crying or whining, (c) weakness, (d) flirting, and (e) relying on someone else to solve problems.

What role is created for women and others is certainly related to the way in which the image makers see the various groups and their sociopsychological perception of the world. By the same token, the child learns about certain roles from his or her perception of the world. That is to say, a worldview, regardless of age, is composed of how a person perceives his or her relationship to nature, institutions, and other persons (Baruth & Manning, 1991). In connection with the term, image makers, it is important to note that the use of marginalized, stereotypical, and positive imagery is assumed today to be created and performed by men and women of all racial and ethnic groups. Although the nature of the psychosocial experiences, artistic motives, professional needs, and financial incentives might differ among creative people, the marginalized and positive images are nevertheless present for teaching and for learning by children. For example, one broad psychosocial hypothesis, beyond financial, creative, and professional considerations, for men and women of color to participate in developing "obvious" marginalized roles might be because younger performers are products of a more integrated society in which their belief is that these images are not used to define their culture and lifestyle. They do not understand or remember when certain images of their racial group were used by the media to retard their economic, social, and political opportunities; they are not aware or do not believe that there are social ramifications to the portrayal of certain roles, and the level of faulty intragroup and intergroup learning that flows out of certain images; and they simply believe that they, like all of their other colleagues in the creative community, have the right to practice their craft without any concern for the images. Indeed, in both younger men and women across the gender and ethnic spectrum, there may be a lack of an institutional, social, and political memory about the use and potential of the various media to define social groups and social roles in American society.

TELEVISION, SOCIAL ROLES, AND MARGINALITY: IMAGES FOR THE FUTURE

Historians have an easier time when they attempt to link theories, issues, and propositions involving both past and present events. I can only suspect that one reason for their ability to deal with a paradox or some levels of contradiction is that the discipline is firmly committed to the proposition that their knowledge of the present is tightly rooted in an understanding of the past. Psychologists and other students of behavior, although also recognizing the role that early experiences have on child, adolescent, and adult behavior, are frequently a little more cautious because of the level of variability found in human nature. The caution can be seen in this chapter as it argued a very modest set of psychological propositions. A major proposition was that early and present-day experiences of the creators of the social roles being portrayed frequently drive, consciously or unconsciously, marginalized images of them. In addition, the social psychological distance, as well as the developmental and psychosocial experiences that the child brings to the images that are created will influence the degree and the quality of their learning and understanding of them. The "experiences" of those who create the social roles and those who learn from and about them are crucial concepts because, like the field of history, many of the images are the products of how people of color and women were perceived in the past and are perceived in the present. Thus, the socializing experiences of the creators of the images, and the children who might receive them, are coupled with the power of television and related media to function as types of legitimizing social agents for learning about one's place and prestige in our society. Past and present experiences and images all come together in television and other powerful media to establish certain concepts or schemas about social groups and their social roles.

If one assumes as a definition of a paradox those statements that are seemingly contradictory and yet perhaps true, it is easy to see why this chapter is somewhat cautious in its propositions. A proposition that is clearly true is that children learn from television and other media. There are, however, complex cognitive processes of attention, perception, comprehension, the nature of reality, and the retrieval of information that add to the need for psychologists and this chapter to be modest in propositions about just what television teaches and how the individual viewer learns. As Condry (1989) put it:

> The world of television drama is different in a multitude of small ways from the world of everyday life that it is attempting to portray. Television is not an exact replica of the world of reality in part because it is a "dramatized" world: scripted, directed, and acted; it is designed with the purpose of attracting and holding attention rather than an accurate portrayal of "reality." (p. 57)

One can readily concede that television dramas are able to take a certain amount of creative license as a natural part of the developmental process.

In an age in which news programs are so efficient in spanning local, national, and international events with various media forms, children are not immune from their positive and negative cross-cultural social role messages. On the local level, for example, many of the news broadcasts are concerned with the issues related to crime and violence. Although these are important areas of concern, professors Gilliam and Iyengar (2000) noted that much of the local news coverage has inextricably linked crime and race in the minds of many Americans. National and international news has so saturated our daily lives about ethnic, gender, religious, and military conflicts through so many different media vehicles that the cross-cultural messages of that content can imperceptibly cause children to filter them through their sociopsychological and develop-mental repertoire of experiences. The results of this filtration process can mean that images and social role messages, if not checked, monitored, or modified, might lead to faulty cross-cultural values and attitudes that can potentially follow children into their next stages of social development.

The future portrayals of various social groups and roles must always be understood within the context of television being a creative entertain-ment medium that is in the process of being transformed into a computer with a series of "bells and whistles," that will give its formal features more power, as well as hundreds of new channels. As we move toward the future, it is always important for the decision makers in the industry, par-ents, and social observers to understand that, although we must not retard the creative process, we do have a sustained obligation to children because they represent a special group in terms of what they learn from this medium. For parents to perform their role of teaching children to use the medium wisely and for broadcasters to be concerned about what children are learning will require an element of trust and open commu-nication between the two publics.

Our basic distrust of television, especially by those groups in our soci-ety who get their information from reading, computers, and other sources, runs high as it relates to meeting the educational and informational needs of children. So often, many people have failed to appreciate the fact that although the content of this creative medium has played a role in mar-ginalizing some social groups and their role in American society, it has been television that has shined its light on the Civil Rights movement, pulled out of the shadows the level of abuse and discrimination against women, and focused on the health and welfare needs of children. Beyond our basic distrust, therefore, there must be the realization that when children are properly schooled to be critical viewers of this medium it can become an important source of knowledge and entertainment. Social action groups must help children in the future to learn how to capitalize on the strengths of television and other media, broadcasters must recognize the special needs of children, and parents must exercise their right to assist in the media education of their boys and girls, which might at times simply mean "turning them off."

Racially diverse and culturally sensitive programming can teach children to learn to value and respect people who belong to groups other than their own. In some current research information from the organization Children Now, it offered the following suggestions for improving culturally diverse content in programming (Media Now, 2002):

- Include people of color in leading roles.
- Represent people of color in positive, nonstereotypical ways.
- Show characters interacting in personal and professional settings, not only with people of their own racial group.
- Cast people of color in a variety of occupations including management, education, business, and other positions of prestige.
- Balance portrayals of different ethnicities in negative roles such as a criminal, comedic sidekick, or cheater. (p. 4)

We know that what children learn from the content of television, the computer, and the emerging media depends on an entire range of psychosocial and developmental factors that make up their worldview. Realizing the complicated nature and unanswered issues about child and adolescent learning related to race, ethnicity, class, religion, gender, disabilities, age, and other misrepresented or underrepresented social roles, it is important to note that when these roles are distorted and inaccurate, television and other media can potentially harm children's social development (Berry & Asamen, 2001). Wartella and Jennings (2001) observed that marketing to children is a year-round activity reaching boys and girls of all ages in multiple venues of television, magazines, in-store displays, direct mail, product placements in movies, video games, and in school. It is fair, therefore, to argue that any real consideration of the positive and negative influences of television on the cross-cultural and even general attitudes of children must be understood and studied within a framework of the multimedia environments in which they are presently growing, learning, and developing. Nevertheless, researchers, parents, teachers, and others should also understand that television is still a major player in the life of the child as an audiovisual portal through which one can acquire access to a variety of other media forms that provide cross-cultural ideas, values, and beliefs about social roles.

All of us in the United States should be concerned with the potential of this medium to be an excellent tool for teaching and learning in a growing multicultural and culturally diverse landscape. In this landscape, television can play a role in helping our children to better understand the real and unreal, as well as the faulty and fair portrayals that are all a part of the creative process. In this landscape people concerned about the social development of children can join with broadcasters concerning the need to be aware of providing roles that will represent culturally balanced images. Balanced portrayals will assist future developing children to gain a more open, civil, and positive worldview of themselves and culturally diverse groups in our society.

Future portrayals on television can be improved when we become sensitive to the types of messages we are providing children. We need to be committed to crafting our portrayals of people from more of an emic perspective that looks at groups from within their own cultural framework as opposed to the etic perspective that views people through the comparative lens outside of their culture (Asamen & Berry, 2003). The development of cultural sensibilities means providing characters that represent people with balanced portrayals of the good and the bad, as well as a variety of physical, social, and emotional attributes. These characters reflect diverse cultural differences within the groups, and have language patterns and social behaviors based on their level of educational and social experiences. These characters should have family interactions and child rearing practices that are reflective of those found in most groups in the country. They should have real cognitive skills, inner beauty, and a variety of believable personality traits. Using these and other criteria when the portrayals call for it can assure us that children of all cultures, when seeing themselves portrayed, will derive a sense of personal worth from the images they see. Moreover, children of cultures other than those depicted will not be misinformed or develop a sense of superiority based on uneven and distorted views (Diamond & Moore, 1995).

One of the current first-rate writers and producers of television programs, David Goldberg, was quoted by Selnow and Gilbert (1993) as saying, "Writers and producers ... breathe in a huge variety of experiences ... and then breathe them out in scripts" (p. 1). In many ways, this statement has been the thesis of this chapter. The creative professionals must have the freedom and responsibility to breathe life into their scripts and characters from their experiences. The corollary to that position is the responsibility we all have to observe the life form being created by them so that we can help children to understand and value themselves as well as culturally diverse people in the United States and the world.

REFERENCES

Academic American Encyclopedia. (1997). Danbury, CT: Grolier.

Action for Children's Television. (1983). *Fighting TV stereotypes and ACT handbook.* Newtonville, MA: Author.

Anderson, D. R., & Lorch, E. P. (1983). Looking at television: Action or reaction? In J. Byrant & D. R. Anderson (Eds.), *Children's understanding of television: Research on attention and comprehension* (pp. 1–33). New York: Academic.

Annenberg Public Policy Center (J. D. Stanger, analyst). (1997). *The 1997 survey of parents and children* (No. 2). Philadelphia: Author.

Asamen, J. K., & Berry, G. L. (2003). The multicultural worldview of children through the lens of television. In E. Palmer & B. Young (Eds.), *Children and the faces of television* (pp. 107–123). Mahwah, NJ: Lawrence Erlbaum Associates.

Baruth, L. G., & Manning, M. L. (1991). *Multicultural counseling and psychotherapy: A lifespan perspective.* New York: Merrill.

Berry, G. L. (1993). Television as a worldwide cultural tapestry. In G. L. Berry & J. K. Asamen (Eds.), *Children and television: Images in a changing sociocultural world* (pp. 1–4). Newbury Park, CA: Sage.

Berry, G. L., & Asamen, J. K. (2001). Television, children, and multicultural awareness: Comprehending the medium in a complex multimedia society. In D. G. Singer & J. L. Singer (Eds.), *Handbook of children and the media* (pp. 359–373). Thousand Oaks, CA: Sage.

Berry, G. L., & Reimert, A. R. (1994). *Marginalization and television.* Unpublished manuscript, University of California, Los Angeles, Graduate School of Education and Information Studies, Los Angeles, CA.

Blocher, D. H. (1987). *The professional counselor.* New York: Macmillian.

Butler, M., & Paisley, W. (1980). *Women and the mass media: Sourcebook for research and action.* New York: Human Sciences Press.

Center for African American Studies Research Report. (2002). *Prime time in Black and White: Making sense of the 2001 fall season.* Los Angeles: University of California, Los Angeles, Center for African American Studies.

Children Now. (1998). *A different world: Children's perceptions of race and class in media.* Oakland, CA: Children Now.

Children Now & The Kaiser Family Foundation (1997). *Reflection of girls in the media.* Oakland, CA: Children Now.

Comstock, G. (1998). Television research: Past problems and present issues. In J. Asamen & G. Berry (Eds.), *Research paradigms, television, and social behavior* (pp. 11–65). Thousand Oaks, CA: Sage.

Condry, J. (1989). *The psychology of television.* Hillsdale, NJ: Lawrence Erlbaum Associates.

Cosby, C. O. (1994). *Television imageable influences: The self-perceptions of young African Americans.* New York: University Press of America.

Dates, J. L., & Barlow, W. (1990). *Split images: African Americans in the mass media*. Washington, DC: Howard University Press.

Davis, D. M. (1990). Portrayals of women in primetime network television: Some demographic characteristics. *Sex Roles, 23*(5–6), 25–332.

Diamond, B. J., & Moore, M. A. (1995). *Multicultural literacy: Mirroring the reality of the classroom*. White Plains, NY: Longman.

Doubleday, C. N., & Droege, K. L. (1993). Cognitive developmental influences on children's understanding of television. In G. L. Berry & J. K. Asamen (Eds.), *Children and television: Images in a changing sociocultural world* (pp. 23–37). Newbury Park, CA: Sage.

Eggen, P., & Kauchak, D. (1997). *Educational psychology: Windows on classrooms*. Columbus, OH: Merrill.

Entman, R. M. (1990). Modern racism: The images of Blacks in local television news. *Critical Studies in Mass Communication, 7*, 332–345.

Fiske, S. T., & Taylor, S. E. (1984). *Social cognition*. Reading, MA: Addison-Wesley.

Fitch, M., Huston, A. C., & Wright, J. C. (1993). From television forms to genre schemata: Children's perceptions of television reality. In G. L. Berry & J. K. Asamen (Eds.), *Children and television: Images in a changing sociocultural world* (pp. 38–52). Newbury Park, CA: Sage.

Geiogamah, H., & Pavel, D. M. (1993). Developing television for American Indian and Alaska Native children in the 20th century. In G. L. Berry & J. K. Asamen (Eds.), *Children and television: Images in a changing sociocultural world* (pp. 191–204). Newbury Park, CA: Sage.

Gilliam, F., & Iyengar, S. (2000). Widening the racial divide: Crime and the local television news. *UCLA Center for African American Studies Report, 16*, (1), 26–27, 38–39.

Goldenson, R. M. (1994). *The encyclopedia of human behavior: Psychology, psychiatry, and mental health*. New York: Doubleday.

Graber, D. (1990). Seeing is remembering: How visuals contribute to learning from television News. *Journal of Communication, 40*, 134–156.

Graves, S. B. (1993). Television, the portrayal of African Americans, and the development of children's attitudes. In G. L. Berry & J. K. Asamen (Eds.), *Children and television: Images in a changing sociocultural world* (pp. 179–190). Newbury Park, CA: Sage.

Hamamoto, D. (1993). They're so cute when they're young: The Asian-American child on television. In G. L. Berry & J. K. Asamen (Eds.), *Children and television: Images in a changing sociocultural world* (pp. 205–228). Newbury Park, CA: Sage.

Hamilton, D. L., & Rose, T. L. (1980). Illusory correlation and the maintenance of stereotypic belief. *Journal of Personality and Social Psychology, 39*, 833–834.

Hauser, P. M. (1981). The census of 1980. *Scientific American, 245*(5), 61.

Huston, A. C., Donnerstein, E., Fairchild, H., Feshbach, N. D., Katz, P. A., Murray, J. P., et al. (1992). *Big world, small screen: The role of television in American society*. Lincoln: University of Nebraska Press.

Johnson, N. (1977). What can we do about television? In M. C. Emergy & T. C. Smythe (Eds.), *Readings in mass communication, concepts, and issues in mass media* (pp. 31–40). Dubuque, IA: Brown.

Jones, J. (1997). *Prejudice and racism*. New York: McGraw-Hill.

Kubey, R., & Donovan, B. W. (2001). Media and the family. In D. G. Singer & J. L. Singer (Eds.), *Handbook of children and the media* (pp. 323–339). Thousand Oaks, CA: Sage.

Leifer, A. D., Gordon, N. J., & Graves, S. B. (1974). Children's television: More than mere entertainment. *Harvard Educational Review, 44*, 213–245.

Lum, D. (1986). *Social work practice and people of color: A process-stage approach.* Monterey, CA: Brooks/Cole.

Mancuso, A. (2001). *An examination of television and real life experiences as sources of children's race schemas.* Unpublished doctoral dissertation proposal, University of California, Los Angeles.

McConnell, J. V. (1980). *Understanding human behavior: An introduction to psychology.* New York: Holt, Rinehart, & Winston.

Media Now. (2002). *Diversity on television.* San Francisco: Children Now.

Murray, J. P. (1980). *Television and youth: 25 years of research and controversy.* Boys Town, NE: Boys Town Center for the Study of Youth Development.

Pedersen, P. B. (1988). *A handbook for developing multicultural awareness.* Alexandria, VA: American Association of Counseling and Development.

Rivlin, H. N. (1973). Preface. In M. C. Stent, W. R. Hazard, & H. N. Rivlin (Eds.), *Cultural pluralism in education* (p. vii). New York: Appleton-Century Crofts.

Selnow, G., & Gilbert, R. (1993). *Society's impact on television: How the viewing public shapes television programming.* Westport, CT: Praeger.

Signorielli, N. (1987). Children and adolescents on television: A consistent pattern of devaluation. *Journal of Early Adolescence, 7*, 255–268.

Signorielli, N. (1993). Television, the portrayal of women, and children's attitudes. In G. L. Berry & J. K. Asamen (Eds.), *Children and television: Images in a changing sociocultural world* (pp. 229–242). Newbury Park, CA: Sage.

Subervi-Vélez, F., & Colsant, S. (1993). The television worlds of Latino children. In G. L. Berry & J. K. Asamen (Eds.), *Children and television: Images in a changing sociocultural world* (pp. 215–228). Newbury Park, CA: Sage.

Sue, D. W., Arrendondo, P., & McDavis, R. (1992). Multicultural counseling competencies and standards: A call to the profession. *Journal of Multicultural Counseling and Development, 20*(2), 64–88.

Wartella, E., & Jennings, N. (2001). Hazards and possibilities of commercial TV in the schools. In D. G. Singer & J. L. Singer (Eds.), *Handbook of children and the media* (pp. 557–570). Thousand Oaks, CA: Sage.

Williams, J. (1974). *Psychology of women: Behavior in a biosocial context.* New York: Norton.

Wilson, C. C., & Gutierrez, F. (1985). *Minority and media: Diversity and the end of mass media.* Beverly Hills, CA: Sage.

Woolf, K. D. (1999). *The fourth annual Annenberg public policy conference on children and television.* Philadelphia: The Annenberg Public Policy Center of the University of Pennsylvania.

5

Is Television Healthy?
The Medical Perspective

Michael Rich

Harvard Medical School
Children's Hospital Boston

Since its introduction in the late 1940s, physicians, psychologists, and other health professionals have expressed concern about the effects of television on the physical and mental health of those who use it. Due to the fact that children are both heavy television viewers and developmentally vulnerable, pediatricians in particular have sought research evidence and clinical interventions for children who are at risk for negative health outcomes. Yet many pediatricians and other physicians also recognize that television is a unique and powerful educational tool. Because much of preventive medicine relies on effective education of patients and their families, many clinicians understand that television can reach more people, often more effectively, than any other health education method. Since its advent, the medical community has regarded television with concern, attraction, and ambivalence.

THE BEGINNINGS—POTENTIALS AND MISGIVINGS

During the early years of television, the American Academy of Pediatrics (AAP) recognized the potential of this new medium to educate the public on health issues. Because pediatricians focus on keeping children healthy, educating children and their parents about normal development is a cornerstone of pediatric practice. The AAP produced several child health education films in the 1930s and 1940s. The response to the films was so positive that prints of *When Bobby Goes to School* were physically worn out by the end of World War II. As the public began buying televisions at the end of the war, the AAP directed its efforts toward developing health education for broadcast on the infant medium.

In 1946, when television was in 6,000 homes, the American Medical Association (AMA) was one of the first professional organizations to utilize its potential, sponsoring broadcast programs such as *Cavalcade of Medicine*, which brought health information to the public. A year later, Johns Hopkins Hospital televised a surgical procedure in a closed-circuit broadcast to 300 physicians, marking the new medium's first use as a tool for medical education. The 1948 AMA national meeting viewed live telecasts of medical and surgical procedures from various locations across Chicago. In 1955, the AMA coproduced a postgraduate medical education program, "Videclinic," that was viewed by 23,000 physicians coast to coast.

In 1954, the AAP created a Committee on Health Education that would "promote research in educational techniques to improve imparting of health knowledge" and "be a source of information for radio and television programs on health education" (Anonymous, 1998). However, because most AAP committees on various aspects of child health pursued public education in their areas of expertise, it was determined in 1957 that the Committee on Health Education was redundant and should be dissolved. Nevertheless, the AAP had set a precedent to use television as an educational tool, and that commitment has lasted to the present (Anonymous, 1998).

Despite their enthusiasm for its power to educate, many health professionals recognized that television had the potential to hurt as well as help their patients. In 1952, a commentary in the *Journal of the American Medical Association* (*JAMA*) worried about the "Influence of Television Crime Programs on Children's Health" (A. Smith, 1952, p. 37).The number of television sets in the United States had increased from a few thousand in 1945 to 17 million 5 years later. Children 7 to 17 years old were averaging 3 hours of viewing each day. The article based its concern on research examining children's reactions to motion picture and radio crime dramas that was published in the *Journal of Pediatrics* 11 years earlier (Preston, 1941). The 1941 study found that 76% of children "habitually exposed" to movies or radio dramas suffered from "increased nervousness" as compared to 40% of children who were not "habitually exposed." Sleep disturbances were found in 85% as compared to 19%, and 51% versus 23% were nail-biters. Fear was found to be five times as prevalent in the habitual viewer or listeners (94%) as in the nonviewer and nonlisteners (17%), resulting in some children "becoming so terrified that they had to go to the mother's bed or screaming from fright until the mother had to waken them" (Preston, 1941, p. 151). The 1952 JAMA article called on the television industry to "acknowledge the adverse medical and psychological implications found in many crime-and-horror programs." The author suggested that, to avoid governmental regulation, the industry should "voluntarily and as rapidly as possible . . . foster research on the impact of television on mind and body and . . . make a sustained effort to avoid programming shows potentially dangerous to the health of the nation's children" (A. Smith, 1952, p. 37).

These early explorations of the interface between television and health illustrate the ambivalence of the medical community. Television was arguably the most effective educational tool and the most pervasive social force of the 20th century. Although it could teach whole populations about proper nutrition, it could also immerse them in violent imagery. Television could be used to share important health information with families or demonstrate innovative medical techniques to practitioners, but for all of its educational potential, television was, first and foremost, a commercial medium. The goal of broadcast television was to sell advertising or, later on, cable subscriptions to the greatest number of customers. In the television industry's efforts to capture the greatest market share for the least production expense, content has often been pushed to be the most edgy, graphic, or titillating, frequently portraying attractive stars engaging in violence, substance use, or other risky health behaviors.

ATTEMPTS TO UNDERSTAND AND CONTROL TELEVISION EFFECTS

There is no question that people learn from television. The lion's share of the advertising industry depends on changing the behavior of television viewers. Yet, as a society, we are reluctant to believe that our young people can be hurt by television viewing. We make a distinction between education and entertainment—we learn important information and values in school, at church, and in the doctor's office, but television is only entertainment, relaxing "down time" for our minds. Unfortunately, this education–entertainment dichotomy is both artificial and incorrect.

Although television had not yet left the laboratory in 1933, Blumer, writing about motion pictures, could easily have been describing television when he called them

> . . . educational in the truer sense of actually introducing [the young person] to and acquainting him with a type of life which has immediate, practical, and momentous significance. In a genuine sense, motion pictures define his role, elicit his direct impulses, and provide substance for his emotions and ideas. Their modes of life are likely to carry an authority and sanction which make them formative of codes of living. (Blumer, 1933, p. 197)

Among the clinical professions, psychology took the lead in researching television exposure and effects in the 1950s, extending and comparing it to work that had been done with motion pictures (Charters, 1933; Dysinger & Ruckmick, 1933; Mackenzie, 1940), radio (Lyness, 1951; Preston, 1941), and comic books (Anderson, 1955; Elmhurst Board of Education, 1954) since the 1930s. Investigations of what children and adolescents were watching indicated that dramatic fiction dominated their tastes, with virtually no educational content watched or desired (Lyness, 1951, 1952; Smythe, 1951).

Television effects research focused almost exclusively on violent content and fear responses in television viewers. The health care community remained silent on the clinical implications of these findings, but the general public and their political representatives did respond, focusing on whether television crime dramas encouraged disrespect for the law. Stating that "juvenile delinquency and disregard for laws have increased in this country because of the laxity in which these problems have been dealt with," Representative E. C. Gathings (D, Arkansas) called for hearings to investigate television programming that was "corrupting the minds and morals of the American people" (*Appendix to the Congressional Record*, 1951). Gathings House Resolution 278 requested that the Subcommittee of the House Committee on Interstate and Foreign Commerce "conduct a full and complete investigation and study to determine the extent to which the radio and television programs currently available to the people of the United States contain immoral and otherwise offensive matter, or place improper emphasis on crime, violence, and corruption." (*Investigation of Radio and Television Programs*, 1952) Chaired by Oren Harris (D, Arkansas), whose opening statement indicated that the subcommittee would not try to define desirable programming or to "clean up" the television industry, the 1952 hearings have been described as congenial, disorganized, and lacking in focus (Hoerrner, 1999).

Network representatives were treated with deference and complimented for their expressions of concern and assurances of self-regulation. Testimony covered television's role in promoting alcohol consumption as well as violence. Unfortunately, no health professionals were among the witnesses, so the health consequences of these risk behaviors were not emphasized. In conclusion, the committee stated that there was too much violence on television, but the television industry was changing too quickly to "pass any conclusive judgment" and they looked forward to the industry removing violent programming from public broadcast under the voluntary controls of the new Television Code. The legislators encouraged the public to criticize broadcasters if they failed to respond and suggested that if the industry was not successful in removing violent content from television, future governmental intervention might be in order.

Little changed. By November 1954, a Gallup Poll indicated that 70% of the American public believed television and comic books contributed to adolescent problems, particularly juvenile delinquency (Gallup, 1954). The Senate Subcommittee to Investigate Juvenile Delinquency had already begun investigating the effects that television had on young people. These hearings were different. Led by the focused, ambitious Senator Estes Kefauver (D, Tennessee), the hearings of 1954 and 1955 established many of the public concerns and the industry responses that would resonate and repeat many times over the ensuing decades. Among the witnesses, Senator Kefauver called health researchers and clinicians. When Dr. Leopold Wexberg, chief of the Mental Health Division of the Bureau of Disease Control in the Department of Public Health, testified in the 1954 hearings that movies, television programs, and comic books may contribute to juvenile delinquency, the investigation was focused on television as one of 12 "special areas" that deserved "concentrated investigation because of their effects" (*Juvenile delinquency*, 1954a).

In response, network executives raised the concern that any governmental regulation of television content would constitute a violation of First Amendment rights to free expression. In addition, they reassured the committee that, "We are aware of no responsible scientific data or opinion which fixes television as the cause of juvenile delinquency. On the contrary, there is a decided body of opinion that television and films have no causal relationship to juvenile delinquency" (*Juvenile delinquency*, 1954b, p. 182). They questioned why Shakespeare and "Jack and the Beanstalk" were not being similarly investigated, explained how the voluntary Television Code would protect the public, and cited examples of positive television programming.

The 1954 hearings concluded with the majority of the Federal Communications Commission (FCC) stating that they were opposed to regulating content on First Amendment grounds, but Commissioner Frieda Hennock disagreed, entering in the record her opinion that the FCC adopt "a firm policy against the future renewal of the licenses of any broadcasters who persist in failure to meet their responsibilities to the public by continuing to subject the children . . . to the concentrated and unbalanced fare of violence" (*Juvenile delinquency*, 1954b, p. 290). The 1954 hearings ended with no legislation, but with calls for more research and for the television industry to improve the Television Code and have child specialists screen programming.

The 1955 hearings, again chaired by Kefauver, called several child health specialists as witnesses. Eleanor Maccoby, PhD, a Harvard child psychologist, presented her research on why children watch television and what activities they are missing during that time, an early version of the displacement theory (Maccoby, 1951). Although she had no research detailing such outcomes, Maccoby speculated whether children's imaginations might be stunted by less fantasy play or whether their cognitive development would be slowed by reduced reading time. Ralph Banay, MD, a Columbia University research psychiatrist, presented his content analysis of 1 week of Washington, DC television programming, stating his opinion, backed by no research, that violent television increased juvenile delinquency (Banay, 1948). Paul Lazarsfeld, PhD, a sociologist from Columbia University, was the only witness who had done any research on the effects of television exposure (Lazarsfeld, 1955). Instead of discussing television effects, however, Lazarsfeld focused on how little was really known about children and television, why so little media research had been conducted, and how difficult it was to secure funding.

Again, television executives testified that this was a complex issue, that no research had indicated any relationship between television and juvenile delinquency, that the industry was broadcasting positive content and voluntarily adhering to the Television Code, and that, above all, the government should not violate the First Amendment.

The subcommittee concluded the 1955 hearings with the opinion that "the FCC is not fully exercising the powers presently vested in it to protect the public interest, and especially to protect the Nation's [sic] children from the multitude of programs dealing with crime and violence" (Clendenen, 1955). They sought recommendations to increase the scope of the FCC mandate to protect television consumers, but only an appeal to use content as a criterion for license renewal survived into the final report.

Although little of substance changed as a result of the 1950s Congressional hearings, the proceedings established lasting patterns of debate among child health professionals, policymakers, and the television industry. Supported by the testimony of health researchers, policymakers reprimanded the industry for television content, scoring political points with the public. The industry disputed the research, but promised voluntary controls and insisted that regulation of content would violate the First Amendment. No legislative or regulatory action was taken and the industry pursued business as usual. Despite repeated calls from witnesses and committee members for more research on television effects, Congress did not move to develop funding for such research.

Interestingly, many issues that would become salient in future debates regarding television effects on children were first introduced during these hearings. Witnesses proposed that television viewing increased aggressive thoughts and behaviors and distracted from the optimal development of reading and cognitive skills. One witness drew attention to linkages between programs and their sponsors' products, calling for no advertising during children's programming. The "catharsis theory," initially advanced at the 1952 hearings, proposed that television violence served as a vicarious release of aggressive tendencies. However, it was not supported by data and, years later, research designed to test the catharsis theory would debunk it, showing that television violence, rather than reducing aggressive thoughts and behaviors, desensitized its viewers to violence. Banay, who presented his 1-week content analysis of violence on television at the 1955 hearings, theorized that emotionally disturbed children would be affected more than normal children, a hypothesis supported nearly 20 years later by research done for the 1972 Surgeon General's Report.

THE MEDICAL LITERATURE ON TELEVISION

Examining both the general medical and health literature (e.g., *The New England Journal of Medicine*, JAMA, and the *American Journal of Public Health*) and appropriate child and adolescent health journals (e.g., *Pediatrics, Archives of Pediatrics and Adolescent Medicine* and its predecessor, *American Journal of Diseases in Children*, and the *Journal of Adolescent Health* and its predecessor, *Journal of Adolescent Health Care*), A. Smith's 1952 article in JAMA represents the only discussion of television in the medical literature in the 1950s and 1960s. During this same period, important research on television effects was being pursued in fields such as psychology and communication. In particular, the experimental work of

Bandura, finding short-term increases in aggression after viewing violent media (Bandura, Ross, & Ross, 1961), and the population epidemiology of Eron, demonstrating television as a significant risk factor for aggressive behavior in children (Eron, 1963), pioneered two critical avenues of investigation in the field. Although these studies would later be "discovered" and cited by those in the medical field as they developed their perspectives and policies on television use, research and advocacy regarding media effects from the medical and public health perspective did not start until the 1970s and 1980s.

Despite the lack of health-specific research, parents and health care clinicians were concerned about television's effects on children from early on. In 1955, the AMA turned to a psychologist, Paul Witty, who had completed five annual surveys of television use, for an article published in their consumer magazine, *Today's Health*. "Comics, Television and Our Children" revealed that children spend "upwards of 20 hours a week with television" and "children read less than before TV." It found "excessive viewing of television . . . to be associated with somewhat lower academic attainment"; the lowest quartile of students averaged 26 hours of television a week and the highest quartile 20 hours a week (Witty, 1955, p. 3). Parents and teachers reported "behavior and adjustment problems associated with TV . . . increased nervousness, fatigue, eyestrain, impoverishment of play and disinterest in school," but concluded "TV alone could not be held responsible." Finally, Witty examined content, finding too few educational programs and too many "undesirable programs for children," indicating that a committee of the National Association for Better Radio and Television was "dismayed over the volume of crime and degree of violence which dominate television programs for children . . . four times greater than in 1951." Witty's article was so popular that it was reprinted by the AMA as a brochure for parents.

MEDICINE EXPLORES TELEVISION'S POTENTIAL FOR HEALTH EDUCATION

While expressing their concern for television's effects on children, however, the medical community still saw television predominantly as an effective means of disseminating information, investing most of its television-related efforts in determining ways to use the medium to educate the general public about health issues, needs, and, of course, ways that physicians could provide solutions for those issues and needs. The AAP convened the first meeting of the Committee on Public Information in

1970, establishing relationships with the major networks so that they could bring child health information to the public through television. The first mention of television in the *New England Journal of Medicine* is a 1972 article on the prevalence of health messages on television (F. Smith, 1972). Planning national public education programs and public service announcements (PSAs) on health issues such as polio immunization, the AAP issued more than 50 press releases annually to networks and local broadcasters as a means of disseminating information on child health issues.

In 1971, the Committee on Public Information collaborated with Action for Children's Television (ACT) to present the National Symposium on Children and Television, featuring presentations by FCC Commissioner Nicholas Johnson and children's television producer and star Fred Rogers. More than 220 pediatricians attended. Later that year, the AAP worked with *Mister Rogers' Neighborhood* on a show about going to the hospital and established an informal advisory role with the producers of *The Little People*, a shortlived network television series about pediatrics. With grant support and the collaboration of the Chicago NBC affiliate, the AAP produced six PSAs on child auto safety restraints, tuberculosis testing, the hyperactive child, polio prevention, rubella, and measles immunization and distributed each of them to between 300 and 500 stations. Ninety-five percent of 250 stations responding to a mail survey indicated that they had aired the PSAs, representing approximately $4 million in donated television airtime.

In 1972, a polio education program produced by the AAP in collaboration with the Centers for Disease Control and Prevention (CDC) and Lederle Laboratories reached 5 million television and radio households; polio PSAs reached an additional 1.4 million people. *Prescription: Food*, a television documentary on child nutrition produced by the AAP, was aired in 1973 in the Boston, Minneapolis, Cleveland, and Washington, DC television markets. This broadcast was credited as being instrumental in helping to obtain supplemental food programs for infants and children in Minneapolis, Cleveland, and Washington, DC.

The AAP made its first foray into series educational television in 1974 with 13 half-hour programs entitled *Ounce of Prevention*, which provided information for parents on topics such as ear infections, tooth decay, nutrition, immunizations, and poisoning. Shown on more than 100 stations nationwide, it reached nearly 49 million viewers. More than 100 AAP pediatricians participated in local follow-up programs, using presentations and interviews on local television to inform the public about and advocate for child health. Collaborating with IBM, the AAP produced the television documentary, *What Makes a Good Father?* shown on all PBS television stations in January 1975. In addition to long forms, the AAP produced PSAs on nutrition and hyperactivity and *Life With Children*, a series of short segments on child health designed to be broadcast by individual television stations during local news.

Due to the success of *Ounce of Prevention*, the AAP obtained a major grant in 1976 to develop a second series of the half-hour programs, this time on topics such as prenatal diagnosis, communicable diseases, the eye, skin disorders, childhood allergies, child abuse and neglect, emergencies, and relationship-building with children at several developmental stages. Encouraged by the numbers of viewers that could be reached through television, the AAP has continued to produce child health education programming to the present, collaborating with independent television producers on series for health-related cable channels.

THE 1972 SURGEON GENERAL'S REPORT ON TELEVISION AND SOCIAL BEHAVIOR

In spite of the medical community's ongoing attraction to the educational potential of television, concern was building among increasing numbers of clinicians about the effects that television viewing was having on children's health and development. The National Commission on the Causes and Prevention of Violence, a presidential commission established by Lyndon B. Johnson after the assassinations of the Kennedys and Martin Luther King to assess the role of violence in American society, issued its 10-volume report in 1969. One of those volumes focused on media violence, reviewing the limited research available at the time, and concluding that there was reason for concern, particularly with television violence seen by children (Baker & Ball, 1969).

It was in this context that Senator John Pastore (D, Rhode Island), chair of the Senate Subcommittee on Communications, convened a hearing in 1969. Inviting the Surgeon General of the United States to the hearing, Pastore asked for the Surgeon General's response to the testimony presented by social scientists, teachers, parents, and television executives. The Surgeon General, who had issued the landmark reports that first linked tobacco smoking and lung cancer, placed media violence in the same public health context as smoking. Asked what he could do about television violence as a public health problem, the Surgeon General requested the formation of the Scientific Advisory Committee on Television and Social Behavior.

As the Surgeon General suggested, the committee was formed, but it generated controversy from the start. The television industry rejected seven of the top violence researchers who were recommended for the committee, replacing them with five network executives. Sixty projects were established across the country, new research was conducted, and 3 years later, the committee released its results. The television executives' presence on the committee had an equivocating effect. The summary statements of the report to the Surgeon General were softened and misleading, using terms such as "preliminary" and "tentative," which fell far short of what was warranted by the research findings. In this context, it is even more concerning that the report concluded that television violence did influence children who viewed it, increasing the likelihood that they would become more aggressive in certain ways. Not all children were affected, and those affected were not all affected in the same way, but there was strong evidence that TV violence could be harmful to young viewers (Murray, 1995).

The medical community was alarmed by the findings. Surgeon General Jesse L. Steinfeld, MD, presenting the report to the Senate Subcommittee on Communications in 1972, stated:

> It is clear to me that the causal relationship between televised violence and anti-social behavior is sufficient to warrant appropriate and immediate remedial action. The data on social phenomena such as television and violence and/or aggressive behavior will never be clear enough for all social scientists to agree on the formulation of a succinct statement of causality. But there comes a time when the data are sufficient to justify action. That time has come. (Higdon, 1976, p. 1)

Concern about television was building among the major medical organizations that care for children. In 1974, the renowned child development expert and a member of the AAP Committee on Public Information, T. Berry Brazelton, wrote to the AAP membership that "a child comes away from a television set believing that physical violence is a perfectly acceptable form of self-expression" (1974, p. 10) but, maintaining his trademark optimism, suggested that "active participation on the part of the parent, as well as the child, may begin to make television the valuable experience it should be" (1974, p. 11). That year, the AAP developed and published *A Family Guide to Children's Television* with ACT.

In 1975, JAMA published what proved to be a political watershed for media effects on health. Reviewing the research, Rothenberg (1975) determined that "one hundred forty-six articles in behavioral science journals, representing 50 studies involving 10,000 children and adolescents from every conceivable background, all showed that violence viewing produces increased aggressive behavior in the young and that immediate remedial action in terms of television programming is warranted" (p. 1043). To compound the problem, the studies showed that children's shows portrayed approximately six times the violence shown in adult programming. Summarizing the studies (p. 1044), Rothenberg addressed four outcomes of interest:

1. Effects on learning—"Novel, aggressive behavior sequences are learned by children through exposure to aggressive actions shown on television or films. A large proportion of the aggressive behaviors learned by observation are retained over long periods of time if the responses have been practiced at least once."

2. Emotional effects—"There is a decreased emotional sensitivity to media violence, as a result of the repetition of violence in the mass media . . . There is decreased aggression anxiety and an increased ability to be violent with others."

3. The question of catharsis—Feshbach's studies "which purported to demonstrate 'aggression catharsis,' have never been replicated and have been disproved by a number of other studies."

4. Effects on aggressive behavior—Aggression is inhibited by (a) reminders that aggression is morally wrong, and (b) awareness of painful outcomes of aggression. Aggression is facilitated by (a) similarities of postobservation experience to observed violence, and (b) the aggressor's state of arousal at time of observing media violence.

From the perspective of three decades, Rothenberg's conclusions appear prescient and provide cause for great concern. At the time he was writing, aggressive behaviors were observed on television, but few viewers went on to practice them, so the learning effect Rothenberg described was less likely to occur. Since then, video games have been invented and are now in 95% of American homes. The graphics, interface transparency, and interactivity of video games have evolved to great sophistication, and players can now participate in and practice behaviors that previously were only witnessed on broadcast television.

THE TELEVISION INDUSTRY ENGAGES WITH THE MEDICAL COMMUNITY

Response to Rothenberg's article was swift and strong, including a criticism from William Rubens of NBC, which stated that NBC "recognizes that television violence may prompt aggressive behavior in some children. We accept the responsibility that places on us" but asserted that Rothenberg's paper contained "distortions" (Rubens, 1976, p. 1551).

After the Rothenberg article, the medical community, led by the AMA, was energized around television. At their House of Delegates meeting in June 1976, the AMA adopted a resolution to oppose television violence and encourage positive programming by the networks: "Television violence is a complex problem. It requires the concerted attention and effort of a variety of individuals and groups, including the medical and other professions, parents and parent surrogates, all segments of the broadcasting industry, and the federal government" (AMA, 1976, p. 79). The resolution authorized the formation of an ad hoc committee to evaluate research and make recommendations for clinicians, as well as the publication of a booklet for clinicians to distribute to parents, emphasizing parental responsibility and guiding their choices of children's programming. The AMA urged television networks, stations, and the FCC to use violence ratings developed by researchers in preparing content and scheduling and to designate violent programming "parental guidance suggested" until the ratings were in place. The AMA sought to explore the possibility of convening joint meetings with the National Association of Broadcasters exploring the effects of television on children, assessing current programming, identifying problem areas, and finding mutually acceptable improvements. The AMA voiced its support of full funding for research on television effects by the National Institute of Mental Health, including the "training of manpower in all appropriate disciplines to perform high quality investigations. Priority should be given to objective and applicable measurements of television violence and its effects, and to the elucidation of how and to what extent various types and degrees of television violence affect children adversely" (AMA, 1976, p. 80).

The 1977 annual meeting of the AMA focused several events on educating its membership about the effects of television on their patients' health. A speech from the Communications Division addressed potential negative and positive effects of television on children, making it explicit that "we're not out to harm the TV industry" and that "positive socially constructive programming can bring it success." Although questioning the health influences of television, the AMA asserted "we emphatically are not calling for censorship or control of TV programming . . . only for reasonable restraint on the part of networks, stations, and sponsors." With this speech, the AMA broadened its concern, "we are concerned not only with violence on TV ... " but with "the medium's overall impact on the social and personal life of our people" (AMA, 1977b, p. 6). A public forum at the meeting on the "Potentials for Positive Programming" discussed both sides of the television issue, providing a document for members entitled "Television: Education for Positive Viewing," which detailed concerns about television, but offered a hopeful set of suggestions for parents on how to select children's television viewing and to generate public programs to discuss the issue, "because we can learn to control our own viewing and our children's viewing and we can turn television into just what it ought to be" (AMA Auxiliary, 1977, p. 1).

In 1977, the AMA House of Delegates stated that "TV violence is an environmental risk factor threatening the health and welfare of young Americans, indeed our future society" and asserted their opposition to "violent programs and their sponsors" and to "television programming that is sexually suggestive or pornographic" (AMA, 1977a, p. 54). The resolution further called for the AMA as an organization and as individual physicians to work with others to deal with this issue and to encourage opposition to television programs containing violence and the companies that sponsor them. They declared their commitment to working with other organizations, particularly the AAP, ACT, the American Academy of Child and Adolescent Psychiatry (AACAP), the American Psychiatric Association, National Parent-Teacher's Association (PTA), and the television industry "on remedial measures and in promoting the development of wholesome and positive programming for children" (AMA, 1977a, p. 54). That same year, the AMA authorized more than $232,000 worth of grants to investigate and determine valid measures of television violence, perform content analysis of sexual behavior portrayed on television, and monitor and rank television violence and the companies that sponsor it. The AMA worked with ACT to upgrade the quality of children's programming; monitor commercials aimed at children; and respond to "distorted" portrayals of racial, ethnic, and sex role models in programming. Finally, the AMA presented "Television Awareness Training" sessions for their pediatrician, psychiatrist, and child psychiatrist members to develop a cadre of clinicians who could teach others about the research demonstrating the potential impact of television on child mental health and development. The intent was to disseminate information and skills through local workshops to parents, community groups, and the press, so that individuals and groups could develop more discerning and discretionary attitudes toward television, and assess the positive and negative ways in which television affected their lives.

In 1977, Robert Stubblefield, MD, a mental health consultant to the AMA, testified about the documented increase in television violence to the House Commerce Subcommittee on Communications: "That television violence represents a serious issue in the mind of the public is a consideration the broadcasting industry can no longer ignore. Television could teach many positive lessons and behavior that would provide alternatives to the violent and anti-social problem-solving so often conveyed in today's programming" (TV violence decried, 1977, p. 1). In response, Alfred R. Schneider, Vice President of the American Broadcasting Company, said that his network "has made a special effort to understand the effects of televised violence on children" (p. 13) by spending $1 million on two 5-year studies that concluded that television viewing did not cause violent or anti-social behavior in children, even though aggressive tendencies increased in psychological testing, fantasies, and play, and some young people were at higher risk for imitative aggression after viewing television. Stubblefield asserted, "The television industry cannot have it both ways—claiming that they entertain, facilitate abreaction and release pent-up emotion, yet denying that they shape and influence behavior. Bluntly stated, shaping and influencing behavior that is stimulating the sale of products is precisely one of the major uses of television" (p. 13).

PEDIATRICIANS STEP FORWARD

Pediatricians were particularly active on the issue of television and children during the late 1970s. In 1976, the AAP expanded the title and purview of the Committee on Communications and Public Information, which prepared an AAP resolution on the effects of television violence on children. Citing research evidence that "viewing violence on television produces increased aggressive behavior in the young" and being "reasonably certain that the causal relationship between televised violence and anti-social behavior is sufficient to warrant appropriate and immediate action," the AAP called for eliminating violence in children's programs and reducing television violence overall. The AAP urged pediatricians to "actively oppose television programs emphasizing high degrees of violence and anti-social behavior which detrimentally affect the attitudes and social behavior of children" (AAP, 1977, p. 1).

On the recommendations of the Committee on Communications and Public Information and the Legislative Issues Committee, the AAP president appointed a Task Force on Television and Advertising, which issued a 1978 recommendation for a ban on television advertising directed at children: "Research indicates that most children do not have the cognitive ability to adequately assess the meaning and intent of commercials. In the face of such evidence, current practices represent commercial exploitation of children for profit" (Academy calls for curbs, 1978, p. 4). The AAP submitted written testimony to the Federal Trade Commission (FTC) for a 1979 hearing on advertising to children: "In a free society, the exercise of responsibility and restraint by advertisers and broadcasters is the ideal remedy. In the absence of such restraint, however, the American Academy of Pediatrics recommends a ban on all television advertisements during programs in which a majority of the audience is composed of children under twelve years of age" (AAP, 1978, Appendix 9). Announcing this policy, Saul J. Robinson, MD, Immediate Past President, explained, "Television advertising directed to children is inherently unfair, since children lack the capacity to understand and evaluate the meaning or intent of television commercials" (Anonymous, 1978). The AMA followed suit in 1979, adopting a resolution that opposed television advertising and programming that commercially exploit children, particularly those advertisements and programs that affect the health and safety of children.

In 1982, the AMA House of Delegates reaffirmed "its vigorous opposition to television violence and its support for efforts designed to increase the awareness of physicians and patients that television violence is a risk factor threatening the health of young people," reinstituting its action program to increase awareness of television violence as a health risk. Having been reaffirmed by action of the House of Delegates twice since that time, this policy remains in effect (AMA, 1982–2003).

In a follow-up to the Surgeon General's 1972 report, the National Institute of Mental Health commissioned a report on television and behavior that was published in 1982. Its findings reinforced those reached by the report 10 years earlier.

> The scientific support for the causal relationship derives from the convergence of findings from many studies, the great majority of which demonstrate a positive relationship between televised violence and later aggressive behavior. (Pearl, Bouthilet, & Lazar, 1982, pp. 89–90)

MEDICAL GROUPS FOCUSING ON THE HEALTH EFFECTS OF TELEVISION

Recognizing that momentum on the issue of television and children was growing, the Executive Board of the AAP recommended formation of an ad hoc Task Force on Children and Television in 1983. At its first meeting, the Task Force defined its function as primarily educational, planning to prepare anticipatory guidance material for parents on television viewing and its effects on children, positive and negative. The Task Force identified critical points that would guide its efforts:

1. Children learn from television.
2. Children's behavior can be altered by television viewing.
3. Effects of television on children are influenced by the child's developmental stage and the context in which he or she views television.
4. Evidence indicates that television adversely affects the behavior of children and adolescents with respect to violence, nutrition, school performance, drugs (including alcohol), sexuality, and stereotype, as well as their worldview.
5. Television has significant potential for beneficial learning.

"The positive effects of television at a motivational level are largely unexploited, and the potential for television meeting its expected values for children is missing" (AAP, 1983, p. 3). Over the next several years, convening biannually, the Task Force met with scientists and network executives, parent groups and scriptwriters, defining and establishing the field of education and advocacy on television as a public health issue.

In 1984, the Task Force on Children and Television issued the first AAP policy statement on television. "Children, Adolescents, and Television" (AAP, 1984, p. 8) states that, next to the family, television may be children's most important source of information and influence on development. It asserts that television "can promote learning, create aspirations, and induce prosocial behavior," but it can also adversely affect learning and behavior of children and adolescents in the following areas: (a) televised violence can promote a tendency toward violence; (b) consumption of high-calorie snacks goes up when viewing television, increasing the prevalence of obesity; (c) learning from television is passive, not active, and takes time away from reading and other active learning; (d) television conveys unrealistic messages about tobacco, alcohol, and other drugs, indirectly encouraging their use; (e) television's portrayal of sex roles and sexuality is unrealistic and without health consequences such as pregnancy or sexually transmitted disease; (f) television reinforces ethnic and racial stereotypes and does not increase understanding of people with disabilities; and (g) television's portrayals of problem solving or conflict resolution are unrealistic. The policy recommended that the AAP (a) educate pediatricians regarding the health implications of television viewing; (b) provide materials and support for appropriate anticipatory guidance regarding television use; (c) encourage legislation to improve children's programming and reduce child-directed advertising; (d) establish relationships with industry groups to improve programming and advertising; (e) continually review new technologies that allow better control of television viewing; and (f) act locally, encouraging television stations to carry quality children's programming and reduce child-directed ads. The policy statement was based on research in psychology and communication; at that point in time, there was little to reference in the medical literature.

MEDICAL AND PUBLIC HEALTH RESEARCH ON MEDIA EFFECTS

This was about to change. Media researchers began to focus more consistently on health effects, resulting in a dramatic increase in research published in the medical and public health literature, starting in the mid-1980s and increasing consistently to the present. After more than two decades of no research in the leading medical and public health journals, *JAMA* printed six articles and *Pediatrics* and the *New England Journal of Medicine* each published three during the 1970s. There continued to be no papers in the *American Journal of Public Health*, *Archives of Pediatrics and Adolescent Medicine*, or *Journal of Adolescent Health*. In the second half of the 1980s, four of the six journals presented 34 papers on media and health. By the 1990s, all six journals were represented, publishing 117 papers on media and their health effects. The first 5 years of the 21st century have produced 159 papers. This increase in medical research on the health effects of media use has resulted in parallel increases in public education and policy statements by major health organizations.

In 1986, the AAP Committee on Adolescence issued a policy statement, "Sexuality, Contraception, and the Media," implicating television as a powerful teacher of unrealistic and irresponsible sexual behavior and indicating its potentially positive role in educating young people about responsible sexuality and in advertising contraception (AAP, 1986). In this statement, the AAP joined the American College of Obstetrics and Gynecology, the Society for Adolescent Medicine, and the American Public Health Association in "supporting and encouraging the airing of advertisements for nonprescription contraceptives on television" (p. 536) as long as the content was "educational, realistic and focused on responsible sexual behavior and decision-making" (p. 536). The AAP urged television producers to "alter the portrayal of sexuality in non-news programming to reflect realistic consequences and responsible behavior and to decrease the association of suggestive and stimulating sexual messages with product advertising" (p. 536).

The Task Force on Children and Television was designed as a temporary means of addressing television as a child health issue, but it became clear that the issue was ongoing and increasing in scope and importance. In 1985, a year before the Task Force was scheduled to be dissolved, the AAP established the Committee on Communications, which would absorb the functions of public education and public relations, as well as address the growing issue of media effects on child health and development. Noting all that had been accomplished in a short period of time, the Task Force on Children and Television expressed concern that its work continue unabated. The 1984 policy statement had given the AAP national recognition as a leading advocate for children on the television issue and they had established vital relationships with researchers and the television industry. Because previous AAP efforts to deal with television had dissipated into inactivity, the Task Force feared that its dispersal would lose the mission and dissipate the momentum that the Task Force had developed. These concerns were unfounded.

In 1988, the Committee on Communications issued its first television policy statement, "The Commercialization of Children's Television and Its Effect on Imaginative Play" (AAP, 1988, p. 900). This statement cautioned about toy-based television programming, warning that it exploited children, promoted violent behavior, caused intellectual passivity, and inhibited imaginative play. It stated that prolonged television viewing was "a major source of inactivity and can cause a variety of adverse health and behavioral disorders," citing the first supporting research from the medical literature, authored by the chair of the now-defunct Task Force on Children and Television (Dietz & Gortmaker, 1985). Recommendations included (a) parents limiting the time their children watch television and monitoring the programs they watch, (b) opposition to television-activated toys and the increasing commercialism of children's television, (c) legislation mandating daily broadcasts of education programs for children, and (d) research on the effects of televised violence and toys that glorify violence.

AACAP approved its only policy statement dealing with media in 1987 (reissued in 1997). "Substance Abuse—The Nature and Extent of the

Problem" (AACAP, 1987/1997) mentioned media exposure as one of the risk factors for substance abuse: "Substance use . . . is often glamorized by the media by associating it with images of being successful, sophisticated, and socially acceptable. Use of alcohol, tobacco, and medication is presented as a part of life without serious regard for the potential consequences." Although the statement decried the influence of television and other media, it did not make recommendations for addressing media as a risk factor. AACAP also published fact sheets on topics of special concern to the child and adolescent psychiatrist. Concerned about the effects of television on the mental and social health of children and adolescents, AACAP issued a fact sheet on children and television violence in 1989, updating it in 1999:

> Extensive watching of television violence by children causes greater aggres-siveness. Sometimes, watching a single violent program can increase aggres-siveness. Children who view shows in which violence is very realistic, frequently repeated or unpunished, are more likely to imitate what they see. The impact of TV violence may be immediately evident in the child's behav-ior or may surface years later, and young people can even be affected when the family atmosphere shows no tendency toward violence. (AACAP, 1989/1999)

In general, the AACAP fact sheets were more inclined to offer solutions for media influence than the policy statement. "Active parenting can ensure that children have a positive experience with television. Parents can help by: viewing programs with your children, selecting develop-mentally appropriate shows, placing limits on the amount of television viewing (per day and per week), turning off the TV during family meals and study time, turning off shows you don't feel are appropriate for your child" (AACAP, 2001).

In 1989, 1 year after its first policy statement, the AAP Committee on Communications published a second one, "Impact of Rock Lyrics and Music Videos on Children and Youth," stating (a) parents should "recog-nize that television is a potent teacher of children and adolescents" (p. 314) and that music videos expose young people to issues such as sexuality, vio-lence, and drug abuse, so parents should control viewing; (b) parents should coview and teach critical viewing of television; (c) music video producers should be influenced to exercise good taste; and (d) the industry should be encouraged to produce videos modeling healthy behavior with prosocial themes. Again, the AAP called for more research (AAP, 1989).

Concern about media influence on adolescents' sexual attitudes and behaviors led the Committee on Communications to form a Task Force on Adolescent Sexuality in 1990. Reviewing the research, they recommended addressing the prevalence of teen pregnancy and sexually transmitted infections by using media to encourage adolescents to decrease their sexual activity and increase their use of contraceptives. Targeting 12- to 15-year-olds, the ongoing message of sexual responsibility would be delivered through pediatricians, music videos, television PSAs, and peer leadership groups. The AAP approved of this program in concept, but the external funding required to implement it never materialized.

In 1990, the AAP Committee on Communications updated "Children, Adolescents and Television" (AAP, 1990), reiterating their concern and directives to the AAP membership and adding recommendations that (a) pediatricians specifically advise parents to limit their children to 1 to 2 hours of television each day, and (b) families participate in selection of television programs, coview, and use prescreened videos as much as possible. They added specifics on their recommendations regarding advertising to children, seeking a ban on toy-based programming, elimination of all alcohol advertising, and the introduction of extensive alcohol counteradvertising. Most important, with this policy statement, and in testimony to the U.S. Congress, the AAP sought strong legislative support for the Children's Television Act. Joined by a diverse coalition of prochild groups, the AAP asked that the Children's Television Act demand 1 hour of quality educational children's programming each day, with strong enforcement of the rule by making compliance a condition of each broadcaster's license renewal. The Children's Television Act was passed into law by Congress in 1990, but in a diluted form, which required only 3 hours of children's television each week.

The AAP Committee on Communications streamlined its policy statement "The Commercialization of Children's Television" in 1992, focusing it on consumerism and advertising, with particular concern paid to advertising of foods with high calories and low nutritional value (AAP, 1992). The Committee recommended that parents teach children that television commercials are designed to sell products, educating them to be "responsible and informed consumers" (p. 344). Increasingly concerned about the effects of television viewing on obesity, the AAP demanded that "food advertisements aimed at children should be eliminated" (p. 344). Because the Children's Television Act had set limits for commercial time during children's programming, the policy statement urged pediatricians to monitor broadcasters' compliance and support the development of more programming alternatives for children. Still able to reference only one research paper from the medical literature, the AAP called for more research.

CONGRESS GETS INVOLVED

In 1993, there was a great deal of congressional activity on television violence, with no fewer than eight Senate and House bills under consideration. As part of this debate, the AAP, now a recognized national leader in advocating for children on media effects, was asked to testify on television violence and its impact on children. William H. Dietz (1993), MD, PhD, chair of the former Task Force on Children and Television, stated to the Subcommittee on Telecommunications and Finance of the House Energy and Commerce Committee and to the Subcommittee on the Constitution of the Senate Judiciary Committee, "We believe that televised violence has a clear and reproducible effect on the behavior of children, that televised violence contributes to the climate in which we live, the frequency with which violence is used to resolve conflict and the passivity with which violence is perceived" (p. 2).

Of most historical importance among the eight bills under consideration by Congress was the Television Violence Reduction Through Parental Empowerment Act of 1993 introduced by Representative Edward Markey (D, Massachusetts). Nicknamed the "V-Chip bill," it mandated that all new televisions be equipped with an electronic device, a violence chip or V-chip, that could be set by parents to block out any show with a rating to which they did not wish their children exposed. The television industry would be responsible for rating the shows and for broadcasting rating information with the shows, triggering the V-chips. "To the fullest extent possible, parents should be empowered with the technology to choose to block the display on their televisions of programs they consider too violent for their children" (Television Violence Reduction through Parental Empowerment Act of 1993, 1993). The AAP endorsed the concept of the bill, because its goal was to increase parental control over their children's media use and exposure. However, the Committee on Communications reviewed the bill and did not believe that the V-chip was a viable solution. The committee thought that parents were unlikely to use it, a perceptive observation given what has occurred since the legislation passed. The V-chip was mandated to be part of every new television with a screen larger than 13 inches sold after January 2000, but in a survey done in 2004, 59% of parents had V-chip-equipped televisions but did not know about or use the device, 26% did not have V-chip-equipped televisions, and only 15% had used the V-chip (Rideout, 2004).

In December 1993, riding the momentum of public and political concern about televised violence, Senator Kent Conrad (D, North Dakota) formed the Citizens Task Force on TV Violence, a coalition of 20 organizations that included the AAP, AMA, AACAP, and the American Psychiatric Association, along with the National Education Association, National PTA and other school organizations, National Association of Social Workers, International Association of Chiefs of Police, and other law enforcement groups. The Citizens Task Force on TV Violence submitted the following recommendations to Attorney General Janet Reno: (a) that a violence code for entertainment media be developed and agreed on by the entertainment industry and the government, (b) that violent-rated programming have warnings superimposed on the television screen, (c) that all televisions have devices for blocking out violent programming, (d) that violent television not be available in prisons, (e) that FCC hearings and a White House conference on media violence be convened, (f) that the Children's Television Act be strengthened and enforced by the FCC, and (g) that antitrust exemptions be continued under the Television Program Improvement Act to permit discussions and collaboration with the television industry in pursuing these initiatives.

In 1994, "in the interest of improving mental health and reducing acts of violence," the AMA Board of Trustees reviewed the body of media effects research and reports generated by the U.S. Surgeon General, the National Institute of Mental Health, American Psychological Association (APA), CDC, National Academy of Science, and Society for Adolescent Medicine. Examining original studies and meta-analyses, their report found that the research supported two conclusions: (a) exposure to televised violence was positively associated with aggression across a wide range of ages and measures of aggressive behavior, and (b) viewing of violent television increased aggressive behavior and decreased prosocial behavior. They noted that these effects remained stable over time, across ages, genders, locations, cultures, and other demographic differences regardless of the outcome measures used. The report quoted Huesmann, a leading researcher in this area: "Aggressive habits seem to be learned early in life, and once established, are resistant to change and predictive of serious adult antisocial behavior. If a child's observation of media violence promotes the learning of aggressive habits, it can have harmful lifelong consequences" (AMA, 1994, p. 80).

Seeking a solution, the AMA examined media rating systems, most notably the Motion Picture Association of America (MPAA) movie ratings on which television and other media ratings are based. The report was critical of the MPAA movie ratings because they were not determined by scientific or objective methods, but by an anonymous and unaccountable ratings board made up of parents, but no experts in child development or health. Social science research on the effects of media exposure was ignored by the ratings board, which was "instructed to focus on how other parents might feel about a film, not on how or whether a film might pose risks for children" (p. 83). The AMA report criticized the structure and implementation of the MPAA rating system on three counts: (a) that its age groupings of 0 to 12 years, 13 to 16, and 17 and older were inconsistent with child developmental stages; (b) that ratings focused on the amount of violence rather than the context, which research indicates has a more potent effect, and (c) that more restrictive ratings were assigned for sexual content and profanity than for violence, a perspective directly contradicted by the research evidence (AMA, 1994).

Concluding that "programming shown by the mass media contributes significantly to aggressive behavior and, in particular, to the aggression-related attitudes of many children, adolescents, and adults" and that "the viewing of televised aggression leads to increases in subsequent aggression that can become part of a lasting behavioral pattern" (p. 80), the AMA called for the development of a valid and usable rating system that would "give consumers more precise information about violent and sexual content of motion pictures, television and cable television programs, and other forms of video and audio entertainment" (p. 88). The AMA offered its expertise in health and child development to work with the entertainment industry on developing a uniform rating system for videos, movies, and television with more detailed content information and several childhood age categories (AMA, 1994). At a hearing of the House Energy and Commerce Subcommittee on Telecommunications and Finance, AMA President Robert E. McAfee, MD, said parents need objective information to make informed decisions regarding their children's media use, "We need a set of minimum, easily understood ratings that allow parents to do the job of parenting" (Jones, 1994, p. 8).

PHYSICIANS TAKE CHARGE ON THE ISSUE OF TELEVISION AND CHILDREN

In the mid-1990s, a number of medical organizations, individually and in coalitions, increased or initiated their efforts to respond effectively to television violence. In 1994, the AAP, AACAP, and the Institute for Mental Health Initiatives discussed collaborating on a number of projects, such as an international conference exploring the effects of exported American entertainment violence on foreign countries. At the

1995 Interim Meeting, the AMA House of Delegates adopted a resolution to expand the Campaign Against Family Violence to address media violence. As a result, in 1996 the AMA published a primer to educate physicians and their patients on media violence (Walsh, Goldman, & Brown, 1996), distributing nearly 50,000 copies. The 1996 AACAP meeting focused on violence, featuring a symposium on media violence. AACAP also issued new and updated versions of its media fact sheets through the mid-1990s, including "Children and TV Violence" (AACAP, 1989/1999), "Influence of Music and Music Videos" (AACAP, 2000), "Children and the News" (AACAP, 2002), and "Children and Watching TV" (AACAP, 2001). Recognizing their responsibility as the long-established leader in advocating for media that are safe for children's health and development, the AAP Committee on Communications invited liaison representatives from the AACAP and the APA to join their meetings from 1995 on.

The AAP, in particular, was a hotbed of activity on the issue of children and television. They issued a number of key policy statements, established a resource office in Los Angeles for the entertainment industry to obtain accurate information on children and their health, and were sought out by a wide variety of entertainment entities to endorse ratings systems or programs. The AAP appointed Donald Shifrin, MD, to represent them on the Council of the National Television Violence Study (Federman, 1996, 1997, 1998), which examined broadcast, independent, and cable television broadcasts over 3 years for both violent content and the context in which the violence is portrayed. Shifrin provided the AAP with overviews of each of the 3 years of the study. After Year 1, he expressed concern about the inappropriate methodology and absence of content analysis, a lack of scientific rigor that was unacceptable to the medical community. Year 2 focused on children's television, finding the prevalence of violence to be greater than in adult television. In addition, the context in which violence is portrayed worsened the effect on children, because violence was perpetrated by attractive characters, appeared justified, had minimal and short-lived consequences for the victim, and went unpunished. Year 3 examined how the television industry responded to the findings and recommendations of Years 1 and 2. There was no measurable response. There was little change in the prevalence of violence on television during the 3 years: 61% of all programs contained violence, much of it trivialized; only 16% showed long-term consequences of violence; and 3% had an antiviolence theme. Antiviolence messages were a rarity in television, and even among them, concrete suggestions for avoiding violence were not offered. Recommendations from the Council included (a) increasing nonviolent programming; (b) showing realistic negative consequences, including punishment, of violence; (c) exploring nonviolent means of resolving conflict; (d) pairing violent portrayals with antiviolence themes; and (e) having on-screen warnings about high-risk behaviors in cartoons and other programs watched by children who may not be able to distinguish fantasy from reality. Unfortunately, the television industry did not respond to any of the Council's recommendations. Without dialogue and cooperation with the television industry, pediatricians found themselves forced to find other ways to keep children healthy and safe in a media-saturated environment.

> If the mammoth amount of research has taught us one thing, it is that television violence is probably here to stay . . . not only must we stress media literacy among our youngest citizens, but increase vigilance as to the job that the television industry will do . . . a significant effort will have to be put forth to the parents of our youngsters in terms of not only the amount of television they watch but where the television set is located, and certainly their own television role modeling within their own family context. (Shifrin, 1998, p. 5)

The AAP continued its advocacy through the 1990s, opposing Whittle Communications' Channel One program, which offered schools televisions in every classroom and a VCR in return for a commitment to show all of their students Channel One's daily broadcasts of 10 minutes of "soft news" programming and 2 minutes of commercials, many of them for snack foods.

In 1995 and 1996, the AAP issued five policy statements addressing various aspects of television's effects on child health and development. A new statement, "Media Violence" (AAP, 1995c), recommended that pediatricians learn about the effects of media violence, incorporate that knowledge into anticipatory guidance of their patients, and advocate with the television producers, networks, and local stations for less violent content and better protections for children. It encouraged parents to monitor and limit their children's television viewing to 1 to 2 hours per day, to coview television and discuss its content, and to ensure that their children become "media literate" and able to protect themselves.

Because pediatricians were increasingly concerned about toy merchandising and junk food commercials on television, the AAP released a second new statement addressing "Children, Adolescents, and Advertising" (AAP, 1995a). In it, the AAP recommended limitations to advertising during children's programming, stricter definitions and enforcement of educational programming, regulation of toy-based programs by the FCC, prime-time antidrug PSAs and tobacco and alcohol counteradvertising, broadcast of condom commercials, a ban on all tobacco and alcohol advertising, and consumer education for children so that they could protect themselves from commercial exploitation.

An update on "Sexuality, Contraception, and the Media" (AAP, 1995d) expanded on the 1986 recommendations, urging parents to discuss with their children the influence of media on sexual behavior, encouraging the television industry to adhere to guidelines for responsible sexual conduct, broadcast PSAs to promote abstinence and the use of condoms to prevent pregnancy and sexually transmitted infections, and air these PSAs as well as commercials for contraception with programs aimed at adolescents.

"Children, Adolescents, and Television" (AAP, 1995b) was also updated in 1995, reinforcing the AAP's concern about the effects of television on child health and development, adding recommendations that (a) parents help children learn critical viewing skills and develop television substitutes such as reading, sports, and hobbies; and (b) pediatricians specifically discuss the effects of media violence on children and that they model appropriate use of television for children and parents by having educational videos, books, and age-appropriate toys in their waiting rooms or by establishing them as television-free zones. "Impact of Music Lyrics and Music Videos on Children and Youth" (AAP, 1996) was reissued in 1996, with many of the same suggestions for pediatricians, parents, and the television industry in relation to music videos, encouraging media literacy and coviewing as protective measures, and adding a recommendation that music and music videos be labeled for content.

MEDICINE REACHES OUT TO THE TELEVISION INDUSTRY

Recognizing the power of television to teach and empower young people, the Committee on Communications sought to improve the content in television programming by encouraging producers to portray children and adolescents as authentic, respected, and valued individuals, and to explore critical issues of health and development in responsible and realistic ways. Therefore, the Committee on Communications recommended that a group of Los Angeles-based pediatricians be formed to offer technical assistance to entertainment industry writers and producers. The AAP Media Resource Team (MRT) was formed in 1994 to work as consultants to the entertainment industry. Its express mission was to (a) increase the number of positive media messages about children and teens; (b) stop negative, harmful, or inaccurate messages aimed at or affecting young people from being broadcast through the media; and (c) serve as a resource for accurate information on child health and development for writers, directors, producers, and other members of the television industry. The AAP hired a part-time consultant, established an office and a doctor's hotline in Los Angeles, and published *Writer Bytes*, a monthly newsletter of tips for writers. The MRT advertised to the television industry that it had 45 pediatricians "on call" for a wide variety of child and adolescent-related questions. MRT representatives met with representatives of the Producers Guild, Directors Guild, and Writers Guild of America, offering their services. Concerned about programming and writing choices, the MRT established dialogues with Fox Network executives and the producers of *Power Rangers*, but had no influence on their programming. The MRT's most effective work may have been with the program *America's Funniest Home Videos* when they convinced the producers, for the purpose of protecting their viewers' safety, not to broadcast potentially dangerous scenes of a child gagging on milk and of one child using another's body as a sled. Over the next 4 years, the MRT worked with ABC, CBS, and PBS on programs including *ER, Home Improvement, Mad About You, Captain Kangaroo,* and *Wimzie's House.* The AAP Board of Directors recognized the importance of the influence and dialogue that the MRT had established with the entertainment industry, but wanted the MRT to make its operations as cost-effective as possible. Because the expense of maintaining a Los Angeles office, publishing a trade newsletter, and paying a part-time consultant were considerable for a dues-supported organization, they requested that MRT generate a quantified evaluation of their operations and achievements for their review.

MEDIA LITERACY AS A HEALTH INTERVENTION

In 1997, the AAP launched *Media Matters*, a national parent empowerment and media literacy campaign to be implemented through pediatricians. Emphasizing the role of media literacy and critical viewing, *Media Matters* planned to educate pediatricians about the effects of media on child health and development, train them in media literacy tools for decreasing negative outcomes, and encourage them to take a media history at each health maintenance visit. The Committee on Communications informed pediatricians of this initiative through a series of media education articles in the *AAP News*, generating great interest among the AAP membership. The *Media Matters* campaign obtained funding from the White House Office of National Drug Control Policy and the Center for Substance Abuse Prevention for two national leadership training courses, physician's and parents' guides to media education, a Media History form, and a speaker's kit on the subject of media and its effects on child health. The training courses were fully enrolled and enthusiastically received by hundreds of pediatricians. A *Media Matters* listserv was established and quickly became an important communication tool for the growing network of pediatricians committed to the issue of children and media. *Media Matters* resource kits, including AAP policy statements on media, speaker's kits, educational brochures, and media history forms, were developed and disseminated to members who requested them. Many of the pediatricians trained by *Media Matters* gave presentations and media literacy workshops to patients, parents, schools, and community groups, providing tools to recognize and address negative outcomes from television and other media use. To date, *Media Matters* remains the most effective large-scale media literacy intervention implemented by any national organization, changing the perspectives and practices of hundreds of its pediatrician members and incorporating media questions and advice as part of the accepted standard of pediatric health care for the future.

At their spring 1997 meeting, the Committee on Communications discussed how much more outreach to the entertainment industry could be done by the MRT if adequate resources were available. They submitted the requested evaluation of the MRT to the AAP Board of Directors with the recommendation that the part-time consultant be offered a 3-year full-time contract and a higher budget for operating expenses. Reviewing the evaluation, the Board of Directors concluded that, although the MRT was making a difference with some writers on some shows, it was not cost-effective. The part-time consultant's contract was terminated as of the end of 1997. As a further costcutting measure, the MRT office was closed and publication of *Writer's Bytes* was suspended. The MRT budget allocation was diverted to other projects. Not to be deterred, however, the pediatrician members of the MRT requested and were permitted to continue as an all-volunteer operation in 1998. To this day, they meet in members' homes, use personal time and resources to maintain the resource hotline, and continue to offer free pediatric advice to the television industry.

THE AAP TAKES LEADERSHIP ON MEDIA
AND CHILD HEALTH

The AAP was asked by the FCC to submit comments on the revised television rating system in 1997, the year that the rating system was coupled with the V-chip. Once the television ratings system was formalized, the AAP was invited to nominate a member to serve on the television ratings board. The AAP has had a member on the television ratings board since that time.

The AAP was one of the sponsors of the 1998 National Media Education Conference, at which AAP members presented one workshop on the negative effects of media on children's physical and mental health and another on an innovative use of television technology to improve child health. Video Intervention/Prevention Assessment (VIA) was a research method developed at Children's Hospital Boston, in which children and adolescents with chronic diseases partnered in their care by making visual illness narratives, video journals of their everyday lives with which they were asked to teach their clinicians about their experiences and needs (Rich, Lamola, Amory, & Schneider, 2000; Rich, Lamola, Gordon, & Chalfen, 2000). The Committee on Communications was renamed and redirected in 1998, becoming the Committee on Public Education, with more of a focus on health education of the general public. That same year, the AAP established the Holroyd-Sherry Award to honor H. James Holroyd and S. Norman Sherry, early leaders in the field of children and media at the AAP. Emphasizing that knowledge of media influences is a critical component of pediatric health care, the award is given each year to the Fellow of the AAP who makes an outstanding contribution to the field of children, adolescents, and the media.

In 1999 and 2000, television was under great scrutiny by pediatricians and child advocates. The AAP had two key annual objectives, of which one was to "reduce the physical and psychosocial consequences of domestic, community, media, and entertainment violence for infants, children, adolescents, and young adults" (AAP, 1998, p. 41). Broadcast television was undergoing a major technical change that would transform the medium—the switch from analog to digital broadcast, which would allow the transmission of much more information—higher quality images, more channels, and two-way interactivity. The top 30 television markets were going digital by the end of 1999, adding as many as 30 to 40 channels per market and allowing broadcasters to track individual viewing habits, preferences, and demographics that could target advertising to children and adolescents. The AAP was concerned about children's safety and privacy. It petitioned the FCC to make the government's gift of the digital airwaves, an estimated value of $70 billion, contingent on broadcasters adopting child-protective obligations, including a ratings system that was objective and content-based, more educational programming, and more public service.

In August 1999, the AAP published "Media Education" (AAP, 1999, p. A1), generating the most controversy and public attention that had been experienced for any AAP policy statement on any subject. A front page *New York Times* story reported:

> Children under 2 years old should not watch television, older children should not have television sets in their bedrooms and pediatricians should have parents fill out a "media history," along with a medical history, on office visits, according to recommendations by the American Academy of Pediatrics. Saying television can affect the mental, social, and physical health of young people, the academy for the first time has laid out a plan for how pediatricians and parents can better manage children's use of television. (Mifflin, 1999)

The AAP had reaffirmed its commitment to addressing television as a critical child health concern, making several new and important recommendations, that pediatricians should: (a) become aware of the health risks posed by media use; (b) ask their patients about media use as part of their check-ups; and (c) advise their patients' parents to limit television and choose programs carefully, coviewing and discussing them with their children, teach critical viewing skills and model responsible media use, create "electronic media-free" environments in children's bedrooms, avoid using television as an "electronic babysitter," emphasize alternative activities, and avoid all television and other screen media use by children under the age of 2 years to optimize this critical period of brain development. Other recommendations charged pediatricians with monitoring television and other media; making children, parents, and communities aware of risks and of positive programming; encouraging the development and implementation of universal media education; and encouraging the government and foundations to increase funding for media effects research (AAP, 1999).

In July 2000, Senator Sam Brownback (R, Kansas), supported by senators and congressmen from both parties, convened the Congressional Public Health Summit in Washington, DC. Starting that "the public has a right to know the truth about the public health risks and dangers of exposing their children to violent entertainment," Senator Brownback

(2005) announced the first consensus statement from the major American health organizations on media violence. *The Joint Statement on the Impact of Entertainment Violence on Children* (AAP, 2000) signed by the AAP, AMA, APA, and AACAP, later joined by the American Academy of Family Physicians and the American Psychiatric Association, asserted, "The conclusion of the public health community, based on over 30 years of research, is that viewing entertainment violence can lead to increases in aggressive attitudes, values and behavior, particularly in children. Its effects are measurable and long-lasting. Moreover, prolonged viewing of media violence can lead to emotional desensitization toward violence in real life."

In 2001, the AAP reissued three key television-related policy statements, bringing them up to date with the research. Noting that unintended injury, homicide, and suicide were the leading causes of death among adolescents, "Media Violence" (AAP, 2001b) included a comprehensive review of the large body of research evidence associating violent content on television and other media with subsequent increases in anxiety, desensitization, and aggressive thoughts and behaviors. It reiterated the roles that pediatricians and parents can play in protecting children and intervening on the effects of violent television, calling for a content-based universal rating system and more child-positive programming, and reminding consumers that if they do not use violent media, violent media will not be made. "Sexuality, Contraception, and the Media" (AAP, 2001c) reiterated earlier recommendations and called for schools to create and implement media education curricula dealing specifically with sexual portrayals. "Children, Adolescents, and Television" (AAP, 2001a) consolidated many of the recommendations made in previous subject-specific statements, urging pediatricians to take media histories as part of their medical evaluations and asking the government to compile a comprehensive report bringing together the current research on media effects on the health and development of children and to provide dedicated research funding.

The success of the AAP's public advocacy and member education led to a growing acceptance that television and other media use should be a key element of the pediatrician's medical history and anticipatory guidance. A survey of the 209 accredited pediatric residency programs in 2001 assessed whether media education had been incorporated into the training of child health professionals (Rich & Bar-on, 2001). Although more than 95% of training directors asserted that media use should be addressed by pediatricians, fewer than one third (28%) of their programs offered one or more lectures on the effects of television and other media on health. Although more than 70% of the programs had specific training on violence, obesity, substance abuse, and other problems that have been associated with television use, fewer than 20% discussed media influence on these disorders. Although over 95% of the program directors were members of the AAP, fewer than 30% had heard of the heavily publicized *Media Matters* initiative. Only *Media Matters* training of the program director was significantly associated with incorporation of media education in pediatric training. Although it was originally hoped that *Media Matters* training could be offered to all AAP members at eight courses across the country, necessary funding was not secured. The third and final *Media Matters* course was conducted in Chicago in November 2001. Despite huge demand from AAP members and research evidence that it was changing how pediatrics was being taught and practiced, the momentum generated by the *Media Matters* initiative was lost and the majority of AAP pediatricians did not receive training.

THE FUTURE OF MEDIA AND CHILD HEALTH

Throughout the first 50 years of television, the medical community struggled with the tension between its potential as an educational tool and its reality as a predominantly negative influence on the physical, mental, and social health of children and adolescents. Physicians used television effectively to keep themselves up to date on medical knowledge and procedures. They worked with health educators, writers, and producers to teach the public about important health issues through dedicated television shows, PSAs, and news and entertainment programming. On balance, however, the medical community was more concerned than enthusiastic about television. Strong, consistent, and growing research evidence linking television viewing with significant health outcomes, such as obesity, substance abuse, risky sexual behavior, anxiety, and violence led individual physicians and medical organizations to warn patients that they should limit and control their television viewing. Some organizations, most notably the AAP, mounted long-term initiatives to educate physicians, patients, and families about the risks and to advocate with government and industry for objective ratings, responsible controls, and research funding.

Considerable efforts yielded mixed results. There was a large body of research evidence bearing on television effects, but it was spread over at least 10 different academic disciplines. The disciplines, which ranged from public health to criminal justice, communication to psychology, and education to sociology, used very different research methods and rarely collaborated with or cross-referenced each other. This allowed television industry lobbyists to discount and even dismiss solid scientific research. Physicians, particularly pediatricians, brought credibility and gravity to those who were concerned about television and its effects, but the political and social agenda on television usually focused on differing lifestyles and values rather than on objective, quantifiable health outcomes. This fragmented the concern and emboldened the industry to take refuge behind the First Amendment. The debate became polarized, with one side Luddite in its denial of television and the revolution of communication technology and the other demanding no limits to creative freedom. The AAP and other organizations that had genuine concerns about television effects were often lumped into the former group, seen as adversaries, and opposed or ignored by the television industry.

It was clear that, to move forward, the debate needed to be reframed. The values on which many who were concerned about television based their objections were subjective and varied from individual to individual. This proved, time and again, to be an untenable paradigm for the debate. However, in the Information Age, when the average American child was exposed to television 30 hours or more each week, there was ample evidence that television and other media could be seen as a pervasive and powerful environmental health influence, one that had concrete, objective, and quantifiable outcomes. In 2002, a group of researchers and clinicians, representing public health, developmental psychology, education, anthropology, communication, and pediatrics, founded the Center on Media and Child Health (CMCH) at Children's Hospital Boston, the pediatric teaching hospital of Harvard Medical School. Their goal was to create an interdisciplinary center of excellence in research, education, and child-positive media production. Through collaboration across disciplines, scientific rigor would be enhanced and findings would be more widely disseminated. Leaving advocacy to others, CMCH would remain neutral, seeking and sharing what science reveals about the effects of media on physical, mental, and social health. By acknowledging that television and other electronic media are a reality, and working with, rather than against, their producers, CMCH had the potential to affect real change in the media environment to which children were exposed.

To ensure that all of the quality research, past and present, be brought to bear on this problem, CMCH was determined to collect and organize a comprehensive database of the extant research on media and health.

The goal is to develop the definitive library of what is known and to offer it, in a form accessible to scientists and parents alike, on the World Wide Web (at www.cmch.tv). In this way, the field of media effects on health can be consolidated and advanced. The "big picture" of what the research shows can be assembled, clarifying what remains to be investigated. CMCH researchers and others can perform meta-analyses of the evidence to date and develop new research to elucidate unexplored areas. CMCH will serve as a training and networking center for researchers in the field and as an information source for clinicians, teachers, policymakers, and parents who want what is healthy and safe for children. CMCH plans to implement pilot projects in media literacy and other interventions, evaluating them on the basis of health outcomes. Child-positive media, such as Video Intervention/Prevention Assessment (VIA), in which sick children use video camcorders to teach their clinicians about their illness experiences and needs (Rich, Lamola, Amory, et al., 2000; Rich, Lamola, Gordon, et al., 2000), will be developed and implemented. In the future, CMCH intends to pursue other health-positive television, including the production of health education videos and consulting on educational and entertainment television series. Ultimately, CMCH seeks to characterize and understand the nature of media effects on health, to offer effective tools for intervening on or preventing media-related health risks, and to educate and empower those who can change our media environment, as producers and as consumers.

ACKNOWLEDGMENTS

Dr. Rich is supported by the National Institute of Child Health and Human Development through Grant K23HD1296. Special thanks are due to Brandy King, MLIS, of the Center on Media and Child Health; John Zwicky, Archivist, Pediatric History Center; Veronica Noland, Public Information Specialist, the American Academy of Pediatrics; and Laura L. Carroll, Archivist, and Allen Podraza, Director of the Records Management and Archives Department of the American Medical Association, for their help in accessing bibliographic and historic material. Thanks also to Norma Pecora, for her patience.

REFERENCES

Academy calls for curbs on children's television advertising. (1978, December). News and Comment, 29, 1, 4.

American Academy of Child and Adolescent Psychiatry. (1997). *Substance abuse—The nature and extent of the problem.* November 4, 2005, from http://www.aacap.org/publications/factsfam/violence.html.(Original work published 1987).

American Academy of Child and Adolescent Psychiatry. (1999). *Fact sheet #13: Children and TV violence.* Retrieved December 1, 2004, from http:// www.aacap.org/publications/factsfam/violence.htm.(Original work published 1989).

American Academy of Child and Adolescent Psychiatry. (2000). *Fact sheet #40: The influence of music and music videos.* Retrieved December 1, 2004, from http://www.aacap.org/publications/factsfam/musicvid.htm.

American Academy of Child and Adolescent Psychiatry. (2001). *Fact sheet #54: Children and watching TV.* Retrieved December 1, 2004, from http:// www.aacap.org/publications/factsfam/tv.htm.

American Academy of Child and Adolescent Psychiatry. (2002). *Fact sheet #67: Children and the news.* Retrieved December 1, 2004, from http://www.aacap.org/publications/factsfam/67.htm.

American Academy of Pediatrics. (1977). *AAP resolution concerning the effects of television violence on children.* Elk Grove Village, IL: Author.

American Academy of Pediatrics. (1978). *Task Force on Television and Advertising—Action memorandum.* Elk Grove Village, IL: Author.

American Academy of Pediatrics. (1983). *Task Force on Children and Television—Meeting minutes September 12–13, 1983.* Elk Grove Village, IL: Author.

American Academy of Pediatrics. (1984). Children, adolescents, and television. *News and Comment, 35*(12), 8.

American Academy of Pediatrics. (1986). Sexuality, contraception, and the media. *Pediatrics, 78,* 535–536.

American Academy of Pediatrics. (1988). The commercialization of children's television and its effect on imaginative play. *Pediatrics, 81,* 900–901.

American Academy of Pediatrics. (1989). Impact of rock lyrics and music videos on children and youth. *Pediatrics, 83,* 314–315.

American Academy of Pediatrics. (1990). Children, adolescents, and television. *Pediatrics, 85,* 1119–1120.

American Academy of Pediatrics. (1992). The commercialization of children's television. *Pediatrics, 89,* 343–344.

American Academy of Pediatrics. (1995a). Children, adolescents, and advertising. *Pediatrics, 95,* 295–297.

American Academy of Pediatrics. (1995b). Children, adolescents, and television. *Pediatrics, 96,* 786–787.

American Academy of Pediatrics. (1995c). Media violence. *Pediatrics, 95,* 949–951.

American Academy of Pediatrics. (1995d). Sexuality, contraception, and the media. *Pediatrics, 95,* 298–300.

American Academy of Pediatrics. (1996). Impact of music lyrics and music videos on children and youth. *Pediatrics, 98,* 1219–1221.

American Academy of Pediatrics. (1998a). *Minutes: Board of directors meeting.* Elk Grove Village, IL: Author.

American Academy of Pediatrics. (1998b). *Running history of the Committee on Public Education* (COPEd). Elk Grove Village, IL: Author.

American Academy of Pediatrics. (1999). Media education. *Pediatrics, 104,* 341–343.

American Academy of Pediatrics. (2000). *Joint statement on the impact of entertainment violence on children: Congressional Public Health Summit, July 26, 2000.* Retrieved February 20, 2004, from http://www.aap.org/advocacy/releases/ jstmtevc.htm.

American Academy of Pediatrics. (2001a). Children, adolescents, and television. *Pediatrics, 107,* 423–426.

American Academy of Pediatrics. (2001b). Media violence. *Pediatrics, 108,* 1222–1226.

American Academy of Pediatrics. (2001c). Sexuality, contraception, and the media. *Pediatrics, 107,* 191–194.

American Medical Association. (1976). *Proceedings, House of Delegates,* Dallas, TX: Author.

American Medical Association. (1977a, December). *Proceedings, House of Delegates.* 31st Interim Meeting of the AMA, Chicago.

American Medical Association. (1977b, January). *Why the AMA is concerned about the effects of television.* Paper presented at the AMA annual meeting, Chicago.

American Medical Association. (1982–2003). *H-485.995 TV violence.* Retrieved July 16, 2004, from http://www.ama-assn.org/apps/pf_new/pf_online?f_n=resultLink& doc=policyfiles/HnE/H-485.995.HTM&s_t=TV+violence&catg=AMA/HnE& catg=AMA/BnGnC&catg=AMA/DIR&&nth=1&&st_p=0&nth= 1&.

American Medical Association. (1994, June). *House of Delegates proceedings: 143rd annual meeting.* American Medical Association, Chicago, IL.

American Medical Association Auxiliary. (1977). *Television: Education for positive viewing.* Paper presented at the AMA annual meeting, Chicago.

Anderson, F. (1955). *Comics, television, and children.* Notre Dame, IN: Ave Maria Press.

Appendix to the Congressional Record. (1951). 82nd Congress, 1st session, A3742. Washington, DC: U.S. Congress.

Baker, R. K., & Ball, S. J. (Eds.). (1969). *Mass media and violence: A report to the National Commission on the Causes and Prevention of Violence.* Washington, DC: U.S. Government Printing Office.

Banay, R. S. (1948). *Youth in despair.* New York: Coward-McCann.

Bandura, A., Ross, D., & Ross, S. A. (1961). Transmission of aggression through imitation of aggressive models. *Journal of Abnormal & Social Psychology, 63,* 575–582.

Blumer, H. (1933). *Movies and conduct.* New York: Macmillan.

Brazelton, T. B. (1974). TV and children: A pediatrician's advice. *News and Comment, 25*(9), 10–11.

Brownback, S. (2005). Retrieved November 1, 2005, from http://brownback.senate. gov/pressapp/record.cfm?id=175741&.

Charters, W. W. (1933). *Motion pictures and youth, a summary.* New York: Macmillan.

Clendenen, R. (1955). Letter to Langdon West (Kefauver Papers, University of Tennessee Library): MS 837, Box 72, Senate Subcommittee Folder.

Dictz, W. H. (1993). *Television violence and its impact on children—Testimony of the American Academy of Pediatrics.* U. S. Senate Hearing.

Dietz, W. H., & Gortmaker, S. L. (1985). Do we fatten our children at the TV set? Television viewing and obesity in children and adolescents. *Pediatrics, 75,* 807–812.

Dysinger, W. S., & Ruckmick, C. A. (1933). *The emotional responses of children to the motion picture situation.* New York: Macmillan.

Elmhurst Board of Education. (1954). A study of comic book and television coverage among school children in Elmhurst, Illinois. New York: Dell.

Eron, L. D. (1963). Relationship of TV viewing habits and aggressive behavior in children. Journal of Abnormal & Social Psychology, 67, 193–196.

Federman, J. (1996). National Television Violence Study: I. Thousand Oaks, CA: Sage.

Federman, J. (1997). National Television Violence Study: II. Thousand Oaks, CA: Sage.

Federman, J. (1998). National Television Violence Study: III. Thousand Oaks, CA: Sage.

Gallup, G. (1954, November 21). The Gallup Poll: Air Waves Share Blame. Washington Post and Times Herald.

Higdon, H. (1976, July 26). Violence on TV. Impact, 1–6.

Hoerrner, K. L. (1999). The forgotten battles: Congressional hearings on television violence in the 1950s. University of Georgia, Athens, GA.

Investigation of radio and television programs. (1952). 82nd Congress, 2nd session, p. 1 Washington, DC: U.S. Congress, House Committee on Interstate and Foreign Commerce.

Jones, L. (1994, July 25). AMA: Give parents tools to judge TV, video violence. American Medical News, p. 8.

Juvenile delinquency. (1954a). Special Rep. No. 1064. Washington, DC: U.S. Congress.

Juvenile delinquency (television programs). (1954b). 83rd Congress, 2nd Session. Washington, DC: U.S. Congress, Senate Committee on the Judiciary.

Lazarsfeld, P. F. (1955). Why is so little known about the effects of television on children and what can be done? Public Opinion Quarterly, 19, 243–251.

Lyness, P. I. (1951). Patterns in the mass communications tastes of the young audience. Journal of Educational Psychology, 42, 449–467.

Lyness, P. I. (1952). The place of the mass media in the lives of boys and girls. Journalism Quarterly, 29, 43–54.

Maccoby, E. E. (1951). Television: Its impact on school children. Public Opinion Quarterly, 15, 421–444.

Mackenzie, C. (1940, June 23). Movies and the child: The debate rages on. The New York Times Magazine, pp. 9–10.

Mifflin, L. (1999, August 4). Pediatricians suggest limits on TV viewing by children. New York Times, pp. A1, A15.

Murray, J. P. (1995). Children and television violence: Violence panel keynote address. Kansas Journal of Law & Public Policy, 4(3), 7–15.

Pearl, D., Bouthilet, L., & Lazar, J. B. (1982). Television and behavior: Ten years of scientific progress and implications for the eighties (Vol. 1: Summary Report). Rockville, MD: U.S. Department of Health and Human Services.

Preston, M. I. (1941). Children's reactions to movie horrors and radio crime. Journal of Pediatrics, 19, 147–168.

Rich, M., & Bar-on, M. (2001). Child health in the Information Age: Media education of pediatricians. Pediatrics, 107, 156–162.

Rich, M., Lamola, S., Amory, C., & Schneider, L. (2000). Asthma in life context: Video Intervention/Prevention Assessment (VIA). Pediatrics, 105, 469–477.

Rich, M., Lamola, S., Gordon, J., & Chalfen, R. (2000). Video Intervention/ Prevention Assessment: A patient-centered methodology for understanding the adolescent illness experience. Journal of Adolescent Health, 27, 155–165.

Rideout, V. (2004). *Parents, media and public policy: A Kaiser Family Foundation study.* Menlo Park, CA: Kaiser Family Foundation.

Rothenberg, M. B. (1975). Effects of television violence on children and youth. *JAMA, 234,* 1043–1046.

Rubens, W. (1976). Violence on television. *JAMA, 235,* 1550–1551.

Shifrin, D. (1998). *National Television Violence Study: A report—Year Three.* Elk Grove Village, IL: American Academy of Pediatrics.

Smith, A. (1952). Influence of TV crime programs on children's health [Comment]. *JAMA, 150,* 37.

Smith, F. (1972). Health messages during a week of television. *New England Journal of Medicine, 286,* 516–520.

Smythe, D. W. (1951). An analysis of television programs. *Scientific American, 184*(6), 15–17.

Television Violence Reduction through Parental Empowerment Act of 1993, 103rd Congress, 1st Sess. (1993).

TV violence decried. (1977, March 7). *American Medical News, 20*(10), 1, 13.

Walsh, D. A., Goldman, L. S., & Brown, R. (1996). *Physician guide to media violence.* Chicago: American Medical Association.

Witty, P. (1955, February). Comics, television, and our children. *Today's Health, 33,* 18–21.

6

Advertising and Consumer Development

Nancy A. Jennings
Ellen A. Wartella
University of Cincinnati
University of California–Riverside

Research of advertising and marketing practices has a relatively short history. Although some theorizing about child consumers began as early as the 1930s and some researchers began to study the topic in the 1950s and 1960s, most of the advertising research began in the 1970s and 1980s with the growth of research on children in general (Pecora, 1998). A brief review of the articles on advertising, consumerism, or marketing in the current database indicates only about 300 citations on this topic, with the majority being published in the 1970s and 1980s (see Table 6.1). The majority of the studies focus on effects of advertising on children (64% of all citations). Very little attention has been dedicated to exploring the content of children's advertising (10%), however, more attention has focused on other types of research, including discussions of regulation and literature reviews (26%). The first citations in this database that mention children's consumerism appear in the 1960s (McNeal, 1969; Wells, 1966). As noted by Wartella (1984), most of the research has been devoted to describing the nature of age-related differences in children's responses and understanding of advertising content. Other factors such as gender, race, and social class seem to be overlooked, although in some cases the research indicates that these factors are not significant. This

TABLE 6.1
Research on Children and Advertising (1950–1998)

	Advertising Articles	Effects	Content Analysis	Other
1950–1959	3	2 (67%)		1 (33%)
1960–1969	6	3 (50%)		3 (50%)
1970–1979	103	62 (60%)	10 (10%)	31 (30%)
1980–1989	117	86 (73%)	8 (7%)	23 (20%)
1990–1998	79	45 (57%)	13 (16%)	21 (27%)
Total	308	198 (64%)	31 (10%)	79 (26%)

chapter explores the nature of research on children's advertising since its growth in the 1970s. It begins with a review of research concerning the socialization of the child consumer and advances to the role of advertising in the socialization process. Next, attention focuses on the nature of advertising content directed to children and then a larger section focuses on the cognitive, affective, and behavioral effects of advertising on children. Finally, as advertising practices move beyond the home, commercial practices in school are reviewed.

SOCIALIZATION OF THE CHILD CONSUMER

Children are often exposed to advertising and consumer behaviors at a very young age. Recently, scholars have proposed various stages or steps of development through which children progress as they become knowledgeable consumers. This section explores two recent reviews of the literature that describe children's understanding of advertising (John, 1999) and different characteristics of consumer behavior (Valkenburg & Cantor, 2001) as well as an earlier proposal regarding how children learn about the consumer environment and their purchasing behaviors (McNeal, 1992; see Table 6.2).

Understanding Advertising Content

In a recent review of the literature concerning children and advertising, John (1999) proposed that children's awareness, knowledge, and understanding of advertising content progresses through several steps as children mature. First, children must be able to distinguish commercials

TABLE 6.2
Stages of Children's Socialization as Consumers

Years of Age	McNeal (1992)	John (1999)	Valkenburg and Cantor (2001)
0–2	Accompany and observe parents		Feeling wants and preferences
2+	Accompany parents and request products		Nagging and negotiating
3–4	Accompany parents and select with permission		
	Accompany parents and make independent purchase		
5	Go to store alone and make independent purchase	Distinguish commercial from TV program	Adventure and the first purchase
7–8		Discern persuasive intent	
8		Perceive bias and perception	Conformity and fastidiousness[a]
11–14		Understand purpose for specific advertising tactics and techniques	

[a] Authors indicate conformity and fastidiousness occurs between ages of 8 and 12.

from other content, which is often acquired by the age of 5 years. Children are able to identify and label commercials even though they may not understand the intent of advertising. This understanding is the second step in building children's knowledge about advertising. Most children can discern the persuasive or selling intent of commercials by the age of 7 or 8 years. As children become aware of the persuasive nature of advertising, they develop the ability to recognize bias and deception in advertising and develop skeptical or negative attitudes in regards to advertising. Therefore, by the age of 8, children have progressed through three steps in understanding advertising and begin to express less trust and liking of advertisements in general. John suggested that children's skepticism and general knowledge of the persuasive intent of advertising is often viewed as a "cognitive defense" against advertising, which would be the next step of children's development. However, research suggests that simply having general knowledge and some skepticism may not be enough for children as old as 8 years of age to employ this mechanism. As children acquire greater knowledge of specific advertising tactics and appeals used to persuade in early adolescence (ages 11–14), they now have a sophisticated knowledge of advertising intent and tactics coupled with a sense of skepticism that allows them to fully appreciate and understand the role and nature of advertising in society.

Developing Consumer Behavior

Valkenburg and Cantor (2001) explored the relationship between developmental theory and marketing models as they suggest four stages of consumer development throughout childhood. They submit that during each phase, a defining characteristic of consumer behavior develops. These characteristics include the ability to "(1) feel wants and preferences, (2) search to fulfill them, (3) make a choice and a purchase, and (4) evaluate the product and its alternatives" (Mowen & Minor, 1998, as cited in Valkenburg & Cantor, 2001, p. 62). The first stage of consumer behavior begins with feeling wants and preferences. Infants and toddlers (ages 0–2 years) can express desire for particular sounds, smells, and tastes, although "their behavior is still primarily reactive and not very intentional" (Valkenburg & Cantor, 2001, p. 64). As children begin to better express themselves in the preschool years (ages 2–5), they enter the next phase of searching to fulfill their wants and preferences. They express their interest in products and begin the nagging and negotiating phase of consumer development. Developmentally, children in this phase begin to express attachment to television personalities, yet they have difficulty distinguishing between fantasy and reality and often think that advertisements are truthful. Also, preschool children prefer shows that are slower paced and contain familiar objects that they can name. In the early elementary years (ages 5–8), children progress through the adventure and first purchase phase. They have a growing interest in fast-paced entertainment compared with the appeal of the slower paced programs in their preschool years, and they begin making purchases, either accompanied by an adult or by themselves. Finally, in the later elementary years (ages 8–12), children begin to evaluate products and their alternatives. Some begin an interest in collecting items such as dolls or baseball cards, which requires careful attention to details and price consciousness. The opinion of peers also becomes valued and may influence purchasing decisions. Valkenburg and Cantor (2001) suggested that although children's consumer behavior continues to grow as they mature, by age 12, most children have experienced all characteristics of consumer behavior as outlined in consumer models.

Learning the Consumer Environment

McNeal (1992) described the manner in which the very young are socialized as consumers. Similar to Valkenburg and Cantor (2001), McNeal's stages of consumer development begin at the earliest of ages, suggesting that consumer education starts at the very beginning of life. The first stage for learning the consumer environment begins with observation. According to McNeal (1992), "by the time a child can sit erect, he or she is placed in his or her culturally defined observation post high atop a shopping cart" (p. 9). From this perch, children first begin to accompany and observe their parents as they make their shopping decisions. By the age of 2, children not only accompany their parents, but also they begin to make requests for products during shopping visits. Children begin to learn which stores have products they prefer and they begin to learn how to get their parents to respond to their desires. By the age of 3 or 4, children begin to explore the stores on foot rather than being confined to a shopping cart and parents begin to allow their children to select some of their favorite products such as cereal or cookies. Around the age of 4, children begin to make their own independent purchases in the presence of their parents. These purchases may be difficult in the beginning due to a lack of understanding of currency and little patience when waiting in long checkout lines. However, in short order, these difficulties are overcome and making the purchase becomes much more rewarding. Finally, between the ages of 5 and 7, children make their first independent purchase by themselves, without their parents nearby. Often these purchases are made at a convenience store or a supermarket for small items such as candy or soda. Just as children are entering formal educational settings, they have already become independent consumers, learning their consumer environment through observation and monitored selecting and purchasing of products.

Negotiating Advertising and Consumerism

A consistent finding from these reviews suggests that children develop knowledge of consumer behaviors at a very young age. Preferences for products followed by requests (even demands) for products are expressed by children very early in life. Developmental theory coupled with marketing and advertising theory suggests that children progress through various stages as they become full-fledged consumers in society. Of concern, however, is the lack of understanding of the persuasive nature of advertising prior to actual participation as a consumer. Children are making independent purchases (McNeal, 1992) and making requests for products through nagging and negotiating (Valkenburg & Cantor, 2001) by the age of 5, yet children do not understand the persuasive intent of advertising until the age of 7 or 8 (John, 1999; Wartella, 1984). Clearly, childhood is just the beginning of a lifetime of consumerism, yet children need clear guidance from parents because many children are already actively engaging in consumer practices, yet do not have the cognitive ability to comprehend the nature of advertising.

ROLE OF ADVERTISING IN SOCIALIZATION PROCESS

Children's potential for exposure to television advertising has increased dramatically over the past three decades. According to Kunkel (2001), the most common calculation of children's exposure to television advertising has been to multiply the average yearly number of hours a typical child watches television (weekly average by 52) by the average number of commercials aired per hour on television. Over time, these calculations have yielded higher and higher estimates of children's exposure to television advertising, doubling from an average of about 20,000 commercials per year in the late 1970s (Adler et al., 1977) to more than 40,000 ads per year in the early 1990s (Kunkel & Gantz, 1992 as cited in Kunkel, 2001).

However, the frequency of children's exposure to commercial content has become increasingly difficult to measure and even harder to define. Kunkel (2001) suggested that it is nearly impossible to account for children's exposure to advertising on television due to (a) changes in the television environment, including differences in the amount of commercials on cable and broadcast channels, the proliferation of program-length commercials, and shorter commercial length with the growth of the 15-second spot; and (b) limitations in measurement of children's television use, particularly differentiating between commercial television and public television exposure. Furthermore, television advertising itself is just one element of a wide variety of marketing strategies directed toward children. Strasburger and Wilson (2002) argued that marketing trends such as toy-based programs, marketing in schools, and online advertising expand children's exposure to marketing messages and may further contribute to children's confusion about the intention of advertising in general. However, it has been suggested that television advertising is perhaps the easiest way to reach children (Strasburger & Wilson, 2002); therefore, our discussion of advertising begins with an exploration of the content of children's television advertising and then focuses on children's cognitive, affective, and behavioral responses to marketing strategies.

CONTENT ANALYSES OF ADVERTISING CONTENT

Not only has the amount of advertising changed over time, so has the nature of advertising content itself. Very few content analyses have been conducted on children's advertising. Early research in the field set a precedent of sampling programs that were specifically targeted to a child audience (Barcus, 1980) rather than exploring all advertising to which children may be exposed, such as that in prime time. Therefore, this review of children's advertising only includes studies with samples from child-oriented programs occurring mostly on Saturday mornings or after-school from as early as the 1970s. Although recent research has explored advertising in children's programming from the 1950s (Alexander, Benjamin, Hoerrner, & Roe, 1999), this review only includes studies from samples of children's programming from the 1970s to the present as a reflection of the growth of research in the field beginning in the 1970s.

Time

The amount of time devoted to commercial content has remained somewhat stable since the early 1970s. Content analyses of children's television as reported in Barcus (1980) indicate only a slight decrease from about 20% to 25% of children's program time in 1971 to 15% in 1975 and 14% in 1977. By the mid- to late 1980s, nonprogram time was on the rise, again, reaching about 20% (or 12 minutes) of children's program time (Condry, Bence, & Schiebe, 1988). According to Condry and his colleagues (1988), on an average Saturday morning in the mid- to late 1980s, children were exposed to "16 to 17 product commercials (66.9% of all nonprogram messages), 4 to 5 program promos (18.4%), 2 to 3 PSAs (11.4%), and 1 drop-in (3.7%)" (p. 259) per hour. (A drop-in is a message of an informational nature.) Promos include program promotions or station identifications and drop-ins are categorized as educational or informative messages (Condry et al., 1988). By 1990, the amount of advertising time had not changed substantially, although some variation can be found by channel type. Kunkel and Gantz (1992) reported that independent stations provide the most nonprogram content, averaging 13:26 minutes per hour, followed by broadcast stations (12:09) and cable networks (10:38).

Of particular interest is the rise in the number of product commercial messages to which children are exposed. Condry and his colleagues (1988) reported that proportion of product commercials per hour increased significantly from 62.8% in 1983 to 78.6% in 1987, although the average nonprogram time per hour had not changed substantially. One suggestion has been that this may be a result of the shortening of other nonprogram content to accommodate more commercial product time (Condry et al., 1988). In the 1980s, the average message size decreased from 30.71 seconds in 1983 to 26.70 seconds in 1987. Two categories of nonprogram content, promos and educational drop-ins, decreased substantially over the same time period, whereas the average number of product commercials increased, suggesting that some messages may be reduced to make room for product commercials (Condry et al., 1988). As a result, a typical hour of Saturday morning children's television in the 1980s consisted of 11.78 minutes of nonprogram material, with product commercials accounting for 8.16 minutes of the hour, Public service announcements (PSAs) 1.45 minutes, promos 1.11 minutes, and drop-ins 1.06 minutes (Condry et al., 1988). By 1990, product ads on children's network television account for 10:05 minutes, 1:08 minutes of promos and station identification, 0:46 minutes of PSAs, and 0:10 minutes of educational drop-ins (Kunkel & Gantz, 1992). Time allocated for product commercials seems to be on the rise, whereas time for PSAs and educational drop-ins has been greatly reduced. This reduction in educational messages and increase in marketing messages may be encouraging consumerism in the child audience.

Products Advertised

This raises the question of what types of products are being advertised to children. For comparison, only reports of broadcast networks (ABC, CBS, and NBC) are discussed in this section. It should be noted that there are differences in the types of products advertised by channel type. Research in the 1970s and 1990s suggested that networks carry more cereal and candies or sweets commercials than independent stations and that independent stations present more toy commercials than the networks (Barcus, 1980; Kunkel & Gantz, 1992). Furthermore, seasonal variations have also been noted in the research concerning the distribution of products advertised.

Research in the 1970s and 1980s indicated that during the pre-Christmas season as early as October toy ads comprise nearly half or more of the child-directed ads (Barcus, 1980; Condry et al., 1988).

Overall, research in the 1970s indicated that four product categories— toys, cereals, candies, and fast-food restaurants—make up the lion's share of the types of products advertised to children, accounting for 80% of all ads (Barcus, 1980). Studies conducted in the 1980s and early 1990s indicated that this practice continued, however, with a redistribution within product categories across time. Advertisements for toys and games appear to have risen from 12.0% in the 1970s to about a third of commercials in the 1980s and then returned to 1970s levels in the early 1990s (17.3%; see Table 6.3). Cereal ads and candy, soda, and snack ads comprised nearly two thirds of children's ads in the 1970s and in the 1990s; however these levels dropped dramatically in the 1980s to a low of 35% in 1985 (see Table 6.3). Ads for restaurants seemed to decrease dramatically in the 1980s and early 1990s from 15.0% in the 1970s to a low of 8.7% in 1990 (see Table 6.3). Finally, ads for "other" products rose in the 1980s to a high of 18.5% in 1985, then dropped again to similar levels reported in the late 1970s (see Table 6.3). Other products include such things as hygiene, clothing, and leisure activities and products such as recreation parks, records, and entertainment.

Clearly the range of products advertised to children has increased in the last forty years. Children are the target of an ever-widening range of product categories, suggesting that their product influence in the family may be expanding.

Nature of Characters in Commercials

Over the past few decades, the nature of the characters depicted in commercials has been of particular interest, especially character gender and race. Ads have been analyzed for presence of male and female characters and the demeanor, activities, language, and production features associated with these depictions. Furthermore, some attention has been drawn to the infrequency of the depiction of children of color and dominance of White males in ads targeted to a young audience (Atkin & Heald, 1977; Barcus, 1980; Doolittle & Pepper, 1975, Riffe, Goldson, Saxton, & Yu, 1989). Because the majority of research has focused on gender, this section discusses these findings since the 1970s.

Early research indicated that males outnumbered females in commercials for children. In four separate samples of children's television from

TABLE 6.3
Distribution of Product Categories

	Barus (1978)[a]	Condry et al., (1988)			Kunkel and Gantz (1992)
	1978	1983	1985	1987	1990
Toys and games	12.0%	19.6%	33.1%	36.2%	17.3%
Cereals	34.0%	31.8%	20.5%	22.8%	31.2%
Candy, soda, and snacks	32.0%	19.6%	14.5%	17.2%	32.4%
Other food and beverage (nonsugared)	1.0%	12.5%	8.8%	7.9%	4.6%[b]
Restaurants	15.0%	1.5%	4.6%	3.4%	8.7%
Other	6.0%	15.0%	18.5%	12.5%	5.8%

[a] As reported in Condry et al. (1988).
[b] Reported in Kunkel & Gantz (1992) as "healthy foods."

1975 to 1977, the majority (60%–70%) of all characters were male (Barcus, 1980). A similar pattern continued in the late 1980s with the percentage of female characters (25%) lagging behind male characters (42%) as well as animated nonhuman characters (32.4%; Riffe et al., 1989). However, research in the late 1990s indicated that the portrayal of girls and boys was much more equitable, with nearly half of the sample being boys (49%) and the other half being girls (51%; Larson, 2001). Although the proportion of females to males may have increased over time, concerns remain regarding how gender is portrayed in children's advertising.

Girls and boys are often portrayed in very stereotyped roles in ads for children and this has not changed significantly over time. Overt factors such as the types of products advertised, the activities in which children engage, the language expressed, and the settings of the advertisements suggest gendered roles for children. Research in the 1980s indicated that the product advertised was related to gender. The male–female ratio in snack food commercials was 3–2 (Riffe et al., 1989). Furthermore, research in the 1990s found that girls were less likely to be found eating together (2.56% of ads) than boys (13.17%; Larson, 2001). Although eating is not necessarily an activity that is traditionally stereotyped, Larson (2001) argued that the absence of girls eating prevents young girls from seeing models of healthy eating habits, which raises concerns of eating disorders, even in school-age girls.

Other activities portrayed in commercials do signify traditional gender roles. Smith (1994) observed that girls engaged in shopping, whereas boys did not, and that only boys performed antisocial behaviors such as stealing or fighting. Aggressive behavior seems to be more visible in male commercials, even as early as the 1970s (Larson, 2001; Macklin & Kolbe, 1984; Welch, Huston-Stein, Wright, & Plehal, 1979). The language used in the ads also is indicative of traditional roles. According to Johnson and Young (2002), feelings and nurturing verbs (e.g., love, cuddle, and care) were more prevalent in girl-oriented ads, whereas competition and destruction verbs (e.g., bash, battle, and wreck) and agency or control verbs (e.g., rule and drive) were more prevalent in boy-oriented ads. Finally, settings of commercials seem to reflect traditional roles for girls and boys. Girl-oriented commercials tend to feature girls at home, whereas boy-oriented ads are more likely to feature a setting away from home (Larson, 2001; Smith, 1994). Even in fantasy settings, Smith (1994) indicated that the most common fantasy setting for girls is a "set in a sort of cotton-candy simple background"(p. 334), whereas fantasy settings for boys include "being inside a video game, in a land of giant dinosaurs, or washing over a chocolate waterfall" (p. 334). These factors tend to serve as signifiers of appropriate behavior and context for girls and boys alike.

More subtle factors such as voiceovers, production features, and even names of toys may also shape the image of femininity and masculinity through children's ads. Early research indicated that male voiceovers were more common, accounting for 91% of commercials where an announcer's voice was clearly identifiable, and that female voiceovers were only used in commercials that presented girl-oriented products (Doolittle & Pepper, 1975). Similar patterns were found in the 1990s, where it was suggested that voiceovers are used to match the orientation of the target for the toy such that boy-oriented commercials feature a male voiceover and girl-oriented commercials feature a female voiceover (Johnson & Young, 2002; Smith, 1994). Moreover, the majority of voiceovers in both boy-oriented (80%) and girl-oriented (87%) toy commercials tend to exaggerate the gender stylization of the voice; that is, female voiceovers tend to be high-pitched or have sing-song qualities, whereas the male voiceovers have masculine or aggressive voice qualities (Johnson & Young, 2002).

These subtle stylistic features of advertising content were first suggested in the 1970s in an examination of the formal features of production in children's advertising. Early research indicated that boys' commercials were more likely to contain highly active toys, higher rates of cuts, more rough cuts, less talking, and louder noise and music than girls' commercials. The latter had more fades and dissolves, smoother transitions, a great deal of talking, and softer background music (Welch et al., 1979). These patterns continued in the 1980s. According to Macklin and Kolbe (1984), ads targeted toward boys were more active than those targeted toward girls. Some research suggests that even the names of the toys may invoke gender stereotypes; for example, names of boy-oriented toys advertised include Big Time Action Hero and Play Doh Demolition Derby, whereas names of girl-oriented toys include Take Care of Me Twins and "Bedtime Bottle Baby" (Johnson & Young, 2002). Taken together, ads present gender stereotypes through more overt factors such as activities and language as well as through more subtle features such as voiceovers and production features.

EFFECTS OF ADVERTISING ON CHILDREN

Considering the high amount of advertising to which children are exposed, what effect does it have? Media researchers historically have analyzed media effect in terms of cognitive (knowledge), affective (attitude), and conative (behavior) outcomes. For instance, Perse (2001) indicated that one framework for discussing media effects is "along a cognitive–affective–behavioral dimension, which marks a distinction between acquisition of knowledge about an action and performance of the action" (p. 17). Children develop cognitive skills to differentiate advertising from program content and discern disclaimers and marketing techniques. Furthermore, children's attitudes and beliefs about advertising change as they mature. Finally, a variety of behavioral outcomes have been associated with advertising exposure.

Cognitive Effects

Much of the early research on children and advertising focused on understanding how children perceived and understood advertising content. A recent literature review of children's understanding and knowledge of advertising suggests that there are several stages in children's comprehension of commercial content (John, 1999). Although the stages have been outlined previously, this section provides more detail of children's abilities to identify advertising content, to understand the selling intent of commercials, and to know specific advertising appeals and tactics. Furthermore, it is important to note the application of different theoretical perspectives regarding advances in the study of children's comprehension of advertising. Early research in the 1970s relied heavily on Piagetian developmental theory as an explanation for age-related differences and focused primarily on younger children, whereas research in the 1980s and 1990s began to turn attention to information-processing theory and to adolescents to understand how children process information over the course of development.

Identifying Advertising Content. As early as 1974, Rossiter and Robertson (1974) argued that there are a number of cognitive distinctions children must make to acquire an understanding of the purpose of commercials. The first of those distinctions is the ability to identify and distinguish between programs and commercials. Early research from the 1970s and 1980s suggested that the majority of children acquire this basic skill by the age of 5 (Blosser & Roberts, 1985; Butter, Popovich, Stackhouse, & Garner, 1981; Levin, Petros, & Petrella, 1982; Stephens & Stutts, 1982). Blosser and Roberts (1985) indicated that only 10% of children under the age of 5 can correctly label a commercial, but over half of children between the ages of 5 and 6 labeled commercials correctly, reaching 100% accuracy by the age of 10. However, it should be noted that the type of distinctions made by the young are very rudimentary. According to Ward (1972), the majority of children age 5 to 8 (65%) display a low level of differentiation between commercial and television content compared to older children (ages 9–12). For example, younger children indicated length ("commercials are shorter than programs") and placement ("before or after show") as the discriminating factors, whereas older children cite that "programs are supposed to entertain" and that "commercials sell, make money" (p. 40). It is the perceptual characteristics of commercials that young children use to make distinctions. Furthermore, it should be noted that in research with preschoolers, some children as young as the age of 3 can distinguish between commercials and programs; however, research indicates that this skill improves dramatically with age (Butter et al., 1981; Levin et al., 1982; Stephens & Stutts, 1982). Of particular interest with the preschool studies is that although age was a significant factor in all analyses, variables such as sex of the child (Butter et al., 1981; Levin et al., 1982) and family variables such as level of mother's education and previous explanations of commercials (Stephens & Stutts, 1982) were not significant, suggesting the truly developmental nature of this skill rather than an artifact of individual differences.

Understanding the Intent of Commercials. Research on children's understanding of the purpose of commercials has relied on children's abilities to articulate the persuasive aspect of advertising. Results of the various survey studies in the 1970s indicated that below age 6 the vast majority of children cannot articulate the selling purpose of advertising (Adler et al., 1977; Bever, Smith, Bengen, & Johnson, 1975; Donohue, Meyer, & Henke, 1978; Meyer, Donohue, & Henke, 1978; Roberts, 1979; Sheikh, Prasad, & Rao, 1974; Ward, Wackman, & Wartella, 1977). Between kindergarten and third grade, between the ages of about 5 and 9 years, the majority of children have usually been shown to be able to articulate the selling intent of advertising. Variations in the different studies in the percentage of children between kindergarten and third grade judged to understand the purpose of commercials appear to be the result of variations in the measurement contexts.

Contextual factors such as the wording of questions and whether or not children had been exposed to television commercials are particularly relevant to assess children's understanding of advertising intent. Wackman, Wartella, and Ward (1979) reported estimates that ranged between one tenth and one half for the proportion of kindergarten-age children who understand that advertising is trying to sell them products based on responses to different questions ("What is a commercial?" vs. "What do commercials try to do?") and whether or not they had just seen a commercial. Open-ended questions also seem to yield different responses than close-ended questions. For instance, of the 108 children in the Stutts, Vance, and Hudleson (1981) study, 78% said that they knew what a commercial was, based on a yes–no answer. There were no significant differences between 3-, 5-, and 7-year-olds in response to this question. When asked to describe what a commercial is and why commercials are shown on television, however, the 3-year-olds were generally unsuccessful, whereas 11% of the 5-year-olds and 64% of the 7-year-olds defined the selling intent of television commercials.

Nonverbal measurements call into question the age at which children understand the intent of advertising. Donohue, Henke, and Donohue (1980) attempted to assess children's comprehension of television through nonverbal measures by having them point to one of two pictures to indicate what the character in the commercial wanted the preschool child (ages 2–6 years) to do. The results indicated that, although the grasp of the concepts improves with age, children as young as 3 demonstrated some understanding of selling intent. In Macklin's (1985) replication of this study, similar results were found; however, as an extension, Macklin used more complex nonverbal measures and found that the majority of children ages 3 to 6 (80%) failed to select even one correct answer when presented with four pictures rather than just two from which to choose. Although there is concern that verbal measures may not allow young children to articulate their thoughts due to performance competencies, great care needs to be taken in the development and employment of nonverbal measures.

Finally, there also has been attention to the type of intent assessed in various studies. Robertson and Rossiter (1974) identified two different attributional intents of advertising—"assistive" and "persuasive." Assistive intent is similar to that of Roberts's (1982, as cited in Macklin, 1987) "informational function" of advertising. Here "television commercials simply show products that are available in the store" (Macklin, 1987, p. 231). In contrast, persuasive intent refers to the fact that advertisements try to persuade consumers to buy products (Robertson & Rossiter, 1974). To understand the persuasive intent of advertising, children need to understand that persuasive messages are, by nature, biased, and that biased messages require different interpretation strategies than informational messages (Roberts, 1982, as cited in Macklin, 1987). The literature suggests that the informational function of advertising may be acquired separately from understanding the persuasive intent of advertising. Blosser and Roberts (1985) indicated that the informational dimension of messages is recognized earliest followed by an emergence of recognition and interpretation of persuasive messages. Even a minority of preschoolers were able to indicate an understanding of the informational intent of commercials using nonverbal measures (Macklin, 1987). However, Robertson and Rossiter (1974) suggested that persuasive intent requires higher cognitive processing skills than assistive intent. This is supported in the findings that those who perceive the persuasive message in advertising are more likely to be older (fifth grade vs. first grade).

Knowing Specific Advertising Appeals and Tactics.   As children develop beyond elementary school, a more complete and fuller understanding of persuasive intent and consumer role develops. Research indicates that knowledge about advertiser tactics becomes more similar to adult knowledge during early adolescence (Boush, Friestad, & Rose, 1994). Other research suggests that teens with greater marketplace knowledge are more likely to recognize techniques advertisers use for persuasion, and are better able to discern when ads are truthful or misleading (Mangleburg & Bristol, 1998).

Sophisticated consumer knowledge also may be used as a defense against advertising tactics. Some research has examined the role and development of cognitive defenses in children. Roedder (1981) proposed an assessment of children's understanding and defenses against advertising using an information processing approach. Roedder identified three types of processors—strategic, cued, and limited. Strategic processors are usually older children who have the ability to store and retrieve information from long-term memory without prompts or cues. Cued processors are younger children who have the capacity to use storage and retrieval strategies, but only when encouraged to do so. Finally, limited processors are very young children who cannot use storage and retrieval strategies even when cued to do so. In her review of the information-processing literature, Roedder (1981) suggested that older children have less difficulty processing and understanding the central persuasive message of commercial content than those with less well-developed storage and retrieval strategies. Further aided learning, or material where the central message is clearly and deliberately identified, was only beneficial for cued processors no matter what the age of the child processing the advertising. Brucks, Armstrong, and Goldberg (1988) supported Roedder's proposal concerning cued processors and found that that "9 to 10-year-old children do not spontaneously retrieve prior knowledge about advertising but can do so when cued" (p. 480). However, Brucks and her colleagues suggest that young children need to be more informed about the nature of advertising and marketing practices and need to be reminded of these tactics to produce counterarguments for advertising in general.

Affective (Emotional) Effects

Wartella (1984) proposed that no model regarding advertising's influence on child viewers would be complete without considering affective as well as cognitive components. Indeed, contemporary advertising theory suggests that emotions and higher cognitive functions are highly interconnected. Consumer response to advertising then must take into account not only cognitive processing but emotions and feelings as well (Vakratsas & Ambler, 1999). Therefore, this section explores research on children's emotions and attitudes toward advertising and children's emotional responses to advertising, particularly in relation to high-risk health behaviors.

Few studies in the 1970s focused on affect because most research was directed toward understanding how children process advertising cognitively. However, intertwined with cognitive processes, the development of skepticism toward ads began to play a part in understanding the socialization of young consumers. In the 1980s and the 1990s, interest shifted away from children's understanding of advertising toward the power of advertising to influence attitudes toward such behaviors as health, smoking, drinking, and eating disorders.

Buijzen and Valkenburg (2000) suggested that two areas of research on the affective outcomes of exposure to advertising involve children's liking of commercials, and children's trust of commercials; therefore, the discussion of children's attitudes about advertising focuses on these two aspects.

Children's Liking of Commercials. A consistent finding of research is that as children mature, they like commercials less and less. Research in the early 1970s indicated that a little over two thirds of first-grade boys (68.5%) reported liking all commercials and this percentage dropped by the fifth grade to only about a quarter (25.3%) of the boys (Robertson & Rossiter, 1974). Barling and Fullagar (1983) reported similar findings. They suggested that as children grow older, they are "less entertained and more bored and irritated" (p. 29) by commercials. Riecken and Yavas (1990) found that older children (ages 8–12) held a negative opinion of commercials with the majority (nearly two thirds of 152 children) finding commercials to be annoying and in poor taste. The research on gender differences is less substantial. Whereas Riecken and Yavas (1990) found no difference in attitudes toward commercials among boys and girls, only one study suggested that fifth-grade girls hold a less favorable opinion of commercials and are less easily persuaded by advertising messages concerning the value of the advertised products than boys (Sheikh & Moleski, 1977).

Researchers also have studied marketing tactics that may impact children's responses to advertisements. Boys who were exposed to the same commercial three to five times within a cartoon program tended to make remarks such as "Oh no, not again" or "not another one," indicating annoyance with the repetitions (Gorn & Goldberg, 1980, p. 424). However, other tactics may lead to increased liking of commercials. Early research indicated that African American children are more likely to express liking a commercial that featured at least one African American child than one that does not contain children of color (Barry & Hansen, 1973). Furthermore, the majority of children indicated that they liked commercials that are entertaining and humorous, whereas they did not like commercials that were dull, scary, or aimed at the opposite sex (Ward, 1972). Finally, Loughlin, and Desmond (1981) found that children indicated liking a televised commercial more if the commercial contained social interactions such as children playing together than if an ad featured a single child playing alone. A wide range of other attributes of commercials such as the type of appeals employed or types of music used have not been investigated for their influence on advertising's appeal to children.

Children's Trust of Commercials (Skepticism). Children's skepticism toward commercials is inversely related to their liking of advertisements. That is, as children grow older, they grow more skeptical and less trusting of commercials at the same time that they begin to dislike advertising in general. Research in the 1970s found that the majority of boys in the first grade expressed trust in all commercials (64.8%), whereas very few (7.4%) fifth-grade boys expressed that same sentiment (Robertson & Rossiter, 1974). Research in the 1980s and 1990s of commercials focused on adolescent skepticism. Research involving high school students revealed that 14-year-olds were the most cynical with 31% indicating that commercials hardly ever tell the truth (Meyer & Hexamer, 1981). Indeed, Boush and his colleagues (1994) found that by age 13 children's knowledge of advertiser tactics resembles adult knowledge and this increased knowledge is related to being more skeptical of advertising.

Other factors also seem to be related to skepticism. Mangleburg and Bristol (1998) suggested that factors such as family communication patterns (concept-oriented family communication), susceptibility to informational peer influence, well-developed marketplace knowledge, and heavy television viewing enhance skepticism in teens. It appears that the more knowledge youth have about advertising and the marketplace, the more skeptical they become.

Research in the 1970s suggested that children develop cognitive and attitude defenses toward advertising. Rossiter and Robertson (1974) defined cognitive defenses as:

> Cognitive defense ... was predicated on the child's ability to discriminate between commercials and programs, to recognize the existence of a sponsor as the source of the commercial message, to recognize the idea of an intended audience for the message, to comprehend the intentionality or purpose of commercials (both persuasive and informative), and to understand the essential symbolic nature of product presentation in commercials. (pp. 138–139)

Furthermore, Rossiter and Robertson (1974) defined attitude defenses as follows: "Attitude defense was based on the child's degree of believability, liking, and motivational tendency to want products he sees advertised in commercials (with disbelief, dislike, and low motivation signifying attitudinal defense)" (p. 139).

Children's abilities to deconstruct advertising messages change dramatically with age and the definition of cognitive defenses just offered spans a wide range of cognitive abilities that are mastered at different development stages. Moreover, as Boush and his colleagues (1994) noted, knowledge of advertiser tactics (a higher order skill) is related to skepticism about advertising, suggesting an interaction between knowledge and attitudes because both are developing simultaneously.

Research suggests that several factors affect the development of cognitive and affective defenses. Rossiter and Robertson (1974) argued that age is the most significant factor contributing to both cognitive and attitudinal defenses; this accounts for 40% and 31% of variance, respectively, in children's measured defenses toward advertising. Socialization (interactions with peers and parents) and experience with television (time spent with television) also seem to contribute to the development of children's defenses, but to a much less significant degree.

Rossiter and Robertson (1974) found that younger children (first graders) only had an attitudinal defense toward advertising. However, by the fifth grade, children were relying on cognitive defenses. This suggested that "generally cynical attitudes of older children and adolescents toward advertising may belie actual persuasive impact" (p. 143). Twenty years later, Boush and his colleagues (1994) found similar results with adolescents. They submitted that beliefs about advertisers' tactics and attempts at persuasion "start with general attitudes and then are filled in with more specific beliefs" (p. 172). However, with younger children, research suggests that both cognitive and attitudinal defenses are "neutralized" (Robertson & Rossiter, 1974, p. 142) by the end of a period of high advertising for toys and games. Furthermore, Brucks and her colleagues (1988) suggested that young children need more than skepticism to counter advertising messages. Indeed, they need to be more informed about the nature of advertising and marketing practices and need to be reminded of these tactics to produce counterarguments for advertising in general. This is consistent with research findings of Boush and his colleagues (1994) and suggests the policy implications of using announcements and warnings to prompt children to use their cognitive and attitudinal defenses just prior to encountering television commercials.

BEHAVIORAL OUTCOMES

Does advertising influence children's consumer behavior? Since the 1970s this question has been explored in different ways. Early research in the 1970s focused on children's preferences for various products, requests for products, and their frequency of shopping. In the 1980s and 1990s, research focused on specific types of product choices, for example, the influence of advertising on children's selection of sugary snacks. This section focuses on children's product preferences and requests.

Children's Preferences for Products

Television advertising can be a source of consumer information for children. Early research indicated that children cite the television as a primary source for learning about products such as toys (Caron & Ward, 1975; Donohue, 1975; Robertson & Rossiter, 1976), and this was a particularly true for heavy viewers of television (Frideres, 1973). Frideres (1973) argued that even children who are light viewers of television are indirectly affected by advertising as a result of a two-step flow through informal communication with trend-setting children who are exposed to more television advertising. Caron and Ward (1975) found that older fifth-grade children both used a variety of mass media as sources of information and were more likely to cite television as the idea source for product requests than third graders. Furthermore, interviews with mothers indicated that young children frequently recognized products they have seen advertised (Burr & Burr, 1977). These studies from the 1970s found that even young grade school children were aware of products, and were developing product preferences.

A variety of factors may lead children to express preferences for advertised products. Early research from the 1970s with African American children found that they expressed a preference for a particular cereal after having seen a commercial that featured an African American child in the advertisement (Barry & Hansen, 1973). Furthermore, children are more likely to express preferences for toys and games following a peak advertising period for such products, such as the pre-Christmas advertising period (Robertson & Rossiter, 1976). Finally, marketing strategies such as premiums also can have an impact on children's expressed preferences for products. Children who were exposed to advertising for a cereal that featured a premium indicated a preference for that cereal when given a choice of other advertised cereals (Heslop & Ryans, 1980). Clearly, early research indicated an impact of advertising on children's preferences for products and that certain advertising strategies and marketing practices could enhance children's preferences.

Children's Requests for Products

Much of the research regarding children's requests for products focused on their requests for toys during the Christmas season, a period of dramatic increase in toy advertising. A common method of data collection is for researchers to examine children's Christmas wish lists in connection with their exposure to television advertising. One consistent finding from this line of research is that heavy exposure to television advertising does have an impact on the types of items children request as Christmas presents. Research conducted in the 1970s found that for children who were heavy television viewers, there was an 8% increase in requests for advertised products compared to requests prior to the pre-Christmas advertising period (Robertson & Rossiter, 1977). Similarly, 20 years later, Buijzen and Valkenburg (2000) found that those brands most frequently advertised were the most often wanted toys and that the number of children's toy wishes consistent with brands in television advertising could be predicted by children's exposure to the network that aired the most commercials. A second consistent finding from these studies is that younger children were more likely to request advertised toys than older children (Buijzen & Valkenburg, 2000; Robertson & Rossiter, 1977).

According to Robertson and Rossiter (1977), the number of requests for advertised products was highest among high-exposure young viewers (first-grade boys) and least among older, light viewers (fifth-grade boys). Buijzen and Valkenburg (2000) reported a general decline in the percentage of requests for advertised products and a change in the types of products requested as children grow older. Specifically, they found that a little over two thirds (67.1%) of younger children (ages 7–8) request advertised products whereas less than half (39.4%) of older children ages 11 or 12 do the same.

In addition to examining children's requests for advertised products, other research has focused on the consequences of such requests and denials of requests among children and parents alike. Early research indicated that advertising can arouse interest in almost all children (over 90%) to request a product; however, fewer (only 57%) actually make the overt request (Sheikh & Moleski, 1977). Parents can respond in a wide variety of ways to such requests. Research in the 1970s indicated that mothers reported they were most likely to buy a product when children say they saw it on television or when they request the product advertised with the premium (Burr & Burr, 1977). Of the mothers who said they would buy the product when the child asked for the premium, nearly three fourths (74%) indicated that they thought the prizes were overemphasized to such an extent that children ask for the product just to get the prize (Burr & Burr, 1977). Maternal responses to requests are of particular interest because research indicates that children are more likely to ask their mother and father together (43%) or just their mother (46.5%) rather than ask just their father (10.3%) for a product (Sheikh & Moleski, 1977).

Parents cannot fulfill all of their children's requests; therefore, research has examined children's responses to denial of their request. Sheikh and Moleski (1977) found that the children's most frequently reported response to a denial were reports of feeling sad or crying, particularly among girls. However, as children grow older, their response changes. Fifth graders were less likely to express feelings of sadness, whereas third graders were less likely to accept denial and were more likely to express aggression such as indicating they would be mad compared to first graders (Sheikh & Moleski, 1977). Children's responses vary greatly depending on their level of development both in the types of requests and responses to denial of such requests. Although these responses may be varied and cause conflict between the parent and child, research with preschoolers suggests that there is "little evidence that exposure to a TV commercial will generate more negative feelings toward a parent who refuses a particular request" (Goldberg & Gorn, 1978, p. 27).

EXTENSION OF ADVERTISING BEYOND HOME AND INTO THE SCHOOL

Marketing to children has expanded beyond television advertising to include such venues as in-store displays, direct mail, kids clubs, and product placement in movies and video games. One of the more controversial marketing strategies has been using schools as a venue for advertising to children. This practice, with roots in the 1920s, has increased substantially since the 1990s (Molnar, 2002). This section explores different marketing activities within the school system, drawing on specific case studies, and discusses the effects of these practices on children.

Types of Advertising Venues and Examples

A variety of marketing strategies are used in schools. Researchers have sorted these activities into a number of categories (Consumers Union,

1995; Molnar, 2002; Richards, Wartella, Morton, & Thompson, 1998; United States General Accounting Office [USGAO], 2000). Four categories of in-school marketing practices are direct advertising, indirect advertising, product sales, and other marketing practices.

Direct Advertising.   The most obvious marketing practice is the advertising of products and services to students in school buildings and facilities such as hallways, scoreboards, buses, and textbooks, along with school publications such as yearbooks, school calendars, school newspapers, and sports programs (USGAO, 2000). Direct advertising includes such activities as the distribution of free sample products and media-based advertising (USGAO, 2000). Examples of free product distribution include such activities as Nike's annual dispersal of new athletic shoes for school sports teams (Glamser, 1997) and packages of hygiene products with items like deodorant and toothpaste from such companies as Procter and Gamble (Jimenez, 1997). Media-based advertising includes advertisements in classroom magazines and television programs such as Channel One, a 12-minute news program that includes 2 minutes of advertising in each daily newscast (Channel One Network, n.d.), or ZapMe!, free computers with a preloaded, permanent interface that features a 2-inch border around the screen where ads appear in a box in the lower left (Bazeley, 1999). Despite controversy over advertising to a captive audience, Channel One continues to be broadcast to 8 million teens in more then 350,000 classrooms nationwide (Channel One Network, n.d.). However, as a result of negative attention to their practices, ZapMe! no longer provides free computers and Internet access to schools (Bell, 2000).

Recently, some schools have even sold the naming rights of their athletic properties and accepted corporate sponsorship in exchange for naming of athletic events. A local telephone company in Colorado bought the naming rights to a school district's athletic stadium for $2 million over 10 years (Seymour, 2001). A high school in Illinois named its football field Rust-Oleum Field after receiving a corporate donation of $100,000 for the construction of the field (Jackson, 2002). When realignment in Arizona created a new high school conference, Wells Fargo Bank paid $12,000 to secure naming of the conference (Trost, 2001). Some school districts are even considering corporate sponsorship to help pay for capital building expenses (Seymour, 2001). The overall extent of such advertising practices is hard to gauge, although they seem to be widespread.

Indirect Advertising. Indirect advertising involves corporate-sponsored activities and training, including production and distribution of curricular materials, contests and incentive programs, teacher training, and grants and other gifts (USGAO, 2000). For example, General Mills has sent teachers "Gushers: Wonders of the Earth" a science lesson about volcanoes that uses the company's Fruit Gushers candy as part of the lesson plan (Stead, 1997), and Procter and Gamble provides a history lesson that teaches students that the company provided soap for Union army soldiers during the Civil War (Applebaum, 2003). As an incentive, children in the Washington, DC area with good grades receive discounts or free products at several businesses including Athlete's Foot, Blockbuster, and Chuck E. Cheese (Kelleher, 2000), and Pizza Hut provides coupons redeemable for a free personal pan pizza for students who reach their teacher's reading goals (Dodge, 1998). Contests, on the other hand, often encourage participants to get involved with products and to use their skills to create award-winning essays, recipes, and the like, such as when Chips Ahoy! had students confirm that there really were 1,000 chocolate chips in every bag of cookies or when Kellogg's had students create sculptures from Rice Krispies and melted butter (Labi, 1999).

Some schools have built corporate relationships with different companies in exchange for equipment and training. Major computer companies have donated computer equipment and advice to schools across the country; Apple Computer donated more than $8 million in equipment and advice in 1990 alone (Larson, 1991). In 1996, Sun Microsystems coordinated "Net Day" in California, where about 200 companies and 20,000 volunteers worked together to wire public schools in California for Internet access (Stead, 1997). More recently, computer companies such as Intel, Microsoft, and Gateway have pledged to provide software, equipment, and computer training for school teachers (Lynem, 2000; Wax, 2000).

Product Sales. Fundraising activities, cash or credit rebate programs, and product sales including exclusive agreements and cafeteria privatization comprise the category of product sales (USGAO, 2000). According to Vickie Mabry, an official with the Association of Fund Raisers and Direct Sellers, U.S. K–12 schools raise about $1.5 billion through fundraising activities (Kittredge, 2000). Some schools are even selling personal seat licenses (PSL), a right to their own seat, in addition to season ticket passes (Trost, 2001). The sale of commercial products has become standard practice in many schools across the country and has lead to the privatization of school lunchrooms and exclusive contracts with soft drink manufacturers. Privatization involves allowing fast-food vendors to provide food service within the school cafeteria. For example, Taco Bell and Pizza Hut sell or deliver products to thousands of schools nationwide (Jacobson, 1995). Additionally, a number of school districts have signed exclusive contracts with soft drink vendors to allow only one vendor on school property. School districts in Seattle (Ervin, 2001) and Colorado Springs (White, Ruskin, Mokhiber, & Weissman, 1999) signed exclusive contracts with Coca-Cola to generate revenue for student activities. Recently, however, Coca-Cola announced changes in their policies toward schools. Specifically, Coca-Cola no longer requires exclusive beverage contracts with school districts; has implemented changes with their vending machines, offering more juices, water, and sugar-free, caffeine-free, and calcium-rich beverages; and installs vending machines without as much commercial signage (Unger & Paul, 2001).

Fundraising has taken on new dimensions with cash and credit rebate programs both online and in stores, where schools get a portion of purchases made by family and friends. Rebate programs take the form of e-shopping through "'support shopping' sites—also known as shop-to-give, virtual fundraising, and cyberscrip" (Poftak, 2000, p. 58). After users log on to these support shopping sites such as www.schoolpop.com, schools can earn money with every e-shopper's purchase from hundreds of online stores, including JCPenney.com, Barnes and Noble.com, and Dell.com (Schoolpop, n.d.). Schoolpop has expanded its operations to include a Schoolpop-affiliated Visa credit card, magazine subscriptions, and rebates for select groceries purchased at participating stores (Schoolpop, n.d.). For those in-store purchases, some retailers have established rebate programs for purchases made in association with special cards such as the Kmart School Spirit Card (Kmartschoolspirit, n.d.) or with a store-affiliated credit card such as a Target Visa Card (Target, n.d.). According to Target's Web site, Target has contributed more than $100 million to schools nationwide through fundraising, scholarships and grants since 1997 (Target, n.d.).

Other Marketing Practices. Recently, schools have been getting involved in market research to generate school income. There are reports of schools conducting market research such as taste tests, and tracking students' Internet behavior, as well as having students conduct product testing for companies such as McDonald's and Toys R Us (Farber, 1999). Schools can earn anywhere from $800 to a few thousand dollars for each market research project (Farber, 1999). Prior to its demise in 2000, ZapMe!

engaged in market research by collecting demographic information on the student users and tracking their Internet use. Each student completed a user profile including the his or her age, sex, and Zip code. When the students used the computers, they logged in with their password and the tracking began. Although these data were collected and shared with advertisers as an aggregate, ZapMe! did offer a program called ZapPoints in which students could acquire points toward prizes while the company gathered personally identifiable information about them (Schwartz, 2000).

Prevalence of Commercial Activities in Schools

Although there have been studies of the presence of reports of commercial activities in education, very little research has been conducted to examine the actual prevalence of these activities in schools. As a component of the 2000 USGAO report, researchers visited 19 schools to evaluate the presence of commercial activities in schools. Results indicated that commercial activities were found in all the schools visited, but high schools had more commercial activities than middle schools or elementary schools. Product sales, direct advertising, and indirect advertising were present in all schools visited, and none of the schools indicated they had participated in any market research. Product sales were the most prevalent form of commercial activity in the visited schools, consisting of exclusive beverage contracts in secondary schools and fundraising sales in elementary schools. Direct advertising was present in many forms in all the schools visited and was most visible as soft drink advertisements on vending machines and corporate names and logos on scoreboards. Teachers and principals limited the amount of indirect advertising in the schools visited such as using corporate-sponsored educational materials as a supplement to the regular classroom curriculum rather than replacing it, or posting information about corporate-sponsored contests rather than promoting them within the classroom. However, many of the elementary schools did engage in a reading incentive program that rewards readers with free pizza (USGAO, 2000).

Effects of Advertising in Schools

Even though commercial activities have been present in schools since the 1920s (Stead, 1997), very little research has been conducted regarding the effects of these activities on children except for research on the effects of the TV news program, Channel One. There is some question regarding how attentively students watch Channel One. According to one study, students are more likely to attend to Channel One if a teacher attends to the program and transmits the expectation that students should do the same (Johnston, 1995). Self-reports of paying attention to the program from a survey of 100 schools with Channel One reveal that 43% say they "usually" pay attention and 37% report that they "occasionally" pay attention. School observations indicate that students "graze" while watching Channel One; that is, students pay attention to stories of personal interest and pay less attention to stories with lower levels of interest (Johnston, 1995).

Researchers have also examined the impact of Channel One on children's consumer behavior. One study indicates that Channel One viewers evaluate products advertised on the program more highly than their nonviewing counterparts (Brand & Greenberg, 1994). Channel One viewers expressed more consumer-oriented attitudes than nonviewers and were more likely than nonviewers to report purchase intentions for Channel One-advertised products. Channel One viewers, however, were no more likely than their nonviewing peers to report actual purchases of Channel One-advertised products (Brand & Greenberg, 1994). However, as Bachen (1998) noted, we do not know whether students' consumer learning in school differs from learning about products in other contexts.

CONCLUSION

Although the literature on children and advertising may be short, it is rich in description, theory, and practical applications. Early studies explored how children process advertising content, primarily from a Piagetian developmental approach. Other theories such as information processing and social influence began to be applied to advertising research. Interest on children's attitudes and behaviors also grew. New approaches such as using nonverbal measures were developed and tested young children's knowledge of advertising intent. Attention began to focus on teens and adolescence and on the impact of advertising on children's lives outside the home. The scope of the research has been wide, but there is still room for new research. We suggest three areas for future research on children and advertising—measurement development, replication, and expansion.

Measurement Development

Some attempts have been made at refining measurement tools, but new research needs to explore these techniques more closely. Nonverbal measurements need further development and enhancement. Although it is obvious that nonverbal measures are more appropriate for younger children, it is still unclear which of these measurement tools provide valid results. Furthermore, a standardized set of attitude measurements needs to be finalized. Although a great deal of research was conducted to evaluate an attitude measurement scale (Bearden, Teel, & Wright, 1979; Giudicatti & Stening, 1980; Lindquist, 1981; Riecken & Samli, 1981; Rossiter, 1977), no convincing evidence has been found regarding the validity of the measures. Also, other measurement scales could be developed to measure comprehension consistently, as well as consumer behavior and skepticism.

Replication

Surprising, among the hundreds of studies conducted since 1970, very few replicate previous research. Several studies examine similar topics, but use different questions or techniques to explore children's responses to advertising. Even among the content analyses, very few variables are measured in the same manner across time. Even among those studies that do measure similar variables, the data sets are collected from different time frames, making comparisons very difficult. Future research should use variables as defined in previous research and collect ads from the same months to evaluate trends and note differences across time.

Expansion

Although replication studies help establish trends, we also need to expand our knowledge as the nature of children's lives change. As we enter into a time of TV-constant households, we need to know more about the impact of advertising and consumerism on the very young and the implications of advertising on family development and communication. Only a handful of studies address children's development as consumers in the preschool years and very few studies explore the family as a unit. Furthermore, we need to turn our attention to other factors besides age, such as race, family income, and consumer experience, that may be influencing children's responses to advertising, particularly when advertising-free channels like PBS and Noggin are scant. Moreover, most of the research focuses on advertising on television. In a society where Internet access is becoming more readily available and electronic commerce has grown, we need to know more about children's electronic consumer behavior and their comprehension of Internet advertisements. Finally, commercialism in schools has become more and more pervasive, yet we still do not know much about the effects of these practices on children.

Advertising appears in almost every aspect of a child's life. From the brand-name characters dangling from an infant's mobile to the corporations that sponsor high school sports, advertising and marketing practices are a large part of youth culture. We have only just begun to understand the impact of advertising on youth. We need to continue this tradition and expand our research to explore the changing environment of contemporary consumerism.

REFERENCES

Adler, R. P., Friedlander, B. Z., Lesser, G. S., Meringoff, L., Robertson, T. S., Rossiter, J. R., et al. (1977). *Research on the effects of television advertising on children.* Washington, DC: U.S. Government Printing Office.

Alexander, A., Benjamin, L. M., Hoerrner, K. L., & Roe, D. (1999). "We'll be back in a moment": A content analysis of advertisements in children's television in the 1950s. In M. C. Macklin & L. Carlson (Eds.), *Advertising to children: Concepts and controversies* (pp. 97–115). Thousand Oaks, CA: Sage.

Applebaum, M. (2003, March 10). Don't spare the brand, *Brandweek, 44*(10), 20+.

Atkin, C., & Heald, G. (1977). The content of children's toy and food commercials. *Journal of Communication, 27*, 107–114.

Bachen, C. M. (1998). Channel One and the education of American youths. *The Annals of the American Academy of Political and Social Science, 557*, 132–147.

Barcus, F. E. (1978). *Commercial children's television on weekend and weekday afternoons.* Newtonville, MA: Action for Children's Television.

Barcus, F. E. (1980). The nature of television advertising to children. In E. L. Palmer & A. Dorr (Eds.), *Children and the faces of television: Teaching, violence and selling* (pp. 273–285). New York: Academic.

Barling, J., & Fullagar, C. (1983). Children's attitudes to television advertisements: A factorial perspective. *Journal of Psychology, 113*(1), 25–30.

Barry, T. E., & Hansen, R. W. (1973). How race affects children's TV commercials. *Journal of Advertising Research, 13*(5), 63–67.

Bazeley, M. (1999, March 21). ZapMe! school role debated: Students get computers; advertisers get a market! [Online] In *Silicon Valley News*, Retrieved March 23, 1999, from http:// www.mercurycenter.com /svtech/news /indepth /docs /zapme032299.htm.

Bearden, W. O., Teel, J. E., & Wright, R. R. (1979). Family income effects on measurement of children's attitudes toward television commercials. *Journal of Consumer Research, 6*, 308–311.

Bell, E. (2000, December 7). Schools lament loss of PCs; Politics persuade firm to pull out. *The San Francisco Chronicle*, p. A19.

Bever, T. G., Smith, M. L., Bengen, B., & Johnson, T. G. (1975). Young viewers' troubling response to TV ads. *Harvard Business Review, 53*, 109–120.

Blosser, B. J., & Roberts, D. F. (1985). Age differences in children's perception of message intent: Responses to television news, commercials, educational spots, and public service announcements. *Communication Research, 12,* 455–484. ·

Boush, D. M., Friestad, M., & Rose, G. M. (1994). Adolescent skepticism toward TV advertising and knowledge of advertiser tactics. *Journal of Consumer Research, 21*(1), 165–175.

Brand, J. E., & Greenberg, B. S. (1994). Commercials in the classroom: The impact of Channel One advertising. *Journal of Advertising Research, 34*(1), 18–27.

Brucks, M., Armstrong, M. E., & Goldberg, M. E. (1988). Children's use of cognitive defenses against television advertising: A cognitive response approach. *Journal of Consumer Research, 14,* 471–482.

Buijzen, M., & Valkenburg, P. M. (2000). The impact of television advertising on children's Christmas wishes. *Journal of Broadcasting and Electronic Media, 44,* 456–470.

Burr, P. L., & Burr, R. (1977). Product recognition and premium appeal. *Journal of Communication, 27,* 115–117.

Butter, E. J., Popovich, P. M., Stackhouse, R. H., & Garner, R. K. (1981). Discrimination of television programs and commercials by preschool children. *Journal of Advertising Research, 2*(2), 53–56.

Caron, A. H., & Ward, S. (1975). Gift decisions by kids and parents. *Journal of Advertising Research, 15*(4), 15–20.

Channel One Network. (n.d.). Retrieved August 1, 2003, from http://www.primedia.com/divisions/tv_group/channelone/.

Condry, J., Bence, P., & Schiebe, C. (1988). Nonprogram content of children's television. *Journal of Broadcasting and Electronic Media, 32,* 255–270.

Consumers Union. (1995). *Captive kids: Commercial pressures on kids at school.* Yonkers, NY: Consumers Union Education Services.

Dodge, S. (1998, December 27). Ads adding up in local schools. *Chicago Sun Times,* p. 1.

Donohue, T. R. (1975). Effect of commercials on black children. *Journal of Advertising Research, 15*(6), 41–47.

Donohue, T. R., Henke, L. L., & Donohue, W. A. (1980). Do kids know what TV commercials intend? *Journal of Advertising, 20*(5), 51–57.

Donohue, T. R., Meyer, T. P., & Henke, L. L. (1978). *Black and white children's perception of the intent and values in specific adult and child oriented television commercials.* Unpublished manuscript, University of Hartford, Hartford, CT.

Doolittle, J., & Pepper, R. (1975). Children's TV ad content: 1974. *Journal of Broadcasting and Electronic Media, 19,* 131–151.

Ervin, K. (2001, November 22). Schools expel Channel One: New policy also limits ads, logos, *The Seattle Times,* p. B1.

Farber, P. J. (1999, October 25). Schools for sale. *Advertising Age,* pp. 22+.

Frideres, J. S. (1973). Advertising, buying patterns and children. *Journal of Advertising Research, 13*(1), 34–36.

Glamser, D. (1997, January 3). This class is brought to you by . . . . *USA Today,* p. 3A.

Goldberg, M. E., & Gorn, G. J. (1978). Some unintended consequences of TV advertising to children. *Journal of Consumer Research, 5,* 22–29.

Gorn, G. J., & Goldberg, M. E. (1980). Children's responses to repetitive television commercials. *Journal of Consumer Research, 6,* 421–424.

Guidicatti, V., & Stening, B. W. (1980). An empirical evaluation of a test measuring children's attitudes toward TV advertisements. *Psychological Reports, 46,* 1222.

Heslop, L. A., & Ryans, A. B. (1980). A second look at children and advertising of premiums. *Journal of Consumer Research, 6,* 414–420.

Jackson, R. (2002, October 18). Naming rights still pure in Warren County. *Dayton Daily News,* p. G1.

Jacobson, M. F. (1995, January 29). Now there's a fourth R: Retailing. *New York Times,* p. F9.

Jimenez, R. (1997, January 8). Freebies in schools get mixed reaction. *The Boston Globe,* p. 1.

John, D. R. (1999). Through the eyes of a child: Children's knowledge and understanding of advertising. In M. C. Macklin & L. Carlson (Eds.), *Advertising to children: Concepts and controversies* (pp. 3–26). Thousand Oaks, CA: Sage.

Johnson, F. L., & Young, K. (2002). Gendered voices in children's television advertising. *Critical Studies in Media Communication, 19,* 461–480.

Johnston, J. (1995). Channel One: The dilemma of teaching and selling. *Phi Delta Kappan, 76,* 436–443.

Kelleher, E. (2000, November 3). Good deals as easy as A-B-C; Some stores will let you cash in on your report card. *The Washington Post,* p. C13.

Kittredge, C. (2000, October 8). New Hampshire weekly: Alarms sounded on commercials in schools. *The Boston Globe,* p. 1.

Kmartschoolspirit (n.d.). Retrieved August 1, 2003, from http://www.kmartschoolspirit.com/faq.asp.

Kunkel, D. (2001). Children and television advertising. In D. G. Singer & J. L. Singer (Eds.), *Handbook of children and the media* (pp. 375–394). Thousand Oaks, CA: Sage.

Kunkel, D., & Gantz, W. (1992). Children's television advertising in the multichannel environment. *Journal of Communication, 42*(3), 134–152.

Labi, N. (1999, April 19). Classrooms for sale. *Time, 153*(15), 44–45.

Larson, J. (1991, October). Computers in school can be habit forming. *American Demographics, 13*(10), 12.

Larson, M. S. (2001). Interactions, activities and gender in children's television commercials: A content analysis. *Journal of Broadcasting and Electronic Media, 45*(1), 41–56.

Levin, S. R., Petros, T. V., & Petrella, F. W. (1982). Preschooler's awareness of television advertising. *Child Development, 53,* 933–937.

Lindquist, J. D. (1981). Measuring children's attitudes toward TV commercials: An instrument reliability test. *Journal of the Academy of Marketing Science, 9,* 9409–9418.

Loughlin, M., & Desmond, R. J. (1981). Social interaction in advertising directed to children. *Journal of Broadcasting, 25,* 303–307.

Lynem, J. N. (2000, January 21). Firms to invest $440 million in teachers. *The San Francisco Chronicle,* p. A19.

Macklin, M. (1985). Do young children understand the selling intent of commercials? *Journal of Consumer Affairs, 19,* 293–304.

Macklin, M. C. (1987). Preschoolers' understanding of the information function of television advertising. *Journal of Consumer Research, 14,* 229–239.

Macklin, M. C., & Kolbe, R. H. (1984). Sex role stereotyping in children's advertising: Current and past trends. *Journal of Advertising, 13*(2), 34–42.

Mangleburg, T. F., & Bristol, T. (1998). Socialization and adolescents' skepticism toward advertising. *Journal of Advertising, 27*(3), 11–21.

McNeal, J. U. (1969). An exploratory study of the consumer behavior of children. In J. McNeal (Ed.), *Dimensions of consumer behavior* (pp.255–276). New York: Appleton-Century-Crofts.

McNeal, J. U. (1992). *Kids as customers: A handbook of marketing to children.* New York: Lexington.

Meyer, T. P., Donohue, T. R., & Henke, L. L. (1978). How Black children see TV commercials. *Journal of Advertising Research, 18*(5), 51–58.

Meyer, T. P., & Hexamer, A. (1981). Perceived truth and trust in television advertising among Mexican-American adolescent: Socialization and developmental consideration. *Journal of Broadcasting, 25*, 139–150.

Molnar, A. (2002). *What's in a name? The corporate branding of America's schools: The fifth annual report on trends in schoolhouse commercialization.* Tempe, AZ: Education Policy Studies Lab, Arizona State University.

Mowen, J. C., & Minor, M. (1998). *Consumer behavior* (5th ed.). London: Prentice-Hall.

Pecora, N. O. (1998). *The business of children's entertainment.* New York: Guilford.

Perse, E. M. (2001). *Media effects and society.* Mahwah, NJ: Lawrence Erlbaum Associates.

Poftak, A. (2000, March). School fundraising goes online. *Technology & Learning, 20*(8), 58.

Richards, J. I., Wartella, E. A., Morton, C., & Thompson, L. (1998). The growing commercialization of schools: Issues and practices. *The Annals of the American Academy of Political and Social Science, 557*, 148–163.

Riecken, G., & Samli, A. C. (1981). Measuring children's attitudes toward television commercials: Extension and replication. *Journal of Consumer Research, 8*(1), 57–61.

Riecken, G., & Yavas, U. (1990). Children's general product and brand-specific attitudes toward television commercials: Implications for public policy and advertising strategy. *International Journal of Advertising, 9*, 136–148.

Riffe, D., Goldson, H., Saxton, K., & Yu, Y. (1989). Females and minorities in TV ads in 1987 Saturday children's programs. *Journalism Quarterly, 66*, 129–136.

Roberts, D. (1979, January). Testimony before the Federal Trade Commission's rulemaking on children and TV advertising, San Francisco, CA.

Roberts, D. F. (1982). Children and commercials: Issues, evidence, interventions. *Prevention in Human Services, 2*(1–2), 19–35.

Robertson, T. S., & Rossiter, J. R. (1974). Children and commercial persuasion: An attribution theory analysis. *Journal of Consumer Research, 1*(1), 13–20.

Robertson, T. S., & Rossiter, J. R. (1976). Short-run advertising effects on children: A field study. *Journal of Marketing Research, 13*(1), 68–70.

Robertson, T. S., & Rossiter, J. R. (1977). Children's responsiveness to commercials. *Journal of Communication, 27*, 101–106.

Roedder, D. L. (1981). Age differences in children's responses to television advertising: An information processing approach. *Journal of Consumer Research, 8*(2), 144–153.

Rossiter, J. R. (1977). Reliability of a short test measuring children's attitudes toward TV commercials. *Journal of Consumer Research, 3*(4), 179–184.

Rossiter, J. R., & Robertson, T. S. (1974). Children's TV commercials: Testing the defenses. *Journal of Communication, 24*(4), 137–145.

Schoolpop. (n.d.). Retrieved August 1, 2003 from http://www.schoolpop.com/cgi/welcome.cgi?pid=40.

Schwartz, J. (2000, November 2). Offer of free computers for schools is withdrawn. *The New York Times,* p. 1C.

Seymour, L. (2001, December 6). It may pay to advertise in Fairfax schools; Officials consider more sponsorship. *The Washington Post,* p. C08.

Sheikh, A. A., & Moleski, L. M. (1977). Children's perception of the value of an advertised product. *Journal of Broadcasting, 21,* 347–354.

Sheikh, A. A., Prasad, V. K., & Rao, T. R. (1974). Children's TV commercials: A review of research. *Journal of Communication, 24*(4), 126–136.

Smith, L. (1994). A content analysis of gender differences in children's advertising. *Journal of Broadcasting and Electronic Media, 38*(3), 91–101.

Stead, D. (1997, January 5). Corporations, classrooms, and commercialism: Some say business has gone too far. *The New York Times,* Section 4A, pp. 30–33+.

Stephens, N., & Stutts, M. A. (1982). Preschoolers' ability to distinguish between television programming and commercials. *Journal of Advertising, 11*(2), 16–26.

Strasburger, V. C., & Wilson, B. J. (2002). *Children, adolescents, & the media.* Thousand Oaks, CA: Sage.

Stutts, M. A., Vance, D., & Hudleson, S. (1981). Program–commercial separators in children's television: Do they help a child tell the difference between Bugs Bunny and the Quik Rabbit? *Journal of Advertising, 10*(2), 16–27.

Target. (n.d.). Retrieved August 20, 2003, from http:// target.com/common/page.jhtml?content=target%5fcg%5ftake%5fcharge%5fof%5feducation&%5frequestid=4214692.

Trost, J. (2001, August 12). Dangerous territory. *Chicago Sun-Times,* p. 114.

Unger, H., & Paul, P. C. (2001, March 14). Coca-Cola learns a lesson in schools; Nutrition is in, exclusivity is out in strategy shift. *The Atlanta Journal and Constitution,* p. 1A.

United States General Accounting Office. (2000). *Commercial activities in schools* (GAO Pub. No. GAO/HEHS-00-156). Washington, DC: Author.

Vakratsas, D., & Ambler, T. (1999). How advertising works: What do we really know? *Journal of Marketing, 63*(1), 26–43.

Valkenburg, P. M., & Cantor, J. (2001). The development of a child into a consumer. *Applied Developmental Psychology, 22,* 61–72.

Wackman, D., Wartella, E., & Ward, S. (1979). *Children's information processing of television advertising.* Unpublished manuscript, University of Minnesota, Minneapolis.

Ward, S. (1972). Children's reactions to commercials. *Journal of Advertising Research, 12,* 37–45.

Ward, S., Wackman, D., & Wartella, E. (1977). *How children learn to buy.* Beverly Hills, CA: Sage.

Wartella, E. (1984). Cognitive and affective factors of TV advertising's influence on children. *Western Journal of Speech Communication, 48,* 171–183.

Wax, E. (2000, May 17). Across the e-divide; Public and private efforts are trying to bridge the gap between Internet haves and have-nots. *The Washington Post*, p. G08.

Welch, R. L., Huston-Stein, A., Wright, J. C., & Plehal, R. (1979). Subtle sex-role cues in children's commercials. *Journal of Communication,29*, 202–209.

Wells, W. D. (1966). Children as consumers. In J. W. Newman (Ed.), *On knowing the consumer* (pp. 138–145). New York: Wiley.

White, A., Ruskin, G., Mokhiber, R., & Weissman, R. (1999). The Cola-ized classroom. *Multinational Monitor, 20*, 16–23.

7

TV Violence: Research and Controversy

John P. Murray
The Mind Science Foundation, San Antonio
Center on Media and Child Health, Children's Hospital Boston
Harvard Medical School

The violent face of television has been presented to audiences from the first broadcasts of this medium. Television broadcasting in the United States began in the early 1940s, with full development following World War II. Although extensive broadcast schedules did not begin until the late 1940s, and violence was not as graphic as it would become in later years, the first public concerns about violence were evident in the 1950s. The early Congressional hearings (U.S. Congress, 1952, 1955) set the stage for similar expressions of public concern that have continued through the 20th century and into the 21st century (U.S. Congress, 2003). What have we learned from all of this research and discussion on the "violent face of television" and what can be done to mitigate the harmful influences?

EARLY RESEARCH AND SOCIAL CONCERNS

The early studies of television's influence began almost simultaneously in England and the United States and Canada in the mid-1950s. In England, a group of researchers at the London School of Economics and Political Science, under the direction of Hilde Himmelweit, a Reader in Social Psychology, began the first study of children's television viewing patterns while TV was still relatively new (only 3 million TV sets were installed in the 15 million households in England). This study was proposed by the Audience Research Department of the British Broadcasting Corporation (BBC) but was conducted by independent researchers. The research, begun in 1955, was published in a 1958 report, *Television and the Child: An Empirical Study of the Effect of Television on the Young* (Himmelweit, Oppenheim, & Vince, 1958). The American and Canadian study was conducted by Wilbur Schramm and his colleagues in communications at Stanford University. This project began in 1957 and was published in a 1961 report, *Television in the Lives of Our Children* (Schramm, Lyle, & Parker, 1961).

The British and American–Canadian surveys provided a very important benchmark for understanding the broad and general effects of television on children. For example, Himmelweit et al.(1958) noted: "We have found a number of instances where viewers and controls differed in their outlook; differences which did not exist before television came on the scene. There was a small but consistent influence of television on the way children thought generally about jobs, job values, success, and social surroundings" (pp. 17–18). With regard to aggression, these correlational studies were less specific, as Himmelweit and her colleagues noted: "We did not find that the viewers were any more aggressive or maladjusted than the controls; television is unlikely to cause aggressive behaviour, although it could precipitate it in those few children who are emotionally disturbed. On the other hand, there was little support for the view that programmes of violence are beneficial; we found that they aroused aggression as often as they discharged it" (p. 20). In the case of the Schramm et al. (1961) study, their conclusions about television violence included the observation that those Canadian and American children who had high exposure to television and low exposure to print were more aggressive than those with the reverse pattern. Thus, the early correlational studies or surveys identified some areas of concern about television violence and set the stage for more focused investigations. Finally, it should be noted that these 1950s studies of viewers and nonviewers took place when television was new in the United States, Canada, and England. Later studies—in the 1970s—would revisit these issues and this research strategy when television was being introduced into isolated communities in Australia (Murray & Kippax, 1977, 1978, 1979) and Canada (Macbeth, 1996; Williams, 1986).

Moving beyond these 1950s surveys, there was another set of studies that emerged in the early 1960s—not surveys or correlational studies but experimental studies that were addressed to cause-and-effect relationships in the

TV violence–aggressive behavior equation. These initial experiments were conducted by Bandura, at Stanford University, who studied preschool-age children, and Berkowitz, at the University of Wisconsin, who worked with college-age youth. In both instances, the studies were experimental in design, which meant that participants were randomly assigned to various viewing experiences and therefore the results of this manipulated viewing could be used to address the issue of causal relationships between viewing and behavior. The early Bandura studies, such as "Transmission of Aggression Through Imitation of Aggressive Models" (Bandura, Ross, & Ross, 1961) or "Imitation of Film-Mediated Aggressive Models" (Bandura, Ross, & Ross, 1963), were set within a social learning paradigm and were designed to identify the processes governing the ways that children learn by observing and imitating the behavior of others. In this context, therefore, the studies used stimulus films (videotape was not generally available) back projected on a simulated television screen, and the behavior of the children was observed and recorded in a playroom setting immediately following the viewing period. Despite the structured nature of these studies, Bandura's research was central to the debate about the influence of media violence. Moreover, the work of Berkowitz and his colleagues, such as "Effects of Film Violence on Inhibitions Against Subsequent Aggression" (Berkowitz & Rawlings, 1963) or "Film Violence and the Cue Properties of Available Targets" (Berkowitz & Geen, 1966), studied the simulated aggressive behavior of youth and young adults following the viewing of segments of violent films, such as a Kirk Douglas boxing film, *The Champion*. The demonstration of increased willingness to use aggression against others following viewing further fueled the debate about the influence of media violence.

Concern about the influence of TV violence began as early as the start of this new medium. The first Congressional hearings were held in the early 1950s (U.S. Congress, 1952, 1955). At these early hearings, developmental psychologist Maccoby (1954) and sociologist Lazarsfeld (1955) presented testimony that relied on some early studies of violence in films, such as the 1930s report, *Boys, Movies and City Streets* (Cressey & Thrasher, 1933), to outline a necessary program of research on the issue of TV violence and its effects on children.

As the 1960s progressed, concern in the United States about violence in the streets and the assassinations of President John F. Kennedy, Martin Luther King, Jr., and Robert Kennedy stimulated continuing interest in media violence. In response, several major government commissions and scientific and professional review committees were established, from the late 1960s through the 1990s, to summarize the research evidence and public policy issues regarding the role of television violence in salving or savaging young viewers.

The five principal commissions and review panels—National Commission on the Causes and Prevention of Violence (Baker & Ball, 1969); Surgeon General's Scientific Advisory Committee on Television and Social Behavior (1972; Murray, 1973); National Institute of Mental Health (1982) Television and Behavior Project; Group for the Advancement of Psychiatry (1982) Child and Television Drama Review; and the American Psychological Association Task Force on Television and Society (Huston et al., 1992)—have been central to setting the agenda for research and public discussion.

In 1982, the National Institute of Mental Health (NIMH) published a 10-year follow-up of the 1972 Surgeon General's study. The two-volume report (National Institute of Mental Health, 1982; Pearl, Bouthilet, & Lazar, 1982), collectively titled *Television and Behavior: Ten Years of Scientific Progress and Implications for the Eighties*, provided a reminder of the breadth and depth of knowledge that has accumulated on the issue of TV violence. In this regard, the NIMH staff and consultants concluded:

> After 10 more years of research, the consensus among most of the research community is that violence on television does lead to aggressive behavior by children and teenagers who watch the programs. This conclusion is based on laboratory experiments and on field studies. Not all children become aggressive, of course, but the correlations between violence and aggression are positive. In magnitude, television violence is as strongly correlated with aggressive behavior as any other behavioral variable that has been measured. (p. 10)

In 1986, the American Psychological Association (APA) empaneled a Task Force on Television and Society to review the research and professional concerns about the impact of television on children and adults. The nine psychologists assigned to this committee undertook reviews of relevant research, conducted interviews with television industry and public policy professionals, and discussed concerns with representatives of government regulatory agencies and public interest organizations. The final report, entitled *Big World, Small Screen: The Role of Television in American Society* (Huston et al., 1992) included the following observation about television violence:

> American television has been violent for many years. Over the past 20 years, the rate of violence on prime time evening television has remained at about

5 to 6 incidents per hour, whereas the rate on children's Saturday morning programs is typically 20 to 25 acts per hour. There is clear evidence that television violence can cause aggressive behavior and can cultivate values favoring the use of aggression to resolve conflicts. (p. 136)

The extent of concern—both social and scientific—is demonstrated by the fact that over the past half-century, about 1,000 reports have been published on the issue of TV violence (Murray, 1980). Of course, only a small percentage of these thousands of pages represent original studies or research reports, but there is an extensive body of research on the impact of TV violence. Nevertheless, the research history is best described in terms of the nature of the research approaches: correlational and experimental and their variants cross-lagged panel studies and field studies.

CORRELATIONAL RESEARCH

The demonstration of a relationship between viewing and aggressive behavior is a logical precursor to studies of the causal role that TV violence may play in promoting aggressive behavior. In this regard, the early surveys of the impact of television on children, conducted by Himmelweit et al. (1958) and Schramm et al. (1961)—discussed earlier — addressed some of these concerns about violence. However, later research was more focused in studying the correlations between TV violence viewing and aggression.

In typical correlational studies, such as those conducted for the Surgeon General's research program (Dominick & Greenberg, 1972; McLeod, Atkin, & Chaffee, 1972a, 1972b; Robinson & Bachman, 1972), the researchers found consistent patterns of significant correlations between the number of hours of television viewed or the frequency of viewing violent programs and various measures of aggressive attitudes or behavior. Also, another study, Atkin, Greenberg, Korzenny, and McDermott (1979), found that heavy TV-violence viewers were more likely to choose physical and verbal aggressive responses to solve hypothetical interpersonal conflict situations (i.e., 45% of the heavy violence viewers chose physical or verbal aggressive responses vs. 21% of the low violence viewers). Similarly, a further study in this genre (Walker & Morley, 1991) found that adolescents who reported enjoying TV violence were more likely to hold attitudes and values favorable to behaving aggressively in conflict situations.

In an approach, a large database, the Cultural Indicators Project, has been used to explore the relationship between television portrayals and the viewer's fearful conception of the world. In a series of studies begun in the 1960s, Gerbner and his colleagues at the University of Pennsylvania (Gerbner, 1970; Gerbner, Gross, Morgan, & Signorielli, 1994) have tracked public perceptions of society in relation to the respondent's extent of television viewing. Of relevance to the violence issue, these researchers have identified differences in the risk-of-victimization perceptions, described as the "mean world syndrome" effect, of light versus heavy viewers. The heavy viewers (usually 5 or more hours per day) are much more fearful of the world around them than are light viewers (about 2 or fewer hours per day). When questioned about their perceptions of risk, heavy viewers are much more likely to overestimate (i.e., greater than the FBI crime reports for their locale would suggest) the chance that they will be the victim of crime in the ensuing six months, have taken greater precautions by changing the security of their homes or restricting their travels at night, and are generally more fearful of the world. As Gerbner et al. (1994) noted, "We have found that long-term exposure to television, in which frequent violence is virtually inescapable, tends to cultivate the image of a relatively mean and dangerous world ... in which greater protection is needed, most people cannot be trusted, and most people are just looking out for themselves" (p. 30).

Special-Case Correlational Research

Studies such as the early surveys clearly demonstrate that violence viewing and aggressive behavior are related but they do not address the issue of cause and effect. And yet, there are some special-case correlational studies in which "intimations of causation" can be derived from the fact that these studies were conducted over several time periods. There have been three major "panel"studies: A study funded by CBS (Belson 1978), one funded by NBC (Milavsky, Kessler, Stipp, & Rubens, 1982), and the third funded by the Surgeon General's Committee and NIMH (Huesmann & Eron, 1986; Huesmann, Eron, Lefkowitz, & Walder, 1984; Lefkowitz, Eron, Walder, & Huesmann, 1972).

The CBS study (Belson, 1978) was conducted in England with 1,565 youths who were a representative sample of 13- to 17-year-old males living in London. The boys were interviewed on several occasions concerning the extent of their exposure to a selection of violent television programs broadcast during the period 1959 through 1971. The level and type of violence in these programs were rated by members of the BBC viewing panel. Thus, it was possible to obtain, for each boy, a measure of both the magnitude and type of exposure to televised violence (e.g., realistic, fictional, etc.). Furthermore, each boy's level of violent behavior was determined by his report of how often he had been involved in any of 53 categories of violence over the previous 6 months. The degree of seriousness of the acts reported by the boys ranged from only slightly violent aggravation, such as taunting, to more serious and very violent behavior such as "I tried to force a girl to have sexual intercourse with me," "I bashed a boy's head against a wall," I burned a boy on the chest with a cigarette while my mates held him down," and "I threatened to kill my father." Approximately 50% of the 1,565 boys were not involved in any violent acts during the 6-month period. However, of those who were involved in violence, 188 (12%) were involved in 10 or more acts during the 6-month period. When Belson compared the behavior of boys who had higher exposure to televised violence to those who had lower exposure (and had been matched on a wide variety of possible contributing factors), he found that the high-violence viewers were more involved in serious interpersonal violence.

The NBC study (Milavsky et al., 1982) was conducted over a 3-year period from May 1970 to December 1973 in two cities, Fort Worth and Minneapolis. Interviews were conducted with samples of second- to sixth-grade boys and girls and a special sample of teenage boys. In the elementary school sample, the information on television viewing and measures of aggression was collected in six time periods over the 3 years. The aggression measure consisted of peer ratings of aggressive behavior based on the work of Eron and his colleagues (Eron, Walder, & Lefkowitz, 1971). In the teenage sample there were only five waves of interviews over the 3 years and the aggression measures were self-report rather than peer-reported aggression. In summarizing the results of this study, the authors concluded, "On the basis of the analyses we carried out to test for such a causal connection there is no evidence that television exposure has a consistently significant effect on subsequent aggressive behavior in the [elementary school] sample of boys" (Milavsky et al., 1982, p. 482). Similar null findings were reported for the elementary school girls and the teenage boys. However, reanalyses of these data by Kenny (1984) and Cook and his associates (Cook, Kendzierski, & Thomas, 1983) have concluded that there are small but clear causal effects in the NBC data and that these effects become stronger when analyzed over longer time periods through successive waves of interviews.

Finally, one of the longest panel studies, 22 years, is the work of Eron and his colleagues (Eron, 1963, 1982; Huesmann & Eron, 1986;

Huesmann et al., 1984; Lefkowitz et al., 1972). In the initial studies, conducted for the Surgeon General's investigation of TV violence (Lefkowitz et al., 1972), the researchers were able to document the long-term effects of violence viewing by studying children over a 10-year period from age 8 to 18. At these two time periods, the youngsters were interviewed about their program preferences and information was collected from peer ratings of aggressive behavior. The violence levels of their preferred TV programs and other media and measures of aggression across these two time periods suggested the possibility that early television violence viewing was one factor in producing later aggressive behavior. In particular, the findings for 211 boys followed in this longitudinal study demonstrated that TV violence at age 8 was significantly related to aggression at age 8 ($r = .21$) and the 8-year-old violent TV preferences were significantly related to aggression at age 18 ($r = .31$) but TV violence preferences at age 18 were not related to aggressive behavior at the earlier time period, age 8 ($r = .01$). When other possible variables, such as parenting practices and discipline style, were controlled it was still clear that early media violence could be part of the cause of later aggressive behavior. Furthermore, in a follow-up study, when these young men were age 30 (Huesmann et al., 1984), the authors found a significant correlation ($r = .41$) between TV violence levels at age 8 and serious interpersonal criminal behavior (e.g., assault, murder, child abuse, spouse abuse, rape) at age 30.

Thus, it seems clear that a correlation between television violence and aggression can be established from diverse studies. Some special cases of longitudinal correlational studies (described as cross-lagged/panel studies) can lead to intimations of causation. However, the issue of causation is best assessed in experimental designs that allow for random assignment of participants to various treatment conditions or, in the case of field studies, take advantage of naturally occurring variations in television viewing experiences.

EXPERIMENTAL STUDIES

The potential role of television violence in the causation of aggressive behavior was, as noted earlier, among the first topics investigated by social scientists. The studies by Bandura (e.g., Bandura, Ross & Ross, 1961, 1963) and Berkowitz (e.g., Berkowitz & Rawlings, 1963) set the stage for later experimental studies in which causal influences of TV violence could be assessed by randomly assigning participants to various viewing conditions. These later studies employed both structured, laboratory-based settings and more naturalistic settings in schools and communities.

One of the earlier studies in this genre (Liebert & Baron, 1972) assessed the effects of viewing segments of a violent television program, *The Untouchables,* on the aggressive behavior of 5- to 9-year-old boys and girls. In this study, the children viewed either *The Untouchables* or a neutral, but active, track race. Following viewing, the child was placed in a playroom setting in which he or she could help or hurt another child who was ostensibly playing a game in another room. The participant could help the other child by pressing a button that would make the game easier to play and allow the other child to win more points. Similarly, the child could hurt the other child by pressing a button that would make the game very difficult play and hence lose points. The results indicated that youngsters who had viewed the violent program manifested a greater willingness to hurt the other child than youngsters who had watched the neutral program. Moreover, an elaboration of this study by Ekman and colleagues (Ekman et al., 1972) included the recording of the facial expressions of these children while they were watching the television violence. In this instance, the children whose facial expressions indicated interest or pleasure while watching TV violence were more willing to hurt the other child than the youngsters whose facial expressions indicated disinterest or displeasure while watching TV violence. Thus, this set of studies identified some potential moderating variables in the violence viewing–aggressive behavior equation.

Other early experiments by researchers using physiological measures of arousal (e.g., galvanic skin response [GSR], heart rate, respiration changes) while watching violent cartoons (Cline, Croft, & Courrier, 1973; Osborn & Endsley, 1971) found that children are emotionally responsive even to cartoon violence. So too, other studies (Ellis & Sekyra, 1972; Hapkiewitz & Roden, 1971; Lovaas, 1961; Mussen & Rutherford, 1961; Ross, 1972) found that exposure to even one violent cartoon leads to increased aggression in the structured playroom settings. Furthermore, studies by Drabman and his colleagues (Drabman & Thomas, 1974; Thomas, Horton, Lippincott, & Drabman, 1977) have shown that children who view violent television programs become desensitized to violence and are more willing to tolerate aggressive behavior in others. Moreover, later studies with emotionally disturbed children (Gadow & Sprafkin, 1993; Grimes, Vernberg, & Cathers, 1997) have found that these youngsters may be more vulnerable to the influence of TV violence. For example, Grimes et al. (1997) found that 8- to 12-year-olds who were diagnosed as having either attention deficit hyperactivity disorder, oppositional defiant disorder, or conduct disorder manifested less emotional concern for victims and were more willing to accept violence as justified than a matched group of children who did not have these disorders.

All of the studies just described were conducted in fairly structured laboratory or playroom settings where the display of aggression or emotional arousal or desensitization was relatively contiguous to the viewing of TV violence. Questions remain about what might happen in more naturalistic settings or field studies of violence viewing and aggressive behavior. One early study that assessed these issues in was the work of Stein and Friedrich (Friedrich & Stein, 1973; Stein & Friedrich, 1972) in which they assessed the impact of viewing aggressive versus prosocial television programs on the behavior of preschoolers in their normal child-care settings. In this study, the preschoolers were assigned to view a diet of either Batman and Superman cartoons, or *Mister Rogers' Neighborhood*, or neutral programming that contained neither aggressive nor prosocial material (i.e., special travel stories for preschoolers). The "diet" consisted of 12 half-hour episodes that were viewed one half-hour per day, 3 days per week, for 4 weeks. The researchers observed the children in the classroom and on the playground for three weeks prior to the start of the viewing period, to establish a baseline for the amount of aggression or prosocial behavior, and continued to observe the children during the 4 weeks of viewing and for an additional 2 weeks. The results were that children who were initially more aggressive and had viewed the diet of Batman and Superman cartoons were more active in the classroom and on the playground, played more roughly with toys, and got into more aggressive encounters. Conversely, youngsters from lower income families who had viewed the *Mister Rogers' Neighborhood* diet increased their prosocial helping behavior. One suggestion from this early field study is that viewing aggressive program content can lead to changes in aggressive behavior, and the opposite is also true for prosocial programming. Moreover, these changes were demonstrated in a relatively short viewing period (12 half-hours) and in the context of other viewing that took place outside of the classroom setting.

Other field studies have used restricted populations such as boys in detention centers or secure residential settings. In one such study, conducted for NBC, Feshbach and Singer (1971) presented preadolescent and adolescent boys in a security facility with a diet of aggressive or nonaggressive television programs over a 6-week period and measured their daily aggressive behavior. They found that the youngsters who watched the nonaggressive programs were more aggressive than the other group. However, this study was criticized on methodological grounds relating to the selection of participants and the assignment of viewing conditions (Liebert, Sobol, & Davidson, 1972) and a subsequent replication (Wells, 1973) failed to duplicate the findings. Moreover, a later study conducted by Berkowitz and his colleagues (Parke, Berkowitz, Leyens, West, & Sebastian, 1977), using aggressive or nonaggressive films presented to adolescent boys living in minimum-security institutions, did demonstrate increases in both verbal and physical interpersonal aggression among the teens viewing the aggressive diet.

Another approach to field studies involved the assessment of the effects of naturally occurring differences in the television exposure available to children in communities with or without television or communities with differing television content. In one set of studies (Murray & Kippax, 1977, 1978) the researchers were able to study the introduction of television in a rural community in Australia, in contrast to two similar communities that had differing experiences with television. In a second set of studies (Macbeth, 1996; Williams, 1986), the research team studied the introduction of television in a rural Canadian community, in contrast to two similar communities with differing television experience. In general, the results of both the Australian and Canadian studies converge in showing that the introduction of television had a major influence on restructuring the social lives of children in these rural communities. In this regard, both studies found that television displaced other media use and involvement in various social activities—a finding not dissimilar to the earlier studies of children in England (Himmelweit et al., 1958) or the United States and Canada (Schramm et al., 1961). However, with regard to the effects of TV violence, these newer field studies provide stronger evidence of negative influence, in differing but complementary ways. Murray and Kippax (Murray, 1980) found changes in perceptions of the seriousness and prevalence of crime among children in the town exposed to higher levels of television violence, whereas Williams and Macbeth (Joy, Kimball, & Zabrack, 1986) found increases in aggression among children following the introduction of television in the town.

WHAT HAVE WE LEARNED?

Research conducted over the past 50 years leads to the conclusion that televised violence does affect viewers' attitudes, values, and behavior

(Hearold, 1986; Murray, 1994; Paik & Comstock, 1994). In general, there seem to be three main classes of effects—aggression, desensitization, and fear.

- *Aggression*. Viewing televised violence can lead to increases in aggressive behavior or changes in attitudes and values favoring the use of aggression to solve conflicts.
- *Desensitization*. Extensive violence viewing may lead to decreased sensitivity to violence and a greater willingness to tolerate increasing levels of violence in society.
- *Fear*. Extensive exposure to television violence may produce the "mean world syndrome" in which viewers overestimate their risk of victimization.

Although the body of research on the effects of viewing television violence is extensive and fairly coherent in demonstrating systematic patterns of influence, we know surprisingly little about the processes involved in the production of these effects. Although we know that viewing televised violence can lead to increases in aggressive behavior or fearfulness and changed attitudes and values about the role of violence in society, it would be helpful to know more about how these changes occur in viewers.

To set the context for the continuing research—within the broad framework of a social learning paradigm—we know that changes in behavior and thoughts can result from observing models in the world around us, be they parents, peers, or other role models, such as those provided by mass media. The processes involved in modeling or imitation and vicarious learning of overt behavior were addressed in social learning theories in the 1960s (Bandura, 1962, 1965, 1969; Berkowitz, 1962, 1965) but we need to expand our understanding of the neurological processes that might govern the translation of the observed models into thoughts and actions.

As a start in this new direction, both Bandura (1994) and Berkowitz (1984) provided some theoretical foundations for the translation of communication events into thoughts and actions. Bandura's social-cognitive approach and Berkowitz's outline of a cognitive-neoassociation analysis posit a role for emotional arousal as an affective tag that may facilitate lasting influences. As Bandura (1994) noted, "People are easily aroused by the emotional expressions of others. Vicarious arousal operates mainly through an intervening self-arousal process. ... That is, seeing others react emotionally to instigating conditions activates emotion-arousing thoughts and imagery in observers" (p. 75). With regard to aggression, we know that viewing television violence can be emotionally arousing (e.g., Cline et al., 1973; Osborn & Endsley, 1971; Zillmann, 1971, 1982) but we lack direct measures of cortical arousal or activation patterns in relation to violence viewing.

The pursuit of neurological patterns of cortical arousal in violence viewing would likely start with the amygdala because it has a well-established role in the control of physiological responses to emotionally arousing or threatening stimuli (Damasio, 1994; 1999; LeDoux, 1996; LeDoux & Hirst, 1986; Ornstein, 1997). Indeed, a National Research Council (1993) report from the Panel on the Understanding and Control of Violent Behavior, concludes:

> All human behavior, including aggression and violence, is the outcome of complex processes in the brain. Violent behaviors may result from relatively permanent conditions or from temporary states . . . Biological research on aggressive and violent behavior has given particular attention to the following in recent years: . . . (2) functioning of steroid hormones such as testosterone and glucocorticoids, especially their action on steroid receptors in the brain; . . . (6) neurophysiological (i.e., brain wave) abnormalities, particularly in the temporal lobe of the brain; (7) brain dysfunctions that interfere with language processing or cognition. (pp. 115–116)

Thus, one suggestion for further research on the impact of media violence is to assess some of the neurological correlates of viewing televised violence. In particular, the use of videotaped violent scenes can serve as the ideal stimulus for assessing activation patterns in response to violence.

It is very likely that the amygdala will be involved in processing violence but the projections to the cortex are not clear. However, development of hypotheses about violence viewing and brain activation needs to start with research on physiological arousal (e.g., Osborn & Endsley, 1971; Zillmann, 1982; Zillmann & Bryant, 1994) and link this to cortical arousal. In this regard, the work of Ekman and Davidson (Davidson, Ekman, Saron, Senulis, & Friesen, 1990; Ekman & Davidson, 1993; Ekman, Davidson, & Friesen, 1990) using EEG recordings while participants viewed gruesome films (a leg amputation) indicate asymmetries in activation patterns in the anterior regions of the left and right hemispheres. In particular, positive affect (indexed by facial expression) has been found to be associated with left-sided anterior activation, whereas negative affect is associated with right-sided activation (Davidson & Tomarken, 1989; Ornstein, 1997).

In our pilot study (Murray et al., 2006; Murray, 2001), we found that both violent and nonviolent viewing activated regions implicated in aspects of visual and auditory processing. In contrast, however, viewing TV violence selectively recruited right precuneus, right posterior cingulate, right amygdala, bilateral hippocampus and parahippocampus, bilateral pulvinar, right inferior parietal and prefrontal, and right premotor cortex. Thus, TV violence viewing appears to activate brain areas involved in arousal and attention, detection of threat, episodic memory encoding and retrieval, and motor programming. These findings are displayed in Fig.7.1 which provides a graphic summary of these data. It can be seen that the regions of interest (ROI) of the composite activations of 8 children, combined in adjusted Talairach space (Talairach & Tournoux, 1988), include the amygdala, hippocampus, and posterior cingulate because these areas are likely indicators of the perception of threat and possible long-term memory storage of the threat event (particularly, these patterns are similar to the memory storage of traumatic events by post-traumatic stress disorder patients. These activation patterns are important because they demonstrate that video violence viewing selectively activates right hemisphere, and some bilateral areas, that collectively suggest significant emotional processing of video violence.

Our continuing research is designed to address these questions about violence viewing in a more robust study that employs a larger and more differentiated sample of children who have had differing experiences with violence (e.g., children who are identified as high or low in aggressive tendencies and children who have been victims of abuse). We will continue to use the methods and procedures that were demonstrated to be effective in the pilot study—we will conjoin measures of physiological arousal (e.g., GSR, heart rate) with neuroimaging techniques (e.g., functional magnetic resonance imaging) to track the emotional and neurological processes involved in viewing televised violence—and we will explore the responses of this larger and more specialized group of children. We anticipate that experience with violence as victims (abused children) would lead to heightened arousal and indications of threat. On the other hand, children who are more aggressive and have had more experience with violence as aggressors may manifest less threat and less arousal in response to the violent scenes.

What we have learned from this broad and diverse compilation of research, conducted over the past 50 years, is that we are all affected by the violence that we encounter on television and in other media. Moreover, our society must come to terms with the effects of media

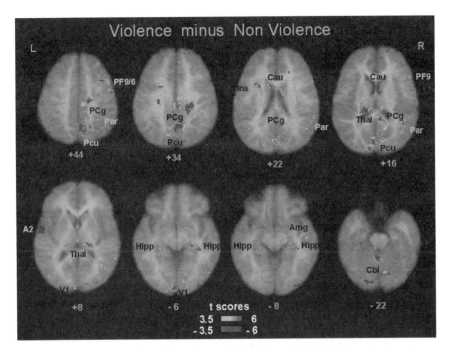

FIG. 7.1   Composite (in Talairach space) of the brains of 8 children viewing violence. (This figure is reproduced in color on the enclosed CD.) Main significant
group average changes in BOLD signal in the Violence minus Nonviolence t-score
image. Cut-off $t = \pm 3.5$, $p < 0.01$, uncorrected. Horizontal axial views are overlaid
on group average T1 images. Labels in Figure: A2 = Secondary Auditory area cortex; V1 = Primary Visual Area; Thal = Thalamus; PcU = Precuneus; PCg =
Posterior Cingulate; PF9/6 = Prefrontal Cortex 9/6; Ins = Insula; Cau = Caudate
Nucleus; Par = Parietal Lobe; Hipp = Hippocampal region; Amg = Amygdala;
Cb = Cerebellum; L = Left Hemisphere; R = Right Hemisphere.

violence and we must begin to develop ways to mitigate the influences of
media mayhem.

One of the ways that we can limit the effects of television violence is
to provide youngsters (and their parents) with "inoculations" or insightful experiences that will help them to understand the workings of
the industry and the role of violence in entertainment programming.
Although this is an additional role for community education, the development of a curriculum on critical viewing skills has been undertaken by
many organizations. For example, groups as diverse as MediaScope (1994,
1996), the George Lucas Educational Foundation (1999), and the Center

for Media Literacy (1995) have provided outstanding educational programs for use in schools and community settings.

REFERENCES

Atkin, C. K., Greenberg, B. S., Korzenny, F., & McDermott, S. (1979). Selective exposure to televised violence. *Journal of Broadcasting, 23*(1), 5–13.

Baker, R. K., & Ball, S. J. (1969). *Mass media and violence: A staff report to the National Commission on the Causes and Prevention of Violence.* Washington, DC: U.S. Government Printing Office.

Bandura, A. (1962). Social learning through imitation. In M. R. Jones (Ed.), *Nebraska symposium on motivation* (pp. 211–269). Lincoln: University of Nebraska Press.

Bandura, A. (1965). Vicarious processes: A case of no-trial learning. In L. Berkowitz (Ed.), *Advances in experimental social psychology* (Vol. 2, pp.1–55). New York: Academic.

Bandura, A. (1969). Social-learning theory of identification processes. In D. A. Goslin (Ed.), *Handbook of socialization theory and research* (pp. 213–262). Chicago: Rand McNally.

Bandura, A. (1994). Social cognitive theory of mass communication. In J. Bryant & D. Zillmann (Eds.), *Media effects: Advances in theory and research* (pp. 61–90). Hillsdale, NJ: Lawrence Erlbaum Associates, Inc.

Bandura, A., Ross, D., & Ross, S. H. (1961). Transmission of aggression through imitation of aggressive models. *Journal of Abnormal and Social Psychology, 63,* 575–582.

Bandura, A., Ross, D., & Ross, S. H. (1963). Imitation of film-mediated aggressive models. *Journal of Abnormal and Social Psychology, 66* (1), 3–11.

Belson, W. (1978). *Television violence and the adolescent boy.* Farnborough, England: Saxon House, Teakfield.

Berkowitz, L. (1962). *Aggression: A social psychological analysis.* New York: McGraw-Hill.

Berkowitz, L. (1965). Some aspects of observed aggression. *Journal of Personality and Social Psychology, 2,* 359–365.

Berkowitz, L. (1984). Some effects of thoughts on anti- and prosocial influences of media events: A cognitive-neoassociation analysis. *Psychological Bulletin, 95,* 110–427.

Berkowitz, L., & Geen, R. G. (1966). Film violence and the cue properties of available targets. *Journal of Personality and Social Psychology, 3,* 525–530.

Berkowitz, L., & Rawlings, E. (1963). Effects of film violence on inhibitions against subsequent aggression. *Journal of Abnormal and Social Psychology, 66,* 405–412.

Center for Media Literacy. (1995). *Beyond blame: Challenging violence in the media.* Los Angeles: Center for Media Literacy.

Cline, V., Croft, R., & Courrier, S. (1973). Desensitization of children to television violence. *Journal of Personality and Social Psychology, 27,* 360–365.

Cook, T. D., Kendzierski, D. A., & Thomas, S. A. (1983). The implicit assumptions of television research: An analysis of the 1982 NIMH report on "Television and Behavior." *Public Opinion Quarterly, 47,* 161–201.

Cressey, P. G., & Thrasher, F. M. (1933). *Boys, movies, and city streets.* New York: Macmillan.

Damasio, A. R. (1994). *Descartes' error: Emotion, reason, and the human brain.* New York: Putnam.

Damasio, A. R. (1999). *The feeling of what happens: Body and emotion in the making of consciousness.* New York: Harcourt Brace.

Davidson, R. J., Ekman, P., Saron, C., Senulis, J., & Friesen, W. V. (1990). Emotional expression and brain physiology I: Approach/withdrawal and cerebral asymmetry. *Journal of Personality and Social Psychology, 58,* 330–341.

Davidson, R. J., & Tomarken, A. J. (1989). Laterality and emotion: An electrophysiological approach. In F. Boller & J. Grafman (Eds.), *Handbook of neuropsychology* (pp. 419–441). Amsterdam: Elsevier.

Dominick, J. R., & Greenberg, B. S. (1972). Attitudes toward violence: The interaction of television exposure, family attitudes, and social class. In G. A. Comstock & E. A. Rubinstein (Eds.), *Television and social behavior: Vol. 3. Television and adolescent aggressiveness* (pp. 314–335). Washington, DC: U.S. Government Printing Office.

Drabman, R. S., & Thomas, M. H. (1974). Does media violence increase children's toleration of real-life aggression? *Developmental Psychology, 10,* 418–421.

Ekman, P., & Davidson, R. J. (1993). Voluntary smiling changes regional brain activity. *Psychological Science, 4,* 342–345.

Ekman, P., & Davidson, R. J. (1994). *The nature of emotion: Fundamental questions.* New York: Oxford University Press.

Ekman, P., Davidson, R. J., & Friesen, W. V. (1990). The Duchenne smile: Emotional expression and brain physiology II. *Journal of Personality and Social Psychology, 58,* 342–353.

Ekman, P., Liebert, R. M., Friesen, W., Harrison, R., Zlatchin, C., Malmstrom, E. V., et al. (1972). Facial expressions of emotion as predictors of subsequent aggression. In G. A. Comstock, E. A. Rubinstein, & J. P. Murray (Eds.), *Television and social behavior: Vol. 5, Television's effects: Further explorations* (pp. 22–58). Washington, DC: U.S. Government Printing Office.

Ellis, G. T., & Sekyra, F. (1972). The effect of aggressive cartoons on behavior of first grade children. *Journal of Psychology, 81,* 37–43.

Eron, L. (1963). Relationship of TV viewing habits and aggressive behavior in children. *Journal of Abnormal and Social Psychology, 67,* 193–196.

Eron, L. (1982). Parent child interaction, television violence and aggression of children. *American Psychologist, 27,* 197–211.

Eron, L. D., Walder, L. O., & Lefkowitz, M. M. (1971). *Learning of aggression in children.* Boston: Little, Brown.

Feshbach, S., & Singer, R. D. (1971). *Television and aggression: An experimental field study.* San Francisco: Jossey-Bass.

Friedrich, L. K., & Stein, A. H. (1973). Aggressive and prosocial television programs and the natural behavior of preschool children. *Monographs of the Society for Research in Child Development, 38*(4), Serial No. 151.

Gadow, K. D., & Sprafkin, J. (1993). Television violence and children with emotional and behavioral disorders. *Journal of Emotional and Behavioral Disorders, 1*(1), 54–63.

George Lucas Educational Foundation. (1999). *Learn & live*. San Rafael, CA: Author.

Gerbner, G. (1970). Cultural indicators: The case of violence in television drama. *Annals of the American Academy of Political and Social Science, 388*, 69–81.

Gerbner, G., Gross, L., Morgan, M., & Signorielli, N. (1994). Growing up with television: The cultivation perspective. In J. Bryant & D. Zillmann (Eds.), *Media effects: Advances in theory and research* (pp. 17–41). Hillsdale, NJ: Lawrence Erlbaum Associates, Inc.

Grimes, T., Vernberg, E., & Cathers, T. (1997). Emotionally disturbed children's reactions to violent media segments. *Journal of Health Communication, 2*(3), 157–168.

Group for the Advancement of Psychiatry. (1982). *The child and television drama: The psychosocial impact of cumulative viewing*. New York: Mental Health Materials Center.

Hapkiewitz, W. G., & Roden, A. H. (1971). The effect of aggressive cartoons on children's interpersonal play. *Child Development, 42*, 1583–1585.

Hearold, S. (1986). A synthesis of 1043 effects of television on social behavior. In G. Comstock (Ed.), *Public communication and behavior* (Vol. 1, pp. 65–133). New York: Academic.

Himmelweit, H. T., Oppenheim, A. N., & Vince, P. (1958). *Television and the child: An empirical study of the effects of television on the young*. London: Oxford University Press.

Huesmann, L. R., & Eron, L. D. (Eds.). (1986). *Television and the aggressive child: A cross-national comparison*. Hillsdale, NJ: Lawrence Erlbaum Associates, Inc.

Huesmann, L. R., Eron, L. D., Lefkowitz, M. M., & Walder, L. O. (1984). Stability of aggression over time and generations. *Developmental Psychology, 20*, 1120–1134.

Huston, A. C., Donnerstein, E., Fairchild, H., Feshbach, N. D., Katz, P. A., Murray, J. P., et al. (1992). *Big world, small screen: The role of television in American society*. Lincoln: University of Nebraska Press.

Joy, L. A., Kimball, M., & Zabrack, M. L. (1986). Television exposure and children's aggressive behavior. In T. M. Williams (Ed.), *The impact of television: A natural experiment involving three towns* (pp. 303–360). New York: Academic.

Kenny, D. A. (1984). The NBC study and television violence. *Journal of Communication, 34*(1), 176–182.

Lazarsfeld, P. F. (1955). Why is so little known about the effects of television and what can be done? *Public Opinion Quarterly, 19*, 243–251.

LeDoux, J. (1996). *The emotional brain: The mysterious underpinnings of emotional life*. New York: Simon & Schuster.

LeDoux, J. E., & Hirst, W. (Eds.). (1986). *Mind and brain: Dialogues in cognitive neuroscience*. New York: Cambridge University Press.

Lefkowitz, M., Eron, L., Walder, L., & Huesmann, L. R. (1972). Television violence and child aggression: A follow up study. In G. A. Comstock & E. A. Rubinstein (Eds.), *Television and social behavior: Vol. 3. Television and adolescent aggressiveness* (pp. 35–135). Washington, DC: U.S. Government Printing Office.

Liebert, R. M., & Baron, R. A. (1972). Short term effects of television aggression on children's aggressive behavior. In J. P. Murray E. A. Rubinstein, & G. A. Comstock (Eds.), *Television and social behavior: Vol. 2. Television and social learning* (pp. 81–201). Washington, DC: U.S. Government Printing Office.

Liebert, R. M., Sobol, M. D., & Davidson, E. S. (1972). Catharsis of aggression among institutionalized boys: Fact or artifact? In G. A. Comstock, E. A. Rubinstein, & J. P. Murray (Eds.), *Television and social behavior: Vol 5. Television's effects: Further explorations* (pp. 351–359). Washington, DC: U.S. Government Printing Office.

Lovaas, O. I. (1961). Effect of exposure to symbolic aggression on aggressive behavior. *Child Development, 32,* 37–44.

Macbeth, T. M. (1996). *Tuning in to young viewers: Social science perspectives on television.* Thousand Oaks, CA: Sage.

Maccoby, E. E. (1954). Why do children watch television? *Public Opinion Quarterly, 18,* 239–244.

McLeod, J. M., Atkin, C. K., & Chaffee, S. H. (1972a). Adolescents, parents, and television use: Adolescent self-report measures from Maryland and Wisconsin samples. In G. A. Comstock & E. A. Rubinstein (Eds.), *Television and social behavior: Vol. 3. Television and adolescent aggressiveness* (pp. 173–238). Washington, DC: U.S. Government Printing Office.

McLeod, J. M., Atkin, C. K., & Chaffee, S. H. (1972b). Adolescents, parents and television use: Self-report and other measures from the Wisconsin sample. In G. A. Comstock & E. A. Rubinstein (Eds.), *Television and social behavior: Vol. 3. Television and adolescent aggressiveness* (pp. 239–313). Washington, DC: U.S. Government Printing Office.

MediaScope. (1994). *The kids are watching* [Video]. Los Angeles: Author.

MediaScope. (1996). *National television violence study—Executive summary, 1994–95.* Thousand Oaks, CA: Sage.

Milavsky, J. R., Kessler, R. C., Stipp, H. H., & Rubens, W. S. (1982). *Television and aggression: A panel study.* New York: Academic.

Murray, J. P. (1973). Television and violence: Implications of the Surgeon General's research program. *American Psychologist, 28,* 472–478.

Murray, J. P. (1980). *Television and youth: 25 years of research and controversy.* Boys Town, NE: The Boys Town Center for the Study of Youth Development.

Murray, J. P. (1994). The impact of televised violence. *Hofstra Law Review, 22,* 809–825.

Murray, J. P. (2001). TV violence and brainmapping in children. *Psychiatric Times, 17*(10), 70–71.

Murray, J. P., & Kippax, S. (1977). Television diffusion and social behavior in three communities: A field experiment. *Australian Journal of Psychology, 29*(1), 31–43.

Murray, J. P., & Kippax, S. (1978). Children's social behavior in three towns with differing television experience. *Journal of Communication, 28*(1), 19–29.

Murray, J. P., & Kippax, S. (1979). From the early window to the late night show: International trends in the study of television's impact on children and adults. In L. Berkowitz (Ed.), *Advances in experimental social psychology* (Vol. 12, pp. 253–320). New York: Academic.

Murray, J. P., Liotti, M., Ingmundson, P., Mayberg, H. S., Pu, Y., Zamarripa, F., et al. (2006). Children's brain activations while viewing televised violence revealed by FMRI. *Media Psychology, 8*(1), 25–37.

Mussen, P., & Rutherford, E. (1961). Effects of aggressive cartoons on children's aggressive play. *Journal of Abnormal and Social Psychology, 62,* 461–464.

National Institute of Mental Health. (1982). *Television and behavior: Ten years of scientific progress and implications for the eighties: Vol. 1. Summary report.* Washington, DC: U.S. Government Printing Office.

National Research Council. (1993). *Understanding and preventing violence.* Washington, DC: National Academy Press.

Ornstein, R. (1997). *The right mind: Making sense of the hemispheres.* New York: Harcourt Brace.

Osborn, D. K., & Endsley, R. C. (1971). Emotional reactions of young children to TV violence. *Child Development, 42,* 321–331.

Paik, H., & Comstock, G. (1994). The effects of television violence on antisocial behavior: A meta-analysis. *Communication Research, 21,* 516–546.

Parke, R. D., Berkowitz, L., Leyens, J. P., West, S., & Sebastian, R. J. (1977). Some effects of violent and nonviolent movies on the behavior of juvenile delinquents. In L. Berkowitz (Ed.), *Advances in experimental psychology Vol. 10,* (pp. 135–172). New York: Academic.

Pearl, D., Bouthilet, L., & Lazar, J. (Eds.). (1982). *Television and behavior: Ten years of scientific progress and implications for the eighties: Vol. 2. Technical reviews.* Washington, DC: U.S. Government Printing Office.

Robinson, J. P., & Bachman, J. G. (1972). Television viewing habits and aggression. In G. A. Comstock & E. A. Rubinstein (Eds.), *Television and social behavior: Vol. 3. Television and adolescent aggressiveness* (pp. 372–382). Washington, DC: U.S. Government Printing Office.

Ross, L. B. (1972). *The effect of aggressive cartoons on the group play of children.* Unpublished doctoral dissertation, Miami University, Oxford, OH.

Schramm, W., Lyle, J., & Parker, E. B. (1961). *Television in the lives of our children.* Palo Alto, CA: Stanford University Press.

Stein, A. H., & Friedrich, L. K. (1972). Television content and young children's behavior. In J. P. Murray, E. A. Rubinstein & G. A. Comstock (Eds.), *Television and social behavior: Vol. 2. Television and social learning* (pp. 202–317). Washington, DC: U.S. Government Printing Office.

Surgeon General's Scientific Advisory Committee on Television and Social Behavior. (1972). *Television and growing up: The impact of televised violence.* Washington, DC: U.S. Government Printing Office.

Talairach, J., & Tournoux, P. (1988). *Co-planar stereotaxic atlas of the human brain.* New York: Thieme Medical.

Thomas, M. H., Horton, R. W., Lippincott, E. C., & Drabman, R. S. (1977). Desensitization to portrayals of real life aggression as a function of television violence. *Journal of Personality and Social Psychology, 35,* 450–458.

U.S. Congress, House Committee on Interstate and Foreign Commerce. (1952). *Investigation of Radio and Television Programs, Hearings and Report, 82nd Congress, 2nd session, June 3–December 5, 1952.* Washington, DC: U.S. Government Printing Office.

U.S. Congress, Senate Committee of the Judiciary, Subcommittee to Investigate Juvenile Delinquency. (1955). *Juvenile Delinquency (Television Programs), Hearings, 83rd Congress, 2nd session, June 5–October 20, 1954.* Washington, DC: U.S. Government Printing Office.

U.S. Congress, Senate Committee on Commerce, Science, and Transportation, Subcommittee on Science, Technology and Space. (2003). Neurobiological Research and the Impact of Media, 108th Congress, April 10, 2003. Washington, DC: U.S. Government Printing Office.

Walker, K. B., & Morley, D. D. (1991). Attitudes and parental factors as intervening variables in the television violence–aggression relation. *Communication Research*, 8(2), 41–47.

Wells, W. D. (1973). *Television and aggression: Replication of an experimental field study.* Unpublished manuscript, Graduate School of Business, University of Chicago, Chicago.

Williams, T. M. (Ed.). (1986). *The impact of television: A natural experiment in three communities.* New York: Academic.

Zillmann, D. (1971). Excitation transfer in communication-mediated aggressive behavior. *Journal of Experimental Social Psychology, 7,* 419–434.

Zillmann, D. (1982). Television viewing and arousal. In D. Pearl, L. Bouthilet, & J. Lazar (Eds.), *Television and behavior: Ten years of scientific progress and implications for the eighties: Vol. 2. Technical reviews* (pp. 53–67). Washington, DC: U.S. Government Printing Office.

Zillmann, D., & Bryant, J. (1994). Entertainment as media effect. In J. Bryant & D. Zillmann (Eds.), *Media effects: Advances in theory and research* (pp. 437–461). Hillsdale, NJ: Lawrence Erlbaum Associates, Inc.

8

Health, Drugs, and Values

Elizabeth P. Lorch
University of Kentucky

As children develop and move through adolescence, they increasingly face choices that influence health and may become part of a long-term lifestyle. In their early years, children's health-related choices may include preferences for particular foods, participation in physical activities, and the extent to which they engage in risky activities. Later in childhood and during adolescence, choices extend to the use of substances with health consequences such as tobacco, alcohol, and illicit drugs, as well as choices about sexual behaviors.

Is there reason to be concerned about the choices some children and adolescents are making? Consider these behaviors that carry substantial risks of negative consequences. According to the American Academy of Child and Adolescent Psychiatry (2001), 16% to 33% of U.S. children and adolescents are obese. Those who are obese between ages 10 and 13 have an 80% chance of being obese as adults, with long-term obesity a leading preventable cause of death and associated with a variety of physical and emotional difficulties. The only preventable cause of death in the United States to outstrip obesity is tobacco-related disease (McGinnis & Foege, 1993). Data from the Monitoring the Future survey indicate that adolescent tobacco use in the United States rose during the early 1990s, with more teen smokers by the middle of the decade than in any previous generation or among the adult population. Even with steady declines in adolescent tobacco use since 1996, 12% of eighth graders and 30% of high school seniors report current cigarette use (i.e., during the past 30 days), with nearly one in five high school seniors reporting established daily use (Johnston, O'Malley, & Bachman, 2001a). Established teen smokers are highly likely to continue smoking as adults (American Academy of Child and Adolescent Psychiatry, 1999), putting these adolescents at risk for long-term health consequences. Alcohol use during adolescence has been relatively stable during the last decade, with about 50% of eighth graders and 80% of high school seniors having used alcohol at some point in their lives. By senior year, about half of students report current use, with one in three seniors reporting they were drunk within the last 30 days. Adolescent use of most illicit drugs increased sharply during the early 1990s, followed by slower increases or leveling off in the latter years of the decade. More than one in four eighth graders and over half of high school seniors report use of some illicit drug (most commonly marijuana) during their lifetimes, with about half of those students reporting current use of an illicit drug (Johnston, O'Malley, & Bachman, 2000, 2001b; Kann et al., 2000). Early use of alcohol or illicit drugs increases the risk of later serious substance use, cognitive impairments and school failure, driving under the influence, involvement in vandalism, and engaging in unplanned and unsafe sex (Siegel & Burgoon, 2002). In terms of sexual activity, about 20% of adolescents report having engaged in sexual intercourse by the end of middle school, with about 80% of adolescents initiating sexual activity by the end of high school (Singh & Darroch, 1999). Initiation of sexual activity during adolescence often is unaccompanied by adequate knowledge of risks and responsibilities (Donohew et al., 2000; McCombie, Hornik, & Anarfi, 2002; Remez, 2000), in the United States resulting in approximately 3 million new cases of sexually transmitted diseases (STDs) and 1 million teenage pregnancies each year (American Academy of Child & Adolescent Psychiatry, 2002). In sum, a substantial number of children and adolescents are engaging in health-related behaviors that pose considerable risks, justifying considerable concern about influences on their choices.

THE ROLE OF TELEVISION IN HEALTH-RELATED CHOICES

There are a variety of important interacting influences on the development of health-related choices; however, the purpose of this chapter is to consider contributions of television viewing during childhood and adolescence to the development of health-related knowledge, attitudes, and behaviors. The review is organized around two general areas, similar to a division used earlier by Brown and Walsh-Childers (1994). The first area concerns potential incidental effects of portrayals of health-related behaviors in entertainment television and accompanying product advertisements. Although persuading adolescents to engage in risky health behaviors certainly is not the purpose of most television programming or even of many commercials, the frequency and context for portraying such behaviors may influence young viewers. In this section, theoretical perspectives that predict and explain such effects are summarized, followed by a review of the nature of television portrayals of nutrition, body image, substance use, and sexual behaviors and of the evidence of effects of such portrayals. The second general area pertains to effects of using television as an intentional intervention to change or reinforce health-related attitudes, beliefs, and behaviors. In this section, theoretical perspectives that guide the use of television in prevention and persuasion are reviewed, followed by an examination of representative successful youth health campaigns and the theoretically guided and empirically supported recommendations that emerge from them.

INCIDENTAL EFFECTS: EXPOSURE TO HEALTH-RELATED BEHAVIORS IN PROGRAMMING

Theoretical Background

Why might viewing entertainment programming lead to effects on children's and adolescents' health-related attitudes, beliefs, and behaviors? Several overlapping theories offer reasons why exposure to television portrayals may influence viewers during childhood and adolescence.

Social Cognitive Theory. Bandura's (e.g., 1989, 1994) social cognitive theory proposes that individuals learn many social behaviors by observing those modeled by others. Children and adolescents are more likely to try a behavior if they perceive a model as similar to themselves or in some other way identify with the model. Another element incorporated into this theory is the existence of an incentive to perform a behavior. Thus, behaviors are more likely to be attempted if the model is perceived as attractive or powerful, if the context for the behavior is appealing, or if the individual modeling the behavior is successful at achieving a goal or obtaining a reward. Finally, social cognitive theory emphasizes the role of *self-efficacy*. An individual's belief in his or her ability to perform a specific behavior also influences the likelihood that the individual will try the behavior. According to social cognitive theory, then, repeated exposure to television characters exhibiting particular health-related behaviors may influence young viewers' health-related choices, especially to the extent that televised portrayals involve attractive characters demonstrating behaviors that are straightforward to imitate and that result in relatively positive consequences.

Script Theories. These theories address ways in which television influences the development of people's knowledge and beliefs about the world (e.g., Huesmann & Miller, 1994). Script theories are not inconsistent with social cognitive theory, but these theories place less stress on characteristics of models and more emphasis on the acquisition of organized scripts for behaviors in certain situations. Based on experiences with real and media events, children and adolescents build representations of what to expect in certain situations or of certain people. In turn, these organized expectations may guide interpretations of real situations and may suggest sequences of behavior that might be used to attain goals. Because scripts begin to form on the basis of a single experience, script theory implies that particularly when children have limited personal experience with a situation, health-related behaviors portrayed on television might play an important role in creating expectations about the context and consequences of these behaviors.

Cultivation Theory. This theory (e.g., Gerbner, Morgan, & Signorielli, 1982), in a sense a specific version of script theory, proposes that heavy viewing leads people to see the world as it is portrayed on television. Cultivation theory emphasizes how cumulative effects of viewing contribute to the construction of norms for a behavior. Thus, to the extent that television programs overrepresent a particular behavior, heavy viewers might be expected to incorporate this overrepresentation into norms for that behavior.

Summary. Some evidence supports each of these theories, and all three perspectives suggest that portrayals of health-related behaviors such as substance use and sexual behaviors may influence children's and adolescents' concepts in a variety of ways. Such portrayals may contribute to concepts of behaviors that are normal in youth culture or in the adult world, behaviors that are acceptable, and behaviors that are associated with positive characteristics or responses from others. Although the three theories are not identical, from all three the frequency and context of such portrayals would be expected to predict effects. Although some of these effects might be positive (e.g., knowledge gained of ways to deal with uncomfortable situations), more research attention has been given to potential negative effects of these portrayals.

Nutrition and Body Image

Nutritional choices and their relation to body image are important aspects of achieving a healthy lifestyle. However, only a brief review of research in this area is reported here to minimize redundancy with other chapters in this volume.

Portrayals of Body Image. It is no surprise that the distribution of body types portrayed in television programming and advertising is markedly different from that found in the general population. The proportion of obese characters is far lower than in the general population of adults or adolescents (Brown & Walsh-Childers, 1994), and the typical woman's body as portrayed on TV has been described as an unattainable ideal (Henderson-King & Henderson-King, 1997). A number of studies of preteens and teens connect experience viewing thin models with less favorable judgments of the self (e.g., Hargreaves & Tiggemann, 2002; Irving, 1990; Kalodner, 1997), and report some association with the development of eating disorders (Henderson-King & Henderson-King, 1997).

Exposure to Advertising. Although children and adolescents are exposed to advertising for a wide variety of products (see Jennings & Wartella, chap. 6, this volume), advertising targeted at children is very likely to emphasize high-fat, high-sugar foods. An examination of advertising over the years indicates that, on average, about 50% of advertisements aimed at children feature highly sugared cereals, candy, snack foods, and fast food (Center for Science in the Public Interest, 1992). If advertising does affect children's food preferences, the emphasis on food low in nutritional value suggests any effect of viewing would be negative. Indeed, the findings of some studies indicate that exposure to television advertisements contributes to children's short-term and long-term food preferences, although parents' food preferences have a stronger influence (Goldberg, Gorn, & Gibson, 1978; Gorn & Goldberg, 1982). However, in a longitudinal study, Anderson, Huston, Schmitt, Linebarger, and Wright (2001) examined different categories of preschool and teen viewing as potential predictors of overweight and obesity during the teen years. Although viewing entertainment television would be expected to produce more exposure to food advertisements than viewing educational or informative television, these authors reported no relation between the content of preschool or teen viewing and the likelihood of teen overweight or obesity. However, there may be effects of child and adolescent television viewing on nutrition and fitness that operate regardless of content.

Effects of Television Viewing Behavior. Although most of the studies reviewed in this chapter focus on relations between specific content and health-related choices, there is evidence that television viewing as a *behavior* may relate to overweight and obesity during childhood and adolescence. Heavy television viewing may result in lessened overall activity (Dietz, 1990, 1993) and may encourage increased calorie consumption (Taras, Sallis, Patterson, Nader, & Nelson, 1989). Positive relations between total viewing time and overweight or obesity have been observed in longitudinal investigations (Anderson et al., 2001; Dietz & Gortmaker, 1985), although one study did not observe such a relation (Robinson et al., 1993).

Summary. Television programs and advertisements communicate a paradox: They are populated largely by thin actors and models, but at the same time advertisements, particularly those directed at children, urge viewers to consume a variety of foods high in fat and sugar. Evidence suggests some immediate effects of viewing specific content, both on self-evaluations and on food preferences. However, long-term effects of repeated exposure to these types of content are less clear. The reduced activity and increased calorie consumption that are likely consequences of heavy television viewing may be stronger long-term predictors of weight problems than specific content viewed.

Portrayals of Substance Use

Substances presenting health concerns for children and adolescents include tobacco, alcohol, and various illicit drugs. There is considerable variation in the degree to which use of tobacco, alcohol, and illicit drugs are portrayed on television, as well as differences in the context and consequences of such use.

Tobacco.   In popular entertainment television programming, portrayal of tobacco use by major characters is relatively low. In a recent analysis of popular television shows (Roberts & Christenson, 2000), 22% of the shows portrayed tobacco use, but there was a low incidence within these shows in terms of the number of characters who smoked and in the amount of time smoking was depicted. Other reviews also report infrequent use by major characters, with somewhat higher incidence in movies shown on television (Strasburger, 1995). When portrayed, the context for smoking generally is incidental and neutral, although Roberts and Christenson (2000) reported that 23% of scenes showing tobacco use included negative statements about smoking. There is little evidence of any relation between television viewing and youth tobacco use. In their longitudinal investigation, Anderson et al. (2001) found no relation between the content of preschool viewing and teen tobacco use. However, the amount of time teens spent watching informative programming was negatively related to tobacco use. Teens who watch more informative programming may be better informed about health issues, or those who choose more informative programming may be less likely to be attracted to tobacco use.

In the United States, there has been no televised advertising of tobacco products since 1971, so direct advertising on television cannot influence youth smoking choices. However, tobacco marketing in other media often has been criticized for its apparent appeal to young smokers. The potency of such marketing receives some documentation from longitudinal evidence that receptivity to tobacco marketing in early adolescence predicts later progression to established smoking (Biener & Siegel, 2000; Pierce, Choi, Gilpin, Farkas, & Merritt, 1996).

Alcohol.   Alcohol occupies a unique position among the risky substances considered in this section. Alcohol use is much more likely to be portrayed in entertainment television programming than tobacco or drug use; unlike the latter substances, there also is direct advertising for beer and wine on television. Historically, alcohol use was depicted with such high frequency in entertainment television of the 1980s that public pressure motivated industry guidelines and reductions in portrayals (Strasburger, 1995). Even with these decreases, content analyses from the 1990s still showed frequent alcohol use. For example, Grube (1993) reported an average of six incidents of drinking per hour. In a recent content analysis of the top 20 shows among teens and the top 20 shows among adults (Roberts & Christenson, 2000), 77% of the episodes of these shows included references to alcohol use, with alcohol consumption common among the shows' major characters. Most commonly, alcohol use was portrayed as incidental, customary, and free of problems (Roberts & Christenson, 2000; Signorielli, 1987; Strasburger, 1995). Roberts and Christenson (2000) did report that 23% of portrayals included negative consequences, but 45% of portrayals were linked to humor. In general, alcohol use seems to be presented as a normative adult behavior, with excesses more likely to be shown humorously than as harmful.

Alcohol advertising also may contribute to an image of alcohol use as normal and attractive adult behavior. Strasburger (1989, 1995) estimated that on average American children and teens are exposed to about 1,500 television commercials for alcohol products each year. These advertisements may contribute to positive expectancies about alcohol use by creating and reinforcing links between use and youth, social activity, involvement with sports, and sexual imagery. Some commercials may be especially attractive to younger audience members when they incorporate humor and "child-friendly" elements such as the famous Budweiser frogs.

What evidence indicates that there are effects on children and adolescents of exposure to alcohol portrayals in programming and advertising? Because alcohol use is shown so commonly in entertainment television and promoted so frequently in advertisements, many studies have investigated the connection between overall viewing and children and teens' alcohol-related beliefs and behaviors. A number of studies have reported that the amount of viewing of entertainment television and alcohol advertising is related to positive alcohol expectancies and alcohol use among adolescents (Aitken, Eadie, Leathar, McNeill, & Scott, 1988; Atkin, 1990; Atkin, Hocking, & Block, 1984; Brown & McDonald, 1995; Connolly, Casswell, Zhang, & Silva, 1994, for adolescent girls only; Neuendorf, 1985; Robinson, Chen, & Killen, 1998; Tucker, 1985, for adolescent boys only). Several experimental studies have reported similar effects on adolescents' attitudes and expectancies after viewing alcohol advertising (Grube & Wallack, 1994) or alcohol use in entertainment programming (Kotch, Coulter, & Lipsitz, 1986; Rychtarik, Fairbank, Allen, Fox, & Drabman, 1983). There are, however, a few exceptions to this pattern. In a national sample, there was no relation between adolescent viewing and alcohol use (Chirco, 1990, cited in Anderson et al., 2001). Further, in their longitudinal study, Anderson et al. (2001) found a negative relation between entertainment TV viewing of female teens and alcohol use by these teens.

Illicit Drug Use.   Over the years, portrayals of illicit drug use have been relatively uncommon (Greenberg, 1981). In the content analysis conducted by Roberts and Christenson (2000), references to illicit drugs were similar in frequency to references to tobacco, in that about 20% of popular television shows contained such references. Similar to alcohol, about 45% of these references were linked to humor. Unlike alcohol and tobacco, however, negative consequences of illicit drug use were more likely to be depicted (67%) and 41% of portrayals included an antidrug statement.

Summary.   There is little reason to believe that televised portrayals of tobacco or illicit drug use contribute to risks for child and adolescent viewers. Use of these substances by major characters is relatively uncommon, and contexts for showing these behaviors are largely incidental for tobacco use and negative for illicit drug use, with the exception of the link to humor for the latter. There may be more cause for concern with regard to portrayals of alcohol use and advertising of alcohol products. Entertainment programming tends to show alcohol use as normative adult behavior, with advertising often presented to be appealing to young viewers and to link alcohol use to status and positive consequences. Television viewing is only one source about alcohol use. However, if "scripts" for alcohol use are facilitated by these portrayals, such scripts are likely to emphasize positive expectancies ("I'll have friends," "We'll have fun") with little appreciation of risks or consequences ("If I drink too much, it will be funny").

Sexual Behavior

Portrayals of Sex.   Over the years, sex as portrayed on television often has been associated with casual relationships and humor, and sometimes with power and violence in action adventure shows and in music videos (Greenberg, Brown, & Buerkel-Rothfuss, 1991). The frequency of sexual references has increased steadily over the last two decades (Greenberg et al., 1991; Kunkel, Cope-Farrar, Biely, Farinola, & Donnerstein, 2001), making sexual content typical fare for children and adolescents viewing virtually any general audience programming. In their content analysis of more than 1,000 programs randomly selected from 10 channels during the 1999–2000 season (excluding newscasts, sports, or children's shows), Kunkel et al. (2001) reported that 68% of all shows contain sexual content, an increase from 56% in a similar analysis conducted 2 years earlier, representing an average rate of approximately four scenes per hour. The proportion of shows including sexual content is highest for situation comedies (84%) and movies shown on television (89%). Characters talking about sex is the most common type of sexual content, but sexual behavior is a major component of 27% of television programs. Consistent with earlier analyses (e.g., Huston, Wartella, & Donnerstein, 1998), sexual behavior most often involves unmarried adults, with only infrequent references to risks or responsibilities associated with sexual intercourse. Kunkel et al. (2001) found that about 10% of shows with sexual content make any reference to risks or responsibilities. Such references are more common in dramas than in comedies and when sexual intercourse is strongly implied or depicted (25% of such shows), but rarely are risks and responsibilities presented as a major issue (2%). Kunkel et al. noted an increase in the frequency of showing teens in intercourse-related scenes, with dramas concerning teens and sex the most likely to include references to risks and responsibilities (32% of scenes portraying teens talking about or engaging in sexual intercourse).

Effects of Portrayals of Sex on Television.   Based on the theoretical perspectives described earlier, exposure to sex on television could be expected to influence knowledge, attitudes, and possibly behaviors of children and adolescents. With regard to social cognitive theory, television portrayals provide attractive models and ample opportunity for observational learning of sexual behaviors and contexts for those behaviors. Script theories suggest that television may help children and adolescents to construct scripts for sexual interactions prior to their own experience, and may contribute to forming concepts of norms for teenage sexual behavior. Huston et al. (1998) noted that television is likely to present more frequent sexual messages than other sources, given that many parents communicate only occasionally and school emphasizes biological information. In fact, teens themselves rank television as an important source of information about sexuality, although they credit schools, parents, and peers as well. For 13- to 15-year-olds, 61% of teens report that they get "a lot" of information about sex from entertainment media (Kaiser Family Foundation, 2000). Among 15- to 17-year-olds, 72% of adolescents believe that sexual content on television influences the behavior of teens their age "somewhat" or "a lot," although only 22% believe sexual content influences their own behavior to this degree (Kaiser Family Foundation, 2002). Some teens report helpful effects from television, including learning how to say "no" to a sexual situation that makes them uncomfortable (60%), learning how to talk to a partner about safer sex (43%), or motivating a conversation with a parent about a sexual issue (33%).

Despite theoretical reasons to expect effects of viewing sexual content and adolescents' self-reports concerning effects, there are relatively few studies that directly evaluate these effects. A small number of experimental studies suggest that sexual content in programs and music videos can result in increases in knowledge (e.g., Greenberg, Linsangan, & Soderman, 1993) and effects on teenagers' judgments about the acceptability of nonmarital sex (Bryant & Rockwell, 1994; Greeson & Williams, 1987). Correlational studies also have reported associations between amount of sexual content viewed and beliefs about sexual attractiveness, the frequency and acceptability of sexual behaviors (Kenrick & Gutierres, 1980), and likelihood of initiating sexual activity (Brown & Newcomer, 1991). One longitudinal study (Peterson, Moore, & Furstenberg, 1991) found no evidence that the amount or content of early adolescent television viewing predicted early initiation of sexual intercourse, but reported that teens who did not talk about television content with parents had higher rates of sexual intercourse.

Summary

Given the likely interest in sexual content among adolescents, the attractive models presented on television, and the high frequency of sexual content on television as compared with other sources, the major theoretical approaches would predict effects of viewing sexual content on knowledge and perhaps on attitudes and behaviors. Research does document some influences, although causal direction is unclear in correlational studies and the degree of influence of naturally occurring viewing is uncertain. Some evidence suggests that family factors such as parental values and communication style may reduce or eliminate any value and attitude changes occurring as a result of exposure to the nature and context of sexual content on television (Huston et al., 1998).

INTENTIONAL EFFECTS: HEALTH-RELATED INTERVENTION THROUGH TELEVISION

Portrayals of health-related behaviors on television are not only incidental to entertainment programming or incorporated in product advertising. Television also is used intentionally as a major medium for public service campaigns aimed at redirecting people's risky choices and reinforcing their healthy choices (Flay & Sobel, 1983; Rogers & Storey, 1987; Schilling & McAlister, 1990). Some campaigns are composed of public service announcements (PSAs) that address a general audience, whereas others have been more specifically targeted at a young audience. Fueled in part by substantial increases in youth smoking in the early 1990s (Johnston et al., 2001a) and the availability of increased funds from tobacco settlements (Hornik, 2002), a number of recent campaigns have been directed at the prevention of smoking initiation and progression to established smoking (Siegel & Biener, 2000; Worden & Flynn, 2002). Similar rises in adolescent illicit drug use in the early 1990s have stimulated new efforts to use television to change these trends (e.g., Palmgreen, Donohew, Lorch, Hoyle, & Stephenson, 2001). Other recent efforts have targeted adolescent alcohol use and risky sexual behaviors (e.g., Donohew et al., 2000; Langer, Zimmerman, Warheit, & Duncan, 1993; McCombie et al., 2002; Priester, 2002).

A review of the effectiveness of these and earlier campaigns presents a mixed picture of success. Although many campaigns appear to increase knowledge relevant to a health-related issue (e.g., Flay, 1987), the consistency and extent of influence on adolescent attitudes and behaviors is less certain (e.g., Brown & Walsh-Childers, 1994). Some studies report no changes in targeted behaviors (Bauman, LaPrelle, Brown, Koch, & Padgett, 1991; Flay et al., 1995; Murray, Prokhorov, & Harty, 1994), whereas others have produced far more encouraging effects on attitudes and behaviors (Flynn et al., 1997; Flynn et al., 1994; Palmgreen et al., 2001; Palmgreen et al., 1995; Perry, Kelder, Murray, & Klepp, 1992; Pierce, Macaskill, & Hill, 2002; Schilling & McAlister, 1990; Siegel & Biener, 2000; Zastowny, Adams, Black, Lawton, & Wilder, 1993). A justifiable conclusion is that public service campaigns directed at young people *can* effect meaningful change but they do not always do so. Thus, an important question to explore concerns identification of reasons why some public service campaigns have been effective, especially at the relatively difficult task of influencing adolescents' risky health-related behaviors.

One possible reason for differential success is the extent to which a PSA campaign is theoretically directed. A number of relevant theories have received empirical support and offer guidance for PSA development and campaign strategies. In general, these theories are not competing explanations, but rather ones that address complementary aspects of health-related choices. Some of the theories place the greatest emphasis on explaining individuals' health-related choices, but have implications for media approaches to change. Others more specifically address aspects of communication, including influences on and individual differences in people's attention to, processing of, and persuasion by messages. These theories are examined in the next section. Following discussion of the theoretical perspectives, two lines of research are discussed in more detail that incorporate theoretical guidance into campaign construction and that have been successful in leading to behavior changes in adolescents. Finally, based on the theories, the two example lines of research, and the results of other studies of PSA effectiveness, factors associated with greater campaign success are summarized.

Theoretical Background

Perspectives Emphasizing the Origins of Health-Related Behaviors. A common theme of these perspectives is the importance of underlying knowledge, beliefs, or attitudes in predicting behaviors. One of these theories, social cognitive theory, was discussed earlier. As applied to health-related persuasion, two elements receive greatest stress (Fishbein et al., 2002). One of these is the concept of self-efficacy (Bandura, 1989, 1994), which includes knowledge about behaviors and people's belief in their ability to carry out these behaviors. The other concerns the nature of incentives that exist to perform relevant behaviors, which includes individuals' beliefs about consequences likely to result from behaviors and their evaluations of these consequences.

A related theoretical perspective, the stages of change model, incorporates social cognitive theory but identifies distinct stages in the behavior change process that begin prior to contemplating change and continue through steps of maintaining change (DiClemente et al., 1991; Prochaska & DiClemente, 1983; Slater, 1999). To move from stage to stage, individuals require relevant information, they need to modify attitudes, and they must acquire new abilities and behaviors to execute change. New behaviors often are complex, and thus are acquired gradually. Attractive models that identify, demonstrate, and encourage specific components of behavior sequences can assist the behavior change process.

Another influential theory, the health belief model (Rosenstock, 1990), also connects to social cognitive theory in terms of a focus on beliefs that function as incentives. According to this model, individuals' behaviors are best predicted by the extent to which they perceive a personal threat (i.e., behaviors and their consequences are personally relevant) and the extent to which they believe benefits of behaviors exceed barriers to them.

Finally, the theory of reasoned action (Ajzen & Fishbein, 1980), is related to script theories, in that it emphasizes the role of expectancies in creating behavioral intentions, which in turn predict behaviors. Expectancies can include concepts of health-related behaviors, expectations about probable consequences of behaviors, and attitudes toward performing the behaviors and experiencing the consequences. In addition, an important type of expectancy from this perspective concerns subjective norms concerning behaviors, including adolescents' perceptions of the prevalence of a behavior in their peer group and perceptions of others' attitudes toward the behavior. That is, an adolescent's perception that a high proportion of peers engage in a particular behavior such as smoking or drug use and do not disapprove of the behavior would increase the risk of the adolescent engaging in that behavior (e.g., Chassin, Presson, & Sherman, 1990; Iannotti, Bush, & Weinfurt, 1996).

Perspectives Emphasizing Message Characteristics in Relation to Individual Differences. Similar to the preceding theoretical perspectives, Petty and Cacioppo's (1986) elaboration likelihood model assumes that changes in attitudes and beliefs precede changes in behaviors. However, this model specifies two routes to persuasion, central processing and peripheral processing, with the dominant route in a given situation dependent both on characteristics of the individual and of the message. Elaboration likelihood is higher and central processing more likely to the extent that individuals have high need for cognition and ample time to consider a message, and to the extent that messages motivate the recipient by being of high personal relevance. Under these conditions, messages that present high-quality arguments are most persuasive, with influences on attitudes and behavior that are relatively likely to persist. When elaboration likelihood is high, a message with low-quality arguments is likely to stimulate counterarguments and reactance. In circumstances in which recipients are unable or unmotivated to think carefully about a message and engage in peripheral processing, positive or negative responses are likely to be superficial (e.g., based on perceived credibility or attractiveness of the source or on the quantity rather than quality of arguments presented), resulting in less persistent attitude or behavior change.

A second model that emphasizes message characteristics in relation to individual differences is the activation model of information exposure

(Donohew, Helm, Lawrence, & Shatzer, 1990; Donohew, Lorch, & Palmgreen, 1998). According to this model, individuals act to achieve or maintain an optimal state of activation when they enter situations in which they may be exposed to information. If the message causes suitable activation, the individual is likely to process and evaluate the message. If the message causes too high (threatening, too exciting) or too low (boring) a level of arousal, the individual is likely to turn away from the message and seek a preferable level of stimulation. Such variations in arousal potential have been termed *message sensation value*, "the degree to which formal and content audiovisual features of a message elicit sensory, affective, and arousal responses" (Palmgreen et al., 1991, p. 219). This model assumes that individuals differ in their optimal level of arousal, consistent with Zuckerman's (1994) concept of sensation seeking. Because individuals higher in sensation seeking also are at greater risk for early substance use and greater problems with substance use (Donohew et al., 1990; Zuckerman, 1994), this model suggests a strategy for reaching children and adolescents with high-sensation value messages (see later). Although the model at first glance might seem to point to a peripheral avenue for persuasion (Petty & Cacioppo, 1986), achieving optimal levels of arousal may be necessary to sustain sufficient attention from high-sensation seekers for a message to be reach the central processing route (Donohew, Palmgreen, Lorch, Zimmerman, & Harrington, 2002).

Two lines of research illustrate the successful integration of several theoretical approaches to influence substance use among children and adolescents. One set of studies emerges from the work of Flynn, Worden, and their colleagues on smoking prevention programs (Flynn, Worden, Secker-Walker, Badger, & Geller, 1995; Flynn et al., 1994; Flynn et al., 1997; Worden & Flynn, 2002). The other line of work represents a collaboration at the University of Kentucky on drug abuse prevention (Donohew, Lorch, & Palmgreen, 1991, 1998; Lorch et al., 1994; Palmgreen, Donohew, Lorch, Hoyle, & Stephenson, 2001, 2002; Palmgreen et al., 1995). Both sets of studies report on the design and use of campaigns that have resulted in behavior changes among targeted adolescents.

In the smoking prevention programs designed by Flynn, Worden, and their colleagues, typically the baseline is a school-based prevention program extending from elementary school through high school, and the media campaign (including television and radio spots) is evaluated in terms of the extent to which it produces an effect over and above the school-based program. This group has used an integration of the theories previously discussed to generate the content of the prevention messages. For example, consistent with the theory of reasoned action, campaign spots are designed to target social norms by demonstrating that most adolescents do not smoke. In line with the health belief model and social cognitive theory, messages reinforce a positive view of nonsmoking and a negative view of smoking. Further building on social cognitive theory and incorporating ideas from the stages of change model, spots demonstrate specific behaviors such as skills for refusing cigarettes and strategies for smoking cessation. The researchers also targeted subgroups according to developmental level, gender, and risk for smoking adoption and conducted formative research to test the appeal of campaign spots to the targeted groups and document preferred outlets for the placement of spots.

Using this approach in the context of long-term studies and with smoking behavior measured both by self-report and salivary analysis, effects of the added media exposure were observed on smoking behavior and on targeted mediators (e.g., social norms). Whereas at baseline there were no differences between the school program only group and the media and school program group in smoking behaviors and in most risk factors, differences between the groups became strong over the course of the 4-year program, with a relative reduction in smoking prevalence of 31% at Grades 10 to 12 for the group with added media exposure. Effects were specific to smoking behavior and targeted mediators and did not generalize to use of nontargeted substances or to nontargeted mediators; persisted at long-term follow-ups; and remained consistent after adjusting for variables such as baseline smoking, age, and gender (e.g., Worden & Flynn, 2002).

The line of research concerned with prevention of adolescent drug use uses the SENTAR approach (e.g., Palmgreen et al., 2002), which is based on the activation model of information exposure and the concept of sensation seeking to guide the definition of an appropriate target audience and the core strategy for how to design messages and structure a campaign to reach this audience. Other theories are integrated with the approach to specify content for campaign spots. For example, consistent with the health belief model and the elaboration likelihood model, negative consequences of drug use are portrayed, but only if they are well documented by research and considered relevant and credible by the target audience.

The centerpiece of the SENTAR strategy is sensation seeking, a powerful risk factor for early drug use and drug abuse problems. Sensation seeking is a biologically based personality trait associated with the need for novelty, emotional intensity, complexity, ambiguity, and the willingness to take risks to obtain these sensations (Zuckerman, 1994). Adolescent high-sensation seekers (HSS) are more likely than low-sensation seekers (LSS) to use a variety of substances, including tobacco, alcohol, and a variety of illicit drugs, and to use substances earlier than LSS (e.g., Barnea, Teichman, & Rahar, 1992; Clayton, Cattarello, & Walden, 1991; Donohew, 1990). Sensation seeking appears to be a stable trait that continues to predict use across long developmental time spans (Caspi et al., 1997; Masse & Tremblay, 1997). As suggested previously, HSS individuals have a higher optimal level of arousal than LSS individuals, and thus prefer messages high in sensation value, which tend to be novel, dramatic, emotionally powerful or physically arousing, graphic or explicit, ambiguous, unconventional, fast-paced, or suspenseful. In experimental studies with HSS older adolescents and young adults, high-sensation value messages were more effective than low-sensation value messages in producing intent to call a prevention hotline, message recall, negative drug attitudes, and lower behavioral intentions to use drugs (Donohew et al., 1991; Everett & Palmgreen, 1995; Palmgreen et al., 1991), messages placed in high-sensation value television programs received more attention from HSS viewers than when they are placed in low-sensation value programs (Lorch et al., 1994), and high-sensation value messages placed into an actual campaign elicited far more calls from HSS callers than from LSS callers, regardless of factors such as gender and drug use status (Palmgreen et al., 1995).

With younger adolescents, a recent study employed the SENTAR approach in three campaigns aired in two different cities to target marijuana use in HSS middle school and high school students. As in the youth smoking prevention research, the design of the television-only campaigns was influenced by extensive formative research with the target audience of HSS youth. The goals of the formative research were to define credible consequences of marijuana use that were salient to members of the target audience (e.g., effects on friendships or romantic relationships, effects on athletic performance, etc.), to evaluate the appeal of concepts and preliminary versions of PSAs, and to gain initial information about favorite television programs of HSS teens. Messages produced for the campaigns were high in sensation value and incorporated consequences prominent in the formative research. A variety of PSAs were included to ensure adequate novelty to sustain the attention of HSS viewers. Using a combination of paid and unpaid time, messages were placed in television programs favored by HSS adolescents, information that was updated throughout the 32-month study. An average of 777 paid and 1,160 unpaid spots were aired in each campaign, with gross rating point data indicating that more than 70% of the targeted age group was exposed to a minimum of three spots per week.

Results of the study were derived from an interrupted time-series analysis based on 32 months of interviews with 100 teens per month in each of two cities. The same age cohort was followed throughout the study, which comprised the seventh through tenth grades at the beginning of the study. The interruptions consisted of three 4-month campaigns, two at different times in one city, with the other city serving as a control location during the first campaign. The major behavioral dependent measure was reported 30-day marijuana use. Although the increase in the age of the cohort across the 32 months resulted in a developmental increase in marijuana use among HSS, this increase in use was reversed during the periods following each campaign. Follow-up analyses confirmed higher campaign exposure in both cities among HSS adolescents (Stephenson et al., 2002). As in the youth smoking prevention research, campaign effects were specific to marijuana use and did not occur for nontargeted substances (Palmgreen et al., 2002).

The findings of these two lines of research demonstrate successful application of theoretically based strategies to use mass media to change adolescent substance use. Extending beyond these lines of research, interventions with clearly defined, reasonable objectives (Rice & Atkin, 1994) and based on an integration of well-tested theoretical principles have been most successful (Atkin, 2002; Derzon & Lipsey, 2002; Donaldson, 2002; Maibach & Parrott, 1995; McAlister, Ramirez, Galavotti, & Gallion, 1989; Rosenstock, 1990; Schilling & McAlister, 1990; Siegel & Biener, 2000). Atkin (2002) raised certain cautions in applying principles based on theories, however. These include inadvertent social norming by giving too much emphasis to a behavior and thus making it seem more typical of a group, making a risky behavior seem too interesting or intriguing (a particular issue for HSS), and redirecting one undesirable or risky behavior to another.

A consideration of the theories, of the characteristics of successful campaigns just described, and the characteristics of other effective campaigns leads to the identification of other recommendations for increasing the effectiveness of televised campaigns. First, a high level of exposure to messages is important to ensuring success. Lack of effects in early television campaigns frequently were linked to failures to ensure widespread, frequent, and prolonged exposure to messages (e.g., Flay & Sobel, 1983).

Many successful campaigns funded extensive exposure and some were able to target exposure to preferred venues or to use multiple channels of exposure (Pierce et al., 2002; Rice & Atkin, 1994; Palmgreen et al., 2002; Siegel & Biener, 2000; Worden & Flynn, 2002). Other related factors often associated with success in changing adolescent attitudes and behaviors include a careful identification of a target audience; formative research and pretesting of campaign messages with that target audience (Atkin & Freimuth, 1989; Palmgreen et al., 2002; Worden & Flynn, 2002); and a tailoring of message format, content, and media channels to the characteristics of that target group (Backer, Rogers, & Sopory, 1992; Derzon & Lipsey, 2002; Slater, 1996; Wartella & Stout, 2002). Finally, there are characteristics of messages that are particularly important in gaining attention and receptivity from adolescent audiences. A variety of messages is important not only when HSS are the target (Palmgreen et al., 2002) but to keep a young audience intrigued (Worden & Flynn, 2002) and to allow for the incorporation of different target audiences, message styles, and tactics for persuasion and change (Atkin, 2002). Messages that are somewhat ambiguous and not "preachy" also appear to increase appeal to adolescents, and they tend to promote elaboration, central processing, and elaboration of risk, while reducing counterarguing and reactance (Atkin, 2002; Palmgreen et al., 2002; Skinner & Slater, 1995; Worden & Flynn, 2002).

CONCLUSIONS

As Smith (2002) argued, contributions of television messages to health-related behaviors are better considered part of continuing "community care" than as a one-time "vaccine" to prevent problem behaviors. This community care perspective is a continuing process of intervention, evaluation, and adjustment of interventions, with success best defined as incremental change over time as "care" continues. Atkin (2002) made a similar point in arguing for a "perpetual campaign" that can always address a new audience and fit the needs of audience members who are changing and subject to other influences in addition to media spots. Media campaigns directed at adolescents also do not have to be confined to brief PSAs only, but may utilize interactive media (Burgoon et al., 2002) or the longer, talk-show-style formats of behavioral journalism (McAlister, Ama, Barroso, Peters, & Kelder, 2000) to increase credibility, present more complex models, and foster elaborative processing of messages. Just as media portrayals of substance use or sexual behavior are only one potential factor among many affecting children's and adolescents' behaviors, media campaigns also are only one influence, and exert their impact within a complex personal, social, and political context (Wartella & Stout, 2002). Campaigns can contribute at the individual level, but problems are not simply ones of individuals knowing enough and making the right choices. Particularly in this area for younger people, the degree to which the family, peer, school, or community context supports risky behavior and unhealthy choices is critically important to understanding the development of health-related behaviors.

REFERENCES

Aitken, P. P., Eadie, D. R., Leathar, D. S., McNeill, R. E. J., & Scott, A. C. (1988). Television advertisements for drinks do reinforce under-age drinking. *British Journal of Addiction, 83*, 1399–1419.

Ajzen, I., & Fishbein, M. (1980). *Understanding attitudes and predicting social behavior.* Englewood Cliffs, NJ: Prentice-Hall.

American Academy of Child and Adolescent Psychiatry. (1999). *Tobacco and kids* (Facts for Families, No. 68). Washington, DC: Author.

American Academy of Child and Adolescent Psychiatry. (2001). *Obesity in children and teens* (Facts for Families, No. 79). Washington, DC: Author.

American Academy of Child and Adolescent Psychiatry. (2002). *Talking to your kids about sex.* (Facts for Families, No. 62). Washington, DC: Author.

Anderson, D. R., Huston, A. C., Schmitt, K. L., Linebarger, D. L., & Wright, J. C. (2001). Early childhood television viewing and adolescent behavior. *Monographs of the Society for Research in Child Development, 66*(1, Serial No. 264), 1–156.

Atkin, C. K. (1990). Effects of televised alcohol messages on teenage drinking patterns. *Journal of Adolescent Health Care, 11*, 10–24.

Atkin, C. K. (2002). Promising strategies for media health campaigns. In W. D. Crano & M. Burgoon (Eds.), *Mass media and drug prevention: Classic and contemporary theories and research* (pp. 35–64). Mahwah, NJ: Lawrence Erlbaum Associates, Inc.

Atkin, C. K., & Freimuth, V. (1989). Formative evaluation research in campaign design. In R. E. Rice & C. K. Atkin (Eds.), *Public communication campaigns* (2nd Ed., pp. 131–150). Newbury Park, CA: Sage.

Atkin, C. K., Hocking, J., & Block, M. (1984). Teenage drinking: Does advertising make a difference? *Journal of Communication, 28*, 71–80.

Backer, T. E., Rogers, E. M., & Sopory, P. (1992). *Designing health communication campaigns: What works?* Newbury Park, CA: Sage.

Bandura, A. (1989). Regulation of cognitive processes through perceived self-efficacy. *Developmental Psychology, 5*, 729–735.

Bandura, A. (1994). Social cognitive theory and exercise of control over HIV infection. In R. J. DiClemente & J. L. Peterson (Eds.), *Preventing AIDS: Theories and methods of behavioral interventions* (pp. 25–59). New York: Plenum.

Barnea, Z., Teichman, M., & Rahar, G. (1992). Personality, cognitive, and interpersonal factors in adolescent substance use: A longitudinal test of an integrative model. *Journal of Youth and Adolescence, 21,* 187–201.

Bauman, K. E., LaPrelle, J., Brown, J. D., Koch, G. G., & Padgett, C. A. (1991). The influence of three mass media campaigns on variables related to adolescent cigarette smoking: Results of a field experiment. *American Journal of Public Health, 81,* 597–604.

Biener, L., & Siegel, M. (2000). Tobacco marketing and adolescent smoking: More support for a causal inference. *American Journal of Public Health, 90,* 407–411.

Brown, J. D., & McDonald, T. (1995). Portrayals and effects of alcohol in television entertainment programming. In S. E. Martin (Ed.), *The effects of the mass media on the use and abuse of alcohol* (pp. 133–150). Bethesda, MD: U.S. Department of Health & Human Services.

Brown, J. D., & Newcomer, S. (1991). Television viewing and adolescents' sexual behavior. *Journal of Homosexuality, 21,* 77–91.

Brown, J. D., & Walsh-Childers, K. (1994). Effects of media on personal and public health. In J. Bryant & D. Zillman (Eds.), *Media effects: Advances in theory and research* (pp. 389–415). Hillsdale, NJ: Lawrence Erlbaum Associates, Inc.

Bryant, J., & Rockwell, S. C. (1994). Effects of massive exposure to sexually oriented prime-time television programming on adolescents' moral judgment. In D. Zillman, J. Bryant, & A. C. Huston (Eds.), *Media, children, and the family: Social scientific, psychodynamic, and clinical perspectives* (pp. 183–195). Hillsdale, NJ: Lawrence Erlbaum Associates, Inc.

Burgoon, M., Alvaro, E. M., Broneck, K., Miller, C., Grandpre, J. R., Hall, J. R., et al. (2002). Using interactive media tools to test substance abuse prevention messages. In W. D. Crano & M. Burgoon (Eds.), *Mass media and drug prevention: Classic and contemporary theories and research* (pp. 67–87). Mahwah, NJ: Lawrence Erlbaum Associates, Inc.

Caspi, A., Dickson, D., Dickson, N., Harrington, H., Langley, J., Moffitt, T. E., et al. (1997). Personality differences predict health-risk behaviors in young adulthood: Evidence from a longitudinal study. *Journal of Personality and Social Psychology, 73,* 1052–1063.

Center for Science in the Public Interest. (1992). *Survey of advertising on children's TV.* Washington, DC: Author.

Chassin, L., Presson, C. C., & Sherman, S. J. (1990). Social psychological contributions to the understanding and prevention of adolescent cigarette smoking. *Personality and Social Psychology Bulletin, 16,* 133–151.

Clayton, R. R., Cattarello, A., & Walden, K. P. (1991). Sensation seeking as a potential mediating variable for school-based prevention intervention: A two-year follow-up of DARE. *Health Communication, 3,* 229–239.

Connolly, G. M., Casswell, S., Zhang, J. F., & Silva, P. A. (1994). Alcohol in the mass media and drinking by adolescents: A longitudinal study. *Addiction, 89,* 1255–1263.

Derzon, J. H., & Lipsey, M. W. (2002). A meta-analysis of mass-communication for changing substance-use knowledge, attitudes, and behavior. In W. D. Crano & M. Burgoon (Eds.), *Mass media and drug prevention: Classic and contemporary theories and research* (pp. 231–258). Mahwah, NJ: Lawrence Erlbaum Associates, Inc.

DiClemente, C. C., Prochaska, J. O., Fairhurst, S. K., Velicer, W. F., Velasquez, M. M., & Rossi, J. S. (1991). The process of smoking cessation: An analysis of pre-contemplation, contemplation and preparation stages of change. *Journal of Consulting and Clinical Psychology, 59*, 295–304.

Dietz, W. H. (1990). You are what you eat—What you eat is what you are. *Journal of Adolescent Health Care, 11*, 76–81.

Dietz, W. H. (1993). Television, obesity, and eating disorders. *Adolescent Medicine, 75*, 543–549.

Dietz, W. H., & Gortmaker, S. L. (1985). Do we fatten our children at the television set? Obesity and television viewing in children and adolescents. *Pediatrics, 75*, 807–813.

Donaldson, S. I. (2002). High-potential mediators of drug-abuse prevention program effects. In W. D. Crano & M. Burgoon (Eds.), *Mass media and drug prevention: Classic and contemporary theories and research* (pp. 215–230). Mahwah, NJ: Lawrence Erlbaum Associates, Inc.

Donohew, L. (1990). Public health campaigns: Individual message strategies and a model. In E. B. Ray & L. Donohew (Eds.), *Communication and health: Systems and applications* (pp. 136–152). Hillsdale, NJ: Lawrence Erlbaum Associates, Inc.

Donohew, L., Helm, D., Lawrence, P., & Shatzer, M. (1990). Sensation-seeking, marijuana use, and responses to drug abuse prevention messages. In R. R. Watson (Ed.), *Drug and alcohol abuse reviews* (pp. 77–93). Clifton, NJ: Humana.

Donohew, L., Lorch, E. P., & Palmgreen, P. (1991). Sensation seeking and targeting of televised anti-drug PSAs. In L. Donohew, H. E. Sypher, W. J. Bukoski (Eds.), *Persuasive communication and drug abuse prevention* (pp. 209–226). Hillsdale, NJ: Lawrence Erlbaum Associates, Inc.

Donohew, L., Lorch, E. P., & Palmgreen, P. (1998). Applications of a theoretic model of information exposure to health interventions. *Human Communication Research, 24*, 454–468.

Donohew, L., Palmgreen, P., Lorch, E., Zimmerman, R., & Harrington, N. (2002). Attention, persuasive communication, and prevention. In W. D. Crano & M. Burgoon (Eds.), *Mass media and drug prevention: Classic and contemporary theories and research* (pp. 119–143). Mahwah, NJ: Lawrence Erlbaum Associates, Inc.

Donohew, L., Zimmerman, R., Cupp, P., Novak, S., Colon, S., & Abell, R. (2000). Sensation-seeking, impulsive decision-making, and risky sex: Implications for risk-taking and design of interventions. *Personality and Individual Differences, 28*, 1079–1091.

Everett, M., & Palmgreen, P. (1995). Influence of sensation seeking, message sensation value, and program context on the effectiveness of anti-cocaine PSAs. *Health Communication, 7*, 239–244.

Fishbein, M., Cappella, J., Hornik, R., Sayeed, S., Yzer, M., & Ahern, R. K. (2002). The role of theory in developing effective antidrug public service announcements. In W. D. Crano & M. Burgoon (Eds.), *Mass media and drug prevention: Classic and contemporary theories and research* (pp. 89–117). Mahwah, NJ: Lawrence Erlbaum Associates, Inc.

Flay, B. R. (1987). Mass media and smoking cessation: A critical review. *American Journal of Public Health, 77*, 153–160.

Flay, B. R., Miller, T. Q., Hedeker, D., Siddiqui, O., Britton, C. F., Brannon, B. R., et al. (1995). The television, school, and family smoking prevention and cessation project: VIII. Student outcomes and mediating variables. *Preventive Medicine, 24,* 29–40.

Flay, B. R., & Sobel, J. L. (1983). The role of mass media in preventing adolescent substance abuse. In T. J. Glynn, C. G. Leukefeld, & J. P. Ludford (Eds.), *Preventing adolescent drug abuse: Intervention strategies* (pp. 5–35). Rockville, MD: National Institute on Drug Abuse.

Flynn, B. S., Worden, J. K., Secker-Walker, R. H., Badger, G. J., & Geller, B. M. (1995). Cigarette smoking prevention effects of mass media and school interventions targeted to gender and age groups. *Journal of Health Education, 26,* 45–51.

Flynn, B. S., Worden, J. K., Secker-Walker, R. H., Pirie, P. L., Badger, G. J., Carpenter, J. H., et al. (1994). Mass media and school interventions for cigarette smoking prevention: Effects 2 years after completion. *American Journal of Public Health, 84,* 1148–1150.

Flynn, B. S., Worden, J. K., Secker-Walker, R. H., Pirie, P. L., Badger, G. J., & Carpenter, J. H. (1997). Long-term responses of higher and lower risk youths to smoking prevention interventions. *Preventive Medicine, 26,* 389–394.

Gerbner, G., Morgan, M., & Signorielli, N. (1982). Programming health portrayals: What viewers see, say, and do. In D. Pearl, L. Bouthilet, & J. Lazar (Eds.), *Television and behavior: Ten years of scientific progress and implications for the eighties* (pp. 291–307). Washington, DC: U.S. Government Printing Office.

Goldberg, M. E., Gorn, G. J., & Gibson, W. (1978). TV messages for snack and breakfast foods: Do they influence children's preferences? *Journal of Consumer Research, 5,* 48–54.

Gorn, G. J., & Goldberg, M. E. (1982). Behavioral evidence of the effects of televised food messages on children. *Journal of Consumer Research, 9,* 200–205.

Greenberg, B. S. (1981). Smoking, drugging, and drinking in top rated TV series. *Journal of Drug Education, 11,* 227–233.

Greenberg, B. S., Brown, J. D., & Buerkel-Rothfuss, N. (1991). *Media, sex, and the adolescent.* Norwood, NJ: Ablex.

Greenberg, B. S., Linsangan, R., & Soderman, A. (1993). Adolescents' reactions to television sex. In B. S. Greenberg, J. D. Brown, & N. L. Buerkel-Rothfuss (Eds.), *Media, sex, and the adolescent* (pp. 196–224). Cresskill, NJ: Hampton.

Greeson, L. E., & Williams, R. A. (1987). Social implications of music videos for youth: An analysis of the content and effects of MTV. *Youth & Society, 18,* 177–189.

Grube, J. W. (1993). Alcohol portrayals and alcohol advertising on television. *Alcohol Health and Research World, 17,* 61–66.

Grube, J. W., & Wallack, L. (1994). Television advertising and drinking knowledge, beliefs, and intentions among school children. *American Journal of Public Health, 84,* 254–259.

Hargreaves, D., & Tiggemann, M. (2002). The effect of television commercials on mood and body dissatisfaction: The role of appearance-schema activation. *Journal of Social and Clinical Psychology, 21,* 287–308.

Henderson-King, E., & Henderson-King, D. (1997). Media effects on women's body esteem: Social and individual difference factors. *Journal of Applied Social Psychology, 27,* 399–417.

Hornik, R. C. (2002). *Public health communication: Evidence for behavior change.* Mahwah, NJ: Lawrence Erlbaum Associates, Inc.

228

LORCH

Huesmann, L. R., & Miller, L. S. (1994). Long-term effects of repeated exposure to media violence in childhood. In L. R. Huesmann (Ed.), *Aggressive behavior: Current perspectives* (pp. 153–183). New York: Plenum.

Huston, A. C., Wartella, E., & Donnerstein, E. (1998). *Measuring the effects of sexual content in the media: A report to the Kaiser Family Foundation.* Menlo Park, CA: Henry J. Kaiser Family Foundation.

Iannotti, R. J., Bush, P. J., & Weinfurt, K. P. (1996). Perceptions of friends' use of alcohol, cigarettes, and marijuana among urban schoolchildren: A longitudinal analysis. *Addictive Behaviors, 21,* 615–633.

Irving, L. M. (1990). Mirror images: Effects of the standard of beauty on the self- and body-esteem of women exhibiting varying levels of bulimic symptoms. *Journal of Social and Clinical Psychology, 9,* 230–242.

Johnston, L. D., O'Malley, P. M., & Bachman, J. G. (2000). *The monitoring of the future: National results on adolescent drug use* (Rep. No. 00–4690). Bethesda, MD: National Institute on Drug Abuse.

Johnston, L. D., O'Malley, P. M., & Bachman, J. G. (2001a). *Cigarette smoking among American teens declines sharply in 2001: Monitoring the future 2001.* Ann Arbor: University of Michigan News and Information Services.

Johnston, L. D., O'Malley, P. M., & Bachman, J. G. (2001b). *Rise in ecstasy use among American teens begins to slow: Monitoring the future 2001.* Ann Arbor: University of Michigan News and Information Services.

Kaiser Family Foundation. (2000). *Teens and sex: The role of popular television fact sheet.* Menlo Park, CA: Author.

Kaiser Family Foundation. (2002). *Teens, sex, and TV.* Menlo Park, CA: Author.

Kalodner, C. R. (1997). Media influences on male and female non-eating-disordered college students: A significant issue. *Eating Disorders, 5,* 47–57.

Kann, L., Kinchen, S. A., Williams, B. I., Ross, J. G., Lowry, R., Grunbaum, J., et al. (2000). Youth risk behavior surveillance—United States, 1999. *MMWR Surveillance Summaries, 49,* 1–96.

Kenrick, D. T., & Gutierres, S. E. (1980). Contrast effects and judgements of physical attractiveness: When beauty becomes a social problem. *Journal of Personality and Social Psychology, 38,* 131–140.

Kotch, J. B., Coulter, M. L., & Lipsitz, A. (1986). Does televised drinking influence children's attitudes toward alcohol? *Addictive Behaviors, 11,* 67–70.

Kunkel, D., Cope-Farrar, K., Biely, E., Farinola, W. J. M., & Donnerstein, E. (2001). *Sex on TV: A biennial report to the Kaiser Family Foundation.* Menlo Park, CA: Henry J. Kaiser Family Foundation.

Langer, L., Zimmerman, R., Warheit, G. J., & Duncan, R. C. (1993). An examination of the relationship between adolescent decision-making orientation and AIDS-related knowledge, attitudes, beliefs, behaviors, and skills. *Health Psychology, 12,* 227–234.

Lorch, E. P., Palmgreen, P., Donohew, L., Harrington, N. G., Dsilva, M. & Helm, D. (1994). Program context, sensation seeking, and attention to televised anti-drug public service announcements. *Human Communication Research, 20,* 390–412.

Maibach, E., & Parrott, R. L. (1995). *Designing health messages: Approaches from communication theory and public health practice.* Thousand Oaks, CA: Sage.

Masse, L. C., & Tremblay, R. E. (1997). Behavior of boys in kindergarten and the onset of substance abuse during adolescence. *Archives of General Psychiatry, 54,* 62–68.

McAlister, A., Ama, E., Barroso, C., Peters, R., & Kelder, S. (2000). Promoting tolerance and moral engagement through students' behavioral journalism. *Cultural Diversity and Minority Psychology, 6,* 363–373.

McAlister, A., Ramirez, A. G., Galavotti, C., & Gallion, K. J. (1989). Anti-smoking campaigns: Progress in the application of social learning theory. In R. E. Rice & C. K. Atkin (Eds.), *Public communication campaigns* (2nd Ed., pp. 291–307). Newbury Park, CA: Sage.

McCombie, S., Hornik, R. C., & Anarfi, J. K. (2002). Effects of a mass media campaign to prevent AIDS among young people in Ghana. In R. C. Hornik (Ed.), *Public health communication: Evidence for behavior change* (pp. 147–161). Mahwah, NJ: Lawrence Erlbaum Associates, Inc.

McGinnis, J. M., & Foege, W. H. (1993). Actual causes of death in the United States. *Journal of the American Medical Association, 270,* 2207–2212.

Murray, D. M., Prokhorov, A. V., & Harty, K. C. (1994). Effects of a statewide anti-smoking campaign on mass media messages and smoking beliefs. *Preventive Medicine, 23,* 54–60.

Neuendorf, K. A. (1985). Alcohol advertising and media portrayals. *Journal of the Institute of Socioeconomic Studies, 10,* 67–78.

Palmgreen, P., Donohew, L., Lorch, E. P., Hoyle, R. H., & Stephenson, M. T. (2001). Television campaigns and adolescent marijuana use: Tests of sensation seeking targeting. *American Journal of Public Health, 91,* 292–296.

Palmgreen, P., Donohew, L., Lorch, E. P., Hoyle, R. H., & Stephenson, M. T. (2002). Television campaigns and sensation seeking targeting of adolescent marijuana use: A controlled time-series approach. In R. Hornik (Ed.), *Public health communication: Evidence for behavior change* (pp. 35–56). Mahwah, NJ: Lawrence Erlbaum Associates, Inc.

Palmgreen, P., Donohew, L., Lorch, E. P., Rogus, M., Helm, D., & Grant, N. (1991). Sensation seeking, message sensation value, and drug use as mediators of PSA effectiveness. *Health Communication, 7,* 217–227.

Palmgreen, P., Lorch, E. P., Donohew, L., Harrington, N. G., Dsilva, M., & Helm, D. (1995). Reaching at-risk populations in a mass media drug abuse prevention campaign: Sensation seeking as a targeting variable. *Drugs and Society, 8,* 29–45.

Perry, C. L., Kelder, S. H., Murray, D. M., & Klepp, K. I. (1992). Communitywide smoking prevention: Long-term outcomes of the Minnesota Heart Health Program and the Class of 1989 Study. *American Journal of Public Health, 82,* 1210–1216.

Peterson, J. L., Moore, K. A., & Furstenberg, F. F. (1991). Television viewing and early initiation of sexual intercourse: Is there a link? *Journal of Homosexuality, 21,* 93–119.

Petty, R. E., & Cacioppo, J. T. (1986). *Communication and persuasion: Central and peripheral routes to attitude change.* New York: Springer-Verlag.

Pierce, J. P., Choi, W. S., Gilpin, E. A., Farkas, A. J., & Merritt, R. K. (1996). Validation of susceptibility as a predictor of which adolescents take up smoking in the United States. *Health Psychology, 15,* 893–899.

Pierce, J. P., Macaskill, P., & Hill, D. (2002). Long-term effectiveness of the early mass media led antismoking campaigns in Australia. In R. Hornik (Ed.), *Public health communication: Evidence for behavior change* (pp. 57–70). Mahwah, NJ: Lawrence Erlbaum Associates, Inc.

Priester, J. R. (2002). Sex, drugs, and attitudinal ambivalence: How feelings of evaluative tension influence alcohol use and safe sex behaviors. In W. D. Crano & M. Burgoon (Eds.), *Mass media and drug prevention: Classic and contemporary theories and research* (pp. 145–162). Mahwah, NJ: Lawrence Erlbaum Associates, Inc.

Prochaska, J. O., & DiClemente, C. C. (1983). *The transtheoretical approach.* Homewood, IL: Dow Jones-Irving.

Remez, L. (2000). *Oral sex among adolescents: Is it sex or is it abstinence? Family planning perspectives.* NY: Alan Guttmacher Institute.

Rice, R. E., & Atkin, C. (1994). Principles of successful public communication campaigns. In J. Bryant & D. Zillmann (Eds.), *Media effects: Advances in theory and research* (pp. 365–387). Hillsdale, NJ: Lawrence Erlbaum Associates.

Roberts, D. F., & Christenson, P. G. (2000). *"Here's looking at you, kid": Alcohol, drugs and tobacco in entertainment media.* Menlo Park, CA: Henry J. Kaiser Family Foundation.

Robinson, T. N., Chen, H. L., & Killen, J. D. (1998). Television and music video exposure and risk of adolescent alcohol use. *Pediatrics, 102,* 54–61.

Robinson, T. N., Hammer, L. D., Killen, J. D., Kraemer, H. C., Wilson, D. M., Hayward, C., et al. (1993). Does television viewing increase obesity among adolescent girls? *Pediatrics, 91,* 273–280.

Rogers, E. M., & Storey, J. D. (1987). Communication campaigns. In C. R. Berger & S. H. Chaffee (Eds.), *Handbook of communication science* (pp. 817–846). Newbury Park, CA: Sage.

Rosenstock, I. (1990). The health belief model: Explaining health behavior through expectancies. In K. Glanz, F. M. Lewis, & B. K. Rymer (Eds.), *Health behavior and health education: Theory, research and practice* (pp. 39–62). San Francisco: Jossey-Bass.

Rychtarik, R. G., Fairbank, J. A., Allen, C. M., Fox, D. W., & Drabman, R. S. (1983). Alcohol use in television programming: Effects on children's behavior. *Addictive Behaviors, 8,* 19–22.

Schilling, R. F., & McAlister, A. L. (1990). Preventing drug use in adolescents through media interventions. *Journal of Consulting and Clinical Psychology, 58,* 415–424.

Siegel, J. T., & Burgoon, J. K. (2002). Expectancy theory approaches to prevention: Violating adolescent expectations to increase the effectiveness of public service announcements. In W. D. Crano & M. Burgoon (Eds.), *Mass media and drug prevention: Classic and contemporary theories and research* (pp. 163–186). Mahwah, NJ: Lawrence Erlbaum Associates, Inc.

Siegel, M., & Biener, L. (2000). The impact of an antismoking media campaign on progression to established smoking: Results of a longitudinal youth study. *American Journal of Public Health, 90,* 380–386.

Signorielli, N. (1987). Drinking, sex, and violence on television: The cultural indicators perspective. *Journal of Drug Education, 17,* 245–260.

Singh, S., & Darroch, J. E. (1999). *Trends in sexual activity among adolescent women: 1982–1995. Family planning perspectives.* New York: Alan Guttmacher Institute.

Skinner, E. R., & Slater, M. D. (1995). Family communication patterns, rebelliousness, and adolescent reactions to antidrug PSAs. *Journal of Drug Education, 25,* 343–355.

Slater, M. (1996). Theory and method in health audience segmentation. *Journal of Health Communication, 1,* 267–283.

Slater, M. (1999). Integrating application of media effects, persuasion, and behavior change theories to communication campaigns: A stages-of-change framework. *Health Communication, 11,* 335–354.

Smith, W. (2002). From prevention *vaccines* to community *care:* New ways to look at program success. In R. C. Hornik (Ed.), *Public health communication: Evidence for behavior change* (pp. 327–356). Mahwah, NJ: Lawrence Erlbaum Associates, Inc.

Stephenson, M. T., Morgan, S. E., Lorch, E. P., Palmgreen, P., Donohew, L., & Hoyle, R. H. (2002). Predictors of exposure from an antimarijuana campaign: Outcome research assessing sensation seeking targeting. *Health Communication, 14,* 23–43.

Strasburger, V. C. (1989). Why just say no won't work. *Journal of Pediatrics, 114,* 676–681.

Strasburger, V. C. (1995). *Adolescents and the media: Medical and psychological impact.* Thousand Oaks, CA: Sage.

Taras, H. L., Sallis, J. F., Patterson, T. L., Nader, P. R., & Nelson, J. A. (1989). Television's influence on children's diet and physical activity. *Developmental and Behavioral Pediatrics, 10,* 176–180.

Tucker, L. A. (1985). Television's role regarding alcohol use among teenagers. *Adolescence, 20,* 593–598.

Wartella, E. A., & Stout, P. A. (2002). The evolution of mass media and health persuasion models. In W. D. Crano & M. Burgoon (Eds.), *Mass media and drug prevention: Classic and contemporary theories and research* (pp. 19–34). Mahwah, NJ: Lawrence Erlbaum Associates, Inc.

Worden, J. K., & Flynn, B. S. (2002). Using mass media to prevent cigarette smoking. In R. C. Hornik (Ed.), *Public health communication: Evidence for behavior change* (pp. 23–33). Mahwah, NJ: Lawrence Erlbaum Associates, Inc.

Zastowny, T. R., Adams, E. H., Black, G. S., Lawton, K. B., & Wilder, A. L. (1993). Sociodemographic and attitudinal correlates of alcohol and other drug use among children and adolescents: Analysis of a large-scale tracking study. *Journal of Psychoactive Drugs, 25,* 224–237.

Zuckerman, M. (1994). *Behavioral expressions and biosocial bases of sensation-seeking.* Cambridge, UK: Cambridge University Press.

Bibliography

1949 to 2005

Abel, J. D. (1968–1969). Television and children: A selective bibliography of use and effects. *Journal of Broadcasting, 13*, 101–105.

Abel, J. D. (1976). The family and child television viewing. *Journal of Marriage and the Family, 38*, 331–335.

Abel, J. D., & Beninson, M. E. (1976). Perceptions of TV program violence by children and mothers. *Journal of Broadcasting, 20*, 355–363.

Abelman, R. (1984). Children and TV: The ABCs of TV literacy. *Childhood Education, 60*, 200–205.

Abelman, R. (1985). Styles of parental disciplinary practices as a mediator of children's learning from prosocial television portrayals. *Child Study Journal, 15*, 131–146.

Abelman, R. (1986a). Children's awareness of television's prosocial fare: Parental discipline as an antecedent. *Journal of Family Issues, 7*, 51–66.

Abelman, R. (1986b). Children, television, and families: An evolution in understanding. *Television & Families, 9*, 2–55.

Abelman, R. (1989). From here to eternity: Children's acquisition of understanding of projective size on television. *Human Communication Research, 15*, 463–481.

Abelman, R. (1990a). Determinants of parental mediation of children's television viewing. In J. Bryant (Ed.), *Television and the American family* (pp. 311–328). Hillsdale, NJ: Lawrence Erlbaum Associates, Inc.

Abelman, R. (1990b). You can't get there from here: Children's understanding of time-leaps on television. *Journal of Broadcasting & Electronic Media, 34*, 469–476.

Abelman, R. (1995a). Gifted, LD, and gifted/LD children's understanding of temporal sequencing on television. *Journal of Broadcasting & Electronic Media, 39*, 297–312.

Abelman, R. (1995b). *Reclaiming the wasteland: TV & gifted children.* Cresskill, NJ: Hampton.

Abelman, R. (1999). Preaching to the choir: Profiling TV advisory ratings users. *Journal of Broadcasting & Electronic Media, 43*, 529–550.

Abelman, R. (2001). Parents' use of content-based TV advisories. *Parenting: Science & Practice*, *1*, 237–265.

Abelman, R., & Atkin, D. (2000). What children watch when they watch TV: Putting theory into practice. *Journal of Broadcasting & Electronic Media*, *44*, 143–154.

Acker, S. R. (1983). Viewers' perceptions of velocity and distance in televised events. *Human Communication Research*, *9*, 335–348.

Acker, S. R., & Tiemens, R. K. (1981). Children's perceptions of changes in size of televised images. *Human Communication Research*, *7*, 340–346.

Acland, C. R. (1992). Textual excess and articulations of gender in Pee-Wee's Playhouse. *Communication*, *13*(1), 21–38.

Adams, D., & Hamm, M. (1988). Video technology and moral development. *Social Studies*, *79*(2), 81–83.

Aday, S. (1998). Newspaper coverage of kids' TV. *Annals of the American Academy of Political Science*, *557*, 96–104.

Adler, R. P. (1975). *Television as a social force: New approaches to criticism*. New York: Praeger.

Adler, R. P. (1980). Children's television advertising: History of the issue. In E. L. Palmer & A. Dorr (Eds.), *Children and the faces of television: Teaching, violence, selling* (pp. 237–250). New York: Academic.

Adler, R. P., & Faber, R. J. (1980). Children's television viewing patterns. In R. P. Adler, G. S. Lesser, L. K. Meringoff, T. S. Robertson, J. R. Rossiter, & F. Ward (Eds.), *The effects of television advertising on children: Review and recommendations* (pp. 13–28). Thousand Oaks, CA: Sage.

Adler, R. P., Lesser, G. S., Meringoff, L. K., Robertson, T. S., Rossiter, J. R., & Ward, F. (1980). *The effects of television advertising on children: Review and recommendations*. Thousand Oaks, CA: Sage.

Adoni, H. (1979). Functions of mass media in the political socialization of adolescents. *Communication Research*, *6*, 84–106.

Aghi, M. (1979). The effectiveness of science education programming. *Journal of Communication*, *29*(4), 104–105.

Alali, A. O. (1991). *Mass media sex and adolescent values*. Jefferson, NC: McFarland.

Albada, K. F. (2000). The public and private dialogue about the American family on television. *Journal of Communication*, *50*(4), 79–110.

Albert, R. S., & Meline, H. (1958). The influence of social status on the uses of television. *Public Opinion Quarterly*, *22*, 145–151.

Alexander, A. (1981). Children, television and sex-role stereotyping. *Journal of Broadcasting*, *25*, 216–217.

Alexander, A. (1985). Adolescents' soap opera viewing and relational perceptions. *Journal of Broadcasting & Electronic Media*, *26*, 295–308.

Alexander, A. (1990). Television and family interaction. In J. Bryant (Ed.), *Television and the American family* (pp. 211–226). Hillsdale, NJ: Lawrence Erlbaum Associates, Inc.

Alexander, A. (1993). Exploring media in everyday life. *Communication Monographs*, *60*(1), 55–64.

Alexander, A. (1994). The effect of media on family interaction. In D. Zillmann, J. Bryant, et al. (Eds.), *Media, children, and the family: Social scientific, psychodynamic, and clinical perspectives* (pp. 51–59). Hillsdale, NJ: Lawrence Erlbaum Associates, Inc.

Alexander, A. (2001). The meaning of television in the American family. J. In Bryant & J. A. Bryant (Eds.), *Television and the American family*. (2nd ed., pp. 273–285). Mahwah, NJ: Lawrence Erlbaum Associates, Inc.

Alexander, A., Benjamin, L. M., Hoerrner, K. L., & Roe, D. (1999). "We'll be back in a moment": A content analysis of advertisements in children's telvision in the 1950s. In M. C. Macklin & L. Carlson (Eds.), *Advertising to children: Concepts and controversies* (pp. 97–115). Thousand Oaks, CA: Sage.

Alexander, A., Hoerrner, K., & Duke, L. (1998). What is quality children's television? *Annals of the American Academy of Political and Social Science, 557*, 70–82.

Alexander, A., & Morrison, M. A. (1995). Electric toyland and the structures of power: An analysis of critical studies on children as consumers. *Critical Studies in Mass Communication, 12*, 344–353.

Alexander, A., Ryan, M. S., & Munoz, P. (1984). Creating a learning context: Investigations on the interaction of siblings during television viewing. *Critical Studies in Mass Communication, 1*, 345–364.

Alexander, A., Wartella, E., & Brown, D. (1981). Estimates of children's television viewing by mother and child. *Journal of Broadcasting, 25*(3), 243–252.

Allen, R. L. (1993). Conceptual models of an African-American belief system: A program of research. In G. L. Berry & J. K. Asamen (Eds.), *Children and television: Images in a changing sociocultural world* (pp. 154–176). Newbury Park, CA: Sage.

Allison, A. (2000). A challenge to Hollywood? Japanese character goods hit the US. *Japanese Studies, 20*(1), 67–88.

Almarsdottir, A. B., & Bush, P. J. (1992). The influence of drug advertising on children's drug use attitudes and behaviors. *Journal of Drug Issues, 22*, 361–376.

Almeida, P. M. (1977). Children's television and modeling of pro-reading behaviors. *Education and Urban Society, 10*(1), 55–60.

Alper, W. S., & Leidy, T. R. (1970). The impact of information transmission through television. *Public Opinion Quarterly, 33*, 556–562.

Altheide, D. L. (1979). The mass media and youth culture. *Urban Education, 14*, 236–253.

Altheide, D. L. (2002). Children and the discourse of fear. *Symbolic Interaction, 25*, 229–250.

Alvarez, M., Huston, A. C., Wright, J. C., & Kerkman, D. D. (1988). Gender differences in visual attention to television form and content. *Journal of Applied Developmental Psychology, 9*, 459–475.

Alwitt, L. F., Anderson, D. R., Lorch, E. P., & Levin, S. R. (1980). Preschool children's visual attention to attributes of television. *Human Communication Research, 7*, 52–67.

Anand, S., & Krosnick, J. A. (2005). Demographic predictors of media use among infants, toddlers, and preschoolers. *American Behavioral Scientist, 48*, 539–561.

Anast, P. (1966). Personal determinants of mass media preferences. *Journalism Quarterly, 43*, 729–732.

Andersen, R. E., Crespo, C., Bartlett, S. J., Cheskin, L. J., & Pratt, M. (1998). Relationship of physical activity and television watching with body weight and level of fatness among children: Results from the third national health and nutrition examination survey. *Journal of the American Medical Association, 279*, 938–942.

Andersen, R. E., Crespo, C., Bartlett, S. J., & Pratt, M. (1998). Television watching and fatness in children. *Journal of the American Medical Association, 280,* 1231–1232.

Anderson, C. (1997). Violence in television commercials during nonviolent programming. The 1996 Major League Baseball playoffs. *The Journal of the American Medical Association, 278,* 1045–1046.

Anderson, C. A., Berkowitz, L., Donnerstein, E., Huesmann, L. R., Johnson, J. D., Linz, D., et al. (2003). The influence of media violence on youth. *Psychological Science in the Public Interest, 4*(3), 81–110.

Anderson, D., & Smith, R. (1984). Young children's TV viewing: The problem of cognitive continuity. In F. Morrison, C. Lord, & D. Keating (Eds.), *Advances in applied developmental psychology* (Vol. 1, pp. 115–163). New York: Academic.

Anderson, D. R. (1998). Educational television is not an oxymoron. *Annals of the American Academy of Political and Social Science, 557,* 24–38.

Anderson, D. R. (2003). Children's Television Act: A public policy that benefits children. *Journal of Applied Developmental Psychology, 24,* 337–340.

Anderson, D. R. (2004). Watching children watch television and the creation of *Blue's Clues.* In H. Hendershot (Ed.), *Nickelodeon nation* (pp. 241–268). New York: New York University Press.

Anderson, D. R., Alwitt, L. F., Lorch, E. P., & Levine, S. R. (1979). Watching children watch television. In G. Hale & M. Lewis (Eds.), *Attention and the development of cognitive skills.* New York: Plenum.

Anderson, D. R., Bryant, J., Wilder, A., Santomero, A., Williams, M., & Crawley, A. M. (2000). Researching Blue's Clues: Viewing behavior and impact. *Media Psychology, 2,* 179–194.

Anderson, D. R., Choi, H., & Lorch, E. P. (1987). Attentional inertia reduces distractability during young children's television viewing. *Child Development, 58,* 798–806.

Anderson, D. R., & Evans, M. K. (2001). Peril and potential of media for infants and toddlers. *Zero to Three, 22*(2), 10–16.

Anderson, D. R., Field, D. E., Collins, P. A., Lorch, E. P., & Nathan, J. G. (1985). Estimates of young children's time with television. *Child Development, 56,* 1345–1357.

Anderson, D. R., Huston, A. C., Schmitt, K. L., Linebarger, D. L., & Wright, J. C. (2001a). Early childhood television viewing and adolescent behavior: The recontact study. *Monographs of the Society for Research in Child Development , 66*(1), vii–147.

Anderson, D. R., Huston, A. C., Schmitt, K. L., Linebarger, D. L., & Wright, J. C. (2001b). *Early childhood television viewing and adolescent behavior: The recontact study.* Boston: Blackwell.

Anderson, D. R., Levin, S. R., & Lorch, E. (1977). The effects of television program pacing in the behavior of preschool children. *Communication Review, 25,* 159–166.

Anderson, D. R., & Lorch, E. P. (1983). Looking at television: Action or reaction? In J. Bryant & D. R. Anderson (Eds.), *Children's understanding of TV: Research on attention and comprehension* (pp. 1–33). New York: Academic.

Anderson, D. R., Lorch, E. P., Field, D. E., Collins, P. A., & Nathan, J. G. (1986). Television viewing at home: Age trends in visual attention and time with television. *Child Development, 57,* 1024–1033.

Anderson, D. R., Lorch, E. P., Field, D. E., & Sanders, J. (1981). The effects of TV program comprehensibility on preschool children's visual attention to television. *Child Development, 52,* 151–157.

Anderson, D. R., Lorch, E. P., Smith, R., Bradford, R., & Levin, S. R. (1981). Effects of peer presence on preschool children's television-viewing behavior. *Developmental Psychology, 17,* 446–453.

Anderson, D. R., & Pempek, T. A. (2005). Television and very young children. *American Behavioral Scientist, 48,* 505–522.

Anderson, J. A. (1972). Television and growing up: Impact of televised violence. *Journal of Broadcasting, 16,* 224–227.

Anderson, J. A. (1981). Research on children and television—a critique. *Journal of Broadcasting, 25,* 395–400.

Anderson, J. A., Meyer, T. P., & Hexamer, A. (1982). An examination of the assumptions underlying telecommunications social policies treating children as a specialized audience. In M. Burgoon (Ed.), *Communication yearbook* (Vol. 6, pp. 369–384). New Brunswick NJ: Transaction Books.

Anderson, J. A., & Ploghoft, M. E. (1993). Children and media in media education. In G. L. Berry & J. K. Asamen (Eds.), *Children and television: Images in a changing sociocultural world* (pp. 89–102). Newbury Park, CA: Sage.

Anderson, J. E. (1950). Psychological aspects of child audiences. *Educational Theatre Journal, 2,* 285–291.

Anderson, K., Comstock, G., & Dennis, H. (1976). Priorities and recommendations: Research on television and the young. *Journal of Communication, 26(2),* 98–107.

Anderson, K. J., & Cavallaro, D. (2002). Parents or pop culture? Children's heroes and role models. *Childhood Education, 78(3),* 161–168.

Anderson, W. H., & Williams, B. M. (1983). Television and the Black child. *Journal of Black Psychology, 9,* 27–42.

Andison, F. S. (1977). Television violence and viewer aggression: A cumulation of study results. *Public Opinion Quarterly, 41,* 314–331.

Andreasen, M. S. (1990). Evolution in the family's use of television: Normative data from industry and academe. In J. Bryant (Ed.), *Television and the American family* (pp. 3–58). Hillsdale, NJ: Lawrence Erlbaum Associates, Inc.

Andreasen, M. S. (1994). Patterns of family life and television consumption . In D. Zillmann, J. Bryant, & A. C. Huston (Eds.), *Media, children, and the family: Social scientific, psychodynamic, and clinical perspectives* (pp. 19–36). Hillsdale, NJ: Lawrence Erlbaum Associates, Inc.

Andreasen, M. S. (2001). Evolution in the family's use of television: An overview. In J. Bryant, & J. A. Bryant (Eds.), *Television and the American family* (2nd ed., pp. 3–32). Mahwah, NJ: Lawrence Erlbaum Associates, Inc.

Andrews, J. (1980). Our eyes are always on television: Deaf teens survey peers. *American Annals of the Deaf, 125,* 1082–1085.

Andsager, J., & Roe, K. (2003). "What's your definition of dirty, baby?": Sex in music videos. *Sexuality and Culture: An Interdisciplinary Quarterly, 7(3),* 79–97.

Andsager, J. L., Austin, E. W., & Pinkleton, B. E. (2001). Questioning the value of realism: Young adults' processing of messages in alcohol-related public service announcements and advertising. *Journal of Communication, 51,* 121–142.

Andsager, J. L., Austin, E. W., & Pinkleton, B. E. (2002). Gender as a variable in interpretation of alcohol-related messages. *Communication Research, 29,* 246–269.

Appell, C. T. (1960). Television's impact upon middle class family life. *Teachers College Record, 61,* 265–274.

Appell, C. T. (1963). Television viewing and the preschool child. *Marriage and Family Living, 25,* 311–318.

Argenta, D. M., Stoneman, Z., & Brody, G. H. (1986). The effects of three different television programs on young children's peer interactions and toy play. *Journal of Applied Developmental Psychology, 7,* 355–371.

Armstrong, C. A., Sallis, J. F., Alcaraz, J. E., Kolody, B., McKenzie, T. L., & Hovell, M. (1998). Children's television viewing, body fat, and physical fitness. *American Journal of Health Promotion, 12,* 363–368.

Armstrong, G. B., Boiarsky, G. A., & Mares, M.-L. (1991). Background television and reading performance. *Communication Monographs, 58,* 235–253.

Armstrong, G. B., & Greenberg, B. S. (1990). Background television as an inhibitor of cognitive processing. *Human Communication Research, 16,* 355–386.

Armstrong, G. B., Neuendorf, K., & Brentar, J. E. (1992). TV entertainment, news, and racial perceptions of college students. *Journal of Communication, 42*(3), 153–176.

Arnett, J. J. (1995). Adolescents' use of media for self-socialization. *Journal of Youth & Adolescence, 24,* 519–533.

Arnett, J. J., Larson, R., & Offer, D. (1995). Beyond effects: Adolescents as active media users. *Journal of Youth & Adolescence, 24*(5), 511–518.

Arnold, A. (1969). *Violence and your child.* New York: Award.

Asamen, J. K., & Berry, G. L. (1993). *Research paradigms, television and social behavior.* Thousand Oaks, CA: Sage.

Atherson, M. J., & Metcalf, J. (2005). Television watching and risk of obesity in American adolescents. *American Journal of Health Education, 36*(1), 2–7.

Atkin, C. K. (1977). Effects of campaign advertising and newscasts on children. *Journalism Quarterly, 54,* 503–508.

Atkin, C. K. (1978a). Broadcast news programming and the child audience. *Journal of Broadcasting, 22*(1), 47–61.

Atkin, C. K. (1978b). Effects of drug commercials on young viewers. *Journal of Communication, 28*(4), 71–79.

Atkin, C. K. (1983). Effects of realistic television violence vs. fictional violence on aggression. *Journalism Quarterly, 60,* 615–621.

Atkin, C. K. (1990). Effects of televised alcohol messages on teenage drinking patterns. *Journal of Adolescent Health Care, 11*(1), 10–24.

Atkin, C. K., & Gantz, W. (1978). Television news and political socialization. *Public Opinion Quarterly, 42,* 183–198.

Atkin, C. K., Greenberg, B., Korzenny, F., & McDermott, S. (1979). Selective exposure to televised violence. *Journal of Broadcasting, 23*(1), 5–13.

Atkin, C. K., Greenberg, B. S., & McDermott, S. T. (1983). Television and race role socialization. *Journalism Quarterly, 60,* 407–414.

Atkin, C. K., & Heald, G. (1977). The content of children's toy and food commercials. *Journal of Communication, 27*(1), 107–114.

Atkin, C. K., Hocking, J., & Block, M. (1984). Teenage drinking: Does advertising make a difference? *Journal of Communication, 34*(1), 157–167.

Atkin, C. K., Murray, J. P., & Nayman, O. B. (1971). The Surgeon General's research program on television and social behavior: A review of empirical findings. *Journal of Broadcasting, 16*(1), 21–35.

Atkin, D. J. (2001). Home ecology and children's television viewing in the new media environment. In J. Bryant & J. A. Bryant (Eds.), *Television and the American family* (2nd ed., pp. 49–74). Mahwah, NJ: Lawrence Erlbaum Associates, Inc.

Atkin, D. J., Greenberg, B. S., & Baldwin, T. F. (1991). The home ecology of children's television viewing: Parental mediation and the new video environment. *Journal of Communication, 41*(3), 40–52.

Atkin, D. J., Heeter, C., & Baldwin, T. (1989). How presence of cable affects parental mediation of TV viewing. *Journalism Quarterly, 66,* 557–578.

Atkin, D. J., & Lin, C. A. (1988). Children's programming reconsidered. *Communications & the Law, 10,* 3–17.

Atwood, J. D., & Donnelly, J. W. (2002). The children's war: Their reactions to devastating events. *Family Journal, 10*(1), 11–18.

Atwood, L. E. (1968). Perception of television program preferences among teenagers and their parents. *Journal of Broadcasting, 12,* 377–388.

Atwood, R., Allen, R., Bardgett, R., Proudlove, S., & Ridr, R. (1982). Children's realities in television viewing: Exploring situation information seeking. In M. Burgoon (Ed.), *Communication Yearbook,* (Vol. 6, pp. 605–626). Beverly Hills, CA: Sage.

Aubrey, J. S. (2004). Sex and punishment: An examination of sexual consequences and the sexual double standard in teen programming. *Sex Roles, 50,* 505–514.

Aubrey, J. S., & Harrison, K. (2004). The gender-role content of children's favorite television programs and its links to their gender-related perceptions. *Media Psychology, 6*(2), 111–146.

Aubrey, J. S., Harrison, K., Kramer, L., & Yeltin, J. (2003). Variety versus timing: Gender differences in college students' sexual expectations as predicted by exposure to sexually-oriented television. *Communication Research, 30,* 432–460.

Aufderheide, P. (1989). Reregulating children's television. *Federal Communications Law Journal, 42*(1), 87–106.

Austin, B. A. (1984). Motivations for television viewing among deaf and hearing students. *American Annals of the Deaf, 129*(1), 17–22.

Austin, E. W. (1992). Parent-child TV interaction: The importance of perspective. *Journal of Broadcasting & Electronic Media, 36,* 359–361.

Austin, E. W. (1993). Exploring the effects of active parental mediation of television content. *Journal of Broadcasting & Electronic Media, 37,* 147–158.

Austin, E. W. (2001). Effects of family communication on children's interpretation of television. In J. Bryant & J. A. Bryant (Eds.), *Television and the American family* (2nd ed., pp. 377–396). Mahwah, NJ: Lawrence Erlbaum Associates, Inc.

Austin, E. W., Bolls, P., Fujioko, Y., & Englebertson, J. (1999). How and why parents take on the tube. *Journal of Broadcasting & Electronic Media, 43,* 175–192.

Austin, E. W., & Johnson, K. K. (1997). Immediate and delayed effects of media literacy training on third graders' decision making for alcohol. *Health Communication, 9,* 323–349.

Austin, E. W., Knaus, C., & Meneguelli, A. (1997). Who talks how to their children about television: A clarification of demographic correlates of parental mediation practices. *Communication Research Reports, 14,* 418–430.

Austin, E. W., & Meili, H. K. (1994). Effects of interpretations of televised alcohol portrayals on children's alcohol beliefs. *Journal of Broadcasting & Electronic Media, 38*, 417–435.

Austin, E. W., & Nach-Ferguson, B. (1995). Sources and influences of young school-age children's general and brand-specific knowledge about alcohol. *Health Communication, 7*(1), 1–20.

Austin, E. W., Roberts, D. F., & Nass, C. I. (1990). Influences of family communication on children's television-interpretation processes. *Communication Research, 17*, 545–564.

Auty, S., & Lewis, C. (2004). Exploring children's choices: The reminder effect of product placement. *Psychology & Marketing, 21*, 697–713.

Avery, R. K. (1979). Adolescents' use of the mass media. *American Behavioral Scientist, 23*(1), 53–70.

Axelson, J. M., & Del Campo, D. S. (1978). Improving teenagers' nutrition knowledge through the mass media. *Journal of Nutrition Education, 10*(1), 30–33.

Ayers, J. B., & Ayers, M. N. (1977). Influence of advertising on spelling in the elementary grades. *Reading Improvement, 14*(2), 116–119.

Babies, toddlers & the media. (2001). *Zero to Three, 22*(2), 4–41.

Babrow, A. S., O'Keefe, B. J., Swanson, D. L., Meyers, R. A., & Murphy, M. A. (1988). Person perception and children's impressions of television and real peers. *Communication Research, 15*, 680–698.

Bachen, C. M. (1998). Channel One and the education of American youths. *Annals of the American Academy of Political Science, 557*, 132–147.

Bailyn, L. (1959). Mass media and children: A study of exposure habits and cognitive effects. *Psychological Monographs, 73*(1). Whole No. 47.

Balance, W. D. G., Coughlin, D., & Bringmann, W. G. (1972). Examiniation of social context effects upon affective responses to "hot" and "cool" communications media. *Psychological Reports, 31*, 793–794.

Ballard, I. M., Jr. (1995). See no evil, hear no evil: Television violence and the First Amendment. *Virginia Law Review, 81*, 175–222.

Balogh, J. K. (1958). Attitudinal and preferential factors of selected male high school students with respect to television viewing. *AV Communication Review, 6*, 203–206.

Balogh, J. K. (1959). Television-viewing habits of high school boys. *Educational Research Bulletin, 38*, 66–71.

Bandura, A. (1965). Vicarious processes: A case on no-trial learning. In L. Berkowitz (Ed.), *Advances in experimental social psychology*. New York: Academic.

Bandura, A. (1968). What TV violence can do to your child. In O. N. Larsen (Ed.), *Violence and the mass media* (pp. 123–130). New York: Harper & Row.

Banet-Weiser, S. (2004). Girls rule! Gender, feminism and Nickelodeon. *Critical Studies in Media Communication, 21*(2), 119–139.

Banet-Weiser, S. (2004). "We pledge allegiance to kids": Nickelodeon and citizenship. In H. Hendershot (Ed.), *Nickelodeon nation* (pp. 209–237). New York: New York University Press.

Banks, M. J. (2004). A boy for all planets: *Roswell, Smallville* and the teen male melodrama. In G. Davis & K. Dickinson (Eds.), *Teen TV: Genre, consumption, identity* (pp. 54–67). London: British Film Institute.

Banks, S. (1980). Children's television viewing behavior. *Journal of Marketing, 44*, 48–55.

Banks, S., & Gupta, R. (1980). Television as a dependent variable, for a change. *Journal of Consumer Research, 7*, 327–330.

Banning, E. L. (1955). Social influences on children and youth. *Review of Educational Research, 25*, 36–47.

Baran, S. J. (1973). TV and social learning in the institutionalized MR. *Mental Retardation, 11*, 36–38.

Baran, S. J. (1974). Prosocial and antisocial television content and modeling by high and low self-esteem children. *Journal of Broadcasting, 18*, 481–495.

Baran, S. J. (1976a). How TV and film portrayals affect sexual gratification in college students. *Journalism Quarterly, 53*, 468–473.

Baran, S. J. (1976b). Sex on TV and adolescent sexual self-image. *Journal of Broadcasting, 20*, 61–68.

Baran, S. J. (1977). Television programs as socializing agents for mentally retarded children. *Communication Review, 25*, 281–289.

Baran, S. J. (1979). Television programs about retarded children and parental attitudes toward their own retarded children. *Mental Retardation, 17*(4), 193–194.

Baran, S. J., Chase, L., & Courtright, J. A. (1979). Television drama as a facilitator of prosocial behavior: "The Waltons." *Journal of Broadcasting, 23*, 277–284.

Baran, S. J., & Meyer, T. P. (1974). Imitation and identification: Two compatible approaches to social learning from the electronic media. *AV Communication Review, 22*, 167–178.

Baran, S. J., & Meyer, T. P. (1976). Retarded children's perceptions of favorite television characters as behavioral models. *Mental Retardation, 13–14*, 28–31.

Baranowski, M. D. (1971). Television and the adolescent. *Adolescence, 6*(23), 369–396.

Barcus, F. E. (1969). Parental influence in children's television viewing. *Television Quarterly, 8*, 63–73.

Barcus, F. E. (1973). Saturday's kidvid ghetto. In R. Glessing & W. P. White (Eds.), *Mass media: The invisible environment* (pp. 142–148). Chicago: Science Research Associates,

Barcus, F. E. (1977). Ethical problems in television advertising to children. In B. Rubin (Ed.), *Questioning media ethics* (pp. 133–148). New York: Praeger.

Barcus, F. E. (1980). The nature of television advertising to children. In E. L. Palmer & A. Dorr (Eds.), *Children and the faces of television: Teaching, violence, selling* (pp. 273–285). New York: Academic.

Barcus, F. E. (1983). *Images of life in children's television: Sex roles, minorities, and families.* New York: Praeger.

Barcus, F. E., & Wolkin, R. (1977). *Children's television: An analysis of programming and advertising.* New York: Praeger.

Barling, J., & Fullagar, C. (1983). Children's attitudes to television advertisements: A factorial perspective. *Journal of Psychology, 113*, 25–30.

Barlow, T., & Wogalter, M. S. (1993). Alcoholic beverage warnings in magazine and television advertisements. *Journal of Consumer Research, 20*, 147–156.

Barner, M. R. (1999). Sex-role stereotyping in FCC-mandated children's educational television. *Journal of Broadcasting & Electronic Media, 43*, 551–564.

Baron, L. J. (1980). Interaction between television and child-related characteristics as demonstrated by eye movement research. *Educational Communication and Technology: A Journal of Theory, Research and Development, 28*, 267–281.

Baron, L. J., & Bernard, R. M. (1982). Children's perception of television time: An exploratory investigation. *Psychological Reports, 50*(3, Part 2), 1275–1283.

Barr, R., & Hayne, H. (1999). Developmental changes in imitation from television during infancy. *Child Development, 70*, 1067–1081.

Barrow, L. C., & Westley, B. H. (1959a). Comparative teaching effectiveness of radio and television. *AV Communication Review, 7*, 14–23.

Barrow, L. C., & Westley, B. H. (1959b). Intelligence and the effectiveness of radio and television. *AV Communication Review, 7*, 193–208.

Barrow, L. C., & Westley, B. H. (1960). Exploring the news: An experiment in the relative effectiveness of radio and TV versions of a children's news program. In W. Schramm (Ed.), *The impact of educational television* (pp. 143–150). Urbana: University of Illinois Press.

Barry, T. E. (1978). Children's television advertising: The attitudes and opinions of elementary school guidance counselors. *Journal of Advertising, 7*(4), 9–16.

Barry, T. E. (1980). A framework for ascertaining deception in children's advertising. *Journal of Advertising, 9*(1), 11–18.

Barry, T. E., & Hansen, R. (1973). How race affects children's TV commercials. *Journal of Advertising Research, 13*(5), 63–67.

Barry, T. E., & Sheikh, A. (1977). Race as a dimension in children's TV advertising: The need for more research. *Journal of Advertising, 6*(3), 5–10.

Bassett, H. T., Cowden, J. E., & Cohen, M. E. (1968). The audiovisual viewing habits of selected subgroups of delinquents. *Journal of Genetic Psychology, 112*, 37–41.

Battin, T. (1953). The use of the diary and survey method involving the question-naire-interview technique to determine the impact of television on school children in regard to viewing habits and formal and informal education. *Speech Monographs, 20*.

Baucum, D. G., Smith, A. E., & Weisberg, P. (1974). Elimination of disturbing nap-time behaviors of preschool children through the withdrawal and representation of TV audio reception. *Psychological Reports, 35*(1, Part 1), 51–56.

Bauman, K. E., La Prelle, J., Brown, J. D., Koch, G. G., & Padgett, C. A. (1991). The influence of three mass media campaigns on variables related to adolescent cigarette smoking: Results of a field experiment. *American Journal of Public Health, 81*, 597–604.

Baxter, W. S. (1960). The mass media and young people. *Journal of Broadcasting, 5*, 49–58.

Beagles-Roos, J., & Gat, I. (1983). Specific impact of radio and television on children's story comprehension. *Journal of Educational Psychology, 75*(1), 128–137.

Bearden, W. O., Teel, J. E., & Wright, R. R. (1979). Family income effects in measurement of children's attitudes toward television commercials. *Journal of Consumer Research, 6*, 308–311.

Bearinger, L. H. (1990). Study group report on the impact of television on adolescent views of sexuality. *Journal of Adolescent Health Care, 11*, 71–75.

Bearison, D. J., Bain, J. M., & Daniele, R. (1982). Developmental changes in how children understand television. *Social Behavior & Personality*, *10*, 133–144.

Beaudoin, C. E. (2002). Exploring antismoking ads: Appeals, themes, and consequences. *Journal of Health Communication*, *7*, 123–137.

Becker, G. (1972). Causal analysis in R-R studies: Television violence and aggression. *American Psychologist*, *27*, 967–968.

Becker, S. L., & Wolfe, G. J. (1960). Can adults predict children's interest in a television program? In W. Schramm (Ed.), *The impact of educational television* (pp. 195–213). Urbana: University of Illinois Press.

Beentjes, J. W. J., & van der Voort, T. H. A. (1988). Television's impact on children's reading skills: A review of the literature. *Reading Research Quarterly*, *23*(4), 57–81.

Beentjes, J. W. J., & van der Voort, T. H. A. (1996). Combining background media with doing homework: Incidence of background media use and perceived effects. *Communication Education*, *45*, 59–72.

Beentjes, J. W. J., Vooijis, M. W. & van der Voort, T. H. A. (1993). Children's recall of televised and printed news as a function of test expectation. *Journal of Educational Television*, *19*, 5–13.

Behnke, R. R., & Miller, P. (1992). Viewer reactions to content and presentational format of television news. *Journalism Quarterly*, *69*, 659–665.

Bell, K. (1980). Young adults and what TV is doing for them. *English Journal*, *69*(9), 82–84.

Belson, W. A. (1960). The effects of television upon family life. *Discovery*, *21*, 426–430.

Belton, T. (2000a). The "Face at the Window" study: A fresh approach to media influence and to investigating the influence of television and videos on children's imagination. *Media, Culture & Society*, *22*, 629–643.

Belton, T. (2000b). Reading beneath the lines of children's stories. *Educational Research*, *42*, 629–644.

Belton, T. (2001). Television and imagination: An investigation of the medium's influence on children's story-making. *Media, Culture & Society*, *23*, 799–820.

Benedek, E. P., & Brown, C. F. (1999). No excuses: Televised pornography harms children. *Harvard Review of Psychiatry*, *7*, 236–240.

Bergen, L., & Grimes, T. (1999). The reification of normalcy. *Journal of Health Communication*, *4*, 211–226.

Berkowitz, L. (1962). Violence in the mass media. In L. Berkowitz (Ed.), *Aggression: A social psychological analysis* (pp. 229–255). New York: McGraw-Hill.

Berkowitz, L. (1964). The effects of observing violence. *Scientific American*, *21*(2), 35–41.

Berkowitz, L. (1984). Some effects of thoughts on anti- and prosocial influences of media events. *Psychological Bulletin*, *95*, 410–427.

Berkowitz, L. (1986). Situational influences on reactions to observed violence. *Journal of Social Issues*, *42*(3), 93–106.

Berkowitz, L. (1988). Frustrations, appraisals, and aversely stimulated aggression. *Aggressive Behavior*, *14*(1), 3–11.

Berman, A. (1988). Fictional depiction of suicide in television films and imitation effects. *American Journal of Psychiatry*, *145*, 982–986.

Berman, D. R., & Stookey, J. A. (1980). Adolescents, television and support for government. *Public Opinion Quarterly*, *44*, 330–340.

Bernard, P. A., Johnston, C., Curtis, S. E., & King, W. D. (1998). Toppled television sets cause significant pediatric morbidity and mortality. *Pediatrics, 102,* E321–E324.

Bernhardt, J. M., Sorenson, J. R., & Brown, J. D. (2001). When the perpetrator gets killed: Effects of observing the death of a handgun user in a televised public service announcement. *Health Education and Behavior, 28*(1), 81–94.

Berry, G. L. (1977). Television and the urban child: Some educational policy implications. *Education and Urban Society, 10*(1), 31–54.

Berry, G. L. (2003). Developing children and multicultural attitudes: The systemic psychosocial influences of television portrayals in a multimedia society. *Cultural Diversity & Ethnic Minority Psychology, 9,* 360–366.

Berry, G. L. (1980a). Children, television and social class roles: The medium as unplanned educational curriculum. In E. L. Palmer & A. Dorr (Eds.), *Children and the faces of television: Teaching, violence, selling* (pp. 71–81). New York: Academic.

Berry, G. L. (1980b). Television and Afro-Americans: Past legacy and present portrayals. In S. B. Withey & R. P. Abeles (Eds.), *Television and social behavior: Beyond violence and children* (pp. 131–248). Hillsdale, NJ: Lawrence Erlbaum Associates, Inc.

Berry, G. L. (1988). Multicultural role portrayals on television as a social psychological issue. *Applied Social Psychology Annual, 8,* 118–129.

Berry, G. L. (1993a). The medium of television and the school curriculum: Turning research into classroom practice. In G. L. Berry & J. K. Asamen (Eds.), *Children & television: Images in a changing sociocultural world* (pp. 103–113). Thousand Oaks, CA: Sage.

Berry, G. L. (1993b). Public television programming and the changing cultural landscape. In G. L. Berry & J. K. Asamen (Eds.), *Children & television: Images in a changing sociocultural world* (pp. 291–295). Thousand Oaks, CA: Sage.

Berry, G. L. (1998). Black family life on television and the socialization of the African American child: Images of marginality. *Journal of Comparative Family Studies, 29,* 233–242.

Berry, G. L., & Asamen, J. K. (1993). *Children and television: Images in a changing sociocultural world.* Newbury Park, CA: Sage.

Berry, G. L., & Mitchell-Kernan, C. (1982). *Television and the socialization of the minority child.* New York: Academic.

Besco, G. S. (1952). Television and its effects on other related interests of high school pupils. *English Journal, 41,* 151–152.

Beuf, A. (1974). Doctor, lawyer, household drudge. *Journal of Communication, 24*(2), 142–145.

Bever, T. G., Smith, M., Bengen, B., & Johnson, T. G. (1975). Young viewers' troubling response to TV ads. *Harvard Business Review, 53*(6), 109–120.

Bickham, D. S., Vandewater, E., Huston, A. C., Lee, J. H., Caplovitz, A. G., & Wright, J. C. (2003). Predictors of children's electronic media use: An examination of three ethnic groups. *Media Psychology, 5,* 107–138.

Bijmolt, T. H. A., Claassen, W., & Brus, B. (1998). Children's understanding of TV advertising: Effects of age, gender, and parental influence. *Journal of Consumer Policy, 21,* 171–194.

Bilowit, D. W., & Ganek, L. B. (1980). Critical television viewing skills for the middle grades. *Television and Children, 3*(2), 40–44.

Birchall, C. (2004). "Feels like home": *Dawson's Creek*, nostalgia and the young adult viewer. In G. Davis & K. Dickinson (Eds.), *Teen TV: Genre, consumption, identity* (pp. 176–189). London: British Film Institute.

Birnbaum, E. (1951). TV programs worthy of our children. *American Teacher, 35*, 6–7.

Bishop, B. R., & Stumphauser, J. S. (1973). Behavior therapy of thumbsucking in children: A punishment (time-out and generalization effect: What's a mother to do?). *Psychological Reports, 33*, 939–944.

Bishop, J. M., & Krause, D. R. (1984). Depictions of aging and old age on Saturday morning television. *Gerontologist, 24*(1), 91–95.

Bishop, L., Boersma, N., & Williams, J. (1969). Teenagers and news media: Credibility canyon. *Journalism Quarterly, 46*, 597–599.

Bishop, R. (2003). The world's nicest grown-up: A fantasy theme analysis of news media coverage of Fred Rogers. *Journal of Communication, 53*(1), 16–32.

Bither, S. W. (1972). Effects of distraction and commitment on the persuasiveness of television advertising. *Journal of Marketing Research, 9*(2), 1–5.

Bittner, J. R., Anatol, K. W., & Seiler, W. J. (1969). College student exposure to mass media news. *College Student Survey, 3*, 46–48.

Blackwell, J., & Yawkey, T. (1975). An investigation of television programming and advertising for young children. *Journal of Instructional Psychology, 2*(1), 28–32.

Blanchard-Fields, F., & Mathews, R. (1986). Inferencing and television: A developmental study. *Journal of Youth & Adolescence, 15*, 453–459.

Blood, R. O., Jr. (1961). Social class and family control of television viewing. *Merrill-Palmer Quarterly, 7*, 205–222.

Bloom, P. M., Hogan, J. E., & Blazing, J. (1997). Sports promotion and teen smoking and drinking: An exploratory study. *American Journal of Health Behavior, 21*(2), 100–109.

Bloome, D., & Ripich, D. (1979). Language in children's television commercials: A sociolinguistic perspective. *Theory Into Practice, 18*, 220–225.

Blosser, B. J. (1988). Ethnic differences in children's media use. *Journal of Broadcasting & Electronic Media, 32*, 453–470.

Blosser, B. J., & Roberts, D. F. (1985). Age differences in children's perception of message intent: Responses to television news, commercials, educational spots, and public service announcements. *Communication Research, 12*, 455–484.

Bluem, A. W. (1967). Media mononucleosis. *Television Quarterly, 6*(4), 45–51.

Bluestone, G. (1966). Life, death and nature in children's TV. In P. D. Hazard (Ed.), *TV as art: Some essays in criticism*. Champaign, IL: National Council of Teachers of English.

Blumenfield, W. S. (1964). Some correlates of TV medical drama viewing. *Psychological Reports, 15*, 901–902.

Blumenfield, W. S., & Remmers, H. H. (1966). Television program preferences and their relationship to self-reported high school grades. *Journal of Educational Research, 59*, 358–359.

Boemer, M. L. (1984). An analysis of the violence content of the radio thriller dramas—And some comparisons with television. *Journal of Broadcasting, 28*, 341–353.

Bogart, L. (1972a). Television and the juvenile audience. In *The age of television: A study of viewing habits and the impact of television on American life* (pp. 245–289). New York: Frederick Ungar. (Original work published 1956)

Bogart, L. (1972b). Warning, the Surgeon General has determined that TV violence is moderately dangerous to your child's mental health. *Public Opinion Quarterly, 36*, 491–521.

Boles, J., & Burton, S. (1992). An examination of free elicitation and response scale measures of feelings and judgments evoked by television advertisements. *Journal of the Academy of Marketing Science, 20*, 225–233.

Bolick, T., & Nowicki, S., Jr. (1984). The incidence of external locus of control in televised cartoon characters. *Journal of Genetic Psychology, 144*, 99–104.

Bolton, R. N. (1983). Modeling the impact of television food advertising in children's diets. *Current Issues and Research in Advertising, 6*, 173–199.

Bontinck, I. (1986). The impact of electronic media on adolescents, their everyday experiences, their learning orientations and leisure time activities. *Communications, 12*(1), 21–30.

Booth, G. D., & Muller, H. (1974). Effectiveness of monochrome and color presentations in facilitating affective learning. *Communication Review, 22*, 409–422.

Booth-Butterfield, M., & Duppstadt, R. D. (1991). Content analysis of shyness portrayals in television advertising. *Communication Research Reports, 8*(1–2), 33–39.

Bordeaux, B. R. (1986). Television viewing patterns of hospitalized school-aged children and adolescents. *Children's Health Care, 15*, 70–75.

Bordeaux, B. R., & Lange, G. (1991). Children's reported investment of mental effort when viewing television. *Communication Research, 18*, 617–635.

Borzekowski, D. L. G., & Robinson, T. N. (1999). Viewing the viewers: Ten video cases of television viewing behaviors. *Journal of Broadcasting & Electronic Media, 43*, 506–528.

Borzekowski, D. L., & Robinson, T. N. (2001). The 30-second effect: An experiment revealing the impact of television commercials on food preferences of preschoolers. *Journal of the American Dietetic Association, 101*, 42–46.

Botta, R. A. (1999). Television images and adolescent girls' body image disturbance. *Journal of Communication, 49*(2), 22–41.

Boudreau, D. (2005). Use of a parent questionnaire in emergent and early literacy assessment of preschool children. *Language, Speech, & Hearing Services in Schools, 36*(1), 33–48.

Boush, D. M. (2001). Mediating advertising effects. In J. Bryant, & J. A. Bryant (Eds.), *Television and the American family* (2nd ed., pp. 397–414). Mahwah, NJ: Lawrence Erlbaum Associates, Inc.

Boush, D. M., Friestad, M., & Rose, G. M. (1994). Adolescent skepticism toward TV advertising and knowledge of advertiser tactics . *Journal of Consumer Research, 21*, 165–175.

Boutwell, W. D. (1962). *Using mass media in the schools.* New York: Appleton-Century-Crofts.

Boyatzis, C. J., Matillo, G., & Nesbitt, K. (1995). Effects of "The Mighty Morphin Power Rangers" on children's aggression with peers. *Child Study Journal, 25*(1), 45–55.

Boynton-Jarrett, R., Thomas, T. N., Peterson, K. E., Wiecha, J., Sobol, A. M., & Gortmaker, S. L. (2003). Impact of television viewing patterns on fruit and vegetable consumption among adolescents. *Pediatrics, 112*, 1321–1327.

Breen, M. P., & Powell, J. T. (1973). The relationship between attractiveness and credibility of television commercials as perceived by children. *Central States Speech Journal, 24,* 97–102.

Brodbeck, A. J., & Jones, D. B. (1963). Television viewing and the norm-violating practices and perspectives of adolescents: A synchronized depth and scope program of policy research. In L. A. Arons & M. A. May (Eds.), *Television and human behavior: Tomorrow's research in mass communication* (pp. 98–137). New York: Appleton-Century-Crofts.

Brodie, J. F. (1972). Drug abuse and television viewing patterns. *Psychology, 9*(2), 33–36.

Brody, G. H., Stoneman, Z., & Sanders, A. K. (1980). Effects of television viewing in family interactions: An observational study. *Family Relations, 29,* 216–220.

Brooker, W. (2001). Living on Dawson's Creek: Teen viewers, cultural convergence, and television overflow. *International Journal of Cultural Studies, 4,* 456–472.

Brooks, P. H., Gaines, L. S., Mueller, R., & Jenkins, S. (1998). Children's television watching and their father's drinking practices. *Addiction Research, 6*(1), 27–34.

Brouwer, M. (1964). Mass communication and the social sciences: Some neglected areas. In L. A. Dexter & D. M. White (Eds.), *People, society, and mass communications* (pp. 547–567). New York: Free Press.

Brown, B. W. (1982). Family intimacy in advertising. *Journal of Communication, 32*(3), 173–183.

Brown, D., & Bryant, J. (1990). Effects of television on family values and selected attitudes and behaviors. In J. Bryant (Ed.), *Television and the American family* (pp. 253–174). Hillsdale, NJ: Lawrence Erlbaum Associates, Inc.

Brown, D., & Hayes, T. (2001). Family attitudes toward television. In J. Bryant & J. A. Bryant (Eds.), *Television and the American family* (2nd ed., pp.111–138). Mahwah, NJ: Lawrence Erlbaum Associates, Inc.

Brown, J. A. (1991). *Television "critical viewing skills" education.* Hillsdale, NJ: Lawrence Erlbaum Associates, Inc.

Brown, J. D. (2002). Mass media influences on sexuality. *Journal of Sex Research, 39*(1), 42–45.

Brown, J. D., Barton White, A., & Nikopoulou, L. (1993). Disinterest, intrigue, resistance: Early adolescent girls' use of sexual media content. In B. S. Greenberg, J. D. Brown, & N. L. Buerkel-Rothfuss (Eds.), *Media, sex and the adolescent* (pp. 177–195). Cresskill, NJ: Hampton.

Brown, J. D., Childers, K. W., Bauman, K. E., & Koch, G. G. (1990). The influence of new media and family structure on young adolescents' television and radio use. *Communication Research, 17,* 65–82.

Brown, J. D., Childers, K. W., & Waszak, C. S. (1990). Television and adolescent sexuality. *Journal of Adolescent Health Care, 11*(1), 62–70.

Brown, J. D., & Newcomer, S. F. (1991). Television viewing and adolescents' sexual behavior. *Journal of Homosexuality, 21*(1–2), 77–91.

Brown, J. D., & Pardun, C. J. (2004). Little in common: Racial and gender differences in adolescents' television diets. *Journal of Broadcasting & Electronic Media, 48,* 266-278.

Brown, J. D., & Schulze, L. (1993). The effects of race, gender, and fandom on audience interpretation of Madonna's music videos. In B. S. Greenberg, J. D. Brown, & N. L. Buerkel-Rothfuss (Eds.), Media, sex and the adolescent (pp. 264–274). Cresskill, NJ: Hampton.

Brown, J. D., & Stern, S. R. (2002). Mass media and adolescent female sexuality: Handbook of women's sexual and reproductive health. In G. M. Wingood & R. J. DiClemente (Eds.), Handbook of women's sexual and reproductive health (pp. 93–112). New York: Kluwer Academic/Plenum.

Brown, J. D., & Witherspoon, E. M. (2002). The mass media and American adolescents' health. Journal of Adolescent Health, 31, 153–170.

Brown, J. R., Cramond, J. K., & Wilde, R. J. (1974). Displacement effects of television and the child's functional orientation to the media. In J. Blumler & E. Katz (Eds.), The uses of mass communications: Current perspectives on gratifications research (pp. 93–112). Beverly Hills, CA: Sage.

Brown, L. K. (1988). Fiction for children: Does the medium matter? Journal of Aesthetic Education, 22(1), 35–44.

Brown, M. H., Skeen, P., & Osborn, D. K. (1979). Young children's perception of the reality of television. Contemporary Education, 50(3), 129–133.

Brown, R. (1976). Children and television. Thousand Oaks CA: Sage.

Brown, W. S. (2002). Ethics and the business of children's public television programming. Teaching Business Ethics, 6(1), 73–81.

Browne, B. A. (1998). Gender stereotypes in advertising on children's television in the 1990's: A cross-national analysis. Journal of Advertising, 27(1), 83–96.

Bruce, D. R. (2001). Notes toward a rhetoric of animation: The Road Runner as cultural critique. Critical Studies in Media Communication, 18, 229–245.

Brucks, M., Armstrong, M. E., & Goldberg, M. E. (1988). Children's use of cognitive defenses against television advertising: a cognitive response approach. Journal of Consumer Research, 14, 471–482.

Brumbaugh, F. N. (1954). What effect does TV advertising have on children? Educational Digest, 19, 32–33.

Bruyn, H. B. (1978). TV's effect on children: An opinion survey of pediatricians. Journal of School Health, 48, 474–476.

Bryan, J. H. (1971). Model affect and children's imitative altruism. Child Development, 42, 2061–2065.

Bryan, J. H., Sherman, R. E., & Fisher, A. (1980). Learning disabled boys' nonverbal behaviors within a dyadic interview. Learning Disability Quarterly, 3(1), 65–72.

Bryant, J. (1990). Television and the American family. Thousand Oaks, CA: Sage.

Bryant, J., & Anderson, D. R. (Eds.). (1983). Children's understanding of television: Research on attention and comprehension . New York: Academic.

Bryant, J., Aust, C. F., Bryant, A., & Benugopalan, G. (2001). How psychologically healthy are America's prime-time television families? In J. Bryant & J. A. Bryant (Eds.), Television and the American family (2nd ed., pp. 247–272). Mahwah, NJ: Lawrence Erlbaum Associates, Inc.

Bryant, J., & Bryant, J. A. (Eds.). (2001). Television and the American family (2nd ed.). Mahwah, NJ : Lawrence Erlbaum Associates, Inc.

Bryant, J., Hezel, R., & Zillmann, D. (1979). Humor in children's educational television. Communication Education, 28, 49–59.

Bryant, J., Parks, S. L., & Zillmann, D. (1983). Children's imitation of a ridiculed model. *Human Communication Research, 10,* 243–255.

Bryant, J., & Rockwell, S. C. (1994). Effects of massive exposure to sexually-oriented primetime television programming on adolescents' moral judgement. In D. Zillmann, J. Bryant, & A. C. Huston (Eds.), *Media, children and the family: Social scientific, psychodynamic, and clinical perspectives* (pp. 183–198). Hillsdale, NJ: Lawrence Erlbaum Associates, Inc.

Bryant, J., Zillmann, D., & Brown, D. (1983). *Entertainment features in children's educational television: Effects on attention and information acquisition.* New York: Academic.

Bryant, J. A., Bryant, J., Mullikin, L., McCollum, J. F., & Love, C. C. (2001). Curriculum-based preschool television programming and the American family: Historical development, impact of public policy, and social and educational effects. In J. Bryant & J. A. Bryant (Eds.), *Television and the American family* (2nd ed., pp. 415–433). Mahwah, NJ: Lawrence Erlbaum Associates, Inc.

Bryant, W. K., & Gremer, J. L. (1981). Television use by adults and children—A multivariate analysis. *Journal of Consumer Research, 8,* 154–161.

Buchholz, L. M., & Smith, R. E. (1991). The role of consumer involvement in determining cognitive response to broadcast advertising. *Journal of Advertising, 20*(1), 4–17.

Buerkel-Rothfuss, N. L. (1993). Background: What prior research shows. In B. S. Greenberg, J. D. Brown, & N. L. Buerkel-Rothfuss (Eds.), *Media, sex and the adolescent* (pp. 5–18). Cresskill, NJ: Hampton.

Buerkel-Rothfuss, N. L., & Buerkel, R. A. (2001). Family mediation. In J. Bryant & J. A. Bryant (Eds.), *Television and the American family* (2nd ed., pp. 355–376). Mahwah, NJ: Lawrence Erlbaum Associates, Inc.

Buerkel-Rothfuss, N. L., Greenberg, B. S., Atkin, C. K., & Nuendorf, K. (1982). Learning about the family from television. *Journal of Communication, 32*(3), 191–201.

Buerkel-Rothfuss, N. L., & Strouse, J. S. (1993). Media exposure and perceptions of sexual behaviors: The cultivation hypothesis moves to the bedroom. In B. S. Greenberg, J. D. Brown, & N. L. Buerkel-Rothfuss (Eds.), *Media, sex and the adolescent* (pp. 225–263). Cresskill, NJ: Hampton.

Buerkel-Rothfuss, N. L., Strouse, J. S., Pettey, G., & Shatzer, M. (1993). Adolescents' and young adults' exposure to sexually oriented and sexually explicit media. In B. S. Greenberg, J. D. Brown, & N. L. Buerkel-Rothfuss (Eds.), *Media, sex and the adolescent* (pp. 99–114). Cresskill, NJ: Hampton.

Buijzen, M., & Valkenburg, P. M. (2000). The impact of television advertising on children's Christmas wishes. *Journal of Broadcasting & Electronic Media, 44,* 456–470.

Buijzen, M., & Valkenburg, P. M. (2003). The unintended effects of television advertising. *Communication Research, 30,* 483–503.

Burr, P. L., & Burr, R. (1977a). Parental responses to child marketing. *Journal of Advertising Research, 17*(6), 17–20.

Burr, P. L., & Burr, R. (1976). Television advertising to children: What parents are saying about government control. *Journal of Advertising, 5*(4), 37–41.

Burr, P. L., & Burr, R. (1977b). Product recognition and premium appeal. *Journal of Communication, 27*(1), 115–117.

Burton, S. G., Calonico, J. M., & McSeveney, D. R. (1979). Effects of preschool television watching on first grade children. *Journal of Communication, 29*(3), 164–170.

Busby, L. J. (1974). Defining the sex-role standard in network children's programs. *Journalism Quarterly, 51*(4), 690–696.

Busby, L. J. (1975). Sex-role research on the mass media. *Journal of Communication, 25*(4), 107–131.

Bush, A. J., Smith, R., & Martin, C. (1999). The influence of consumer socialization variables on attitude toward advertising: A comparison of African-Americans and Caucasians. *Journal of Advertising, 28*(3), 13–24.

Bushman, B. J., & Bonacci, A. M. (2002). Violence and sex impair memory for television ads. *Journal of Applied Psychology, 87,* 557–564.

Bushman, B. J., & Cantor, J. (2003). Media ratings for violence and sex: Implications for policymakers and parents. *American Psychologist, 58,* 130–141.

Bushman, B. J., & Huesmann, L. R. (2001). Effects of televised violence on aggression. In D. G. Singer & J. L. Singer (Eds.), *Handbook of children and the media* (pp. 223–254). Thousand Oaks, CA: Sage.

Busselle, R. W. (2003). Television exposure, parents' precautionary warnings and young adults' perceptions of crime. *Communication Research, 30,* 530–557.

Butsch, R. (2001). A history of research on movies, radio, and television. *Journal of Popular Film & Television, 29*(3), 112–120.

Butter, E. J., Popovich, P. M., Stackhouse, R. H., & Garner, R. K. (1981). Discrimination of television programs and commercials by preschool children. *Journal of Advertising Research, 2*(2), 53–56.

Butter, E. J., Weikel, K. B., Otto, V., Wright, K. P., & Deinzer, G. (1991). TV advertising of OTC medicines and its effects on child viewers. *Psychology & Marketing, 8,* 117–128.

Bybee, C., Robinson, J. D., & Turow, J. (1982). Determinants of parental guidance of children's television viewing for a special subgroup: Mass media scholars. *Journal of Broadcasting, 26,* 697–710.

Bybee, C., Robinson, J. D., & Turow, J. (1985). The effects of television on children: What the experts believe. *Communication Research Reports, 2,* 149–155.

Byrd-Bredbenner, C. (2002). Saturday morning children's television advertising: A longitudinal content analysis. *Family and Consumer Sciences Research Journal, 30,* 382–403.

Byrd-Bredbenner, C., & Grasso, D. (2000a). Health, medicine, and food messages in television commercials during 1992 and 1998. *Journal of School Health, 70,* 61–65.

Byrd-Bredbenner, C., & Grasso, D. (2000b). What is television trying to make children swallow? Content analysis of the nutrition information in prime-time advertisements. *Journal of Nutrition Education, 32,* 187–195.

Byrne, G. C. (1969). Mass media and political socialization of children and pre-adults. *Journalism Quarterly, 46,* 140–142.

Cagley, J. (1974). Children's preferences of selected print appeals. *Journal of Advertising, 3*(4), 34–39.

Calder, B. J., Robertson, T. S., & Rossiter, J. R. (1975). Children's consumer information processing. *Communications Research, 2,* 307–316.

Calder, B. J., & Sternthal, B. (1980). Television commercial wear out: An information processing view. *Journal of Marketing Research, 27,* 173–186.

Caldwell, D. C. (1973). Use of graded captions with instructional television for deaf learners. *American Annals of the Deaf, 118*, 500–507.

Calfin, M. S., Carroll, J. L., & Schmidt, J. (1993). Viewing music-video tapes before taking a test of premarital sexual attitudes. *Psychological Reports, 72*, 475–481.

Calvert, S. L. (1988). Television production feature effects on children's comprehension of time. *Journal of Applied Developmental Psychology, 9*, 263–273.

Calvert, S. L. (1999a). *Children's journeys through the information age.* Boston: McGraw-Hill College.

Calvert, S. L. (1999b). The form of thought. In I. Sigel (Ed.), *Development of mental representation: Theories and applications* (pp. 453–470). Mahwah NJ: Lawrence Erlbaum Associates, Inc.

Calvert, S. L. (2001). Impact of televised songs on children's and young adults' memory of educational content. *Media Psychology, 3*, 325–342.

Calvert, S. L., & Gersh, T. L. (1987). The selective use of sound effects and visual inserts for children's television story comprehension. *Journal of Applied Developmental Psychology, 8*, 363–375.

Calvert, S. L., & Huston, A. C. (1987). Television and children's gender schemata. *New Directions for Child Development, 38*, 75–88.

Calvert, S. L., Huston, A. C., Watkins, B. A., & Wright, J. C. (1982). The relation between selective attention to television forms and children's comprehension of content. *Child Development, 53*, 601–610.

Calvert, S. L., Huston, A. C., & Wright, J. C. (1987). Effects of television preplay formats on children's attention and story comprehension. *Journal of Applied Developmental Psychology, 8*, 329–342.

Calvert, S. L., Kondla, T. A., Ertel, K. A., & Meisel, D. S. (2001). Young adult's perceptions and memories of a televised woman hero. *Sex Roles, 45*(1–2), 31–53.

Calvert, S. L., & Kotler, J. A. (2003a). The Children's Television Act: Can media policy make a difference. *Journal of Applied Developmental Psychology, 24*, 375–380.

Calvert, S. L., & Kotler, J. A. (2003b). Lessons from children's television: The impact of the Children's Television Act on children's learning. *Journal of Applied Developmental Psychology, 24*, 275–336.

Calvert, S. L., Kotler, J., Kuhl, A., & Riboli, M. (2001). *Impact of the Children's Television Act on children's learning.* Greensboro, NC: Smith Richardson Foundation.

Calvert, S. L., Kotler, J. A., Murray, W. F., Gonzales, E., Savoye, K., Hammack, P., et al. (2001). Children's online reports about educational and informational television programs. *Journal of Applied Developmental Psychology, 22*, 103–117.

Calvert, S. L., Kotler, J. A., Zehnder, S. M., & Shockey, E. M. (2003). Gender stereotyping in children's reports about educational and informational television programs. *Media Psychology, 5*, 139–173.

Calvert, S. L., & Scott, C. (1989). Sound effects for children's temporal integration of fast-paced television content. *Journal of Broadcasting & Electronic Media, 33*, 233–246.

Calvert, S. L., & Tart, M. (1993). Song versus verbal forms for very-long-term, long term and short term verbatim recall. *Journal of Applied Developmental Psychology, 14*, 245–260.

Cameron, G. T., Schleuder, J., & Thorson, E. (1991). The role of news teasers in processing TV news and commercials. *Communication Research, 18*, 667–684.

Campbell, N. (2004). "Teensomething": American youth programming in the 1990s. In N. Campbell (Ed.), *American youth cultures* (pp. 155–181). Edinburgh, Scotland: Edinburgh University Press.

Campbell, R. (2001). Demons, aliens, teens and television. *Television Quarterly, 31*(4), 56–64.

Campbell, T. A., Wright, A. C., & Huston, A. C. (1987). Form cues and content difficulty as determinants of children's cognitive processing of televised educational messages. *Journal of Experimental Child Psychology, 43*, 311–327.

Cantor, J. (1978). Research on television's effects on children. *Phaedrus, 5*(1), 9–13.

Cantor, J. (1981). Modifying children's eating habits through television ads—Effects of humorous appeals in a field setting. *Journal of Broadcasting, 25*(1), 37–47.

Cantor, J. (1991). Fright responses to mass media productions. In J. Bryant & D. Zillmann (Eds.), *Responding to the screen: Reception and reaction processes* (pp. 169–197). Hillsdale, NJ: Lawrence Erlbaum Associates, Inc.

Cantor, J. (1992). Children's emotional responses to technological disasters conveyed by the mass media. In J. M. Wober (Ed.), *Television and nuclear power: Making the public mind* (pp. 31–53). Norwood, NJ: Ablex.

Cantor, J. (1994). Confronting children's fright responses to mass media. In D. Zillmann & J. Bryant (Eds.), *Media, children, and the family: Social scientific, Psychodynamic, and clinical perspectives* (pp. 139–150). Hillsdale, NJ: Lawrence Erlbaum Associates, Inc.

Cantor, J. (1996). Television and children's fear. In T. M. MacBeth (Ed.), *Tuning into young viewers: Social science perspectives on television* (pp. 87–115). Thousand Oaks, CA: Sage.

Cantor, J. (1998a). Children's attraction to violent television programming. In J. H. Goldstein (Ed.), *Why we watch: The attractions of violent entertainment* (pp. 88–115). New York: Oxford University Press.

Cantor, J. (1998b). *"Mommy, I'm scared"; How TV and movies frighten children and what we can do to protect them.* New York: Harcourt Brace.

Cantor, J. (1998c). Ratings for program content: The role of research findings. *Annals of the American Academy of Political Science, 557*, 54–69.

Cantor, J. (2000). Media violence. *Journal of Adolescent Health, 27*(Suppl.), 30–34.

Cantor, J., & Hoffner, C. (1990). Children's fear reactions to a televised film as a function of perceived immediacy of depicted threat. *Journal of Broadcasting & Electronic Media, 34*, 421–442.

Cantor, J., & Mares, M.-L. (2001). Effects of television on child and family emotional well-being. In J. Bryant & J. A. Bryant (Eds.), *Television and the American family* (2nd ed., pp. 317–332). Mahwah, NJ: Lawrence Erlbaum Associates, Inc.

Cantor, J., Mares, M.-L., & Hyde, J. S. (2003). Autobiographical memories of exposure to sexual media content. *Media Psychology, 5*, 1–31.

Cantor, J., Mares, M. L., & Oliver, M. B. (1993). Parent's and children's emotional reactions to TV coverage. In B. S. Greenberg & W. Gantz (Eds.), *Desert Storm and the mass media* (pp. 325–340). Cresskill, NJ: Hampton.

Cantor, J., & Nathanson, A. I. (1996). Children's fright reactions to television. *Journal of Communication, 46*(4), 139–152.

Cantor, J., & Nathanson, A. I. (1997). Predictors of children's interest in violent television programs. *Journal of Broadcasting & Electronic Media, 41*, 155–167.

Cantor, J., & Omdahl, B. (1991). Effects of fictional media depictions of realistic threats on children's emotional responses, expectations, worries, and liking for related activities. *Communication Monographs, 58*, 384–401.

Cantor, J., & Omdahl, B. L. (1999). Children's acceptance of safety guidelines after exposure to televised dramas depicting accidents. *Western Journal of Communication, 63*(1), 57–71.

Cantor, J., & Reilly, S. (1982). Adolescents' fright reactions to television and films. *Journal of Communication, 32*(1), 87–99.

Cantor, J., & Sparks, G. (1984). Children's fear responses to mass media: Testing some Piagetian predictions. *Journal of Communication, 34*(1), 90–103.

Cantor, J., Sparks, G. G., & Hoffner, C. (1988). Calming children's television fears: Mr. Rogers vs. the Incredible Hulk. *Journal of Broadcasting & Electronic Media, 32*, 271–288.

Cantor, J., & Wilson, B. J. (1984). Modifying fear responses to mass media in preschool and elementary school children. *Journal of Broadcasting, 28*, 432–443.

Cantor, J., & Wilson, B. J. (1988). Helping children cope with frightening media presentations. *Current Psychological Research and Reviews, 7*(1), 58–75.

Cantor, J., & Wilson, B. J. (2003). Media and violence: Intervention strategies for reducing aggression. *Media Psychology, 5*, 363–403.

Cantor, J., Wilson, B. J., & Hoffner, C. (1986). Emotional responses to a televised nuclear holocaust film. *Communication Research, 13*, 257–277.

Cantor, M. G. (1971). *The Hollywood TV producer.* New York: Basic Books.

Cantor, M. G. (1974). Producing television for children. In G. Tuchman (Ed.), *The TV establishment.* (pp. 103–118). Englewood Cliffs, NJ: Prentice-Hall.

Cantor, M. G., & Orwant, J. (1980). Differential effects of television violence on girls and boys. *Studies in Communications, 1*, 63–68.

Cappella, J. N., Fishbein, M. H., Ahern, R., Kirkland, R., & Sayeed, S. (2001). Using theory to select messages in antidrug media campaigns: Reasoned action and media priming. In R. E. Rice & C. K. Atkin (Eds.), *Public communication campaigns* (3rd ed., pp. 214–230). Thousand Oaks, CA: Sage.

Carlson, J. M. (1983). Crime show viewing by preadults: The impact on attitudes toward civil liberties. *Communication Research, 10*, 529–552.

Carlson, L., Grossbart, S., & Walsh, A. (1990). Mother's communication orientation and consumer-socialization tendencies. *Journal of Advertising, 19*(3), 27–38.

Carlson, L., Laczniak, R. N., & Muehling, D. D. (1994). Understanding parental concern about toy-based programming: New insights from socialization theory. *Journal of Current Issues and Research in Advertising, 16*(2), 58–72.

Carlson, L., Laczniak, R. N., & Walsh, A. (2001). Socializing children about television: An intergenerational study. *Journal of the Academy of Marketing Science, 29*, 276–288.

Caron, A. H. (1979). First time exposure to television—effects on Inuit children's cultural images. *Communication Research, 6*, 135–154.

Caron, A. H., & Ward, S. (1975). Gift decisions by kids and parents. *Journal of Advertising Research, 15*(4), 15–20.

Carpenter, C. R. (1955). Psychological research using television. *American Psychologist, 10*, 606–610. ·

Carpenter, C. J., Huston, A. C., & Spera, L. (1989). Children's use of time in their every day activities during middle childhood In M. Bloch & A. Pellegrini (Eds.), *The ecological context of Children's play* (pp. 165–190). Norwood NJ: Ablex.

Carruth, B. R., Goldberg, D., & Skinner, J. (1991). Do parents and peers mediate the influence of television advertising on food related purchases. *Journal of Adolescent Research, 6*, 253–271.

Cassidy, K. L., Reid, G. J., McGrath, P. J., Finley, G. A., Smith, D. J., Morley, C., et al. (2002). Watch needle, watch TV: Audiovisual distraction in preschool immunization. *Pain Medicine, 3*, 108–118.

Cater, D., & Strickland, S. (1975). *TV violence and the child: The evolution and fate of the Surgeon General's Report*. New York: Russell Sage Foundation.

Caution, G. (1984). The effects of television advertisements on Black children. *Psychiatric Forum, 12*(2), 72–81.

Celozzi, M. J., Kazelskis, R., & Gutsch, K. V. (1981). The relationship between viewing televised violence in ice hockey and subsequent levels of personal aggression. *Journal of Sport Behavior, 4*, 157–162.

Centerwall, B. S. (1989a). *Exposure to television as a cause of violence*. New York: Academic.

Centerwall, B. S. (1989b). Exposure to television as a risk factor for violence. *American Journal of Epidemiology, 129*, 643–652.

Centerwall, B. S. (1994). Television and the development of the superego: Pathways to violence. In C. Chiland & J. G. Young (Eds.), *Children and violence*. The Child in the Family: The Monograph Series of the International Association for Child and Adolescent Psychiatry and Allied Professions (Vol. 11, pp. 178–197). Northvale, NJ: Aronson.

Certain, L. K., & Kahn, R. S. (2002). Prevalence, correlates, and trajectory of television viewing among infants and toddlers. *Pediatrics, 109*, 634–642.

Chaffee, S. H., & Atkin, C. K. (1971). Parental influences on adolescent media use. In F. G. Kline & P. Clarke (Eds.), *Mass communication and youth: Some current perspectives* (pp. 21–38). Beverly Hills, CA: Sage.

Chaffee, S. H., McLeod, J. M., & Atkin, C. K. (1972). Parental influences in adolescent media use. *American Behavioral Scientist, 14*, 323–340.

Chaffee, S. H., McLeod, J. M., & Wackman, D. B. (1973). Family communication patterns and adolescent political participation. In J. Dennis (Ed.), *Socialization to politics: A reader* (pp. 349–364). New York: Wiley.

Chaffee, S. H., & Tims, A. (1976). Interpersonal factors in adolescent television use. *Journal of Social Issues, 32*(4), 98–115.

Chaffee, S. H., Ward, L. S., & Tipton, L. P. (1973). Mass communication and political socialization. In J. Dennis (Ed.), *Socialization to politics: A reader* (pp. 391–409). New York: Wiley.

Chan-Olmsted, S. M. (1996). From Sesame Street to Wall Street: An analysis of market competition in commercial children's television. *Journal of Broadcasting & Electronic Media, 40*, 30–44.

Chandler, D. (1997). Children's understanding of what is 'real' on television: A review of the literature. *Journal of Educational Media, 23*(1), 65–80.

Chandler, M., Greenspan, S., & Barenboim, C. (1973). Judgments of intentionality in response to videotaped and verbally presented moral dilemmas: The medium is the message. *Child Development, 44,* 315–320.

Chandler, T. M., & Heinzerling, B. M. (1999). *Children and adolescents in the market place: Twenty-five years of academic research.* Ann Arbor, MI: The Pierian Press.

Chaney, D. C. (1970). Involvement, realism and the perception of aggression in television programs. *Human Relations, 23,* 373–381.

Chang, N. (2000). Reasoning with children about violent television shows and related toys. *Early Childhood Education Journal, 28*(2), 85–89.

Chapin, J. R. (1999). Third-person perception and sexual risk taking among minority "at-risk" youth. *Mass Communication & Society, 2,* 163–173.

Chapin, J. R. (2000). Adolescent sex and mass media: A developmental approach. *Adolescence, 35,* 799–811.

Charren, P., Gelber, A., & Arnold, M. (1994). Media, children, and violence—A public policy perspective. *Pediatrics, 94,* 631–637.

Chavez, E. L., Hamilton, S. B., & Keilin, W. G. (1986). The day after: A preliminary report on its effects on children. *American Psychologist, 41,* 722–723.

Cheles-Miller, P. (1975). Reactions to marital roles in commercials. *Journal of Advertising Research, 15*(4), 45–49.

Cheng, T. L., Brenner, R. A., Wright, J. L., Sachs, H. S., Moyer, P., & Rao, M. R. (2004). Children's violent television viewing: Are parents monitoring? *Pediatrics, 114,* 94–99.

Chiland, C., Young, J. G., & Kaplan, D. (1994). *Children and violence.* Northvale, NJ: Aronson.

Childers, P. R., & Ross, J. (1973). The relationship between viewing television and student achievement. *Journal of Educational Research, 66,* 317–319.

Children, adolescents, and television. (2001). *Pediatrics, 107,* 423–426.

Chisholm, A. (2002). Acrobats, contortionists, and cute children: The promise and perversity of U.S. women's gymnastics. *Signs: Journal of Women in Culture & Society, 27,* 415–450.

Choate, R. B. (1980). The politics of change. In E. L. Palmer & A. Dorr (Eds.), *Children and the faces of television: Teaching, violence, selling* (pp. 323–338). New York: Academic.

Choate, R. B., & Debevoise, N. M. (1976). Caution! Keep this commercial out of reach of children. *Journal of Drug Issues.*

Choi, H. P., & Anderson, D. R. (1991). A temporal analysis of free toy play and distractibility in young children. *Journal of Experimental Child Psychology, 52,* 41–69.

Christakis, D. A., Zimmerman, F. J., DiGuiseppe, D. L., & McCarty, C. A. (2004). Early television exposure and subsequent attentional problems in children. *Pediatrics, 113,* 708–714.

Christenson, P. G. (1982). Children's perceptions of TV commercials and products: The effects of PSA's. *Communication Research, 9,* 491–524.

Christenson, P. G. (1985). Children and commercials: The relationship between general trust and specific influence. *Communication Research Reports, 2*(1), 41–45.

Christenson, P. G. (1992). Preadolescent perceptions and interpretations of music videos. *Popular Music and Society, 16*(3), 63–74.

Christenson, P. G., & Roberts, D. F. (1983). The role of television in the formation of children's social attitudes. In M. J. A. Howe (Ed.), *Learning from television* (pp. 79–99). New York: Academic.

Christiansen, J. B. (1979). Television role models and adolescent occupational goals. *Human Communication Research, 5*, 335–337.

Churchill, G. A., Jr., & Moschio, G. P. (1979). Television and interpersonal influences in adolescent consumer learning. *Journal of Consumer Research, 6*, 23–35.

Cirino, P. (1977). *Mass media for the young: We're being more than entertained.* Honolulu, HI: Lighthouse Press.

Clancy-Hepburn, K., Hickey, A., & Neville, G. (1974). Children's behavior responses to TV food advertisements. *Journal of Nutrition Education, 6*(3), 93–96.

Clark, C. C. (1969). Television and social control: Some observations on the portrayal of ethnic minorities. *Television Quarterly, 8*, 18–122.

Clarke, A. T., & Kutz-Costes, B. (1997). Television viewing, educational quality of the home environment and school readiness. *Journal of Educational Research, 90*, 279–285.

Clarke, P. (1971a). Children's response to entertainment. In F. G. Kline & P. Clarke (Eds.), *Mass communication and youth: Some current perspectives* (pp. 51–67). Beverly Hills, CA: Sage.

Clarke, P. (1971b). Children's response to entertainment: Effects of co-orientation on information-seeking. *American Behavioral Scientist, 14*, 353–369.

Clarke, P. (1971c). Introduction: Some proposals for continuing research on youth and the mass media. *American Behavioral Scientist, 14*, 313–322.

Cline, V. (1974). *Where do you draw the line?* Provo, UT: Brigham Young University Press.

Cline, V., Croft, R., & Courrier, S. (1973). Desensitization of children to television violence. *Journal of Personality and Social Psychology, 27*, 360–365.

Clinton, S. (1975). Television as a behavior model: Results of research with children. *American Education, 11*, 40.

Coates, F. (1954). Parents and America's first TV generation. *National Council Outlook, 4*, 9–10.

Coats, E. J., & Feldman, R. S. (1995). The role of television in the socialization of nonverbal behavioral skills. *Basic & Applied Social Psychology, 17*, 327–341.

Coats, E. J., Feldman, R. S., & Philippot, P. (1999). The influence of television on children's nonverbal behavior. In P. Philippot & R. S. Feldman (Eds.), *The social context of nonverbal behavior* (pp. 156–181). New York: Cambridge University Press.

Cobb, N. J., Stevens-Long, J., & Goldstein, S. (1982). The influence of televised models on toy preference in children. *Sex Roles, 8*, 1075–1080.

Coffey, S., & Stipp, H. (1997). The interactions between computer and television usage. *Journal of Advertising Research, 37*(2), 61–67.

Coffin, T. E. (1955). Television's impact on society. *American Psychologist, 10*, 630–641.

Coffin, T. E., & Tuchman, S. (1973). Rating television programs for violence: Comparison of five surveys. *Journal of Broadcasting, 17*(1), 3–20.

Cohen, A., & Adoni, H. (1980). Children's fear responses to real-life violence on television: The cast of the 1973 Middle East War. *Communications, 6*(1), 81–93.

Cohen, A., Adoni, H., & Drori, G. (1983). Adolescents' perceptions of social conflicts in television news and social reality. *Human Communication Research, 10,* 203–225.

Cohen, A., & Salomon, G. (1979). Children's literate television viewing: Surprises and possible explanations. *Journal of Communication, 29*(3), 156–163.

Cohen, A., Wigand, R. T., & Harrison, R. (1976). The effects of emotion-arousing events of children's learning from TV news. *Journalism Quarterly, 52,* 204–210.

Cohen, A., Wigand, R. T., & Harrison, R. (1977). The effects of type of event proximity and retention in children's attention to and learning from television news. *Communications, 3*(1), 30–46.

Cohen, J. (1997). Parasocial relations and romantic attraction: Gender and dating status. *Journal of Broadcasting & Electronic Media, 41,* 516–529.

Collins, R. L., Elliot, M. N., Berry, S. H., Kanouse, D. E., & Hunter, S. B. (2003). Entertainment television as a healthy sex educator: The impact of condom efficacy information in an episode of *Friends. Pediatrics, 112* (5), 1115–1122.

Collins, R. L., Elliot, M. N., Berry, S. H., Kanouse, D. E., Kunkel, D., Hunter, S. B., et al. (2004). Watching sex on television predicts adolescent initiation of sexual behavior. *Pediatrics, 114,* e280–e289.

Collins, R. L., Schell, T., Ellickson, P. L., & McCaffrey, D. (2003). Predictors of beer advertising awareness among eighth graders. *Addiction, 98,* 1297–1306.

Collins, W. A. (1970). Learning of media content: A developmental study. *Child Development, 41,* 1133–1142.

Collins, W. A. (1973). Effect of temporal separation between motivation, aggression, and consequences: A developmental study. *Developmental Psychology, 8,* 215–221.

Collins, W. A. (1975). The developing child as viewer. *Journal of Communication, 25*(4), 35–44.

Collins, W. A. (1978). Temporal integration and children's understanding of social information on television. *American Journal of Orthopsychiatry, 48,* 198–204.

Collins, W. A. (1979). Children's comprehension of television content. In E. Wartella (Ed.), *Children communicating: Media and development of thought, speech and understanding* (pp. 21–52). Beverly Hills, CA: Sage.

Collins, W. A. (1981a). Recent advances in research on cognitive processing of television viewing. *Journal of Broadcasting, 25,* 327–334.

Collins, W. A. (1981b). Schemata for understanding television. In H. Kelly & H. Gardner (Eds.), *Viewing children through television* (pp. 31–46). San Francisco: Jossey-Bass.

Collins, W. A. (1982). Children's processing of television content: Implications for prevention of negative effects. *Prevention in Human Services, 2*(1, Suppl. 2), 53–66.

Collins, W. A. (1983). Social antecedents, cognitive processing, and comprehension of social portrayals on television. In E. T. Higgins, D. N. Ruble, & W. W. Hartup (Eds.), *Social cognition and social behavior: Developmental perspectives* (pp. 110–133). New York: Cambridge University Press.

Collins, W. A., Berndt, T. J., & Hess, V. L. (1974). Observational learning of motives and consequences for television aggression: A developmental study. *Child Development, 45,* 799–802.

Collins, W. A., & Getz, S. (1976). Children's social responses following modeled reactions to provocation: Prosocial effects of a television drama. *Journal of Personality, 44,* 488–500.

Collins, W. A., Sohol, B. L., & Westby, S. (1981). Effects of adult commentary on children's comprehension and inferences about a televised aggressive portrayal. *Child Development, 52*(1), 158–163.

Collins, W. A., & Wellman, H. M. (1982). Social scripts and developmental patterns in comprehension of televised narratives. *Communication Research, 9,* 380–398.

Collins, W. A., Wellman, H. M., Keviston, A., & Westley, S. D. (1978). Age related aspects of comprehension and inference from a televised dramatic narrative. *Child Development, 49,* 389–399.

Collins, W. A., & Zimmerman, S. A. (1975). Convergent and divergent social cues: Effects of televised aggression on children. *Communication Research, 2*(4), 331–346.

Comstock, G. (1975). The effects of television on children and adolescents: The evidence so far. *Journal of Communication, 25*(4), 25–34.

Comstock, G. (1977a). *Priorities for action-oriented psychological studies of television and behavior.* Santa Monica, CA: Rand.

Comstock, G. (1977b). Types of portrayal and aggressive behavior. *Journal of Communication, 27*(3), 189–198.

Comstock, G. (1978). The impact of television on American institutions. *Journal of Communication, 28*(2), 12–28.

Comstock, G. (1979). Television and the children of ethnic minorities. *Journal of Communication, 29*(1), 104–115.

Comstock, G. (1980a). New emphases in research on the effects of television and film violence. In E. L. Palmer & A. Dorr (Eds.), *Children and the faces of television: Teaching, violence, selling* (pp. 129–148). New York: Academic.

Comstock, G. (1980b). Television entertainment: Taking it seriously; what does the research show about television and the young? What are its implications? *North Carolina Medical Journal, 4*(1), 1–8.

Comstock, G. (1981). Influence of mass media on child health behavior. *Health Education Quarterly, 8*(1), 32–38.

Comstock, G. (1986). Television and film violence. In S. J. Apter & A. P. Goldstein (Eds.), *Youth violence: Programs and prospects* (pp. 178–218). Elmsford, NY: Pergamon.

Comstock, G. (1993). The medium and the society: The role of television in American life. In G. L. Berry & J. K. Asamen (Eds.), *Children and television: Images in a changing sociocultural world* (pp. 117–131). Newbury Park, CA: Sage.

Comstock, G. (1995). Television and the American child. In C. N. Hedley, P. Antonacci, & M. Rabinowitz (Eds.), *Thinking and literacy: The mind at work* (pp. 101–123). Hillsdale, NJ: Lawrence Erlbaum Associates, Inc.

Comstock, G., & Cobbey, R. E. (1976). The role of social and behavioral science in policymaking for television. *Journal of Social Issues, 32*(4), 157–178.

Comstock, G., & Fisher, M. (1975). *Television and human behavior: A guide to the pertinent scientific literature.* Santa Monica, CA: Rand.

Comstock, G., & Scharrer, E. (Eds.). (1999). *Television: What's on, who's watching, and what it means.* San Diego, CA: Academic.

Comstock, G., & Scharrer, E. (2001). The use of television and other film-related media. In D. G. Singer & J. L. Singer (Eds.), *Handbook of children and the media* (pp. 47–72). Thousand Oaks, CA: Sage.

Comstock, G., & Strasburger, V. C. (1990). Deceptive appearances: Television violence and aggressive behavior. *Journal of Adolescent Health Care, 11,* 31–44.

Condry, J. C. (1971). Contemporary broadcasting as related to the needs of children. *Clinical Pediatrics, 10,* 459–461.

Condry, J. C. (1989). *The psychology of television.* Hillsdale, NJ: Lawrence Erlbaum Associates, Inc.

Condry, J. C., Bence, P., & Scheibe, C. (1988). Nonprogram content of children's television. *Journal of Broadcasting & Electronic Media, 32,* 255–270.

Connolly, G. M., Casswell, S., Zhang, J. F., & Silva, P. A. (1994). Alcohol in the mass media and drinking by adolescents: A longitudinal study. *Addiction, 89,* 1255–1263.

Conway, M. M., Ahern, D., & Wickoff, M. L. (1981). Mass media and changes in adolescents' political knowledge during an election cycle. *Political Behavior, 3*(1), 69–80.

Conway, M. M., Stevens, A. J., & Smith, R. G. (1975). The relationship between media use and children's civic awareness. *Journalism Quarterly, 52,* 531–538.

Conway, M. M., Wykoff, M. L., Feldbaum, E., & Ahern, D. (1981). The news media in children's political socialization. *Public Opinion Quarterly, 45,* 164–178.

Cook, D. T. (2000). The other "child study": Figuring children as consumers in market research, 1910–1990s. *Sociological Quarterly, 41,* 487–507.

Cook, T. D., Kendzierski, D. A., & Thomas, S. V. (1983). The implicit assumptions of television research: An analysis of the 1982 NIMH report on television and behavior. *Public Opinion Quarterly, 47,* 161–201.

Cool, V. A., Yarbrough, D., Patton, J., Runde, R., & Keith, T. (1994). Experimental effects of radio and television distractors on children's performance on mathematics and reading assignments. *Journal of Experimental Education, 62,* 181–194.

Coon, K. A., Goldberg, J., Rogers, B. L., & Tucker, K. L. (2001). Relationships between the use of television during meals and children's food consumption patterns. *Pediatrics, 107*(1), e7.

Cooper, H., Valentine, J. C., Nye, B., & Lindsay, J. J. (1999). Relationships between five after-school activities and academic achievement. *Journal of Educational Psychology, 91,* 369–378.

Cope-Farrar, K. M., & Kunkel, D. (2002). Sexual messages in teens' favorite prime-time television programs. In J. D. Brown & J. R. Steele (Eds.), *Sexual teens, sexual media: Investigating media's influence on adolescent sexuality* (pp. 59–78). Mahwah, NJ: Lawrence Erlbaum Associates, Inc.

Corcoran, F., & Schneider, M. J. (1985). Correlates of the interpretation of televised drama: A study of young children's abilities. *Early Childhood Development and Care, 20,* 301–313.

Corder-Bolz, C. R. (1980). Mediation: The role of significant others. *Journal of Communication Research, 30*(3), 106–118.

Corder-Bolz, C. R., & O'Bryant, S. (1978). Teacher vs. program: Can people affect television? *Journal of Communication, 28*(1), 97–103.

Cordua, G. D., McGraw, K. O., & Drabman, R. S. (1979). Doctor or nurse: Children's perception of sex-typed occupations. *Child Development, 50,* 590–593.

Corteen, R. S., & Williams, T. M. (1986). *Television and reading skills.* Orlando, FL: Academic.

Cortes, C. E. (2000). *The children are watching: How the media teach about diversity.* New York: Teachers College Press.

Cosmas, S. C., & Yannopoulos, N. (1981). Advertising directed to children: A look at the mother's point of view. *Journal of the Academy of Marketing Science, 9*, 174–190.

Costabile, A., Genta, M. L., Zucchini, E., Smith, P. K., & Harker, R. (1992). Attitudes of parents toward war play in young children. *Early Education and Development, 3*, 356–369.

Cottle, T. J. (2001). *Mind fields: Adolescent consciousness in a culture of distractions* New York: Peter Lang.

Courtwright, J. A., & Baran, S. J. (1980). The acquisition of sexual information by young people. *Journalism Quarterly, 57*, 107–114.

Cowden, J. E., Bassett, H. T., & Cohen, M. F. (1969). An analysis of some relationships between fantasy-aggressive and aggressive behavior among institutionalized delinquents. *Journal of Genetic Psychology, 114*, 179–183.

Craig, J. R., & Smith, B. R. (1999). Implementing the FCC's three-hour children's television rule: A first look. *Feedback, 40*, 14–19.

Craig, K. D., & Wood, K. (1971). Autonomic components of observers' responses to pictures of homicide victims and nude females. *Journal of Experimental Research in Personality, 5*, 304–309.

Cramer, P., & Mecham, M. B. (1982). Violence in children's animated television. *Journal of Applied Developmental Psychology, 3*, 23–39.

Crane, V. (1980). Content development for children's television programs. In E. L. Palmer & A. Dorr (Eds.), *Children and the faces of television: Teaching, violence, selling* (pp. 33–48). New York: Academic.

Crawley, A. M., Anderson, D. R., Santomero, A., Wilder, A., Williams, M., Evans, M. K., et al. (2002). Do children learn how to watch television? The impact of extensive experience with Blues Clues on preschool children's television viewing behavior. *Journal of Communication, 52*, 264–280.

Crawley, A. M., Anderson, D. R., Wilder, A., Williams, M., & Santomero, A. (1999). Effects of repeated exposures to a single episode of the television program Blue's Clues on the viewing behaviors and comprehension of preschool children. *Journal of Educational Psychology, 91*, 630–637.

Crespo, C. J., Smit, E., Troiano, R. P., Bartlett, S. J., Macera, C. A., & Andersen, R. E. (2001). Television watching, energy intake, and obesity in US children: Results from the third National Health and Nutrition Examination Survey, 1988–1994. *Archives of Pediatrics & Adolescent Medicine, 155*, 360–365.

Crocker, E. (1986). Television for hospitalized children: The issue of control. *Children's Health Care, 15*(2), 76–78.

Croghan, I. T., Campbell, H. M., Patten, C. A., Croghan, G. A., Schroeder, D. R., & Novotny, P. J. (2004). A contest to create media messages aimed at recruiting adolescents for stop smoking programs. *Journal of School Health, 74*, 325–329.

Cronen, V. E. (1973). Belief, salience, media exposure, and summation theory. *Journal of Communication, 23*(1), 86–94.

Crowell, D. C., & Au, K. H. (1981). Developing children's comprehension in listening, reading, and television viewing. *The Elementary School Journal, 82*, 128–135.

Crowell, D. H., Evans, I. M., & O'Donnell, C. R. (1987). *Childhood aggression and violence: Sources of influence, prevention, and control.* New York: Plenum.

Cruise-O'Brien, R. (1980). Mass media, education and the transmission of values. *Prospects: Quarterly Review of Education, 10*(1), 61–67.

Culkin, J. M. (1970). New directions in children's television [Special Issue]. *Television Quarterly, 9*(3).

Culley, J. D., Lazar, W., & Atkin, C. K. (1976). The experts look at children's television. *Journal of Broadcasting, 29*(1), 3–21.

Curry, N. E. (1996). The reality of make-believe. In M. Collins & M. M. Kimmel (Eds.), *Mister Rogers' Neighborhood: Children, television, and Fred Rogers* (pp. 51–66). Pittsburgh, PA: University of Pittsburgh Press.

Cushing, W. G., & Lemert, J. B. (1973). Has TV altered students' news media preferences? *Journalism Quarterly, 50*, 138–140.

Czikszentmihalyi, M., Larson, R., & Prescott, S. (1977). The ecology of adolescent activity and experience. *Journal of Youth & Adolescence, 6*, 281–294.

Daane, D. M. (2003). Child and adolescent violence. *Orthopaedic Nursing, 22*(1), 23–32.

Dail, P. W., & Way, W. L. (1985). What do parents observe about parenting from prime time television. *Family Relations, 34*, 491–499.

Dalfonzo, G. R. (1999). Children in charge. *The Responsive Community, 10*(1), 59–68.

Dardenne, R. (1994). Student musings on life without mass media. *Journalism Educator, 49*(3), 72–79.

Dates, J. (1980). Race, racial attitudes and adolescent perceptions of Black television characters. *Journal of Broadcasting, 24*, 549–560.

Dates, J. L., & Stroman, C. A. (2001). Portrayals of families of color on television. In J. Bryant & J. A. Bryant (Eds.), *Television and the American family* (2nd ed., pp. 207–228). Mahwah, NJ: Lawrence Erlbaum Associates, Inc.

Daven J., O'Conner F. J., & Briggs, R. (1976). The consequences of imitative behavior in children: The "Evel Knievel syndrome." *Pediatrics, 57*, 418–419.

Davidson, E. S., Yasuna, A., & Tower, A. (1979). The effects of television cartoons in sex-role stereotyping in young girls. *Child Development, 50*, 597–600.

Davies, J. (1996). *Educating students in a media-saturated culture.* Lancaster, PA: Technomic.

Davies, H., Buckingham, D., & Kelley, P. (2004). In the worst possible taste: Children, television and cultural value. In R. C. Allen & A. Hill (Eds.), *The television studies reader* (pp. 479–493). New York: Routledge.

Davis, G. (2004). "Saying it out loud": Revealing television's queer teens. In G. Davis & K. Dickinson (Eds.), *Teen TV: Genre, consumption, identity* (pp. 127–140). London: British Film Institute.

Davis, S. N. (2003). Sex stereotypes in commercials targeted toward children: A content analysis. *Sociological Spectrum, 23*, 407–426.

Davis, D. K., & Abelman, R. (1983). Families and television: An application of frame analysis theory. *Journal of Family Issues, 4*, 385–404.

Dawson, B., Jefferey, B. D., & Peterson, P. E. (1985). Television commercials as a symbolic representation of reward in the delay of gratification paradigm. *Cognitive Therapy and Research, 9*, 217–224.

Dawson, B. L., Walsh, J. A., & Jeffrey, D. B. (1988). Television food commercials' effect on children's resistance to temptation. *Journal of Applied Social Psychology, 18*, 1353–1360.

DeFleur, M. L. (1963). Children's knowledge of occupational roles and prestige: Preliminary report. *Psychological Reports, 13*, 760.

DeFleur, M. L. (1964). Occupational roles as portrayed on television. *Public Opinion Quarterly, 28*, 57–74.

DeFleur, M. L., & DeFleur, L. B. (1967). The relative contribution of television as a learning source for children's occupational knowledge. *American Sociological Review, 32*, 777–789.

DeFoe, J. F., & Breed, W. (1980). The mass media and alcohol education: A new direction. *Journal of Alcohol and Drug Education, 25*(3), 48–58.

DeJong, W., & Hoffman, K. D. (2000). A content analysis of television advertising for the Massachusetts Tobacco Control Program media campaign, 1993–1996. *Journal of Public Health Management and Practice, 6*(3), 27–39.

Deleon, D. L., & Naon, R. L. (1974). The regulation of televised violence. *Stanford Law Review, 26*, 1241–1325.

DeLoache, J. S., & Korac, N. (2003). Video-based learning in the very young. *Developmental Science, 6*, 245–247.

DeMars, T. R. (2000). *Modeling behavior from images of reality in television narratives: Myth-information and socialization.* Lewiston, NY: E. Mellon Press.

Denney, D. R. (1972). Modeling and eliciting effects upon conceptual strategies. *Child Development, 43*, 810–823.

Dennison, B. A., Erb, T. A., & Jenkins, P. L. (2002). Television viewing and television in bedroom associated with overweight risk among low-income preschool children. *Pediatrics, 109*, 1028–1035.

Derbaix, C., & Pecheux, C. (2003). A new scale to assess children's attituted toward TV advertising. *Journal of Advertising Research, 43*, 390–400.

Derdeyn, A. P., & Turley, J. M. (1994). Television, films, and the emotional life of children. In D. Zillmann, J. Bryant, & A. C. Huston (Eds.), *Media, children, and the family: Social scientific, psychodynamic, and clinical perspectives* (pp. 131–138). Hillsdale, NJ: Lawrence Erlbaum Associates, Inc.

Derksen D. J., & Strasburger V. C. (1994). Children and the influence of the media. *Primary Care, 21*, 747–758.

Derksen, D. J., & Strasburger, V. C. (1996). Media and television violence: Effects on violence, aggression, and antisocial behaviors in children. In A. M. Hoffman (Ed.), *Schools, violence, and society* (pp. 61–77). Westport, CT: Praeger.

Dervin, B., & Greenberg, B. S. (1972). The communication environment of the urban poor. In F. G. Kline & P. J. Tichenor (Eds.), *Current perspectives in mass communication research* (pp. 195–233). Beverly Hills, CA: Sage.

Derzon, J. H., & Lipsey, M. W. (2002). A meta-analysis of the effectiveness of mass-communication for changing substance-use knowledge, attitudes, and behavior. In W. D. Crano & M. Burgoon (Eds.), *Mass media and drug prevention: Classic and contemporary theories and research* (pp. 231–258). Mahwah, NJ: Lawrence Erlbaum Associates, Inc.

Desmond, R. J. (1978). Cognitive development and television comprehension. *Communication Research, 5*, 202–220.

Desmond, R. J., & Donohue, T. R. (1981). The role of the 1976 televised presidential debates in the political socialization of adolescents. *Communication Quarterly, 29*, 302–308.

Desmond, R. J., Hirsch, B., Singer, D., & Singer, J. (1987). Gender differences, mediation and disciplinary styles in children's responses to television. *Sex Roles, 16,* 375–389.

Desmond, R. J., & Jeffries-Fox, S. (1983). Elevating children's awareness of television advertising: The effects of a critical viewing program. *Communication Education, 32*(1), 107–115.

Desmond, R. J., Singer, J. L., & Singer, D. G. (1990). Family mediation: Parental communication patterns and the influences of television on children. In J. Bryant (Ed.), *Television and the American family* (pp. 293–310). Hillsdale, NJ: Lawrence Erlbaum Associates, Inc.

Desmond, R. J., Singer, J. L., Singer, D. G., Calam, R., & Colimore, K. (1985). Family mediation patterns and television viewing: Young children's use and grasp of the medium. *Human Communication Research, 11,* 461–480.

De Sousa, A. (1974). Causes of behavior problems in children. *Child Psychology Quarterly, 7*(1), 3–8.

Dessart, G. (1966). A twenty-one inch medium for thirty-six receivers. In P. D. Hazard (Ed.), *TV as art: Some essays in criticism.* Champaign, IL: National Council of Teachers of English.

Dexter, L. A., & White, D. M. (Eds.). (1964). *People, society and mass communication.* New York: The Free Press.

Dickens, M., & Williams, F. (1964). Mass communication: Effects of television on children. *Educational Research, 34,* 215–216.

Dienstbier, R. A. (1977). Sex and violence: Can research have it both ways? *Journal of Communication, 27*(3), 176–188.

Dietrich, D., & Ladevish, L. (1977). Medium and message—Effects of television on children. *Language Arts, 54,* 196–204.

Dietz, W. H. (1986). Prevention of childhood obesity. *Pediatric Clinics of North America, 33,* 823–833.

Dietz, W. H. (1990). You are what you eat: What you eat is what you are. *Journal of Adolescent Health Care, 11*(1), 76–81.

Dietz, W. H. (1993). Television, obesity, and eating disorders. *Adolescent Medicine, 75,* 543–549.

Dietz , W. H. J., & Gortmaker, S. L. (1985). Do we fatten our children at the television set? Obesity and television viewing in children and adolescents. *Pediatrics, 75,* 807–812.

Dietz, W. H., & Strasburger, V. C. (1991). Children, adolescents, and television. *Current Problems in Pediatrics, 21*(1), 8–32.

DiLillo, D., Potts, R., & Himes, S. (1998). Predictors of children's risk appraisals. *Journal of Applied Developmental Psychology, 19,* 415–427.

Dimmick, J. (1976). Family communication and TV program choice. *Journalism Quarterly, 53,* 720–723.

DiScala, C., Barthel, M., & Sege, R. (2001). Outcomes from television sets toppling onto toddlers. *Archives of Pediatrics & Adolescent Medicine, 155,* 145–148.

Dittmar, M. L. (1994). Relations among depression, gender, and television viewing of college students. *Journal of Social Behavior and Personality, 9,* 317–328.

Dobrow, J. R., & Gidney, C. L. (1998). The good, the bad, and the foreign: The use of dialect in children's animated television. *Annals of the American Academy of Political and Social Science, 557,* 105–119.

Dobson, J. (1977). Children, death, and the media. *Counseling Values, 21*, 172–179.

Dohrmann, R. (1975). A gender profile of children's educational TV. *Journal of Communication, 25*, 56–65.

Dominick, J. R. (1974). Children's viewing of crime shows and attitudes of law enforcement. *Journalism Quarterly, 51*, 5–12.

Dominick, J. R. (1984). Videogames, television violence, and aggression in teenagers. *Journal of Communication, 43*(2), 136–147.

Dominick, J. R., & Greenberg, B. S. (1970). Mass media functions among low-income adolescents. In B. S. Greenberg & B. Dervin (Eds.), *Uses of the mass media by the urban poor*. New York: Praeger.

Dominick, J. R., Richman, S., & Wurtzel, A. (1979). Problem solving in TV shows popular with children: Assertion vs. aggression. *Journalism Quarterly, 56*, 455–463.

Domino, G. (1982). Get high on yourself: The effectiveness of a campaign on self-esteem, drug use, and drug attitudes. *Journal of Drug Education, 12*, 163–171.

Donagher, P. C., Poulos, R. W., Liebert, R. M., & Davidson, E. S. (1980). Race, sex, and social example: An analysis of character portrayals on inter-racial television entertainment. *Sociological Reports, 39*, 269–277.

Donaldson, J. (1981). The visibility and image of handicapped people on television. *Exceptional Children, 47*, 413–416.

Donner, L. (1990). Television and violence. In L. J. Hertzbeg & G. F. Ostrum (Eds.), *Violent behavior: Vol. 1. Assessment & intervention* (pp. 151–166). Costa Mesa, CA: PMA.

Donnerstein, E. (1980). Aggressive erotica and violence against women. *Journal of Personality and Social Psychology, 39*, 269–277.

Donnerstein, E., Wilson, B. J., & Linz, D. (1992). On the regulation of broadcast indecency to protect children. *Journal of Broadcasting & Electronic Media, 36*, 111–117.

Donohue, T. R. (1975a). Black children's perceptions of favorite TV characters as models of antisocial behavior. *Journal of Broadcasting, 19*, 153–167.

Donohue, T. R. (1975b). Effect of commercials on Black children. *Journal of Advertising Research, 15*(6), 41–47.

Donohue, T. R. (1977). Favorite TV characters as behavioral models for the emotionally disturbed. *Journal of Broadcasting, 21*, 333–335.

Donohue, T. R. (1978). Television's impact on emotionally disturbed children's value systems. *Child Study Journal, 8*, 187–201.

Donohue, T. R., Henke, L. L., & Donohue, W. A. (1980a). Do kids know what TV commercials intend? *Journal of Advertising, 20*(5), 51–57.

Donohue, T. R., Henke, L. L., & Donohue, W. A. (1980b). Non-verbal assessment of children's understanding of television commercial intent and program market segmentation. *Journal of Advertising Research, 20*(5), 51–57.

Donohue, T. R., Henke, L. L., & Meyer, T. P. (1983). Learning about television commercials: The impact of instructional units on children's perceptions of motive and intent. *Journal of Broadcasting, 27*, 251–261.

Donohue, T. R., Henke, L. L., & Morgan, L. A. (1988). The impact of television's role on physically abused children. *Child Study Journal, 18*, 233–247.

Donohue, T. R., Meyer, T., & Henke, L. (1978). Black and White children: Perceptions of TV commercials. *Journal of Marketing, 42*(4), 34–40.

Donohue, W. A., & Donohue, T. R. (1977). Black, white, white gifted and emotionally disturbed children's perceptions of the reality in television programming. *Human Relations, 30,* 609–621.

Doob, A. N., & Macdonald, G. E. (1979). Television viewing and fear of victimization: Is the relationship causal? *Journal of Personality and Social Psychology, 37,* 170–179.

Doolittle, J. C. (1980). Immunizing children against the possible antisocial effects of viewing violence: A curricular intervention. *Perceptual & Motor Skills, 51,* 498.

Doolittle, J. C., & Pepper, R. (1975). Children's TV ad content. *Journal of Broadcasting, 19,* 131–142.

Dorr, A. (1980). When I was a child I thought as a child. In S. B. Withey & R. P. Abeles (Eds.), *Television and social behavior: Beyond violence and children* (pp. 191–230). Hillsdale, NJ: Lawrence Erlbaum Associates, Inc.

Dorr, A. (1981). Television and affective development and functioning: Maybe this decade. *Journal of Broadcasting, 25,* 335–345.

Dorr, A. (1986). *Television and children: A special medium for a special audience.* Beverly Hills, CA: Sage.

Dorr, A., Graves, S. B., & Phelps, E. (1980). Television literacy for young children. *Journal of Communication, 30*(3), 71–80.

Dorr, A., & Kovaric, P. (1980). Televised violence and its effects. In E. L. Palmer & A. Dorr (Eds.), *Children and the faces of television: Teaching, violence, selling* (pp. 183–199). New York: Academic.

Dorr, A., Kovaric, P., & Doubleday, C. (1989). Parent–child coviewing of television. *Journal of Broadcasting, 33,* 35–51.

Dorr, A., Kovaric, P., & Doubleday, C. (1990). Age and content influences on children's perceptions of the realism of television families. *Journal of Broadcasting & Electronic Media, 34,* 377–397.

Dorr, A., & Kunkel, D. (1990). Children and the media environment: Change and consistency amid change. *Communication Research, 17*(1), 5–25.

Dorr, A., & Lesser, G. (1980). Career awareness in young children. *Communication Research & Broadcasting, 3,* 76–84.

Dorr, A., & Rabin, B. E. (1995). Parents, children, and television. In M. H. Bornstein (Ed.), *Handbook of Parenting: Vol. 4. Applied and practical parenting* (pp. 323–351). Mahwah, NJ: Lawrence Erlbaum Associates, Inc.

Dotson, M. J., & Hyatt, E. M. (2005). Major influence factors in children's consumer socialization. *Journal of Consumer Marketing, 22*(1), 35–42.

Doubleday, C. N., & Droege, K. L. (1993). Cognitive developmental influences on children's understanding of television. In G. L. Berry & J. K. Asamen (Eds.), *Children & television: Images in a changing sociocultural world* (pp. 23–37). Thousand Oaks, CA: Sage.

Douglas, W. (1996). The fall from grace? The modern family on television. *Communication Research, 23,* 675–702.

Douglas, W. (2001). Subversion of the American television family. In J. Bryant & J. A. Bryant (Eds.), *Television and the American family* (2nd ed. pp. 229–246). Mahwah, NJ: Lawrence Erlbaum Associates, Inc.

Douglas, W., & Olson, B. M. (1996). Subversion of the American family? An examination of children and parents in television families. *Communication Research, 23*, 73–99.

Downs, A. C. (1990). Children's judgements of televised events: The real versus pretend distinction. *Perceptual & Motor Skills, 70*, 779–782.

Drabman, R. S., & Thomas, M. H. (1974). Does media violence increase children's toleration of real-life aggression? *Developmental Psychology, 10*, 418–421.

Drabman, R. S., & Thomas, M. H. (1975). Does television violence breed the difference. *Journal of Communication, 25*(4), 86–89.

Drabman, R. S., & Thomas, M. H. (1976). Does watching violence on television cause apathy? *Pediatrics, 57*, 329–331.

Drabman, R. S., & Thomas, M. H. (1977). Children's imitation of aggressive and prosocial behavior when viewing alone and in pairs. *Journal of Communication, 27*(3), 199–205.

Drabman, R. S., & Thomas, M. H. (1981). Children's perceptions of media-portrayed sex roles. *Sex Roles, 7*, 379–389.

Drabman, R. S., Thomas, M. H., & Jarvie, G. (1977). Will our children care? New evidence concerning the effects of televised violence on our children. *Journal of Clinical Child Psychology, 6*, 44–46.

Drew, D. G., & Reese, S. D. (1984). Children's learning from a television newscast. *Journalism Quarterly, 61*, 83–88.

Drew, D. G., & Reeves, B. (1980a). Children and television news. *Journalism Quarterly, 57*, 45–54, 114.

Drew, D. G., & Reeves, B. (1980b). Learning from a television news story. *Communication Research, 7*, 121–135.

Dubanoski, R. A., & Parton, D. A. (1971). Imitative aggression in children as a function of observing a human model. *Developmental Psychology, 4*, 489.

Dubow, E. F., & Miller, L. S. (1996). Television violence viewing and aggressive behavior. In T. M. MacBeth (Ed.), *Tuning in to young viewers: Social science perspectives on television* (pp. 117–147). Thousand Oaks, CA: Sage.

Duggal, H. S., Berezkin, G., & John, V. (2002). PTSD and TV viewing of World Trade Center. *Journal of the American Academy of Child and Adolescent Psychiatry, 41*, 494–495.

Duncan, M. C. (1989). Television portrayals of children's play and sport. *Play and Culture, 2*, 235–252.

Duncan-Andrade, J. (2004). Your best friend or your worst enemy: Youth popular culture, pedagogy, and curriculum in urban classrooms. *Review of Education, Pedagogy & Cultural Studies, 26*, 313–338.

Dunham, F. (1952). Effect of television on school achievement of children. *School Life, 34*, 88–89.

Dunn, T. P., & Cardwell, J. D. (1984). Television and children: A symbolic interactionist perspective. *Psychology, 21*(2), 30–35.

DuRant, R. H., Baranowski, T., Johnson, M., & Thompson, W. O. (1994). The relationship among television watching, physical-activity and body composition of young children. *Pediatrics, 94*, 449–455.

DuRant, R. H., Rome, E., Rich, M., Allred, E., Emans, J., & Woods, E. (1997). Tobacco and alcohol use behaviors portrayed in music videos: A content analysis. *American Journal of Public Health, 87*, 1131–1135.

DuRant, R. H., Thompson, W. O., Johnson, M., & Baranowski, T. (1996). The relationship among television watching, physical activity, and body composition of 5- or 6-year old children. *Pediatric Exercise Science, 8*(1), 15–26.

Durkin, K. (1984). Children's accounts of sex-role stereotypes in television. *Communication Research, 11*, 341–362.

Durkin, K. (1985). *Television, sex roles and children: A developmental social psychological account.* Philadelphia: Taylor & Francis.

Durkin, K., & Nugent B. (1998). Kindergarten children's gender-role expectations for television actors. *Sex Roles, 38*, 387–402.

Dussich, J. P. J. (1970). Violence and the media. *Criminology, 8*(1), 80–94.

Dworetz, S. M. (1987). Before the age of research: Liberalism and the media socialization of children. *Social Theory and Practice, 13*, 187–218.

Dye, R. P. (1966). Video violence. *Journal of Broadcasting, 10*, 97–102.

Dyson, A. H. (1997). *Writing superheroes: Contemporary childhood, popular cultures, and classroom literacy.* New York: Teachers College Press.

Dyson, A. H. (2001). Donkey Kong in Little Bear country: A first grader's composing development in the media spotlight. *The Elementary School Journal, 101*, 417–433.

Eakin, M. K. (1951). Television in education. *The Elementary School Journal, 52*, 129–131.

Eakin, M. K. (1955). Commercial television programs for children. *The Elementary School Journal, 56*, 53.

Easterlin, R. A. (1982). The changing circumstances of child rearing. *Journal of Communication, 32*(3), 86–98.

Eastman, H. A., & Liss, M. B. (1980a). Ethnicity and children's TV preferences. *Journalism Quarterly, 57*(2), 277–280.

Eastman, H. A., & Liss, M. B. (1980b). TV preferences of children from four parts of the United States. *Journalism Quarterly, 57*, 488–491.

Eaton, B. C., & Dominick, J. R. (1991). Product-related programming and children's TV: A content analysis. *Journalism Quarterly, 68*, 67–75.

Edgar, P. (1977). Families without television. *Journal of Communication, 27*(2), 73–77.

Edwardson, M., Kent, K., Engstrom, E., & Hofman, R. (1992). Audio recall immediately following video change in television news. *Journal of Broadcasting & Electronic Media, 36*, 395–410.

Efron, E., & Hickey, N. (1969). *TV and your child: In search of an answer.* New York: Triangle Publications.

Egan, L. (1978). Children's viewing patterns of television news. *Journalism Quarterly, 55*, 337–342.

Eisenstock, B. A. (1984). Sex-role differences in children's identification with counterstereotypical televised portrayals. *Sex Roles, 10*, 417–430.

Eisler, R. T., & Loye, D. (1980). Childhood and the chosen future. *Journal of Clinical Child Psychology, 9,* 102–106.

Eleey, M. F., Gerbner, G., & Tedesco, N. (1972). Apples, oranges, and the kitchen sink: An analysis and guide to the comparison of "violence ratings." *Journal of Broadcasting, 17,* 21–31.

Elias, M. J. (1974). How to win friends and influence kids on television. *Human Behavior, 3*(4), 16–23.

Elias, M. J. (1979). Helping emotionally disturbed children through prosocial television. *Exceptional Children, 46,* 217–218.

Elias, M. J. (1983). Improving coping skills of emotionally disturbed boys through television-based social problem solving. *American Journal of Orthopsychiatry, 53,* 61–72.

Elias, M. J., & Maher, C. A. (1983). Social and affective development of children: A programmatic perspecitve. *Exceptional Children, 49,* 339–346.

Ellickson, P. L., McCaffrey, D. F., Ghosh-Dastidar, B., & Longshore, D. L. (2003). New inroads in preventing adolescent drug use: Results from a large-scale trial of Project ALERT in middle schools. *American Journal of Public Health, 93,* 1830–1836.

Ellickson, P. L., Collins, R. L., Hambarsoomians, K., & McCaffrey, D. F. (2005). Does alcohol advertising promote adolescent drinking? Results from a longitudinal assessment. *Addiction, 100*(2), 235–247.

Elliot, T., & Byrd, E. K. (1983). Attitude change toward disability through television portrayal. *Journal of Applied Rehabilitation Counseling, 14*(2), 35–37.

Elliott, W. R., & Slater, D. (1980). Exposure, experience and perceived TV reality for adolescents. *Journalism Quarterly, 57,* 409–414, 431.

Elliott, W. Y. (1956). *Television's impact on American culture.* Lansing: Michigan State University.

Ellis, G. T., & Sekyra, F. (1972). The effect of aggressive cartoons on the behavior of first grade children. *Journal of Psychology, 81,* 37–43.

Emmers-Sommer, T. M., & Allen, M. (1999). Surveying the effect of media effects: A meta-analytic summary of media effects research in "Human Communication Research." *Human Communication Research, 25*(4), 478–497.

Emmett, B. P., & Osborn, D. K. (1970). Children's reactions to TV violence: A review of research. *Young Children, 25*(1), 4–11.

Enis, B. M., Spencer, D. R., & Webb, R. R. (1980). Television advertising and children: Regulatory vs. competitive perspectives. *Journal of Advertising, 9*(1), 19–26.

Epstein, L. H., Paluch, R. A., Gordy, C. C., & Dorn, J. (2000). Decreasing sedentary behaviors in treating pediatric obesity. *Archives of Pediatrics & Adolescent Medicine, 154,* 220–226.

Epstein, L. H., Valoski, A. M., Vara, L. S., McCurley, J., Wisniewski, L., Kalarchian, M. A., et al. (1995). Effects of decreasing sedentary behavior and increasing activity on weight change in obese children. *Health Psychology, 14*(2), 109–115.

Erickson, H. (1998). *Sid and Marty Krofft: A critical study of Saturday morning children's television.* Jefferson, NC: McFarland.

Eron, L. D. (1963). Relationship of TV viewing habits and aggressive behavior in children. *Journal of Abnormal and Social Psychology, 67,* 193–196.

Eron, L. D. (1982). Parent–child interaction, television violence, and aggression of children. *American Psychologist, 37*, 197–211.

Eron, L. D. (1986). Interventions to mitigate the psychological effects of media violence on aggressive behavior. *Journal of Social Issues, 42*(3), 155–169.

Eron, L. D. (1992). Gender differences in violence: Biology and/or socialization? In K. Bjoerkqvist & P. Niemelae (Eds.), *Of mice and women: Aspects of female aggression* (pp. 89–97). San Diego, CA: Academic.

Eron, L. D., Brice, P., Fisher, P., & Mermelstein, R. (1983). Age trends in the development of aggression, sex typing and related television habits. *Developmental Psychology, 19*(1), 71–77.

Eron, L. D., Huesmann, L. R., Lefkowitz, M. M., & Walder, L. O. (1972). Does television violence cause aggression? *American Psychologist, 27*, 253–263.

Eron, L. D., Walder, L. O., & Lefkowitz, M. M. (1971). *Learning of aggression in children.* Boston: Little, Brown.

Ervy, H. (1952). TV murder causes bad dreams. *Film World, 8*, 247.

Etzioni, A. (2002). Suffer the children. *Education Week, 22*(9), 56, 42.

Evans, C. C. (1955). Television for the pre-school child. *Elementary English, 32*, 541–542.

Evans, C. C. (1957). Tots and TV. *Childhood Education, 33*, 316.

Evans, R. I., Rozelle, R., Mittlemark, M., Hansen, W., Bang, A., & Havis, J. (1978). Deterring onset of smoking in children—Knowledge of immediate physiological effects and coping with peer pressure, media pressure, and parent modeling. *Journal of Applied Social Psychology, 8*(2), 126–135.

Faber, R. J., Brown, J. D., & McLeod, J. M. (1979). Coming of age in the global village. In E. Wartella (Ed.), *Children communicating: Media development and thought, speech, understanding* (pp. 215–249). Beverly Hills, CA: Sage.

Faber, R. J., Meyer, T. P., & Miller, M. M. (1984). The effectiveness of health disclosures within children's television commercials. *Journal of Broadcasting, 28*, 463–476.

Faber, R. J., Perloff, R., & Hawkins, R. (1982). Antecedents of children's comprehension of television advertising. *Journal of Broadcasting, 26*, 575–584.

Fairchild, H. H. (1988). *Creating positive television images.* Thousand Oaks, CA: Sage.

Faith, M., Berman, N., Heo, M., Pietrobelli, A., Gallagher, D., Epstein, L. H., et al. (2001). Effects of contingent television on physical activity and television viewing in obese children. *Pediatrics, 107*, 1043–1048.

Farrar, K., Kunkel, D., Biely, E., Eyal, K., & Fandrich, R. (2003). Sexual messages during prime-time primary programming. *Sexuality & Culture: An Interdisciplinary Quarterly, 7*(2), 7–37.

Fechter, J. V., Jr. (1971). Modeling and environmental generalization by mentally retarded subjects of televised aggressive of friendly behavior. *American Journal of Mental Deficiency, 76*, 266–267.

Feeley, J. T. (1974). Interest patterns and media preferences of middle-grade children. *Reading World, 13*, 224–237.

Feilitzen, C. V., & Linne, O. (1975). Identifying with television characters. *Journal of Communication, 25*(4), 51–55.

Feinberg, S. (1977). The classroom's no longer prime time. *Today's Education, 66*(3), 78–79.

Feinbloom, R. I. (1976). Children and television. *Pediatrics, 57,* 301–303.

Feinbloom, R. I. (1977). Children and television. *School Media Quarterly, 5,* 171–174.

Feingold, P. C., & Knapp, M. L. (1977). Anti-drug abuse commercials. *Journal of Communication, 27*(1), 20–28.

Feldman, R. S., Coates, E. J., & Spielman, D. A. (1996). Television exposure and children's decoding of nonverbal behavior. *Journal of Applied Social Psychology, 26,* 1718–1733.

Feldman, S., & Wolf, A. (1974). What's wrong with children's commercials? *Journal of Advertising Research, 14*(1), 39–43.

Feldman, S., Wolf, A., & Warmouth, D. (1977). Parental concern about child-directed commercials. *Journal of Communication, 27*(1), 125–137.

Feldstein, J. H., & Feldstein, S. (1982). Sex differences on televised toy commericals. *Sex Roles, 8,* 581–587.

Ferguson, D. A. (1994). Measurement of mundane TV behaviors: Remote control device flipping frequency. *Journal of Broadcasting & Electronic Media, 38,* 35–47.

Fernandez-Collado, C. F., Greenberg, B., Korzenny, F., & Atkin, C. (1978). Sexual intimacy and drug use in TV series. *Journal of Communication, 28*(3), 30–37.

Feshbach, N. D. (1973). The effects of violence in childhood. *Journal of Clinical Child Psychology, 2*(3), 28–31.

Feshbach, N. D. (1988). Television and the development of empathy. *Applied Social Psychology Annual, 8,* 261–269.

Feshbach, N. D., Dillman, A., & Jordan, T. (1979). Children and television advertising: Some research and some perspectives. *Journal of Clinical Child Psychology, 8*(1), 26–30.

Feshbach, S. (1961). The stimulating versus cathartic effects of a vicarious aggressive activity. *Journal of Abnormal and Social Psychology, 63,* 381–385.

Feshbach, S. (1963). The effects of aggressive content in television upon the aggressive behavior of the audience. In L. Arons & M. A. May (Eds.), *Television and human behavior* (pp. 32–97). New York: Appleton-Century-Crofts.

Feshbach, S. (1976). The role of fantasy in the response to television. *Journal of Social Issues, 32*(4), 71–85.

Feshbach, S. (1988). Television research and social policy: Some perspectives. *Applied Social Psychology Annual, 8,* 198–213.

Feshbach, S., Feshbach, N. D., & Cohen, S. E. (1982). Enhancing children's discrimination in response to television advertising: The effects of psychoeducational training in two elementary school age groups. *Developmental Review, 2,* 385–403.

Feshbach, S., & Singer R. D. (1971). *Television and aggression: An experimental field study.* San Francisco: Jossey-Bass.

Fetler, M. (1984). Television viewing and school achievement. *Journal of Communication, 34,* 104–118.

Field, D. E., & Anderson, D. R. (1985). Instruction and modality effects on children's television attention and comprehension. *Journal of Educational Psychology, 77,* 91–100.

Film World. (1954a). Crime pattern in TV films for children shown in annual study. *Film World, 10,* 456.

Film World. (1954b). National Council of Churches makes a study of parent's opinions of TV. *Film World, 10,* 280, 314.

Fingerson, L. (1999). Active viewing: Girls' interpretations of family television programs. *Journal of Contemporary Ethnography, 28,* 389–418.

Finn, J. D. (1953). Television and education: A review of research. *Communication Review, 1,* 106–126.

Finn, P. (1980). Developing critical viewing skills. *Educational Forum, 44,* 473–482.

Fischer, M. A. (1985). A developmental study of preference for advertised toys. *Psychology & Marketing, 2*(1), 3–12.

Fisher, D. A., Hill, D. L., Grube, J. W., & Gruber, E. L. (2004). Sex on American television: An analysis across program genres and network types. *Journal of Broadcasting & Electronic Media, 48,* 529–554.

Fisherkeller, J. (1997). Everyday learning about identities among young adolescents in television culture. *Anthropology and Education Quarterly, 28,* 467–492.

Fisherkeller, J. (2000). "The writers are getting kind of desperate": Young adolescents, television, and literacy. *Journal of Adolescent & Adult Literacy, 43,* 596–606.

Fitch, M., Huston, A. C., & Wright, J. C. (1993). From television forms to genre schemata: Children's perceptions of television reality. In G. L. Berry & J. K. Asamen (Eds.), *Children and television: Images in a changing sociocultural world* (pp. 38–52). Newbury Park, CA: Sage.

Fitzsimmons, S. J., & Osburn, H. G. (1968). The impact of social issues and public affairs television documentaries. *Public Opinion Quarterly, 32,* 379–397.

Flanders, J. P. (1968). A review of research on imitative behavior. *Psychological Bulletin, 69,* 316–337.

Flavell, J. H., Flavell, E. R., & Green, F. L. (1987). Young children's knowledge about the apparent-real and pretend-real distinctions. *Developmental Psychology, 23,* 816–822.

Flavell, J. H., Flavell, E. R., Green, F., & Korfmacher, J. (1990). Do young children think of television images as pictures or real objects? *Journal of Broadcasting & Electronic Media, 34,* 399–419.

Fleming, K., Thorson, E., & Atkin, C. K. (2004). Alcohol advertising exposure and perceptions: Links with alcohol expectancies and intentions to drink or drinking in underaged youth and young adults. *Journal of Health Communication, 9*(1), 3–30.

Fletcher, A. D. (1969). Negro and White children's television program preferences. *Journal of Broadcasting, 13,* 359–366.

Fogler, S. (1950). Prometheus or Frankenstein? *Journal of Educational Sociology, 24,* 154–166.

Fogler, S. (1953). Progress reports on TV. *The Elementary School Journal, 53,* 513–516.

Ford, B. S., McDonald, T. E., Owens, A. S., & Robinson, T. N. (2002). Primary care interventions to reduce television viewing in African-American children. *American Journal of Preventive Medicine, 22,* 106–109.

Ford, M. P. (1973). Imagery and verbalization as mediators in tactal-visual information processing. *Perceptual & Motor Skills, 36,* 815–822.

Forge, K. L., & Phemister, S. (1987). The effect of prosocial cartoons on preschool children. *Child Study Journal, 17*(2), 83–88.

Forsey, S. D. (1963). The influence of family structures upon the patterns and effects of family viewing. In L. Arons & M. A. May (Eds.), *Television and human behavior: Tomorrow's research in mass communication* (pp. 64–80). New York: Appleton-Century-Crofts.

Fosarelli, P. D. (1984). Television and children: A review. *Journal of Developmental and Behavioral Pediatrics*, 5(1), 30–37.

Fosarelli, P. D. (1986). Advocacy for children's appropriate viewing of television: What can we do? *Children's Health Care*, 15(2), 79–81.

Foster, J. E. (1964). Father images: Television and ideal. *Journal of Marriage and the Family*, 26, 353–355.

Fouts, G. T., & Glick, M. (1979). Effects of live and TV models on observational and extroverted children. *Perceptual & Motor Skills*, 48, 863–867.

Fouts, G. T., & Liikanen, P. (1975). The effects of age and developmental level on imitation in children. *Child Development*, 46, 555–558.

Fowles, B. (1976). Teaching children to read: An argument for television. *Urban Review*, 9, 114–120.

Fowles, B. (1977). A child and his television set: What is the nature of the relationship? *Education and Urban Society*, 10(1), 89–102.

Fowles, B., & Horner, V. (1975). The effects of television on children and adolescents: A suggested research strategy. *Journal of Communication*, 25(4), 98–101.

Fox, R. F. (1998). "Got-to-be, got-to-be, Dom-in-o's!": The semantics of student responses to TV commercials. In S. P. Kodish & R. P. Holston (Eds.), *Developing sanity in human affairs* (pp. 268–276). Westport, CT: Greenwood.

Fox, R. F. (2000). *Harvesting minds: How TV commercials control kids*. Westport, CT: Praeger.

Frank, J. (1969). *Television: How to use it wisely with children*. New York: Child Study Association of America.

Frank, P. R. (1978). Drug abuse is alive and well. *Educational Forum*, 42, 459–467.

Frazer, C. F., & Reid, L. N. (1979). Children's interaction with commercials. *Symbolic Interaction*, 2, 79–96.

Frazier, C. (1981). The social character of children's television viewing. *Communication Research*, 8, 307–322.

Freedman, J. L. (1984). Effect of television violence on aggressiveness. *Psychological Bulletin*, 96, 227–246.

Freedman, J. L. (1986). Television and aggression: A rejoinder. *Psychological Bulletin*, 100, 372–378.

Freedman, J. L. (1988). Television violence and aggression: What the evidence shows. *Applied Social Psychology Annual*, 8, 144–162.

Freedman, L. Z. (1961). Daydream in a vacuum tube: A psychiatrist's comment on the effects of television. In W. Schramm, J. Lyle, & E. B. Parker (Eds.), *Television in the lives of our children* (pp. 189–194). Stanford, CA: Stanford University Press.

Freidson, E. L. (1953). Adult discount: An aspect of children's changing taste. *Child Development*, 24, 39–49.

Freidson, E. L. (1954). Consumption of mass media by Polish-American children. *Quarterly of Film, Radio and Television*, 9, 92–101.

French, J., & Pena, S. (1991). Children's hero play of the 20th century: Changes resulting from television's influence. *Child Study Journal*, 21, 79–95.

Frenette, M. (1999). Explorations in adolescents' sense-making of anti-smoking messages. *Electronic Journal of Communication*, 9.

Frideres, J. S. (1973). Advertising, buying patterns and children. *Journal of Advertising Research, 13*(1), 34–36.

Friedlander, B. Z. (1993). Community violence, children's development, and mass media: In pursuit of new insights, new goals, and new strategies. *Psychiatry, 56*, 66–81.

Friedlander, B. Z., Weston, H. S., & Scott, C. S. (1974). Suburban preschool children's comprehension of age-appropriate informational television programs. *Child Development, 45*, 561–565.

Friedman, L. J. (1977). *Sex role stereotyping in the media: An annotated bibliography.* New York: Garland.

Friedrich-Cofer, L., & Huston, A. (1986). Television violence and aggression: The debate continues. *Psychological Bulletin, 100*, 364–371.

Friedrich-Cofer, L. K., Huston-Stein, A., Kipnis, D. M., Susman, E. J., & Clewett, A. S. (1979). Environmental enhancement of prosocial television content: Effects on interpersonal behavior, imaginative play, and self-regulation in a natural setting. *Developmental Psychology, 15*, 637–646.

Friedrich, L. K., & Huston-Stein A. (1973). Aggressive and prosocial television programs and the natural behavior of preschool children. *Monographs of the Society for Research in Child Development, 38*(4), 1–64.

Friedrich, L. K., & Huston-Stein, A. (1975). Prosocial television and young children: The effects of verbal labeling and role playing on learning and behavior. *Child Development, 46*, 27–38.

Friedson, E. (1953). The relations of social situation of contact to the media of mass communication. *Public Opinion Quarterly, 17*, 230–238.

Friedstad, M., & Thorson, E. (1993). Remembering ads: The effects of coding strategies, retrieval cues, and emotional response. *Journal of Consumer Psychology, 2*(1), 1–23.

Frost, J. L., Shin, D., & Jacobs, P. J. (1998). Physical environments and children's play. In O. N. Saracho & B. Spodek (Eds.), *Multiple perspectives on play in early childhood education* (pp. 255–294). Albany: State University of New York Press.

Frueh, T., & McGhee, P. E. (1975). Traditional sex role development and amount of time spent watching television. *Developmental Psychology, 11*(1), 109.

Fryear, J. L., & Thelen, M. H. (1969). Effect of sex of model and sex of observer on the imitation of affectionate behavior. *Developmental Psychology, 1*, 298.

Fujioka, Y., & Austin, E. W. (2002). The relationship of family communication patterns to parental mediation style. *Communication Research, 29*, 642–665.

Fujioka, Y., & Austin, E. W. (2003). The implications of vantage point in parental mediation of television and child's attitudes toward drinking alcohol. *Journal of Broadcasting & Electronic Media, 47*, 418–435.

Funk, J. B., Baldacci, H. B., Pasold, T., & Baumgardner, J. (2004). Violence exposure in real-life, video games, television, movies, and the Internet: Is there desensitization. *Journal of Adolescence, 27*, 23–39.

Furno Lamude, D. (1991). Dimensions of psychological time and favorite TV personalities. *Social Behavior & Personality, 19*, 277–288.

Furstenberg, F. F., Jr. (1999). Children and family change: Discourse between social scientists and the media. *Contemporary Sociology, 28*(1), 10–17.

Gable, S., & Lutz, S. (2000). Household, parent, and child contributions to childhood obesity. *Family Relations, 49*, 293–300.

Gadberry, S. (1974). Television as a baby-sitter: A field comparision of preschoolers' behavior during playtime and during television viewing. *Child Development, 45*, 1132–1136.

Gadberry, S. (1980). Effects of restricting first graders' TV-viewing on leisure time use, IQ change, and cognitive style. *Journal of Applied Developmental Psychology, 1*, 45–57.

Gaddy, G. (1986). Television's impact on high school achievement. *Public Opinion Quarterly, 50*, 340–359.

Gadow, K. D., & Sprafkin, J. (1987). Effects of viewing high versus low aggression cartoons on emotionally disturbed children. *Journal of Pediatric Psychology, 12*, 413–427.

Gadow, K. D., & Sprafkin, J. (1989). Field experiments of television violence with children: Evidence for an environmental hazard? *Pediatrics, 83*, 399–405.

Gadow, K. D., & Sprafkin, J. (1993). Television violence and children with emotional and behavioral disorders. *Journal of Emotional & Behavioral Disorders, 1*, 54–63.

Gadow, K. D., Sprafkin, J., & Ficarrotto, T. J. (1987). Effects of viewing aggression-laden cartoons on preschool aged emotionally disturbed children. *Child Psychiatry and Human Development, 17*, 257–274.

Gadow, K. D., Sprafkin, J., Kelly, E., & Ficarrotto, T. J. (1988). Reality perceptions of television: A comparision of social-labeled learning-disabled and nonhandicapped children. *Journal of Clinical Child Psychology, 17*, 25–33.

Galst, J. P. (1980). Television food commercials and pro-nutritional public service announcements as determinants of young children's snack choices. *Child Development, 51*, 935–938.

Galst, J. P., & White, M. (1976). The unhealthy persuader: The reinforcing value of television and children's purchase-influencing attempts at the supermarket. *Child Development, 47*, 1089–1096.

Gamble, M., & Cotugna, N. (1999). A quarter century of TV food advertising targeted at children. *American Journal of Health Behavior, 23*, 261–267.

Gans, H. J. (1968). *The uses of television and their educational implications: Preliminary findings from a survey of adult and adolescent New York television viewers.* New York: The Center for Urban Education.

Gantz, W. (2001). Conflicts and resolution strategies associated with television in marital life. In J. BrFyant & J. A. Bryant (Eds.), *Television and the American family* (2nd ed., pp. 289–316). Mahwah, NJ: Lawrence Erlbaum Associates, Inc.

Gantz, W., & Masland, J. (1986). Television as babysitter: TV ranked lowest on preferred activity lists for busy mothers, but use of TV as "sitter" is extensive. *Journalism Quarterly, 63*, 530–536.

Gantz, W., & Schwartz, N. C. (2000). Promotion in children's programming. In S. T. Eastman (Ed.), *Research in media promotion* (pp. 163–201). Mahwah, NJ: Lawrence Erlbaum Associates, Inc.

Garbarino, J. A. (1972). A note on the effects of television viewing. In U. Bronfenbrenner (Ed.), *Influences on human development* (pp. 397–400). Hinsdale, IL: Dryden.

Gardner, H., & Krasney Brown, L. (1984). Symbolic capabilities and children's television. In J. P. Murray & G. Salomon (Eds.), *The future of children's television* (pp. 45–51). Boys Town, NE: Father Flanagan's Boys Town.

Garner, H. G. (1975). An adolescent suicide, the mass media, and the educator. *Adolescence, 10,* 241–246.

Garramone, G. M. (1983). TV news and adolescent political socialization. In R. W. Bostrum & B. H. Westley (Eds.), *Communication Yearbook* (Vol. 7, pp. 651–669). Beverly Hills, CA: Sage.

Garramone, G. M., Atkin, C. K., Pinkleton, B. E., & Cole, R. T. (1990). Effects of negative political advertising on the political process. *Journal of Broadcasting & Electronic Media, 34,* 299–311.

Garry, R. (1967). Television for children. *Journal of Education, 150*(1), 1–46.

Garry, R., Rainsberry, F. B., & Winick, C. (1962). *For the young viewer: Television programming for children . . . at the local level.* New York: McGraw-Hill.

Geen, R. G. (1968). Effects of frustration, attack, and prior training in aggressiveness upon aggressive behavior. *Journal of Personality and Social Psychology, 9,* 316–321.

Geen, R. G. (1994). Television and aggression: Recent developments in research and theory. In D. Zillmann & J. Bryant (Eds.), *Media, children, and the family: Social scientific, psychodynamic, and clinical perspectives* (pp. 151–162). Hillsdale, NJ: Lawrence Erlbaum Associates, Inc.

Geen, R. G., & Berkowitz, L. (1967). Some conditions facilitating the occurrence of aggression after the observations of violence. *Journal of Personality, 35,* 666–676.

Geen, R. G., & O'Neal, E. C. (1969). Activation of cue elicited aggression by general arousal. *Journal of Personality and Social Psychology, 11,* 289–292.

Geen, R. G., & Stonner, D. (1972). Context effects in observed violence. *Journal of Personality and Social Psychology, 25,* 145–150.

Geen, R. G., Stonner, D., & Kelley, D. R. (1974). Aggression anxiety and cognitive appraisal of aggression-threat stimuli. *Journal of Personality and Social Psychology, 29,* 196–200.

Geen, R. G., & Thomas, S. L. (1986). The immediate effects of media violence on behavior. *Journal of Social Issues, 42*(3), 7–27.

Geiogamah, H., & Pavel, D. M. (1993). Developing television for American Indian and Alaska native children in the late 20th century. In G. L. Berry & J. K. Asamen (Eds.), *Children and television: Images in a changing sociocultural world* (pp. 191–204). Newbury Park, CA: Sage.

Geiser-Getz, G. C. (1995). "Cops" and the comic frame: Humor and meaning-making in reality-based television. *Electronic Journal of Communication, 5*(1).

Geist, E. A., & Gibson, M. (2000). The effect of network and public television programs on four and five year olds ability to attend to educational tasks. *Journal of Instructional Psychology, 27,* 250–261.

Geller, H., & Young, G. (1977). Family viewing: An FCC tumble from the tightrope? *Journal of Communication, 27*(2), 193–201.

Gentile, D. A., & Walsh, D. A. (2002). A normative study of family media habits. *Journal of Applied Developmental Psychology, 23,* 157–178.

Gerbner, G., & Gross, L. (1976). Living with television: The violence profile. *Journal of Communication, 26*(2), 173–199.

Gerbner, G., & Gross, L. (1980). The violent face of television and its lessons. In E. L. Palmer & A. Dorr (Eds.), *Children and the faces of television: Teaching, violence, selling* (pp. 149–162). New York: Academic.

Gerbner, G., Gross, L., Signorelli, N., & Morgan, M. (1980). Aging with television: Images on television drama and conceptions of social reality. *Journal of Communication, 30*(1), 37–47.

Gerend, M. A., MacKinnon, D. P., & Nohre, L. (2000). High school students' knowledge and beliefs about television advisory warnings. *Journal of Applied Communication Research, 28,* 291–308.

Gerhardstein, P., & Rovee-Collier, C. (2002). The development of visual search in infants and very young children. *Journal of Experimental Child Psychology, 81,* 194–215.

German, D. B. (1994). The role of the media in political socialization and attitude formation toward racial/ethnic minorities in the US. In R. F. Farnen (Ed.), *Nationalism, ethnicity, and identity: Cross national and comparative perspectives* (pp. 285–297). New Brunswick, NJ: Transaction.

Gerson, W. M. (1966). Mass media socialization behavior: Negro–white differences. *Social Forces, 45,* 40–50.

Gesselman, D. (1951). Television and reading. *Elementary English, 28,* 385–391.

Gibbons, J., Anderson, D. R., Smith, R., Field, D. E., & Fischer, C. (1986). Young children's recall and reconstruction of audio and audiovisual narratives. *Child Development, 57,* 1014–1023.

Gidwani, P. P., Sobol, A., DeJong, W., Perrin, J. M., & Gortmaker, S. L. (2002). Television viewing and initiation of smoking among youth. *Pediatrics, 110,* 505–508.

Gilkison, P. (1965). What influences the buying decisions of teenagers? *Journal of Retailing, 41,* 48.

Gilpin, E., Distefan, J. M., & Pierce, J. P. (2004). Population receptivity to tobacco advertising/promotions and exposure to anti-tobacco media: Effect of master settlement agreement in California: 1992–2002. *Health Promotion Practices, 5*(Suppl. 1), 91–99.

Ginsburg, H. J., Jenkins, C., Walsh, R., & Peck, B. (1989). Visual superiority effect in televised prevention of victimization programs for preschool children. *Perceptual & Motor Skills, 68,* 1179–1182.

Giudicatti, V., & Stening, B. W. (1980). Socioeconomic background and children's cognitive abilities in relation to television advertisements. *Journal of Psychology, 106,* 153–155.

Goff, D. H., & Goff, L. D. (1982). Regulation of television advertising to children: The policy dispute in its second decade. *Southern Speech Communication Journal, 48*(1), 38–50.

Goldberg, D. L., Carruth, B. R., & Skinner, J. (1993). Television viewing and dietary-intake of pregnant adolescents. *Nutrition Research, 13,* 621–632.

Goldberg, M. E. (1990). A quasi-experiment assessing the effectiveness of TV advertising directed to children. *Journal of Marketing Research, 27,* 445–454.

Goldberg, M. E., & Gorn, G. J. (1974). Children's reactions to television advertising: An experimental approach. *Journal of Consumer Research, 1*(2), 69–75.

Goldberg, M. E., & Gorn, G. J. (1978). Some unintended consequences of television advertising to children. *Journal of Consumer Research, 5*(1), 22–29.

Goldberg, M. E., & Gorn, G. J. (1983). Researching the effects of television advertising on children: A methodological critique. In M. J. A. Howe (Ed.), *Learning from television* (pp. 125–151). New York: Academic.

Goldberg, M. E., Gorn, G. J., & Gibson, W. (1978). TV messages for snack and breakfast foods: Do they influence children's preferences? *Journal of Consumer Research, 5*(2), 73–81.

Goldsen, R. K. (1978). Why television advertising is deceptive and unfair. *ETC: A Review of General Semantics, 35*, 354–375.

Goodman, E. (1981). Children as consumers: The subtle (and not so subtle) marketing of sex. *Childhood Education, 58*(2), 74–75.

Goodman, F. L., & To, C. Y. (1979). The future of television in the lives of children. *Viewpoints in Teaching and Learning, 55*(4), 36–40.

Goranson, R. E. (1970). Media violence and aggressive behavior: A review of experimental research. In L. Berkowitz (Ed.), *Advances in experimental social psychology* (Vol. 1, pp. 1–31). New York: Academic.

Gordon, T. F. (1969). An exploration into television violence. *Educational Broadcasting Review, 3*, 44–48.

Gordon, T. F., & Verna, M. E. (1978). *Mass communication effects and processes: A comprehensive bibliography, 1950–1975.* Beverly Hills, CA: Sage.

Gorn, G. J., & Goldberg, M. E. (1977). The impact of television advertising on children from low income families. *Journal of Communication Research, 4*, 86–88.

Gorn, G. J., & Goldberg, M. E. (1980). Children's responses to repetitive TV commercials. *Journal of Consumer Research, 6*, 421–424.

Gorn, G. J., & Goldberg, M. E. (1982). Behavioral evidence of the effects of televised food messages on children. *Journal of Consumer Research, 9*, 200–205.

Gorn, G. J., & Goldberg, M. E. (1987). Television and children's food habits: A big brother/sister approach. In M. E. Manley-Casimir & C. Luke (Eds.), *Children and television: A challenge for education* (pp. 34–48). New York: Praeger.

Gorn, G. J., Goldberg, M. E., & Kanugo, R. N. (1976). The role of educational television in changing the intergroup attitudes of children. *Child Development, 47*, 277–280.

Gortmaker, S. L., Must, A., Sobol, A. M., Peterson, K., Colditz, G. A., & Dietz, W. H. (1996). Television viewing as a cause of increasing obesity among children in the United States, 1986–1990. *Archives of Pediatrics & Adolescent Medicine, 150*, 356–362.

Gortmaker, S. L., Salter, C. A., Walker, D. K., & Deitz, W. H. Jr. (1990). The impact of television viewing on mental aptitude and achievement: A longitudinal study. *Public Opinion Quarterly, 54*, 594–604.

Gotz, I. I. (1975). On children and television. *The Elementary School Journal, 75*, 415–418.

Götz, M., Lemish, D., Aidman, A., & Moon, H. (2005). *Media and the make-believe worlds of children: When Harry Potter meets Pokémon in Disneyland.* Mahwah NJ: Lawrence Erlbaum Associates, Inc.

Gould, M. S., & Schaffer, M. (1986). The impact of suicide in television movies. *The New England Journal of Medicine, 315*, 690–694.

Gould, M. S., Shaffer, D., & Kleinman, M. (1988). The impact of suicide in television movies: Replication and commentary. *Suicide and Life-Threatening Behavior, 18* (1), 90–99.

Granberg, D. (1971). Selectivity in exposure and the effect of attitudes on judgments of the mass media coverage of the King assassination. *Journal of Social Psychology, 85*, 147–148.

Granello, D. H. (1997). Using *Beverly Hills, 90210* to explore developmental issues in female adolescents. *Youth & Society, 29*(1), 24–53.

Graves, S. B. (1993). Television, the portrayal of African Americans, and the development of children's attitudes. In G. L. Berry & J. K. Asamen (Eds.), *Children & television: Images in a changing sociocultural world* (pp. 179–190). Thousand Oaks, CA: Sage.

Graves, S. B. (1996). Diversity on television. In T. M. MacBeth (Ed.), *Tuning in to young viewers: Social science perspectives on television* (pp. 61–86). Thousand Oaks, CA: Sage.

Graves, S. B. (1999). Television and prejudice reduction: When does television as a vicarious experience make a difference? *Journal of Social Issues, 55,* 707–727.

Gray, O. P. (1987). Violence and children. *Archives of Disease in Childhood, 62,* 428–430.

Green, M. (1972). Television and violence: Who's doing what to whom. *Human Behavior, 1,* 73–78.

Green, J. M. (1978). Research on the effects of television advertising on children: A review of literature and recommendations for future research. A report prepared for the National Science Foundation. *American Journal of Psychiatry, 135,* 1121.

Greenberg, B. S. (1964). The effects of communicator incompatibility on children's judgments of television programs. *Journal of Broadcasting, 8,* 157–171.

Greenberg, B. S. (1965). Television for children: Dimensions of communicator and audience perceptions. *AV Communication Review, 13,* 385–396.

Greenberg, B. S. (1972). Children's reactions to TV Blacks. *Journalism Quarterly, 49,* 5–14.

Greenberg, B. S. (1993). Race differences in television and movie behaviors. In B. S. Greenberg, J. D. Brown, & N. L. Buerkel-Rothfuss (Eds.), *Media, sex and the adolescent* (pp. 145–152). Cresskill, NJ: Hampton.

Greenberg, B. S. (1994). Content trends in media sex. In D. Zillmann J. Bryant, & A. C. Huston et al. (Eds.), *Media, children, and the family: Social scientific, psychodynamic, and clinical perspectives* (pp. 165–182). Hillsdale, NJ: Lawrence Erlbaum Associates, Inc.

Greenberg, B. S., & Brand, J. E. (1993a). Cultural diversity on Saturday morning television. In G. L. Berry & J. K. Asamen (Eds.), *Children & television: Images in a changing sociocultural world* (pp. 132–142). Thousand Oaks, CA: Sage.

Greenberg, B. S., & Brand, J. E. (1993b). Television news and advertising in schools: The "Channel One" controversy. *Journal of Communication, 43*(1), 143–151.

Greenberg, B. S., Brown, J. D., & Buerkel-Rothfuss, N. (1993). *Media, sex, and the adolescent.* Cresskill, NJ: Hampton.

Greenberg, B. S., Dervin, B., Dominick, J. R., & Bowes, J. (1970). *Use of the mass media by the urban poor: Findings of the three research projects with an annotated bibliography.* New York: Praeger.

Greenberg, B. S., & Dominick, J. R. (1969). Racial and social class difference in teen-agers use of television. *Journal of Broadcasting, 13,* 331–344.

Greenberg, B. S., Fernando-Collado, C., Graef, D., Korzenny, F., & Atkin, C. (1979). Trends in use of alcohol and other substances on television. *Journal of Drug Education, 9,* 243–253.

Greenberg, B. S., & Linsangan, R. (1993). Gender differences in adolescents' media use, exposure to sexual content and parental mediation. In B. S. Greenberg, J. D. Brown, & N. L. Buerkel-Rothfuss (Eds.), *Media, sex and the adolescent* (pp. 134–144). Cresskill, NJ: Hampton.

Greenberg, B. S., Linsangan, R., & Soderman, A. (1993). Adolescents' reactions to television sex. In B. S. Greenberg, J. D. Brown, & N. L. Buerkel-Rothfuss (Eds.), *Media, sex and the adolescent* (pp. 196–224). Cresskill, NJ: Hampton.

Greenberg, B. S., Linsangan, R., Soderman, A., Heeter, C., Lin, C., Stanley, C., et al. (1993). Adolescents' exposure to television and movie sex. In B. S. Greenberg, J. D. Brown, & N. L. Buerkel-Rothfuss (Eds.), *Media, sex and the adolescent* (pp. 61–98). Cresskill, NJ: Hampton.

Greenberg, B. S., Perry, K. L., & Covert, A. M. (1983). The body human: Sex education, politics, and television. *Family Relations, 32*, 419–425.

Greenberg, B. S., & Reeves, B. (1976). Children and the perceived reality of television. *Journal of Social Issues, 32*(4), 86–97.

Greenberg, B. S., Stanley, C., Siemicki, M., Heeter, C., Soderman, A., & Linsangan, R. (1993). Sex content on soaps and prime-time television series most viewed by adolescents. In B. S. Greenberg, J. D. Brown, & N. L. Buerkel-Rothfuss (Eds.), *Media, sex and the adolescent* (pp. 29–44). Cresskill, NJ: Hampton.

Greenberg, H. R. (1967). Cutting them down to size. *Psychiatric Quarterly Supplement, 41*, 281–283.

Greenfield, P., & Beagles-Roos, J. (1988). Radio vs. television: Their cognitive impact on children of different socioeconomic and ethnic groups. *Journal of Communication, 38*(2), 71–92.

Greenfield, P., Farrar, D., & Beagles-Roos, J. (1986). Is the medium the message? An experimental comparison of the effects of radio and television on imagination. *Journal of Applied Developmental Psychology, 7*, 201–218.

Greenfield, P. M., Bruzzone, L., & Koyamatsu, K. (1987). What is rock music doing to the minds of our youth? A first experimental look at the effects of rock music lyrics and music videos. *Journal of Early Adolescence, 7*, 315–329.

Greenfield, P. M., Yut, E., Chung, M., Land, D., Kreider, H., Pantoja, M., et al. (1990). The program-length commercial: A study of the effects of television/toy tie-ins on imaginative play. *Psychology & Marketing, 7*, 237–255.

Greenhalgh, D. G., & Palmieri, T. L. (2003). The media glorifying burns: A hindrance to burn prevention. *Journal of Burn Care & Rehabilitation, 24*, 159–163.

Greenstein, J. (1954). Effects of television upon elementary school grades. *Journal of Educational Research, 48*, 161–176.

Greer, D., Potts, R., Wright, J. C., & Huston, A. C. (1982). The effects of television commercial form and commercial placement on children's social behavior and attention. *Child Development, 53*, 611–619.

Greeson, L. E. (1991). Recognition and ratings of television music videos: Age, gender, and sociocultural effects. *Journal of Applied Social Psychology, 21*, 1908–1920.

Greeson, L. E., & Williams, R. (1987). Social implications of music videos for youth: An analysis of the content and effects of MTV. *Youth & Society, 18*, 177–189.

Grieve, R., & Williamson, K. (1977). Aspects of auditory and visual attention to narrative material in normal and mentally handicapped children. *Journal of Child Psychiatry and Allied Disciplines, 18*, 251–262.

Griffin, E. (1976). What's fair to children? The policy need for new research on children's perceptions of advertising content. *Journal of Advertising, 5*(2), 14–18.

Griffin, E. (1980). The future is inevitable: But can it be shaped in the interests of children? In E. L. Palmer & A. Dorr (Eds.), *Children and the faces of television: Teaching, violence, selling* (pp. 339–352). New York: Academic.

Griffin, M. (1985). What young filmmakers learn from television: A study of structure in films made by children. *Journal of Broadcasting & Electronic Media, 29*, 79–92.

Griffin, R., Shaikat, S., & Plotkin, R. (1994). Sex, schemata, and social status: TV character identification and occupational aspirations among adolescents. In L. H. Turner, & H. M. Sterk (Eds.), *Differences that make a difference: Examining the assumptions in gender research* (pp. 85–97). Westport, CT: Bergin & Garvey.

Griffiths, M. (2005). Children drawing toy commercials: Re-imagining television production features. *Visual Communication, 4*(1), 21–38.

Griffiths, M., & Machin, D. (2003). Television and playground games as part of children's symbolic culture. *Social Semiotics, 13*, 147–161.

Griffore, R. J., & Phenice, L. A. (1996). Rules and television viewing. *Psychological Reports, 78*, 814.

Grimes, T. (1991). Mild auditory-visual dissonance in television news may exceed viewer attentional capacity. *Human Communication Research, 18*, 268–298.

Grimes, T., & Bergen, L. (2001). The notion of convergence as an epistemological base for evaluating the effect of violent TV programming on psychologically normal children. *Mass Communication & Society, 4*, 183–198.

Grimes, T., Bergen, L., Nichols, K., Vernberg, E., & Fonagy, P. (2004). Is psychopathology the key to understanding why some children become aggressive when they are exposed to violent television programming? *Human Communication Research, 30*, 153–181.

Groffman, S. (2003). TV or not TV, that is the question? *Journal of Optometric Vision Development, 34*(4), 167–170.

Gross, L. S., & Walsh, R. P. (1980). Factors affecting parental control over children's television viewing—A pilot study. *Journal of Broadcasting, 24*, 411–419.

Grossman, D. (2000). Teaching kids to kill: In R. S. Moser & C. E. Frantz (Eds.), *Shocking violence: Youth perpetrators and victims* (pp. 17–32). Springfield, IL: Charles C. Thomas.

Grube, J. W. (1993). Alcohol portrayals and alcohol advertising on television: Content and effects on children and adolescents. *Alcohol Health & Research World, 17*(1), 54–60.

Grube, J. W., & Wallack, L. (1994). Television beer advertising and drinking knowledge beliefs, and intentions among school children. *American Journal of Public Health, 84*(2), 254–259.

Gruber, E., & Thau, H. (2003). Sexually related content on television and adolescents of color: Media theory, Physiological development, and psychological impact. *Journal of Negro Education, 72*, 438–457.

Guba, E., Wolf, W., de Groot, S., Knemeyer, M., Van Atta, R., & Light, L. (1964). Eye movements and TV viewing in children. *AV Communication Review, 12*, 386–401.

Guest, L. P. (1955). Brand loyalty, twelve years later. *Journal of Applied Psychology, 39*, 405–408.

Guidicatti, V., & Stening, B. W. (1980). An empirical evaluation of a test measuring children's attitudes toward TV advertisements. *Psychological Reports, 46*, 1222.

Gunter, B. (1981). Measuring children's comprehension of television commercials. *Current Psychological Research and Reviews, 1*(2), 159–170.

Gunter, B., Furnham, A., & Griffiths, S. (2000). Children's memory for news: A comparison of three presentation media. *Media Psychology, 2*, 93–118.

Gussow, J. (1972). Counternutritional messages of TV ads aimed at children. *Journal of Nutrition Education, 4*(2), 48–52.

Guttentag, D. N., Albritton W. L., & Kettner, R. B. (1983). Daytime television viewing by hospitalized children: The effect of alternative programming. *Pediatrics, 71*, 620–625.

Haefner, M. J. (1991). Ethical problems of advertising to children. *Journal of Mass Media Ethics, 6*, 83–92.

Haefner, M. J., & Comstock, J. (1990). Compliance gaining on prime time family programs. *Southern Communication Journal, 55*, 402–420.

Haefner, M. J., Metts, S., & Wartella, E. A. (1989). Siblings' strategies for resolving conflict over television program choice. *Communication Quarterly, 37*, 223–230.

Haefner, M. J., & Wartella, E. A. (1987). Effects of sibling coviewing on children's interpretations of television programs. *Journal of Broadcasting & Electronic Media, 31*, 153–168.

Hae-Kyong, B., & Reece, B. B. (2003). Minorities in children's television commercials: New, improved, and stereotyped. *Journal of Consumer Affairs, 37*(1), 42–68.

Haines, K. C. (1984). Eye–hand coordination as related to television watching among preschool children. *Early Childhood Development and Care, 13*, 391–397.

Haines, W. H. (1955). Juvenile delinquency and television. *Journal of Social Theory, 1*, 192–198.

Hake, K. (2001). Five-year-olds' fascination for television: A comparative study. *Childhood: A Global Journal of Child Research, 8*, 423–441.

Hall, B. H. (1980). Critical television viewing skills for high school students. *Television and Children, 3*(2), 45–48.

Halpern, W. I. (1975). Turned-on toddlers. *Journal of Communication, 25*(4), 66–70.

Hamamoto, D. Y. (1993). They're so cute when they're young: The Asian-American child on television. In G. L. Berry & J. K. Asamen (Eds.), *Children and television: Images in a changing sociocultural world* (pp. 205–214). Newbury Park, CA: Sage.

Hampl, J. S. , Wharton, C. M., Taylor, C. A., Winham, D. M. , Block, J. L., & Hall, R. (2004). Primetime television impacts on adolescents' impressions of bodyweight, sex appeal, and food and beverage consumption. *Nutrition Bulletin, 29*(2), 92–99.

Hanratty, M. A., O'Neal, E., & Sulzer, J. L. (1972). The effects of frustration upon the imitation of aggression. *Journal of Personality and Social Psychology, 21*, 30–34.

Hapkiewicz, W. G. (1979). Children's reactions to cartoon violence. *Journal of Clinical Child Psychology, 8*(1), 30–34.

Hapkiewicz, W. G., & Roden, A. H. (1971). The effect of aggressive cartoons on children's interpersonal play. *Child Development, 42*, 1583–1585.

Hapkiewicz, W. G., & Stone, R. D. (1974). The effect of realistic versus imaginary aggressive models on children's interpersonal play. *Child Study Journal, 4*(2), 47–58.

Hargis, C. H., Gickling, E. E., & Mahmoud, C. C. (1975). The effectiveness of TV in teaching sight words to students with learning disabilities. *Journal of Learning Disabilities, 8*, 37–39.

Hargreaves, D., & Tiggemann, M. (2002). The effect of television commercials on mood and body dissatisfaction: The role of appearance-schema activation. *Journal of Social and Clinical Psychology, 21*, 287–308.

Hargreaves, D., & Tiggemann, M. (2003). The effect of "thin ideal" television commercials on body dissatisfaction and schema activation during early adolescence. *Journal of Youth & Adolescence, 32*, 367–374.

Harmon, J. M., Jr. (1950). Television and the leisure-time activities of children. *Education, 71*, 126–128.

Harrell, J. S., Gansky, S., Bradley, C. B., & McMurray, R. G. (1997). Leisure time activities of elementary school children. *Nursing Research, 46*, 246–253.

Harris, M. B. (1992). Television viewing, aggression and ethnicity. *Psychological Reports, 70*(1), 137–138.

Harris, M. B., Harris, R. J., & Davis, S. M. (1991). Ethnic and gender differences in Southwestern students' sources of information about health. *Health Education Research, 6*(1), 31–42.

Harris, M. B., & Voorhees, S. D. (1981). Sex-role stereotypes and televised models of emotion. *Psychological Reports, 48*(3), 826.

Harrison, K. (1997). Does interpersonal attraction to thin media personalities promote eating disorders? *Journal of Broadcasting & Electronic Media, 41*, 478–500.

Harrison, K. (2000a). The body electric: Thin-ideal media and eating disorders in adolescents. *Journal of Communication, 50*(3), 119–143.

Harrison, K. (2000b). Television viewing, fat stereotyping, body shape standards, and eating disorder symptomatology in grade school children. *Communication Research, 27*, 617–640.

Harrison, K. (2001). Ourselves, our bodies: Thin-ideal media, self-discrepancies, and eating disorder symptomatology in adolescents. *Journal of Social & Clinical Psychology, 20*, 289–323.

Harrison, K. (2005). Is "fat free" good for me? A panel study of television viewing and children's nutritional knowledge and reasoning . *Health Communication, 17*, 117–132.

Harrison, L., & Williams, T. M. (1986). Television and cognitive development. In T. M. Williams (Ed.), *The impact of television: A natural experiment in three communities* (pp. 87–142). Orlando, FL: Academic.

Harter, S. (2000). Is self-esteem only skin-deep? The inextricable link between physical appearance and self-esteem. *Reclaiming Children and Youth, 9*(3), 133–138.

Hartnagel, T. F., Teevan, J. J., & McIntyre, J. J. (1975). Television violence and violent behavior. *Social Forces, 54*, 341–351.

Harwood, R. L., & Weissberg, R. P. (1987). The potential of video in the promotion of social competence in children and adolescents. *Journal of Early Adolescence, 7*, 345–363.

Hashizume, S. (1970). The structure of the family education as seen in terms of TV-watching behavior. *Journal of Educational Sociology, 25*, 32–44.

Hawkins, R. P. (1977). The dimensional structure of children's perceptions of television reality. *Communication Research, 4*, 299–320.

Hawkins, R. P., & Pingree, S. (1980). Some processes in the cultivation effect. *Communication Research, 7*, 193–226.

Hawkins, R. P., & Pingree, S. (1981). Using television to construct social reality. *Journal of Broadcasting, 25*, 347–364.

Hawkins, R. P., & Pingree, S. (1986). Activity in the effects of television on children. In J. Bryant & D. Zillmann (Eds.), *Perspectives on media effects* (pp. 233–250). Hillsdale, NJ: Lawrence Erlbaum Associates, Inc.

Hawkins, R. P., Tapper, J., Bruce, L., & Pingree, S. (1995). Strategic and nonstrategic explanations for attentional inertia. *Communication Research, 22*, 188–206.

Hawkins, R. P., Yong-Ho, K., & Pingree, S. (1991). The ups and downs of attention to television. *Communication Research, 18*, 53–76.

Hayes, D. A. (1994). The children's hour revisited: The Children's Television Act of 1990. *Federal Communications Law Journal, 46*, 293–328.

Hayes, D. S., & Birnbaum, D. W. (1980). Preschoolers' retention of televised events: Is a picture worth a thousand words? *Developmental Psychology, 16*, 410–416.

Hayes, D. S., & Casey, D. M. (1992). Young children and television: The retention of emotional reactions. *Child Development, 63*, 1423–1436.

Hayes, D. S., Chemelski, B. E., & Birnbaum, D. W. (1981). Young children's incidental and intentional retention of televised events. *Developmental Psychology, 17*, 230–232.

Hayes, D. S., & Kelly, S. B. (1984). Young children's processing of television: Modality differences in the retention of temporal relations. *Journal of Experimental Psychology, 38*, 505–514.

Hayes, D. S., & Kelly, S. B. (1985). Sticking to syntax: The reflection of story grammar in children's and adult's recall of radio and television shows. *Merrill-Palmer Quarterly, 31*, 345–360.

Hayes, D. S., Kelly, S. B., & Mandel, M. (1986). Media differences in children's story synopses: Radio and television contrasted. *Journal of Educational Psychology, 78*, 341–346.

Hayes, E. J., Hill, J., & Young, H. (1975). Superfly, the Mack, Black youth, and counselors. *School Counselor, 22*, 174–179.

Hayes, E. J., McWilliams, J., & Hayes, J. C. (1977). Blaxploitation films and their effects on aggressive behavior in children. *Journal of Non-White Concerns in Personnel and Guidance, 5*, 175–179.

Hayner, H., Herbert, J., & Simcock, G. (2003). Imitation from television by 24- and 30-month olds. *Developmental Science, 6*, 254–261.

Haynes, R. B. (1978). Children's perceptions of "comic" and "authenthic" cartoon violence. *Journal of Broadcasting, 22*(1), 63–70.

Head, S. (1954). Content analysis of television drama programs. *Quarterly of Film, Radio and Television, 9*, 175–194.

Heald, G. R. (1980). Television viewing guides and parental recommendations. *Journalism Quarterly, 57*(1), 141–144.

Healy, J. M. (2004). Early television exposure and subsequent attentional problems in children. *Pediatrics, 113*, 917–919.

Hearold, S. (1986). A synthesis of 1043 effects of television on social behavior. In G. Comstock (Ed.), *Public communication and behavior* (pp. 65–133). Orlando, FL: Academic.

Heath, L., Bresolin, L., & Rinaldi, R. (1989). Effects of media violence on children: A review of the literature. *Archives of General Psychiatry, 46*, 376–379.

Heeren, J., & Shichor, D. (1984). Mass media and delinquency prevention: The case of "scared straight". *Deviant Behavior, 5,* 375–386.

Heeter, C. (1988). Watching Saturday morning cartoons. In C. Heeter & B. S. Greenberg (Eds.), *Cableviewing* (pp. 89–96). Norwood, NJ: Ablex.

Heeter, C., & Greenberg, B. S. (1985). Profiling the zappers. *Journal of Advertising Research, 25*(2), 15–19.

Heeter, C., Greenberg, B. S., Baldwin, T. F., Paugh, R., Srigley, R., & Atkin, D. (1988). Parental influences on viewing style. In C. Heeter & B. S. Greenberg (Eds.), *Cableviewing* (pp. 140–150). Norwood, NJ: Ablex.

Hein, K. (1980). Impact of mass media on adolescent sexual behavior. *American Journal of Disordered Child, 13*(4), 133–134.

Heineman, G. (1971). A network's point of view toward programming for children. *Clinical Pediatrics, 10,* 466.

Heins, M. (2001). *Not in front of the children: "Indecency," censorship and the innocence of youth.* New York: Hill and Wang.

Heintz, K. E. (1992). Children's favorite television families: A descriptive analysis of role interactions. *Journal of Broadcasting & Electronic Media, 36,* 443–451.

Heintz-Knowles, K. E. (2001). Balancing acts: Work–family issues on prime-time TV. In J. Bryant & J. A. Bryant (Eds.), *Television and the American family* (2nd ed., pp. 177–206). Mahwah, NJ: Lawrence Erlbaum Associates, Inc.

Hendershot, H. (1994). Media reform in the age of toasters: "Strawberry Shortcake," The continuum of gender construction and the deregulation of children's television. *Wide Angle, 16*(4), 57–82.

Hendershot, H. (1998). *Saturday morning censors: Television regulation before the V-chip.* Durham, NC: Duke University Press.

Hendershot, H. (2000). Teletubby trouble. *Television Quarterly, 31*(1), 19–25.

Hendershot, H. (2002). Great expectations: The rise and fall of the v-chip; The TV equivalent of the human appendix, it has failed to change children's viewing habits. *Television Quarterly, 33*(2–3), 70–75.

Hendershot, H. (2004). *Nickelodeon nation.* New York: New York University Press.

Henderson, R. W., Swanson, R., & Zimmerman, B. (1975). Inquiry response induction in preschool children through televised modeling. *Developmental Psychology, 11,* 523–524.

Hendry, L. B., & Patrick, H. (1977). Adolescents and television. *Journal of Youth & Adolescence, 6,* 325–336.

Henricksen, L. (1996). Naive theories of buying and selling: Implications for teaching critical-viewing skills. *Journal of Applied Communication Research, 24,* 93–109.

Henson, J. (1971). A producer's point of view on television for children. *Clinical Pediatrics, 10,* 465.

Heslop, L. A., & Ryans, A. B. (1980). A second look at children and the advertising of premiums. *Journal of Consumer Research, 6,* 414–420.

Hess, R. D., & Goldman, H. (1962). Parents' views of the effect of television on their children. *Child Development, 33,* 411–426.

Hesse, P., & Mack, J. E. (1991). The world is a dangerous place: Images of the enemy on children's television . In R. W. Rieber (Ed.), *The psychology of war and peace: The image of the enemy* (pp. 131–153). Thousand Oaks, CA: Sage.

Hetherington, E. M. (1964). Humor preferences in normal and physically handicapped children. *Journal of Abnormal and Social Psychology, 69,* 694–696.

Hills, M. (2004). *Dawson's Creek:* "Quality teen TV" and "mainstream cult"? In G. Davis & K. Dickenson (Eds.), *Teen TV: Genre, consumption, identity* (pp. 17–28). London: British Film Institute.

Himmelweit, H. T. (1963). Plan 4: An experimental study of taste development in children. In L. Arons & M. A. May (Eds.), *Television and human behavior* (pp. 46–62). New York: Appleton-Century-Crofts.

Himmelweit, H. T. (1966). Television and the child. In B. Berelson & M. Janowitz (Eds.), *Reader in public opinion and communication* 2nd ed., (pp. 418–445). New York: The Free Press.

Himmelweit, H. T., & Bell, N. (1980). Television as a sphere of influence on the child's learning about sexuality. In E. Roberts (Ed.), *Childhood sexual learning: The unwritten curriculum* (pp. 113–137). Cambridge, MA: Ballinger.

Hindin, T. J., Contento, I., & Gussow, J. D. (2004). A media literacy nutrition education curriculum for Head Start parents about the effects of television advertising on their children's food requests. *Journal of the American Dietetic Association, 104,* 192–198.

Hirsch, B., & Kulberg, J. M. (1987). Television and temporal development. *Journal of Early Adolescence, 7,* 331–344.

Hirsch, K. W. (1960). TV program selection as a function of prestige. *AV Communication Review, 8,* 284–285.

Hitchings, E., & Moynihan, P. (1998). The relationship between television food advertisements recalled and actual foods consumed by children. *Journal of Human Nutrition & Dietetics, 11,* 511–517.

Hite, C. F., & Hite, R. E. (1995). Reliance on brand by young children. *Journal of Marketing Research Society, 37,* 185–193.

Hoffman, D. (1998). TV, inactivity, and kids' obesity. *Physician & Sportsmedicine, 26*(11), 32–33.

Hoffman, M. L. (1979). Development of moral thought, feeling, and behavior. *American Psychologist, 34,* 958–966.

Hoffmann, R. J., & Flook, M. A. (1980). An experimental investigation of the role of television in facilitating shape recognition. *Journal of Genetic Psychology, 136,* 305–306.

Hoffner, C. (1996). Children's wishful identification and parasocial interaction with favorite television characters. *Journal of Broadcasting & Electronic Media, 40,* 389–402.

Hoffner, C., & Buchanan, M. (2002). Parents' responses to television violence: The third-person perception, parental mediation, and support for censorship. *Media Psychology, 4,* 231–252.

Hoffner, C., & Cantor, J. (1985). Developmental differences in responses to a television character's appearance and behavior. *Developmental Psychology, 21,* 1065–1074.

Hoffner, C., Cantor, J., & Thorson, E. (1988). Children's understanding of a televised narrative: Developmental differences in processing video and audio content. *Communication Research, 15,* 227–245.

Hoffner, C., Cantor, J., & Thorson, E. (1989). Children's responses to conflicting auditory and visual features of a televised narrative. *Human Communication Research, 16,* 256–278.

Hoffner, C., & Haefner, M. J. (1994). Children's news interest during the Gulf War: The role of negative affect. *Journal of Broadcasting & Electronic Media, 38,* 193–204.

Hoffner, C., & Haefner, M. J. (1997). Children's comforting of frightened coviewer: Real and hypothetical television-viewing situations. *Communication Research, 24,* 136–152.

Hollander, N. (1971). Adolescents and the war: The sources of socialization. *Journalism Quarterly, 58,* 472–479.

Hollander, S. W., & Jacoby, J. (1973). Recall of crazy mixed-up commercials. *Journal of Advertising Research, 13*(3), 39–42.

Hollenbeck, A. R. (1978). Television viewing patterns of families with young infants. *Journal of Social Psychology, 105,* 259–264.

Hollenbeck, A. R., & Slaby, R. G. (1979). Infant visual and vocal responses to television. *Child Development, 50,* 41–45.

Hollenbeck, A. R., & Slaby, R. G. (1982). Influence of a televised model's vocalization pattern on infants. *Journal of Applied Developmental Psychology, 3,* 57–65.

Holly, E. (1979). The role of media in the programming of an underclass. *Black Scholar, 10*(5), 31–37.

Holroyd, H. J. (1985). Children, adolescents, and television. *American Journal of Diseases of Children, 139,* 549–550.

Holtzman, J. M., & Akiyama, H. (1985). What children see: The aged on television in Japan and the United States. *Gerontologist, 25*(1), 62–68.

Honig, A. S. (1983). Television and young children. *Young Children, 38*(4), 63–76.

Hooper, M.-L., & Chang, P. (1998). Comparison of demands of sustained attentional events between public and private children's television programs. *Perceptual & Motor Skills, 86,* 431–434.

Hopkins, N. M., & Mullis, A. (1985). Family perceptions of television viewing habits. *Journal of Applied Family and Child Studies, 34,* 177–181.

Horn, O., Paradis, G., Potvin, L., Macaulay, A. C., & Desrosiers, S. (2001). Correlates and predictors of adiposity among Mohawk children. *Preventive Medicine, 33,* 274–281.

Hornick, R. C. (1977). Mass media use and the revolutions of using frustrations: A reconsideration of the theory. *Communication Research, 4,* 387–414.

Hornick, R. C. (1978). Television access and the slowing of cognitive growth. *American Educational Research Journal, 15*(1), 1–15.

Horton, R. W., & Santogrossi, D. A. (1978). The effect of adult commentary on reducing the influence of television violence. *Personality and Social Psychology Bulletin, 4,* 337–440.

Houle, R., & Feldman, R. S. (1991). Emotional displays in children's television programming. *Journal of Nonverbal Behavior, 15,* 261–271.

Hoven, C. W., Duarte, C. S., Wu, P., Erickson, E., Musa, G. J., & Mandell, D. J. (2004). Exposure to trauma and separation anxiety in children after the WTC attack. *Applied Developmental Science, 8,* 172–183.

Howitt, D. (1972). Television and aggression: A counterargument. *American Psychologist, 27*, 969–970.

Howitt, D., & Cumberbatch, G. (1973). The parameters of attraction to mass media figures. *Journal of Moral Education, 2*, 269–281.

Hoy, M. G., Young, C. E., & Mowen, J. C. (1986). Animated host-selling advertisements: Their impact on young children's recognition, attitudes, and behavior. *Journal of Public Policy and Marketing, 5*, 171–184.

Hoyt, J. L. (1970). Effect of mass media violence "justification" on aggression. *Journal of Broadcasting, 14*, 455–464.

Huesmann, L. R. (1986). Psychological processes promoting the relation between exposure to media violence and aggressive behavior by the viewer. *Journal of Social Issues, 42*, 125–139.

Huesmann, L. R. (1988). An information processing model for the development of aggression. *Aggressive Behavior, 14*, 13–24.

Huesmann, L. R., & Eron, L. D. (1986). *Television and the aggresive child: A cross-national comparison.* Hillsdale, NJ: Lawrence Erlbaum Associates, Inc.

Huesmann, L. R., Eron, L. D., Klein, R., Brice, P., & Fischer, P. (1983). Mitigating the imitation of aggressive behavior by changing children's attitudes about media violence. *Journal of Personality and Social Psychology, 44*, 899–910.

Huesmann, L. R., Eron, L. D., Lefkowitz, M. M., & Walder, L. O. (1973). Television violence and aggression: The causal effect remains. *American Psychologist, 28*, 617–620.

Huesmann, L. R., Fischer, P., Eron, L., Mermelstein, R., Kaplain-Shain, E., & Morikawa, S. (1979). Children's sex-role preference, sex of television model, and imitation of aggressive behavior. *Aggressive Behavior, 5*, 217–218.

Huesmann, L. R., Lagerspetz, K., & Eron, L. D. (1984). Intervening variables in the television violence–aggression relation: Evidence from two countries. *Developmental Psychology, 20*, 746–775.

Huesmann, L. R., & Malamuth, N. M. (1986). Media violence and antisocial behavior. *Journal of Social Issues, 42*(3), 1–6.

Huesmann, L. R., & Miller, L. S. (1994). Long-term effects of repeated exposure to media violence in childhood. In L. R. Huesmann (Ed.), *Aggressive behavior: Current perspectives* (pp. 153–186). New York: Plenum.

Huesmann, L. R., Moise, J. F., & Podolski, C. (1997). The effects of media violence on the development of anti-social behavior. In D. M. Stoff & J. Breiling (Eds.), *Handbook of antisocial behavior* (pp. 181–193). New York: Wiley.

Huesmann, L. R., Moise-Titus, J., Podolski, C. L., & Eron, L. (2003). Longitudinal relations between children's exposure to TV violence and their aggressive and violent behavior in young adulthood: 1977–1992. *Developmental Psychology, 39*, 201–221.

Hughes, J. N., & Hasbrouck, J. E. (1996). Television violence: Implications for violence prevention. *School Psychology Review, 25*, 134–151.

Hume, H., O'Connor, W. A., & Lowery, C. R. (1977). Family adjustment, and the psychosocial ecosystem. *Psychiatric Annals, 7*(7), 32–49.

Hur, K. K. (1978). Impact of "Roots" on Black and White teenagers. *Journal of Broadcasting, 88*, 289–298.

Hur, K. K., & Baran, S. H. (1979). One-parent children's identification with television characters and parents. *Communication Quarterly, 27*(3), 31–36.

Huskey, L., Jackstadt, S. L., & Goldsmith, S. (1991). Economic literacy and the content of television network news. *Social Education*, 55, 182–185, 194.

Husson, W. (1981). Theoretical issues in the study of children's attention to television. *Communication Research*, 9(3), 31–36.

Husson, W., & Krull, R. (1983). Nonstationarity in children's attention to television. In R. W. Bostrum & B. H. Westley (Eds.), *Communication yearbook* (Vol. 7, pp. 304–314). Beverly Hills, CA: Sage.

Huston, A. C., & Alvarez, M. M. (1990). The socialization context of gender role development in early adolescence. In R. Montemayor & G. R. Adams (Eds.), *From childhood to adolescence: A transitional period* (pp. 156–179). Newbury Park, CA: Sage.

Huston, A. C., Donnerstein, E., Fairchild, H. H., Feschbach, N. D., Katz, P. A., Murray, J. P., et al. (1992). *Big world, Small screen: The role of television in American society.* Lincoln: University of Nebraska Press.

Huston, A. C., Green, D., Wright, J. C., Welch, R., & Ross, R. (1984). Children's comprehension of televised formal features with masculine and feminine connotations. *Developmental Psychology*, 20, 707–716.

Huston, A. C., Watkins, B. A., & Kunkel, D. (1989). Public policy and children's television. *American Psychologist*, 44, 424–433.

Huston, A. C., & Wright, J. C. (1983). Children's processing of television: The informative functions of formal features. In J. Bryant & D. R. Anderson (Eds.), *Children's understanding of television* (pp. 35–68). New York: Academic.

Huston, A. C., & Wright, J. C. (1989). The forms of television and the child viewer. In G. Comstock (Ed.), *Public communication and behavior* (pp. 103–158). New York: Academic.

Huston, A. C., & Wright, J. C. (1994). Educating children with television: The forms of the medium. In D. Zillmann & J. Bryant (Eds.), *Media, children, and the family: Social scientific, psychodynamic, and clinical perspectives* (pp. 73–84). Hillsdale, NJ: Lawrence Erlbaum Associates, Inc.

Huston, A. C., & Wright, J. C. (1996). Television and socialization of young children. In T. M. MacBeth (Ed.), *Tuning in to young viewers: Social science perspectives on television* (pp. 37–60). Thousand Oaks, CA: Sage.

Huston, A. C., & Wright, J. C. (1998). Television and the informational needs of children. *Annals of the American Academy of Political and Social Science*, 557, 9–23.

Huston, A. C., Wright, J. C., Alvarez, M., Truglio, R., Fitch, M., & Piemyat, S. (1995). Perceived television reality and children's emotional and cognitive responses to its social content. *Journal of Applied Developmental Psychology*, 16, 231–251.

Huston, A. C., Wright, J. C., Fitch, M., Wroblewski, R., & Piemyat, S. (1997). Effects of documentary and fictional television formats on children's acquisition of schemata for unfamiliar occupations. *Journal of Applied Developmental Psychology*, 18, 563–583.

Huston, A. C., Wright, J. C., Marquis, J., & Green, S. B. (1999). How young children spend their time: Television and other activities. *Developmental Psychology*, 35, 912–925.

Huston, A. C., Wright, J. C., Rice, M. L., Kerkman, D., & St. Peters, M. (1990). Development of television viewing patterns in early childhood: A longitudinal investigation. *Developmental Psychology*, 26, 409–420.

Huston, A. C., Wright, J. C., Wartella, E., Rice, M., Watkins, B., Campbell, T., et al. (1981). Communicating more than content-formal features of children's television programs. *Journal of Communication, 33,* 32–48.

Huston-Stein, A. (1967). Imitation of resistance to temptation. *Child Development, 38,* 157–169.

Huston-Stein, A., Fox, S., Greer, D., Watkins, B. A., & Whitaker, J. (1981). The effects of action and violence in television programs on the social behavior and imaginative play of preschool children. *Journal of Genetic Psychology, 138,* 183–191.

Huston-Stein, A., & Friedrich, L. K. (1975). Impact of television on children and youth. In E. M. Hetherington (Ed.), *Review of child development research* (Vol. 5, pp. 183–256). Chicago: University of Chicago Press.

Huston-Stein, A., & Wright, J. C. (1979). Children and television: Effects of the medium, its content and its form. *Journal of Research and Development in Education, 13*(1), 20–31.

Hutchinson, J. R. (1949). Television, a cure for delinquency. *Secondary Education, 14,* 3.

Hymowitz, K. S. (2001). The teening of childhood. *Arts Education Policy Review, 102*(6), 13–21.

Hyung-Jim, W., & Kim, Y. (2003). Modern gladiators: A content analysis of televised wrestling. *Mass Communication & Society, 6,* 361–379.

Ingelfinger, E. J. (1976). Violence on TV: An unchecked environmental hazard. *New England Journal of Medicine, 294,* 837–838.

Isler, L., Popper, E. T., & Ward, S. (1987). Children's purchase requests and parental responses: Results from a diary study. *Journal of Advertising Research, 27*(5), 28–39.

Jackman, J. (1975). Drug abuse: Barriers to care: Continuity of care. *Drug Forum, 4,* 209–216.

Jackson-Beeck, M. (1979). Interpersonal and mass communication in children's political socialization. *Journalism Quarterly, 566,* 48–53.

Jacobvitz, R. S., Wood, M. R., & Albin, K. (1991). Cognitive skills and young children's comprehension of television. *Journal of Applied Developmental Psychology, 12,* 219–235.

Jacoby, J., & Kyner, D. B. (1973). Brand loyalty vs. repeat purchasing behavior. *Journal of Marketing Research, 10*(1), 1–9.

Jaglom, L., & Gardner, H. (1981a). Decoding the worlds of television. *Studies in Visual Communication, 7*(1), 33–47.

Jaglom, L., & Gardner, H. (1981b). The preschool viewer as anthropologist. In H. Kelly & H. Gardner (Eds.), *Viewing children through television* (pp. 9–30). San Francisco: Jossey-Bass.

Jambor, E. (2001). Media involvement and the idea of beauty. In J. J. Robert-McComb (Ed.), *Eating disorders in women and children: Prevention, stress management, and treatment* (pp. 179–183). Boca Raton, FL: CRC.

James, N. C., & McCain, T. A. (1982). Television games preschool children play: Patterns, themes, and uses. *Journal of Broadcasting, 26,* 783–800.

Jarvis, C. (2001). School is hell: Gendered fears in teenage horror. *Educational Studies, 27,* 257–267.

Jason, L. A. (1983). Self monitoring in reducing children's excessive television monitoring. *Psychological Reports, 53,* 1280.

Jason, L. A. (1987). Reducing children's excessive television viewing and assessing secondary changes. *Journal of Clinical Child Psychology, 16*(3), 245–250.

Jason, L. A., & Fries, M. (2004). Helping parents reduce children's television viewing. *Research on Social Work Practice, 14,* 121–132.

Jason, L. A., & Johnson, S. Z. (1995). Reducing excessive television while increasing physical activity. *Child & Family Behavior Therapy, 17*(2), 35–45.

Jason, L. A., Johnson, S. Z., & Jurs, A. (1993). Reducing children's television viewing with an inexpensive lock. *Child & Family Behavior Therapy, 15*(3), 45–54.

Jason, L. A., Kennedy Hanaway, L., & Brackshaw, E. (1999). Television violence and children: Problems and solutions. In T. P. Gullotta & S. J. McElhaney (Eds.), *Violence in homes and communities: Prevention, intervention, and treatment* (pp. 133–156). Thousand Oaks, CA: Sage.

Jassem, H., & Glasser, T. L. (1983). Children, indecency, and the perils of broadcasting. *Journalism Quarterly, 60,* 509–512, 579.

Jayaratne, T. E., Flanagan, C., & Anderman, E. (1996). Predicting college students attitudes toward the Persian Gulf War: The role of gender and television exposure. *Peace & Conflict: Journal of Peace Psychology, 2,* 151–171.

Jeffrey, D. B., McLellarn, R. W., & Fox, D. T. (1982). The development of children's eating habits: the role of television commercials. *Health Education Quarterly, 9,* 174–189.

Jeffries-Fox, S., & Jeffries-Fox, B. (1981). Gender differences in socialization through television to occupational roles: An exploratory approach. *Journal of Early Adolescence, 1,* 293–302.

Jellinek, M. (2001). Impact of media. *Journal of the American Academy of Child & Adolescent Psychiatry, 40,* 1124–1124.

Jenkins, G. G. (1977). Families, mass communications and the marketplace. *Childhood Education, 54*(2), 67–70.

Jenkins, H. (1998). *The children's culture reader.* New York: New York University Press.

Jing, X., Soyeon, S. & Lotz, S. (2004). Ethnic identity, socialization factors, and culture-specific consumption behavior. *Psychology & Marketing, 21,* 93–113.

John, D. R. (1999). Through the eyes of a child: Children's knowledge and understanding of advertising. In M. C. Macklin & L. Carlson (Eds.), *Advertising to children: Concepts and controversies* (pp. 3–26). Thousand Oaks, CA: Sage.

Johnson, F. L., & Young, K. (2002). Gendered voices in children's television advertising. *Critical Studies in Media Communication, 19,* 461–480.

Johnson, J. (1982). Using television to change stereotypes. *Prevention in Human Services, 2*(1–sup–2), 67–81.

Johnson, J. G., Cohen, P., Smailes, E. M., Kasen, S., & Brook, J. S. (2002). Television viewing and aggressive behavior during adolescence and adulthood. *Science, 295,* 2468–2471.

Johnson, M. O. (1996). Television violence and its effect on children. *Journal of Pediatric Nursing, 11*(2), 94–99.

Johnson, R. T. (1990). The videobased setting as a context for learning story information. *Childhood Education, 66,* 168–171.

Johnston, J., & Ettema, J. S. (1986). Using television to best advantage: Research for prosocial television. In J. Bryant & D. Zillmann (Eds.), *Perspectives on media effects* (pp. 143–164). Hillsdale, NJ: Lawrence Erlbaum Associates, Inc.

Johnstone, J. W. C. (1974). Social integration and mass media use among adolescents: A case study. In J. G. Blumer & E. Katz (Eds.), *The uses of mass communications: Current perspectives on gratifications research* (pp. 35–48). Beverly Hills, CA: Sage.

Jones, G. (2002). *Killing monsters: Why children need fantasy, and make-believe violence.* New York: Basic Books.

Jones, R. S. (1981). New media and politicization: American youth. *Journal of Early Adolescence, 1*(1), 60–71.

Jones, S. (2005). MTV: The medium was the message. *Critical Studies in Media Communication, 22*(1), 83–89.

Jordan, A. B. (1997). Children and television: A conference summary. *Annals of the American Academy of Political and Social Science, 550,* 153–167.

Jordan, A. B. (2003). Children remember prosocial program lessons but how much are they learning? *Journal of Applied Developmental Psychology, 24,* 341–345.

Jordan, A. B. (2004a). The role of media in children's development: An ecological perspective. *Journal of Developmental & Behavioral Pediatrics, 25,* 196–207.

Jordan, A. B. (2004b). The three-hour rule and educational television for children. *Popular Communication, 2,* 103–118.

Jordan, A. B., & Woodard, E. H. (1998). Growing pains: Children's television in the new regulatory environment. *Annals of the American Academy of Political and Social Science, 557,* 83–95.

Jordan, A. B., & Woodard, E. H. (2001). Electronic childhood: The availability and use of household media by 2- to 3-year-olds. *Zero to Three, 22*(2), 4–9.

Josephson, W. L. (1987). Television violence and children's aggression: Testing the priming, social script and disinhibition predictions. *Journal of Personality and Social Psychology, 53,* 882–892.

Joy, L. A., Kimball, M. M., & Zabrack, M. L. (1986). Television exposure and children's aggressive behavior. In T. M. Williams (Ed.), *The impact of television: A natural experiment in three communities* (pp. 303–360). Orlando, FL: Academic.

Kacerguis, M. A., & Adams, G. (1979). Implications of sex typed child rearing practices, toys, and mass media materials in restricting occupational choices of women. *Family Coordinator, 28,* 369–375.

Kachgal, T. (2004). "Look at *The Real World.* There's always a gay teen on there": Sexual citizenship and youth-targeted reality television. *Feminist Media Studies, 4,* 361–365.

Kahn, K. F., & Geer, J. G. (1994). Creating impressions: An experimental investigation of political advertising on television. *Political Behavior, 16*(1), 93–116.

Kaid, L. L. (1997). Effects of the television spots on images of Dole and Clinton. *American Behavioral Scientist, 40,* 1085–1094.

Kaid, L. L., Chanslor, M., & Hovind, M. (1992). The influence of program and commercial type on political advertising effectiveness. *Journal of Broadcasting & Electronic Media, 36,* 303–320.

Kalamas, A. D., & Gruber, M. L. (1998). Electrodermal responses to implied versus actual violence on television. *Journal of General Psychology, 125*(1), 31–37.

Kaliebe, K., & Sondheimer, A. (2002). The media: Relationships to psychiatry and children: A seminar. *Academic Psychiatry, 26,* 205–215.

Kamins, M. A., Marks, L. J., & Skinner, D. (1991). Television commercial evaluation in the context of program induced mood: Congruency versus consistency effects. *Journal of Advertising, 20*(2), 1–14.

Kaplan, D. (1985). The world according to television. *Instructor, 94*(9), 52–54.

Kaplan, R. M. (1972). On television as a cause of aggression. *American Psychologist, 27,* 968–969.

Katzman, N. I., & Nyenhuis, J. (1972). Color vs. black-and-white effects on learning, opinion, and attention. *AV Communication Review, 20,* 16–28.

Kaune, W. T., Miller, M. C., Linet, M. S., Hatch, E. E., Kleinerman, R. A., Wacholder, S., et al. (2000). Children's exposure to magnetic fields produced by U.S. television sets used for viewing programs and playing video games. *Bioelectromagnetics, 21,* 214–227.

Kavoori, A., & Matthews, D. (2004). Critical media pedagogy: Lessons from the Thinking Television Project. *Howard Journal of Communications, 15,* 99–115.

Kay, H. (1972). Weaknesses in the television-causes-aggression analysis by Eron et al. *American Psychologist, 27,* 970–973.

Kaye, B. K., & Sapolsky, B. S. (2004). Watch your mouth! An analysis of profanity uttered by children on prime-time television. *Mass Communication & Society, 7,* 429–452.

Kefauver, E. (1956). Effects of mass media on children: Television and juvenile delinquency. *Religious Education, 51,* 456–461.

Keith, T. Z., Reimers, T. M., Fehrmann, P. G., Pottebaum, S. M., & Aubery, L. W. (1986). Parental involvement, homework, and TV time: Direct and indirect effects on high school achievement. *Journal of Educational Psychology, 35,* 912–925.

Keller, S. (1963). The social world of the urban slum child: Some early findings. *American Journal of Orthopsychiatry, 33,* 823–831.

Kellermann, K. (1985). Memory processes in media effects. *Communication Research, 12*(1), 83–131.

Kelley, B. R., & Beauchesne, M. A. (2001). The impact of violence on children and adolescents. *School Nurse News, 18*(4), 38–42.

Kelley, P., Buckingham, D., & Davies, H. (1999). Talking dirty: Children, sexual knowledge and television. *Childhood: A Global Journal of Child Research, 6,* 221–242.

Kelly, A. E., & Spear, P. S. (1991). Intraprogram synopses for children's comprehension of television content. *Journal of Experimental Child Psychology, 52*(1), 87–98.

Kelly, H., & Gardner, H. (1981). *Viewing children through television.* San Francisco: Jossey-Bass.

Kelly, K., & Edwards, R. (1992). Observations: Does discussion of advertising transform its effects? Yes . . . sometimes: A case among college students and their responses to anti-drug advertising. *Journal of Advertising Research, 32*(4), 79–83.

Kelly, P. T. (Ed.). (1999). *Television violence: A guide to the literature* (2nd ed.). Commack, NY: Nova Science.

Kennedy, C. M. (2000). Television and young Hispanic children's health behaviors. *Pediatric Nursing, 26,* 283–291.

Kennedy, C. M., Strzempko, F., Danford, C., & Kools, S. (2002). Children's perceptions of TV and health behavior effects. *Journal of Nursing Scholarship, 34,* 289–294.

Kenny, C. T., & Elliott, L., Jr. (1972). Selective exposure and the "active group effect." *Journal of Psychology, 82*, 197–199.

Kent, R. J., & Machleit, K. A. (1990). The different effects of within-brand and between-brand processing on the recall and recognition of television commercials. *Journal of Advertising, 19*(2), 4–14.

Kerkman, D. D., Kunkel, D. H. A. C., Wright, J. C., & Piñon, M. F. (1990). Children's television programming and the free market solution. *Journalism Quarterly, 67*, 147–156.

Kerkman, D. D., Piñon, M. F., Wright, J. C., & Huston, A. C. (1996). Children's reasoning about video and real balance-scale. *Early Education and Development, 7*, 237–252.

Kessler, R. C., Downey, G., Milavsky, J. R., & Stipp, H. (1988). Clustering of teenage suicides after television news stories about suicides: A reconsideration. *American Journal of Psychiatry, 145*, 1379–1383.

Kielwasser, A. P., & Wolf, M. A. (1992). Mainstream television, adolescent homosexuality, and significant silence. *Critical Studies in Mass Communication, 9*, 350–373.

Kimball, M. M. (1986). Television and sex-role attitudes. In T. M. Williams (Ed.), *The impact of television: A natural experiment in three communities* (pp. 265–302). New York: Academic.

Kimball, M. M., & Joy, L. A. (1987). Television violence: Does it promote aggressive behavior? In M. E. Manley-Casimir & C. Luke (Eds.), *Children and television: A challenge for education* (pp. 49–75). New York: Praeger.

Kinder, M. (1984). Music video and the spectator: Television, ideology, and dream. *Film Quarterly, 38*, 2–15.

Kinder, M. (1991). *Playing with power in movies, television, and video games.* Berkeley: University of California Press.

Kinder, M. (Ed.). (1999). *Kids' media culture.* Durham NC: Duke University Press.

King, D. L. (1994). *Captain Planet and the Planeteers:* Kids, environmental crisis, and competing narratives of the new world order. *Sociological Quarterly, 35*(1), 103–120.

King, J., & Hayslip, B. (2001). The media's influence on college students' views of death. *Omega: Journal of Death & Dying, 44*(1), 37–56.

King, M. M., & Multon, K. D. (1996). The effects of television role models on the career aspirations of African American junior high school students. *Journal of Career Development, 23*, 111–125.

Kinsey, J. (1987). The use of children in advertising and the impact of advertising aimed at children. *6*, 169–175.

Kippax, S., & Murray, J. P. (1980). Using the mass media—Need gratification and perceived utility. *Communication Research, 7*, 335–360.

Klapper, H. L. (1978). Childhood socialization and television. *Public Opinion Quarterly, 42*, 426–430.

Klapper, J. T. (1960). *The effects of mass communication.* New York: Free Press.

Klapper, J. T. (1968). The impact of viewing "aggression": Studies and problems of extrapolation. In O. N. Larsen (Ed.), *Violence and the mass media* (pp. 131–138). New York: Harper & Row.

Klein, H., Shiffman, K. S., & Welka, D. A. (2000). Gender-related content of animated cartoons, 1930 to the present. *Advances in Gender Research, 4*, 291–317.

Klein, J., Brown, J. D., Childers, K. W., Oliveri, J., Porter, C., & Dykers, C. (1992). Adolescents risky behavior and mass-media use. *Pediatrics, 90,* 24–31.

Klesges, R. C., Shelton, M. L., & Klesges, L. M. (1993). Effects of television on metabolic rate: Potential implications for childhood obesity. *Pediatrics, 91,* 281–286.

Kline, F. G., & Clarke, P. (1971). *Mass communications and youth: Some current perspectives.* Beverly Hills, CA: Sage.

Kline, F. G., Miller, P. V., & Morrison, A. J. (1974). Adolescents and family planning information: An exploration of audience needs and media effects. In J. G. Blumer & E. Katz (Eds.), *The uses of mass communications: Current perspectives on gratifications research* (pp. 113–136). Beverly Hills, CA: Sage.

Kline, S. (1993). *Out of the garden: Toy, TV, and child culture in the age of marketing.* New York: Verso.

Kline, S. (1995). The promotion and marketing of toys: Time to rethink the paradox? In A. D. Pellegrini (Ed.), *The future of play theory* (pp. 165–186). Albany: State University of New York Press.

Kline, S., & Pentecost, D. (1990). The characterization of play: Marketing children's toys. *Play and Culture, 3,* 235–255.

Klinger, L. J., Hamilton, J. A., & Cantrell, P. J. (2001). Children's perceptions of aggressive and gender-specific content in toy commercials. *Social Behavior & Personality, 29*(1), 11–20.

Knell, G. E. (1995). The Children's Television Act: Encouraging positive television for our children. *Comm/Ent: Hastings Communications and Entertainment Law Journal, 17,* 699–704.

Knight, S. (1979). Children's advertising—behind the candy-coated message. *Technology Review, 81*(7), 74–75.

Kniveton, B. H. (1973). Social class and imitation of aggression adult and peer models. *Journal of Social Psychology, 89,* 311–312.

Kolbe, R. H. (1990). Gender roles in children's television advertising: A longitudinal analysis. In J. Leigh & C. R. Martin, Jr. (Eds.), *Current issues and research in advertising* (pp. 197–206). Ann Arbor: Graduate School of Business Administration, University of Michigan.

Kolbe, R. H., & Langefeld, C. D. (1993). Appraising gender role portrayals in TV commercials. *Sex Roles, 28,* 393–417.

Kolbe, R. H., & Muehling, D. D. (1995). An investigation of the fine print in children's television advertising. *Journal of Current Issues and Research in Advertising, 17*(2), 77–95.

Korn, J. H. (1978). The concept of a drug in first and third grade children. *Journal of Drug Education, 8*(1), 59–67.

Kotch, J. B., Coulter, M. L., & Lipsitz, A. (1986). Does televised drinking influence children's attitudes towards alcohol? *Addictive Behavior, 11*(1), 67–70.

Kotler, J. A., Wright, J. C., & Huston, A. C. (2001). Television use in families with children. In J. Bryant & J. A. Bryant (Eds.), *Television and the American family* (2nd Ed., pp. 33–48). Mahwah, NJ: Lawrence Erlbaum Associates, Inc.

Kotz, K., & Story, M. (1994). Food advertisements during children's Saturday morning television programming: Are they consistent with dietary recommendations? *Journal of American Diet Association, 94,* 1296–1300.

Kovaric, P. M. (1993). Television, the portrayal of the elderly, and children's attitudes. In G. L. A. Samen & J. K. Berry (Eds.), *Children & television: Images in a changing sociocultural world* (pp. 243–254). Thousand Oaks, CA: Sage.

Kraus, S. (1973). Mass communication and political socialization: Re-assessment of two decades of research. *Quarterly Journal of Speech, 59*, 390–400.

Krcmar, M. (1996). Family communication patterns, discourse behavior, and child television viewing. *Human Communication Research, 23*, 251–277.

Krcmar, M. (1998). The contribution of family communication patterns to children's interpretations of television violence. *Journal of Broadcasting & Electronic Media, 42*, 250–264.

Krcmar, M. (2001). The effect of television policy on children and families. In J. Bryant & J. A. Bryant (Eds.), *Television and the American family* (2nd Ed., pp. 435–448). Mahwah, NJ: Lawrence Erlbaum Associates, Inc.

Krcmar, M., & Albada, K. F. (2000). The effect of an educational/informational rating on children's attraction to and learning from an educational program. *Journal of Broadcasting & Electronic Media, 44*, 674–689.

Krcmar, M., & Cantor, J. (1997). The role of television advisories and ratings in parent–child discussions of television viewing choices. *Journal of Broadcasting & Electronic Media, 41*, 393–411.

Krcmar, M., & Cooke, M. C. (2001). Children's moral reasoning and their perceptions of television violence. *Journal of Communication, 51*, 300–316.

Krcmar, M., & Curtis, S. (2003). Mental models: Understanding the impact of fantasy violence on children's moral reasoning. *Journal of Communication, 53*, 460–478.

Krcmar, M., & Valkenburg, P. M. (1999). A scale to assess children's moral interpretations of justified and unjustified violence and its relationship to television viewing. *Communication Research, 26*, 608–634.

Krcmar, M., & Vieira, E. T., Jr. (2005). Imitating life, imitating television: The effects of family and television models on children's moral reasoning. *Communication Research, 32*, 267–294.

Krendl, K., Clarke, G. Dawson, R., & Dawson, C. (1993). Preschoolers and VCRs in the home: A multiple methods approach. *Journal of Broadcasting & Electronic Media, 37*, 293–312.

Krendl, K., & Watkins, B. (1983). Understanding television: An exploratory inquiry into the reconstruction of narrative content. *Educational Communication and Technology Journal, 31*, 201–212.

Kronenberger, W. G., Matthews, V. P., Dunn, D. W., Yang, W., Wood, E. A., Giauque, A. L., et al. (2005). Media violence exposure and executive functioning in aggressive and control adolescents. *Journal of Clinical Psychology, 61*, 725–738.

Krosnick, J. A. (2003). Psychosocial predictors of heavy television viewing among preadolescents and adolescents. *Basic and Applied Social Psychology, 25*, 87–111.

Krugman, D. M., Cameron, G. T., & White, C. M. (1995). Visual attention to programming and commercials: The use of in-home observations. *Journal of Advertising, 24*(1), 1–12.

Krugman, D. M., Quinn, W. H., Sung, Y., & Morrison, M. (2005). Understanding the role of cigarette promotion and youth smoking in a changing marketing environment. *Journal of Health Communication, 10*, 261–279.

Krull, R. (1983). Children learning to watch television. In J. Bryant & D. R. Anderson (Eds.), *Children's understanding of television* (pp. 103–123). New York: Academic.

Krull, R., & Husson, W. (1979). Children's attention: The case of TV viewing. In E. Wartella (Ed.), *Children communicating: Media and development of thought, speech and understanding* (pp. 83–114). Beverly Hills, CA: Sage.

Krull, R., & Husson, W. (1980). Children's anticipatory attention to the TV screen. *Journal of Broadcasting, 24*(1), 35–47.

Kruttschnitt, C., Heath, L., & Ward, D. (1986). Family violence, television viewing habits, and other adolescent experiences related to violent criminal behavior. *Criminology, 24*, 235–267.

Kubey, R. W. (1990). Television and family harmony among children, adolescents, and adults: Results from the experience sampling method. In J. Bryant (Ed.), *Television and the American family* (pp. 73–88). Hillsdale, NJ: Lawrence Erlbaum Associates, Inc.

Kubey, R. W. (1996). Television dependence, diagnosis, and prevention: With commentary on video games, pornography, and media education. In T. M. MacBeth (Ed.), *Tuning in to young viewers: Social science perspectives on television* (pp. 221–260). Thousand Oaks, CA: Sage.

Kubey, R. W., & Larson, R. (1990). The use and experience of the new video media among children and young adolescents. *Communication Research, 17*(1), 107–130.

Kubey, R. W., & Peluso, T. (1990). Emotional response as a cause of interpersonal news diffusion: The case of the space shuttle tragedy. *Journal of Broadcasting & Electronic Media, 34*, 69–76.

Kundanis, R. M. (2003). *Children, teens, families, and mass media: The millennial generation.* Mahwah, NJ: Lawrence Erlbaum Associates, Inc.

Kundanis, R. M. (2004). The faces of televisual media: Teaching, violence, selling to children. *American Journal of Psychology, 117*, 643–649.

Kunkel, D. (1988a). Children and host-selling television commercials. *Communication Research, 15*(1), 71–92.

Kunkel, D. (1988b). From a raised eyebrow to a turned back: The FCC and children's product-related programming. *Journal of Communication, 38*(4), 61–90.

Kunkel, D. (1991). Crafting media policy: The genesis and implications of the Children's Television Act of 1990. *American Behavioral Science, 35*, 181–202.

Kunkel, D. (1992). Children's television advertising in the multichannel environment. *Journal of Communication, 42*(3), 134–152.

Kunkel, D. (1993). Policy and the future of children's television. In G. L. Berry & J. K. Asamen *Children & television: Images in a changing sociocultural world* (pp. 273–290). Thousand Oaks, CA: Sage.

Kunkel, D. (1998). Policy battles over defining children's educational television. *Annals of the American Academy of Political and Social Science, 557*, 39–53.

Kunkel, D. (2003). The truest metric for evaluating the Children's Television Act. *Journal of Applied Developmental Psychology, 24*, 347–354.

Kunkel, D., & Canepa, J. (1994). Broadcasters' license renewal claims regarding children's educational programming. *Journal of Broadcasting & Electronic Media, 38*, 397–416.

Kunkel, D., Cope, K. M., & Biely, E. (1999). Sexual messages on television: Comparing findings from three studies. *Journal of Sex Research, 36*, 230–236.

Kunkel, D., & Farianola, W. J. (2001). Underestimating our own weight? The scope and impact of communication research on public policy. In W. B. Gudykuns (Ed.), *Communication Yearbook* (Vol. 25, pp. 411–431). Mahwah, NJ: Lawrence Erlbaum Associates.

Kunkel, D., Farinola, W., Jo, M., Farrar, K., Donnerstein, E., Biely, E., et al. (2002). Deciphering the V-chip: An examination of the television industry's program rating judgments. *Journal of Communication, 52*(1), 112–138.

Kunkel, D., & Gantz, W. (1993). Assessing compliance with industry self-regulation of television advertising to children. *Journal of Applied Communication Research, 21*, 148–162.

Kunkel, D., & Goette, U. (1997). Broadcasters' response to the Children's Television Act. *Communication Law & Policy, 2*, 289–308.

Kunkel, D., & Murray, J. (1991). Television, children, and social policy, issues and resources for child advocates. *Journal of Clinical Psychology, 20*, 88–95.

Kunkel, D., & Roberts, D. (1991). Young minds and marketplace values: Issues in children's television advertising. *Journal of Social Issues, 47*(1), 57–72.

Kunkel, D., & Watkins, B. (1987). Evolution of children's television regulatory policy. *Journal of Broadcasting & Electronic Media, 31*, 367–389.

Kunkel, D., Wilson, B. J., Donnerstein, E., Linz, D., Smith, S., Gray, T., et al. (1995). Measuring television violence: The importance of context. *Journal of Broadcasting & Electronic Media, 39*, 284–291.

Kuribayashi, A., Roberts, M. C., & Johnson, R. J. (2001). Actual nutritional information of products advertised to children and adults on Saturday. *Children's Health Care, 30*, 309–322.

Lake, S. (1981). *Television's impact on children and adolescents.* Phoenix, AZ: Oryx.

Lambert, W. E., & Klineberg, O. (1967). *Children's views of foreign peoples.* New York: Appleton-Century-Crofts.

Lambo, A. M. (1981). Children's ability to evaluate television commercial messages for sugared products. *American Journal of Public Health, 71*, 1060–1062.

Landau, S., Lorch, E., & Milich, R. (1992). Visual attention to and comprehension of television in attention-deficit hyperactivity disordered and normal boys. *Child Development, 63*, 928–937.

Lande, R. G. (1993). The video violence debate. *Hospital and Community Psychiatry, 44*, 347–351.

Lang, A., Geiger, S., Strickerda, M., & Sumner, J. (1993). The effects of related and unrelated cuts on television viewer's attention, processing capacity, and memory. *Communication Research, 20*(1), 4–29.

Lang, A., Schwartz, N., Yongkuk, C., & Seungwhan, L. (2004). Processing substance abuse messages: Production pacing, arousing content and age. *Journal of Broadcasting & Electronic Media, 48*, 61–89.

Laosa, L. M. (1976). Viewing bilingual multicultural educational television: An empirical analysis of children's behaviors during television viewing. *Journal of Educational Psychology, 68*, 133–142.

Larsen, O. N. (1962). Innovators and early adopters of television. *Sociological Inquiry, 32*, 16–34.

Larsen, O. N. (1966). Controversies about the mass communication of violence. *Annals of the American Academy of Political and Social Science, 364*, 37–49.

Larsen, O. N., Gray, L. N., & Fortis, J. G. (1963). Goals and goal-achievement in television content: Models for anomie. *Sociological Inquiry, 33*, 180–196.

Larsen, O. N., Gray, L. N., & Fortis, J. G. (1968). Achieving goals through violence on television. In O. N. Larsen (Ed.), *Violence and the mass media* (pp. 97–114). New York: Harper & Row.

Larson, M. S. (1989). Interaction between siblings in primetime television families. *Journal of Broadcasting & Electronic Media, 33,* 305–315.

Larson, M. S. (1993). Family communication on prime-time television. *Journal of Broadcasting & Electronic Media, 37,* 349–357.

Larson, M. S. (1996). Sex roles and soap operas: What adolescents learn about single motherhood. *Sex Roles, 35,* 97–110.

Larson, M. S. (2001a). Interactions, activities and gender in children's television commercials: A content analysis. *Journal of Broadcasting & Electronic Media, 45,* 41–56.

Larson, M. S. (2001b). Sibling interaction in situation comedies over the years. In J. Bryant & J. A. Bryant (Eds.), *Television and the American family* (pp. 163–176).

Larson, M. S. (2002). Race and interracial relationships in children's television commercials. *Howard Journal of Communications, 13,* 223–235.

Larson, M. S. (2003). Gender, race, and aggression in television commercials that feature children. *Sex Roles, 48,* 67–75.

Larson, R. (1995). Secrets in the bedroom: Adolescents' private use of media. *Journal of Youth & Adolescence, 24,* 535–550.

Larson, R. (2001). Children and adolescents in a changing media world. *Monographs of the Society for Research in Child Development, 66*(1), 148–154.

Larson, R., & Kubey, R. (1983). Television and music: Contrasting media in adolescent life. *Youth & Society, 15*(1), 13–31.

Lasky, K. (1990). Perceptions of television programming among college students with varying degrees of video production experience. *Educational Research Quarterly, 14,* 48–52.

Lavalekar, A. (2000). Social awareness in relation to media among high school students. *Psychological Studies, 45,* 178–180.

Lawrence, F. C., Trasker, G. E., Daly, C. T., Orhiel, A. L., & Wozniak, P. H. (1986). Adolescents' time spent viewing television. *Adolescence, 21,* 431–436.

Lawrence, F. C., & Wozniak, P. H. (1989). Children's television viewing with family members. *Psychological Reports, 65,* 395–400.

Lazar, B. A. (1994a). Under the influence: An analysis of children's television regulation. *Social Work, 39,* 67–74.

Lazar, B. A. (1994b). Why social work should care: Television violence and children. *Child & Adolescent Social Work Journal, 11,* 3–19.

Lazar, B. A. (1996). Old battles, new frontiers: A study of television violence and social work with children. *Child & Adolescent Social Work Journal, 13,* 527–540.

Lazar, B. A. (1998). The lull of tradition: A grounded theory study of television violence, children and social work. *Child & Adolescent Social Work Journal, 15,* 117–131.

Lazarsfeld, P. F. (1955). Why is so little known about the effects of television on children and what can be done? *Public Opinion Quarterly, 19,* 242–251.

Lazarus, A. L. (1956). Pupils' TV habits. *Educational Leadership, 13,* 242.

Leaper, C., Breed, L., Hoffman, L., & Perlman, C. A. (2002). Variations in the gender-stereotyped content of children's television cartoons across genres. *Journal of Applied Social Psychology, 32,* 1653–1662.

Ledingham, J. (1999). Nutrition, health and safety: The effects of media violence on children. *Journal of Early Education and Family Review, 6*(5), 37–42.

Lee, B. (1980). Prime time in the classroom. *Journal of Communication, 30*(1), 175–180.

Lee, D. J., Trapido, E., Weatherby, N., & Rodriguez, R. (2001). Correlates of participation and willingness to participate in anti-tobacco activities. *Journal of Community Health, 26,* 447–457.

Lee, E. B., & Browne, L. A. (1981). Television uses and gratifications among Black children, teenagers, and adults. *Journal of Broadcasting, 25,* 203–208.

Lee, E. B., & Browne, L. A. (1995). Effects of television advertising on African-American teenagers. *Journal of Black Studies, 25,* 523–536.

Lee, J. (1991). Integrating popular culture in a pedagogy of resistance: Students respond to the sitcom "Roseanne". *Feminist Teacher, 5*(3), 19–24.

Lee, R. E. (1971). Inquiry into children's programming—A call for action. *The Notre Dame Lawyer, 47,* 230–246.

Lee, R. G., Taylor, V. A., & McGetrick, R. (2004). Toward reducing youth exposure to tobacco messages: Examining the breadth of brand and nonbrand communications. *Journal of Health Communication, 9,* 461–479.

Lees, G. E. (1978). Unsafe for little ears—Regulation of broadcast advertising to children. *UCLA Law Review, 25,* 1131–1186.

Lefkowitz, M. M., Eron, L., Walder, L., & Huesmann, L. R. (1977). *Growing up to be violent.* New York: Pergamon.

Lefkowitz, M. M., Walder, L. O., Eron, L. D., & Huesmann, L. R. (1973). Preference for televised contact sports as related to sex differences in aggression. *Developmental Psychology, 9,* 417–420.

Leifer, A. D., Collins, W. A., Gross, B. M., Taylor, P. H., Andrews, L., & Blackmer, E. R. (1971). Developmental aspects of variables related to observational learning. *Child Development, 42,* 1509–1516.

Leifer, A. D., Gordon, N. J., & Graves, S. B. (1974). Children's television more than mere entertainment. *Harvard Educational Review, 44,* 213–245.

Lejins, P. (1960). *Crime, violence, and horror movies and TV shows and juvenile delinquency.* New York: National Council on Crime and Delinquency.

Lemert, J. B., & Nestvold, K. J. (1970). Television news and status conferral. *Journal of Broadcasting, 14,* 491–497.

Lemish, D. (1982). The rules of viewing television in public places. *Journal of Broadcasting, 26,* 757–781.

Lemish, D. (1987). Viewers in diapers: The early development of television viewing. In T. R. Lindlof (Ed.), *Natural audiences: Qualitative research of media uses and effects* (pp. 33–57). Norwood, NJ: Ablex.

Lemish, D. (1997). Kindergartners' understanding of television: A cross-cultural comparison. *Communication Studies, 48*(2), 109–126.

Lemish, D., & Rice, M. L. (1986). Television as a talking picture book: A prop for language acquisition. *Journal of Child Language, 13,* 251–274.

Lemon, J. (1977). Women and Blacks on prime-time television. *Journal of Communication, 27*(4), 70–79.

Lerner, L., & Weiss, R. L. (1972). Role of value of reward and model affective response in vicarious reinforcement. *Journal of Personality and Social Psychology, 21,* 93–100.

Lesser, G. S. (1976). Application of psychology to television programming: Formulation of program objectives. *American Psychologist, 31*, 135–136.

Lesser, H. (1977). *Television and the preschool child.* New York: Academic.

Levi, R. P. (1979). Violence on television: An old problem with a new picture. *North Carolina Law Review, 58*, 97–136.

Levin, D. E. (1998). *Remote control childhood? Combating the hazards of media culture.* Washington, DC: National Association for the Education of Young Children.

Levin, D. E., & Carlsson-Paige, N. (2003). Marketing violence: The special toll on young children of color. *Journal of Negro Education, 72*, 427–438.

Levin, S. R., Petros, T. V., & Petrella, F. W. (1982). Preschooler's awareness of television advertising. *Child Development, 53*, 933–937.

Levin, S. T., & Anderson, D. R. (1976). The development of attention. *Journal of Communication, 26*(2), 126–135.

Levine, L. E., & Waite, B. M. (2000). Television viewing and attentional abilities in fourth and fifth grade children. *Journal of Applied Developmental Psychology, 21*, 667–679.

Levine, M. (1996). *Viewing violence: How media violence affects your child's and adolescent's development.* New York: Doubleday.

Levinson, R. M. (1975). From Olive Oyl to Sweet Polly Purebread: Sex role stereotypes and televised cartoons. *Journal of Popular Culture, 9*, 561–572.

Levonian, E. (1969). Personality and communication-mediated opinion change: The influence of control. *Journal of Communication, 19*, 217–226.

Lewin, Z. G. (1990). Children, television advertising, policy issues and practices: A cognitive developmental perspective. *Interdisciplinaria, 9*(2), 71–82.

Lewis, C. E., & Lewis, M. A. (1974). The impact of television commercials on health-related beliefs and behaviors of children. *Pediatrics, 3*, 431–435.

Lewis, L. A. (1990). *Gender, politics and MTV: Voicing the difference.* Philadelphia: Temple University Press.

Lewis, M. A., & Lewis, C. E. (1975). Kids vs. commercials. *American Family Physician, 12*(5), 126–127.

Lewis, P. (1949). TV and teenagers. *Educational Screen, 28*, 159–161.

Lewis, P. (1950). TV takes a test. *Educational Screen, 29*, 196–198.

Lewis, P. (1951a). Child TV fans, and superfans. *Science Digest, 29*, 39.

Lewis, P. (1951b). Teenagers tame TV. *Educational Screen, 30–31*, 174–175.

Li-Vollmer, M. (2002). Race representation in child-targeted television commercials. *Mass Communication & Society, 5*, 207–226.

Libow, J. A. (1992). Traumatized children and the news media: Clinical considerations. *American Journal of Orthopsychiatry, 62*, 379–386.

Lichter, S. R., Lichter, L. S., Rothman, S., & Amundson, D. (1988). TV and the family: The parents prevail. *Public Opinion, 10*, 51–54.

Liebert, D. E., Sprafkin, J. N., Liebert R. M., & Rubinstein, E. A. (1977). Effects of television commercial disclaimers on the product expectations of children. *Journal of Communication, 27*(1), 118–124.

Liebert, R. M. (1974). Television and children's aggressive behavior: Another look. *American Journal of Psychoanalysis, 34*(2), 99–107.

Liebert, R. M. (1975). Modeling and the media. *School Psychology Digest, 4*(1), 22–29.

Liebert, R. M. (1986). Effects of television on children and adolescents. *Journal of Developmental and Behavioral Pediatrics, 7*(1), 43–48.

Liebert, R. M., & Baron, R. A. (1972). Some immediate effects of televised violence on children's behavior. *Developmental Psychology, 6*, 469–475.

Liebert, R. M., Cohen, L. A., Joyce, C., Murrel, S., Nisonoff, L., & Sonnenschein, S. (1977). Effects of television: Predispositions revisited. *Journal of Communication, 27*(3), 217–221.

Liebert, R. M., Davidson, E. S., & Neale, J. M. (1974). Aggression in childhood: The impact of television. In V. B. Cline (Ed.), *Where do you draw the line?* Provo, UT: Brigham Young University Press.

Liebert, R. M., Neale, J. M., & Davidson, E. S. (1973). *The early window: Effects of television on children and youth.* Elmsford, NY: Pergamon.

Liebes, T. (1992). Television, parents, and the political socialization of children. *Teachers College Record, 94*, 73–86.

Lin, C. A. (1993). Modeling the gratification-seeking process of television viewing. *Human Communication Research, 20*, 224–244.

Lin, C. A. (2001). The VCR, home video culture, and new video technologies. In J. Bryant & J. A. Bryant (Eds.), *Television and the American family* (2nd Ed., pp. 91–107). Mahwah, NJ: Lawrence Erlbaum Associates, Inc.

Lin, C. A., & Atkin, D. J. (1989). Parental mediation and rulemaking for adolescent use of television and VCRs. *Journal of Broadcasting & Electronic Media, 33*, 53–67.

Lindlof, T. R., & Copeland, G. A. (1982). Television rules of prepartum new families. In M. Burgoon (Ed.), *Communication Yearbook* (Vol. 6, pp. 555–582). Beverly Hills, CA: Sage.

Lindquist, J. D. (1981). Measuring children's attitudes toward TV commercials: An instrument reliability test. *Journal of the Academy of Marketing Science, 9*, 409–418.

Lindquist, C. H., Reynolds, K. D., & Goran, M. I. (1999). Sociocultural determinants of physical activity among children. *Preventive Medicine, 29*, 305–312.

Linebarger, D. L. (2001). Learning to read from television: The effects of using captions and narration. *Journal of Educational Psychology, 93*, 288–298.

Linebarger, D. L., Kosanic, A. Z., Greenwood, C. R., & Doku, N. S. (2004). Effects of viewing the television program "Between the Lions" on the emergent literacy skills of young children. *Journal of Educational Psychology, 96*, 297–308.

Linebarger, D. L., & Walker, D. (2005). Infants' and toddlers' television viewing and language outcomes. *American Behavioral Scientist, 48*, 624–646.

Linn, M. C., de Benedictis, T., & Delucchi, K. (1982). Adolescent reasoning about advertisements: Preliminary investigations. *Child Development, 53*, 1599–1613.

Linn, S., & Poussaint, A. F. (1999). Watching television: What are children learning about race and ethnicity? *Child Care Information Exchange, 128*, 50–52.

Linton, S. (1992). Analysis of information about television in developmental psychology textbooks. *Teaching of Psychology, 19*, 82–86.

Lipsitz, A., Brake, G., Vincent, E. J., & Winters, M. (1993). Another round for the brewers: Television ads and children's alcohol expectancies. *Journal of Applied Social Psychology, 23*, 439–450.

Lisosky, J. M. (2001). For all kids' sakes: Comparing children's television policy-making in Australia, Canada and the United States. *Media, Culture & Society, 23*, 821–842.

Liss, M. B. (1981). Children's television selections: A study of indicators of same-race preferences. *Journal of Cross-Cultural Psychology, 12*(1), 103–110.

Liss, M. B., & Price, D. (1981). What, when, and why deaf children watch television. *American Annals of the Deaf, 126,* 493–498.

Liss, M. B., & Reinhardt, L. C. (1980). Aggression on prosocial television programs. *Psychological Reports, 46,* 1065–1066.

Liss, M. B., Reinhardt, L. C., & Fredriksen, S. (1983). TV heroes: The impact of rhetoric and deeds. *Journal of Applied Developmental Psychology, 4,* 175–187.

List, J. A., Collins, A. W., & Westby, S. D. (1983). Comprehension and inferences from traditional and nontraditional sex-role portrayals on television. *Child Development, 54,* 1579–1587.

Littner, N. A. (1969). A psychiatrist looks at television and violence. *Television Quarterly, 8,* 7–23.

Long, B. H., & Henderson, E. H. (1973). Children's use of time: Some personal and social correlates. *The Elementary School Journal, 72,* 193–199.

Long, M. L., & Simon, R. J. (1974). The roles and statuses of women on children and family TV programs. *Journalism Quarterly, 51,* 107–110.

Lonner, W. J., Thorndike, R. M., Forbes, N. E., & Ashworth, C. (1985). The influence of television on measured cognitive abilities: A study with Native Alaskan children. *Journal of Cross Cultural Psychology, 16,* 355–380.

Lopiparo, J. J. (1977). Aggression on TV could be helping our children. *Intellect, 105,* 345–346.

Lorch, E. P. (1994). Measuring children's cognitive processing of television. In A. Lang (Ed.), *Measuring psychological responses to media messages* (pp. 209–226). Hillsdale, NJ: Lawrence Erlbaum Associates, Inc.

Lorch, E. P., Anderson, D. R., & Levin, S. R. (1979). The relationship of visual attention to children's comprehension of television. *Child Development, 50,* 722–727.

Lorch, E. P., Bellack, D. R., & Augsback, L. H. (1987). Young children's memory for televised stories: Effects of importance. *Child Development, 58,* 453–463.

Lorch, E. P., Castle V. J. (1997). Preschool children's attention to television: Visual attention and probe response times. *Journal of Experimental Child Psychology, 66*(1), 111–127.

Lorch, E. P., Milich, R., Sanchez, R. P., van den Broek, P., Baer, S., Hooks, K., et al. (2000). Comprehension of televised stories in boys with attention deficit/hyperactivity disorder and nonreferred boys. *Journal of Abnormal Psychology, 109,* 321–330.

Lorch, E. P., & Sanchez, R. P. (1997). Children's memory for televised events. In P. W. van den Broek & P. J. Bauer (Eds.), *Developmental spans in event comprehension and representation: Bridging fictional and actual events* (pp. 271–291). Hillsdale, NJ: Lawrence Erlbaum Associates, Inc.

Lorch, E. P., Sanchez, R. P., van den Broek, P., Milich, R., Murphy, E. L., Lorch, R. F., Jr., et al. (1999). The relation of story structure properties to recall of television stories in young children with attention-deficit hyperactivity disorder and nonreferred peers. *Journal of Abnormal Child Psychology, 27,* 293–309.

Loughlin, M., & Desmond, R. J. (1981). Social interaction in advertising directed to children. *Journal of Broadcasting, 25,* 303–307.

Lovaas, O. I. (1961). Effect of exposure to symbolic aggression on aggressive behavior. *Child Development, 32,* 37–44.

Lovelace, V. O., & Huston, A. C. (1982). Can television teach prosocial behavior? *Prevention in Human Services, 2*(1–sup-2), 93–106.

Lovibond, S. H. (1967). The effect of media stressing crime and violence upon children's attitudes. *Social Problems, 15,* 91–100.

Lovil, D. D., & Padderud, A. B. (1981). Video disclaimers in television advertising: Are they effective? *Journal of Communication, 31*(2).

Low, J., & Durkin, K. (2001). Children's conceptualization of law enforcement on television and in real life. *Legal & Criminal Psychology, 6,* 197–214.

Lowe, P. J., & Durkin, K. (1999). The effect of flashback on children's understanding of television crime content. *Journal of Broadcasting & Electronic Media, 43,* 83–97.

Lowenstein, L. F. (1978). Television violence and its effect on the young mind. *News & Views, 3*(8), 25–27.

Lowney, K. S. (2003). Wrestling with criticism: The World Wrestling Federation's ironic campaign against the Parents Television Council. *Symbolic Interaction, 26,* 427–446.

Luecke-Aleksa, D., Anderson, D. R., Collins, P., & Schmitt, K. L. (1995). Gender constancy and television viewing. *Developmental Psychology, 31,* 773–780.

Luke, C. (1987). Television discourse and schema theory: Toward a cognitive model of information processing. In M. E. Manley-Casimir & C. Luke (Eds.), *Children and television: A challenge for education* (pp. 76–107). New York: Praeger.

Luke, C. (1990). *Constructing the child viewer: A history of the American discourse on television and children 1950–1980.* New York: Praeger.

Luke, C. (1991). The making of the child TV viewer: A post culturalist agenda for conducting the history of research on mass media and children. *Howard Journal of Communications, 3*(1–2), 14–35.

Lull, J. (1978). Choosing television programs by family vote. *Communication Quarterly, 26,* 53–57.

Lull, J. (1980a). Family communication patterns and the social uses of television. *Communication Research, 7,* 319–334.

Lull, J. (1980b). Girl's favorite TV females. *Journalism Quarterly, 57,* 146–150.

Lull, J. (1980c). The social uses of television. *Human Communication Research, 6,* 197–209.

Lull, J. (1982). How families select television programs: A mass-observational study. *Journal of Broadcasting, 26,* 801–811.

Lull, J. (1985). The naturalistic study of media use and youth culture. In K. E. Rosengren, L. A. Wenner, & P. Palmgreen (Eds.), *Media gratifications research: Current perspectives* (pp. 209–224). Beverly Hills, CA: Sage.

Lull, J. (1988). *World families watch television.* Thousand Oaks, CA: Sage.

Lull, J. (1990). Families' social uses of television as extensions of the household. In J. Bryant (Ed.), *Television and the American Family* (pp. 59–72). Hillsdale, NJ: Lawrence Erlbaum Associates, Inc.

Lull, J., Hanson, C. A., & Marx, M. J. (1977). Recognition of female stereotypes in TV commercials. *Journalism Quarterly, 54,* 153–156.

Lury, K. (2002). Chewing gum for the ears: Children's television and popular music. *Popular Music, 21*, 291–307.

Lyle, J., & Hoffman, H. R. (1972). Television in the lives of our children—The 1970s. *Educational and Industrial Television, 5*(5), 10.

Lyness, P. I. (1951). Patterns in the mass communication tastes of the young audience. *Journal of Educational Psychology, 42*, 449–467.

Lyness, P. I. (1952). The place of the mass media in the lives of boys and girls. *Journalism Quarterly, 29*, 43–54.

MacBeth, T. M. (1996a). Indirect effects of television: Creativity, persistence, school achievement, and participation in other activities. In T. M. MacBeth (Ed.), *Tuning in to young viewers: Social science perspectives on television* (pp. 149–219). Thousand Oaks, CA: Sage.

MacBeth, T. M. (1996b). *Tuning into young viewers: Social science perspectives on television.* Thousand Oaks, CA: Sage.

MacBeth, T. M. (1998). Quasi-experimental research on television and behavior: Natural and field experiments. In J. K. Asamen & G. L. Berry (Eds.), *Research paradigms, television and social behavior* (pp. 109–152). Thousand Oaks, CA: Sage.

Maccoby, E. E. (1951). Television: Its impact on school children. *Public Opinion Quarterly, 15*, 421–444.

Maccoby, E. E. (1954). Why do children watch television? *Public Opinion Quarterly, 18*, 239–244.

Maccoby, E. E. (1963). The effects of television on children. In W. Schramm (Ed.), *The science of human communication* (pp. 116–127). New York: Basic Books.

Machin, D., & Davies, M. M. (2003). Future generations: The implied importance of the fantasy world in development of a child's imagination. *Childhood: A Global Journal of Child Research, 10*(1), 105–117.

Mackey, M. (2003). Television and the teenage literate: Discourses of *Felicity. College English, 65*(4), 389–410.

Macklin, M. C. (1983). Do children understand television ads? *Journal of Advertising Research, 23*(1), 63–70.

Macklin, M. C. (1984). Psychometric investigations of Rossiter's short test measuring children's attitudes toward television commercials. *Psychological Reports, 54*, 623–627.

Macklin, M. C. (1985). Do young children understand the selling intent of commercials. *Journal of Consumer Affairs, 19*, 293–304.

Macklin, M. C. (1987). Preschoolers' understanding of the information function of television advertising. *Journal of Consumer Research, 14*, 229–239.

Macklin, M. C. (1988). The relationship between music in advertising and children's responses: An experimental investigation. In S. Hecker & D. W. Stewart (Eds.), *Nonverbal communication in advertising* (pp. 225–244). Lexington, MA: Heath.

Macklin, M. C. (1990). The influence of model age in children's reactions to advertising stimuli. *Psychology & Marketing, 7*, 295–310.

Macklin, M. C. (1994a). The effects of an advertising retrieval cue on young children's memory and brand evaluations. *Psychology & Marketing, 11*, 291–311.

Macklin, M. C. (1994b). The impact of audiovisual information on children's product-related recall. *Journal of Consumer Research, 21*(1), 154–164.

Macklin, M. C., & Carlson, L. (Eds.). (1999). *Advertising to children: Concepts and controversies.* Thousand Oaks, CA: Sage.

Macklin, M. C., & Kolbe, R. H. (1984). Sex role stereotyping in children's advertising: Current and past trends. *Journal of Advertising, 13*(2), 34–42.

Maclean, M. S., & Crane, E. (1961). Program preferences: Their implications for the educational broadcaster. *AV Communication Review, 9*, 85–98.

Maher, J. K., & Childs, N. M. (2003). A longitudinal content analysis of gender roles in children's television advertisements: A 27-year review. *Journal of Current Issues & Research in Advertising, 25*, 71–82.

Mahoney, K. (1953). Elementary school pupils TV habits and choices. *Catholic Education Review, 51*, 234–245.

Makas, E. (1993). Changing channels: The portrayal of people with disabilities on television. In G. L. Berry & J. K. Asamen (Eds.), *Children & television: Images in a changing sociocultural world* (pp. 255–268). Thousand Oaks, CA: Sage.

Maldonado, N. S. (1992). Making TV environmentally safe for children. *Childhood Education, 68*, 229–230.

Mallalieu, L., Palan, K. M., & Laczniak, R. N. (2005). Understanding children's knowledge and beliefs about advertising: A global issue that spans generations. *Journal of Current Research in Advertising, 27*(1), 53–65.

Mangleburg, T. F., & Bristol, T. (1998). Socialization and adolescents' skepticism toward advertising. *Journal of Advertising, 27*(3), 11–21.

Manley-Casimir, M. E. (1987). Children, culture, and the curriculum of television: The challenge for education. In M. E. Manley-Casimir & C. Luke (Eds.), *Children and television: A challenge for education* (pp. 236–245). New York: Praeger.

Manley-Casimir, M. E., & Luke, C. (1987). *Children and television: A challenge for education.* Thousand Oaks, CA: Sage.

Manno, C. J., Bantz, J., & Kauffman, J. M. (2000). Cultural causes of rage and violence in children and youth. *Reaching Today's Youth: The Community Circle of Caring Journal, 4*(2), 54–59.

Manrai, L. A., Broach, V. C., & Manrai, A. K. (1992). Advertising appeal and tone: Implications for creative strategy in television commercials. *Journal of Business Research, 25*(1), 43–58.

Manrai, L. A., Manrai, A. K., & Murray, N. (1994). Comprehension of info-aid supers in television advertising for social ideas: Implications for public policy. *Journal of Business Research, 30*(1), 75–84.

Manusco, J. C., Morrison, J. K., & Aldrich, C. C. (1978). Developmental changes in social-moral perception: Some factors affecting children's evaluations and predictions of the behavior of a transgressor. *Journal of Genetic Psychology, 132*(1), 121–136.

Mares, M.-L., Cantor, J., & Steinbach, J. B. (1999). Using television to foster children's interest in science. *Science Communication, 20*, 283–297.

Mares, M.-L., & Woodard, E. (2005). Positive effects of television on children's social interactions: A meta-analysis. *Media Psychology, 7*, 301–322.

Markham, D. (1968). The dimensions of source credibility of television newscasters. *Journal of Communication, 18*, 57–64.

Marshall, S. J., Biddle, S. J. H., Gorely, T., Cameron, N., & Murdey, I. (2004). Relationships between media use, body fatness and physical activity in children and youth: A meta analysis. *International Journal of Obesity, 28*, 1238–1247.

Marshall, T. R. (1981). The benevolent bureaucrat: Political authority in children's literature and television. *Western Political Quarterly, 34*, 389–398.

Martin, C. A., & Benson, L. (1970). Parental perceptions of the role of television in parent–child interaction. *Journal of Marriage and the Family, 32*, 410–444.

Martin, C. E., & Duncan, D. F. (1984). Televised OTC drug ads as surrogate dope pushers among young people: Fact or fiction. *Journal of Alcohol and Drug Education, 29*(3), 19–30.

Martin, M. C. (1997). Children's understanding of the intent of advertising: A meta-analysis. *Journal of Public Policy and Marketing, 16*, 205–216.

Marton, J. P., & Acker, L. E. (1982). Television provoked aggression: Effects of gentle, affection-like training prior to exposure. *Child Study Journal, 12*(1), 27–43.

Marx, H. L. (1953). *Television and radio in American life.* New York: Wilson.

Masson, G. E. (1965). Children learn words from commercial TV. *The Elementary School Journal, 65*, 318–320.

Mastro, D. E. (2003). A social identity approach to understanding the impact of television messages. *Communication Monographs, 9*, 360–366.

Mastronardi, M. (2003). Adolescence and media. *Journal of Language & Social Psychology , 22*, 83–94.

Mates, B. F. (1980). Current emphases and issues in planned programming for children. In E. L. Palmer & A. Dorr (Eds.), *Children and the faces of television: Teaching, violence, selling* (pp. 19–32). New York: Academic.

Mathes, S. (1976). Channeling children: Sex stereotyping on prime time TV. *Journal of Learning Disabilities, 9*, 459–460.

Mattern, K. K., & Lindholm, B. W. (1985). Effect of maternal commentary in reducing aggressive impact of televised on preschool children. *Journal of Genetic Psychology, 146*, 133–134.

Matthews, D. (2003). Media memories: The first cable/VCR generation recalls their childhood and adolescent media viewing. *Mass Communication & Society, 6*, 219–241.

Maxon, A. B., & Welch, A. J. (1992). The role of language competence on comprehension of television messages by children with hearing impairments. *Volta Review, 94*, 315–326.

Mayer, V. (2003). Living telenovelas/telenovelizing life: Mexican American girls' identities and transnational telenovelas. *Journal of Communication, 53*, 479–495.

Mayes, S. L., & Valentine, K. B. (1979). Sex role stereotyping in Saturday morning cartoon shows. *Journal of Broadcasting, 23*(1), 41–50.

McAbee, T. A., Miller, B. J., & Burnside, V. (1986). The "feelings just are" children's television project. *Community Mental Health Journal, 22*(1), 56–60.

McAllister, M. P., & Giglio, J. M. (2005). The commodity flow of U.S. children's television. *Critical Studies in Media Communication, 22*(1), 26–35.

McArthur, L. Z., & Eisen, S. (1976). Television and sex-role stereotyping. *Journal of Applied Social Psychology, 6*, 329–351.

McCall, R. B., Parke, R. D., & Kavanaugh, R. D. (1977). Imitation of live and televised models by children one to three years of age. *Monographs of the Society for Research in Child Development, 45*.

McCarthy, E. D., Lagner, T. S., Gersten, J. C., Eisenberg, J. G., & Orzeck, L. (1975). Violence and behavior disorders. *Journal of Communication, 25*(4), 71–85.

McClure, L. F., Chinsky, J. M., & Larcen, S. W. (1978). Enhancing social problem-solving performance in an elementary school setting. *Journal of Educational Psychology, 70,* 504–513.

McCollum, J. F., Jr., & Bryant, J. (2003). Pacing in children's television programming. *Mass Communication & Society, 6,* 115–137.

McCombs, M. E., & Mullins, L. E. (1973). Consequences of education: Media exposure, political interest, and information-seeking orientations. *Mass Communication Review, 1*(1), 27–31.

McCorkle, S. (1982). An analysis of verbal language in Saturday morning children's programs. *Communications Quarterly, 30,* 210–216.

McCormack, T. H. (1962). The context hypothesis and TV learning. *In Studies in public communications.* Chicago: University of Chicago Press.

McCroskey, J. C., & Prichard, S. V. O. (1967). Selective-exposure and Lyndon B. Johnson's 1966 "State of the Union" address. *Journal of Broadcasting, 11,* 331–337.

McDermott, S. T., & Greenberg, B. S. (1984). Black children's esteem: Parents, peers, television. In R. W. Bostrum & B. H. Westley (Eds.), *Communication Yearbook* (Vol. 8, pp. 164–177). Beverly Hills, CA: Sage.

McDevitt, M., & Chaffee, S. (2000). Closing gaps in political communication and knowledge: Effects of a school intervention. *Communication Research, 27,* 259–292.

McDonald, D. G. (1986). Generational aspects of television coviewing. *Journal of Broadcasting & Electronic Media, 30,* 75–85.

McDowell, S. D., & Maitland, C. (1998). The V-chip in Canada and the United States: Themes and variations in design and deployment. *Journal of Broadcasting & Electronic Media, 42,* 401–422.

McGhee, P. E. (1980). Toward the integration of entertainment and educational functions of television: The role of humor. In P. H. Tannenbaum (Ed.), *The entertainment functions of television* (pp. 183–208). Hillsdale, NJ: Lawrence Erlbaum Associates, Inc.

McGhee, P. E., & Freuh, T. (1980). Television viewing and the learning of sex-role stereotypes. *Sex Roles, 6,* 179–188.

McGillicuddy-DeLisi, A., & Bullock, M. (2003). Children's learning from television: Applied developmental psychology at its best. *Journal of Applied Developmental Psychology, 24,* 273–275.

McGoldrick, K. E. (1986). Children and television. *Journal of the American Medical Women's Association, 41*(4), 99.

McGregor, M. A. (1986). Assessing FCC response to report of Children's Television Task Force. *Journalism Quarterly, 63,* 481–487.

McGuire, K. M. (2002). The relationship between the availability of a children's television program and song recognition. *Journal of Research in Music Education, 50,* 227–245.

McHale, S. M., Crouter, A. C., & Tucker, C. J. (2001). Free-time activities in middle childhood: Links with adjustment in early adolescence. *Child Development, 72,* 1764–1779.

McKenna, M. W., & Ossoff, E. P. (1998). Age differences in children's comprehension of a popular television program. *Child Study Journal, 28*(1), 53–68.

McKenzie, T. L., Sallis, J. F., Nader, P. R. & Broyles, S. L., (1992). Anglo- and Mexican-American preschoolers at home and at recess: Activity patterns and environmental influences. *Journal of Developmental and Behavioral Pediatrics, 13*(3), 173–180.

McLeod, D. M. (1995). Communicating deviance: The effects of television news coverage of social protest. *Journal of Broadcasting & Electronic Media, 39*, 4–19.

McNeal, J. (1969). An exploratory study of the consumer behavior of children. In J. McNeal (Ed.), *Dimensions of consumer behavior* (pp. 225–275). New York: Appleton-Century-Crofts.

McVey, M. D. (1999). Violence on television: How teachers can help parents affect positive change. *Journal of Early Education and Family Review, 7*(2), 36–45.

Meadowcroft, J. M. (1986). Family communication patterns and political development: The child's role. *Communication Research, 13*, 603–624.

Meadowcroft, J. M. (1996). Attention span cycles. In J. H. Watt & C. A. Van Lear (Eds.), *Dynamic patterns in communication processes* (pp. 255–276). Thousand Oaks, CA: Sage.

Meadowcroft, J. M., & McDonald, D. G. (1986). Meta-analysis of research on children and the media: Atypical development. *Journalism Quarterly, 63*, 474–481.

Meadowcroft, J. M., & Reeves, B. (1989). Influence of story scheme development on children's attention to television. *Communication Research, 16*, 352–374.

Medrich, E. A. (1979). Constant television: A background to daily life. *Journal of Communication, 29*(3), 171–176.

Meerlo, J. A. M. (1954). Television addiction and reactive apathy. *Journal of Nervous and Mental Diseases, 120*, 290–291.

Mehling, R. (1960). Television's value to the American family member. *Journal of Broadcasting, 4*, 307–313.

Mehmet-Radji, O. (2004). Early television exposure and subsequent attentional problems in children. *Child: Care, Health & Development, 30*, 559–561.

Meline, C. W. (1976). Fostering creativity in children: Does the medium matter? *Journal of Communication, 26*(3), 81–89.

Melody, W. (1973). *Children's television: The economics of exploitation.* New Haven, CT: Yale University Press.

Melody, W. H., & Ehrlich, W. (1974). Children's TV commercials: The vanishing policy options. *Journal of Communication, 24*(4), 113–125.

Meltzoff, A. N. (1988). Imitation of televised models by infants. *Child Development, 59*, 1221–1229.

Meringoff, L. K. (1980a). The effects of volume and repetition on advertising. In R. P. Adler, G. S. Lesser, L. K. Meringoff, T. S. Robertson, J. R. Rossiter, & F. Ward (Eds.), *The effects of television advertising on children: Review and recommendation* (pp. 123–152). Lexington, MA: Lexington Books.

Meringoff, L. K. (1980b). Influence of the medium on children's story apprehension. *Journal of Educational Psychology, 72*, 240–249.

Meringoff, L. K., & Lesser, G. S. (1980a). Children's ability to distinguish television commercials from program material. In R. P. Adler, G. S. Lesser, L. K. Meringoff, T. S. Robertson, J. R. Rossiter, & F. Ward (Eds.), *The effects of television advertising on children: Review and recommendation* (pp. 29–42). Lexington, MA: Lexington Books.

Meringoff, L. K., & Lesser, G. S. (1980b). The influence of format and audio-visual techniques on children's perceptions of commercial messages. In R. P. Adler, G. S. Lesser, L. K. Meringoff, T. S. Robertson, J. R. Rossiter, & F. Ward (Eds.), *The effects of television advertising on children: Review and recommendation* (pp. 43–60). Lexington, MA: Lexington Books.

Meringoff, L. K., Vibbert, M. M., Char, C. A., Fernie, D. E., Banker, G. S., & Gardner, H. (1983). How is children's learning from television distinctive? Exploiting the medium methodologically. In J. Bryant & D. R. Anderson (Eds.), *Children's understanding of television* (pp. 151–179). New York: Academic.

Merrill, I. (1961). Broadcast viewing and listening by children. *Public Opinion Quarterly, 25,* 262–276.

Merritt, B., & Stroman, C. A. (1993). Black family imagery and interaction on television. *Journal of Black Studies, 23,* 492–499.

Messaris, P. (1983). Family conversations about television. *Journal of Family Issues, 4,* 293–308.

Messaris, P., & Kerr, D. (1983). Mothers' comments about TV: Relation to family communication patterns. *Communication Research, 10,* 175–194.

Messaris, P., & Kerr, D. (1984). TV-related mother–child interaction and children's perceptions of television characters. *Journalism Quarterly, 61,* 662–666.

Messaris, P., & Sarrett, C. (1981). On the consequences of television-related parent–child interaction. *Human Communication Research, 7,* 226–244.

Messenger Davies, M., & Machin, D. (2000). "It helps people make their decisions": Dating games, public service broadcasting and the negotation of identity in middle-childhood. *Childhood, 7,* 173–191.

Meyer, M., & Nissen, U. (1981). Effects and functions of television—Children and adolescents: A bibliography of selected research literature 1970–1978. *Communication Research & Broadcasting, 2,* 172.

Meyer, M. D. E. (2003). "It's me, I'm it": Defining adolescent sexual identity through relational dialectics in *Dawson's Creek. Communication Quarterly, 51,* 262–276.

Meyer, T. P. (1973). Children's perceptions of favorite television characters as behavioral models. *Educational Broadcasting Review, 7*(1), 25–33.

Meyer, T. P. (1976). Impact of "All in the Family" on children. *Journal of Broadcasting, 20,* 23–33.

Meyer, T. P., Donohue, T. R., & Henke, L. L. (1978). How Black children see TV commercials. *Journal of Advertising Research, 18*(5), 51–58.

Meyer, T. P., & Hexamer, A. (1981). Perceived truth and trust in television advertising among Mexican-American adolescents: Socialization and developmental consideration. *Journal of Broadcasting, 25,* 139–150.

Mielke, K. W. (1994). On the relationship between television viewing and academic achievement. *Journal of Broadcasting & Electronic Media, 38,* 361–366.

Milavsky, J. R., Pekowski, B., & Stipp, H. (1975–1976). TV drug advertising and proprietary and illicit drug use among teenage boys. *Public Opinion Quarterly, 39*(4), 457–481.

Milavsky, J. R., Rubens, W. S., Kessler, R. C., & Stipp, H. H. (1982). *Television and aggression: A panel study.* New York: Academic.

Miles, B. (1975). *Channeling children: Sex stereotyping in prime-time TV.* Princeton, NJ: Women on Words and Images.

Milgram, S., & Shotland, R. L. (1973). *Television and antisocial behavior: Field experiments.* New York: Academic.

Milich, R., & Lorch, E. P. (1994). Television viewing methodology to understand cognitive processing of ADHD children. *Advances in Clinical Child Psychology, 16*, 177–201.

Milkie, M. A. (1994). Social world approach to cultural studies: Mass-media and gender in the adolescent peer group. *Journal of Contemporary Ethnography, 23*, 354–380.

Miller, B. M., O'Connor, S., & Sirignano, S. (1995). Out-of-school time: A study of children in three low-income neighborhoods. *Child Welfare, 74*, 1249–1280.

Miller, J. H., Jr., & Busch, P. (1979). Host selling vs. premium TV commercials: An experimental evaluation of their influence on children. *Journal of Marketing Research, 16*, 323–332.

Miller, K. E. (2001). Television viewing time increases risk for obesity in children. *American Family Physician, 64*, 1251–1252.

Miller, K. E. (2003). Children's behavior correlates with television viewing. *American Family Physician, 67*, 593–595.

Miller, K. E. (2004). Reducing television viewing by preschool children. *American Family Physician, 70*, 1784–1788.

Miller, K. R., & Wheeler-Scruggs, K. (2002). Entertainment television and hearing students' attitudes regarding the pediatric cochlear implant. *American Annals of the Deaf, 147*(3), 20–24.

Miller, M. M., & Reeves, B. (1976). Dramatic TV content and children's sex-role stereotypes. *Journal of Broadcasting, 20*, 35–50.

Miller, T. W. (1977). Impact of television programming for children on family life: Issues for family therapy. *American Journal of Family Therapy, 5*(2), 40–47.

Miller, T. W. (1983). Identification process and sensory impact of children's television programming on the preschool child. *Child Study Journal, 13*, 203–207.

Miller, W. C., & Beck, T. (1976). How do TV parents compare to real parents? *Journalism Quarterly, 53*, 324–328.

Minow, N. N., & LaMay, C. L. (1995). *Abandonded in the wasteland: Children, television, and the first amendment.* New York: Hill and Wang.

Mishara, B. L. (1999). Conceptions of death and suicide in children ages 6–12 and their implications for suicide prevention. *Suicide and Life-Threatening Behavior, 29*, 105–18.

Mitchell, J. M., O'Brien, R. W., Semansky, R. M., & Iannotti, R. J. (1995). Sources of AIDS information for parents and children. *Medical Care, 33*, 423–431.

Mitroff, D. (2003). On the horns of a dilemma. *Journal of Applied Developmental Psychology, 24*, 355–361.

Moeller, S. D. (2002). A hierarchy of innocence: The media's use of children in the telling of international news. *Harvard International Journal of Press/Politics, 7*(1), 36–56.

Mohr, P. J. (1979a). Efficacy of the family viewing concept: A test of assumptions. *Central States Speech Journal, 30*, 342–351.

Mohr, P. J. (1979b). Parental guidance of children's viewing of evening television programs. *Journal of Broadcasting, 23*, 213–228.

Molitor, F., & Hirsch, K. W. (1994). Children's toleration of real-live aggression after exposure to media violence: A replication of the Drabman and Thomas studies. *Child Study Journal, 24*, 191–207.

Monosmith, S. W., Shute, R. E., St. Pierre, R. W., & Alles, W. F. (1981). Opinion of seventh to twelfth graders regarding the effectiveness of pro- and anti-smoking message. *Journal of Drug Education, 11*, 213–225.

Monsen, R. B. (2002). Children and the media. *Journal of Pediatric Nursing, 17*, 309–310.

Moody, K. (1999). *The children of Telstar: Early experiments in school television production.* New York: Vantage.

Moore, E. S. (2004). Children and the changing world of advertising. *Journal of Business Ethics, 52*, 161–167.

Moore, M. L. (1992). The family as portrayed on prime-time television, 1947–1990: Structure and characteristics. *Sex Roles, 26*, 41–61.

Moore, R. L. (1990). Effects of television on family consumer behavior. In J. Bryant (Ed.), *Television and the American family* (pp. 275–292). Hillsdale, NJ: Lawrence Erlbaum Associates, Inc.

Moore, R. L., & Moschis, G. P. (1981). The role of family communication in consumer learning. *Journal of Communication, 31*(4), 3–20.

Moore, R. L., & Moschis, G. P. (1983). Role of mass media and the family in the development of consumption norms. *Journalism Quarterly, 60*, 67–73.

Moore, R. L., & Stephens, L. F. (1975). Some communication and demographic determinants of consumer learning. *Journal of Consumer Research, 2*, 80–92.

Moore, S. G. (1977). The effects of television on the prosocial behavior of young children. *Young Children, 32*, 60–64.

Moreno, L. A., Fleta, J., & Mur, L. (1998). Television watching and fatness in children. *Journal of the American Medical Association, 280*, 1230–1231.

Morgan, D. (1951). Television versus reading: Teenager's discussion. *Wilson Library Bulletin, 26*, 327.

Morgan, M. (1980). Television viewing and reading: Does more equal better? *Journal of Communication, 30*(1), 159–165.

Morgan, M. (1982). Television and adolescents sex-role stereotypes: A longitudinal study. *Journal of Personality and Social Psychology, 43*, 947–955.

Morgan, M. (1987). Television, sex-role attitudes, and sex-role behavior. *Journal of Early Adolescence, 7*, 269–282.

Morgan, M., & Gross, L. (1980). Television viewing, IQ and academic achievement. *Journal of Broadcasting, 24*, 117–133.

Moriarty, D., & McCabe, A. (1979). Studies of television and youth sports laboratory—Field research on the effects of prosocial and antisocial TV models on children and youth. *Aggressive Behavior, 5*, 190–191.

Morison, P., McCarthy, M., & Gardner, H. (1979). Exploring the realities of television with children. *Journal of Broadcasting, 23*, 453–463.

Morris, W. N., Marshall, H. M., & Miller, R. S. (1973). The effect of vicarious punishment on prosocial behavior in children. *Journal of Experimental Child Psychology, 15*, 222–236.

Morrison, T. G., Kalin, R., & Morrison, M. A. (2004). Body-image evaluation and body-image investment among adolescents: A test of sociocultural and social comparison theories. *Adolescence, 39*, 571–592.

Morrow, J., & Suid, M. (1977). *Media and kids: Real-world learning in the schools.* Rochelle Park, NJ: Hayden.

Moschis, G. P. (1989). Point of view: Cigarette advertising and young smokers. *Journal of Advertising Research*, 29(2), 51–60.

Moschis, G. P., & Moore, R. L. (1979). Decision-making among the young: A socialization perspective. *Journal of Consumer Research*, 6, 101–111.

Moschis, G. P., & Moore, R. L. (1982). A longitudinal study of television advertising effects. *Journal of Consumer Research*, 9, 279–286.

Moschis, G. P., & Moore, R. L. (1987). An analysis of the acquisition of some consumer competencies among adolescents. *Journal of Consumer Affairs*, 12, 277–291.

Mosse, H. L. (1966). The influence of mass media on the sex problems of teenagers. *Journal of Sex Research*, 2(1), 27–35.

Mosse, H. L. (1977). Terrorism and mass media. *New York State Journal of Medicine*, 77, 2294–2296.

Mundorf, N., & Brownell, W. (1990). Media preferences of older and younger adults. *Gerontologist*, 30, 685–691.

Mundorf, N., & Zillmann, D. (1991). Effects of story sequencing on affective reactions to broadcast news. *Journal of Broadcasting & Electronic Media*, 35, 197–211.

Mundorf, N., Zillmann, D., & Drew, D. (1991). Effects of disturbing televised events on the acquisition of information from subsequently presented commercials. *Journal of Advertising*, 20(1), 46–53.

Munn, M. (1958). The effect on parental buying habits of children exposed to children's television programs. *Journal of Broadcasting*, 2, 253–258.

Murphy-Bergman, V., & Whobrey, L. (1983). The impact of captions on hearing impaired children's affective reactions to television. *Journal of Special Education*, 17(1), 47–62.

Murray, F. S., & Stanley, R. L. (1980). Perceptual learning of cartoon faces by young children. *Bulletin of the Psychonomic Society*, 16, 367–370.

Murray, J. P. (1973). Television and violence: Implications of the Surgeon General's research program. *American Psychologist*, 28, 472–478.

Murray, J. P. (1980). *Television and youth: 25 years of research & controversy*. Boys Town, NE: Boys Town Center for the Study of Youth Development.

Murray, J. P. (1993). The developing child in a multimedia society. In G. L. Berry & J. K. Asamen (Eds.), *Children and television: Images in a changing sociocultural world* (pp. 9–22). Newbury Park, CA: Sage.

Murray, J. P. (1994). The impact of television violence. *Hofstra Law Review*, 22, 809–825.

Murray, J. P. (1995). Children and television violence. *Kansas Journal of Law and Public Policy*, 4, 7–14.

Murray, J. P. (1997). Media violence and youth. In J. D. Osofsky (Ed.), *Children in a violent society* (pp. 72–96). New York: Guilford.

Murray, J. P. (1998). Studying television violence: A Research agenda for the 21st century. In J. K. Asamen & G. L. Berry (Eds.), *Research paradigms, television and social behavior* (pp. 369–412). Thousand Oaks, CA: Sage.

Murray, J. P., & Kippax, S. (1978). Children's social behavior in three towns with differing television's experience. *Journal of Communication*, 28(1), 19–29.

Murray, J. P., & Kippax, S. (1979). From the early window to the late night show: International trends in the study of television's impact on children and adults. In L. Berkowitz (Ed.), *Advances in experiemental social psychology* (Vol. 12, pp. 254–320). New York: Academic.

Murray, J. P., Nayman, O., & Atkin, C. (1971). Television and the child: A comprehensive research bibliography. *Journal of Broadcasting, 16,* 3–20.

Murray, J. P., & Salomon G. (1984). *The future of children's television: Results of the Markle Foundation/Boys Town Conference.* Boys Town, NE: Father Flanagan's Boys Town.

Murray, J. P., & Wartella, E. A. (1999). The reification of irrelevancy: A comment on "The reification of normalcy." *Journal of Health Communication, 4,* 227–231.

Murray, R. L., Cole, R. R., & Fedler, F. (1970). Teenagers and TV violence: How they rate and view it. *Journalism Quarterly, 47,* 247–255.

Murry, J. P., Jr., & Dacin, P. A. (1995). Cognitive moderators of negative-emotion effects: Implications for understanding media context. *Journal of Consumer Research, 22,* 439–447.

Murry, J. P., Jr., Lastovicka, J. L., & Singh, S. N. (1992). Feeling and liking responses to television programs: An examination of two explanations for media-context effects. *Journal of Consumer Research, 18,* 441–451.

Musgrave, P. W., & Reid, G. R. (1971). Some measures of children's values. *Social Science Information, 10*(1), 137–153.

Mussen, P., & Rutherford, E. (1961). Effects of aggressive cartoons on children's aggressive play. *Journal of Abnormal and Social Psychology, 62,* 461–464.

Mutz, D. C., Roberts, D. F., & Van Vuuren, D. P. (1993). Reconsidering the displacement hypothesis: Television's influence on children's time use. *Communication Research, 20,* 51–75.

Myers, P. N., Jr., & Biocca, F. A. (1992). The elastic body image: The effect of television advertising and programming on body image distortions in young women. *Journal of Communication, 42*(3), 108–133.

Nadel, M. S. (2000). Empower parents to choose quality children's television. *Journal of Policy Analysis & Management, 19*(1), 145–147.

Naidu, B. R., & Wallace, B. (1993). Television's effect on cognitive development. *Gifted Educational International, 9*(1), 5–11.

Nathan, J. G., Anderson, D. R., Field, D. E., & Collins, P. (1985). Television viewing at home: Distances and visual angles of children and adults. *Human Factors, 27,* 467–476.

Nathanson, A. I. (1999). Identifying and explaining the relationship between parental mediation and children's aggression. *Communication Research, 26,* 124–143.

Nathanson, A. I. (2001a). Parent and child perspectives on the presence and meaning of parental television mediation. *Journal of Broadcasting & Electronic Media, 45,* 201–220.

Nathanson, A. I. (2001b). Parents versus peers: Exploring the significance of peer mediation of antisocial television. *Communication Research, 28,* 251–274.

Nathanson, A. I. (2002). The unintended effects of parental mediation of television on adolescents. *Media Psychology, 4,* 207–230.

Nathanson, A. I. (2004). Factual and evaluative approaches to modifying children's responses to violent television. *Journal of Communication, 54,* 321–336.

Nathanson, A. I., & Botta, R. A. (2003). Shaping the effects of television on adolescents' body image disturbance: The role of parental mediation. *Communication Research, 30,* 304–331.

Nathanson, A. I., & Cantor, J. (2000). Reducing the aggression-promoting effect of violent cartoons by increasing children's fictional involvement with the victim: A study of active mediation. *Journal of Broadcasting & Electronic Media, 44,* 125–142.

Nathanson, A. I., Eveland, W. P. J., Park, H.-S., & Paul, B. (2002). Perceived media influence and efficacy as predictors of caregivers' protective behaviors. *Journal of Broadcasting & Electronic Media, 46,* 385–410.

Nathanson, A. I., & Lemish, D. (2001). Mediation of children's television. In W. B. Gudykunst (Ed.), *Communication Yearbook* (Vol. 25, pp. 115–151). Mahwah, NJ: Lawrence Erlbaum Associates, Inc.

Nathanson, A. I., Wilson, B. J., McGee, J., & Sebastian, M. (2002). Counteracting the effects of female stereotypes on television via active mediation. *Journal of Communication, 52,* 922–937.

Nathanson, A. I., & Yang, M. S. (2003). The effects of mediation content and form on childen's response to violent television. *Human Communication Research, 29,* 111–134.

National Educational Association. (1953). Ninety-three murders a week. *Journal of the National Educational Association, 42,* 266.

Neeley, J. J., Heckel, R. V., & Leichtman, H. M. (1973). The effect of race of model and response consequences to the model on imitation in children. *Journal of Social Psychology, 89,* 225–231.

Neeley, S. M., & Schumann, D. W. (2004). Using animated spokes-characters in advertising to young children. *Journal of Advertising, 33*(3), 7–23.

Neuman, S. B. (1980). Television: Its effects on reading and school achievement. *Reading Teacher, 33,* 801–805.

Neuman, S. B. (1982). Television viewing and leisure reading: A qualitative analysis. *Journal of Educational Research, 75,* 299–304.

Neuman, S. B. (1986). Television, reading, and the home environment. *Reading Research & Instruction, 25,* 173–183.

Neuman, S. B. (1988). The displacement effect: Assessing the relation between television viewing and reading performance. *Reading Research Quarterly, 23,* 414–440.

Neuman, S. B. (1991). *Literacy in the television age: The myth of the TV effect.* Norwood, NJ: Ablex.

Neuman, S. B., Burden, D., & Holden, E. (1990). Enhancing children's comprehension of a televised story through previewing. *Journal of Educational Research, 83,* 258–265.

Neumark-Sztainer, D., Goeden, C., Story, M., & Wall, M. (2004). Associations between body satisfaction and physical activity in adolescents: Implications for programs aimed at preventing a broad spectrum of weight-related disorders. *Eating Disorders, 12,* 125–138.

Newby, T. J., Robinson, P. W., & Hill, R. D. (1980). Preferences of Mexican-American children for parents on television. *Journal of Psychology, 105,* 239–245.

Newcomb, A. F., & Collins, W. A. (1979). Children's comprehension of family role portrayals in televised dramas: Effects of socioeconomic status, ethnicity, and age. *Developmental Psychology, 15,* 417–423.

Newhagen, J. E. (1994). Effects of censorship disclaimers in Persian Gulf War television news on negative thought elaboration. *Communication Research, 21*, 232–248.

Newhagen, J. E., & Reeves, B. (1992). The evening's bad news: Effects of compelling negative television news images on memory. *Journal of Communication, 42*(2), 25–41.

Nias, D. K. (1979). The classification and correlates of children's academic and recreational interests. *Journal of Child Psychology and Psychiatry and Allied Disciplines, 20*(1), 73–79.

Nicholas, K. B., McCarter, R. E., & Heckel, R. V. (1971a). The effects of race and sex on the imitation of television models. *Journal of Social Psychology, 85*, 315–316.

Nicholas, K. B., McCarter, R. E., & Heckel, R. V. (1971b). Imitation of adult and peer television models by white and Negro children. *Journal of Social Psychology, 85*, 317–318.

Nikken, P., & Peeters, A. L. (1988). Children's perceptions of television reality. *Journal of Broadcasting & Electronic Media, 32*, 441–452.

Nikken, P., & Van Der Voort, T. H. A. (1999). Quality standards for children's programs in the writings of television critics. *Journal of Educational Media, 24*(1), 17–23.

Nippold, M. (1988). Explanation of ambiguous advertisements: A developmental study with children and adolescents. *Journal of Speech and Hearing Research, 31*, 466–474.

Nippold, M. A., Duthie, J. K., & Larsen, J. (2005). Literacy as a leisure activity: Free-time preferences of older children and young adolescents. *Speech & Hearing Services in Schools, 36*, 93–103.

Niven, H. (1960). Who in the family selects the TV program? *Journalism Quarterly, 37*, 110–111.

Noble, G. (1970). Concepts of order and balance in a children's TV program. *Journalism Quarterly, 47*, 101–108.

Noble, G. (1973). Effects of different forms of filmed aggression on children's constructive and destructive play. *Journal of Personality and Social Psychology, 26*, 54–59.

Nolan, J. D., Galst, J. P., & White, M. A. (1977). Sex bias on children's television programs. *Journal of Psychology, 96*, 197–204.

Nolan, L. L., & Patterson, S. J. (1990). The active audience: Personality type as an indicator of TV program preference. *Journal of Social Behavior and Personality, 5*, 697–710.

Norris, S. (2002). The implication of visual research for discourse analysis: Transcription beyond language. *Visual Communication, 1*(1), 97–121.

Nostbakken, D. (1987). The power of television: Enrichment of the television experience by parents and teachers. In M. E. Manley-Casimir & C. Luke (Eds), *Children and television: A challenge for education* (pp. 111–144). New York: Praeger.

Nowicki, S. (1984). The proactive role for researchers on children's television: A commentary on Ward's study. *Merrill-Palmer Quarterly, 30*, 265–267.

Nystrom, C. L. (1983). What television teaches about sex. *Educational Leadership, 40*(6), 20–25.

O'Bryan, K. G. (1980). The teaching face: An historical perspective. In E. L. Palmer & A. Dorr (Eds.), *Children and the faces of television: Teaching, violence, selling* (pp. 5–17). New York: Academic.

O'Bryant, S. L. (1978). Black children's learning of work roles from television commercials. *Psychological Reports, 42,* 227–230.

O'Bryant, S. L., & Corder-Bolz, C. R. (1978). The effects of television on children's stereotyping of women's work roles. *Journal of Vocational Behavior, 12,* 233–244.

O'Connor, L. A., Brooks-Gunn, J., & Graber, J. (2000). Black and White girls' racial preferences in media and peer choices and the role of socialization for Black girls. *Journal of Family Psychology, 14,* 510–521.

Ogletree, S. M., Martinez, C. N., Turner, T. R., & Mason, B. (2004). Pokemon: Exploring the role of gender. *Sex Roles, 50,* 851–861.

Ogletree, S. M., Williams, S. W., Raffeld, P., Mason, B., & Fricke, K. (1990). Female attractiveness and eating disorders: Do children's television commercials play a role? *Sex Roles, 22,* 791–797.

Ogura, C. (1979). Effects of TV heroes on sex-related personality formation in preschool children. *Journal of Child Development, 15,* 1–7.

O'Keefe, M. T. (1971). The anti-smoking commercials: A study of television's impact on behavior. *Public Opinion Quarterly, 35,* 242–248.

O'Kelly, C. G. (1974). Sexism in children's television. *Journalism Quarterly, 51,* 722–724.

O'Kelly, C. G., & Bloomquist, L. E. (1976). Women and Blacks on TV. *Journal of Communication, 26*(4), 179–184.

Olfman, S. (2002). Asperger's disorder in cultural context. *Encounter, 15*(1), 50–58.

Oppliger, P. A., & Sherblom, J. C. (1992). Humor: Incongruity, disparagement, and David Letterman. *Communication Research Reports, 9*(1), 99–108.

Orange, C. M., & George, A. M. (2000). Child sacrifice: Black America's price of paying the media piper. *Journal of Black Studies, 30,* 294–314.

Orlandi, M. A. (1989). The effects of alcohol and tobacco advertising on adolescents. *Drugs and Society, 3*(1–2), 77–97.

Osburne, D. K., & Endsley, R. C. (1971). Emotional reactions of young children to TV violence. *Child Development, 42,* 321–331.

Osburne, D. K., & Hale, W. (1969). Television violence. *Childhood Education, 45,* 505–507.

Osgerby, B. (2004). "So who's got time for adults!": Femininity, consumption and the development of teen TV—From *Gidget* to *Buffy*. In G. Davis & K. Dickinson (Eds.), *Teen TV: Genre, consumption, identity* (pp. 71–86). London: British Film Institute.

Owen, D., & Dennis, J. (1992). Sex differences in politicization: The influence of mass media. *Women & Politics, 12*(4), 19–41.

Owens, J. A. (2004). The electronic sandman: The impact of the media on adolescent sleep. *Sleep: Journal of Sleep & Sleep Disorder Research, 27*(1), 15–16.

Owens, J., Maxim, R., McGuinn, M., Nobile, C., Msall, M., & Alario, A. (1999). Television-viewing habits and sleep disturbance in school children. *Pediatrics, 104*(3), e27.

Page, R. M. (1991). Loneliness as a risk factor in adolescent hopelessness. *Journal of Research in Personality, 25*, 189–195.

Page, R. M., Hammermeister, J., Scanlan, A., & Allen, O. (1996). Psychosocial and health-related characteristics of adolescent television viewers. *Child Study Journal, 26*, 319–331.

Paget, K. F., Kritt, D., & Bergemann, L. (1984). Understanding strategic interactions in television commercials: A developmental study. *Journal of Applied Developmental Psychology, 5*, 145–161.

Paik, H., & Comstock, G. (1994). The effects of television violence on antisocial behavior: A meta-analysis. *Communication Research, 21*, 516–546.

Paine, L. S. (1984). Children as consumers: An ethical evaluation of children's television advertising. *Business and Professional Ethics Journal, 3*, 119–145.

Palermo, G. B. (1995). Adolescent criminal behavior: TV violence one of the culprits. *International Journal of Offender Therapy & Comparative Criminology, 39*(1), 11–22.

Palmer, E. L. (1973). Formative research in the production of television for children. In G. Gerbner, L. P. Gross, & W. H. Melody (Eds.), *Communications technology and social policy* (pp. 229–245). New York: Wiley.

Palmer, E. L. (1984). Providing quality television for America's children. In J. P. Murray & G. Salomon (Eds.), *The future of children's television* (pp. 103–122). Boys Town, NE: Father Flanagan's Boys Town.

Palmer, E. L. (1986a). The day after "The Day After": A look at parent response. *Marriage & Family Review, 10*(2), 37–49.

Palmer, E. L. (1986b). The flower and the mushroom: Young children encounter "The Day After." *Marriage & Family Review, 10*(2), 51–58.

Palmer, E. L. (1987a). *Children in the cradle of television.* Lexington, MA: Lexington Books.

Palmer, E. L. (1987b). U.S. children's television in crisis: Problems of tradition, vision, and value. In M. E. Manley-Casimir & C. Luke (Eds.), *Children and television: A challenge for education* (pp. 165–184). New York: Praeger.

Palmer, E. L. (1988). *Television and America's children: A crisis of neglect.* New York: Oxford University Press.

Palmer, E. L. (1998). Major paradigms and issues in television research: Field of dreams, world of realities. In J. K. Asamen & G. L. Berry (Eds.), *Research paradigms, television and social behavior* (pp. 39–66). Thousand Oaks, CA: Sage.

Palmer, E. L., & Carr, K. (1991). Dr. Rogers, meet Mr. Rogers: The theoretical and clinical similarities between Carl and Fred Rogers. *Social Behavior & Personality, 19*(1), 39–44.

Palmer, E. L., & Dorr, A. (Eds.) (1980). *Children and the faces of television: Teaching, violence, selling.* New York: Academic.

Palmer, E. L., Hockett, A. B., & Dean, W. W. (1983). The television family and children's fright reactions. *Journal of Family Issues, 4*, 279–292.

Palmer, E. L., & MacNeil, M. (1991). Children's comprehension processes: From Piaget to public policy. In J. Bryant & D. Zillmann (Eds.), *Responding to the small screen: Reception and reaction processes* (pp. 27–44). Hillsdale, NJ: Lawrence Erlbaum Associates, Inc.

Palmer, E. L., & McDowell, C. N. (1979). Program commercial separators in children's television programming. *Journal of Communication, 29*(3), 197–201.

Palmer, E. L., & McDowell, C. N. (1981). Children's understanding of nutritional information presented in breakfast cereal commercials. *Journal of Broadcasting, 25,* 295–301.

Palmer, E. L., Smith, K. T., & Strawser, K. S. (1993). Rubik's tube: Developing a child's television worldview. In G. L. Berry & J. K. Asamen (Eds.), *Children & television: Images in a changing sociocultural world* (pp. 143–154). Thousand Oaks, CA: Sage.

Palmer, E. L., & Young, B. M. (2003). *The faces of televisual media: Teaching, violence, selling to children* (2nd ed.). Mahwah, NJ: Lawrence Erlbaum Associates, Inc.

Palmgreen, P., Donohew, L., Lorch, E. P., Hoyle, R. H., & Stephenson, M. T. (2001). Television campaigns and adolescent marijuana use: Tests of sensation seeking targeting. *American Journal of Public Health, 91,* 292–296.

Palmgreen, P., Donohew, L., Lorch, E. P., Hoyle, R. H., & Stephenson, M. T. (2002). Television campaigns and sensation seeking targeting of adolescent marijuana use: A controlled time series approach. In R. C. Hornik (Ed.), *Public health communication: Evidence for behavior change* (pp. 35–56). Mahwah NJ: Lawrence Erlbaum Associates, Inc.

Papazain, E. (1967). Teenagers and broadcast media. *Media/Scope, 11,* 109–115.

Parasuraman, A. (1979–1980). Social acceptance of children's commercials on television: Some suggestions for marketers. *Baylor Business Studies, 10,* 29–39.

Pardun, C. J., L'Engle, K. L., & Brown, J. D. (2005). Linking exposure to outcomes: Early adolescents' consumption of sexual content in six media. *Mass Communication & Society, 8,* 75–91.

Parke, R. D., Berkowitz, L., Leyens, J. P., West, S. G., & Sebastian, R. J. (1977). Some effects of violent and nonviolent movies on the behavior of juvenile delinquents. In L. Berkowitz (Ed.), *Advances in experimental social psychology* (Vol. 10, pp. 135–172). New York: Academic.

Parker, E. B. (1961a). Changes in the function of radio with the adoption of television. *Journal of Broadcasting, 5,* 39–48.

Parker, E. B. (1961b). Television and the process of cultural change. *Journalism Quarterly, 38,* 537–540.

Parker, E. B. (1963). The effects of television on library circulation. *Public Opinion Quarterly, 27,* 578–589.

Patterson, A. C., & Neustader, C. (1978). How to cope with violence on the tube. *Audiovisual Instruction, 23*(6), 40–42.

Patterson, J. L. (2002). Relationships of expressive vocabulary to frequency of reading and television experience among bilingual toddlers. *Applied Psycholynguistics, 23,* 493–508.

Pauker, M. (1978). The dire health consequences of television advertising aimed at children. *Children in Contemporary Society, 12*(1).

Paul, N. (1971). How does television influence the emotional world of children? *Clinical Pediatrics, 10,* 452–454.

Payne, D. E. (1976). The relationship between television advertising and drug abuse among youth. *Journal of Drug Education, 6,* 215–220.

Pearl, A., & Weston, J. (2003). Attitudes of adolescents about cosmetic surgery. *Annals of Plastic Surgery, 50*, 628–631.

Pearl, D. (1987). Familial, peer, and television influences on aggressive and violent behavior. In D. H. Crowell, I. M. Evans, & C. O'Donnell (Eds.), *Childhood aggression and violence: Sources of influence, prevention, and control* (pp. 231–247). New York: Plenum.

Pecora, N. (1995). Children & television advertising from a social science perspective. *Critical Studies in Mass Communication, 12*, 354–364.

Pecora, N. O. (1998). *The business of children's entertainment.* New York: Guilford.

Pecora, N. (2004). Nickelodeon grows up: The economic evolution of a network. In H. Hendershot (Ed.), *Nickelodeon nation* (pp. 15–44). New York: New York University Press.

Peevers, B. H. (1979). Androgyny on the TV screen? An analysis of sex-role portrayal. *Sex Roles, 5*, 797–809.

Pena, S., French, J., & Doerann, J. (1990). Heroic fantasies: A cross-generational comparison of two children's television heroes. *Early Childhood Research Quarterly, 5*, 393–406.

Pepper, R. (1984). Cable and the future of children's television. In J. P. Murray & G. Salomon (Eds.), *The future of children's television* (pp. 135–147). Boys Town, NE: Father Flanagan's Boys Town.

Peracchio, L. A. (1993). Young children's processing of a televised narrative: Is a picture really worth a thousand words? *Journal of Communication Research, 20*, 281–293.

Peracchio, L. A., & Luna, D. (1998). The development of an advertising campaign to discourage smoking initiation among children and youth. *Journal of Advertising, 27*(3), 49–56.

Perkins, K. R. (1996). The influence of television images on Black females' self perceptions of physical attractiveness. *Journal of Black Psychology, 22*, 453–469.

Perloff, R. M. (1977). Some antecedents of children's sex-role stereotypes. *Psychological Reports, 40*, 463–466.

Perloff, R. M. (1982). Mass media and sex-typing: Research perspectives and policy implications. *International Journal of Women's Studies, 5*, 265–273.

Perse, E. M. (1986). Soap opera viewing patterns of college students and cultivation. *Journal of Broadcasting & Electronic Media, 30*, 175–193.

Perse, E. M., Burggraf, C. S., & Pavitt, C. Q. (1993). College students' views of marriage on television. *New Jersey Journal of Communication, 1*, 103–116.

Perse, E. M., Pavitt, C., & Burggraf, C. S. (1990). Implicit theories of marriage and evaluations of marriage on television. *Human Communication Research, 16*, 387–408.

Perse, E. M., & Rubin, A. M. (1990). Chronic loneliness and television use. *Journal of Broadcasting & Electronic Media, 34*, 37–53.

Persson, A., & Musher-Eizenman, D. (2003). The impact of a prejudice-prevention television program on young children's ideas about race. *Early Childhood Research Quarterly, 18*, 530–546.

Peters, K. M., & Blumberg, F. C. (2002). Cartoon violence: Is it as detrimental to preschoolers as we think? *Early Childhood Education Journal, 29*, 143–148.

Peterson, J. L., Moore, K. A., & Furstenberg, F. F. (1991). Television viewing and early initiation of sexual intercourse: Is there a link? *Journal of Homosexuality*, *21*(1–2), 93–118.

Peterson, L. (1985). Preventive consumer education in children's judgement of televised advertisements. *Education and Treatment of Children*, *8*, 199–219.

Peterson, L., & Lewis, K. E. (1988). Preventive intervention to improve children's discrimination of the persuasive tactics in televised advertising. *Journal of Pediatric Psychology*, *13*, 163–170.

Peterson, P. E., Balfour, J. D., Bridgmater, C. A., & Dawson, B. (1984). How pronutrition television programming affects children's dietary habits. *Developmental Psychology*, *20*, 55–63.

Pezdek, K. (1985). Is watching television passive, uncreative, or addictive? Debunking some myths. *Television and Families*, *8*(2), 41–46.

Pezdek, K., & Hartman, E. F. (1983). Children's television viewing: Attention and comprehension of auditory versus visual information. *Child Development*, *54*, 1015–1023.

Pezdek, K., Lehrer, A., & Simon, S. (1984). The relationship between reading and cognitive processing of television and radio. *Child Development*, *55*, 2072–2082.

Pezdek, K., & Stevens, E. (1984). Children's memory for auditory and visual information on television. *Developmental Psychology*, *20*, 212–218.

Pfefferbaum, B., & Nixon, S. J. (1999). Posttraumatic stress responses in bereaved children after the Oklahoma City bombing. *Journal of the American Academy of Child & Adolescent Psychiatry*, *38*, 1372–1379.

Pfefferbaum, B., Nixon, S. J., Tivis, R. D., Doughty, D. E., Pynoos, R. S., Gurwitch, R. H., et al. (2001). Television exposure in children after a terrorist incident. *Psychiatry*, *64*, 202–211.

Phillips, D., Prince, S., & Schiebelhut, L. (2004). Elementary school children's responses 3 months after the September 11 terrorist attacks: A study in Washington D.C. *American Journal of Orthopsychiatry*, *74*, 509–528.

Phillips, D. P., & Carstensen, L. L. (1986). Clustering of teenage suicides after television news stories about suicides. *The New England Journal of Medicine*, *315*, 685–689.

Phillips, D. P., & Paight, D. J. (1987). The impact of televised movies about suicide: A replicative study. *The New England Journal of Medicine*, *317*, 809–811.

Pierce, C. M. (1978). *Television and education*. Beverly Hills, CA: Sage.

Pierce, C. M. (1984). Television and violence: Social psychiatric perspectives. *American Journal of Social Psychiatry*, *4*(3), 41–44.

Pierce, K. (1983). Relation between time spent viewing television and children's writing skills. *Journalism Quarterly*, *60*, 445–448.

Pierce, K. (1989). Sex-role stereotyping of children on television: A content analysis of the roles and attributes of child characters. *Sociological Spectrum*, *9*, 321–328.

Pike, J. J., & Jennings, N. A. (2005). The effects of commercials on children's perceptions of gender appropriate toy use. *Sex Roles*, *52*, 83–91.

Pinderhughes, C. A. (1972). Televised violence and social behavior. *Psychiatry Opinion*, *9*(2), 28–36.

Pingree, S. (1978). The effects of nonsexist television commercials and perceptions of reality on children's attitudes about women. *Psychology of Women Quarterly*, *2*, 262–277.

Pingree, S. (1986). Children's activity and television comprehensibility. *Communication Research, 13*, 239–256.

Pingree, S., & Hawkins, R. P. (1982). What children do with television: Implications for communication research. In P. J. Dervin & M. J. Voight (Eds.), *Progress in communication science* (Vol. 3 pp. 225–244). Norwood, NJ: Ablex.

Pingree, S., Hawkins, R. P., Rouner, D., Burns, J., Gikonyo, W., & Newwirth, C. (1984). Another look at children's comprehension of television. *Communication Research, 11*, 477–496.

Pinkleton, B. E., Austin, E. W., & Fujioka, Y. (2001). The relationship of perceived beer ad and PSA quality to high school students' alcohol-related beliefs and behaviors. *Journal of Broadcasting & Electronic Media, 45*, 575–597.

Piñon, M. (1999). Video imagery and children's acquisition of televised geographic information: Affecting more than . . . *Journal of Instructional Psychology, 26*, 226–237.

Pittman, D. (1958). Mass media and juvenile delinquency. In J. Roucek (Ed.), *Juvenile delinquency* (pp. 230–250). New York: Philosophical Library.

Plomin, R., Corley, R., DeFries, J. C., & Fulker, D. W. (1990). Individual differences in television viewing in early childhood: Nature as well as nurture. *Psychological Science, 1*(6), 371–377.

Polce-Lynch, M., Myers, B. J., Kliewer, W., & Kilmartin, C. (2001). Adolescent self-esteem and gender: Exploring relations to sexual harrassment, body image, media influence, and emotional expression. *Journal of Youth & Adolescence, 30*, 225–244.

Polley, D. C., Spicer, M. T., Knight, A. P., & Hartley, B. L. (2005). Intrafamilial correlates of overweight and obesity in African-American and Native-American grandparents, parents, and children, in rural Oklahoma. *Journal of the American Dietetic Association, 102*, 262–265.

Poloff, M. E., & Greenberg, B. S. (1979). Resolving conflict: Methods used by TV characters and teenage viewers. *Journal of Broadcasting, 23*, 285–300.

Ponder, S. W., & Beach, P. S. (1988). Television, children and the pediatrician: Impact on health practices. *Texas Medicine, 84*(3), 21–25.

Pool, M. M., Koolstra, C. M., & van der Voort, T. H. A. (2003). The impact of background radio and television on high school students' homework performance. *Journal of Communication, 53*(1), 74–87.

Pool, M. M., van der Voort, T. H. A., Beentjes, J. W. J., & Koolstra, C. M. (2000). Background television as an inhibitor of performance on easy and difficult homework assignments. *Communication Research, 27*, 293–326.

Posavac, H. D., Posavac, S. S., & Weigel, R. G. (2001). Reducing the impact of media images on women at risk for body image disturbance: Three targeted interventions. *Journal of Social & Clinical Psychology, 20*, 324–340.

Posner, J. K., & Vandell, D. L. (1999). After-school activities and the development of low-income urban children: A longitudinal study. *Developmental Psychology, 35*, 868–879.

Postman, N. (1985). The disappearance of childhood. *Childhood Education, 61*, 286–293.

Postman, N. (1987). The blurring of childhood and the media. *Religious Education, 82*, 293–95.

Potter, R. L. (1979). Is children's programming improving? *Teacher, 96*(7), 34, 40–43.

Potter, W. J. (1990). Adolescents' perceptions of the primary values of television programming. *Journalism Quarterly, 67*, 843–851.

Potter, W. J. (1992). How do adolescents' perceptions of television reality change over time? *Journalism Quarterly, 69*, 392–405.

Potter, W. J., & Smith, S. (1999). Consistency of contextual cues about violence across narrative levels. *Journal of Communication, 49*(4), 121–133.

Potter, W. J., & Warren, R. (1996). Considering policies to protect children from TV violence. *Journal of Communication, 46*(4), 116–138.

Potts, R., Doppler, M., & Hernandez, M. (1994). Effects of television content on physical risk-taking in children. *Journal of Experimental Child Psychology, 58*, 321–331.

Potts, R., & Henderson, J. (1991). The dangerous world of television: A content analysis of physical injuries in children's television programming. *Children's Environments Quarterly, 8*(3–4), 7–14.

Potts, R., Huston, A. C., & Wright, J. C. (1986). The effects of television form and violent content on boys' attention and social behavior. *Journal of Experimental Child Psychology, 41*(1), 1–17.

Potts, R., & Martinez, I. (1994). Television viewing and children's beliefs about scientists. *Journal of Applied Developmental Psychology, 15*, 287–300.

Potts, R., Runyan, D., Zerger, A., & Marchetti, K. (1996). A content analysis of safety behaviors of television characters: Implications for children's safety and injury. *Journal of Pediatric Psychology, 21*, 517–528.

Potts, R., & Swisher, L. (1998). Effects of televised safety models on children's risk taking and hazard identification. *Journal of Pediatric Psychology, 23*, 157–163.

Poulos, R. W., Harvey, S. E., & Liebert, R. L. (1976). Saturday morning television: A profile of the 1974–75 children's season. *Psychological Reports, 39*, 1047–1057.

Poulos, R. W., Rubinstein, E. A., & Liebert, R. M. (1975). Positive social learning. *Journal of Communication, 25*(4), 90–97.

Powell, K. A., & Abels, L. (2002). Sex-role stereotypes in TV programs aimed at the preschool audience: An analysis of Teletubbies and Barney & Friends. *Women & Language, 25*(1), 14–22.

Powell, M. (2001). Children's play and television. *Montessori Life, 13*(2), 36–39.

Prabhu, N. P., Duffy L. C., & Stapleton, F. B. (1996). Content analysis of prime-time television medical news: A pediatric perspective. *Archives of Pediatrics & Adolescent Medicine, 150*(1), 46–49.

Prasad, V. K., Rao, T. R., & Sheikh, A. A. (1978). Can people affect television? Mother vs. commercial. *Journal of Communication, 28*(1), 91–96.

Prasad, V. K., & Smith, L. J. (1994). Television commercials in violent programming: An experimental evaluation of their effects on children. *Journal of the Academy of Marketing Science, 22*, 340–351.

Pratt, C. (1982). How media credibility ratings of African and United States students compare. *Journalism Quarterly, 59*, 581–587.

Prawat, D. M., & Prawat, R. S. (1975). Preschoolers' viewing behavior while watching two types of television fare. *Perceptual & Motor Skills, 40*, 575–582.

Preston, E., & White, C. L. (2004). Commodifying kids: Branded identities and the selling of adspace on kids' networks. *Communication Quarterly, 52*, 115–128.

Prince, P., & Lazarus, M. (1975). Junior consumer protection. *Educational Broadcasting, 8*, 13–15, 30.

Prisuta, R. H. (1979). Televised sports and political values. *Journal of Communication*, 29(1), 94–102.

Proctor, M. H., Moore, L. L., Gao, D., Cupples, L. A., Bradlee, M. L., Hood, M. Y., et al. (2003). Television viewing and change in body fat from preschool to early adolescence: The Framingham Children's Study. *International Journal of Obesity*, 27, 827–834.

Proman, J. M. (2004). Liability of media companies for the violent content of their products marketed to children. *St. John's Law Review*, 78(2), 427–448.

Prosuite, R. H. (1979). The adolescent and television news: A viewer profile. *Journalism Quarterly*, 56, 277–282.

Purdie, S. I., Collins, W. A., & Westby, S. (1981). Effect of plot organization on children's comprehension of evaluative cues about televised aggressive portrayal. *Journal of Applied Developmental Psychology*, 2, 179–190.

Quarforth, J. M. (1979). Children's understanding of the nature of television characters. *Journal of Communication*, 29(3), 210–218.

Quisenberry, J. D. (1982). Television commercials: Effects on children. *Childhood Education*, 58, 316–318, 320–322.

Quisenberry, N. L., & Klasek, C. B. (1976). Should teachers watch TV after the family viewing hour? *Audiovisual Instruction*, 21(9), 13–14.

Quisenberry, N. L., & Klasek, C. B. (1977). Can watching TV be good for children? *Audiovisual Instruction*, 22(3), 56–57.

Ra, J. B. (1977). A comparison of preschool children's preferences for television and their parents. *Journal of Social Psychology*, 102(1), 163–164.

Rabinovitch, M. S. (1972). Violence perception as a function of entertainment value and TV violence. *Psychonomic Science*, 29, 360–362.

Rajecki, D. W., Dame, J. A., Creek, K. J., Barrickman, P. J., Reid, C., & Appleby, D. C. (1993). Gender casting in television toy advertisements: Distributions, message content analysis and evaluations. *Journal of Consumer Psychology*, 2, 307–327.

Rajecki, D. W., McTavish, D. G., Rasmussen, J. L., Schreuders, M., Byers, D. C., & Jessup, K. S. (1994). Violence, conflict, trickery, and other story themes in TV ads for food for children. *Journal of Applied Social Psychology*, 24, 1685–1700.

Rapaczynski, W., Singer, D. G., & Singer, J. L. (1982). Teaching television: A curriculum for young child. *Journal of Communication*, 32(2), 46–55.

Rapport, L. J., & Meleen, M. (1998). Childhood celebrity, parental attachment, and adult adjustment: The young performers study. *Journal of Personality Assessment*, 70, 484–505.

Rarick, D. L., Townsend, J. E., & Boyd, D. A. (1973). Adolescent perceptions of police: Actual and as depicted in TV drama. *Journalism Quarterly*, 50, 438–446.

Ravi, S. D., Dorus, W., & Borge, G. F. (1985). Adolescent suicides modeled after television movie. *American Journal of Psychiatry*, 142, 989.

Reeves, B. (1978). Perceived TV reality as a predictor of children's social behavior. *Journalism Quarterly*, 55, 682–689, 695.

Reeves, B. (1979). Children's understanding of television people. In E. Wartella (Ed.), *Children communicating: Media and development of thought, speech and understanding* (pp. 115–155). Beverly Hills, CA: Sage.

Reeves, B., & Garramone, G. M. (1982). Children's person perception: The generalization from television to real people. *Human Communication Research*, 8, 317–326.

Reeves, B., & Garramone, G. M. (1983). Television's influence on children's encoding of personal information. *Human Communication Research, 10*, 257–268.

Reeves, B., & Greenberg, B. S. (1977). Children's perception of television characters. *Human Communication Research, 3*, 113–127.

Reeves, B., & Lometti, G. E. (1979). The dimensional structure of children's perceptions of television characters: A replication. *Human Communication Research, 5*, 247–256.

Reeves, B., & Miller, M. M. (1978). A multidimensional measure of children's identification with television characters. *Journal of Broadcasting, 22*, 71–86.

Reeves, B., & Thorson, E. (1986). Watching television: Experiments of the viewing process. *Communication Research, 13*, 343–361.

Reeves, B., Thorson, E., & Scheuder, J. (1986). Attention to television: Psychological theories and chronometric measures. In J. Bryant & D. Zillmann (Eds.), *Perspectives on media effects* (pp. 251–279). Hillsdale, NJ: Lawrence Erlbaum Associates, Inc.

Rehage, K. J. (1949). Notes on television and the schools. *The Elementary School Journal, 50*, 128–130.

Reid, L. N. (1979a). The impact of family group interaction on children's understanding of television advertising. *Journal of Advertising, 8*(3), 13–19.

Reid, L. N. (1979b). Viewing rules as mediating factors of children's responses to commercials. *Journal of Broadcasting, 23*, 15–26.

Reid, L. N., Bearden, W. O., & Teel, J. E. (1980). Family income, TV viewing, and children's cereal ratings. *Journalism Quarterly, 57*, 327–330.

Reid, L. N., & Frazer, C. F. (1979). Studying the child/television advertising relationship: A symbolic interactionist approach. *Journal of Advertising, 8*(4), 13–19.

Reid, L. N., & Frazer, C. F. (1980a). Children's use of television commercials to initiate social interaction in family viewing situations. *Journal of Broadcasting, 24*, 149–158.

Reid, L. N., & Frazer, C. F. (1980b). Television at play. *Journal of Communication, 30*(4), 66–73.

Reid, L. N., & Rotfield, H. S. (1981). How informative are ads on children's TV shows? *Journalism Quarterly, 58*, 108–111.

Reidel, L. (1975). Simultaneous TV and radio broadcasts teach children in their homes. *Audiovisual Instruction, 20*(5), 19–20.

Reinking, D., & Wu, J.-H. (1990). Reexamining the research on television and reading. *Reading Research & Instruction, 29*(2), 30–43.

Reitzes, K. A., & White, M. A. (1982). Children's expectations for television entertainment versus television news events. *Journal of Applied Communication Research, 10*, 168–173.

Remafedi, G. (1990). Study group report on the impact of television portrayals of gender roles on youth. *Journal of Adolescent Health Care, 11*(1), 59–61.

Repetti, R. L. (1984). Determinants of children's sex stereotyping: Parental sex role traits and television viewing. *Personality and Social Psychology Bulletin, 10*, 457–468.

Resnick, M. D. (1990). Study group report on the impact of televised drinking and alcohol advertising on youth. *Journal of Adolescent Health Care, 11*, 25–30.

Resnik, A. J., & Stern, B. L. (1977). Children's television advertising and brand choice: A laboratory experiment. *Journal of Advertising, 6*(3), 11–17.

Resnik, A. J., Stern, B. L., & Alberty, B. (1979). Integrating results from children's television advertising research. *Journal of Advertising, 8*(3), 3–12.

Resnik, H. S., & Smith, D. M. (1979). Career awareness: They're never too young to start. *Audiovisual Instruction, 24*(2), 41–42, 61.

Revelle, G. L., Wellman, H. M., & Karabenick, J. D. (1985). Comprehension monitoring in preschool children. *Child Development, 56,* 654–663.

Rice, M. L. (1983). The role of television in language aquisition. *Developmental Review, 3,* 211–224.

Rice, M. L. (1984a). Television language and child language. In J. P. Murray & G. Salomon (Eds.), *The future of children's television* (pp. 53–58). Boys Town, NE: Father Flanagan's Boys Town.

Rice, M. L. (1984b). The words of children's television. *Journal of Broadcasting, 28,* 445–461.

Rice, M. L., & Haight, P. L. (1986). Motherese of Mr. Rogers: A description of the dialogue of educational television programs. *Journal of Speech and Hearing Disorders, 51,* 282–287.

Rice, M. L., Huston, A. C., & Wright, J. C. (1986). Replays as repetitions: Young children's interpretation of television forms. *Journal of Applied Developmental Psychology, 7,* 61–76.

Rice, M. L., & Wartella, E. A. (1981). Television as a medium of commercials: Implications for how to regard young viewers. *Journal of Broadcasting, 25*(4).

Rice, M. L., & Woodsmall, L. (1988). Lessons from television: Children's word learning when viewing. *Child Development, 59,* 420–429.

Richards, J. E., & Turner, E. D. (2001). Extended visual fixation and distractibility in children from six to twenty-four months of age. *Child Development, 72,* 963–972.

Ridder, J. M. (1963). Pupil opinions and the relationship of television viewing to academic achievement. *Journal of Educational Research, 57,* 204–206.

Ridley-Johnson, R., Chance, J. E., & Cooper, H. (1984). Correlates of children's television viewing: Expectancies, age and sex. *Journal of Applied Developmental Psychology, 5,* 225–235.

Ridley-Johnson, R., Cooper, H., & Chance, J. (1983). The relation of children's television viewing to school achievement and IQ. *Journal of Educational Research, 76,* 294–297.

Ridley-Johnson, R., Surdy, T., & O'Laughlin, E. (1991). Parent survey on television violence viewing: Fear, aggression, and sex differences. *Journal of Applied Developmental Psychology, 12,* 63–71.

Riecken, G., & Samli, A. C. (1981). Measuring children's attitudes toward television commercials: Extension and replication. *Journal of Consumer Research, 8,* 57–61.

Riecken, G., & Yavas, U. (1990). Children's general product and brand-specific attitudes toward television commercials: Implications for public policy and advertising strategy. *International Journal of Advertising, 9,* 136–148.

Riffe, D., Goldson, H., Saxton, K., & Yu, Y. (1989). Females and minorities in TV ads in 1987 Saturday children's programs. *Journalism Quarterly, 66,* 129–136.

Riley, J., Cantwell, F., & Ruttiger, K. (1949). Some observations on the social effects of TV. *Public Opinion Quarterly, 13,* 223–234.

Ritchie, D., Price, V., & Roberts, D. F. (1987). Television, reading, and reading achievement: A reappraisal. *Communication Research, 14,* 292–315.

Rivadeneyra, R., & Ward, L. M. (2005). From Ally McBeal to Sabado Gigante: Contributions of television viewing to the gender role attitudes of Latino adolescents. *Journal of Adolescent Research, 20,* 453–475.

Roberson, D. (1981). Mandatory programming rules for children's television. *Comm/Ent: Hastings Communication and Entertainment Law Journal, 3,* 701–718.

Roberts, D. F. (1973). Communication and children: A developmental approach. In I. de Sola Pool & W. Schramm (Eds.), *Handbook of communication* (pp. 174–215). Chicago: Rand McNally.

Roberts, D. F. (1982). Children and commercials: Issues, evidence, interventions. *Prevention in Human Services, 2*(1–Sup–2), 19–35.

Roberts, D. F., & Bachen, C. M. (1981). Mass communication effects. *Annual Review of Psychology, 32,* 307–356.

Roberts, D. F., Bachen, C. M., Hornby, C., & Hernandez-Ramos, P. (1984). Reading and television: Predictors of reading achievement of different age levels. *Communication Research, 11,* 9–49.

Roberts, D. F., Christenson, P., Gibson, W. A., Mooser, L., & Goldberg, M. E. (1980). Developing discriminating consumers. *Journal of Communication, 30*(3), 94–105.

Roberts, D. F., & Foehr, U. G. (2004). *Kids and media in America.* New York: Cambridge University Press.

Roberts, D. F., & Schramm, W. (1971). Children's learning from the mass media. In W. Schramm & D. F. Roberts (Eds.), *The process and effects of mass communication* (pp. 598–611). Urbana: University of Illinois Press.

Roberts, K. P., & Blades, M. (1999). Children's memory and source monitoring of real-life and televised events. *Journal of Applied Developmental Psychology, 20,* 575–596.

Roberts, K. P., & Blades, M. (2000). *Discriminating between memories of television and real life.* In K. P. Roberts & M. Blades (Eds.), *Children's source monitoring.* (147–169). Mahwah, NJ: Lawrence Erlbaum Associates, Inc.

Roberts, S., & Howard, S. (2005). Children and technology—Watching *Teletubbies*: Television and its very young audience. In J. Marsh (Ed.), *Popular culture, new media and digital literacy in early childhood* (pp. 91–107). New York: Routledge-Falmer

Robertson, T. S. (1979). Parental mediation of television advertising effects. *Journal of Communication, 29*(1), 12–25.

Robertson, T. S. (1980a). The impact of proprietary medicine advertising on children. In R. P. Adler, G. S. Lesser, L. K. Meringoff, T. S. Robertson, J. R. Rossiter, & F. Ward (Eds.), *The effects of television advertising on children: Review and recommendation* (pp. 111–122). Lexington, MA: Lexington Books.

Robertson, T. S. (1980b). Television advertising and parent–child relations. In R. P. Adler, G. S. Lesser, L. K. Meringoff, T. S. Robertson, J. R. Rossiter, & F. Ward (Eds.), *The effects of television advertising on children: Review and recommendation* (pp. 195–212). Lexington, MA: Lexington Books.

Robertson, T. S., Gatignon, H., & Klees, D. M. (1989). Advertising and children: A cross-cultural study. *Communication Research, 16,* 459–485.

Robertson, T. S., & Rossiter, J. R. (1974). Children and commercial persuasion: An attribution theory analysis. *Journal of Consumer Research, 1*, 13–20.

Robertson, T. S., & Rossiter, J. R. (1976a). Children and commercial persuasion: A reply to Ryans and Deutscher. *Journal of Consumer Research, 3*(1), 68–70.

Robertson, T. S., & Rossiter, J. R. (1976b). Short-run advertising effects on children: A field study. *Journal of Marketing Research, 13*(1), 68–70.

Robertson, T. S., & Rossiter, J. R. (1977). Children's responsiveness to commercials. *Journal of Communication, 27*(1), 101–106.

Robertson, T. S., Rossiter, J. R., & Gleason, T. C. (1979a). Children's receptivity to proprietary medicine advertising. *Journal of Consumer Research, 6*, 247–255.

Robertson, T. S., Rossiter, J. R., & Gleason, T. C. (1979b). *Televised medicine advertising and children.* New York: Praeger Special Studies.

Robinson, D. C. (1977). Television, children and censorship. In S. L. Wasby (Ed.), *Civil liberties: Policy and policy making* (pp. 25–35). Carbondale: Southern Illinois University Press.

Robinson, J. D., & Skill, T. (2001). Five decades of families on television: From the 1950s through the 1990s. In J. Bryant & J. A. Bryant (Eds.), *Television and the American family* (2nd ed., pp. 139–162). Mahwah, NJ: Lawrence Erlbaum Associates, Inc.

Robinson, J. P. (1990). Television's effects on families' use of time. In J. Bryant (Ed.), *Television and the American family* (pp. 195–210). Hillsdale, NJ: Lawrence Erlbaum Associates, Inc.

Robinson, T. N. (1998). Does television cause childhood obesity? *Journal of the American Medical Association, 279*, 959–960.

Robinson, T. N. (1999). Reducing children's television viewing to prevent obesity: A randomized controlled trial. *Journal of the American Medical Association, 282*, 1561–1567.

Robinson, T. N. (2001). Television viewing and childhood obesity. *Pediatric Clinics of North America, 48*, 1017–1025.

Robinson, T. N., Chen, H. L., & Killen, J. D. (1998). Televison and music video exposure and risk of adolescent alcohol use. *Pediatrics, 102*(5).

Robinson, T. N., Hammer, L. D., Killen, J. D., Kraemer, H. C., Wilson, S. M., Hayward, C., et al. (1993). Does television viewing increase obesity and reduce physical activity: Cross-sectional and longitudinal analyses among adolescent girls. *Pediatrics, 91*, 273–280.

Robinson, T. N., & Killen, J. D. (1995). Ethnic and gender differences in the relationship between television viewing and obesity, physical activity, and dietary fat intake. *Journal of Health Education, 26*, 91–98.

Robinson, T. N., Killen, J. D., Kraemer, H. C., Wilson, D. M., Matheson, D. M., Haskell, W. L., et al. (2003). Dance and reducing television viewing to prevent weight gain in African-American girls: The Stanford GEMS pilot study. *Ethnicity & Disease, 13*, S65–S77.

Robinson, T. N., Saphir, M. N., Kraemer, H. C., Varady, A., & Haydel, K. F. (2001). Effects of reducing television viewing on children's requests for toys: A randomized controlled trial. *Journal of Developmental and Behavioral Pediatrics, 22*, 179–184.

Robinson, T. N., Wilde, M. L., Navracruz, L. C., Haydel, K. F., & Varady, A. (2001). Effects of reducing children's television and video game use on aggressive behavior:

A randomized controlled trial. *Archives of Pediatrics & Adolescent Medicine, 155*(1), 17–23.

Roderick, J. A., & Jackson, P. (1986). TV viewing habits, family rules, reading grades, heroes and heroines of gifted and nongifted middle school students. *Roeper Review, 9*, 114–119.

Roedder, D. L. (1981). Age differences in children's responses to television advertising: An information processing approach. *Journal of Consumer Research, 8*, 144–153.

Roedder, D. L., Sternthal, B., & Calder, B. J. (1983). Attitude behavior consistency in children's responses to television advertising. *Journal of Marketing, 20*, 337–349.

Rogers, F. (1971). Communicating with children through television. *Clinical Pediatrics, 10*, 456–458.

Rohrer, J. C. (1996). "We interrupt this program to show you a bombing": Children and schools respond to televised war. *Childhood Education, 72*, 201–205.

Rolandelli, D. R. (1989). Children and television: The visual superiority effect reconsidered. *Journal of Broadcasting & Electronic Media, 33*, 69–81.

Rolandelli, D. R., Sugihara, K., & Wright, J. C. (1992). Visual processing of televised information by Japanese and American children. *Journal of Cross Culture Psychology, 23*(1), 5–24.

Rolandelli, D. R., Wright, J. C., Huston, A. C., & Eakins, D. (1991). Children's auditory and visual processing of narrated and nonnarrated television programming. *Journal of Experimental Child Psychology, 51*, 90–122.

Roloff, M. E., & Greenberg, B. S. (1980). TV, peer, and parent models for pro- and antisocial conflict behaviors. *Human Communication Research, 6*(4), 340–351.

Rones, B. (1949). Does television damage the eyes? *Sight-Saving Research, 19*, 127–131.

Roody, S. I. (1952). Effects of radio, television and motion pictures on the development of maturity. *English Journal, 41*, 245–250.

Rose, A. (1995). Metaphor with an attitude: The use of The Mighty Morphin' Power Rangers television series as a therapeutic metaphor. *International Journal of Play Therapy, 4*(2), 59–72.

Rosen, C. S., Schwebel, D. C., & Singer, J. L. (1997). Preschoolers' attributions of mental states in pretense. *Child Development, 68*, 1133–1142.

Rosenbaum, W. B., Rosenbaum, L. L., & McGinnies, E. (1974). Sex differences in selective exposure. *Journal of Social Psychology, 92*, 85–89.

Rosenblatt, P. C., & Cunningham, M. R. (1976). Television watching and family tensions. *Journal of Marriage and the Family, 38*(1), 105–111.

Rosenfeld, A. A. (1993). Children living through Desert Storm. *Child Abuse & Neglect: The International Journal, 17*, 821–829.

Rosengren, K. E., Windahl, S., Hakansson, P. A., & Johnsson-Smargadi, U. (1976). Adolescent's TV relations: Three scales. *Communication Research, 3*, 347–366.

Rosenkoetter, L. I. (1999). The television situation comedy and children's prosocial behavior. *Journal of Applied Social Psychology, 29*, 979–993.

Rosenkoetter, L. I., Huston, A. C., & Wright, J. C. (1990). Television and the moral judgment of the young child. *Journal of Applied Developmental Psychology, 11*, 123–137.

Rosenkoetter, L. I., Rosenkoetter, S. E., Ozretich, R. A., & Acock, A. C. (2004). Mitigating the harmfull effects of television violence. *Journal of Applied Developmental Psychology, 25, 25–47.*

Rosenthal, N. (1962). Crime and violence in television programs: Their impact on children and adolescents. *Audio-Visual Aids Review, 3, 5–9.*

Rosenwasser, S. M., Lingenfelter, M., & Harrington, A. (1989). Nontraditional gender role portrayals on television and children's gender role perceptions. *Journal of Applied Developmental Psychology, 10, 97–105.*

Ross, R. P., Campbell, T., Huston-Stein, A., & Wright, J. (1981). Nutritional misinformation of children: A developed and experimental analysis of the effects of televised food commercials. *Journal of Applied Developmental Psychology, 1, 329–347.*

Ross, R. P., Campbell, T., Wright, J. C., Huston, A. C., Rice, M. L., & Turk, P. (1984). When celebrities talk, children listen: An experimental analysis of children's responses to television ads with celebrity endorsement. *Journal of Applied Developmental Psychology, 5, 185–202.*

Ross, S. (2004). Dormant dormitory friendships: Race and gender in *Felicity*. In G. Davis & K. Dickinson (Eds.), *Teen TV: Genre, consumption, identity* (pp. 141–150). London: British Film Institute.

Rossiter, G. (1999). The shaping influence of film and television on the spirituality and identity of children and adolescents. *International Journal of Children's Spirituality, 4, 207–224.*

Rossiter, J. R. (1977). Reliability of a short test measuring children's attitudes toward TV commercials. *Journal of Consumer Research, 3, 179–184.*

Rossiter, J. R. (1979). Does TV advertising affect children? *Journal of Advertising Research, 19(1), 49–53.*

Rossiter, J. R. (1980a). The effects of volume and repetition on television commercials. In R. P. Adler, G. S. Lesser, L. K. Meringoff, T. S. Robertson, J. R. Rossiter, & F. Ward (Eds.), *The effects of television advertising on children: Review and recommendation* (pp. 153–184). Lexington, MA: Lexington Books.

Rossiter, J. R. (1980b). Children and television advertising policy issues, perspectives, and the status of research. In E. L. Palmer & A. Dorr (Eds.), *Children and the faces of television: Teaching, violence, selling* (pp. 251–272). New York: Academic.

Rossiter, J. R. (1980c). Source effects and self-concept appeals in children's television advertising. In R. P. Adler, G. S. Lesser, L. K. Meringoff, T. S. Robertson, J. R. Rossiter, & F. Ward (Eds.), *The effects of television advertising on children: Review and recommendation* (pp. 61–94). Lexington, MA: Lexington Books.

Rossiter, J. R., & Robertson, T. S. (1974). Children's TV commercials: Testing the defenses. *Journal of Communication, 24(4), 137–145.*

Rossiter, J. R., & Robertson, T. S. (1975). Children's television viewing: An examination of parent–child consensus. *Sociometry, 38, 308–326.*

Rossiter, J. R., & Robertson, T. S. (1976). Canonical analysis of developmental, social, and experimental factors in children's comprehension of television advertising. *Journal of Genetic Psychology, 129, 317–327.*

Rossiter, J. R., & Robertson, T. S. (1980). Children's dispositions toward proprietary drugs and the role of TV drug advertising. *Public Opinion Quarterly, 44(3), 316–329.*

Rossler, P., & Brosius, H.-B. (2001). Do talk shows cultivate adolescents' views of the world? A prolonged-exposure experiment. *Journal of Communication, 51*(1), 143–163.

Rotfeld, H. J., & Reid, L. N. (1979). Potential secondary effects of regulating children's television advertising. *Journal of Advertising, 8*(4), 9–14.

Rothenberg, M. B. (1975). Effect of television violence on children and youth. *Journal of the American Medical Association, 234*, 1043–1046.

Rothenberg, M. B. (1983). The role of television in shaping the attitudes of children. *Journal of the American Academy of Child Psychiatry, 22*, 86–87.

Rothenberg, M. B. (1985). Role of television in shaping the attitudes of children. *Children's Health Care, 13*, 148–149.

Rothschild, M. L., Thorson, E., Reeves, B., Hirsch, J. E., & Goldstein, R. (1986). EEG activity and the processing of television commercials. *Communication Research, 13*, 182–220.

Rothschild, N., & Morgan, M. (1987). Cohesion and control: Adolescents' relationships with parents as mediators of television. *Journal of Early Adolescence, 7*, 299–314.

Rouner, D., Slater, M. D., & Domenech-Rodriguez, M. (2003). Adolescent evaluation of gender role and sexual imagery in television advertisements. *Journal of Broadcasting & Electronic Media, 47*, 435–454.

Rovinelli, L., & Whissell, C. (1998). Emotion and style in 30–second television advertisements targeted at men, women, boys, and girls. *Perceptual & Motor Skills, 86*, 1048–1050.

Rozin, P., Riklis, J., & Margolis, L. (2004). Mutual exposure or close peer relationships do not seem to foster increased similarity in food, music or television program preferences. *Appetite, 42*(1), 41–48.

Rubin, A. M. (1976). Television in children's political socialization. *Journal of Broadcasting, 20*, 51–60.

Rubin, A. M. (1977). Television usage, attitudes and viewing behaviors of children and adolescents. *Journal of Broadcasting, 21*, 355–369.

Rubin, A. M. (1978). Child and adolescent television use and political socialization. *Journalism Quarterly, 55*, 125–129.

Rubin, A. M. (1979). Television use by children and adolescents. *Human Communication Research, 5*, 109–120.

Rubin, A. M. (1981). An examination of television viewing motivations. *Communication Research, 8*, 141–165.

Rubin, A. M. (1984). Ritualized and instrumental television viewing. *Journal of Communication, 34*(3), 67–77.

Rubin, A. M. (1986). Age and family control influences on children's television viewing. *Southern Speech Communication Journal, 52*, 35–51.

Rubin, A. M., & Perse, E. (1987). Audience activity and television news gratifications. *Communication Research, 14*, 58–84.

Rubin, R. S. (1974). Effects of cognitive development on children's responses to television advertising. *Journal of Business Research, 2*, 409–419.

Rubinstein, E. A. (1972). Television and social behavior: Social science research for social policy. *Educational Broadcasting Review, 6*, 409–415.

Rubinstein, E. A. (1974). The TV violence report: What's next? *Journal of Communication, 24*(1), 80–88.

Rubinstein, E. A. (1976). Warning: The Surgeon General's research program may be dangerous to preconceived notions. *Journal of Social Issues, 32*(4), 18–34.

Rubinstein, E. A. (1978). Television and the young viewer. *American Scientist, 66,* 685–693.

Rubinstein, E. A. (1980). Television violence: An historical perspective. In E. L. Palmer & A. Dorr (Eds.), *Children and the faces of television: Teaching, violence, selling* (pp. 113–127). New York: Academic.

Rubinstein, E. A. (1981). Research on children and television—A critique. *Journal of Broadcasting, 25,* 389–393.

Rubinstein, E. A. (1983). Television and behavior: Research conclusions of the 1982 NIMH report and their policy implications. *American Psychologist, 38,* 820–825.

Rubinstein, E. A., & Brown, J. D. (1985a). *The media, social science, and social policy for children.* Norwood, NJ: Ablex.

Rubinstein, E. A., & Brown, J. D. (1985b). Television and children: A public policy dilemma. In E. A. Rubinstein & J. D. Brown (Eds.), *The media, social science and social policy for children* (pp. 93–117). Norwood, NJ: Ablex.

Ruble, D. N., Balaban, T., & Cooper, J. (1981). Gender constancy and the effects of sex-typed televised toy commercials. *Child Development, 52,* 667–673.

Rue, V. M. (1974). Television and the family: The question of control. *Family Coordinator, 23*(1), 72–81.

Ruff, H. A., Capozzoli, M., & Weissberg, R. (1998). Age, individuality, and context as factors in sustained visual attention during the preschool years. *Developmental Psychology, 34,* 454–464.

Rule, B. G., & Ferguson, T. J. (1986). The effects of media violence on attitudes, emotions, and cognitions. *Journal of Social Issues, 42*(3), 29–50.

Runco, M. A., & Pezdek, K. (1984). The effect of television and radio on children's creativity. *Human Communication Research, 11,* 109–120.

Rush, W. S. (1965). Some factors influencing children's use of the mass media of communication. *Journal of Experimental Education, 33,* 301–304.

Rushton, J. P. (1975). Generosity in children: Immediate and long-term effects of modeling, preaching, and moral judgment. *Journal of Personality and Social Psychology, 31,* 459–466.

Rushton, J. P. (1979). Effects of prosocial television and film material on the behavior of viewers. In L. Berkowitz (Ed.), *Advances in experimental social psychology* (Vol. 12, pp. 321–351). New York: Academic.

Rust, L., & Watkins, T. A. (1975). Children's commercials: Creative development. *Journal of Advertising Research, 15*(5), 21–26.

Ryans, A. B., & Deutscher, T. (1975). Children and commercial persuasion: Some comments. *Journal of Consumer Research, 2,* 237–239.

Rychtarik, R. G., Fairbank, J. A., Allen C. M., Foy, D. W., & Drabman, R. S. (1983). Alcohol-use in television programming—Effects on children's behavior. *Addictive Behavior, 8*(1), 19–22.

Saelens, B. E., Sallis, J. F., Nader, P. R., Broyles, S. L., Berry, C. C., & Taras, H. L. (2002). Home environmental influences on children's television watching from early to middle childhood. *Journal of Developmental and Behavioral Pediatrics, 23,* 127–132.

Saffer, H. (2002). Alcohol advertising and youth. *Journal of Studies on Alcohol, 114* (Suppl. 14), 173–181.

Salomon, G. (1972). Can we affect cognitive skills through visual media: Explication of an hypothesis and initial findings. *AV Communication Review, 20,* 401–423.

Salomon, G. (1979). Shape, not only content: How media symbols partake in the development of abilities. In E. Wartella (Ed.), *Children communicating: Media and development of thought, speech and understanding* (pp. 53–82). Beverly Hills, CA: Sage.

Salomon, G. (1984a). Investing effort in television viewing. In J. P. Murray & G. Salomon (Eds.), *The future of children's television* (pp. 59–64). Boys Town, NE: Father Flanagan's Boys Town.

Salomon, G. (1984b). Television is "easy" and print is "tough": The differential investment of mental effort in learning as a function of perceptions and attributions. *Journal of Educational Psychology, 76,* 647–658.

Salomon, G. (1987). Television and reading: The roles of orientations and reciprocal relations. In M. E. Manley-Casimir & C. Luke (Eds.), *Children and television: A challenge for education* (pp. 15–33). New York: Praeger.

Salomon, G., & Leigh, T. (1984). Predispositions about learning from print and television. *Journal of Communication, 34*(2), 119–135.

Salomon, G., & Murray, J. P. (1984). Researching children's television and the new technologies. In J. P. Murray & G. Salomon (Eds.), *The future of children's television* (pp. 125–133). Boys Town, NE: Father Flanagan's Boys Town.

Sanchez, R. P., Lorch, E. P., Milich, R., & Welsh, R. (1999). Comprehension of televised stories by preschool children with ADHD. *Journal of Clinical Child Psychology, 28,* 376–385.

Sardo-Brown, D., & Beeghly, D. (1996). The reading and television viewing habits of a sample of pre-service education majors. *College Student Journal, 30*(1), 37–44.

Sarlo, G., Jason, L. A., & Lonak, C. (1988). Parents' strategies for limiting children's television watching. *Psychological Reports, 63,* 435–438.

Sawin, D. B. (1981). The fantasy–reality distinction in television violence: Modifying influences on children's aggression. *Journal of Research in Personality, 15,* 323–330.

Saylor, C. F., Cowart, B. L., Lipovsky, J. A., Jackson, C., & Finch, A. J., Jr. (2003). Media exposure to September 11: Elementary school students' experiences and symptoms. *American Behavioral Scientist, 46,* 1622–1642.

Scharrer, E. (2001). Men, muscles, and machismo: The relationship between television violence exposure and aggression and hostility in the presence of hypermasculinity. *Media Psychology, 3,* 159–188.

Scharrer, E. (2002). Third-person perception and television violence: The role of out-group stereotyping in perceptions of susceptibility to effects. *Communication Research, 29,* 681–704.

Scheibe, C. (1979). Sex roles in TV commercials. *Journal of Advertising Research, 19*(1), 23–27.

Scheidler, M. G., Shultz, B. L., Schall, L., Vyas, A., & Barksdale, E. M. J. (2002). Falling televisions: The hidden danger for children. *Journal of Pediatric Surgery, 37,* 572–575.

Scherer, K. E. (1971). Stereotype change following exposure to counter-stereotypical media heroes. *Journal of Broadcasting, 15,* 91–100.

Schippa, E., Gregg, P. B., & Hewes, D. E. (2004). Can a television series change attitudes about death? A study of college students and *Six Feet Under. Death Studies, 28,* 459–474.

Schleuder, J. D., White, A. V., & Cameron, G. T. (1993). Priming effects of television news bumpers and teasers on attention and memory. *Journal of Broadcasting & Electronic Media, 37,* 437–452.

Schmidt, J. (2003). Let's just play. *Teaching Tolerance, 24,* 19–25.

Schmitt, K. L., & Anderson, D. R. (2002). Television and reality: Toddlers' use of visual information from video to guide behavior. *Media Psychology, 4,* 51–76.

Schmitt, K. L., Anderson, D. R., & Collins, P. A. (1999). Form and content: Looking at visual features of television. *Developmental Psychology, 35,* 1156–1167.

Schmitt, K. L., Woolf, K. D., & Anderson, D. R. (2003). Viewing the viewers: Viewing behaviors by children and adults during television programs and commercials. *Journal of Communication, 53,* 265–283.

Schmitz, K. H., Harnack, L., Jacobs, D. R., Jr., Gao, S. , Lytle, L. A., Coevering, P. V., et al. (2004). Reliability and validity of a brief questionnaire to assess television viewing and computer use. *Journal of School Health, 74,* 370–378.

Schneider, L. B. (1994). Warning: Television violence may be harmful to children; but the First Amendment may foil Congressional attempts to legislate against it. *University of Miami Law Review, 49,* 477–530.

Schrag, R. L. (1982). Teach your children well: Method and rationale in the criticism of adolescent-oriented television programming. *Western Journal of Speech Communication, 46,* 98–108.

Schrag, R. L. (1991a). Narrative rationality and "first stories": Pedagogical implications for children's television. *Communication Education, 40,* 313–324.

Schrag, R. L. (1991b). Sugar and spice and everything nice versus snakes and snails and puppy dog tails: Selling social stereotypes on Saturday morning television. In L. Vande Berg & L. Wenner (Eds.), *Television criticism* (pp. 220–235). White Plains, NY: Longman.

Schramm, W. (1968). What TV is doing to our children. In D. M. White & R. Averson (Eds.), *Sight, sound and society* (pp. 57–67). Boston: Beacon Press.

Schramm, W., Lyle, J., & Parker, E. B. (1960). Patterns in children's reading of newspapers. *Journalism Quarterly, 37,* 35–40.

Schramm, W., Lyle, J., & Parker, E. B. (1961a). Children's learning from television. *Studies in Public Communication, 3,* 86–98.

Schramm, W., Lyle, J., & Parker, E. B. (1961b). *Television in the lives of our children.* Stanford, CA: Stanford University Press.

Schuetz, S., & Sprafkin, J. (1978). Spot messages appearing within Saturday morning television programs. In G. Tuchman, A. K. Daniels, & J. Benet (Eds.), *Hearth and home* (pp. 69–77). New York: Oxford University Press.

Schuetz, S., & Sprafkin, J. (1979). Portrayal of prosocial and aggressive behaviors in children's TV commercials. *Journal of Broadcasting, 23,* 33–40.

Schuh, K. (2004). Students' spontaneous use of information from media sources: What and how do they link? *International Journal of Instructional Media, 31,* 333–344.

Schwartz, L. A., & Markham, W. T. (1985). Sex stereotyping in children's toy advertisements. *Sex Roles*, *12*, 157–170.

Schweitzer, K., Zillmann, D., Weaver, J. B., & Luttrell, E. S. (1992). Perception of threatening events in the emotional aftermath of a televised college football game. *Journal of Broadcasting & Electronic Media*, *36*, 75–82.

Scott, L. F. (1954). Social attitudes of children revealed by responses to television programs. *California Journal of Elementary Education*, *22*, 176–179.

Scott, L. F. (1958). Relationships between elementary school children and television. *Journal of Educational Research*, *52*, 134–137.

Scott, R. K. (1990). Effect of sex on excitation transfer and recall of television news. *Psychological Reports*, *66*, 435–441.

Seagoe, M. V. (1951a). Children's television habits and preferences. *Quarterly of Film, Radio and Television*, *6*, 143–152.

Seagoe, M. V. (1951b). A score sheet for children's television. *Quarterly of Film, Radio and Television*, *6*, 327–337.

Seagoe, M. V. (1952a). Issues and criteria for children's television. *Educational Theatre Journal*, *4*, 231–237.

Seagoe, M. V. (1952b). Some current research in television for children. *California Journal of Educational Research*, *3*, 151–153.

Seal-Wanner, C. (2002). Can children's television increase cultural understanding? *Television Quarterly*, *33*(2–3), 64–69.

Searls, D. T., Mead, N. A., & Ward, B. (1985). The relationship of students' reading skills to TV watching leisure time reading, and homework. *Journal of Reading*, *29*, 158–162.

Seasonwein, R., & Sussman, L. R. (1972). Can extremists using TV move an audience? *Journalism Quarterly*, *49*, 61–64.

Sege, R. (1998). Life imitating art: Adolescents and television violence. In T. P. Gullotta, G. R. Adams & R. Montemayor (Eds.), *Delinquent violent youth: Theory and interventions* (pp. 129–143). Thousand Oaks, CA: Sage.

Sege, R., & Dietz, W. (1994). Television viewing and violence in children: The pediatrician as an agent for change. *Pediatrics*, *94*, 600–607.

Seidenberg, R. (1974). Images of health, illness and women in drug advertising. *Journal of Drug Issues*, *4*, 264–267.

Seiter, E. (1990). Different children, different dreams: Racial representation in advertising. *Journal of Communication Inquiry*, *14*(1), 31–47.

Seiter, E. (1993). *Sold separately: Children and parents in consumer culture*. New Brunswick, NJ: Rutgers University Press.

Seiter, E., & Mayer, V. (2004). Diversifying representation in children's TV: Nickelodeon's model. In H. Hendershot (Ed.), *Nickelodeon nation* (pp. 120–133). New York: New York University Press.

Selnow, G. W. (1990). The influence of television on language production: Rules, culture and Benjamin Whorf. *Communications*, *15*, 163–170.

Selnow, G. W., & Bettinghaus, E. P. (1982). Television exposure and language development. *Journal of Broadcasting*, *26*, 469–479.

Selnow, G. W., & Reynolds, H. (1984). Some opportunity costs of television viewing. *Journal of Broadcasting & Electronic Media*, *28*, 315–322.

Sendelbaugh, J. W. (1978). Television viewing habits of hearing-impaired teenagers in Chicago metropolitan area. *American Annals of the Deaf, 123*, 536–541.

Shanahan, J., & Morgan, M. (1992). Adolescents, families and television in five countries: Implications for cross-cultural educational research. *Journal of Educational Television, 18*, 35–55.

Shanahan, K. J., Hermans, C. M., & Hyman, M. R. (2003). Violent commercials in television programs for children. *Journal of Current Issues & Research in Advertising, 25*, 71–82.

Shane, H. (1950). Impact of television on schools and home. *Nation's Schools, 45*, 23–24.

Shann, M. H. (2001). Students' use of time outside of school: A case for after school programs for urban middle school youth. *Urban Review, 33*, 339–356.

Shannon, B., Peacock, J., & Brown, M. J. (1991). Body fatness, television viewing and caloric intake of a sample of Pennsylvania sixth grade children. *Journal of Nutrition Education, 23*, 262–268.

Shannon, P., & Fernie, D. E. (1985). Print and television: Children's use of the medium is the message. *The Elementary School Journal, 85*, 663–672.

Sharapan, H. (1977). "Mister Roger's Neighborhood." Dealing with death on a children's television series. *Death Education, 1*(1), 131–136.

Shatzer, M., Korzenny, F., & Griffis-Korzenny, B. (1985). Adolescents viewing "Shogun": Cognitive and attitudinal effects. *Journal of Broadcasting & Electronic Media, 29*, 341–346.

Shayon, R. L. (1951). *Television and our children*. New York: Longman, Green & Company.

Sheikh, A. A., & Moleski, L. M. (1977a). Children's perception of the value of an advertised product. *Journal of Broadcasting, 21*, 347–354.

Sheikh, A. A., & Moleski, L. M. (1977b). Conflict in the family over commercials. *Journal of Communication, 27*(1), 152–157.

Sheikh, A. A., Prasad, V. K., & Rao, T. R. (1974). Children's TV commercials: A review of research. *Journal of Communication, 24*(4), 126–136.

Sheiman, D. J. (1980). Effects of televised drug commercials on children. *Pediatrics, 65*, 678.

Shelby, M. E., Jr. (1964). Children's programming trends on network television. *Journal of Broadcasting, 8*, 247–256.

Shim, S. (1996). Adolescent consumer decision-making styles: The consumer socialization perspective. *Psychology & Marketing, 13*, 547–569.

Shim, S., & Koh, A. (1997). Profiling adolescent consumer decision-making styles: Effects of socialization agents and social-structural variables. *Clothing & Textiles Research Journal, 15*(1), 50–59.

Shimp, T. A., Dyer, R. F., & Divita, S. F. (1976). An experimental test of the harmful effects of premium-oriented commercials on children. *Journal of Consumer Research, 3*, 1–11.

Shin, N. (2004). Exploring pathways from television viewing to academic achievement in school-age children. *Journal of Genetic Psychology, 165*, 367–382.

Shrum, L. J., & O'Guinn, T. C. (1993). Processes and effects in the construction of social reality: Construct accessibility as an explanatory variable. *Communication Research, 20*, 436–471.

Shrum, L. J., Wyer, R. S., Jr., & O'Guinn, T. C. (1998). The effects of television consumption on social perceptions: The use of priming procedures to investigate psychological processes. *Journal of Consumer Research, 24,* 447–458.

Shukula, S. (1979). The impact of SITE on primary school children. *Journal of Communication, 29*(4), 99–105.

Siegel, A. E. (1958). The influence of violence in the mass media upon children's role expectations. *Child Development, 29,* 35–36.

Siegel, A. E. (1975). Communicating with the next generation. *Journal of Communication, 25*(4), 14–24.

Siegel, J. T., & Burgoon, J. K. (2002). Expectancy theory approaches to prevention: Violating adolescent expectations to increase the effectiveness of public service announcements. In W. D. Crano & M. Burgoon (Eds.), *Mass media and drug prevention: Classic and contemporary theories and research* (pp. 163–186). Mahwah, NJ: Lawrence Erlbaum Associates, Inc.

Siemicki, M. (1986). Nationally distributed children's shows: What cable TV contributes. *Journalism Quarterly, 63,* 710–718.

Sigel, R. S. (1965). Television and the reactions of school children to the assassination. In B. S. Greenberg & E. B. Parker (Eds.), *The Kennedy assassination and the American public* (pp. 199–219). Stanford, CA: Stanford University Press.

Signorielli, N. (1987). Children and adolescents on television: A consistent pattern of devaluation. *Early Adolescence, 7,* 255–268.

Signorielli, N. (1989). Television and conceptions about sex roles: Maintaining conventionality and the status quo. *Sex Roles, 21,* 341–360.

Signorielli, N. (1990). Children, television, and gender roles. *Journal of Adolescent Health Care, 11*(1), 50–58.

Signorielli, N. (1991a). Adolescents and ambivalence toward marriage: A cultivation analysis. *Youth & Society, 23,* 121–149.

Signorielli, N. (1991b). *A sourcebook on children and television.* Thousand Oaks, CA: Sage.

Signorielli, N. (1993a). Television and adolescents' perceptions about work. *Youth & Society, 24,* 314–341.

Signorielli, N. (1993b). Television, the portrayal of women, and children's attitudes. In G. L. Berry & J. K. Asamen (Eds.), *Children & television: Images in a changing sociocultural world* (pp. 229–242). Thousand Oaks, CA: Sage.

Signorielli, N., & Lears, M. (1992a). Children, television, and conceptions about chores: Attitudes and behaviors. *Sex Roles, 27,* 157–170.

Signorielli, N., & Lears, M. (1992b). Television and children's conceptions of nutrition: Unhealthy messages. *Health Communication, 4,* 245–257.

Signorielli, N., & Morgan, M. (1990). *Cultivation analysis: New directions in media effects research.* Thousand Oaks, CA: Sage.

Signorielli, N., & Morgan, M. (2001). Television and the family: The cultivation perspective. In J. Bryant & J. A. Bryant (Eds.), *Television and the American family* 2nd ed., (pp. 333–351). Mahwah, NJ: Lawrence Erlbaum Associates, Inc.

Signorielli, N., & Staples, J. (1997). Television and children's conceptions of nutrition. *Health Communication, 9,* 289–301.

Silverman-Watkins, L. T., & Sprafkin, J. M. (1983). Adolescents' comprehension of televised sexual innuendos. *Journal of Applied Developmental Psychology, 4,* 359–369.

Simmons, B. J., Stalsworth, K., & Wentzel, H. (1999). Television violence and its effects on young children. *Early Childhood Education Journal, 26,* 149–153.

Simonson, H. (1992). Interaction effects of television and socioeconomic status on teenage aggression. *International Journal of Adolescence and Youth, 3,* 333–343.

Simpson, B. (2004). *Children and television.* In F. Corcoran (Ed.), *RTE and the Globalisation of Irish Television* (pp. 149–176). Portland, OR: Intellects.

Singer, D. G. (1978a). Reading, imagination, and television. *School Library Journal, 2*(1), 145–164.

Singer, D. G. (1978b). Television and imaginative play. *Journal of Mental Imagery, 2*(1), 145–164.

Singer, D. G. (1983). A time to reexamine the role of television in our lives. *American Psychologist, 38,* 815–816.

Singer, D. G. (1985). Does violent television produce aggressive children? *Pediatric Annals, 14,* 804, 807–810.

Singer, D. G. (1989a). Caution: Television may be hazardous to a child's mental health. *Journal of Developmental and Behavioral Pediatrics, 10,* 259–261.

Singer, D. G. (1989b). Children, adolescents, and television—1989: I. Television violence: A critique. *Pediatrics, 83,* 445–446.

Singer, D. G. (1993). Creativity of children in a television world. In G. L. Berry & J. K. Asamen (Eds.), *Children & television: Images in a changing sociocultural world* (pp. 73–88). Thousand Oaks, CA: Sage.

Singer, D. G., & Singer, J. L. (1976). Family television viewing habits and the spontaneous play of preschool children. *American Journal of Orthopsychiatry, 46,* 496–502.

Singer, D. G., & Singer, J. L. (1980). Television viewing and aggressive behavior in preschool children: A field study. *Forensic Psychology and Psychiatry, 347,* 289–303.

Singer, D. G., & Singer, J. L. (1981). Television and the developing imagination of the young child. *Journal of Broadcasting, 25,* 373–387.

Singer, D. G., & Singer, J. L. (1983). Learning how to be intelligent consumers of television. In M. J. A. Howe (Ed.), *Learning from television* (pp. 203–222). New York: Academic.

Singer, D. G., & Singer, J. L. (1987). Television and the popular media in the world of the early adolescent [Special Issue]. *Journal of Early Adolescence.*

Singer, D. G., & Singer, J. L. (1994). Evaluating the classroom viewing of a television series: "Degrassi Junior High." In D. Zillmann, J. Bryant, & A. C. Huston (Eds.), *Media, children, and the family: Social scientific, psychodynamic, and clinical perspectives* (pp. 97–115). Hillsdale, NJ: Lawrence Erlbaum Associates, Inc.

Singer, D. G., & Singer, J. L. (Eds.). (2001). *Handbook of children and the media.* Thousand Oaks, CA: Sage.

Singer, D. G., & Singer, J. L. (2005). *Imagination and play in the electronic age.* Cambridge, MA: Harvard University Press.

Singer, D. G., Zuckermen, D. M., & Singer, J. L. (1980). Helping elementary school children learn about TV. *Journal of Communication, 30*(3), 84–93.

Singer, J. L. (1980). The power and limits of television. In P. Tannenbaum (Ed.), *The entertainment function of television* (pp. 31–66). Hillsdale, NJ: Lawrence Erlbaum Associates, Inc.

Singer, J. L. (1986). Is television bad for children? *Social Science, 71,* 178–182.

Singer, J. L., & Singer, D. G. (1976). Can TV stimulate imaginative play? *Journal of Communication, 26*(3), 74–80.

Singer, J. L., & Singer, D. G. (1981). *Television, imagination and aggression.* Hillsdale, NJ: Lawrence Erlbaum Associates, Inc.

Singer, J. L., & Singer, D. G. (1983). Implications of childhood television viewing for cognition, imagination, and emotion. In J. Bryant & D. R. Anderson (Eds.), *Children's understanding of television* (pp. 265–295). New York: Academic.

Singer, J. L., & Singer, D. G. (1984a). Intervention strategies for children's television. In J. P. Murray & G. Salomon (Eds.), *The future of children's television* (pp. 93–102). Boys Town, NE: Father Flanagan's Boys Town.

Singer, J. L., & Singer, D. G. (1984b). Psychologists look at television: Cognitive, developmental, personality, and social policy implications. *Annual Progress in Child Psychiatry and Child Developmental, 38,* 826–834.

Singer, J. L., & Singer, D. G. (1986a). Family experiences and television viewing as predictors of children's imagination, restlessness and aggression. *Journal of Social Issues, 42*(3), 107–124.

Singer, J. L., & Singer, D. G. (1986b). Television viewing and family communication style as predictors of children's emotional behavior. *Journal of Children in Contemporary Society, 17*(4), 75–91.

Singer, J. L., & Singer, D. G. (1988). Some hazards of growing up in a television environment: Children's aggression and restlessness. *Applied Social Psychology Annual, 8,* 171–188.

Singer, J. L., & Singer, D. G. (1998). Barney & Friends as entertainment and education: Evaluating the quality and effectiveness of a television series for preschool children. In J. K. Asamen & G. L. Berry (Ed.), *Research paradigms, television, and social behavior* (pp. 305–367). Thousand Oaks, CA: Sage.

Singer, J. L., Singer, D. G., Desmond, R., & Hirsch, B. (1988). Family mediation and children's cognition, aggression, and comprehension of television: A longitudinal study. *Journal of Applied Developmental Psychology, 9,* 329–347.

Singer, J. L., Singer, D. G., & Rapaczynski, W. (1984a). Children's imagination as predicted by family patterns and television viewing: A longitudinal study. *Genetic Psychology Monographs, 110*(1), 43–69.

Singer, J. L., Singer, D. G., & Rapaczynski, W. S. (1984b). Family patterns and television viewing as predictors of children's beliefs and aggression. *Journal of Communication, 34*(2), 73–89.

Singer, J. L., Singer, D. G., & Sherrod, L. R. (1980). A factor analytic study of preschooler's play behavior. *Academic Psychology Bulletin, 2,* 143–156.

Singer, M. I., Flannery, D. J., Shenyang, G., Miller, D., & Leibbrandt, S. (2004). Exposure to violence, parental monitoring, and television viewing as contributors to children's psychological trauma. *Journal of Community Psychology, 32,* 489–505.

Singer, M. I., & Miller, D. B. (1999). Contributors to violent behavior among elementary and middle school children. *Pediatrics, 104,* 878–884.

Singer, M. I., Slovak, K., Frierson, T., & York, P. (1998). Viewing preferences, symptoms of psychological trauma, and violent behaviors among children who watch television. *Journal of the American Academy of Child & Adolescent Psychiatry, 37*, 1041–1048.

Singh, S. N., & Cole, C. A. (1993). The effects of length, content, and repetition on television commercial effectiveness. *Journal of Marketing Research, 30*, 91–104.

Sister Mary Peter. (1956). Television for teachers and teenagers. *Catholic School Journal, 56*, 308–309.

Skeen, P., Brown, M. H., & Osborn, D. K. (1982). Young children's perception of "real" and "pretend" on television. *Perceptual & Motor Skills, 54*, 883–887.

Skill, T. (1994). Family images and family actions as presented in the media: Where we've been and what we've found. In D. Zillmann & J. Bryant (Eds.), *Media, children, and the family: Social scientific, psychodynamic, and clinical perspectives* (pp. 37–50). Hillsdale, NJ: Lawrence Erlbaum Associates, Inc.

Slade, C. (2000). Why not lie? Television talk and moral debate. *Television & New Media, 1*, 419–430.

Slater, D., & Elliott, W. R. (1975). Television's influence on social reality. *Quarterly Journal of Speech, 52*(1), 44–49.

Slater, M., Beauvais, F., Rounder, D., Van Luuen, J., Murphy, K., & Domenech-Rodriquez, M. (1996). Adolescent counterarguing of TV beer advertisments: Evidence for effectiveness of alcohol education and critical viewing discussions. *Journal of Drug Education, 26*, 143–158.

Slater, M., Rouner, D., Domenech-Rodriquez, M., Beauvais, F., Muphy, K., & VanLeuven, J. K. (1996). Adolescent perceptions of underage drinkers in TV beer ads. *Journal of Alcohol and Drug Education, 42*(1), 43–56.

Slater, M., Rouner, D., Domenech-Rodriquez, M., Beauvais, F., & Murphy, K., & Van Leuven J. K. (1997). Adolescent responses to TV beer ads and sports content/context: Gender and ethnic differences. *Journalism & Mass Communication Quarterly, 74*, 108–122.

Slater, M. D., Henry, K. L., Swaim, R. C., & Anderson, L. L. (2003). Violent media content and aggressiveness in adolescents: A downward spiral model. *Communication Research, 30*, 723–736.

Slater, M. D., Henry, K. L., Swaim, R. C., & Cardador, J. M. (2004). Vulnerable teens, vulnerable times: How sensation seeking, alienation, and victimization moderate the violent media content-aggressiveness relation. *Communication Research, 31*, 642–668.

Slavenas, R. (1984). T.V. or not T.V., is that the question? *Early Child Development and Care, 13*, 377–389.

Smidt, S. (2001). "All stories that have happy endings have a bad character": A young child responds to televisual texts. *English in Education, 35*(2), 25–33.

Smith, D. M. (1971). Some uses of mass media by 14 year olds. *Journal of Broadcasting, 16*, 37–50.

Smith, D. M. (1975). Mass media as a basis for interaction: An empirical study. *Journalism Quarterly, 52*, 44–49.

Smith, F. (1964). Comparison of televiewing and non-televiewing children's explanations of natural phenomenon. *Science Education, 48*, 90–93.

Smith, K. H., & Rogers, M. (1994). Effectiveness of subliminal messages in television commercials: Two experiments. *Journal of Applied Psychology, 79*, 866–874.

Smith, L. J. (1994). A content analysis of gender differences in children's advertising. *Journal of Broadcasting & Electronic Media, 38*, 323–337.

Smith, M. E., & Gevins, A. (2004). Attention and brain activity while watching television: Components of viewer engagement. *Media Psychology, 6*, 285–305.

Smith, R., Anderson, D., & Fischer, C. (1985). Young children's comprehension of montage. *Child Development, 56*, 962–971.

Smith, R. D., Fosarelli, P. D., Palumbo, F., Loening, V., & Melmed, R. (1986). The impact of television on children: Current pediatric training practices. *American Journal of Diseases in Children, 140*, 78–79.

Smith, R. J., & Schutte, N. S. (1982). Children's television experience in two cultures. *Educational Psychology, 2*, 137–146.

Smith, S. L., & Donnerstein, E. (1998). Harmful effects of exposure to media violence: Learning of aggression, emotional desensitization, and fear. In R. G. Geen & E. Donnerstein (Ed.), *Human aggression: Theories, research, and implications for social policy* (pp. 167–202). San Diego, CA: Academic.

Smith, S. L., & Wilson, B. J. (2000). Children's reactions to a television news story: The impact of video footage and proximity of the crime. *Communication Research, 27*, 641–673.

Smith, S. L., & Wilson, B. J. (2002). Children's comprehension of and fear reactions to television news. *Media Psychology, 4*, 1–26.

Smith-Miller, C. A. (2004). Is watching television making kids fat? *American Journal of Nursing, 104*(12), 12–25.

Smythe, D. W. (1950a). Television and its educational implications. *Elementary English, 27*, 41–52.

Smythe, D. W. (1950b). TV danger for U. S. youth. *Science Digest, 27*, 36.

Smythe, D. W. (1954). Reality as presented by television. *Public Opinion Quarterly, 18*, 143–156.

Smythe, D. W. (1955). Dimensions of violence. *AV Communication Review, 3*, 58–63.

Sneed, C., & Runco, M. A. (1992). The beliefs adults and children hold about television and video games. *Journal of Psychology, 126*, 1706–1718.

Sneegas, J. E., & Plank, T. A. (1998). Gender differences in pre-adolescent reactance to age-categorized television advisory labels. *Journal of Broadcasting & Electronic Media, 42*, 423–434.

Snow, R. P. (1974). How children interpret TV violence in play context. *Journalism Quarterly, 51*, 13–21.

Snow, R. P. (1987). Youth, rock 'n roll, and the electronic media. *Youth & Society, 4*, 326–343.

Snyder, R. J. (1995). First-year effects of the 1990 Children's Television Act on Saturday morning commercial time. *Communications & the Law, 17*(4), 67–74.

Sobczak, P. M., & Bowers, M. R. (1993). An experimental design for measuring the effects of source credibility and goal behavior estimate in health promotion television commercials. *Psychology, 30*(2), 30–43.

Sobieraj, S. (1998). Taking control: Toy commercials and the social construction of patriarchy. In L. H. Bowker (Ed.), *Masculinities and violence* (pp. 15–28). Thousand Oaks, CA: Sage.

Soderman, A., Greenberg, B. S., Linsangan, R. (1993). Pregnant and non-pregnant adolescents' television and movie experiences. In B. S. Greenberg, J. D. Brown, & N. L. Buerkel-Rothfuss (Eds.), *Media, sex and the adolescent* (pp. 163–174). Cresskill, NJ: Hampton.

Soldow, G. F. (1983). The processing of information in the young consumer: The impact of cognitive developmental stage on television, radio, and print advertising. *Journal of Advertising, 12*(3), 4–14.

Somers, A. R. (1976). Violence, television and the health of American youth. *The New England Journal of Medicine, 294*, 811–817.

Somers, A. R. (1978). Television and children: Issues involved in corrective action. *American Journal of Orthopsychiatry, 48*, 205–213.

Sparks, G. G. (1986). Developmental differences in children's reports of fear induced by the mass media. *Child Study Journal, 16*(1), 55–66.

Sparks, G. G., & Cantor, J. (1986). Developmental differences in fright responses to a television program depicting a character transformation. *Journal of Broadcasting & Electronic Media, 30*, 309–323.

Spence, M. J., Jerger, S., & Rollins, P. R. (2002). Children's recognition of cartoon voices. *Journal of Speech, Language, and Hearing Research, 45*(1), 214–222.

Spigel, L. (1993). Seducing the innocent: Childhood and television in postwar America. In L. Spigel (Ed.), *Ruthless criticism: New perspectives in U.S. communication history* (pp. 259–290). Minneapolis: University of Minnesota Press.

Spirek, M. M. (1993). Parent and child perceptions of strategy effectiveness for reducing children's television-induced fear. *Journal of Social Behavior and Personality, 8*(6), 51–65.

Splaine, J. E. (1978). Television and its influence on reading. *Educational Technology, 18*(6), 15–19.

Sprafkin, J., & Gadow, K. D. (1986). Television viewing habits of emotionally-disturbed, learning disabled, and mentally retarded children. *Journal of Applied Developmental Psychology, 7*, 45–59.

Sprafkin, J., & Gadow, K. D. (1988). The immediate impact of aggressive cartoons on emotionally disturbed and learning disabled children. *Journal of Genetic Psychology, 149*(1), 35–44.

Sprafkin, J., Gadow, K. D., & Abelman, R. (1992). *Television and the exceptional child.* Hillsdale, NJ: Lawrence Erlbaum Associates, Inc.

Sprafkin, J., Gadow, K. D., & Dussault, M. (1986). Reality perceptions of television: A preliminary comparison of emotionally disturbed and nonhandicapped children. *American Journal of Orthopsychiatry, 56*(1), 147–152.

Sprafkin, J., Gadow, K. D., & Grayson, P. (1987). Effects of viewing aggressive cartoons on the behavior of learning disabled children. *Journal of Child Psychology and Psychiatry and Allied Disciplines, 28*, 387–398.

Sprafkin, J., Gadow, K. D., & Kant, G. (1987). Teaching emotionally disturbed children to discriminate reality from fantasy on television. *Journal of Special Education, 21*(4), 99–107.

Sprafkin, J., Kelly, E., & Gadow, K. D. (1987). Reality perceptions of television: A comparison of emotionally disturbed, learning disabled, and nonhandicapped children. *Journal of Developmental and Behavioral Pediatrics, 8*, 149–153.

Sprafkin, J., Liebert, R. N., & Poulos, R. W. (1975). Effects of a prosocial televised example on children's helping. *Journal of Experimental Child Psychology, 20*(1), 119–126.

Sprafkin, J., & Rubinstein, E. (1979). Children's television viewing habits and prosocial behavior: A field correlational study. *Journal of Broadcasting, 23,* 265–276.

Sprafkin, J., & Rubinstein E. (1982). Using television to improve the social behavior of institutionalized children. *Prevention in Human Services, 2*(1–2), 107–114.

Sprafkin, J., Silverman, L. T., & Rubinstein, E. A. (1980). Reactions to sex on television: An exploratory study. *Public Opinion Quarterly, 44,* 303–315.

Sprafkin, J., Swift, C., & Hess, R. (1983). *Television: Enhancing the preventive impact of television.* New York: Hayworth.

Sprafkin, J., Watkins, L. T., & Gadow, K. D. (1990). Efficacy of a television literacy curriculum for emotionally disturbed and learning disabled children. *Journal of Applied Developmental Psychology, 11,* 225–244.

Srygley, S. K. (1978). Influence of mass media on today's young people. *Educational Leadership, 35,* 526–529.

St. Peters, M., Fitch, M., Huston, A. C., Wright, J. C., & Eakins, D. J. (1991). Television and families: What do young children watch with their parents? *Child Development, 62,* 1409–1423.

Stack, S. (1990). The impact of fictional television films on teenage suicide, 1984–85. *Social Science Quarterly, 71,* 391–399.

Stacy, A. W., Zogg, J. B., Unber, J. B., & Dent, C. W. (2004). Exposure to televised alcohol ads and subsequent adolescent alcohol use. *American Journal of Health Behavior, 28,* 498–509.

Stafford, M., Wells, J. C., & Fewtrell, M. (1998). Television watching and fatness in children. *Journal of the American Medical Association, 280,* 1231–1232.

Stampfl, R. M., Moschis, G., & Lawton, J. T. (1978). Consumer education and the pre-school child. *Journal of Consumer Affairs, 12,* 12–29.

Stanley, C., & Greenberg, B. S. (1993). Family structure and adolescents' orientation to TV and movie sex. In B. S. Greenberg, J. D. Brown, & N. L. Buerkel-Rothfuss (Eds.), *Media, sex and the adolescent* (pp. 153–162). Cresskill, NJ: Hampton.

Steede, K. K., & Range, L. M. (1989). Does television induce suicidal contagion with adolescents? *Journal of Community Psychology, 17,* 166–172.

Stein, G. M., & Bryan, J. H. (1972). The effect of a television model upon rule adoption behavior of children. *Child Development, 43,* 268–273.

Steinberg, S., & Kincheloe, J. L. (2004). *Kinderculture: The corporate construction of childhood* (2nd ed.). Boulder, CO: Westview.

Steinke, J. (1998). Connecting theory and practice: Women and scientist role models in television programming. *Journal of Broadcasting & Electronic Media, 42,* 142–151.

Steinke, J., & Long, M. (1996). A lab of her own? Portrayals of female characters on children's educational science programs. *Science Communication, 18,* 91–115.

Stephens, N., & Stutts, M. A. (1982). Preschooler's ability to distinguish between television programming and commercials. *Journal of Advertising, 11*(2), 16–26.

Stephenson, M. T. (2003). Examining adolescents responses to antimarijuana PSAs. *Human Communication Research, 29,* 343–370.

Stericker, A. B., & Kurdek, L. A. (1982). Dimensions and correlates of third through eighth graders' sex role self-concepts. *Sex Roles, 8*, 915–929.

Stern, B. L., & Harmon, R. R. (1984). The incidence and characteristics of disclaimers in children's television advertising. *Journal of Advertising, 13*(2), 12–16.

Stern, S. R., & Mastro, D. E. (2004). Gender portrayals across the life span: A content analytic look at broadcast commercials. *Mass Communication & Society, 7*, 215–236.

Sterne, G. (1991). TV making children obese and cognitively compromised. 8(2), 10.

Sternglanz, S. H., & Serbin, L. A. (1974). Sex role stereotyping in children's television programs. *Developmental Psychology, 10*, 710–715.

Sternheimer, K. (2003). *It's not the media: The truth about pop culture's influence on children.* Boulder, CO: Westview.

Steuer, F. B., Applefield, J. M., & Smith, R. (1971). Televised aggression and the interpersonal aggression of preschool children. *Journal of Experimental Child Psychology, 11*, 442–227.

Stilling, E. A. (1997). The electronic melting pot hypothesis: The evaluation of acculturation among Hispanics through television viewing. *Howard Journal of Communications, 8*, 77–100.

Stipp, H. (1993). The challenge to improve television for children: A new perspective. In G. L. Berry & J. K. Asamen (Eds.), *Children & television: Images in a changing sociocultural world* (pp. 296–302). Thousand Oaks, CA: Sage.

Stipp, H. (2003). How children can learn from television. *Journal of Applied Developmental Psychology, 24*(3), 363–365.

Stipp, H., & Milavsky, J. R. (1988). U.S. television programming's effects on aggressive behavior of children and adolescents. *Current Psychological Research and Reviews, 7*(1), 76–92.

Stipp, H., Scott-Hill, K., & Dorr, A. (1987). Using social science to improve children's television. *Journal of Broadcasting & Electronic Media, 31*, 461–473.

Stockman, T. (1994). Discrediting the past, rubbishing the future: A critical comparison of the Flintstones and the Jetsons. *Journal of Educational Television, 20*(1), 27–38.

Stone, V. A. (1974). Attitudes toward television newswomen. *Journal of Broadcasting, 18*, 49–62.

Stoneman, Z., & Brody, G. H. (1981). Peers as mediators of television food advertisements aimed at children. *Developmental Psychology, 17*, 853–858.

Stoneman, Z., & Brody, G. H. (1983a). Family interaction during three programs: Contextualist observations. *Journal of Family Issues, 4*, 349–365.

Stoneman, Z., & Brody, G. H. (1983b). Immediate and long term recognition and generalization of advertised products as a function of age and presentation mode. *Developmental Psychology, 19*, 56–61.

Stoneman, Z., Brody, G. H., Davis, C. H., & Crapps, J. M. (1989). Role relations between children who are mentally retarded and their older siblings: Observations in three in-home contexts. *Research in Developmental Disabilities, 10*, 61–76.

Stout, D. A., Jr., & Mouritsen, R. H. (1988). Prosocial behavior in advertising aimed at children: A content analysis. *Southern Speech Communication Journal, 53*, 159–174.

Strasburger, V. C. (1985). Television and adolescents. *Pediatric Annals, 14,* 814–820.

Strasburger, V. C. (1986). Does television affect learning and school performance? *Pediatrician, 13,* 141–147.

Strasburger, V. C. (1989). Children, adolescents, and television—1989: II. The role of pediatricians. *Pediatrics, 83,* 446–448.

Strasburger, V. C. (1992). Children, adolescents, and television. *Pediatrics in Review, 13*(4), 144–151.

Strasburger, V. C. (1995). *Adolescents and the media: Medical and psychological impact.* Thousand Oaks, CA: Sage.

Strasburger, V. C. (1997). Children, adolescents, and television. A call for physician action. *Western Journal of Medicine, 166,* 353–354.

Strasburger, V. C. (2001). Children and TV advertising: Nowhere to run, nowhere to hide. *Journal of Developmental and Behavioral Pediatrics, 22,* 185–187.

Strasburger, V. C., & Donnerstein, E. (1999). Children, adolescents, and the media: Issues and solutions. *Pediatrics, 103,* 129–139.

Strasburger, V. C., & Wilson, B. J. (2002). *Children, adolescents, and the media.* Thousand Oaks, CA: Sage.

Streicher, H. W. (1974). The girls in the cartoons. *Journal of Communication, 24*(2), 125–129.

Streicher, L. H., & Bonney, N. L. (1974). Children talk about television. *Journal of Communication, 24,* 54–61.

Streifel, S. (1974). Isolating variables which affect TV preferences of retarded children. *Psychological Reports, 35,* 115–122.

Streifel, S., & Smeets, P. M. (1974). Determining TV preferences and its implications for educating retarded children. *Exceptional Children, 40,* 285–286.

Strickler, D. S., & Farr, B. (1979). TV as a tool to improve basic communication. *Language Arts, 56,* 634–640.

Stroman, C. A. (1984). The socialization influence of television on Black children. *Journal of Black Studies, 15*(1), 79–100.

Stroman, C. A. (1986). Television viewing and self-concept among Black children. *Journal of Broadcasting & Electronic Media, 30,* 87–93.

Stroman, C. A. (1991). Television's role in the socialization of African American children and adolescents. *Journal of Negro Education, 60,* 314–327.

Strouse, J. S., & Buerkel-Rothfuss, N. (1993). Media exposure and the sexual attitudes and behaviors of college students. In B. S. Greenberg, J. D. Brown, & N. L. Buerkel-Rothfuss (Eds.), *Media, sex and the adolescent* (pp. 277–292). Cresskill, NJ: Hampton.

Strouse, J. S., Buerkel-Rothfus, N., & Long, E. C. J. (1995). Gender and family as moderators of the relationship between music video exposure and adolescent sexual permissiveness. *Adolescence, 30,* 505–521.

Strouse, J. S., & Fabes, R. (1985). Formal versus informal sources of sex education: Competing forces in the sexual socialization of adolescents. *Adolescence, 20,* 251–263.

Stryker, J. E. (2003). Media and marijuana: A longitudinal analysis of news media effects on adolescents' marijana use and related outcomes, 1977–1999. *Journal of Health Communication, 8,* 305–328.

Stumphauzer, J. S., & Bishop, B. R. (1969). Saturday morning television cartoons: A simple apparatus for the reinforcement of behavior in children. *Developmental Psychology, 1,* 763–764.

Stutts, M. A., & Hunnicutt, G. G. (1987). Can young children understand disclaimers in television commercials? *Journal of Advertising, 16*(1), 41–46.

Stutts, M. A., Vance, D., & Hudleson, S. (1981). Program-commercial separators in children's television: Do they help a child tell the difference betwee Bugs Bunny and the Quik Rabbit. *Journal of Advertising, 10*(2), 16–27.

Subervi-Velez, F., & Colsant, S. (1993). The television worlds of Latino children. In G. L. Berry & J. K. Asamen (Eds.), *Children and television: Images in a changing sociocultural world* (pp. 215–228). Newbury Park, CA: Sage.

Subervi-Velez, F., & Necochea, J. (1990). Television viewing and self-concept among Hispanic American children: A pilot study. *Howard Journal of Communications, 2,* 315–329.

Subrahmanyam, K. (2003). Youth and media: Opportunities for development or lurking dangers? Children, adolescents, and media. *Journal of Applied Developmental Psychology, 24,* 381–387.

Sudano, G. R. (1978). Television and development of aesthetic literacy in children. *Contemporary Education, 49,* 223–227.

Sullivan, J. L., & Jordan, A. B. (1999). Playing by the rules: Impact and implementation of children's educational television regulations among local broadcasters. *Communication Law & Policy, 4,* 483–511.

Sullivan, J. M. (1978). TV newsmen—Stop cheating my children. *Intellect, 106,* 393–394.

Sullivan, M. F. (1979). Soap opera in the classroom. *Educational Leadership, 37*(1), 78–80.

Sundelin, C., Rasmussen, F., et al. (1999). Information through television: Does it promote child safety? *Journal of Safety Research, 30*(1), 82–84.

Surbeck, E., & Endsley, R. C. (1979). Children's emotional reactions to TV violence: Effects of film, character, reassurance, age, and sex. *Journal of Social Psychology, 109,* 269–281.

Surette, R. (2002). Self-reported copycat crime among a population of serious and violent juvenile offenders. *Crime & Delinquency, 48*(1), 46–69.

Surlin, S. H., & Dominick, J. R. (1970). Television's function as a "third parent" for Black and White teenagers. *Journal of Broadcasting, 15,* 55–64.

Susman, E. J. (1978). Visual and verbal attributes of television and selective attention in preschool children. *Developmental Psychology, 14,* 565–566.

Swan, K., Meskill, C., & DeMaio, S. (1998). *Social learning from broadcast television.* Cresskill, NJ: Hampton.

Swanson, R. A., & Henderson, R. W. (1977). Effects of televised modeling and active participation on rule-governed question production among Native American preschool children. *Contemporary Educational Psychology, 2,* 345–352.

Swanson, R. A., & Henderson, R. W. (1979). Induction of a concrete operational concept through televised modeling: Evidence and speculation on mediational processes. *Contemporary Educational Psychology, 4,* 202–210.

Sweetser, F. L., Jr. (1955). Home television and behavior: Some tentative conclusions. *Public Opinion Quarterly, 19,* 79–84.

Tan, A. S. (1979). TV beauty ads and role expectations of adolescent female viewers. *Journalism Quarterly, 56*, 283–288.

Tan, A. S. Fujioka, Y., Bautista, D., Maldonado, R., Tan, G., & Wright, L. (2000). Influence of television use and parental communication on educational aspirations of Hispanic children. *Howard Journal of Communications, 11*, 107–125.

Tan, A. S., & Gunter, D. (1979). Media use and academic achievement of Mexican-American high school students. *Journalism Quarterly, 56*, 827–831.

Tan, A. S., & Kinner, D. (1982). Television role models and anticipated social interaction. *Journalism Quarterly, 59*, 654–656.

Tan, A. S., Nelson, L., Dong, Q., & Tan, G. (1997). Value acceptance in adolescent socialization: A test of a cognitive-functional theory of television effects. *Communication Monographs, 64*, 82–97.

Tan, A. S., Randy, J., Huff, C., & Miles, J. (1980). Children's reactions to male and female newscasters: Effectiveness and believability. *Quarterly Journal of Speech, 66*, 201–205.

Tan, A. S., & Tan, G. (1979). Television youth and self-esteem of Blacks. *Journal of Communication, 29*(1), 129–135.

Tan, A. S., & Vaughn, P. (1976). Mass media exposure, public affairs knowledge, and Black militancy. *Journalism Quarterly, 53*, 271–279.

Tangney, J. P. (1988). Aspects of the family and children's television viewing content preferences. *Child Development, 59*, 1070–1079.

Tangney, J. P., & Feshbach, S. (1988). Children's television viewing frequency: Individual differences and demographic correlates. *Personality and Social Psychology Bulletin, 14*, 145–158.

Tannenbaum, P. H. (1985). "Play it again, Sam": Repeated exposure to television programs. In D. Zillmann & J. Bryant (Eds.), *Selective exposure to communications* (pp. 225–241). Hillsdale, NJ: Lawrence Erlbaum Associates, Inc.

Tannenbaum, P. H., & Gaer, E. P. (1965). Mood changes as a function of stress of protagonist and degree of identification in a film viewing situation. *Journal of Personality and Social Psychology, 2*, 612–616.

Tannenbaum, P. H., & Zillmann, D. (1984). Emotional arousal in the facilitation of aggression through communication. *Advances in Experimental Social Psychology, 8*, 148–192.

Taras, H. L., & Gage, M. (1995). Advertised foods on children's television. *Archives of Pediatrics & Adolescent Medicine, 149*, 649–652.

Taras, H. L., Sallis, J. F., Patterson, T., & Nader, P. (1989). Television's influence on children's diet and physical activity. *Journal of Developmental and Behavioral Pediatrics, 10*(4), 176–180.

Tasker, G. (1957). *Videotown: The first decade of television.* New York: Cunningham & Walsh.

Tavassoli, N. T., Shultz, C. J., & Fitzsimons, G. J. (1995). Program involvement? Are moderate levels best for ad memory and attitude toward the ad? *Journal of Advertising Research, 35*(5), 61–72.

Teachman, G., & Orme, M. (1981). Effects of aggressive and pro-social film material on altruistic behavior of children. *Psychological Reports, 48*, 699–702.

Tedeschi, J. T., & Felson, R. B. (1994). *Violence, aggression, and coercive actions.* Washington, DC: American Psychological Association.

Teevan, J. J., Jr., & Hartnagel, T. F. (1976). The effect of television violence on the perceptions of crime by adolescents. *Sociology and Social Research, 60,* 337–348.

Telfer, R. J., & Kann, R. S. (1984). Reading achievement, free reading, watching television, and listening to music. *Journal of Reading, 27,* 536–539.

Tennant, F. S., Jr. (1979). Awareness of substance abuse and other health-related behaviors among preschool children. *Journal of Drug Education, 9,* 119–128.

Terr, L. C., Bloch, D., Michel, B. A., Shi, H., Reinhardt, J. A., & Metayer, S. (1996). Children's memories in the wake of Challenger. *American Journal of Psychiatry, 153,* 618–625.

Terr, L. C., Bloch, D., Michel, B. A., Shi, H., Reinhardt, J. A., & Metayer, S. (1997). Children's thinking in the wake of Challenger. *American Journal of Psychiatry, 154,* 744–751.

Thayer, J. R. (1963). The relationship of various audience composition factors to television programs types. *Journal of Broadcasting, 7,* 217–225.

Thelen, M. H. (1971). The effect of subject race, model race, and vicarious praise on vicarious learning. *Child Development, 42,* 972–977.

Thelen, M. H., & Soltz, W. (1969). The effect of vicarious reinforcement on imitation in two social-racial groups. *Child Development, 40,* 879–887.

Thomas, M. H., & Drabman, R. S. (1975). Toleration of real life aggression as a function of exposure to televised violence and age of subject. *Merrill-Palmer Quarterly, 21,* 227–232.

Thomas, M. H., & Drabman, R. S. (1978). Effects of television violence on expectations of other's aggression. *Personality and Social Psychology Bulletin, 4,* 73–76.

Thomas, M. H., Horton, R. W., Lippincott, E. C., & Drabman, R. S. (1977). Desensitization to portrayals of real-life aggression as a function of televised violence. *Journal of Personality and Social Psychology, 35,* 450–458.

Thompson, F. T., & Austin, W. P. (2003). Television viewing and academic achievement revisited. *Education, 124,* 194–202.

Thompson, G. W. (1964). Children's acceptance of television advertising and the relation of televiewing to school achievement. *Journal of Educational Research, 52,* 171–174.

Thompson, K. (2002). Border crossings and diasporic identities: Media use and leisure practices of an ethnic minority. *Qualitative Sociology, 25,* 409–418.

Thompson, M., Walsh-Childers, K., & Brown, J. D. (1993). The influence of family communication patterns and sexual experience on processing of a movie video. In B. S. Greenberg, J. D. Brown, & N. L. Buerkel-Rothfuss (Eds.), *Media, sex and the adolescent* (pp. 248–263). Cresskill, NJ: Hampton.

Thompson, T. L., & Zerbinos, E. (1995). Gender roles in animated cartoons: Has the picture changed in 20 years? *Sex Roles, 32,* 651–673.

Thompson, T. L., & Zerbinos, E. (1997). Television cartoons: Do children notice it's a boy's world? *Sex Roles, 37,* 415–432.

Thorburn, A. L. (1990). Regulating television for the sake of children. *University of Detroit Law Review, 67,* 413–441.

Thornton, W., & Voigt, L. (1984). Television and delinquency: A neglected dimension of social control. *Youth & Society, 15,* 445–468.

Thorson, E., Christ, W. G., & Caywood, C. (1991). Effects of issue-image strategies, attack and support appeals, music, and visual content in political commercials. *Journal of Broadcasting & Electronic Media, 35,* 465–486.

Tidhar, C. E. (1984). Children communicating in cinematic codes: Effects on cognitive skills. *Journal of Educational Psychology, 76*, 957–965.

Tiemens, R. K. (1970). Some relationships of camera angle to communicator credibility. *Journal of Broadcasting, 14*, 483–490.

Tierney, J. D. (1983). A study of the influence of television heroes on adolescents. *Communications, 9*, 113–141.

Tiggemann, M. (2005). Television and adolescent body image: The role of program content and viewing motivation. *Journal of Social & Clinical Psychology, 24*, 361–381.

Timmer, J. (2002). When a commercial is not a commercial: Advertising of violent entertainment and the First Amendment. *Communication Law & Policy, 7*, 157–186.

Tinkham, S. F., & Weaver-Lariscy, R. A. (1993). A diagnostic approach to assessing the impact of negative political television commercials. *Journal of Broadcasting & Electronic Media, 37*, 377–399.

Tinkham, S. F., & Weaver-Lariscy, R. A. (1994). Ethical judgments of political television commercials as predictors of attitude toward the ad. *Journal of Advertising, 23*(3), 43–57.

Tobin, J. J. (2000). *"Good guys don't wear hats": Children's talk about the media.* New York: Teachers College Press.

Tobin, J. (2004). *Pikachu's global adventure: The rise and fall of Pokémon.* Durham, NC: Duke University Press.

Tognoli, J., & Storch, J. L. (1980). Inside and outside: Setting locations of female and male characters in children's television. *EDRA: Environmental Design Research Association, 11*, 288–297.

Tolley, H. (1973). *Children and war: Political socialization to international conflict.* New York: Teachers College Press, Columbia University.

Toomey, T. C. (1972). Alteration of a perceptual mode correlate through a televised model. *Journal of Experimental Research in Personality, 6*, 52–59.

Tower, R. B., Singer, D. G., & Biggs, J. L. (1979). Differential effects of television programming on preschoolers' cognition, imagination, and social play. *American Journal of Orthopsychiatry, 49*, 265–281.

Troseth, G. L. (2003). Getting a clear picture: Young childen's understanding of a televised image. *Developmental Science, 6*, 247–253.

Troseth, G. L., & DeLoache J. S. (1998). The medium can obscure the message: Young children's understanding of video. *Child Development, 69*, 950–965.

Truglio, R. T., Murphy, K. C., Oppenheimer, S., Huston, A. C., & Wright, J. C. (1996). Predictors of children's entertainment television viewing: Why are they tuning in? *Journal of Applied Developmental Psychology, 17*, 475–493.

Trumbo, C. W. (2004). Mass-mediated information effects on testicular self-examination among college students. *Journal of American College Health, 52*(6), 257–261.

Tucker, D. E., & Saffelle, J. (1982). The Federal Communication Commission and the regulation of children's television. *Journal of Broadcasting, 26*, 657–669.

Tucker, L. A. (1985). Television's role regarding alcohol use among teenagers. *Adolescence, 20*, 593–598.

Tucker, L. A., & Hager, R. L. (1996). Television viewing and muscular fitness of children. *Perceptual & Motor Skills, 82*, 1316–1318.

Tucker, L. R. (1998). The framing of Calvin Klein: A frame analysis of media discourse about the August 1995 Calvin Klein jeans advertising campaign. *Critical Studies in Mass Communication, 15*, 141–157.

Turk, P. (1979). Children's advertising: An ethical morass for business and government. *Journal of Advertising, 8*(4), 4–8.

Turner, C. W., Hesse, B. W., & Peterson, L. (1986). Naturalistic studies of the long-term effects of television violence. *Journal of Social Issues, 42*(3), 51–73.

Turow, J. (1980). Non-fiction on commercial children's television—Trends and policy implications. *Journal of Broadcasting, 24*, 437–448.

Turow, J. (1981). *Entertainment, education and the hard sell: Three decades of children's television.* New York: Praeger.

Tutolo, D. (1981). Critical listening/reading of advertisements. *Language Arts, 58*, 679–683.

Unger, J. B., Schuster, D., Zogg, J., Dent, C. W., & Stacy, A. W. (2003). Alcohol advertising exposure and adolescent alcohol use: A comparison of exposure measures. *Addiction Research & Theory, 11*, 177–193.

Uscinski, H. J. (1984). Deregulating commercial television: Will the marketplace watch our for children? *The American University Law Review, 34*(1), 141–173.

Utter, J., Neumark-Sztainer, D., & Jeffery, R. (2003). Couch potatoes or french fries: Are sedentary behaviors associated with body mass index, physical activity, and dietary behaviors among adolescents? *Journal of the American Dietetic Association, 103*, 1298–1305.

Valdez, A. (1981). The economic context of U.S. children's television: Parameters for reform. In E. McAnany, J. Schnitman, & N. Janus (Eds.), *Communication and social structure: Critical studies in mass media research* (pp. 145–180). New York: Praeger.

Valkenburg, P. M., & Cantor, J. (2001). The development of a child into a consumer. *Applied Developmental Psychology, 22*, 61–72.

Valkenburg, P. M., Cantor, J., & Peeters, A. L. (2000). Fright reactions to television: A child survey. *Communication Research, 27*, 82–99.

Valkenburg, P. M., & Janssen, S. C. (1999). What do children value in entertainment programs? A cross-cultural investigation. *Journal of Communication, 49*(2), 3–21.

Valkenburg, P. M., & van der Voort, T. H. A. (1994). Influence of TV in daydreaming and creative imagination—A review of research. *Psychological Bulletin, 116*, 316–339.

Valkenburg, P. M., & Vroone, M. (2004). Developmental changes in infants' and toddlers' attention to television entertainment. *Communication Research, 31*, 288–311.

Van Auken, S., & Lonial, S. C. (1985). Children's perceptions of characters: Human versus animate assessing implications for children's advertising. *Journal of Advertising, 14*(2), 13–22.

Van Camp, S. S. (1978). The world through five-year-old eyes. *Childhood Education, 54*, 246–250.

van den Broek, P., Lorch, E. P., & Thurlow, R. (1996). Children's and adults' memory for television stories: The role of causal factors, story-grammar categories, and hierarchical level. *Child Development, 67*, 3010–3028.

van den Bulck, J. (2004). Television viewing, computer game playing, and Internet use and self-reported time to bed and time out of bed in secondary-school children. *Sleep: Journal of Sleep & Sleep Disorder Research, 27*(1), 101–104.

van den Bulck, J., & van den Bergh, B. (2000). The influence of perceived parental guidance patterns on children's media use: Gender differences and media displacement. *Journal of Broadcasting & Electronic Media, 44,* 329–348.

van der Voort, T. H. A. (2001). Television's impact on children's leisure-time reading and reading skills. In L. Verhoeven & C. Snow (Eds.), *Literacy and motivation* (pp. 95–124). Mahwah, NJ: Lawrence Erlbaum Associates, Inc.

van der Voort, T. H. A., & Valkenburg, P. M. (1994). Television's impact on fantasy play: A review of research. *Developmental Review, 14*(1), 27–51.

Van Evra, J. P. (1995). Advertising's impact on children as a function of viewing purpose. *Psychology & Marketing, 12,* 423–432.

Van Evra, J. P. (1998). *Television and child development* (2nd ed.). Mahwah, NJ: Lawrence Erlbaum Associates, Inc.

Van Hoose, J. J. (1980). The impact of television usage on emerging adolescents. *High School Journal, 63,* 239–243.

Vandewater, E. A., Bickham, D. S., Lee, J. H., Cummings, H. M., Wartella, E. A., & Rideout, V. J. (2005). When the television is always on: Heavy television exposure and young children's development. *American Behavioral Scientist, 48,* 562–578.

Vandewater, E. A., Lee, J. H., & Shim, M. (2005). Family conflict and violent electronic media use in school-aged children. *Media Psychology, 7,* 73–87.

Vandewater, E. A., Park, S., Huang, X., & Wartella, E. A. (2005). "No—You can't watch that": Parental rules and young children's media use. *American Behavioral Scientist, 48,* 608–623.

Vandewater, E. A., Shim, M., & Caplovitz, A. G. (2004). Linking obesity and activity level with children's television and video game use. *Journal of Adolescence, 27,* 71–85.

Vaughn, K. K., & Fouts, G. T. (2003). Changes in television and magazine exposure and eating disorder. *Sex Roles, 49,* 313–320.

Verbal imaging of gender in television ads for kids—Teaching ideology through Potty Dotty and electronic karate fighters. (2001). *Women & Language, 24,* 42–45.

Verna, M. E. (1975). The female image in children's TV commercials. *Journal of Broadcasting, 19,* 301–309.

Versfelt, D. S. (1989). Constitutional considerations of the Children's Television Act of 1988: Why the president's veto was warranted. *Comm/Ent: Hastings Communication and Entertainment Law Journal, 11,* 625–642.

Vidmar, N., & Rokeach, M. (1974). Archie Bunker's bigotry: A study in selective perception and exposure. *Journal of Communication, 24,* 36–47.

Villani, S. (2001). Impact of media on children and adolescents: A 10-year review of the research. *Journal of the American Academy of Child & Adolescent Psychiatry, 40,* 392–401.

Vincent, R. C., & Basil, M. D. (1997). College students' news gratifications, media use and current events knowledge. *Journal of Broadcasting & Electronic Media, 41,* 380–392.

Wackman, D. B., & Wartella, E. (1977). A review of cognitive development theory and research and the implication for research on children's responses to television. *Communication Research, 4,* 203–224.

Wackman, D. B., Wartella, E., & Ward, S. (1977). Learning to be consumers: The role of the family. *Journal of Communication, 27,* 138–151.

Wade, S. E. (1971a). Adolescents, creativity, and media. In F. G. Kline & P. Clarke (Eds.), *Mass communication and youth: Some current perspectives* (pp. 39–49). Beverly Hills, CA: Sage.

Wade, S. E. (1971b). Adolescents, creativity, and media: An exploratory study. *American Behavioral Scientist, 14,* 341–351.

Wade, S. E. (1973). Interpersonal discussion: A critical predictor of leisure activity. *Journal of Communication, 23,* 426–445.

Wadsworth, A. J. (1989). The uses and effects of mass communication during childhood. In J. F. Nussbaum (Ed.), *Life-span communication: Normative processes* (pp. 93–116). Hillsdale, NJ: Lawrence Erlbaum Associates, Inc.

Wagner, C. A. (1979). Meeting the perceived needs of children and parents. *Elementary School Guidance and Counseling, 13,* 232–242.

Wagner, L. (1980). Effects of TV on reading. *Journal of Reading, 24,* 201–206.

Wakefield, M., Flay, B., Nichter, M., & Giovino, G. (2003a). Effects of anti-smoking advertising on youth smoking: A review. *Journal of Health Communication, 8,* 229–248.

Wakefield, M., Flay, B., Nichter, M., & Giovino, G. (2003b). Role of the media in influencing trajectories of youth smoking. *Addiction, 98,* 79–104.

Wakshlag, J. J. (1982). Stability in the popularity of television programs among children and adolescents. *Journal of Broadcasting, 26,* 711–716.

Wakshlag, J. J., & Greenberg, B. S. (1979). Programming strategies and the popularity of television programs for children. *Human Communication Research, 6,* 58–68.

Walker, J. R., & Bellamy, R. V., Jr. (2001). Remote control devices and family viewing. In J. Bryant & J. A. Bryant (Eds.), *Television and the American family* (2nd ed., pp. 75–89). Mahwah, NJ: Lawrence Erlbaum Associates, Inc.

Walker, K. B., & Morley, D. D. (1991). Attitudes and parental factors as intervening variables in the television violence–aggression relation. *Communication Research Reports, 8,* 41–47.

Walma Van Der Molen, J. H., & Van Der Voort, T. H. A. (2000). The impact of television, print, and audio on children's recall of the news. *Human Communication Research, 26,* 24–26.

Walsh, A. D., Laczniak, R. N., & Carlson, L. (1998). Mothers' preferences for regulating children's television. *Journal of Advertising, 27*(3), 23–36.

Walsh, D. A., & Gentile, D. A. (2001). A validity test of movie, television and video-game ratings. *Pediatrics, 107,* 1302–1310.

Walsh-Childers, K., & Brown, J. D. (1993). Adolescents' acceptance of sex-role stereotypes and television viewing. In B. S. Greenberg, J. D. Brown, & N. L. Buerkel-Rothfuss (Eds.), *Media, sex and the adolescent* (pp. 117–133). Cresskill, NJ: Hampton.

Walters, R. H. (1966). Implications of laboratory studies of aggression for the control and regulation of violence. *Annals of the American Academy of Political and Social Science, 364,* 60–72.

Walters, R. H., & Parke, R. D. (1964). Influence of response consequences to a social model on resistance to deviation. *Journal of Experimental Child Psychology, 1,* 269–280.

Walters, R. H., Parke, R. D., & Cane, V. A. (1965). Timing of punishment and the observation of consequences to others as determinants of response inhibition. *Journal of Experimental Child Psychology, 2,* 10–30.

Wand, B. (1968). Television viewing and family choice differences. *Public Opinion Quarterly, 32,* 84–94.

Wanzenried, J. W., Smith-Howell, D., & Powell, F. C. (1992). Source credibility and presidential campaigns: Governor Clinton and the allegation of marital infidelity. *Psychological Reports, 70,* 992–994.

Ward, C. D., Seboda, B. L., & Morris, V. B. (1974). Influence through personal and nonpersonal channels of communication. *Journal of Psychology, 88,* 135–140.

Ward, L. M. (1995). Talking about sex: Common themes about sexuality in the prime time television programs children and adolescents view most. *Journal of Youth & Adolescence, 24,* 595–615.

Ward, L. M. (2002). Does television exposure affect emerging adults' attitudes and assumptions about sexual relationships? Correlational and experimental confirmation. *Journal of Youth & Adolescence, 31,* 1–15.

Ward, L. M. (2003). Understanding the role of entertainment media in the sexual socialization of American youth: A review of empirical research. *Developmental Review, 23,* 347–388.

Ward, L. M. (2004). Wading through the stereotypes: Positive and negative associations between media use and Black adolescents' conceptions of self. *Developmental Psychology, 40,* 284–294.

Ward, L. M., Gorvine, B., & Cytron-Walker, A. (2002). Would that really happen? Adolescents' perceptions of sexual relationships according to prime-time television. In J. D. Brown & J. R. Steele (Eds.), *Sexual teens, sexual media: Investigating media's influence on adolescent sexuality* (pp. 95–123). Mahwah, NJ: Lawrence Erlbaum Associates, Inc.

Ward, L. M., & Greenfield, P. M. (1998). Designing experiments on television and social behavior: Developmental perspectives. In J. K. Asamen & G. L. Berry (Eds.), *Research paradigms, television and social behavior* (pp. 67–108). Thousand Oaks, CA: Sage.

Ward, L.M., Hansbrough, E., & Walker, E. (2005). Contributions of music video exposure to Black adolescents' gender and sexual schemas. *Journal of Adolescent Research, 20,* 143–166.

Ward, L. M., & Rivadeneyra, R. (1999). Contributions of entertainment television to adolescents' sexual attitudes and expectations: The role of viewing amount versus viewer involvement. *Journal of Sex Research, 36,* 237–249.

Ward, S. (1972a). Advertising and youth: Two studies. *Sloan Management Review, 14,* 63–82.

Ward, S. (1972b). Children's reactions to commercials. *Journal of Advertising Research, 12*(2).

Ward, S. (1972c). Kid's TV—Marketers on a hot seat: Research evidence helps clarify burning consumerist issue of children's television advertising. *Harvard Business Review, 50,* 16–18.

Ward, S. (1978). Compromise in commercials for children. *Harvard Business Review, 56*(6), 128–136.

Ward, S. (1980a). The effects of premium offers in children's television advertising. In R. P. Adler, G. S. Lesser, L. K. Meringoff, T. S. Robertson, J. R. Rossiter, & F. Ward (Eds.), *The effects of television advertising on children: Review and recommendation* (pp. 95–110). Lexington, MA: Lexington Books.

Ward, S. (1980b). The effects of television advertising on consumer socialization. In R. P. Adler, G. S. Lesser, L. K. Meringoff, T. S. Robertson, J. R. Rossiter, & F. Ward (Eds.), *The effects of television advertising on children: Review and recommendation* (pp. 185–194). Lexington, MA: Lexington Books.

Ward, S., & Wackman, D. B. (1971). Family and media influences on adolescent consumer learning. *American Behavioral Scientist, 14,* 415–427.

Ward, S., & Wackman, D. B. (1973). Children's information processing of television advertising. In P. Clarke (Ed.), *New models for mass communication research.* Beverly Hills, CA: Sage.

Ward, S., Wackman, D. B., Faber, R., & Lesser, G. S. (1974). *Effects of television advertising on consumer socialization.* Cambridge, MA: Marketing Science Institute.

Ward, S., Wackman, D. B., & Wartella, E. (1977). *How children learn to buy: The development of consumer information-processing skills.* Beverly Hills, CA: Sage.

Ward, T. B. (1984). Opinions on television advertising to children: A content analysis of letters to the Federal Trade Commission. *Merrill-Palmer Quarterly, 30,* 247–259.

Warren, R. (2001). In words and deeds: Parental involvement and mediation of children's television viewing. *Journal of Family Communication, 1,* 211–231.

Warren, R. (2003). Parental mediation of preschool children's television viewing. *Journal of Broadcasting & Electronic Media, 47,* 394–418.

Warren, R., Gerke, P., & Kelly, M. A. (2002). Is there enough time on the clock? Parental involvement and mediation of children's television viewing. *Journal of Broadcasting & Electronic Media, 46,* 87–111.

Wartella, E. (Ed.). (1979). *Children communicating: Media and development of thought, speech and understanding.* Beverly Hills, CA: Sage.

Wartella, E. (1980a). Children's impression of television mothers. In M. Greve-Partsch (Eds.), *Women, communication, and careers* (pp. 76–84). New York: K. G. Saur.

Wartella, E. (1980b). Individual differences in children's responses to television advertising. In E. L. Palmer & A. Dorr (Eds.), *Children and the faces of television: Teaching, violence, selling* (pp. 307–322). New York: Academic.

Wartella, E. (1984). Cognitive and affective factors of TV advertising's influence on children. *Western Journal of Speech Communication, 48,* 171–183.

Wartella, E. (1987a). Commentary on qualitative research on children's mediated communication. In T. Lindlof (Ed.), *Natural audiences* (pp. 109–120). Norwood, NJ: Ablex.

Wartella, E. (1987b). Television, cognition, and learning. In M. E. Manley-Casimir & C. Luke (Eds.), *Children and television: A challenge for education* (pp. 3–14). New York: Praeger.

Wartella, E. (1988). The public context of debates about television and children. *Applied Social Psychology Annual, 8,* 59–68.

Wartella, E. (1994). Producing children's television programs. In J. Etteman & D. C. Whitney (Eds.), *Audiencemaking: How the media created the audience* (pp. 38–56). Thousand Oaks, CA: Sage.

Wartella, E. (1999). Children and media: On growth and gaps. *Mass Communication & Society, 2*, 81–87.

Wartella, E., Alexander, A., & Lemish, D. (1979). The mass media environment of children. *American Behavioral Scientist, 23*, 33–53.

Wartella, E., & Ettema, J. (1974). A cognitive developmental study of children's attention to television commercials. *Communication Research, 1*, 69–88.

Wartella, E. A., & Reeves, B. (1984). Trends in research on children's television. In J. P. Murray & G. Salomon (Eds.), *The future of children's television* (pp. 23–35). Boys Town, NE: Boys Town Center.

Wartella, E. A., & Reeves, B. (1985). Historical trends in research on children and the media: 1900–1960. *Journal of Communication, 25*(2), 118–133.

Wartella, E., Wackman, D. B., Ward, S., Shamir, J., & Alexander, A. (1979). The young child as consumer. In E. Wartella (Ed.), *Children communicating: Media and development of thought, speech and understanding* (pp. 251–282). Beverly Hills, CA: Sage.

Wass, H., Raup, J., & Sisler, H. (1989). Adolescents and death on television. *Death Studies, 13*, 161–173.

Watkins, B. (1985). Television viewing as a dominant activity of childhood: A developmental theory of television effects. *Critical Studies in Mass Communication, 2*, 323–337.

Watkins, B. (1987). Improving educational and informational television for children: When the marketplace fails. *Yale Law and Policy Review, 5*, 345–381.

Watkins, B. (1988). Children's representation of television and real life stories. *Communication Research, 15*, 159–184.

Watkins, B., Calvert, S., Huston-Stein, A., & Wright, J. C. (1980). Children's recall of television material: Effects of presentation mode and adult labeling. *Developmental Psychology, 16*, 672–674.

Watkins, B., Huston-Stein, A., & Wright, J. C. (1980). Effects of planned television programming. In E. L. Palmer & A. Dorr (Eds.), *Children and the faces of television: Teaching, violence, selling* (pp. 49–70). New York: Academic.

Watt, J. H., Jr., & Krull, R. (1974). An information theory measure for television programming. *Communication Research, 1*, 44–68.

Watt, J. H., Jr., & Krull, R. (1977). An examination of three models of television viewing and aggression. *Human Communication Research, 3*, 99–112.

Waxmonsky, J., & Beresin, E. V. (2001). Taking professional wrestling to the mat: A look at the appeal and potential effects of professional wrestling on children. *Academic Psychiatry, 25*, 125–131.

Weaver, B., & Barbour, N. (1992). Mediation of children's televiewing. *Families in Society: The Journal of Contemporary Human Services, 73*, 236–242.

Weaver, J. B., Walker, J. R., McCord, L. L., & Bellamy, R. V., Jr., (1996). Exploring the links between personality and television remote control device use. *Personality & Individual Differences, 20*, 483–489.

Weber, D. S., & Singer, D. (2004). The media habits of infants and toddlers: Findings from a parent survey. *Zero to Three, 25*(1), 30–36.

Weber, L. J., & Fleming, D. B. (1984). Black adolescents and the news. *Journal of Negro Education, 53*, 85–90.

Webster, J. G., & Coscarelli, W. C. (1979). The relative appeal to children of adult versus children's television programming. *Journal of Broadcasting, 23*, 437–451.

Webster, J. G., Pearson, J. C., & Webster, D. S. (1986). Children's television viewing as affected by contextual variables in the home. *Communication Research Reports, 3*, 1–8.

Wee, V. (2004). Selling teen culture: How American multimedia conglomeration reshaped teen television in the 1990s. In G. Davis & K. Dickinson (Eds.), *Teen TV: Genre, consumption, identity* (pp. 87–98). London: British Film Institute.

Weigel, R. H., & Howes, P. (1982). Race reactions on children's television. *Journal of Psychology, 111*, 109–112.

Weigel, R. H., & Jessor, R. (1973). Television and adolescent conventionality: An exploratory study. *Public Opinion Quarterly, 37*, 76–90.

Weintraub, J. S. (1988). The protection of commercial speech and the regulation of children's television: Throwing out the baby with the bathwater? *New York Law School Journal of Human Rights, 6*, 63–98.

Weiss, A. J., & Wilson, B. J. (1996). Emotional portrayals in family television series that are popular among children. *Journal of Broadcasting & Electronic Media, 40*, 1–29.

Weiss, A. J., & Wilson, B. J. (1998). Children's cognitive and emotional responses to the portrayal of negative emotions in family-formatted situation comedies. *Human Communication Research, 24*, 584–609.

Welch, A. J., & Watt, J. H., Jr. (1982). Visual complexity and young children's learning from television. *Human Communication Research, 8*, 133–145.

Welch, R. L., Huston-Stein, A., Wright, J. C., & Plehal, R. (1979). Subtle sex-role cues in children's commercials. *Journal of Communication, 29*(3), 202–209.

Wells, L. (1974). Television versus books for preschoolers. *Child Study Journal, 4*, 93–97.

Wells, W. D. (1965). Communicating with children. *Journal of Advertising Research, 5*, 2–14.

Wells, W. D. (1966). Children as consumers. In J. W. Newman (Ed.), *On knowing the consumer*. New York: Wiley.

Werner, A. (1975). The effects of television on children and adolescents: A case of sex and class socialization. *Journal of Communication, 25*(4), 45–50.

Werner-Wilson, R. J., Fitzharris, J. L., & Morrissey, K. M. (2004). Adolescent and parent perceptions of media influence on adolescent sexuality. *Adolescence, 39*, 303–313.

Wertham, F. (1966). *A sign for Cain: An exploration of human violence*. New York: Macmillan.

Wharton, R., & Mandell, F. (1985). Violence on television and imitative behavior: Impact on parenting practices. *Pediatrics, 75*, 1120–1123.

White, D. M., & Averson, R. (1968). *Sight, sound and society: Motion pictures and television in America*. Boston: Beacon.

White, M. A., & Pollack, J. (1985). Within and across modality comprehension of electronic media in children. *International Journal of Man-Machine Study, 22*, 209–214.

Wicks, R. H. (1992). Improvement over time in recall of media information: An exploratory study. *Journal of Broadcasting & Electronic Media, 36*, 287–302.

Wilcox, B. L. (2003). The research/policy nexus: The Children's Television Act as a case in point. *Journal of Applied Developmental Psychology, 24*, 367–373.

Wilcox, B. L., & Kunkel, D. (1996). Taking television seriously: Children and television policy. In E. F. Zigler & S. L. Kagan (Eds.), *Children, families, and government: Preparing for the twenty-first century* (pp. 333–352). Thousand Oaks, CA: Sage.

Wildman, B. G., & Kelly, J. A. (1980). Group news watching and discussion to increase the current affairs awareness of retarded adolescents. *Child Behavior Therapy, 2*(1), 25–36.

Wilgosh, L. (2001). Enhancing gifts and talents of women and girls. *High Ability Studies, 12*(1), 45–59.

Wilkins, J. L., Scharff, W. H., & Schlottmann, R. S. (1974). Personality type, reports of violence, and aggressive behavior. *Journal of Personality and Social Psychology, 30*, 243–247.

Williams, B. T. (2003). What they see is what we get: Television and middle school writers. *Journal of Adolescent & Adult Literacy, 46*, 546–554.

Williams, F. (1973). Social class differences in how children talk about television. In C. D. Mortenson & K. K. Sereno (Eds.), *Advances in communication research*. New York: Harper & Row.

Williams, F., & Natalicio, D. S. (1972). Evaluating "Carrascolendas": A television series for Mexican-American children. *Journal of Broadcasting, 16*, 299–309.

Williams, F., Smart, M. E., & Epstein, R. H. (1979). Use of commercial television in parent and child interaction. *Journal of Broadcasting, 23*, 229–235.

Williams, M. E., & Hall, E. R. (1994). Creating educational television programs that are relevant to the lives of children. *Youth & Society, 26*, 243–255.

Williams, P. A., Haertel, E. H., Haertel, G. D., & Walberg, H. J. (1982). The impact of leisure-time television on school learning: A research synthesis. *American Educational Research Journal, 19*, 19–50.

Williams, T. M. (1979). Differential impacts of TV on children—Natural experiment in communities with and without TV. *Aggressive Behavior, 5*, 203–204.

Williams, T. M. (1981). How and what do children learn from television? *Human Communication Research, 7*, 180–192.

Willis, E., & Strasburger, V. C. (1998). Media violence. *Pediatric Clinics of North America, 45*, 319–.

Wilson, B. J. (1989). Desensitizing children's emotional reactions to the mass media. *Communication Research, 16*, 723–745.

Wilson, B. J., & Cantor, J. (1985). Developmental differences in empathy with a television protagonist's fear. *Journal of Experimental Child Psychology, 39*, 284–299.

Wilson, B. J., Cantor, J., Gordon, L., & Zillmann, D. (1986). Affective response of nonretarded and retarded children to the emotions of a protagonist. *Child Study Journal, 16*, 77–93.

Wilson, B. J., Colvin, C. M., & Smith, S. L. (2002). Engaging in violence on American television: A comparison of child, teen, and adult perpetrators. *Journal of Communication, 52*(1), 36–60.

Wilson, B. J., Hoffner, C., & Cantor, J. (1987). Children's perceptions of the effectiveness of techniques to reduce fear from mass media. *Journal of Applied Developmental Psychology, 8*, 39–52.

Wilson, B. J., & Smith, S. L. (1998). Children's responses to emotional portrayals on television. In P. A. Andersen & L. K. Guerrero (Eds.), *Handbook of communication and emotion: Research, theory, applications, and contexts* (pp. 533–569). San Diego, CA: Academic.

Wilson, B. J., Smith, S. L., Potter, W. J., Kunkel, D., Linz, D., Colvin, C. M., et al. (2002). Violence in children's television programming: Assessing the risks. *Journal of Communication, 52*(1), 5–35.

Wilson, B. J., & Weiss, A. J. (1992). Developmental differences in children's reactions to a toy advertisement linked to a toy-based cartoon. *Journal of Broadcasting & Electronic Media, 36*, 371–394.

Wilson, C. E. (1974). The effect of medium on loss of information. *Journalism Quarterly, 51*, 111–115.

Wilson, M. (1977). Can a consumer quiz show be educational? *Journal of Business Education, 53*(3), 124–125.

Wiman, A. R. (1983). Parental influence and children's responses to television advertising. *Journal of Advertising, 12*(1), 11–18.

Wimmer, R. D. (1979). Students as active viewers of television. *Communication Education, 28*, 147–150.

Winett, R. A., & Kramer, K. D. (1989). A behavioral systems framework for information design and behavior change. In J. L. Salvaggio & J. Bryant (Eds.), *Media use in the informational age: Emerging patterns of adoption and consumer use* (pp. 237–257). Hillsdale, NJ: Lawrence Erlbaum Associates, Inc.

Wingood, G. M., DiClemente, R., Bernhardt, J. M., Harrington, K., Davies, S. L., Robillard, A., et al. (2003). A prospective study of exposure to rap music videos and African American female adolescents' health. *American Journal of Public Health, 93*, 437–440.

Winick, C. (1966). Television and the culture of the child. In P. D. Hazard (Ed.), *TV as art: Some essays on criticism*. Champaign, IL: National Council of Teachers of English.

Winick, C., Wiliamson, L. G., Chuzmir, S. F., & Winick, M. P. (1971). *Children's television commercials: A content analysis*. New York: Praeger.

Winick, C., Williamson, L. G., Chuzmir, S. F., & Winick, M. P. (1974). Children's television commercials: A content analysis. *Public Opinion Quarterly, 38*, 309–310.

Winick, M. P., & Winick, C. (1979). *The television experience: What children see*. Beverly Hills, CA: Sage.

Winston, F. K., Duyck Woolf, K., Jordan, A., & Bhatia, E. (2000). Actions without consequences: Injury-related messages in children's programs. *Archives of Pediatrics & Adolescent Medicine, 154*, 366–369.

Withey, S. B., & Abeles, R. P. (1980). *Television and social behavior: Beyond violence and children*. Hillsdale, NJ: Lawrence Erlbaum Associates, Inc.

Witt, S. D. (2000). The influence of peers on children's socialization to gender roles. *Early Child Development and Care, 162*, 1–7.

Witty, P. A. (1950). Children's, parent's, and teacher's reactions to television. *Elementary English, 27*, 349–355.

Witty, P. A. (1951a). Interest in TV and success in school. *Educational Administration and Supervision, 37*, 193–210.

Witty, P. A. (1951b). Television and the educative process. *School and Society, 74*, 369–372.

Witty, P. A. (1951c). Television and the high school student: Surveys of elementary, junior, and senior high school pupils. *Education, 74*, 273–276.

Witty, P. A. (1952a). Children's interest in comics, radio, motion pictures and TV. *Educational Administration and Supervision, 38*, 138–147.

Witty, P. A. (1952b). Children's reactions to TV—A third report. *Elementary English*, 469–473.

Witty, P. A. (1952c). Two studies of children's interest in TV. *Elementary English, 29*, 251–257.

Witty, P. A. (1953). Children's reaction to TV—A fourth report. *Elementary English, 30*, 444–451.

Witty, P. A. (1954a). Children and TV: A fifth report. *Elementary English, 31*, 348–357.

Witty, P. A. (1954b). Comparative studies of interest in TV. *Educational Administration and Supervision, 40*, 321–335.

Witty, P. A. (1954c). Televiewing by pupils, parents, teachers, 1950–1953. *School and Society, 79*, 150–152.

Witty, P. A. (1954d). Television and children. *Journal of the National Education Association, 43*, 92.

Witty, P. A. (1955). Children and TV: A sixth report. *Elementary English, 38*, 309–310.

Witty, P. A. (1956a). A seventh report on TV. *Elementary English, 33*, 523–528.

Witty, P. A. (1956b). A sixth report on TV. *School and Society, 83*, 166.

Witty, P. A. (1961). Televiewing by children and youth. *Elementary English, 38*, 528–554.

Witty, P. A. (1966). Studies of the mass media, 1949–1965. *Science Education, 50*, 119–126.

Witty, P. A. (1967). Children of the television era. *Elementary English, 44*, 528–535, 554.

Witty, P. A., & Bricker, H. (1952). *Your child and radio, TV, comics and movies*. Chicago: Science Research Associates.

Witty, P. A., & Kinsella, P. (1959). Children and the electronic Pied Piper. *Education, 80*, 48–56.

Wolf, M. A., Hexamer, A., & Meyer, T. P. (1981). Research on children and television: A review of 1980. In M. Burgoon (Ed.), *Communication Yearbook* (Vol. 6, pp. 353–368). New Brunswick, NJ: Transaction Books.

Wolf, T. M. (1972). A developmental investigation of televised modeled verbalizations on resistance to deviation. *Developmental Psychology, 6*, 537.

Wolf, T. M., & Cheyne, H. (1972). Persistence of effects of live behavioral, televised behavioral, and live verbal models on resistance to deviation. *Child Development, 43*, 1429–1436.

Wolfe, D. E., & Jellison, J. A. (1995). Interviews with preschool children about music videos. *Journal of Music Therapy, 32*, 265–285.

Wong, N. D., Hei, T. K., Qaqundah, P. Y., Davidson, D. M., Bassin, S. L., & Gold, K. (1992). Television viewing and pediatric hypercholesterolemia. *Pediatrics, 90*, 75–79.

Wood, W., Wong, F. Y., & Chachere, J. G. (1991). Effects of media violence on viewers aggression in unconstrained social interaction. *Psychological Bulletin, 109*, 371–383.

Woodrick, C., Chissom, B., & Smith, D. (1977). Television-viewing habits and parent-observed behaviors of third-grade children. *Psychological Reports, 40*, 830.

Worden, J. K., & Flynn, B. S. (2002). Using mass media to prevent cigarette smoking. In R. C. Hornik (Ed.), *Public health communication: Evidence for behavior change* (pp. 23–33). Mahwah, NJ: Lawrence Erlbaum Associates, Inc.

Wotring, C. E., & Greenberg, B. S. (1973). Experiments in televised violence and verbal aggression: Two exploratory studies. *Journal of Communication, 23*, 446–460.

Wright, J. C., & Huston, A. C. (1983). A matter of form: Potentials of television for young viewers. *American Psychologist, 38*, 835–843.

Wright, J. C., Huston, A. C., Murphy, K. C., St. Peters, M., Piñon, M., Scantlin, R., et al. (2001). The relations of early television viewing to school readiness and vocabulary of children from low-income families: The early window project. *Child Development, 72*, 1347–1366.

Wright, J. C., Huston, A. C., Reitz, A. L., & Piemyat, S. (1994). Young children's perceptions of television reality: Determinants and developmental differences. *Developmental Psychology, 30*, 229–239.

Wright, J. C., Huston, A. C., Truglio, R., Fitch, M., Smith, E., & Piemyat, S. (1995). Occupational portrayals on television: Children's role schemata, career aspirations, and perceptions of reality. *Child Development, 66*, 1706–1718.

Wright, J. C., Huston, A. C., Vandewater, E. A., Bickham, D. S., Scantlin, R. M., Kotler, J. A., et al. (2001). American children's use of electronic media in 1997: A national survey. *Journal of Applied and Developmental Psychology, 22*, 31–47.

Wright, J. C., Kunkel, D., Piñon, M., & Huston, A. C. (1989). How children reacted to televised coverage of the space shuttle disaster. *Journal of Communication, 39*, 27–45.

Wright, J. C., St. Peters, M., & Huston, A. C. (1990). Family television use and its relation to children's cognitive skills and social behavior. In J. Bryant (Ed.), *Television and the American family* (pp. 227–252). Hillsdale, NJ: Lawrence Erlbaum Associates, Inc.

Wroblewski, R., & Huston, A. C. (1987). Televised occupational stereotypes and their effects on early adolescents: Are they changing? *Journal of Early Adolescence, 7*, 283–297.

Wulfemeyer, K. T., & Mueller, B. (1992). Channel One and commercials in the classrooms—Advertising content aimed at students. *Journalism Quarterly, 69*, 724–742.

Wurtzel, A. (1977). Research: Television violence and aggressive behavior. *ETC: A Review of General Semantics, 2*, 212–225.

Wurtzel, A., & Dominick, J. R. (1971). Evaluation of television drama: Interaction of acting styles and shot selection. *Journal of Broadcasting, 16*, 103–110.

Wurtzel, A., & Surlin, S. (1978). Viewer attitudes toward television advisory warnings. *Journal of Broadcasting, 22*, 19–31.

Yates, G. C. R. (1974). Influence of televised modeling and verbalization on children's delay of gratification. *Journal of Experimental Child Psychology, 18*, 333–339.

Yoon, J. S., & Somers, C. (2003). Aggressive content of high school students' TV viewing. *Psychology Reports, 93*, 949–953.

Young, E. A., McFatter, R., & Clopton, J. R. (2001). Family functioning, peer influence, and media influence as predictors of bulimic behavior. *Eating Behaviors, 2*, 323–337.

Young, R. (1969). Television in the lives of our parents. *Journal of Broadcasting, 14,* 37–46.

Zagona, S., & Kelly, M. (1966). The resistance of the closed mind to a novel and complex audio-visual experience. *Journal of Social Psychology, 70,* 123–131.

Zajonc, R. B. (1954). Some effects of the "space" serials. *Public Opinion Quarterly, 18,* 367–374.

Zentall, S. S., & Stormont, M. (1999). Assessment of setting in the behavioral ratings of preschoolers with and without high levels of activity. *Psychology in the Schools, 36,* 109–115.

Zhu, J. H., Milavsky, J. R., & Biswas, R. (1994). Do televised debates affect image perception more than issue-knowledge? A study of the first 1992 presidential debate. *Human Communication Research, 20,* 302–333.

Ziegler, S. K. (1970). Attention factors in televised messages: Effects on looking behavior and recall. *Journal of Broadcasting, 14,* 307–315.

Zielinska, I. E., & Chambers, B. (1995). Using group viewing of television to teach preschool children social skills. *Journal of Educational Television, 21,* 85–99.

Zillmann, D. (1971). Excitation transfer in communication-mediated aggressive behavior. *Journal of Experimental Social Psychology, 7,* 419–434.

Zillmann, D., & Bryant, J. (1985). Affect, mood, and emotion as determinants of selective exposure. In D. Zillmann & J. Bryant (Eds.), *Selective exposure to communication* (pp. 157–190). Hillsdale, NJ: Lawrence Erlbaum Associates.

Zillmann, D., Bryant, J., & Huston, A. C. (1994). *Media, children, and the family: Social scientific, psychodynamic, and clinical perspectives.* Hillsdale, NJ: Lawrence Erlbaum Associates, Inc.

Zillmann, D., & Cantor, J. (1977). Affective responses to the emotions of a protgonist. *Journal of Experimental Social Psychology, 13,* 155–165.

Zillmann, D., Hoyt, J. L., & Day, K. D. (1974). Strength and duration of the effect of aggressive, violent, and erotic communications on subsequent aggressive behavior. *Communication Research, 1,* 286–306.

Zillmann, D., Johnson, R. C., & Hanrahan, J. (1973). Pacifying effect of happy ending of communications involving aggression. *Psychological Reports, 32,* 967–970.

Zimmerman, F. J., Glew, G. M., Christakis, D. A., & Katon, W. (2005). Early cognitive stimulation, emotional support, and television watching as predictors of subsequent bullying among grade-school children. *Archives of Pediatrics & Adolescent Medicine, 159,* 384–388.

Zohoori, A. R. (1988). A cross cultural analysis of children's television use. *Journal of Broadcasting & Electronic Media, 32,* 105–113.

Zohoori, A. R. (1990). Children, television, and the acculturation process. In S. Thomas (Ed.), *Communication and culture: Language, performance, technology, and media* (pp. 255–264). Norwood, NJ: Ablex.

Zoog, J. B., Ma, H., & Dent, C. W. (2004). Self-generated alcohol outcomes in 8th and 10th graders: Exposure to vicarious sources of alcohol information. *Addictive Behaviors, 29,* 3–16.

Zuckerman, D. M., Singer, D. G., & Singer, J. L. (1980a). Children's television viewing, racial and sex-role attitudes. *Journal of Applied Social Psychology, 10,* 281–294.

Zuckerman, D. M., Singer, D. G., & Singer, J. L. (1980b). Television viewing, children's reading, and related classroom behavior. *Journal of Communication, 30*(1), 166–174.

Zuckerman, D. M., & Zuckerman, B. S. (1985). Television's impact on children. *Pediatrics*, *75*, 233–240.

Zuckerman, P., Ziegler, M., & Stevenson, H. (1978). Children's viewing of television and recognition memory of commercials. *Child Development*, *49*, 96–104.

Zusne, L. (1968). Measuring violence in children's cartoons. *Perceptual & Motor Skills*, *27*, 901–902.

Zylke, J. W. (1988). More voices join medicine in expressing concern over amount, content of what children see on TV. *Journal of the American Medical Association*, *260*, 1831, 1835.

Author Index

Subject Index